KU-615-345

Civil Litigation Handbook

University of Liverpool

Withdrawn from stock

putyourknowledgeintopractice

Business Law
J. Scott Slorach and Jason G. Ellis

Foundations for the LPC
George Miles *et al.*

Lawyers' Skills
Julian Webb *et al.*

Criminal Litigation Handbook
Martin Hannibal and Lisa Mountford

Civil Litigation Handbook
Susan Cunningham-Hill and Karen Elder

Property Law Handbook
Robert Abbey and Mark Richards

A Practical Approach to Civil Procedure
Stuart Sime

A Practical Approach to Conveyancing
Robert Abbey and Mark Richards

A Practical Approach to ADR
Susan Blake *et al.*

Commercial Law
Robert Bradgate and Fidelma White

Employment Law
James Holland and Stuart Burnett

Family Law Handbook
Jane Sendall

Interactive online resources
www.oxfordinteract.com

LPC Skills Online
Liz Polding and Jill Cripps

LPC Accounts Online
James Catchpole

For more vocational law titles please visit www.oxfordtextbooks.co.uk

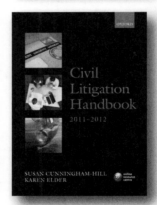
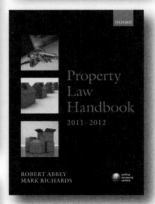

Civil
Litigation
Handbook

SUSAN CUNNINGHAM-HILL

KAREN ELDER

OXFORD

UNIVERSITY PRESS

OXFORD

UNIVERSITY PRESS

Great Clarendon Street, Oxford OX2 6DP

Oxford University Press is a department of the University of Oxford.
It furthers the University's objective of excellence in research, scholarship,
and education by publishing worldwide in

Oxford New York

Auckland Cape Town Dar es Salaam Hong Kong Karachi
Kuala Lumpur Madrid Melbourne Mexico City Nairobi
New Delhi Shanghai Taipei Toronto

With offices in

Argentina Austria Brazil Chile Czech Republic France Greece
Guatemala Hungary Italy Japan Poland Portugal Singapore
South Korea Switzerland Thailand Turkey Ukraine Vietnam

Oxford is a registered trademark of Oxford University Press
in the UK and in certain other countries

Published in the United States
by Oxford University Press Inc., New York

© S. Cunningham-Hill & K. Elder 2011

The moral rights of the authors have been asserted
Database right Oxford University Press (maker)
Contains public sector information licensed under the Open Government Licence v1.0
(http://www.nationalarchives.gov.uk/doc/opengovernment-licence/
open-government-licence.htm)
Crown Copyright material reproduced with
the permission of the Controller, HMSO (under
the terms of the Click Use licence.)

First edition 2008
Second edition 2010

All rights reserved. No part of this publication may be reproduced,
stored in a retrieval system, or transmitted, in any form or by any means,
without the prior permission in writing of Oxford University Press,
or as expressly permitted by law, or under terms agreed with the appropriate
reprographics rights organization. Enquiries concerning reproduction
outside the scope of the above should be sent to the Rights Department,
Oxford University Press, at the address above.

You must not circulate this book in any other binding or cover
and you must impose the same condition on any acquirer

British Library Cataloguing in Publication Data

Data available

Typeset by Laserwords Private Limited, Chennai, India
Printed in Great Britain on acid-free paper by
Ashford Colour Press Limited, Gosport, Hampshire

ISBN 978-0-19-960936-9

10 9 8 7 6 5 4 3 2 1

CONTENTS

ONLINE RESOURCE CENTRE CONTENTS

STUDENT RESOURCES

☻ Case study documentation

Documentation in support of the two fictional case studies in the book

☻ Three additional chapters

Chapter A: Injunctions and other Equitable Remedies
Chapter B: Assessment of Costs Proceedings
Chapter C: Guide to Preparing Instructions to Counsel

☻ Annotated forms

Key forms from the litigation process, with useful annotations to help you understand how they should be completed correctly

- N1 Claim Form
- N150 Allocation Questionnaire
- Form N244 Application Notice

☻ Litigation train

An interactive timeline to help put the litigation process in context

☻ Podcasts

Recorded by the authors, these audio files will accompany and supplement your understanding of topics in Chapters 3, 4, 16 and 20.

- First client meeting
- Part 36 overview
- Consent orders

☻ Updates

Updates to cases and legislation since book publication

☻ Web links

Direct links to some useful websites relating to civil litigation

LECTURER RESOURCES (FOR REGISTERED ADOPTERS)

☻ Answers to the self-test questions

Answers to the self-test questions that appear at the end of a number of chapters in the book

☻ Case study materials

Suggested answers to the questions in relation to the two fictional case studies in the book

☻ Video clips

Four video scenarios to accompany the two fictional case studies featured in the book

- Andrew James Pike – Mediation. Chapter 5
- Andrew James Pike – Interim Payment. Chapters 13 and 14
- Andrew James Pike – Part 36 client meeting. Chapter 16
- Bollingtons Limited – Telephone application. Chapter 13

PREFACE

Our aim when preparing the fourth edition of this book has been to provide a primarily practical but comprehensive text on the areas of civil litigation that any legal practitioner or student on the Legal Practice Course will encounter during his time in the dispute resolution department or in his studies for the core Civil Litigation element of this core subject area. This text is designed for use by all practitioners in litigation including student, paralegal, trainee or newly qualified practitioners and to act as a refresher for any practitioner re-entering the world of litigation in practice.

We believe that this book provides a comprehensive guide for the study of Civil Litigation, enabling such a student to engage with the method of study required to prepare for practice, and advise his notional 'client'. It will also prepare and guide any legal practitioner about to undertake those early tentative steps advising 'real clients', ensuring that the principles of the Solicitors' Code of Conduct 2007 are maintained, and furnish that young litigator with the skills to engage in the tasks that are likely to fall to him. Please note that a new Code of Conduct has been drafted and will come into force in the Autumn of 2011. We refer to the basic principles of the new Code in this edition. The January online update will deal with the final approved Code.

There are five important parts to the innovative approach of this book. They include:

1. The 'Litigation Train'—a diagrammatic flow line that we illustrate at the beginning of relevant chapters in the book that represents a stage of the litigation process. By the time a student of litigation in practice, including any student on a Legal Practice Course, has studied through to the end of the book, the sections of this diagrammatic 'train journey' will together form a complete diagrammatic illustration of the path an action may take, from the first meeting with his legal representative, to trial and enforcement of any judgment.

2. This Litigation Train is also reproduced in the Online Resource Centre, created for use with this book, and is represented by three visual levels. Level 1 marks the main stages of litigation. By clicking on one of these stages, the student will be brought into level 2. Level 2 of each stage is represented by 6 headings—'Client Issues and Funding', 'Professional Conduct', 'CPR and Practice', 'ADR', 'Costs—Proportionality and Reasonableness', and 'Time'. Clicking on each of these headings brings the student into Level 3 where details will be given of the main factors arising within the heading selected for the stage of the action selected.

We believe that the diagrammatic Litigation Train will enable students, and enable practitioners, to see 'at a glance' how an action may progress, what might arise at that stage not only in terms of practice and procedure but also the other considerations that a legal practitioner must engage with. These include professional conduct, the relationship with the client, other professionals and other persons involved in the litigation at that stage. It will give the student a visual image and, in note form, a review of the action at that stage. It will also enable a student to see, and remind the practitioner, what might have taken place before that stage and what might be taking place later in the litigation. In this way a student will be able to focus his work and in so doing act in the best interests of his client at all times. A practitioner may be reminded of these steps or a para-legal may use the diagrammatic train as an aide memoire.

3. The wholly practical elements of the book enable a student to understand and anticipate the activities and skills that he will need when undertaking the work of a legal representative. Notably these include the chapters 'Trainee's Guide to Interim Applications', 'Trial Preparation', 'First Client Meeting and Initial Considerations', and 'Drafting'.

4. Included in the chapters there are 'text boxes'. These are called, 'Practical Considerations' text boxes, 'Costs' text boxes, 'Professional Conduct' text boxes and 'ADR' text boxes. These highlight notable examples of how each of these elements might arise in practice at that part of the litigation.

5. The Online Resource Centre. In addition to the Litigation Train noted in '2' above, this resource includes:

   • video clips of parts of litigation 'in action';

   • suggested solutions to the case study and general questions contained at the end of most chapters will also give additional exercises to aid learning or act as a review for young practitioners. These are available for lecturers to provide to their students;

   • some forms completed and with notes to assist in the understanding of the detail and content of these forms as they are used in practice;

   • several new podcasts to aid understanding, and give an alternative medium to learn from in two complex areas;

   • additional chapters on the assessment of costs, and the law, practice, and procedure of injunctions and a guide to preparing instructions to counsel.

   For students of legal practice these online resources will, in part, be tutor controlled.

In this fourth edition we have attempted to include additional features and make the amendments suggested by our readers. Once again we ask for, and welcome, any constructive comments from lecturers, young practitioners, supervising partners, and students about how the text and the online resources can be improved.

 Civil practice is fast moving and practice can change quickly. Updates to law, practice, and procedure will be uploaded to the Online Resource Centre in January 2012. We endeavour to keep this as up-to-date as we can but again, we welcome feedback from lecturers, practitioners, and students alike of new developments that they feel should be uploaded to the site each year.

The writing of the first edition of this book and the production of the video case studies and online resources and the preparations for this fourth edition could not have been achieved without the cooperation and assistance of many friends and colleagues.

In relation to the case study video clips: Ne'ema Bowen, Ian Cartlidge, Kate Clarke, Chris Dale, Malcolm Hacking, Peter Robinson, HH Judge John Rubery and Jon Gotham. For valuable help in the preparation of the practical and substantive elements of this book we have to thank:

• from Stoke on Trent Combined Court: HH Judge John Rubery, District Judge Peter Rank and the other members of the Judiciary at Stoke on Trent Combined Court Centre.

• from Staffordshire University: Lucy Crompton, Helen Fox, Simon Gilbert, Martin Hannibal, Peter Jordan, Lisa Mountford, and Alison Pope.

We would also like to thank the following universities who have reviewed this book in development. We have found your comments and suggestions constructive and invaluable:

• Pamela Abrams of The University of Westminster;

• Ralph Camp of Hertfordshire University;

• Ian Doerfler of Leeds Metropolitan University;

• Lucy Floyd of the Oxford Institute of Legal Practice;

- Deborah Grove of BPP Professional Education, Law School;
- Vaughan Hall of De Montfort University;
- Charlotte Hart of the University of the West of England;
- Maggie Hemsworth of the University of Plymouth;
- Edward Iredale of The City Law School;
- Susan Lazer of Huddersfield University;
- Jackie Panter of Manchester Metropolitan University;
- Liz Pugh of London Metropolitan University;
- Julia Ramsay of Anglia Ruskin University;
- Amanda Rees of Swansea University;
- Sonya Smith of Birmingham City University.

We also thank the team at OUP for their patient help and guidance.

Very sadly we report the death in June 2010 of Ralph Lewis QC. He had taken a great interest in the book and offered both advice and inspiration. As a result his enthusiastic foreword is not part of this edition.

Lastly, but very gratefully, we thank our families and our children for their continued support.

To all these people we are extremely grateful and give our heartfelt thanks.

For any errors or omissions, we apologise and take full responsibility for them.

The law is as stated in April 2011. Refer to the Online Resource Centre for important changes in the law during 2011/2012.

Susan Cunningham-Hill
Karen Elder
Staffordshire University Law School

GUIDED TOUR OF THE BOOK

The *Civil Litigation Handbook* by Cunningham-Hill & Elder is a pedagogically rich text which has been designed to facilitate your learning and understanding of civil litigation. This 'Guided tour of the book' will explain how to get the best from this book by illustrating each of the features used by the authors to explain the practical processes involved in civil litigation.

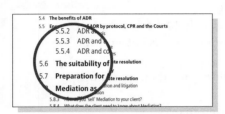

CHAPTER CONTENTS

A detailed contents list at the start of each chapter enables you to anticipate what will be covered and identify what the main topics of the chapter will be. Also use this feature to gain an understanding of how the topics fit together in the wider subject area.

LIST OF RELEVANT COURT FORMS

At the start of relevant chapters, look out for the lists of these, to help you know which forms should be used and when.

'LITIGATION TRAIN' DIAGRAMS

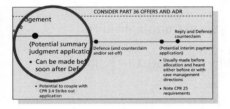

At the start of relevant chapters, these useful diagrams illustrate where you are in the overall litigation process and help you to see the 'bigger picture'. Use these diagrams to put your learning into context. By seeing these litigations trains as continuous you will see more clearly the progression of cases through the litigation process and be able to see, at a glance, where steps most commonly arise.

EXAMPLES

Look for the example icon to find relevant, practical examples of how the law has been or could be applied in common situations. These examples bring the subject to life and allow you to examine how principles, rules, and statutes work in practice.

PROFESSIONAL CONDUCT BOXES

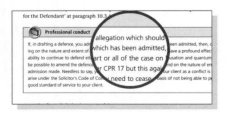

These boxes are used to highlight areas where you need to be mindful of professional conduct issues, and give guidance on how to apply the Solicitors' Code of Conduct in litigation situations.

PRACTICAL CONSIDERATIONS BOXES

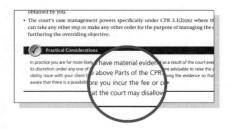

It can sometimes be difficult to see how the various rules and processes would work in practice. These boxes will help you gain an understanding of how things work in the day-to-day practical situations are likely to come across as a trainee solicitor.

COSTS BOXES

In practice, it is vital to consider your client's costs and when any fees need to be paid. These boxes highlight any costs issues that apply at various times within the litigation process.

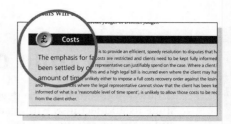

ONLINE RESOURCE CENTRE ICON

Wherever this icon appears in the margin, more information is available on the online resource centre which accompanies this text. This may be video footage, case study documentation or links to other useful web sites or guidance. See the 'Guided tour of the online resource centre' at p.xxvi for more information.

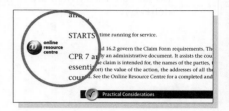

END OF CHAPTER FEATURES

CASE STUDIES

Throughout the book, the authors refer to two fictional case studies, which provide a practical focus to the law and procedures described in the text. The documentation for these case studies appears on the online resource centre. See the 'Guided tour of the website' at p.xxvi for more information.

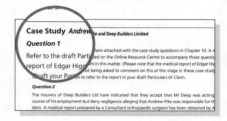

KEY POINTS SUMMARY

The key points covered are summarized in a user-friendly list at the end of each chapter. Look to these summaries to help you consolidate your learning or to check your knowledge at revision time.

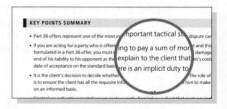

SELF-TEST QUESTIONS

These questions allow you to test yourself on particular areas of the law in preparation for your exams or to assess your learning throughout the duration of the course. Use these questions to highlight areas where you might need to improve your understanding by re-reading the text or asking your lecturer.

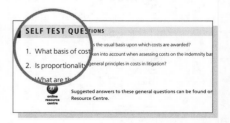

FIGURES

Flowcharts, shaded boxes or example forms provide a visual representation of what has been described within the chapter.

GUIDED TOUR OF THE WEBSITE

Online resource centres are developed to provide students and lecturers with ready-to-use teaching and learning resources. They are free-of-charge, designed to complement the text and offer additional materials which are well-suited to electronic delivery.

STUDENT RESOURCES

All the resources in this area of the site are freely accessible to all, with no password required. Simply visit the site at:
www.oxfordtextbooks.co.uk/orc/civilhandbook11_12/.

PODCASTS

Access podcasts created by the authors and designed to give you short overviews of key aspects of the civil litigation process. Use them to assimilate your knowledge or learn on the move.

UPDATES

Updates are posted on the web when the law changes or when an important case passes through the courts, allowing you to keep fully informed of developments. The updates are freely accessible to all and offer an easy way to keep abreast of changes in this rapidly changing subject area.

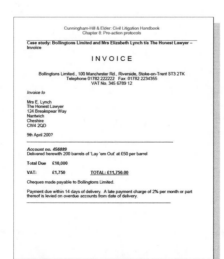

CASE STUDY DOCUMENTATION

Click on the case study section to see the case study questions from the book and any documentation necessary to help you answer them. Your lecturer can access the answers to these questions — ask them to download these on your behalf.

ANNOTATED FORMS

Key forms from the litigation process are featured here, along with useful annotations to help you understand how they should be correctly completed.

ADDITIONAL CHAPTERS

Chapters containing detailed information on assessment of costs, preparing instructions to counsel and injunctions are available, providing extra information on these topics for those who require it.

LINKS TO LEGISLATION, RULES, AND OTHER DOCUMENTATION

This part of the web provides links to useful information which is freely accessible elsewhere on the internet. Use this resource to find relevant guidelines, statutes, codes of practice, and other documentation quickly and easily.

INTERACTIVE 'LITIGATION TRAIN'

An interactive version of the litigation train diagrams featured throughout the book helps you to see how the whole litigation process fits together and the issues that you need to keep in mind at any particular point.

LECTURER RESOURCES

These resources are available solely to lecturers who are adopting the text. To obtain a username and password, complete the registration form at:
www.oxfordtextbooks.co.uk/orc/civilhandbook11_12/; All of the resources on this part of the site can be downloaded into your institutions' virtual learning environment (VLE).

VIDEO CLIPS

High resolution video footage relating to the case studies within the book allows you to emphasize the practical application of what you describe in your teaching. (Low resolution sample video clips are available for viewing by all.)

CASE STUDY MATERIALS

You can download answers to the case study questions within the book and any documentation relating to those answers, including sample documents. You can then choose when to provide these to your students, making it possible to integrate the case studies within the book fully into your teaching.

GLOSSARY

Below is a chart of the most common terms introduced or amended by the CPR.

NEW TERMINOLOGY	OLD TERMINOLOGY
Overriding Objective	No equivalent
Allocation (to track)	No equivalent
Interim Application Notice	Interlocutory Summons
Authorized Cost Officer	Taxing Officer
Child	Minor/Infant
Protected party	Patient
Claimant	Plaintiff
Claim Form	Writ/Default Summons
Alternative service	Substituted service
Statements of case	Pleadings
Case Management Conference (CMC)	Summons for Directions
Clinical Negligence	Medical Negligence
Costs Judge	Taxing Master
Detailed Assessment	Taxation
Senior Court Costs Office (SCCO)	Supreme Court Taxing Office
Disclosure and Inspection	Discovery and Inspection
In Private	In camera
Hearing rooms	Chambers/courtrooms
Further Information	Further and Better Particulars
Freezing Injunction	Mareva Injunction
Litigation Friend	Next friend/Guardian *ad Litem*
Parts	RSC/CCR Orders
Counterclaims and Additional Claims	Third-Party Proceedings
Part 36 Offer	Calderbank letter
Claimant's Part 24 application	Order 14 Summons
Defendant's Part 24 application	No equivalent
Particulars of Claim	Statement/Particulars of Claim
Schedule of Past and Future Loss and Expense	Schedule of Special Damages

NEW TERMINOLOGY	OLD TERMINOLOGY
Listing for trial	Setting down for trial
Permission of the Court	Leave of the Court
Statement of Truth	No equivalent
High Court Witness summons	Subpoena
Single joint expert	No equivalent
Search Order	Anton Piller order
Summary Assessment	No equivalent
With Notice	*Inter Partes*
Without Notice	*Ex Parte*

TABLE OF CASES

TABLE OF CIVIL PROCEDURE RULES

TABLE OF PROFESSIONAL CONDUCT RULES

TABLE OF STATUTES

TABLE OF STATUTORY INSTRUMENTS

1.1 INTRODUCTION

This brief introductory chapter serves several purposes. Its aims are to:

- explain the philosophy of the book and its pedagogical features;
- assist in broadening your research skills and knowledge;
- introduce you to the Civil Procedure Rules (CPR);
- review the civil court system and its designated judges;
- highlight professional conduct considerations and how they are dealt with in this book.

1.2 CIVIL LITIGATION—A NEW APPROACH

1.2.1 WHY A NEW APPROACH?

This civil litigation book provides an innovative and vocational approach to those studying civil litigation and those new to practice.

It has been our intention, whilst writing this book, to provide a practical yet informative approach to the study and practice of civil litigation. As experienced tutors and litigators, we are aware of the need for a book that gives students and practitioners an accessible and comprehensive explanation of the fundamental substantive and procedural issues whilst also providing a learning resource that illustrates, through practice-based case studies, diagrams, self test questions, video clips, and podcasts, how civil litigation is conducted in practice.

Our experience of university student-centred learning has demonstrated that utilizing a wide range of interrelated learning resources is the most effective method of facilitating and reinforcing the understanding of key legal issues both progressively and holistically.

This assists both students, in the preparation of their civil litigation assessments, and new practitioners, in their transition to becoming experienced litigators.

1.2.2 HOW IS THIS APPROACH ACHIEVED?

This innovative approach is reflected in our belief that students and practitioners should be aware that resolving disputes for clients encompasses not only a working knowledge of the CPR, but also an awareness of the alternatives to litigation, coupled with an understanding of professional conduct obligations and legal skills. The overall picture is therefore one of integration of all of those. To enable those using this book to gauge their progress and level of understanding, the Online Resource Centre (ORC) accompanying this book contains case study questions, and general questions.

There are also text boxes dispersed through the chapters that highlight practical considerations, alternative dispute resolution (ADR) processes, professional conduct, and costs issues, all of which enhance the existing substantive text on these matters.

We have also selected relevant court forms that are used frequently in practice, along with other important relevant documents for you to consider. Some of the more common court forms have been annotated to help you to understand better how to complete them. All of these court forms and documents appear in the Online Resource Centre.

The vocational approach is achieved in a number of ways. Our writing style seeks to explain the law and procedure in an accessible and reader-friendly way. In general, we have not reproduced the actual CPR, although clearly the text explaining the law, practice, and procedure has evolved from the CPR and the way in which the court has interpreted these rules in the years since April 1999. Any student or practitioner will need to examine the text of the relevant CPR in dealing with any matter in litigation. This book is intended to be used as a manual to aid your understanding of the rules. The book aims to lead you to the CPR. The CPR can be accessed at http://www.justice.gov.uk/guidance/courts-and-tribunals/courts/procedure-rules.

The substantive parts of each chapter are supplemented by practical examples, charts, and templates, as well as a summary of key points, some general questions, and podcasts. We have also included two case studies that feature as stand-alone cases in the book. These are an essential part of our practical approach because the case studies, which follow the paths of two actions through litigation, can be used to check your understanding at the end of each chapter. These case studies are:

- the personal injury case study—*Andrew James Pike v Deep Builders Ltd*;
- the debt/breach of contract case study—*Bollingtons Ltd v Mrs Elizabeth Lynch t/a The Honest Lawyer*.

The case study questions appear at the end of most chapters. The information and materials relevant to the case study questions, along with the suggested answers to these, appear in the Online Resource Centre.

The case studies are designed to be studied progressively as you follow the reading of the chapters. Because these case studies are progressive, you will need to keep the 'path' of each action in your mind as you move on to the next set of questions between consecutive chapters. To get the most from the case study questions, in terms of the application of substantive knowledge and procedure, the key is to contextualize each case study in terms of what has gone before and what is likely to come next. This will help to develop your proactive skills as a practitioner and engender 'thinking outside the box'. Treat these fictional characters as your own clients!

To further assist in this contextualization, we have devised a teaching tool illustrated at the beginning of chapters and in the Online Resource Centre called the 'litigation train'. This depicts diagrammatically the fundamental steps to be taken in a case from start to finish, as well as highlights important considerations at various stages of the action. As such, the 'train' is not associated in any way with the case studies, but rather offers a neutral 'checklist' of the likely procedural and practical steps that may be taken as a case proceeds to trial. The diagrammatic litigation train enables you to see 'at a glance' where the case sits in its path to trial and will therefore allow you to see the steps that may be taken at that stage. It will also enable you to contextualize your case, and see what has gone before and what may happen next.

As indicated above, the litigation train features both at the beginning of chapters, commencing in Chapter 6, and in the Online Resource Centre. The former illustrates a small section of the train relevant to the chapter, whilst the latter denotes three different levels of detail of the train, as follows, uncovered by the click of the mouse.

1. The first level displays the train in its entirety.

2. The second level sets out a variety of generic subheadings for each individual stage on the train.

3. The third level details the substantive information for each subheading.

The final part of the vocational approach—linked to both case studies—is the video clips that appear on the Online Resource Centre. All of the participants in the video clips very kindly agreed to give up their valuable time in order to assist us in making the films. The clips should be viewed as learning aids in that they seek to illustrate, in a practical way, aspects of civil practice. The videos are not necessarily a depiction of how cases always proceed, and they should not be regarded as definitive examples of how advocacy and client relations should be conducted. Commentary is included on the clips, as well as 'top tips' from the advocate's and the court's perspectives. The participants relied on the documentation and information provided for the case studies as presented at the end of chapters and as featured in the Online Resource Centre. The filming was based around a 'general framework for filming' document, but all participants devised the detail of their own script.

1.3 THE ONLINE RESOURCE CENTRE (ORC)

The Online Resource Centre that accompanies this book can be accessed at http://www.oxfordtextbooks.co.uk/orc/civilhandbook11_12/. Features included on the website are fully explained in the 'Guided tour of the website' (see pp xxvi–xxvii), but it is also useful to introduce the resource here.

The website is divided into useful sections to help the individual reader and includes the following resources:

Section 1   Student resources
These are freely available resources and include the litigation train, annual updates to cover recent developments in civil litigation, useful web links, online chapters, and podcasts. No password is required to access this part of the website. Here, you will also find a selection of annotated court forms and additional documents to support the case studies in the book.

Section 2   Open-access video clips
Selected video clips of the case studies are available here for online browsing and may be used to review specific aspects of litigation in practice.

Section 3   Password-protected lecturer resources
Your lecturer will have access to these and can provide them to you. The resources include:

• high-quality video clips of the two case studies that bring the case studies to life and illustrate some key features of modern-day litigation including those areas in which you, as a practitioner, are likely to become involved;

• case study information, materials, questions, and suggested answers;

• answers to the self-test questions in the book.

Wherever you see this symbol, there is a link to the Online Resource Centre. In order to derive maximum benefit from this book, we recommend that you make full use of the learning and information resources available on the Online Resource Centre.

1.4 RESEARCH SOURCES

Legal research is an important part of your studies, but it is also a crucial skill that you will be required to exercise in practice. An accurate, relevant, and up-to-date research report to your supervising fee earner will reflect well on you and provide essential information regarding the conduct of a case as it moves forward. The Online Resource Centre provides invaluable links to related websites from which you can access further useful information. Here, we include a summary of useful practitioner resources.

1.4.1 PRACTITIONER WORKS

In recent years, there has been a proliferation of new resources for civil litigators. We seek to mention those works most commonly used by civil litigators in practice.

1.4.1.1 *Blackstone's Civil Practice* (Oxford University Press)

This is an established leading research source for civil litigators. This is published annually with a CD-ROM and updates in the form of supplements. It provides an accessible and user-friendly detailed explanation of the CPR, along with the CPR themselves replicated in their entirety, plus related Practice Directions (PDs), Protocols, guides, and relevant legislation.

1.4.1.2 *The White Book* (Sweet and Maxwell)

This work is otherwise known as *Civil Procedure*, and appears both in paper format and on CD-ROM. The Westlaw UK database also contains the full text of the *White Book*. It is an annual publication, with regular updates. It comes in two volumes: volume one containing the CPR and PDs, Rules of the Senior Court (RSC), County Court Rules (CCR), miscellaneous Practice Directions and Practice Statements, Protocols, procedural guides, a guide to time limits under the CPR, and a glossary; volume two containing the Court Guides.

1.4.1.3 *The Green Book* (Butterworths)

This work is otherwise known as *The Civil Court Practice*, and is available in paper format, on CD-ROM, and online. This publication overlaps with the White Book, because it comprises two volumes containing similar information. It is updated annually with further periodic reviews.

1.4.1.4 *The Blue Book* (Legislation.gov.uk)

This publication is also known as the definitive version of the CPR. Whilst it contains much of the same information as the White and Green Books, and is offered both in paper format and on CD-ROM, it is updated monthly and so is a valuable source of up-to-date information.

1.4.2 JOURNALS AND NEWSLETTERS

Articles contained in journals and newsletters allow practitioners to keep up to date with current issues in all areas of the law. There are general legal journals, such as the *Solicitor's Journal* and the *Law Society Gazette*, which contain legal news, letters, commentaries, and a legal update on a variety of topical legal matters. The journals and newsletters pertinent to civil litigation are as follows.

1.4.2.1 *Litigation Funding* **(Law Society Publishing)**

This is a sister journal to the *Law Society Gazette* detailing the current trends and developments on funding litigation in this country.

1.4.2.2 *Civil Procedure News* **(Sweet and Maxwell)**

This journal focuses primarily on cases dealing with CPR points and interpretation. It also contains a costs section, which is helpful when looking for a costs-only decision.

1.4.3 ELECTRONIC RESEARCH SOURCES

In undertaking any research, you should be aware of the difference between 'primary sources' and 'secondary sources'. Journals and newsletters will essentially contain secondary sources, but are a valuable resource to aid the understanding of certain procedural points. However, primary sources should always be reviewed in any aspect of research.

1.5 A MATTER OF STYLE

The use of the masculine he/his should be taken to include she/her. It is not intended to cause offence by adopting the masculine as the general descriptive phrase in this book. Further, in using the masculine, we do not want to give the impression that all advocates and judges are male; far from it—the female stake in litigation practice on both sides of the bench is ever increasing and is set to continue to do so.

1.6 THE CIVIL PROCEDURE RULES (CPR)

The CPR now represent the cornerstone of the English and Welsh civil legal system today. They include, as well as the substantive rules themselves, Pre-Action Protocols (the guidance in relation to the pre-action behaviour of parties) and High Court Guides (the supplemental information in respect of court practice in the High Court).

All of these aim to provide a comprehensive procedural code that will govern the conduct of all civil cases in all courts in this country, and will represent your primary source for the study and practice of civil litigation. The CPR have an explicit foundation in the concept of the 'overriding objective', which is looked at in some detail in Chapter 2, along with the whole philosophy of the civil courts system.

1.7 THE COMPOSITION OF THE HIGH COURT AND COUNTY COURTS OF ENGLAND AND WALES AND APPEALS

This section aims to provide you with a reminder of the hierarchy of the civil courts that you will have examined during your academic studies.

1.7.1 THE HIGH COURT

The High Court comprises three divisions:

- the Chancery Division;
- the Queen's Bench Division; and
- the Family Division.

Business is allocated between the divisions under the provisions of the Senior Courts Act 1981, s. 61 and Sched. 1. The High Court deals with higher level civil disputes. Figure 1.1

provides an 'at a glance' table of the business undertaken in the Chancery and Queen's Bench Division only, because family matters are outside the scope of this book. Both the Queen's Bench and Chancery Divisions have a number of specialist courts the business of which is also outside the scope of this book. It is sufficient for you to be aware of the court structure and the identity of the courts, the business of some of which is self-evident from their names.

As a new practitioner, the majority of High Court matters that you are likely to come across will be heard in the non-specialist courts. However, any division has jurisdiction to deal with any business suitable for the High Court. Each division has wide powers of transfer of a case to another division or to retain a case even if started in the 'wrong' division. In general, business will be allocated according to the expertise of the judicial officers in each division.

The High Court's main administrative offices and court facilities are located at the Royal Courts of Justice (RCJ), The Strand, London. In addition, there are 131 district registries, which have been established under ss. 99–102 of the Senior Courts Act 1981. Any High Court matter can be issued out of the RCJ, but it is usually more convenient for those practising outside London to issue out of one of the district registries. These are most commonly found in cities and larger towns.

Most trials in the High Court are conducted by High Court judges, who must be practitioners of at least ten years' standing, although, under s. 9 of the Senior Courts Act 1981, the Lord Chief justice may request a circuit judge or recorder to sit as a High Court judge. Such a judge is usually known as a 's. 9 judge'. Interim applications in the High Court are heard by masters in the RCJ or by district judges outside London. Masters or district judges must be practitioners with a relevant legal qualification for a relevant period and have gained legal experience during that relevant period.

FIGURE 1.1

QUEEN'S BENCH DIVISION	CHANCERY DIVISION
Non-specialist matters	*Non-specialist matters*
• General contract matters, including debt	• Sale, exchange, or partition of land
• General matters of tort, including damages for personal injuries and clinical negligence in excess of £50,000	• Mortgages
	• Execution of trusts
• Recovery of land and goods	• Administration of estates
• Judicial review	• Bankruptcy
	• Taking of partnership accounts
	• Rectification of deeds
	• Probate claims
	• Intellectual property
Specialist courts	*Specialist courts*
• Technology and Construction (TCC)	• Companies
• Commercial	• Patents
• Admiralty	
• Mercantile	
• Administrative	

1.7.2 THE COUNTY COURTS

The county courts derive jurisdiction and powers from the County Courts Act 1984. There are 216 county courts throughout England and Wales, each exercising jurisdiction for a geographical area. The county court deals with the lower level (and value) debt, personal injury, and general breach of contract cases, although some technology and construction (TCC) and patent work can also be conducted in particular county courts up to a limit of £30,000.

In many county court administrative offices, there may also be housed the district registry for that region (and perhaps for a greater geographical region than that of the county court), a family court, a probate division, and sometimes also a Crown Court. If this is the case, the court is described as a 'Combined Court Centre'. Further, if you are dealing with a matter that has been run in one of the smaller county courts, then common practice is for the trial of that matter to be transferred to a trial centre, usually housed in one of the larger nearby county courts in a different geographical area.

The principal judicial officers of the county courts are circuit judges and district judges. Circuit judges are professional judges with at least ten years' professional experience. Circuit judges will often sit in the civil courts (and the Crown Court) and they may be supplemented by recorders, who are part-time judges. As stated above, a circuit judge or recorder may be 'ticketed' to sit as a High Court judge for a specific action or for specific days. Circuit judges hear most county court trials that are not heard by the district judges. Much of the administrative judicial work of the county courts is conducted by district judges. Again, these district judges may sit as county court district judges or may be allocated to High Court business.

Circuit judges may exercise all of the powers of the county court. The powers of the district judges are fewer. They usually try all small claims track cases, many of the fast-track cases, and interim applications, although they may be empowered to administer the work of the court beyond their normal duties.

In practice, it may be important to know the geographical area covered by a county court or district registry if you are not to issue out of your local court. A search can be made on the website of Her Majesty's Courts Service—http://www.hmcourts-service.gov.uk—which contains a full list of courts, work types, and geographical regions. This can be very useful in cases in which you have only a local county court and no district registry.

1.7.3 APPEALS

It is important to know to which court to appeal. With the creation of the Supreme Court in October 2009, the appeals process in this country has been modified somewhat.

1.7.3.1 Which court do you appeal to?

The identity of an appellate court is governed by the Access to Justice Act 1999 (Destination of Appeals) Order 2000, SI 2000/1071. The appellate courts are as follows:

- appeals from a High Court district judge are to a High Court judge;
- appeals from a High Court judge are to the Court of Appeal;
- appeals from the Court of Appeal are to the Supreme Court;
- appeals from a county court district judge are to a county court circuit judge;
- appeals from a county court circuit judge are to a High Court judge.

The exception to this is that the final decision by a circuit judge in a multi-track case or in one of the specialist courts will be appealed to the Court of Appeal.

1.7.3.2 Appeals in the county courts, High Court and the Court of Appeal

As a result of the creation of the Supreme Court, the rules on appeals to the county court, High Court and the Court of Appeal contained in CPR 52 and its PD are still in the process of being restructured predominantly to include five distinct PDs rather that one long and rather complex one containing five sections. The authors understand that the new PDs are expected to come into force in July 2011.

A brief commentary on how to make an appeal is contained in Chapter 20 at paragraph 20.7.3.

1.7.3.3 Appeals to the Supreme Court

The Supreme Court replaced the appellate committee of the House of Lords. Section 40 of the Constitutional Reform Act 2005 states that any civil appeal from any order or judgment of the Court of Appeal in England and Wales lies only to this new Supreme Court.

It has now been defined that the Supreme Court will:

- hear appeals on arguable points of law of general public importance;
- act as the final court of appeal in England, Wales and Northern Ireland;
- hear appeals from civil cases in England, Wales, Northern Ireland and Scotland;
- hear appeals from criminal cases in England, Wales and Northern Ireland.

As a result of the new Supreme Court coming into existence, there are a new set of rules: the Supreme Court Rules 2009, SI 2009/1603. These replace in their entirety the old rules for appeals to the House of Lords although are not entirely different in substance.

Finally and somewhat confusingly, a far-reaching change in terminology has also come about since 1 October 2009. Firstly, what used to be known as the 'Supreme Court of England and Wales'—namely the Court of Appeal, the High Court and the Crown Court—will now be collectively known as the 'Senior Courts of England and Wales'. Secondly there has been a retrospective amendment to the name of the Supreme Court Act 1981, from now on known as the Senior Courts Act 1981. This second change is onerous as it requires amending many statements of case that state interest pursuant to this statute; for example chapters 9 and 11.

The judges of the new Supreme Court are called Supreme Court Justices. There are no more 'Law Lords'.

1.8 PROFESSIONAL CONDUCT

A very important and pervasive area of practice is the professional conduct rules that govern the solicitors' profession and other legal practitioners alike. The rules are currently set out in the Solicitors' Code of Conduct 2007. There are six core duties and 25 separate rules, each with a detailed guidance note. The Code of Conduct can be accessed online at http:// www. sra.org.uk/rules/. A failure to abide by the Code may result in disciplinary proceedings being brought against you or even in you being struck off the Roll.

Because professional conduct is a pervasive aspect of being a practitioner, we have aimed to achieve an integrated approach to this difficult area. We have sought to do this in three different ways:

- by dispersing text boxes dealing with professional conduct issues throughout the chapters at appropriate intervals;
- in later chapters, by dealing substantively with key areas of the CPR that feature in general litigation practice, including client relations (particularly costs information to the client, conflict, disclosure, confidentiality, and advocacy) and litigation services; and
- by integrating conduct issues into the case study questions.

At the time of updating this handbook, the Solicitors' Regulation Authority is currently consulting on a revised 'Code of Practice' that is proposed to be introduced by October 2011 to replace the Code of Conduct in its entirety. It is thought that the new Code will comprise ten principles. These are expected to be:

- Principle 1: Uphold the rule of law and the proper administration of justice.
- Principle 2: Act with integrity.
- Principle 3: Not allow your independence to be compromised.
- Principle 4: Act in the best interests of each client.
- Principle 5: Provide a proper standard of service to your clients.
- Principle 6: Behave in a way that maintains the trust the public places in you and in the provision of legal services.
- Principle 7: Comply with your legal and regulatory obligations and deal with your regulators and ombudsmen in an open, timely and co-operative manner.
- Principle 8: Run your business/carry out your role in the business effectively and in accordance with proper governance and sound financial management principles.
- Principle 9: Run your business/carry out your role in the business in a way that promotes equality and diversity and does not discriminate unlawfully in connection with the provision of legal services.
- Principle 10: Protect client money and assets.

Legal representatives should be aware of the changes and look out for press reports on the detail and timing of the implementation of the changes.

2 THE ETHOS OF MODERN CIVIL LITIGATION

2.1 INTRODUCTION

Civil litigation has seen some fundamental procedural and practical changes over the past ten years or so, not only in relation to the method of conducting cases through the courts, but also regarding the resolution of disputes by other processes. The study and practice of what is commonly referred to as 'civil litigation' is probably therefore somewhat misleading. A more accurate description would be 'dispute resolution', as there is now an emphatic move away from resolving disputes through the court system. Consequently, whilst students and practitioners are required to know how to conduct a case within the court framework, they are also expected to have an understanding of the philosophy and alternatives to litigation if they are to act in accordance with their professional obligations. Chapter 5 will detail these alternative dispute resolution (ADR) methods.

This chapter addresses the following:

- the fundamental changes to civil litigation;
- an introduction to the Civil Procedure Rules (CPR);
- the concept of the overriding objective; and
- human rights and civil litigation.

2.2 CIVIL LITIGATION REFORM

2.2.1 WHAT IS THE PURPOSE OF CIVIL LITIGATION?

Civil litigation encompasses the 'machinery' and the 'mechanics' of how legal and equitable rights are asserted, determined, and enforced through the courts. The processes perform the function of resolving disputes that cannot be resolved by agreement, and provide a mechanism whereby rights may be upheld by enforcing certain conduct on some members of society who infringe basic rules of conduct. The rules being upheld have their base in Christian and commercial ethics: what is good, but also what may have been agreed.

The courts therefore exist to do justice between persons who come to them. This aim appears simple. It has, however, been a long-term criticism of the courts that the very processes designed to ensure that justice may be achieved play a part in the delays that are often created in taking a case through the courts. It has long been recognized that where justice is delayed, justice may not be achieved.

Disputes often are not straightforward and considerable investigation is needed to make a case ready for trial. The time at which the bulk of these investigations are done has also played a part in the delay.

Litigants are often unable to cope with the complexities of the law on their own and have to seek the assistance of the legal profession. The amount that a legal representative charges will be largely controlled by the amount of work done. The experience of the legal representative undertaking the work also affects the charges. Litigation can be very expensive.

All of these issues played a part in the need for reform of the procedures. These reforms culminated in the CPR.

2.2.2 THE BACKGROUND TO THE CPR—THE WOOLF REPORT

In 1994, Lord Woolf was tasked with creating a new procedural code for civil litigation in England and Wales.

In his final report, at p. 2, Lord Woolf identified that:

> The defects I identified in our present system were that it is *too expensive* in that the costs often exceed the value of the claim; *too slow* in bringing cases to a conclusion and *too unequal*: there is a lack of equality between the powerful, wealthy litigant and the under-resourced litigant. It is *too uncertain*: the difficulty of forecasting what litigation will cost and how long it will last induces the fear of the unknown; and, it is *incomprehensible* to many litigants. Above all it is *too fragmented* in the way it is organised since there is no-one with clear overall responsibility for the administration of civil justice; and *too adversarial* as cases are run by the parties, not by the courts and the rules of the court, all too often, are ignored by the parties and not enforced by the court. [Emphasis added]

It should be remembered that all these criticisms are those of civil litigation before the CPR came into force. 12 years on and you will see from your study of civil litigation in practice now that many of these criticisms have – largely – been addressed. This does not mean that there are no criticisms of the CPR in practice!

Now, the issue of proceedings has been designated as the starting point for file management and investigation, but the issuing of proceedings should now only take place when no other solution is possible or prior efforts to resolve the dispute have failed. This means that investigation and analysis should take place before issue.

At p. 4, Lord Woolf intended that the CPR would be

> *fundamentally different* from what it is was. That the CPR would be underpinned by an *'overriding ethos'* [this became the overriding objectives set out in CPR Part1] which imposes an obligation on the courts and the parties to further the overriding objective of the rules so as *to deal with cases justly*. The rule provides a definition of dealing with a case justly, embodying the principle of *equality, economy, proportionality and expedition* which are fundamental to an effective contemporary system of justice. [Emphasis added]

2.2.3 AN OVERVIEW OF THE CIVIL PROCEDURE RULES (CPR)

The Woolf reforms came into force on 26 April 1999. Some of the changes in procedure introduced by the CPR have taken the form of very radical changes to our court system. The effect of the CPR has been profound.

The fundamental changes that led to the CPR include the following.

- Most of the 'old rules' contained in the Rules of the Senior Courts (RSC) (The White Book) and the County Court Rules (CCR) (The Green Book) were revoked on 26 April 1999, and were replaced by the CPR.
- Rules governing some specialist litigation have largely been continued, but they have needed to adapt to fit with the CPR.
- The CPR have a fundamental objective—that is, a stated reason for their existence: the 'overriding objective'. For this reason, all previous decisions of the court need to be applied with some caution, as they did not have a formal 'aim' and thus may not be useful in interpreting the new rules.
- Financial considerations are now a key factor to take into account—the issue of 'proportionality' has become a keyword.
- There are fundamental changes in the way in which litigation is funded.
- Both the county court and the High Court now apply the same set of rules. Practice Directions will be used to supplement and clarify the CPR, so standardizing the practice of the courts throughout England and Wales.
- Documentation has been standardized and more modern terminology has been introduced.
- Pre-Action Protocols now indicate what steps (of 'best practice') should be taken *before* an action is commenced.
- The whole culture, or ethos, of litigation has changed—the aim being that it should be less adversarial.
- The new systems of judicial management ensure that the courts now govern the progress of an action.
- Cases are now 'tracked' by the court—to either the small claims track, the fast track or the multi-track.
- Trials are expected to deal with relevant issues only.

The CPR are constantly being amended and updated, and thus any legal representative needs to keep a careful eye on the regular updates issued by the Ministry of Justice, available online at http://www.justice.gov.uk/civil/procrules_fin/index.htm, usually in April and October each year.

2.3 **THE OVERRIDING OBJECTIVE**

Lord Woolf's conclusion has become embodied in the very first (and fundamental) Part of the CPR, entitled '*The Overriding Objective*':

> *1.1 (1) The Overriding Objective of these Rules is to enable the court to deal with cases justly.*
>
> *(2) Dealing with a case justly includes, so far as is practicable—*
>
> *(a) ensuring that the parties are on an equal footing;*
>
> *(b) saving expense;*
>
> *(c) dealing with the case in ways which are proportionate—*
>
> > *(i) to the amount of money involved;*
> >
> > *(ii) to the importance of the case;*
> >
> > *(iii) to the complexity of the issues; and*
> >
> > *(iv) to the parties' financial position;*
>
> *(d) ensuring that it is dealt with expeditiously and fairly; and*
>
> *(e) allotting to it an appropriate share of the court's resources, while taking into account the need to allot resources to other cases.*

This 'overriding objective' is critical. It is the cornerstone of the CPR. The overriding objective is to be the starting point for all proceedings commenced and as the case proceeds. It is the rule to which all legal representatives will return whenever assistance is required in interpreting the CPR or in seeking to justify a step in the action.

2.3.1 **A NEW PROCEDURAL CODE OR A NEW CODE OF PRACTICE?**

It is important to remember that the CPR are a new 'procedural code' not directly a new 'code of practice'. The CPR do not override existing rules of evidence: although the CPR specifically do not create a new code of practice, the impact of the changes brought in by the CPR have indirectly created an entirely new litigation 'ethos' and this, in turn, has caused significant changes in the way in which legal representatives conduct litigation in practice.
   This change of 'ethos' (or attitude) has been brought about by:

- the court having the power, and being required, to manage cases actively;
- the expectation that time limits imposed by the court will be adhered to;
- the expectation that parties will conduct their pre-action work in accordance with the Protocols (see Chapter 8) and conduct their pre-action exchanges within a more cooperative, rather than adversarial, forum;
- the expectation that the courts should be seen as a forum of last resort dispute resolution and that ADR should be considered by the parties at all stages of the action, including pre-action and throughout the whole path of the action up until, and including, the trial;
- the impact that the new costs regime has had on the way in which litigants proceed and behave in litigation;
- the impact that some of the more significant procedural changes have had on practice—significantly, these are: the new regime of 'offers to settle' under CPR 36; the greater responsibility transferred to litigants to state the truth of their allegations; the provisions offering both parties the option of seeking summary judgment or summary 'dismissal' of the action when it is appropriate (summary judgment was previously only available to

claimants); and the provisions requiring parties to undertake personal obligations and duties to search for and disclose documents;

- providing rules that encourage parties to cooperate towards the use of single experts (whilst at the same time clarifying the obligations and duties of the experts to the court);

- the powers that the court now has to restrict expert evidence.

Each of the above has had a significant impact on the way in which litigation is now conducted, but the 'overriding objective' set out in the CPR at Part 1, r. 1 (that is, CPR 1.1) encompasses all of the above and creates the focus for the way in which all litigation should now be conducted.

This is the first time that litigation in England and Wales has had an overriding and focused 'aim'. The 'overriding objective' gives an all-encompassing aim to the way in which the rules of procedure should be interpreted, applied, and justified. The application of the CPR must (at all times) give effect to the overriding objective. This means that all steps taken in litigation must enable the case to be conducted:

- justly;

- expeditiously;

- fairly; and

- proportionately.

2.3.2 WHAT IS THE EFFECT OF THE OVERRIDING OBJECTIVE?

The effect of the aims set out in the overriding objective means that interpretation of the rules must be purposive rather than a close analysis of individual words. The application of the rules and the use made of them by litigants must 'in general' be justifiable in terms of the aims of the overriding objective. Words will, wherever possible, be given their natural meaning.

Words such as 'may' clearly imply a discretion, but words such as 'must' or 'should' do not. Care needs to be taken, however, even when seeing such words in a rule.

For example, it may be that the word 'may' is included in a rule and this implies that there is a discretion—but what may not be clear from the rule is who has that discretion. It became clear from *McPhilemy v Times Newspapers Ltd (No 2)* [2000] 1 WLR 1732 that the discretion in the word 'may' in CPR 32.5(5)—'any other party may put the witness statement in as evidence' (the rule relates to provisions applying when a party has served a witness statement, but later elects not to call that witness or use the statement at trial)—is with the court, not the 'other party', as mentioned in the rule. This is not obvious from the words of the CPR.

 Practical Considerations

The need to consider the natural meaning of words used as well as (but not contrary to) the overriding objective means that great care must always be taken to look at all of the words of a CPR when applying it. Mistakes in understanding the clear meaning of a rule will rarely be an excusable mistake by any legal representative. Examples that might be given here of an 'easy' mistake to make as the result of a less-than-thorough look at the rule being applied might be that, in CPR 24.2, there is an unobtrusive, but very important, little word—'and'—contained at the end of CPR 24.2(a)(ii). Any legal representative who drafted a witness statement in support of an application for summary judgment would find his application defective unless the evidence were to cover both aspects of the rule that are quietly, but clearly, intended by the inclusion of that little word 'and' in the rule. Mistakes caused by a less than careful look at the rules can be costly!

2.3.2.1 Dealing with a case justly, expeditiously, fairly, and proportionately

The court's primary concern must be to create justice, but this 'justice' must be further defined in terms of the need for a case to be: conducted without undue delay; fair to the parties; and proportionate to the value (or importance or complexity) of the action. Where the aims of the overriding objective seem, in certain circumstances, to contradict each other, the need to achieve 'justice' will override any apparent contradiction. So, for example, if a party requires an extension of time, this may contradict the aim to deal with cases expeditiously. In these circumstances, the aim to give 'justice' will override the need for expeditiousness if, on the particular facts, it is appropriate and 'just' to do so.

It is the interaction of the meaning of these words that has taken up considerable judicial time since 1999.

We can generally say that dealing with a case 'justly' involves an analysis of the remaining aims. Dealing with a case 'proportionately' will sometimes mean that what may be appropriate or 'just' in one case will not be appropriate or 'just' in another: for example, where the value or importance of one case is less than that of another. Proportionality is most often applied to the financial value of an action and the costs that should be utilized to seek justice, but it can equally be applied to situations concerning the importance of the case or the availability of judicial time.

Where cases are to be dealt with 'expeditiously', this means not only 'efficiently', but also in a way that saves costs. 'Saving costs' incorporates the concept of what is proportionate—that is, what is a suitable level of expenditure for that case.

We could add a further 'aim' to the CPR: that of requiring the parties and their legal representatives to cooperate wherever possible. This need to have a less adversarial, more cooperative litigation system is clearly anticipated in the impetus that other forms of dispute resolution have been given by the CPR. It also implies a need for legal representatives to be less combative in their dealings with one another, and to be cooperative with each other and the court in assisting a case to proceed efficiently. The impact of these consequences of the CPR can be clearly seen in the following two cases.

- ***Hertsmere Primary Care Trust v Administrators of Balasubramanium's Estate* [2005] EWHC 320 (Ch), [2005] 3 All ER 274** In this case, the claimant had made a Part 36 offer, but the response to it from the defendant was that the offer 'was defective', although the defendant declined to explain why. This behaviour was seen by the court as a refusal to 'cooperate' and the court treated the offer as if it had been properly made.

- ***Hateley v Morris* [2004] EWHC 252 (Ch), [2004] 1 BCLC 582** In this case, a striking out order made by the court was overturned on appeal because although there had been considerable delay (eight months) in seeking to relist the matter for a case management conference (CMC), either side could have taken this step as part of its duty to cooperate in progressing proceedings.

 Practical Considerations

The need to be cooperative does not mean that parties have the obligation to further the interests of the court to progress the matter at 'the expense' of the legal representative's obligations to act in 'the best interests of their client'. There is a balance to be had in accepting when a step will take place as against those steps that the court may or may not order. When progress is impeded, it is best for parties to be aware that both sides have an obligation to assist the court. To this end, it is expected that legal representatives will resist taking issue with minor technical points or using obstructive tactics. It is always possible to be 'cooperative', but at the same time rigorous in protecting the client's interests.

2.3.2.2 What advice should be given to clients concerning the overriding objective?

It is important that clients should be advised at an early stage (perhaps in the retainer or client care letter) of their obligations and duties, and the expectations of the court in conducting actions within the aims of the overriding objectives. In advising clients about these aims, the client should also be advised of the possible consequences of a failure to abide by the overriding objective. These may include costs and/or interest sanctions, which may be applied as a penalty for the failure.

Also, and indirectly related to the aims of the overriding objective, the client should be advised of:

- his duties arising from the need to make a statement of truth in all statements of case and other documents supporting the action;
- his duties of disclosure; and
- the duties that any expert witness will have. An expert witness will have an overriding duty to the court and an obligation to further the aims encompassed in the overriding objective, regardless of whether the expert is being instructed by, and being paid by, the client. (This is discussed in some detail later in this book, in Chapter 19.)

2.4 A BRIEF OVERVIEW OF THE IMPACT OF THE CPR ON LITIGATION PRACTICE

In this short overview, we have summarized the key areas in which the CPR have had the greatest impact on the way in which civil litigation is conducted under the CPR and as listed in paragraph 2.3.1 above. Each of the areas covered in this overview is considered in greater depth in this book in the relevant chapters.

2.4.1 PRE-ACTION PREPARATION

A far greater level of preparation will be essential before proceedings are issued, and will be desirable even before a 'letter before claim' or 'letter of claim' (see Chapter 8) is sent. Once a claim is commenced, then the court will take it through all of the stages to trial. At commencement, the court will expect the parties to have defined the issues of the case and to have undertaken pre-action work in such a way that the case is ready for 'management by the court' and will follow the strict timetable that the courts are likely to impose to make the case ready for trial in a reasonable timescale. This timescale is likely to be relaxed only if the parties wish to attempt to resolve the dispute by ADR. A claimant or his legal representative will not be permitted to conduct the action in the timescale that would best suit his workload or in the timescale that would best suit the client in order that he might have more time to pay for the legal costs incurred in proceedings. Above all, parties will be unlikely to be able to adjourn the trial date without showing good cause, and that the cause is both 'just', 'proportionate' and 'fair' (to meet the aims of the overriding objective).

2.4.2 THE CONTROL AND MANAGEMENT OF THE ACTION AFTER PROCEEDINGS ARE COMMENCED

Since the introduction of the CPR, the parties (or their legal representatives) do not have control of the conduct and progress of a claim. The courts no longer perform a reactive role, because the CPR vests the judges with the task of active case management. The judges will be proactive. A 'procedural judge' will be responsible for bringing an action to a resolution either by settlement or final judgment with all swiftness. Early on in the litigation process, he will fix a trial 'window' and give such directions as are necessary to ensure that the trial occurs within that period. The first key task awaiting the procedural judge will be the decision as to which 'track' to allocate the claim to: 'small claims track'; 'fast track'; or 'multi-track'. Generally, the small claims track will apply to straightforward claims up to a financial value of not more than £5,000; the fast track will apply to claims up to a financial value of not more than £25,000; and the multi-track will apply to the remainder of claims.

Apart from track allocation, the procedural judge will use the 'allocation questionnaires' completed by each party to help him to decide how to start the case management process. The allocation questionnaire is a party's first opportunity to influence the management decisions that the procedural judge makes to progress the action to trial. Often, the directions set by the court after allocation will remain the timetable for the whole action, but in more complex actions, there may be further hearings to manage the case by way of CMCs and, sometimes, a 'pre-trial directions hearing' and/or 'pre-trial review'.

Where an extension of time is required for any significant procedural step governed by specific or standard directions, or the CPR itself, an application must be made to the court for permission to extend the time. Usually, the court will expect the application to be made before the relevant time limit has expired. Generally, the parties will be unable simply to agree any significant extension themselves. The court itself will need to be persuaded to grant an extension. Again, any order extending the time limits for steps in the action will have to be 'proportionate', 'fair', and 'cost-efficient'.

2.4.3 THE COMMENCEMENT OF AN ACTION—A NEW STYLE OF DRAFTING WITH THE INCORPORATION OF A STATEMENT OF TRUTH

The CPR are intended to dispense with the traditional style of what were often very lengthy and sometimes obscure 'pleadings'. They have been replaced by 'statements of case'. The CPR encourage more concise drafting in all statements of case. The claim form, Form N1, replaces nearly all forms of originating process (there are some exceptions for specialist proceedings). Statements of case should, in general, become more informative than had been the case prior to the CPR: for example, a defendant cannot now simply deny something that is claimed; he must positively set out why he denies it and set out, in detail, the substance of his defence. Statements of case may contain evidence and may exhibit documents.

All statements of case will have to contain a 'statement of truth' signed by the litigant, or one of its officers or its legal representative. This has never been required before in statements of case, and the necessity of declaring the truth of the allegations and statements in a party's case will have the effect of better engaging that party with the truth of allegations that he wishes to pursue. There are clear penalties within the common law and the CPR for a party pursuing statements that he knows to be untrue.

2.4.4 THE DISCLOSURE OF DOCUMENTS

A party's duty to disclose documents will generally be limited to the documents within his *control*. Of these, he must disclose *those on which he relies, or which could either adversely affect his own or another party's case or support another party's case* (this definition is called 'standard disclosure'). A party will not be required to search for and disclose documents, irrespective of the cost, effort, and disruption that it entails to locate them. The level of the search for documents, within the standard set (usually standard disclosure), will be gauged by reference to what is proportionate (as well as fair and just) in the circumstances of the case. A 'reasonable search' is all that will be required. A litigant who wants disclosure going beyond the above will only get it if it is thought by the court to be necessary to dispose fairly of the claim or save costs.

Litigants themselves will also be personally engaged in the disclosure process and will need to make a declaration that they have:

- understood their obligations to give disclosure; and
- carried out that search reasonably.

Again, the CPR contains penalties and sanctions when there is a breach of these duties and a failure to disclose.

2.4.5 SUMMARY JUDGMENT APPLICATIONS

The CPR makes summary judgment available to claimants and defendants alike, disposing of whole claims or particular issues within claims at an early stage. The court also has power to list summary judgment hearings on its own initiative. Before the CPR, only the claimant had the power to make applications for summary judgment. This was a useful tool for disposing early of actions in which there was no reasonable prospect of the defence, or a part of it, proceeding successfully. The CPR has now also made this useful tool available to defendants who are able to establish the fact that the claim, or a part of it, has no reasonable prospect of being successfully pursued.

2.4.6 ALTERNATIVE DISPUTE RESOLUTION (ADR), SETTLEMENT, AND COSTS

The CPR encourage parties to compromise. They provide the incentive for parties to consider ADR at the earliest opportunity and to continue to consider whether ADR is an option all the way to trial. The encouragement to consider ADR is given impetus by:

- early, pre-action preparation (Protocols) putting parties in a better position in the early days of the dispute to consider terms of settlement;
- the CPR giving the court the power to order a stay of the action for the purposes of investigating whether ADR could resolve the dispute;
- the CPR enabling the court to impose costs and other penalties for any perceived intransigence on the part of a party who unreasonably refuses to cooperate in ADR; and
- the CPR creating a powerful tool to all litigants to make formal offers to settle (both pre-action and during the action). Under the provisions of CPR 36, such offers can put enormous pressure on a party as a result of the costs and interest sanctions that the courts will impose when a reasonable offer has been rejected by a party.

2.4.7 WITNESSES

2.4.7.1 Witnesses of fact
Key witnesses will need to be identified very early on, with concise statements taken (using their own words) and their availability during the 'trial window' ensured. Depositions may be used more widely in relation to proceedings in this country.

2.4.7.2 Expert witnesses
The days of the partisan expert witness are over. Any expert witness needs to give the court balanced evidence and, when the evidence of one expert contradicts that of another, the court will expect the experts to meet and to provide assistance to the court that will enable the judge to understand the differences of opinion. A Pre-Action Protocol concerning the instruction of expert witnesses has been incorporated into the CPR and some significant clarification of the way the courts will approach the use of expert evidence has also recently provided. Wherever possible the courts will promote the use of a single joint expert. Judges will very much expect legal representatives and witnesses to comply with that Protocol.

Some clear principles can generally be identified, as follows.

- Experts should be identified and instructed early on.
- Regard should be had to the *overriding objective* in deciding whether an expert on an issue is required at all and, if so, whether a jointly instructed expert would be appropriate.
- If a party acts unreasonably in retaining an expert, he may be penalized in costs (possibly having to pay both parties' costs).
- Whether an expert is instructed jointly or only by one party, his paramount duty is to assist the court.

2.4.8 COSTS

The courts will apply CPR Part 44 robustly. This deals with the court's powers to make costs orders and is intended to support the overriding objective. The court will consider the parties' conduct both pre-action and during the progress of the action. Parties and legal representatives who fail to conduct litigation efficiently and reasonably and with regard to the overriding objective will find that costs orders will come to haunt them in the form either of interim costs orders, payable forthwith, or of unsatisfactory costs orders, payable at the end of the action.

Following the Protocols and seeking the court's approval before significant expense is incurred is sensible practice.

 Costs

There are altogether too many occasions on which a legal representative's dealings with 'costs' are insufficient and lack in foresight. This is remarkable, bearing in mind that 'profitability' is at the forefront of the minds of all practice managers. An example of this lack of foresight that occurs very frequently is the degree of thoroughness that is (not) applied to preparing costs schedules. In the fast track, costs are usually assessed summarily—that is, the judge will consider the costs order at the end of the hearing based on the costs schedules filed by the parties before the hearing. Where the schedule contains insufficient detail of the claim for time spent, then it is all too easy for the opposing party simply to state that the sum of the claim is too lacking in any real detail to be justified, or to question the content of the work done in the time. When it is further considered that fast-track trials may be conducted by a barrister or solicitor-advocate who has not had the day-to-day control of the file, then questions of 'what was done in the time' cannot satisfactorily be answered. Often, in those circumstances, the sum claimed will be significantly reduced by the judge assessing those costs. Where it was simply a case of briefing the barrister or solicitor-advocate properly on the issues within the costs schedule, or in preparing a better and more detailed costs schedule, the sum of costs orders will be unsatisfactory—for you and for your client.

2.4.9 TRIAL

The CPR aim to reduce the number of cases going to trial and where a trial is the only option, the CPR will aim to limit the time of trials. Many of the matters set out in paragraphs 2.4.1–2.4.8 above have an impact in ensuring that cases that are capable of settlement do settle. The rules also ensure (as far as possible) that trials deal with only the real issues remaining between the parties. This will result in shorter trials becoming shorter. Trial dates will be difficult to vacate and so the parties will need to plan properly to ensure that they and their witnesses are ready for trial. Although the risk of a party being 'ambushed' (with new issues or matters) at trial had already been much reduced over the years, the CPR has continued that trend. Expert evidence is now controlled and directed towards assisting the court to understand the technical matters that the court had identified as needed. Outstanding issues that require determination at trial will need to be agreed; skeleton arguments, chronologies, and reading plans are commonly ordered to be provided to the court after agreement between the parties. Also, the court will determine which witnesses are required to give oral evidence at trial after hearing reasons for their essential presence. Any witness evidence that has not been exchanged will rarely be permitted to be adduced. The court may also require a timetable for the conduct of the trial itself and the advocates are usually required to adhere to the set timetable.

2.5 THE COMPUTATION OF TIME

Litigation is frequently about working within a framework of rules with associated time limits. As a legal representative, you will therefore need to know how to calculate a period of time for filing (lodging with the court) or serving (on a third party) that is either specified by the CPR and its Practice Direction (PD) or a judgment or order of the court.

We intend to deal with general time computation and not specific time limits imposed by the CPR, statute, or any service requirements. Those time limits are dealt with in the appropriate chapters later in the book.

2.5.1 PERIODS OF TIME EXPRESSED AS A NUMBER OF MONTHS

If you must do something within 'four months', this implicitly means four calendar months (CPR 2.10).

For example, if you were to issue a claim form on 1 March, it would have to be served within four months after the date of issue—that is, on or before 1 July.

2.5.2 PERIODS OF TIME EXPRESSED AS A NUMBER OF DAYS

The key issues for you to be aware of here are the meaning of 'clear days' and the difference between 'more than five days' or 'less than five days'.

2.5.2.1 'Clear days'
Periods of time expressed in days, whether more or less than five days, implicitly mean 'clear days'. What this means is that in calculating the number of days in which you must do something, you must not include the day on which the period begins, and if the end of the period is defined by reference to an event such as a hearing, then you must not include the day of the event (CPR 2.8(2) and (3)).

For example, if your particulars of claim must be served within 14 days of service of the claim form and the claim form was served on 2 November, then the last day for service of the particulars of claim is 16 November.

2.5.2.2 'More than five days'
If a time period is stated to be more than five days then bank holidays and Saturdays and Sundays are included.

For example, taking the case of the Particulars of Claim above the weekends in November are included in the 14-day calculation.

2.5.2.3 'Less than five days'
Some periods of time are expressed to be five days or less, but bank holidays, Christmas Day, Good Friday and weekends are excluded (CPR 2.8(4)).

For example, if you are to serve an application notice three days before a hearing and the hearing is on 20 February (a Monday), then the last day for service will be 14 February (a Tuesday).

Practical Considerations

Calculating time in these instances can be crucial, so ensure that you read the part of the CPR, judgment, or order carefully. There are occasions on which a step has to be taken within a period of days described as being 'beginning with' a certain day. If that is the case, then that start day is included in the computation of time.

2.5.2.4 An important exception

The main exception to the above points is where you are calculating the deemed date of service (see Chapter 9, paragraph 9.7.1).

2.5.2.5 Filing documents when the court office is closed

CPR 2.8(5) states that where the period of time for filing a document ends on a day on which the court office is closed, the document will be filed in time if it is done on the next day on which the court is open.

2.6 THE IMPACT OF HUMAN RIGHTS LEGISLATION ON CIVIL LITIGATION

2.6.1 HOW ARE THE CPR INTERPRETED?

The CPR have been drafted in 'plain English', the intention being to make them intelligible to a layperson using the courts (representing increased 'access to justice'). When construing the rules, the courts primarily seek to give the words their natural meaning. Where the meaning is clear, the courts do not have the power to interpret a different meaning. However, if the application of the natural meaning of a rule applying traditional rules of construction means that a party's human rights would be infringed, the Human Rights Act 1998, s. 3(1), provides that 'so far as it is possible to do so, . . . (the words) must be read and be given effect in a way that is comparable with the Convention Rights'. The court therefore has the power to interpret the CPR in the light of human rights legislation.

2.6.2 WHAT ARE THE MAIN PROVISIONS OF THE EUROPEAN CONVENTION ON HUMAN RIGHTS (ECHR) THAT HAVE A DIRECT IMPACT ON THE CPR AND THE LITIGATION PROCESS?

Articles 6, 8, and 10 of the European Convention on Human Rights (ECHR) are those that have the most direct impact on the CPR and across which you, as a legal representative, will come most frequently in litigation practice.

2.6.2.1 Article 6—the right to a fair hearing

The provisions under Art. 6 make it clear that any provision that restricts a person's right to submit his claim to a judge may breach the 'right to a fair hearing'. There are many situations in which a person's rights are restricted in this way: for example, where the dispute must be submitted to a tribunal (such as in employment disputes) or to an administrative process (that is, in setting the sum of maintenance that a parent must pay to the other parent with care of the child where the parents are divorced). When this occurs, three questions need to be considered to establish whether the restriction is one that contravenes the right to a fair hearing, as follows.

1. Does the case involve a determination of the person's civil rights and obligations?
2. Is the administrative determination of the person's rights subject to control by the courts?
3. Is the restriction of the person's right to access to the courts proportionate?

In nearly all of the situations in which we see the law apparently restricting a person's right to a fair hearing, we will see that they do not breach Art. 6 once the above three questions are considered.

In *Paul Stretford v The Football Association* [2007] EWCA Civ 238, the Court of Appeal held that a valid clause to submit a dispute to arbitration was not a breach of Art. 6. The Court further stated that the existence of a valid arbitration clause in an agreement constituted a waiver of the right to a 'public' hearing where the arbitration clause was voluntary and not compulsory.

2.6.2.2 Article 8—the right to respect for private and family life

Private and family life includes the relationship between spouses, parents and children, unmarried couples and their children, grandparents and grandchildren, a person's sexual orientation, personal identity, and private space.

Article 8 may be invoked to protect personal and private information, correspondence, telephone conversations, and relationships between people. A balance sometimes has to be struck between the protection provided by Art. 8 and the right to a fair hearing under Art. 6. Where the confidentiality involves children (for example, in a family law hearing), it is generally thought that Art. 8 will take precedence, but where the confidentiality involves adults (for example, in the need for proper and fair disclosure in a civil action), Art. 6 will take precedence. In the latter situation, there are clear limits to any precedence of Art. 6. This has been clearly demonstrated in *Jones v University of Warwick* [2003] 1 WLR 954, in which video evidence of the claimant in personal injury actions has been held to be 'fair' where the video evidence is obtained secretly, but in public places, but not fair if obtained secretly and of the claimant in his own home.

In *Long Beach Ltd and Denis Christel Sassou Nguesso v Global Witness Ltd* [2007] EWHC 1980 (QB), the court examined the balance to be achieved between the claimants' right to privacy under Art. 8 and the rights of the defendant to freedom of expression under Art. 10. The findings in this case were significantly influenced by the fact that the documents (over which the claimants sought the right to privacy) had already come into the 'public' domain as a result of the court proceedings and the public interest in publication.

2.6.2.3 Article 10—the right to freedom of expression

Article 10 provides a qualified right to freedom of expression. The right is qualified by the need to protect another individual's rights or reputation. This Article has altered the common law test applied in the grant of injunctions. Whilst injunctions are outside the scope of this book in its text form, a stand-alone chapter on injunctions appears in the Online Resource Centre.

Also, in defamation claims, there may be proceedings to restrain publication of information that would invade the privacy of another person. *Douglas v Hello! Ltd* [2001] QB 967, the case involving Michael Douglas and Catherine Zeta Jones, involved a breach of the couple's right to privacy of photographs taken of their wedding. In these cases, a balance has to be made between the potentially competing interests of protecting private and family life under Art. 8, and the right to freedom of expression and the protection of the rights and reputation of persons under Art. 10.

In *Ash v McKennitt* [2006] EWCA Civ 1714, the Court of Appeal upheld a judgment preventing publication of certain material in a book. It was considered that the respondent singer's right to privacy under Art. 8 outweighed the right of freedom of expression of the singer's former friend writing the book. The case provides helpful clarification of the law of privacy and breach of confidence, and the basis for balancing the right of privacy with the right of freedom of expression. This balancing exercise was also considered in detail in the case *HRH Prince of Wales v Associated Newspapers Ltd* [2006] EWCA Civ 1776, concluding that where it was obvious that the information was private (as it was here, being contained within a private diary), Art. 8 will prevail.

2.6.3 RAISING HUMAN RIGHTS LEGISLATION IN CIVIL LITIGATION

2.6.3.1 Jurisdiction

Claims under the Human Rights Act 1998, s. 7(1)(a), in respect of a judicial act must be brought in the High Court. Other civil claims under the Human Rights Act 1998 can be brought in the county court or the High Court.

Deputy district judges and masters (whether sitting in the High Court or in a county court) cannot hear claims under the Human Rights Act 1998.

2.6.3.2 Statements of case

Form N1 (the claim form) and notices of appeal have boxes on the printed form in which the claimant must state whether a Human Rights Act 1998 point is being raised in the action or in the appeal. If it is, then full particulars of the point must be set out in the particulars of claim or appeal claim.

2.6.3.3 A declaration of incompatibility

The court may not make a declaration of incompatibility under the Human Rights Act 1998, s. 4, unless 21 days' notice has been given to the Crown (Human Rights Act 1998, s. 5, and CPR 19.4A(1)). Directions requiring notice will usually be made at the first CMC and a Minister, or other person permitted by the Human Rights Act 1998, is entitled to be joined on application by the Minister or by direction of the court.

2.6.3.4 In claims for damages for a breach of a human right

Where a claim is made for damages for a breach of a human right, notice must be given to the Crown.

KEY POINTS SUMMARY

- Understand that litigation today is underpinned by the overriding objective.

- Be aware of the impact of the CPR on how you conduct the resolution of a dispute for your clients.

- Check your time limits when calculating periods of time.

- Take account of human rights issues when proceeding with a claim.

SELF-TEST QUESTIONS

1. What role does the court have in the conduct of litigation?

2. The implementation of the CPR resulted in a significant change in the way in which practitioners approach dispute resolution. Name two of the most significant changes that the CPR have brought about.

3. When a part of the CPR indicates when an order should be complied with by reference to a number of days, is the date of the order and/or the date by which the order must be complied with included in calculating the number of days?

online
resource
centre

Suggested answers to these general questions can be accessed by adopting lecturers on the Online Resource Centre. Your lecturer can provide these to you.

3 COSTS INFORMATION TO THE CLIENT AND FUNDING OPTIONS

3.1 INTRODUCTION

When a legal representative takes instructions from a client at the outset of a new matter, he is obliged to give to the client the best information possible about the likely costs of pursuing and ultimately resolving the dispute, as well as discussing with the client the best way of funding the action.

In both of these areas of advice to the client, there have been recent reforms to the regulatory framework that govern the costs information and funding advice given, including the Solicitors' Code of Conduct 2007 and the abolition of the Conditional Fee Agreements (CFAs) Regulations.

But beware, with the Ministry of Justice having recently published a consultation on Lord Jackson's costs review, and the Solicitors' Regulation Authority currently consulting on a revised 'Code of Practice' (see Chapter 1 paragraph 1.8), there could be some far-reaching reforms to come later this year.

This chapter will focus on the current regime in relation to professional conduct and CFAs and will cover the following:

- what information your client needs to know about costs, including a review of Rule 2.03 of the Solicitors' Code of Conduct 2007 and its impact on the advice to be given;

- the different types of funding options currently available to a client, predominantly concentrating on CFAs and 'after the event' (ATE) insurance.

A brief overview of Lord Jackson's proposals relevant to funding is set out later in this chapter. This will help you identify the trend of any possible future changes.

3.2 **THE SOLICITORS' CODE OF CONDUCT 2007**

The Solicitors' Code of Conduct 2007 contains, amongst other things, the rules setting out what information a solicitor should give to his client about costs. The Code is particular to solicitors, but essentially applies to all those in legal practice. Rule 2, 'Client relations', is the relevant rule for this chapter and we are going to focus on Rule 2.03 on information about the cost. The Code is supplemented by detailed Guidance Notes relating to each individual rule within the Code.

 Professional Conduct

The Code must be taken seriously and its rules are mandatory. The Guidance Notes are not mandatory, but it is likely that they will be used to interpret the mandatory rules contained in the Code. Additionally, the Code has statutory force. (See later for the full effect on a solicitor in breach of the Code.)

3.2.1 **RULE 2.03—INFORMATION ABOUT THE COST**

3.2.1.1 **Rule 2.03(1)**

(1) As a legal representative, you must give your client the best possible information about the likely overall cost of a matter both at the outset and, where appropriate, as the matter progresses. In particular you must:

(a) advise the client of the basis and terms of your charges;

(b) advise the client if charging rates are to be increased;

(c) advise the client of likely payments which you or your client may need to make to others;

(d) discuss with the client how the client will pay, in particular:

  (i) whether the client may be eligible and should apply for public funding; and

  (ii) whether the client's own costs are covered by insurance or may be paid by someone else such as an employer or trade union;

(e) advise the client that there are circumstances where you may be entitled to exercise a lien for unpaid costs; [A lien is an equitable charge exercisable over property—in this case, the file of papers. It is the charge that allows the solicitor to retain the file until all outstanding costs have been paid. Whilst the file technically belongs to the client, he is not entitled to possession of it until he has cleared all of his bills.]

(f) advise the client of the potential liability for any other party's costs; and

(g) discuss with the client whether their liability for another party's costs may be covered by existing insurance or whether specially purchased insurance may be obtained.

 Costs

It is extremely difficult to provide an estimate of the overall likely cost of a matter to the client. The Guidance Notes to Rule 2.03 suggest that the legal representative only provides the client with as much information as possible at the outset and then keeps the client updated. If a precise figure cannot be given at the outset, the legal representative should explain the reason to the client and agree a maximum figure.

3.2.1.2 Rule 2.03(2)

(2) Where you are acting for the client under a conditional fee agreement [CFA], (including a collective conditional fee agreement) in addition to complying with 2.03(1) above and 2.03(5) and (6) below, you must explain the following, both at the outset and, when appropriate, as the matter progresses:

(a) the circumstances in which your client may be liable for your costs and whether you will seek payment of these from the client, if entitled to do so;

(b) if you intend to seek payment of any or all of your costs from your client, you must advise your client of their right to an assessment of those costs; and

(c) where applicable, the fact that you are obliged under a fee sharing agreement to pay to a charity any fees which you receive by way of costs from the client's opponent or other third party.

3.2.1.3 Rule 2.03(3)

(3) Where you are acting for a publicly funded client, in addition to complying with 2.03(1) above and 2.03(5) and (6) below, you must explain the following at the outset:

(a) the circumstances in which they may be liable for your costs;

(b) the effect of the statutory charge;

(c) the client's duty to pay any fixed or periodic contribution assessed and the consequence of failing to do so; and

(d) that even if your client is successful, the other party may not be ordered to pay costs or may not be in a position to pay them.

3.2.1.4 Rule 2.03(4)

(4) Where you agree to share your fees with a charity in accordance with 8.01(h) you must disclose to the client at the outset the name of the charity.

3.2.1.5 Rule 2.03(5)

(5) Any information about the costs must be clear and confirmed in writing.

3.2.1.6 Rule 2.03(6)

(6) You must discuss with your client whether the potential outcomes of any legal case will justify the expense or risk involved including, if relevant, the risk of having to pay an opponent's costs.

3.2.1.7 Rule 2.03(7)

(7) If you can demonstrate that it was inappropriate in the circumstances to meet some or all of the requirements in 2.03(1) and (5) above, you will not breach 2.03.

 Practical Considerations

Rule 2.03(7) can be a tricky rule to satisfy. However, it is generally accepted that you will not be in breach of 2.03(7) if you do repeat work for a client on agreed terms (although increases in charge-out rates and changes in fee earners should still be notified in writing) or if you are an in-house legal representative.

3.2.2 **HOW DOES THE LEGAL REPRESENTATIVE IN PRACTICE COMPLY WITH RULE 2.03?**

In order not to fall foul of your professional conduct obligations here, the Code's requirements should be dealt with at the outset of a new matter. This is discussed at Chapter 6, paragraph 6.2.

As the matter progresses, the legal representative has a continuous duty to update the client about costs, as well as to ensure that he complies with the specific requirements under the Civil Procedure Rules (CPR) on costs, such as providing costs estimates at any stage of the litigation (particularly at allocation in multi track cases, most case management hearings, and at the pre-trial stage—see Chapter 12), under CPR 44.2 in relation to adverse costs orders made against the client in his absence and CPR 44.14(3) regarding wasted costs orders.

In addition to focusing on the Code, clients involved in litigation need to be aware of the following issues, which have an impact on the costs information that needs to be given to them:

- the loser generally pays the winner's costs—but this is not always the case, because costs are ultimately in the discretion of the court;

- the court will look at the conduct of the parties when making a decision about who pays costs;

- what options there are for resolving their dispute, such as mediation or another form of alternative dispute resolution (ADR);

- the fact that litigation is expensive;

- there should be a review of the cost-benefit analysis at key stages, such as disclosure and witness statement exchange—an analysis that is fundamentally based on the underlying principle of proportionality when undertaking work on behalf of a client and may include reviewing the merits of the case, the total costs of the action at particular stages and to trial, the client's resources or the terms of a funding or insurance agreement, the opponent's ability to pay any judgment against him, and the likelihood of enforcing a judgment against the opponent;

- costs are quantified on two bases: standard and indemnity (defined in Chapter 4, paragraph 4.3.2);

- costs are assessed pursuant to either a summary assessment or a detailed assessment. (These procedures are set out in the Online Resource Centre chapter on 'Assessment of Costs'.)

online resource centre

3.2.3 WHAT ARE THE CONSEQUENCES IF YOU BREACH THE CODE?

As indicated above, the Code has a statutory effect, as well as a disciplinary effect. Essentially, this means that a breach of the requirements of the Code renders you liable to pay damages to the client and to a reduction of the bill, as well as to conditions being placed on your practising certificate (if you are a solicitor), a fine, a suspension, or even being struck off the Roll. These sanctions are all separate from the client's right to pursue a negligence claim against you, if appropriate. This occurred in the case of *Eversheds v Michael and Simone Cuddy* [2009] EWHC 90154 (Costs), which serves as a reminder of the importance of keeping clients informed of the costs position on their cases. It emphasized the need for solicitors to comply with both their professional conduct obligations and their own terms of business and highlighted the importance of keeping detailed attendance notes of any discussions about costs as well as a written record of the costs information that has been provided to the client.

3.3 DIFFERENT METHODS OF FUNDING A CLAIM

When you take initial instructions from your client, you will need to consider in some detail with him how he is going to fund his claim or his defence of a claim. There are a number of options that may or may not be available to your client, but it is best to sit down with your client and discuss each option with him, so as to find the most appropriate method of funding.

Below are listed the different methods. Each will be discussed in turn, but CFAs and ATE insurance will be dealt with in some detail, because these feature heavily in the current litigation climate.

3.3.1 'BEFORE THE EVENT' (BTE) INSURANCE

Many clients have existing insurance in respect of motor vehicles and property. Under the terms of these policies, the client may have (sometimes unbeknown to him) legal expenses insurance that may cover payment of some/all of his own and his opponent's legal costs of a civil action, if necessary.

A legal representative should ask his client to check all existing insurance policies to ascertain whether such cover is provided, the extent of the cover, and whether it is appropriate. If your client is relying on such a policy to fund an action, it will be appropriate for the legal representative himself to look at the terms of the policy. (See paragraph 3.3.7.2 below for a fuller discussion of this.)

3.3.2 PRIVATE FUNDS

Private funds are the traditional method of paying for litigation, and the client's ability to pay privately very much depends on his own resources available from capital and income. It is more usual for commercial clients to pay privately than individuals.

The client will pay the legal representative's costs of conducting the case at an agreed hourly rate, plus disbursements and VAT. (For a full discussion on how those costs are made up and assessed, see Chapter 4, paragraphs 4.3.2 and 4.4.) In accordance with the terms of the retainer set out in the client care letter, the client will usually be billed on an interim basis every month for work done.

 Professional Conduct

The client should be informed that, if he is successful, his costs are likely to be more than any amount of costs recoverable from his opponent. This is for several reasons:

- the opponent will always attempt to compromise your costs as a matter of principle;

- you will usually advise your client to accept, with your client's express authority, a lesser amount for your costs to avoid the further expense and time commitment of a detailed assessment of those costs;

- in pursuing a claim on behalf of your client in accordance with your professional conduct obligations and doing the best for your client, you will almost certainly spend time on the case that will simply be irrecoverable if the matter proceeds to a detailed assessment: for example, attending on the client for an hour when your opponent would argue that 30 minutes was reasonable, or spending six hours drafting and reviewing your client's witness statement, when three-and-a-half hours may have been reasonable.

In litigation, when a costs recovery order has been made in your client's favour, this will not generally cover the time spent on certain aspects of the case and thus, although it is work properly done on the file (for example, interviewing or taking a statement from a witness that you ultimately decide not to use) and is work for which your client should pay, it will not be part of the costs of the action.

In practice, there is an unwritten rule that there is usually to be expected, in most cases, a shortfall of 20–30 per cent in the recovery of costs.

3.3.3 UNION AND ASSOCIATION FUNDING

If your client is a member of a trade union or other association, he may have funding in place by virtue of his membership to cover his own, and possibly his opponent's, legal fees if he loses. It is incumbent on the legal representative to ask the client at the first meeting whether he is a member of a union or association.

It may well be that further enquiries are needed to ascertain relevant cover, but care must be taken by the legal representative to ask the client in a clear and unambiguous manner about membership details. If it is the case that the client has union funding, it is very likely that the union will insist, in accordance with the terms of membership, that panel solicitors be appointed to represent the client. In this case, you must inform the client that if he is to take advantage of this, then he must terminate any retainer that he has with you and you must forward to the client any relevant documentation.

3.3.4 PUBLIC FUNDING

Public funding in civil matters is effected through the Legal Services Commission (LSC), which runs a scheme known as the 'Community Legal Service' that began in April 2000.

The way in which public funding works today is that it is only solicitors' practices that have a contract with the LSC that can undertake publicly funded work. As has already been seen from Rule 2.03(3) of the Code, legal representatives have a specific professional conduct duty in terms of information given to the client on costs.

In order to be eligible for public funding, the client has to satisfy a financial eligibility test and a merits test before the level of service from the LSC is decided upon. Details of all of the materials governing public funding can be found in the Legal Services Commission Manual and on the LSC website—http://www.legalservices.gov.uk. If public funding is available, it can be offered, subject to the satisfaction of the means and merits test, on a partial contribution basis by the client out of his disposable capital or income paid to the LSC on a monthly basis, or the client can be wholly publicly funded with no contribution.

However, there are a number of excluded categories of work that cannot be funded by the LSC and these include (not exhaustively) all personal injury work and matters of a property, trust, probate, or commercial nature—that is, essentially, most areas of civil and commercial litigation. Due to these far-reaching exclusions, LSC funding is not looked at in any detail in this book.

3.3.5 CONDITIONAL FEE AGREEMENTS (CFAS)

3.3.5.1 When did CFAs come about?

CFAs have existed in England and Wales since 1995, and are a common method of funding for most types of civil action—in particular, personal injury matters. However, the regulatory framework that governed CFAs changed in November 2005 and this is dealt with below.

3.3.5.2 What are CFAs?

A CFA is essentially an agreement for litigation services under which the legal representative's fees and expenses, or any part of them, are payable only in particular circumstances (Courts and Legal Services Act 1990, s. 58). CFAs are available to claimants and defendants, and can stand alone or be used in conjunction with ATE insurance.

There are a number of different types of CFA, depending on the fee agreement between the client and the law firm. The most common types of CFA are those with a success fee, a discounted CFA with no success fee, and a hybrid CFA, which provides for a discounted fee in the event of losing, but a success fee in the event of winning. These are looked at below.

However, there is also a fourth type of CFA without a success fee (also known as a 'Thai Trading agreement'), whereby the law firm agrees to forgo all of its fees if the client loses, but will recover base costs if he wins.

3.3.5.2.1 *CFA with a success fee*

A CFA with a success fee is the most common agreement and is very often used in personal injury claims. Basically, the client pays no legal costs to his legal representative throughout the duration of his case. If the client wins, the legal representative is entitled to charge an agreed percentage uplift to his base costs (these are the normal legal costs based on an hourly rate), known as an 'additional liability', or 'success fee'. If the client loses, there is no charge to the client for the base costs incurred and no success fee is levied. In both cases, win or lose, the legal representative is entitled to the payment of disbursements.

(See the 'Case study documentation' section of the Online Resource Centre for an example of a CFA with success fee.)

 Practical Considerations

The terms of payment from the client to the legal representative whether he wins or loses will ultimately depend on the terms of the CFA. For example, some CFAs will require payment of disbursements to be paid by the client as the case progresses. Other firms may make a decision to pay the disbursements as they arise and recoup them from the client or the opponent, depending on whether the case is successful or not.

3.3.5.2.2 *Discounted CFAs*

A discounted CFA more commonly features in commercial cases, and operates on the basis that an enhanced percentage on base costs is charged to the client as the litigation progresses and that the client pays as he goes along. If the client is successful, then there is no further enhancement, but if the client loses, then the legal costs are reduced and a reimbursement may be made to the client. (See the 'Case study documentation' section of the Online Resource Centre for an example of a discounted CFA.)

With the demise of public funding in civil litigation, part of the aim of the expansion of the use of CFAs for funding purposes was to provide access to justice, and to encourage the risks of litigation to be shared between the client litigant and the person most able to assess the level of that risk—the legal representative. A legal representative is unlikely to take on an action if he stands too great a risk of not being paid if the action is lost.

3.3.5.2.3 *The hybrid CFA*

Whilst hybrid CFAs have been in existence for some time, in *Gloucestershire County Council v Evans* [2008] EWCA Civ 21, the Court of Appeal has now confirmed that it is possible to have this type of CFA notwithstanding that CFA legislation has failed to refer to them. The Court of Appeal has also helpfully given some guidance on the amount that would be subject to the success fee if the funded party were to be successful here.

It held that the success fee should be applied to the basic charges, and not the difference between the discounted charges and the basic charges (that is, the costs at risk) as argued by the defendant. In *Gloucestershire County Council*, the basic charges were £145 per hour and the discounted rate was £95 per hour, with the costs at risk according to the defendant being £50 per hour.

The rationale behind the Court's decision was that the success fee should be applied to the hourly rate that would have been in place had the retainer not been a CFA—or a collective conditional fee agreement (CCFA), as in this case—which would, of course, be the basic and not the discounted charges.

Whether your client enters into a CFA with or without a success fee or a hybrid CFA, these funding agreements can introduce a tactical advantage to your client as against his opponent, especially when accompanied by ATE insurance. The message sent is that the client's legal representative believes that the case is strong enough to persuade him to enter into a CFA under which there is always a litigation risk that he may lose some or all of his legal costs incurred. If the risk were too high, the legal representative would not agree to act.

3.3.5.2.4 *What about 'no win, no fee'?*

In this country, any CFA is commonly known as a 'no win, no fee' agreement. This is not an accurate description of a retainer on this basis.

Let us consider the example of a CFA with a success fee. This allows a legal representative to undertake a case for a client without receiving payment in respect of his legal costs throughout the duration of the case. If the case is lost, the legal representative is entitled to the payment of disbursements from his client and, as such, there is a financial consequence to the client. If the case is won, the legal representative is entitled to charge base costs, plus a success fee—the idea being that the success fee is compensation for running the risk of not being paid at all and for postponing payment. Some of these costs may be recoverable from the opponent, but not all—particularly the cost of the postponement element of the success fee. Therefore, whether your client wins or loses his case, when being funded by a CFA with a success fee, he is likely to have to make some type of payment to his legal representative. This will be discussed in more detail in paragraph 3.3.5.5 below.

3.3.5.3 The regulation of CFAs

3.3.5.3.1 *What governs CFAs?*

There are three sources of authority by which CFAs are to be regulated:

- the Courts and Legal Services Act 1990;
- the Conditional Fee Agreements Order 2000, SI 2000/823; and
- the Solicitors' Code of Conduct 2007.

3.3.5.3.2 *What does the legal representative need to discuss when advising his client on entering into a CFA?*

There are only six mandatory requirements that a legal representative must bring to his client's attention and these are as follows.

- It must be in writing.
- It must not relate to proceedings that cannot be the subject of an enforceable CFA (that is, criminal and family proceedings).
- The maximum amount of the success fee must not exceed 100 per cent of the base costs.
- You must explain to your client when he may be liable for his own and his opponent's costs.
- You must explain the client's entitlement to an assessment of costs when you intend to seek payment of costs from your client.
- You must disclose to your client whether you have any interest in any funding policy.

 Practical Considerations

Practically, it is advisable to consider matters from your client's perspective: a client receiving a standard Solicitors' Regulation Authority (SRA) CFA with a success fee, plus the nine-page leaflet such as that which appears on the Online Resource Centre, will be very much at a loss if he is expected to read and understand all of this material on his own. Additionally, he needs to know that this is still a legally binding contract, and that it represents the retainer between himself and the firm.

The six requirements noted above make no mention of explaining to the client how the success fee works and is calculated. We deal with this below in paragraph 3.3.5.5.1. Essentially, you should explain the terms of the CFA to your client in detail, probably at a meeting, and back up important aspects in writing. The aspects that you may wish to discuss are likely to include:

- what happens on termination of the agreement;
- why the success fee has been set at a certain level;
- the extent to which the success fee reflects an allowance for delayed payment (as opposed to simply the risk of losing); and
- what provisions for the reasons behind the success fee need to be disclosed to the court (including provisions that any shortfall between the success fee and that ordered to be recovered from the losing party may be recovered only with the permission of the court).

 online resource centre

3.3.5.4 What happens if you fail to adhere to these requirements?

If you fail to explain the requirements under the Courts and Legal Services Act 1990 to your client (that is, that the CFA must be in writing, that it must not relate to criminal and family proceedings, and that the maximum amount of the success fee must not exceed

100 per cent of the base costs), then the CFA is very likely to be held unenforceable. What this means is that you may be deemed to have had an unenforceable contract with your client and therefore to have had no legal basis upon which to charge for the work done, effectively preventing you from recovering your legal costs from either your client or his opponent.

If you fail to comply with Rule 2.03 of the Solicitors' Code of Conduct 2007 (that is, that you must explain to your client when he may be liable for his own and his opponent's costs, that you must explain the client's entitlement to an assessment of costs when you intend to seek payment of costs from your client, and that you must disclose to your client whether you have any interest in any funding policy), then you may face disciplinary charges and sanctions, but the Guidance Notes to the Rule seem to suggest that it is unlikely that the CFA will be invalid.

Any breach in this particular situation will not, however, prevent you from recovering, if your client wins, any disbursements and the insurance premium. It is only the legal costs that will remain irrecoverable.

3.3.5.5 The success fee

As discussed above, the success fee is the additional liability or enhancement of the legal representative's base costs and this cannot represent more than 100 per cent of the base costs. For example, if the winning party's base costs were £20,000, the success fee could not exceed £20,000, making a maximum legal costs figure of £40,000. Under the provisions of s. 29 of the Access to Justice Act 1999, the success fee is recoverable from the losing party.

 Practical Considerations

The issue of whether the client suffers the burden of the success fee is usually dependent on the form of the costs order made by the court (the court may not order a total recovery), the contract for the recovery of the success fee from his legal representative, and any insurance premium (see below) that may pay any shortfall. It is therefore very difficult ever to give clients a definitive answer to the question, 'how much will it cost me?' The form of the costs order made by the court is entirely within the discretion of the court; therefore, it is not possible to tell a client exactly, or with certainty, what the costs consequences will be of the litigation contemplated. In advising clients about the costs risks of litigation, it is advisable to use words such as 'most likely', 'likely', 'probably', or similar. Words of certainty should not be used when advising any client about the extent of costs recoverable or payable by the client.

3.3.5.5.1 *How is the success fee calculated?*

There are two aspects to the calculation of the success fee. The success fee represents the risk factor to the legal representative of taking on the litigation (Practice Direction 43–48.11.8) and the fact that the legal representative is, in effect, postponing being paid his legal costs until the resolution of the claim. Whatever percentage is attached to each, the global success fee must not total more than 100 per cent of the base costs. It is important to note here that if the client wins, it is only the part of the success fee that relates to the risk assessment that is recoverable from the opponent if a favourable costs order is made. The part of the success fee that relates to the cost of postponement is payable by the client and not the opponent (CPR 44.3B(1)(a)). The client therefore needs to understand that if he wins, he will be required to pay to his legal representative an amount to reflect this and that this percentage will have been set out in the CFA itself. Obviously, if the client loses, no part of the success fee becomes payable by the client.

Professional Conduct

In *Utting v McBain* [2007] EWHC 90085 (costs), under the abolished Regulations, the court considered that even if the solicitor for the successful party had allocated a nil percentage to the postponement element of the success fee, that solicitor was still obliged to explain how the global success fee is, or could be, made up. Under the new regime and the Solicitors' Code of Conduct 2007, the authors believe that it will be good practice to do the same, even though there are now no legal requirements to explain how the success fee is made up.

How this global success fee is actually calculated will depend on each case and firms may have their own policy on this. Some firms will undertake the risk assessment based on a case-by-case basis, while others will look at a cross-section of similar cases and consider the probability of success in that way. Further guidance is also given in sections 11.7–11.10 of PD 43–48, which stipulate what is a reasonable amount for a success fee.

There have, however, been a plethora of cases on the overall percentage of success fees recoverable—in particular, in road traffic accidents. Some helpful guidance has been given as a result of these cases and the suggested success fee ranges from 12.5 per cent in fast-track value road traffic accident cases that settle early, to 100 per cent in more complex personal injury litigation. Each case should be considered with reference to its particular facts. (For details of these cases and the success fees, see Chapter 4, paragraph 4.4.5.1.)

It is also possible, and indeed popular, to have staged success fees, starting low and increasing as the case progresses, or starting high and decreasing if admissions of liability are made (again, see Chapter 4, paragraph 4.4.5.1).

3.3.6 'AFTER THE EVENT' (ATE) INSURANCE

3.3.6.1 What is ATE insurance?

ATE insurance generally works in one of two ways within the realms of litigation. Its most popular use is to supplement a CFA. It can provide insurance to cover the case in which the client loses and is ordered to pay some or all of his opponent's legal costs and disbursements, as well as his own disbursements. The second way in which it is used is as a stand-alone insurance policy without a CFA, whereby the client is seeking funding from a reputable insurer against his own and his opponent's legal costs and disbursements.

ATE insurance is only available after the dispute has arisen and should only be obtained if there is no other insurance or funding option available to the client. (See paragraphs 3.3.6.3 and 3.3.7 below for discussions on the consequences of taking out ATE insurance where BTE insurance is already in place.) ATE insurance will never cover the payment of a court order or judgment in respect of damages.

3.3.6.2 The premium

As with all insurance policies, the client is responsible for payment of the premium, and the level of the premium is usually based on the strength of the case and the level of cover required. In the ATE market for personal injury claims, the premium is not too onerous, usually totalling less than £500. However, in commercial cases, it is not uncommon for premiums to be as much as 20–30 per cent of the amount of cover required. For example, if the client seeks cover in respect of an adverse costs order only, and his legal representative believes that the opponent's likely legal costs and disbursements are in the region of £20,000, then the premium will be approximately £4,000–6,000. Insurance providers will generally fix the premium of ATE insurance in commercial matters on a case-by-case basis.

As you can see, premiums can be expensive, but some insurers will allow the staged payment of premiums, or for premiums to be paid at the conclusion of proceedings. Otherwise, you may need to consider with your client whether he should take out a loan to pay for the premium and claim the interest back from the opponent if successful in his claim.

 Professional Conduct

Legal representatives must exercise care when discussing with the client which ATE policy and insurer should be used, because they do not want to be found to have been in breach of Rule 19 of the Solicitors' Code of Conduct. The legal representative should therefore expressly give no guarantees that the means of funding adopted will be the most appropriate and inform the client of any constraints. In practice, there are now many specialist ATE brokers who, for a small fee, will locate a selection of policies for the client's needs and the client can then choose. However, there is a cost implication, because the application forms are detailed, and require the legal representative to give a full review of the case and his views on the prospects of success. If the prospects are lower than 50–60 per cent, it is unlikely that an insurer will underwrite the policy, unless in exchange for an extremely high premium.

3.3.6.3 The recoverability of the premium

The premium, in principle, in respect of ATE cover is recoverable (Access to Justice Act 1999, s. 29), although in accordance with CPR 44.4 and 44.5, it must be reasonably incurred, and reasonable and proportionate in amount. PD 43–48.11.10, sets out the court's specific considerations relating to insurance cover as follows:

(1) where the insurance cover is not purchased in support of a conditional fee agreement with a success fee, how its cost compares with the likely cost of funding the case with a conditional fee agreement with a success fee and supporting the insurance cover;

(2) the level and extent of the cover provided;

(3) the availability of any pre-existing insurance cover;

(4) whether any part of the premium would be rebated in the event of an early settlement;

(5) the amount of commission payable to the receiving party or his legal representatives or other agents.

In recent years, there has been much case law and discussion focusing on the circumstances in which a premium can be recovered. The main issues raised by the losing party relate to the timing of the policy—that is, whether it is ever reasonable to assert that the ATE was taken out too early (*Callery v Gray Nos 1 and 2* [2002] UKHL 28) and whether it is reasonable for a claimant to use an ATE policy in place of a BTE policy (*Sarwar v Alam* [2001] EWCA Civ 1401). In *Callery*, the House of Lords held that the ATE premium was recoverable pre-issue if the amount was reasonable. In *Sarwar*, the Court of Appeal established that a legal representative is under a duty to make reasonable enquiries to identify whether there is a BTE policy, although there may be circumstances in which it may be inappropriate to use it.

The issue of the recoverability of an ATE premium is often tied up in arguments raised by the losing party on the enforceability of the CFA that accompanies the ATE. This is discussed further below.

3.3.7 THE ENFORCEABILITY OF CFAS BOTH WITH AND WITHOUT A SUCCESS FEE

The pre-November 2005 era created much case law relating to the enforceability of CFAs. The main reasons for these CFAs being ultimately rendered unenforceable were the onerous duty on legal representatives to comply with 'information to the client' and failing to enquire as to alternate sources of funding. These cases are currently still of importance although the notable lack of significant judgments on this aspect since the rule changes in 2005 demonstrate fewer cases being contested on these issues—a good thing for claimants!

3.3.7.1 Information to the client

The key case on this is *Hollins v Russell* [2003] EWCA Civ 718, in which it was established that if there were a material breach that had an adverse effect on the client, then the CFA would be unenforceable. The Court of Appeal went further in *Jones v Caradon Catnic Ltd* [2006] EWCA 3 (Costs LR 427), in which it held that the CFA was unenforceable even though there was no material adverse affect to the client. It is still yet to be seen how the court will tackle the issue of material breach in the post-November 2005 CFAs.

3.3.7.2 Enquiries in relation to BTE

There is some debate as to how far a legal representative must go to ascertain whether there is any pre-existing insurance, public funding, or trade union membership cover, and whether this constitutes a material breach so as to render the associated CFA unenforceable. *Myatt v NCB* [2006] EWCA Civ 1017 suggested that the overall test was that there was now an implied obligation on a legal representative to take reasonable steps to ascertain BTE cover and that what was reasonable would depend on the circumstances of the case. As suggested in paragraph 3.3.7.1 above, the court had given this a strict interpretation so as to render a CFA unenforceable if 'adequate enquiries' had not been made. However, in *Woolley v Haden Building Services Ltd* [2008] EWHC 90097 (Costs), the court held that despite the claimant's solicitor's decision to ask his client to check her household contents insurance for legal expenses cover without checking it himself, he had done enough to avoid a material breach of the regulations.

This case can, however, be contrasted with *Kilby v Gawith* [2008] EWCA Civ 812, in which the Court of Appeal held that the claimant—who had BTE, but nevertheless entered into a CFA with a success fee in her personal injury claim—was entitled to recover the fixed success fee of 12.5 per cent because there was no discretion under CPR 45.11(2) to enable the Court to decide whether a success fee was allowed and, if so, how much. This is a good example of court rules overriding the court's discretion in particular types of predictable costs case (see Chapter 4, paragraphs 4.4.5 and 4.7.1).

These latter two cases seem to demonstrate a willingness on the part of the court to allow CFAs with success fees to stand irrespective of legitimate challenges to their enforceability on a variety of grounds.

3.3.8 THIRD-PARTY FUNDING AND CHAMPERTY

Third-party funding, whilst now an acceptable option for litigation funding, is partly born out of the principle of 'champerty'.

Champerty involved the funding of a party's case by a non-party on the basis of the funder's financial interest in the damages awarded. For example, a commercial entity may offer to fund either the prosecution or defence of a dispute in return for a share of the damages awarded. This type of arrangement was known as 'champertous' and contrary to public policy, and otherwise illegal. An illegal contract is therefore unenforceable, which would prevent the recovery of any legal costs as against the opponent, in line with the indemnity principle.

However, the Court of Appeal in *Arkin v Bourchard Lines* [2005] EWCA Civ 655 decided that an individual's right to access to justice must override the doctrine of champerty, but with a 'penalty' to the funder (see below).

Third-party funding is now legal and essentially involves the provision of funds by individuals or companies who have no other connection with the litigation. A funder may provide the full legal costs of the proceedings, may partly fund the proceedings, or may fund only disbursements. Protection from adverse costs orders is often, but not always, provided and, in some circumstances, the funder may provide no direct funding at all, but instead agree to cover a party's potential exposure to adverse costs. In return, the funder would expect to make a financial profit for its outlay.

This profit is usually calculated on a contingency fee basis, perhaps in addition to any costs recovered from the opponent, or is assessed based on a multiplier of the investment provided—that is, if the funder puts in £50,000, it may require £50,000 to be multiplied by a specified figure as a return on its investment.

The 'penalty' to the funder if the funded party loses is that the court has a discretion to order that the funder—effectively, a non-party to the litigation—be ordered to pay the costs of the successful opponent, rather than the funded party. The court derives its authority from s. 51(1) and (3) of the Senior Courts Act 1981. The discretion, it would seem from *Arkin,* is only exercised in exceptional circumstances—such as where the funder seeks to control the litigation and/or benefits from its outcome. Conversely, a funder who has no personal interest in the litigation, who seeks to derive no benefit, and who retains no control over it is unlikely to find itself the subject of such a costs order.

There is however a presumption against making a s. 51 order against a 'pure' funder, as opposed to a professional funder, such as an insurance company. In *Jackson v Thakrar* [2007] EWHC 626 (TCC), the court held that such orders were exceptional and, for the court to exercise its discretion in favour of an order, there needed to be a causational element: did the funding provided by the non-party cause the opponent to incur costs that would not otherwise have been incurred? If those costs would have been incurred in any event, then it is unlikely that the court will make an order under s. 51. For the courts to make these orders, applications will need to be made on notice. (See *Hitachi Capital (UK) plc v V-12 Finance Ltd* [2009] EWHC 2432 (Comm).)

 Practical Considerations

Because third-party funding is now a real alternative to CFAs in the litigation market, when discussing funding options with your client, you will need to raise the possibility of this type of funding. A competent legal representative should also consider seeking costs against a non-party, especially in situations in which an unsuccessful opponent does not 'look good for the money'. Equally, a person considering supporting the litigation of another will require careful advice to avoid making himself a potential target for a costs application.

Third-party funding is a developing area and the Civil Justice Council (CJC) is currently looking at the regulation of third-party funding agreements. A code for third party funders is within the remit of Lord Justice Jackson's review of litigation costs. This is dealt with below.

3.3.9 WHAT NEXT FOR FUNDING?

Lord Jackson completed his wide-ranging review of the civil litigation costs system in January 2010. His recommendations covered aspects of funding highlighted below in Figure 3.1.

The current impetus behind the implementation of some/all of the recommendations lies with the Ministry of Justice who, at the time of updating the handbook, are still consulting. It is the authors' view that it is only those recommendations, with clear cost-cutting attributes, that will be implemented. The potential changes are tentatively thought to be as follows:

- Further consultation into the recovery of the success fee and ATE premium.

- The introduction of contingency fee agreements. A step in this direction has tentatively been taken by the Court of Appeal in the case of *Regina Sibthorpe v London Borough of Southwark* [2011] EWCA Civ 25 where it was held that the claimants' solicitor's funding arrangements were not champertous: the claimants' solicitors had entered into a CFA with a success fee but had agreed that if the claimants lost and an adverse costs order was made against them, then the solicitor would indemnify the claimants in respect of their costs not covered by insurance. The reasoning behind this judgment is thought to be twofold: firstly, there had been no cases where such an arrangement had previously been held to be champertous (despite the fact that the solicitor clearly had a financial interest in the outcome of the litigation); and, secondly, it would probably be inappropriate to extend the law of champerty when there is a clear drive to curtail it.

FIGURE 3.1

CURRENT POSITION	LORD JACKSON'S PROPOSALS
1. No current policy on push towards BTE by insurers.	The take up of BTE should be encouraged by insurers when individuals take out motor or household policies, and by the Department for Business, Innovation and Skills in respect of small- and medium-sized businesses. The aim is not to make BTE compulsory but to increase the extent of these policies.
2. The success fee (only the risk element) is recoverable from the opponent where a party has secured a favourable costs order.	The recoverability of the success fee should be abolished and linked to this to reflect the potential imbalance to the claimant, the level of general damages for personal injury claims, nuisance and other civil wrongs should be increased by 10 per cent. As a fall-back position Lord Jackson has recommended that there should be a regime of regulated fixed success fees.
3. The ATE premium (as long as this is reasonable in amount and reasonably and proportionately incurred) is recoverable from the opponent where a party has secured a favourable costs order.	The recoverability of ATE premiums should be abolished or at the very least, there should be restrictions on the circumstances in which it can be recovered and the amount of the premium.
4. Tentative moves towards the use of third party funding as a legitimate method of funding claims and defences. It is currently unregulated and third party funders have limited liability in respect of an adverse costs order against them.	Third party funding should continue to develop. To aid this development, there should be a voluntary code for all litigation funders and regulation by the FSA should be encouraged. Further the judgment in *Arkin* above should be repealed allowing third party funders to face the full potential for adverse costs orders against them. Additionally the extent of their liability should not be limited by the amount of their investment.
5. Contingency fees, otherwise known as damage-based contingency fees (these are defined as fees which are payable if your client wins but which are calculated as a percentage of the damages recovered) for contentious work between all legal representatives and their clients are illegal.	Both solicitors and counsel should be permitted to enter into contingency fee arrangements but with restrictions. Again this should be regulated and the client should receive independent legal advice.
6. There is currently very limited access to public funds for most types of litigious cases.	There should be a Contingent Legal Aid Fund or Supplementary Legal Aid Scheme to promote access to justice. These should be self-funding and non-profit-making.

3.4 **WHAT DO YOU TELL YOUR OPPONENT ABOUT FUNDING?**

ATE insurance, either on its own or coupled with a CFA with or without a success fee, is very likely to increase your client's opponent's costs if your client is successful. Therefore, notice must be given to the opponent of both the CFA with the success fee and/or any ATE insurance, in order to warn him of this cost implication. This must be done both pre-action in accordance with section IV para. 9.3 of the Practice Direction on Pre-Action Conduct (this must also be done for union-backed funding), and in accordance with CPR 44.15(1), where it stipulates that a notice of funding (N251) must be filed and served on issue of proceedings if funding is already in place (or with the acknowledgement of service or the defence if no acknowledgement has been filed), or within seven days of entering into the funding if after the issue of proceedings. Details of the sum or percentage of the success fee element are not required and no direct notice is required of this.

The consequence of not giving notice is that the party in receipt of the funding is unlikely to recover the success fee and/or premium for the time period over which the funding was not declared (CPR 44.3B(1))—at least, this was the position until *Birmingham City Council v Rose Forde* [2009] EWHC 12 (QB), in which it was held that a retrospective success fee, in some circumstances, was not contrary to public policy despite the fact that no notice would have been given to the opponent. The paying party would be safeguarded by the fact that the court would assess the reasonableness of the success fee. It is yet to be seen what those 'circumstances' are, but it would now seem that it is possible for a legal representative to assess the risk and enter into a CFA with the client on one basis, and then reassess the risk with the benefit of hindsight and enter into another CFA with retrospective effect. There has also been a spate of cases where 'relief from sanctions' for failure to give information about funding was considered (see *Haydon v Strudwick* [2010] EWHC 90164 (Costs) and others). In these cases, the claimants failed to give the defendants information about funding in accordance with paragraph 19.4 of PD 43–48. In these cases, relief was given under CPR 3.9 because the defendants suffered no prejudice and had in fact known about the funding position notwithstanding the fact that the claimants had no good reasons not to comply with the PD!

If you review the notice of funding available among the court forms presented in the Appendices, you will see that it only concerns the disclosure of a CFA with a success fee and ATE, and requires details only of the date of the CFA and the claim to which it relates, along with the name of the ATE insurer, the date of the policy, the policy number, and the claim to which it relates. Similar notification is required for a publicly funded client.

Therefore, if your client enters into any type of CFA without a success fee and does not take out ATE, then there is no requirement to give any notice to your opponent. For all other types of funding, there is no mandatory requirement to give notice to your opponent, although it is professionally courteous to inform your opponent if there is an independent funder.

3.5 **MISCELLANEOUS POINTS**

3.5.1 **BARRISTERS AND CFAS**

It is usual to invite any barrister (known as counsel) instructed in an action in which the legal representative has a CFA with his client, to enter into a similar CFA with the legal representative. A model CFA also exists between these legal professionals for personal injury cases. The Bar Council has prepared a guideline manual about these CFAs, which is available at www.barcouncil.org.uk.

It has to be appreciated, however, that the barrister is being asked to share the risk of the action in the same way as the client's legal representative, but that the barrister is probably taking on a greater risk, because it is the riskier cases that go all the way to trial.

It should also be noted here that there is no requirement for the disclosure of a CFA with a success fee made between the legal representative and counsel.

3.5.2 COLLECTIVE CONDITIONAL FEE AGREEMENTS (CCFAS)

CCFAs are based on exactly the same principle as CFAs, both with and without success fees, and are used by legal representatives who act for clients who are routinely involved in litigation, such as trade unions and other associations or corporations. Instead of entering into a separate CFA with each new matter for the client, there will be one CCFA, which does not specify each individual matter, but instead provides for fees to be paid on a common basis in relation to a type of claim: for example, a tripping claim or a road traffic accident. Accompanying a CCFA with a success fee will be a risk assessment document in respect of each individual claim. In practice, however, many CCFAs are without success fees and this therefore removes the requirement to comply with the disclosure of the funding arrangements.

KEY POINTS SUMMARY

- Before bringing a claim, consider ADR or, if available, whether the dispute might be resolved by a trade body or another means.

- If litigation is the only feasible option, undertake a quantification and risk assessment whether acting on behalf of the claimant or defendant.

- On the basis of the value and risk assessment, consider whether a CFA is suitable or available, or whether some other method of paying legal costs might be more desirable.

- Discuss whether the client needs or wants insurance to bring or defend the claim and the timing of both.

- Consider whether insurance is available and, if so, at what cost.

- Review with the client what court fees, witness fees, or expert fees will be payable and when.

- Keep in mind your professional conduct obligations in relation to client care and information on costs.

- Maintain a detailed written account of the costs advice and information that you give to your client, and review it periodically.

- Keep an eye out for the potential implementation of Lord Jackson's review of costs and funding.

SELF-TEST QUESTIONS

1. Can ATE insurance be used to fund a claim in the absence of a CFA?

2. What does a legal representative take into account when calculating a success fee?

3. What are the sanctions if you fail to provide costs information to your client in accordance with Rule 2 of the Solicitors' Code of Conduct 2007?

online resource centre Suggested answers to these general questions can be accessed by adopting lecturers on the Online Resource Centre. Your lecturer can provide these to you.

4.1   INTRODUCTION

The term 'legal costs', for the purposes of litigation, is intended to cover the amount of time that a legal representative spends on a matter. These are otherwise known as 'profit costs'. The terms 'disbursements' covers counsel's fees, court fees, expenses, and payments to other third parties, such as experts, incurred from the outset of the retainer until it is terminated or concluded. For the sake of clarity, the term 'costs' is intended to cover both legal costs and disbursements.

The client has a contractual obligation to pay for all of his costs incurred in bringing or defending a claim. These costs are known as 'solicitor and client costs' and are discussed in Chapter 6, paragraph 6.2.2.2. However, the client may be able to recover a proportion of those costs from his opponent either by agreement or by an order of the court. Once the client has established an entitlement to the recovery of his costs, the parties will endeavour to agree the amount. If they cannot agree, then the court will assess those costs. The procedures for assessing costs are detailed in the Online Resource Centre chapter on 'Assessment of Costs'.

online
resource
centre

The way in which the court will deal with the recovery of costs is primarily based on the 'overriding objective' contained in CPR 1, the aim of which is to deal with cases justly. The overriding objective was discussed at some length in Chapter 2. However, three of the methods that the court is specifically encouraged to use to meet that objective have an obvious bearing on costs and are worth looking at again.

To deal with a case justly, the court must, so far as is practicable:

- ensure that the parties are on an equal footing;
- save expense; and
- deal with the case in ways that are proportionate to the amount of money involved and to the parties' financial positions.

Therefore, as a starting point, it should be borne in mind that whoever pays the costs at the end of the day, those costs should be kept, overall, within sensible proportions, having regard to the case in question.

Against the background of the overriding objective, this chapter will focus on the recovery of costs including:

- the discretionary nature of costs awards;
- the general principle that the loser pays;
- the basis upon which costs orders are made;
- the aspects of a legal representative's work that are recoverable and how they are formulated; and
- the different types of costs order.

The proposed changes set out in Lord Jackson's Review of civil costs will also be considered at the end of this chapter to help you identify the extent of the potential amendments that may be implemented.

4.2 THE GENERAL PRINCIPLES OF COSTS IN LITIGATION

There are two fundamental principles that underpin costs within the litigation framework:

- the payment of costs by one party to another is at the discretion of the court; and
- a general rule has emerged that the loser should pay the winner's costs.

4.2.1 THE DISCRETIONARY NATURE OF COSTS

The court's discretion in the award of costs is founded on s. 51 of the Senior Courts Act 1981 and CPR 44.3(1), and is wide-reaching. The court is required to take into account all of the circumstances of the case, particularly regarding the following (CPR 44.3(4) and (5)):

- the parties' conduct before (as well as during) the proceedings, especially concerning compliance with Pre-Action Protocol;
- whether it was reasonable for the parties to raise, pursue, or contest any allegation or issue within the litigation;
- the way in which a party pursued or defended his case, or any specific allegation or issue;
- whether the winner exaggerated his claim;
- whether a party was only partly successful; and
- any valid offers to settle.

As can be seen, it is the parties' conduct in virtually every aspect of litigation that is under scrutiny by the courts in the exercise of its discretion. This conduct issue should be highlighted to the client at the outset in order that he understands how the recovery of his costs could be affected by his behaviour both before and during proceedings.

There is, however, one situation in which the court has no discretion in whether to make an award of costs between parties: that is, where a valid CPR 36 offer has been accepted (see Chapter 16, paragraphs 16.7.1 and 16.8.1).

4.2.2 THE LOSER PAYS THE WINNER'S COSTS

This second general principle is only a starting point and the courts frequently depart from it when considering costs at the end of a hearing, sometimes ordering only a partial costs recovery or no cost recovery at all. The main reason why the court may not order the loser to pay the winner's costs is, again, due to the conduct of one or both parties. CPR 44.3 and 44.5 require the court to take into account the conduct of the parties to the litigation both pre- and post-issue.

 Costs

In practice, there have been cases in which the trial judge has made a deduction from the winner's costs to be paid by the loser, because the winner had, for example, inflated his claim. However, the costs judge on assessment has further reduced the winner's costs because of the requirement on assessment that he take into account conduct when assessing costs. This is, in effect, a double reduction and potentially unfair. *Northstar Systems Ltd (1), Seaquest Systems Ltd (2) and Ultraframe (UK) Ltd v Fielding and Ors* [2006] EWCA Civ 1660 gave guidance on this and suggested that conduct is relevant to both CPR 44.3 and 44.5. The Court held that whilst the assessing judge must avoid this 'double jeopardy' in order to try to achieve this, the trial judge should spell out, when making the order for costs, whether the assessing judge should take into account conduct under CPR 44.5.

There is always a plethora of cases demonstrating how the court will exercise its discretion on conduct and so it is worth keeping abreast of these cases, because some decisions on costs will more significantly affect the way in which you advise your client on the issue of costs recovery.

The remainder of this section will deal with instances in which the court frequently departs from the general rules, as stated above, and makes a different costs order. The situations set out below do not represent an exhaustive list of the occasions on which the court will exercise its discretion, but illustrate how wide the court's discretion can be and, in some instances, how conflicting that can be.

4.2.3 INSTANCES IN WHICH THE COURT MAY PENALIZE A PARTY IN COSTS

Below are detailed some instances in which the court has exercised its discretion on costs and moved away from the general rules on costs, as stated above. The penalties that are ultimately sanctioned by the court are set out in the cases below, but are born out of CPR 44.3(6). (See paragraph 4.6 below for details of the additional penalties.)

4.2.3.1 Failure to comply with Pre-Action Protocol

In *Charles Church Developments Ltd v Stent Foundations Ltd* [2007] EWHC 855, the court held that a costs penalty was to be imposed at an interim stage even though the proceedings were stayed after the defence had been filed to allow negotiations to take place. The Construction and Engineering Protocol had been breached according to the judge, despite the fact that proceedings had been issued to protect against limitation, and the claimant was ordered to pay 50 per cent of its own costs and 50 per cent of the defendant's costs up to the stay.

The court in this instance felt that the claimant should have followed the Protocol 'to the letter' and so it was severely penalized at an early stage in the litigation rather than once the case had been concluded. Tactically, this was a sensible step for the court to take, because by making an interim costs order before the parties embarked upon their chosen method of dispute resolution—that is, mediation—the parties went into the mediation with one less issue to argue about. Contrast that decision with *TJ Brent and Anor v Black and Veatch* [2008] EWHC 1497 (TCC), in which the same court dismissed an application for a costs sanction to be imposed for failure to comply with a Pre-Action Protocol because the court should be only concerned with substantial compliance, not 'minor departures'. Where do we go from here?

4.2.3.2 Failure to negotiate

Successful parties have been criticized for failing to engage in negotiations and penalized accordingly in costs. Any form of alternative dispute resolution (ADR) should be attempted within the spirit of any Protocol, but *Straker v Tudor Rose (A Firm)* [2007] EWCA Civ 368 has suggested that whilst this is the case, a successful party's costs should not, in fact, be penalized to the extent that their costs are reduced to nil.

The reason why the Court of Appeal came to this decision on costs is that the claimant had not acted unreasonably in the pursuit of his case and there was no finding of dishonesty or exaggeration, which may have led to a more punitive costs order. It was simply not necessary in this particular case. The case also illustrates the right to pursue a legitimate claim provided that, when such a claim is pursued, it is done so proportionately.

4.2.3.3 Refusal to enter into an alternative dispute resolution (ADR) process

In deciding the level of costs to award, the court must have regard to the 'the efforts made, if any, before and during the proceedings in order to try and resolve the dispute' (CPR 44.5(3)(a)(ii)).

There have been many costs awards made based on a party's refusal to mediate and what is to be taken into account by the court. The most prominent of these was *Dunnett v Railtrack* [2002] 2 All ER 850, which was the first case in the courts to seriously penalize a successful party for refusing appropriately to mediate, and *Halsey v Milton Keynes NHS Trust* [2004] EWCA Civ 576, which still provides the most comprehensive guidelines on what the court will take into account when assessing whether a party was justified in refusing to mediate.

The court will consider in such circumstances:

- the nature of the dispute;
- the merits of the case;
- the extent to which other settlement methods were attempted;
- whether the cost of ADR would be disproportionately high;
- whether any delay in setting up the ADR would have been prejudicial; and
- whether ADR had reasonable prospects of success.

 Practical Considerations

Based on these recent decisions, best practice would suggest that it is a question of knowing the strengths and weakness of your client's case, and balancing those with proportionality in terms of time and costs. It is not simply a matter of railroading your client's case to trial if it is strong, but nor is it necessary to agree to an ADR process where it is clearly inappropriate. Examples of the former would be if, rather than risk trial, you were to consider an application for summary judgment or a strike-out at an early stage (where your opponent's case is weak or misconceived); an example of the latter would if you were to evaluate your client's conduct against the *Halsey* guidelines. In both cases, it is apparent that, as a matter of course, all members of the legal profession should now routinely consider with their clients whether their disputes are suitable for ADR. In view of the extent of the cost consequences, it is advisable that this is evidenced in writing.

4.2.3.4 Rejection of CPR 36 offers

Since the April 2007 amendment to CPR 36, how the courts deal practically with costs orders on CPR 36 offers is still developing. *Lisa Carver v BAA* [2008] EWCA Civ 412, has created much comment. This and other cases on CPR 36 can be found in Chapter 16 at paragraph 16.9.

4.2.3.5 Exaggeration of a successful party's claim

Where a claimant exaggerates his claim, recent cases have held that he should be deprived of part of his costs even where he has beaten the defendant's CPR 36 offer. (See *Jackson v Ministry of Defence* [2006] EWCA Civ 548, in which the Court of Appeal held that despite the fact that the claimant had reduced its claim from £1,000,000 to £240,000, because he was only awarded £150,000 at trial, beating the defendant's CPR 36 offer, his costs should be reduced by 25 per cent for exaggeration.) However, the courts have taken a slightly different view in how to approach the issue of exaggeration in *Martine Widlake v BAA Ltd* [2009] EWCA Civ 1256 where the Court of Appeal overturned the first instance decision that the claimant pay the defendant's costs even though she had been awarded damages, by making no order for costs. The basis of the Court of Appeal's rationale was that despite the exaggeration by the claimant, this was not to be seen as an issue won or lost but just something that needed to be taken into consideration when trying to identify which party should pay the costs. The Court of Appeal obviously felt in this case that some degree of exaggeration does not always merit a punitive costs order.

4.2.3.6 Failure to succeed on the whole claim

Costs orders made on partial success cases are difficult to predict. It is not clear who the winner is, because some issues that were raised at the outset of the case are either dropped or dismissed at trial. Costs orders in these cases are often overturned on appeal and it is difficult to offer guidance as to how the court is likely to deal with such cases, because they seem to deal with each case differently. However, the courts are likely to concentrate on whether a party was successful on an issue not the reasonableness of raising the issue in the first place. Further, if the 'lost issues' had a negligible impact on costs, it may be appropriate to award the winning party all of its costs.

The courts are trying to be more prescriptive here and some further guidance has been given in the landmark case of *Multiplex Construction (UK) Ltd v Cleveland Bridge UK Ltd* [2008] EWHC 2280 (TCC), which established eight key principles in the award of costs. This case sends a strong message that litigation—particularly complex, high-value litigation—should be compromised, but that, in the absence of settlement, there can be no certainty about the ultimate costs order. These principles have been followed in *Fitzroy Robinson Ltd v Mentmore Towers Ltd* [2010] EWHC 98 where the TCC judge carved up the case to enable him to make almost a 'piecemeal' costs order that detrimentally affected both parties to the action as follows. This case involved a dispute between an architect and its property developer client. The court held that whilst the architect had won on liability, the costs order was to be as follows:

• The architect was only to recover 75 per cent of its costs due to the fact that the property developer had successfully proved an important issue against it.

• The property developer was punished by being ordered to pay some of the architect's costs on the indemnity basis to reflect the fact that they had acted unreasonably by delaying the action and had dealt with expert evidence poorly.

 Practical Considerations

When advising a client on the recovery of costs in litigation, whether claiming or defending, it is best to reinforce with him that the primary obligation for payment of his own legal costs rests with him, but that the court has a discretion to order that some—but, most probably, not all—of those costs be paid for by his opponent in certain circumstances. It is better for the client to see the recovery of legal costs as a 'bonus' rather than 'the norm', because judges have such a wide discretion in the award of legal costs that it is becoming increasingly difficult to predict when and how much will be recovered. Clients should also be made aware that their conduct both before and during the litigation may also be called into question and, if thought not to be in accordance with their duty to the court, then they may in fact be punished by costs orders against them.

4.2.4 THE PUBLICLY FUNDED LITIGANT

Despite the fact that community legal services funding is restricted in civil matters, in cases in which it has been awarded and the publicly funded litigant is unsuccessful in the litigation, what happens to the legal costs of the winning party?

The Community Legal Service (Costs) Regulations 2000, SI 2000/441, state that a publicly funded litigant is generally protected against adverse costs orders. This is known as 'costs protection', but only extends to the ambit of the publicly funded certificate and to the duration of the proceedings in which the litigant was publicly funded. Therefore if your client is successful against a publicly funded opponent with full costs protection, he will rarely recover any of his legal costs.

A publicly funded litigant can lose his costs protection in the following circumstances:

- when, on the report of his instructing solicitor informing the Legal Services Commission (LSC) of a change in the merits of his case or his income, the certificate is withdrawn, leaving the remainder of the action without funding and consequently the litigant unprotected; or
- where the opponent of a of publicly funded litigant contacts the LSC, making representations about the conduct and/or merits of the publicly funded party to the extent that the certificate is also withdrawn.

 Practical Considerations

It is therefore very important that your client is made aware as soon as an opponent is in receipt of a publicly funded certificate that he is very unlikely to secure any costs recovery in respect of that part of the proceedings in the event of a successful outcome to the dispute, whether at trial or otherwise. This may affect your client's decision to pursue the litigation or to accept (or reject) offers.

4.3 THE BASIS ON WHICH COSTS ARE AWARDED

In paragraph 4.2 above, we have looked at the basic principles and how the court decides who is to pay the costs of an action. Underlying those principles are two further considerations that the court and the parties have to bear in mind when deciding how much the winning party is entitled to recover.

4.3.1 THE INDEMNITY PRINCIPLE

The indemnity principle is a long-standing principle that the winning party cannot recover more from his opponent than he has paid to his solicitor in the course of the litigation. To this end, if a client care retainer letter is not sent to the client, it could be argued that, in the absence of a formal contract, the client has no liability to pay his legal representative's costs and therefore the losing party has no liability to pay the winning party's costs.

Example

You act for a client in a personal injury matter and send a client care letter. You make a successful application to the court for an interim payment. The court also awards you your costs. When the court is assessing those costs at the end of the hearing, the amount that you are seeking to recover cannot exceed the amount of costs that you have incurred on behalf of your client in respect of the application. Consequently, if the total cost of making the application was £750, you are limited to recovering that amount from your opponent.

There are, however, four notable exceptions to the indemnity principle, as follows.

- Conditional fee agreements (CFAs) had the potential to breach the indemnity principle on the basis that the purpose of the agreement is that the client pays the legal representative only nominal legal fees (see Chapter 3, paragraph 3.3.5, for more on the nominal amount that the client may have to pay if he loses) should he lose the case. However, this potential trouble spot was catered for by s. 31 of the Access to Justice Act 1999, which permitted the winning CFA client to recover his base legal costs plus a success fee if the CFA was in the prescribed form.

- In-house legal representatives are presumed to cost the same as instructing an independent firm to act, although, in practice, this is hardly ever the case. Nevertheless, the case of *Re Eastwood* [1975] 1 Ch 112 established this pragmatic approach and it has remained ever since.

- A publicly funded party's legal representative is only entitled to prescribed rates, although he is entitled to a full recovery of costs from a losing opponent.

- Pro bono representation, whilst free of charge to the client, can, in certain circumstances, be paid for by the unsuccessful opponent in accordance with s. 194 of the Legal Services Act 2007.

4.3.2 **THE TWO BASES OF ASSESSMENT**

The two bases of assessment are known as the 'standard basis' and the 'indemnity basis', and the court has the discretion to award costs using either one. The word 'indemnity' is used here again, but it takes on a different meaning when used in assessing costs.

The 'indemnity principle' and 'indemnity costs' are two separate issues that those new to practice often find confusing: the former is the global background against which costs are assessed, as described above; the latter is a formula that the court will use to calculate costs.

The same fundamental rule applies to costs assessed on the standard and indemnity bases: in each case, they must be reasonably incurred and reasonable in amount. Costs are usually awarded on the standard basis unless the court feels that there has been some culpable behaviour, in which case, indemnity costs may be awarded. Such instances of unreasonable behaviour on the part of the paying party have not been specifically categorized, although in *JP Morgan Chase Bank (formerly known as the Chase Manhattan Bank) (a body corporate) v Springwell Navigation Corporation (a body corporate)* [2008] EWHC 2848 (Comm), the court commented on the importance of complying with the overriding objective and that indemnity costs were awarded here because the case was 'out of the norm'.

Practical Considerations

Such instances of situations in which an indemnity costs order may be made include pursuing an unjustified claim, rejecting a CPR 36 offer, an abuse of court process, dishonesty, or repeated flouting of court orders. A party who is faced with an intransigent or obstructive opponent can increase his chances of securing a costs recovery order on the indemnity basis if, before proceeding with any application or step (that the party now has to take because of the opponent's intransigence or obstructive behaviour), a letter is written to that opponent, warning him that an application for costs on the indemnity basis will be sought.

4.3.2.1 The standard basis

If the court awards costs to be assessed on the standard basis, CPR 44.4(2) states that only costs that are proportionate are to be allowed, but that if there is any doubt, then the doubt will be resolved in favour of the paying party. The key point here is that the costs must be reasonably incurred, reasonable in amount, and proportionate. (A discussion on proportionality merits its own stand-alone section and this is dealt with in paragraph 4.3.2.4 below.)

4.3.2.2 The indemnity basis

If the court awards costs on the indemnity basis, CPR 44.4(3) provides that if there is any doubt as to whether a cost has been incurred reasonably or is reasonable in amount, then the doubt is resolved in favour of the receiving party. The key point here is that proportionality is not taken into account under the strict interpretation of the CPR.

4.3.2.3 What does the court take into account when deciding the amount of costs on either basis?

In deciding what costs have been reasonably incurred, are reasonable in amount, and are proportionate for a standard basis assessment, and what costs have been unreasonably incurred or are unreasonable in amount for an indemnity basis assessment, the court, in accordance with CPR 44.5, will take into account the following (subject to the indemnity principle):

- the conduct of the parties at all times, including how the parties behaved and whether they attempted to settle the dispute;
- the value of money or property involved;
- the importance of the matter to the parties;
- the particular complexity of the matter, or the difficulty or novelty of the questions that it raised;
- the skill, effort, specialized knowledge, and responsibility involved;
- the time spent on the case; and
- the place and the circumstances in which the work or any part of it was done.

4.3.2.4 Proportionality in relation to costs

As mentioned in paragraph 4.3.2.1, costs on the standard basis must be proportionate as well as reasonable. The guidance received on this is derived from the decision of the Court of Appeal in *Lownds v Home Office* [2002] All ER (D) 329, and cannot be overemphasized. The Lord Chief Justice laid down a twofold revised test, as follows.

1. In a case in which proportionality is likely to be an issue, a preliminary decision on the proportionality of the costs as a whole must be made at the outset.

2. If the costs are not disproportionate as a whole, the court can consider the second stage, which will include the consideration of the reasonableness of each item—that is, whether it was reasonable to incur the cost of that item.

If the costs are not held to be proportionate, the court must consider at the second stage whether the costs were necessary, not only reasonable. The court will first consider whether an item was necessarily incurred and, if so, a reasonable amount is then normally to be allowed. In deciding what is 'necessary', the conduct of the parties is highly relevant.

Practical Considerations

Remember that, when deciding the question of proportionality, the court will also look to the factors identified under CPR 44.5. For example, the court will consider whether the appropriate level of fee earner or counsel was used, whether offers to settle were made, and whether experts were instructed. If assessing proportionality in a CFA matter, the court should not reduce a success fee simply on the ground that, when added to the base costs, the total cost appears disproportionate.

4.4 HOW LEGAL COSTS AND DISBURSEMENTS ARE FORMULATED

Now that we have looked at the fundamental costs provisions, we need to ascertain exactly what can be charged for and ultimately recovered from the opponent if a favourable costs order is made.

4.4.1 WHAT WORK CAN BE INCLUDED?

A legal representative's work is calculated and ultimately assessed by reference to time spent on a variety of tasks, including various attendances either by telephone or at face-to-face meetings with clients, opponents, counsel, experts, the court, and others. Time spent considering and preparing documentation, including statements of case, letters, reports, advices, schedules, and perusing original documentation, is also allowable. Much of a legal representative's work is taken up with these items of work in the run-up to an interim hearing or trial, and added to the above will be time spent at the hearing. At paragraph 4.1 above, we discussed disbursements: these are to be added to the overall statement of costs or bill to be presented to the opponent at the conclusion of a successful action or application.

4.4.2 HOURLY RATES

Once you have identified what items of work have been done and what disbursements have been incurred, you will need to consider what hourly rate will be applied to the hours spent in undertaking those tasks. These are considered periodically by the Advisory Committee on Costs. At the time of writing, the Master of the Rolls was considering increases for 2011 but had made no final decision. When he has, the new rates can be found at http://www.judiciary. gov.uk/publications-and-reports. For the time being see Table 4.1 for the rates in force.

You can see that there are zonal rates in England and Wales that include groups of towns and cities: National 1 and National 2. These involve two bands covering the whole country, except London, with a further three bands for the City of London, Central London, and Outer London. The rates for London 3, Bands A and B are presented as ranges following the format of *The Guide to the Summary Assessment of Costs*. These ranges go some way towards reflecting the wide range of work types transacted in these areas.

TABLE 4.1 GUIDELINE HOURLY RATES FOR 2010

	Band A	Band B	Band C	Band D
London 1	409	296	226	138
London 2	317	242	196	126
London 3	229–67	172–229	165	121
National 1	217	192	161	118
National 2	201	177	146	111

In addition, there are four levels of fee earner within these bands:

- Grade A—solicitors with over eight years' post-qualification experience (PQE), including at least eight years' litigation experience;
- Grade B—solicitors and legal executives with over four years' PQE, including at least four years' litigation experience;
- Grade C—other solicitors and legal executives, and fee earners of equivalent experience;
- Grade D—trainee solicitors, paralegals, and fee earners of equivalent experience.

It is further recognized that, in certain complex, major litigation, the appropriate rate may exceed the guideline—sometimes by a significant margin. It is within the court's inherent discretion whether it is prepared to allow a greater hourly rate. This often arises when a party instructs a legal representative from outside his locality, in which case charging rates are much higher.

 Practical Considerations

The client needs to be aware that the figure to which he agrees in his retainer with his legal representative at the outset of the case (and any subsequent increase, decrease, or change in fee earner as the matter moves along) may be higher or lower than these guideline hourly rates. If it is the case that the client care letter denotes a higher hourly rate than the guideline figure, unless the court can be persuaded, it is likely that the SCCO guideline figure will be adhered to. If the retainer letter figure is lower than the guideline figure, then, because of the indemnity principle, the client will be stuck with a costs recovery based on the lower figure in his client care letter.

4.4.3 WORK DONE BY COUNSEL

Work undertaken by counsel, including advocacy, drafting or amending documentation, and written, telephone, or conference advices, can be recovered as against an opponent. However, it is essential that the solicitor negotiate the 'fee note' with counsel's clerk in advance of incurring the fee—particularly if it will have to be justified in detailed assessment proceedings. Counsel also operates on an hourly rate basis, denoted by experience and seniority.

4.4.4 EXPERTS' FEES

It is important that the terms of engagement with the expert are agreed in writing before any work is undertaken. The Online Resource Centre contains a sample retainer letter to an expert. If these fees are to be recovered from another party, then the expert will need to prepare an account of the time spent and an hourly charging rate for the work done.

4.4.5 CFA SUCCESS FEES AND AFTER THE EVENT INSURANCE PREMIUMS

As can be seen from Chapter 3, paragraph 3.3.5, cases can be funded by way of a CFA with a success fee and/or after-the-event (ATE) insurance, in respect of which a premium must be paid. In this section, we are concerned with dealing with how the success fee and premium are formulated. If the CFA has no success fee, then the courts will take the same approach to the assessment of costs as if the work had been done under an ordinary retainer.

4.4.5.1 The success fee

4.4.5.1.1 *Discretionary success fees*

The actual assessment of the success fee does not occur until the conclusion of the case at a detailed assessment hearing (if the parties cannot agree). For details of the detailed assessment proceedings, see the Online Resource Centre chapter on 'Assessment of Costs'. Remember that it is only that part of the success fee which relates to the risk element of the litigation and not the postponement of payment of fees that is recoverable from an opponent. Guidance on what the court takes into account when assessing the success fee is set out in Practice Direction (PD) 43–48.11. The court will look at matters as they appeared to the legal representative at the time that the CFA was entered into when coming to its decision and exercise its discretion. Consider the following cases.

In *Spiralstem Ltd v Marks and Spencers plc* [2007] EWHC 90084 (Costs), the court held that the claimant was not entitled to recover a 100 per cent success fee provided for in the CFA because it was unrealistic to suppose that a firm such as the claimant's legal representatives would have invested so much in such a speculative claim. However, two recent cases depart from the *Spiralstem* judgment. Firstly, *Oliver v Whipps Cross University Hospital NHS Trust* [2009] EWHC 1104 (QB) at first instance reduced the success fee from 100 per cent to 67 per cent in line with the *Spiralstem* argument. On appeal, the success fee was restored to 100 per cent clarifying that a legal representative is entitled to enter into a CFA at an early stage when in a position of relevant ignorance of the prospects of success. Secondly, *Matthew Peacock v MGN Ltd* [2010] EWHC 90174 (Costs) also allowed a 100 per cent success fee. The claimant's success fee was staged so that it was ultimately 100 per cent if the claim proceeded to 28 days after service of the defence and beyond. It was held here that the decision to enter into a staged success fee was reasonable even if it was fixed at 100 per cent early on in the litigation. Furthermore, it was up to the claimant when to choose the stage and the 100 per cent was in fact stage 3. This in effect gave the defendant every opportunity to settle at a lower success fee.

It is the authors' view that there will be more conflicting cases of this nature.

4.4.5.1.2 *Fixed success fees*

Whilst the courts will not give specific guidance on the amount of the success fee to be granted, the CPR specify fixed success fees in certain cases, although there are provisos to these.

- Fixed success fees for road traffic accidents (RTAs) after October 2003 (CPR 45, sections II and III) are confined to claims that settle before the issue of proceedings and which do not exceed £10,000. As well as fixed costs in accordance with CPR 45.9(1) and a fixed choice of disbursements, the success fee is fixed at 12.5 per cent of those fixed recoverable costs in CPR 45.9(1).

- Fixed success fees for employers' liability claims in accidents, not disease claims, after October 2004 (CPR 45, section IV) range from 25 per cent to 100 per cent.

- In both RTAs and employers' liability disease cases, it is possible to have a fixed percentage increase in the success fee in accordance with CPR 45.15–45.19 for the RTA claims and CPR 45.23–45.26 for the disease cases.

 Practical Considerations

There have been a number of cases in recent years dealing with the level of success fees, mainly in respect of RTAs (excluding the three bullet points above)—in particular, *Callery v Gray* [2001] EWCA Civ 1117 and *Halloran v Delaney* [2002] EWCA Civ 1258. However, it would be unwise to try to adopt these judgments or any of these cases above as general principles, because each case should be dealt with on its own merits. Nevertheless, it is clearly emerging that a two-stage success fee is likely to be the way in which the courts will look at the assessment of the success fee as a whole: a lower success fee where claims are settled in the Protocol phase and a higher one (to be negotiated with the client at the appropriate time) where the matter proceeds to trial, with the fees varying depending on the type of claim.

4.4.5.2 The insurance premium

In practice, the issues surrounding the assessment of the insurance premium are often tied in with the issue of its recoverability: whether the premium is reasonable and whether it should, in fact, have been taken out in the first place (see Chapter 3, paragraph 3.3.6.3, for further discussions on recoverability). However, in *Kris Motor Spares Ltd v Fox Williams LLP* [2010] EWHC 1008 (QB), on an appeal, the costs judge emphasized that when it comes to a party challenging the amount of the premium, the paying party should adduce evidence of the level that they believe is appropriate and must do so promptly. There is no question of reversing the burden of proof, even where, as in this case, the premium was expensive (£95,000 to obtain cover of £130,000!)

4.5 THE DIFFERENT TYPES OF COSTS ORDER MADE BY THE COURT

As litigation progresses, the court can make a variety of costs orders at interim hearings and at trial. The Costs Practice Direction 43–48, section 8.5, lists some frequently made orders (see Figure 4.2 at the end of this chapter).

4.6 THE COURT'S POWERS TO CONTROL COSTS RECOVERED BY ONE PARTY AGAINST ANOTHER

The courts are constantly looking at ways of reducing the cost of litigation and making it less unpredictable. In addition to the court's discretion in the award of costs set against the background of basic costs principles, as highlighted in paragraphs 4.2 and 4.3 above, the court has developed a number of alternative costs orders that can be made, usually in multi-track cases in which matters are particularly complicated.

CPR 44.3(6) permits the court to make the following orders of costs recovery:

(a) a proportion of another party's costs;

(b) a stated amount in respect of another party's costs;

(c) costs from or until a certain date only;

(d) costs incurred before proceedings have begun;

(e) costs relating to particular steps taken in the proceedings;

(f) costs relating only to a distinct part of proceedings; and

(g) interest on costs from or until a certain date, including a date before judgment.

Below, we focus on just two approaches by the court born out of these possible orders.

4.6.1 COST CAPPING

'Cost capping' refers to when the court places a limit on the amount that a party can recover from its opponent. It can do this prospectively or retrospectively, although the latter is rare. The court derives its general powers under s. 51 of the Senior Courts Act 1981 and CPR 3.1(2)(m).CPR 44.18–20 contains the rules on costs capping and PD 43–48 at section 23A provides further guidance.

The process of cost capping involves making an application to the court under CPR 23 (although oral applications can be made), usually at an early stage in the action, such as allocation or a subsequent early case management conference (CMC).

The evidence in support of the application usually takes the form of a witness statement detailing why the costs should be capped. It is usual to suggest that, without cost capping, costs will be unreasonably or disproportionately incurred. Along with the witness statement will be required a detailed costs estimate of the party whose costs are intended to be capped.

The court will exercise its inherent discretion as to whether to cap a party's cost in accordance with the overriding objective and CPR 44.18. Recent case law suggests that there has to be a significant and real risk that disproportionate and unreasonable costs will be incurred, and that the conventional case management powers will not prevent that *(Knight v Beyond Properties PTY Ltd* [2006] EWHC 1242 (Ch)). Judges are, however, shying away from making cost capping orders because of the time and cost consequences involved in having the court determine what the cap should be. In *Barr v Biffa Waste Services Ltd (No 2)* [2009] EWHC 2444 (TCC), a cost-capping order was refused because the court felt that disproportionate costs could be dealt with adequately by the courts' general case management powers or at a detailed assessment.

If a costs cap is ordered, the court will have regard to CPR 44.5 and the circumstances to be taken into account, as well as to a party's right to continue his proceedings under Art. 6 of the European Convention on Human Rights. Once a cost capping order is made, as with any other type of costs order, the party is not limited to what he spends on litigation, but simply to what he can recover from the other party if he wins and obtains a costs order in his favour.

4.6.2 PERCENTAGE-BASED AND ISSUES-BASED COSTS ORDERS

Percentage-based and issues-based orders are considered where there are a number of issues in the case upon which the judge at trial has to make a ruling. Often, there will be a clear and significant cost attached to either proving or disproving the issue. What the court is inclined to do in the circumstances in which both parties are successful on some, but not all, of the issues, instead of awarding all of the costs of the action to the ultimately successful party, the court will award costs of proving the issues and disproving other issues to the respective parties. This is done by either making a party pay a percentage of its or its opponent's costs, or allowing costs incurred on the issues proved or disproved.

 Practical Considerations

In practice, the courts favour making percentage-based costs orders rather than issues-based costs orders because, once the trial judge has made the order (having had the advantage of hearing all of the issues in the case in detail), it is then for the costs judge to decipher the issues before deciding whether individual items are attributable to certain issues that have been allowed or disallowed. This takes time and could lengthen the detailed assessment hearing, which will ultimately have an impact on the time and costs of assessment.

4.7 PREDICTABLE COSTS, THE NEW ROAD TRAFFIC CLAIM PROCESS AND FIXED COSTS

Not all costs fall to be assessed by the court. The CPR deal with four kinds of fixed or predictable costs. The fixed levels detailed below can only be exceeded in exceptional circumstances (CPR 45.12(1)):

(a) undisputed claims, small claims, and enforcement proceedings in which the costs are fixed in accordance with CPR 45.1–45.6, supplemented by section 24 of PD 43–48 and CPR 27.14(2)(a);

(b) predictable costs for certain road traffic claims that settle prior to proceedings under CPR 45.7–45.14;

(c) fixed success fee uplifts for road traffic claims and some employers' liability claims pursuant to CPR 45.15–45.26; and

(d) fixed trial costs in the fast track, under CPR 46 and PD 43–48, paras 26 and 27.

This section will focus on the predictable costs element in (b) and fast-track trial costs in (d). See the relevant sections of the CPR as set out above for the miscellaneous costs provisions in (a). In respect of (c), see paragraph 4.4.5.1.2 above on fixed success fees. We also deal with the new road traffic claim process.

4.7.1 PREDICTABLE COSTS

CPR 45.7–45.14 set out a predictable costs regime for road traffic claims that settle in the total sum of £10,000 before the issue of proceedings. The rules are supplemented by PD 43–48.25A.

The costs that are recoverable are limited to:

- fixed costs relating to the agreed damages—that is, £800 plus 20 per cent of the damages up to £5,000, plus 15 per cent of the damages between £5,000 and £10,000, and a 12.5 per cent London weighting (CPR 45.9(2));
- VAT;
- a fixed success fee if relevant (for details as to how the court assesses the success fee, see paragraph 4.4.5.1 above); and
- disbursements from a specified list in CPR 45.10.

 Example

You practise in Exeter and have negotiated a settlement during the Personal Injury (PI) Protocol phase of your client's PI claim arising out of an RTA earlier in the year. During your handling of the claim, you obtained your client's doctor (GP) and hospital notes, and instructed a consultant orthopaedic surgeon to prepare a report, which was disclosed to the defendant. You also obtained a copy of the police accident report book, on receipt of which, you instructed an enquiry agent to locate witnesses, but none were found.

Damages have been agreed at £8,000.

Your fixed costs are as follows:

- £800; plus
- £1000 (being 20 per cent of £5,000); plus
- £450 (being 15 per cent of £3,000); plus
- VAT on £2,250; plus
- recovery of the GP and hospital note fee, the fee for the medical report, and that for the police accident report book.

Unfortunately, you are unlikely to recover the enquiry agent's fee, because it does not fall within any of the disbursements in CPR 45.10.

The predictable costs regime is directed at eliminating a costs assessment, and at providing certainty for both parties' legal representatives and insurers. However, it does not deal with limiting the insurance premium or the amount of a specified disbursement and, as such, there remain potential areas for disagreement.

4.7.2 THE NEW ROAD TRAFFIC CLAIM PROCESS

This process applies only to road traffic cases from April 2010 worth between £1,000 and £10,000 where there has been an admission of liability. The whole process is undertaken online until settlement is no longer possible and then it reverts to the court system. There is a new Protocol for these types of cases. (see Chapter 8 on Protocol and Chapter 9, paragraph 9.2.7 for further detail) The base costs are divided into stages as follows:

- Stage 1—legal representatives will be paid £400 where they complete a new notification form and send this to the insurer for a decision on liability.

- Stage 2—where liability is admitted and the process continues to settlement within a strict timetable, the fee will be set at £800.

- Stage 3—where no settlement on quantum has been reached and the matter proceeds to a disposal hearing, legal representatives will be paid £250 for a paper hearing or £500 for an oral hearing.

There are provisions for a second medical report in more complex cases and an extra £500 in cases involving children. Additionally, the success fee will be 12.5 per cent for stages 1 and 2 and up to 100 per cent where cases reach stage 3.

4.7.3 FAST-TRACK FIXED COSTS

CPR 46 deals with fast-track trial costs.

It is only the costs of the fast-track trial that are fixed; the costs of the rest of the matter from date of instruction are not, unless your client's claim fell within (b) in paragraph 4.7 above and settled before issue.

These trial costs that the court may award are based on the value of the claim, although the court does have the power to award more or less than the fixed amounts. A common example of this is where your client asks you to attend the trial with him, in addition to your trial advocate. This is often for comfort or a 'belt and braces' approach. CPR 46.3(2) indicates that the additional fee of £345 will only be recoverable by your client if it was 'necessary' for you to attend to assist your trial advocate.

4.7.4 FIXED COSTS ON A SPECIFIED MONEY CLAIM

Fixed costs can be recovered in an action in which a defendant to a money claim admits the whole sum claimed, and pays it on receipt of the claim form and particulars of claim. Details of the fixed costs allowed can be found in CPR 45.2 and a further discussion on this in Chapter 10, paragraph 10.5.1.

4.8 WASTED COSTS ORDERS

Wasted costs orders are governed by s. 51(6) of the Senior Courts Act 1981, as substituted by s. 4 of the Courts and Legal Services Act 1990 and CPR 48.7.

These are costs orders whereby the court has held that the conduct of a legal representative has been shown to have been improper, unreasonable, or negligent. The result of this is that the legal representative is ordered to pay either his own client's costs by way of an indemnity, where those costs have been disallowed as against the other party, or to pay the costs of his opponent.

The Practice Direction to CPR 48 sets out the principles to be considered by the court in hearing such an application. The test is essentially threefold, as follows.

1. The legal representative must have acted improperly, unreasonably, or negligently.

2. His conduct must have caused a party to incur unnecessary costs.

3. It must be just, in all of the circumstances, to make the order.

The case of *Ridehalgh v Horsefield and Anor* [1994] Ch 205 suggested that wasted costs orders are only designed to apply to a small number of cases. The case also helpfully defined improper, unreasonable, and negligent as being a breach of professional duty, vexatious, and incompetent, respectively.

In so far as the test for 'unnecessary' is concerned, the way in which the court will deal with this is by looking to the 'but for' test—that is, 'but for' the conduct of the legal representative, would the costs, on a balance of probability, have been incurred?

The court's discretion to make a wasted costs order follows a formula:

- whether, on the evidence of the applicant alone, a wasted costs order is likely; and
- whether such a costs order is justified, notwithstanding the cost involved.

The respondent adviser to the application is given the opportunity to object to the application, but the burden rests with the applicant, although there is no burden on the respondent to excuse himself.

As for the timing of the application, wasted costs orders are usually dealt with at the end of the trial when the judge is hearing cost applications. The reason for this is that the conduct can be scrutinized in the context of the whole proceedings and the issue of proportionality can also be considered.

Practical Considerations

It is not always clear when to proceed with a wasted costs order. Conduct that might be considered appropriate for wasted costs orders probably includes failing to attend a court appointment, breaching court orders, negligently mispleading a case, continuing with an action after it has become hopeless, and where a real loss has been suffered as a result of the legal representative's conduct. This is not a complete list of the occasions on which the court might consider a wasted costs order.

Professional Conduct

Where a wasted costs order is made and the client is not present in court to hear the order, the party's legal representative must notify the client in writing of the costs order no later than seven days after the legal representative receives notice of the order (CPR 44.2). If the legal representative fails to do so, he will be in breach of Rule 2.03.

4.9 WHAT NEXT FOR COSTS? LORD JACKSON'S REVIEW

Lord Jackson's review of costs was requisitioned with a view to reducing the increasing costs of litigation whilst trying to maintain and improve access to justice. One of the main features of the Review was to address the issue of proportionality that spans many aspects of litigation.

As you have seen from Chapter 3, some of his recommendations concern changing the way in which cases are funded. Most of his recommendations focus on costs, but in order to reduce costs and ensure litigation is proportionate, he has proposed that some of the stages of litigation be re-examined. These include disclosure, witness statements and experts' reports, case management and Part 36 offers. Later chapters will chart these recommendations. Here, we set out what the current position is on the area of costs at which Lord Jackson has looked and what he is envisaging will take place if the Ministry of Justice implements his findings. The online chapter on the Assessment of Costs also contains some reference to Lord Jackson's findings in relation to summary and detailed assessment proceedings.

Since Lord Jackson's review was published in January 2010, it is thought that the Ministry of Justice are only seriously considering implementing, from the above table, the one-way costs-shifting regime and they are, at the time of updating the handbook, still consulting on this.

However, what has quite forcibly been launched into action since the review are the changes below that have been borne out of a growing concern for costs:

- the Low Value RTA Cases Protocol (see above);
- a pilot of costs budgeting and management in all Mercantile and Technology and Construction Courts.

FIGURE 4.1

CURRENT POSITION	LORD JACKSON'S PROPOSALS
1. Working towards a proportionate ratio of costs to damages recovered. Proportionality of costs is underpinned by the overriding objective and the twofold test in *Lownds* (paragraph 4.3.2.4).	The CPR should be amended to include a definition of proportionality and the decision in *Lownds* should be reversed so that costs that are said to be necessarily incurred are not in fact proportionate. In essence, if parties wish to pursue claims or defences at a disproportionate cost, they will have to do so at their own expense. He has recommended that the issue of disproportionate costs should be at the forefront of reform and many of his proposals have their roots in overcoming the issue of disproportionate costs in litigation.
2. The indemnity principle: the winning party cannot recover more from his opponent than he has paid to his solicitor in the course of the litigation.	The abolition of the indemnity principle but with the proviso that it is unlikely that the winning party will recover costs at an hourly rate which is higher than they paid to their legal representatives.
3. No current body in place to give guidance on legal fees.	A Costs Council (a free-standing body that reports to the Master of the Rolls) should be established to give guidance on recoverable fees for counsel, to ensure guideline hourly rates are proportionate and to review fast track costs.
4. There are a number of fixed and predicable costs regimes as well as the new road traffic claim process but these are only relevant where very specific criteria apply (see paragraph 4.7 above).	The recoverable costs of fast track cases to be limited to £12,000 (or £13,500 for London) with other specific categories of fast track cases still being fixed.
5. In all types of litigation, the basis for the recovery of costs is that the payment of costs by one party to another is discretionary but that the starting point is that the loser generally pays the winner's costs.	In personal injury claims, there should be qualified one-way costs-shifting. What this means is that each party will bear their own costs regardless of their conduct.
6. In personal injury litigation, the payment of referral fees is legally permitted by the Solicitors' Code of Conduct 2007.	Lord Jackson proposes the banning, or at the very least, the capping of referral fees.
7. Parties, along with their legal representatives, are responsible for the management of their own costs. The courts can, to some degree, control those costs by costs orders such as costs-capping, issue-based or percentage-based costs orders.	Costs budgeting and costs management should be included in litigation training for judges and legal representatives. Rules should set out a standard costs management procedure to follow, on a compulsory basis in certain types of litigation and on a non-mandatory basis in other types of litigation. The CPR provisions on costs capping should be amended to allow such orders not just in 'exceptional circumstances'.

KEY POINTS SUMMARY

- Bear in mind the overriding objective, reasonableness, and proportionality.

- Costs orders are discretionary.

- The principle 'the winner is awarded his costs against the loser' is the starting point against which the discretion can be exercised.

- Remember the wide variety of costs orders that can be made and advise your client accordingly.

- Understand the difference between 'standard' and 'indemnity' costs.
- Note the potential changes to the current costs regime as suggested by Lord Jackson.

SELF-TEST QUESTIONS

1. What basis of costs is the usual basis upon which costs are awarded?

2. Is proportionality taken into account when assessing costs on the indemnity basis?

3. What are the two general principles in costs in litigation?

4. In which types of case are there fixed success fees?

online resource centre

Suggested answers to these general questions can be accessed by adopting lecturers on the Online Resource Centre. Your lecturer can provide these to you.

FIGURE 4.2 THE DIFFERENT TYPES OF COSTS ORDER MADE BY THE COURT

Costs in any event	These can be made at trial (and are often known as costs of proceedings) or at interim hearings. It means that whatever other costs orders are made at trial or other interim hearings, a party in receipt of this costs order has an absolute entitlement to the costs of that particular application or hearing.
Costs in the case/ application	These are usually made at interim hearings, particularly CMCs and PTRs. A party in receipt of this costs order will only get his costs of the application or hearing if he gets a cost order in his favour at trial.
Costs reserved	Here the court postpones making a decision on costs, usually until trial or another substantive hearing. If it does not make a later costs order regarding the reserved costs then the costs will be costs in the case.
Claimant's/ Defendant's costs in the case/application	This is often used where one party has been successful at an interim hearing but the court is not minded to give that party a costs in any event order but neither is it minded to make costs in the case order. What the court does is to make this order which has the effect of allowing the party who was successful on the application, costs in any event order only if he secures a costs of proceedings order at trial. If he does not obtain a costs of proceedings order at trial then each party bears their own costs of the application to which this order relates.
Costs thrown away	Where a judgment or order is set aside, or the whole or part of any proceedings are adjourned, the party in whose favour the costs order is made is entitled to costs he has incurred as a consequence.
Costs of and occasioned by the amendment	This is the usual order the court makes in respect of an application to amend a statement of case. The order requires the party making the amendment to pay the other party's costs of preparing for and attending the hearing and any consequential amendments to his own statement of case.
Costs here and below	This order is often made on appeals and allows the party who is successful on the appeal to recover his costs of the appeal and the lower court.
No order as to costs/ each party bear their own costs	Each party is to bear its own costs of the part of the proceedings to which the order relates whatever costs order the court makes at trial.

5.1 INTRODUCTION

Alternative dispute resolution (ADR) has been available in this country for many years, and has now become an important and necessary consideration as an alternative to litigation. The court now has a duty, as part of its active management of cases, to further the overriding objective, which includes, under CPR 1.4(2)(e), encouraging ADR as a method of dispute resolution.

This chapter will deal with the methods by which the Civil Procedure Rules (CPR) encourage parties to settle their disputes at an early stage and, ultimately, without proceeding to trial. It will also look at the methods of dispute resolution that may be available, including a more detailed look at the most common of them. This chapter covers:

- the different types of ADR;

- the integration of ADR into the CPR;

- the philosophy of ADR; and
- a detailed look at mediation.

5.2 A DEFINITION OF ALTERNATIVE DISPUTE RESOLUTION (ADR)

There is no single overarching definition of ADR, but it has been said that a starting premise must be that it is a voluntary process and must therefore be consented to by the parties to a dispute. However, the Glossary to the CPR defines ADR simply as a 'collective description of methods of resolving disputes otherwise than through the normal trial process'. Another more recent description of ADR was put forward in *Halsey v Milton Keynes NHS Trust* [2004] EWCA Civ 576, in which Dyson LJ said 'references to ADR are usually understood as being references to some form of mediation by a third party'. But these descriptions are of limited help, because it appears that they exclude negotiations between parties and their legal representatives, and arbitration.

For the purposes of this book, we seek to include any process as an ADR process. All of these are looked at below.

 Practical Considerations

Whilst it has been stated that submission to an ADR process is voluntary, the decision in a Chancery case, *Shirayama Shokusan Co v Danovo Ltd* [2003] EWHC 390, would seem to suggest otherwise. It was held that the court does have jurisdiction to order parties to attempt ADR even if one party is unwilling. However, this does not seem to have been followed, and best practice would suggest that there would be little to be gained from an unwilling and aggrieved opponent in an ADR process such as mediation.

5.3 THE DIFFERENT TYPES OF ADR

5.3.1 NEGOTIATIONS, OR ROUND TABLE DISCUSSIONS

Whether you negotiate over the telephone or arrange a meeting to sit around a table to try to resolve a dispute, this can be done at any time, but should always be conducted on a 'without prejudice' basis. The solicitor for each party usually carries out telephone negotiations. 'Round table' meetings more commonly involve each party attending with his solicitor and, possibly, counsel. Breaks can be taken during the negotiation to give each party the opportunity to have confidential discussions with its legal team.

This forum gives the client the opportunity to have his case aired, and to appreciate the strengths and weakness of his opponent's case. It is usually—but not always—the first step taken in trying to resolve a dispute before proceeding with one of the other alternatives listed below.

5.3.2 MEDIATION

The process of mediation is confidential and conducted without prejudice to impending or continuing litigation between parties. It may take place at any time before or during litigation and can normally be set up at very short notice, although, like other forms of negotiation, the timing may be critical. The process is also non-binding until a final written agreement has been signed by the parties. The parties can walk away from it at any time before a settlement is concluded, although the court may, to a degree, investigate their behaviour during any mediation, as well as their attitude towards it.

The parties appoint a neutral intermediary who endeavours to facilitate a settlement. The mediator does not act as judge or arbitrator, nor does he rule on the merits and neither will he suggest or impose the settlement terms. Rather, by shuttling between the parties, exploring their positions, and bringing them together as and when appropriate, the mediator helps the parties to find common ground. As the settlement emerges from consensus, one of the key advantages is that the parties then 'own' the settlement and do not see it as having been forced upon them by a court or third party.

It is often capable of achieving commercially sensible solutions, which can leave both parties satisfied—not something that a court decision following great expenditure and a 'gloves off' approach can often achieve. The solution may also be in the form of relief that the court itself had no power to order. If successful, it will probably be a great deal cheaper than a trial. Even if unsuccessful, both parties are likely to benefit by knowing more about the strengths and weaknesses of each other's position, and this may promote settlement at a later date.

There is no formal regulation of mediation as yet in this country but the Civil Mediation Council exists to drive mediation forward in the UK in terms of accreditation of mediators. The EU Mediation Directive has however defined five key provisions relating to mediation in cross-border disputes for civil and commercial matters. It is the authors' view that mediation in the UK complies with the Directive.

5.3.3 CONCILIATION

As with mediation, conciliation is based on a neutral intermediary liaising with the parties, but usually the conciliator will be more proactive and may suggest his own solutions. This method of dispute resolution is common in employment disputes, often through the Advisory, Conciliation and Arbitration Service (ACAS).

5.3.4 THE EXECUTIVE TRIBUNAL

The 'executive table' is usually used to resolve commercial disputes. A panel is formed from senior representatives of the parties who have not themselves been involved in the dispute. The representatives sit together with a neutral adviser. The process is similar to a mini-trial, although, in reality, it is not a trial at all. The parties present their cases to the executives, who then have an opportunity to evaluate the respective claims. Rather than making a determination, however, the panel members then retire and endeavour to negotiate a settlement on a commercial basis. If the executives struggle to come to an agreement, the independent adviser issues a non-binding advisory opinion.

5.3.5 EARLY NEUTRAL EVALUATION (ENE)

Under early neutral evaluation (ENE), a third party—usually an independent legal representative or, in some cases, a judge who has been 'released' by the judiciary for this purpose—considers the issues and advises on the likely outcome. If a judge is chosen to provide the evaluation, he will not determine the action if it goes ahead. Having the view of an independent arbiter, respected by both parties, may then act as a spur to settlement—or at least enable the parties to re-evaluate their cases or appreciate the critical issues and the likely outcome if they do not settle.

5.3.6 JUDICIAL OR EXPERT DETERMINATION

If pursuing judicial or expert determination, the parties jointly instruct and make written submissions to a senior judge (often one who has retired) or Queen's Counsel (QC), who then makes a written appraisal. The parties are required to agree the form and extent of the instruction in advance, and whether the appraisal is to be binding or not. It is extremely important that the client understands the nature and extent of the instruction, especially if it is to be binding, because this will ultimately determine the case. These decisions cannot generally be appealed, but can be challenged on limited grounds—usually where the expert has materially departed from his instructions.

In *Doughty Hanson and Co Ltd v Bruce Patrick Roe; and Bruce Patrick Roe v (1) Doughty Hanson and Co Ltd (2) Nigel Edward Doughty (3) Richard Peter Hanson* [2007] EWHC 2212 (Ch), the court examined the circumstances under which the conclusions of an expert appointed for an expert determination could be challenged. The case highlights that 'non-speaking' decisions are harder to challenge. A 'non-speaking' determination is one for which the expert does not need to give his reasons. However, parties can provide that the expert give a 'speaking' determination. This will give a party a more ready means of challenging the outcome, but such an expert determination is more expensive. The court does, however, take the view that it should not readily interfere with the outcome of a process of dispute resolution in which the parties have willingly engaged.

In practice, expert determination can be on a preliminary issue, such as liability, leaving the parties to negotiate or mediate the quantum part of the claim.

5.3.7 ARBITRATION

Arbitration features heavily in the construction industry, and appears commonly as the dispute resolution clause in many national and international commercial agreements. The 1996 Arbitration Act governs current arbitration practice in this country, and introduces mandatory and non-mandatory provisions.

The arbitrator is usually a solicitor, barrister, architect, or quantity surveyor, who conducts the arbitration on a private basis according to a timetable set by him in discussion with the parties, with a view to coming to a final and binding decision known as a 'final award'. The process involves meetings between the arbitrator and the parties, as well as the presentation of statements of case, written submissions, and documentary evidence.

Once the award has been made, the arbitrator does not release it until he has been paid by the parties. The award can be enforced in the High Court if not paid, or set aside by a High Court judge, on the application of the disgruntled party to a specialist division of the High Court. (See Chapter 1, Figure 1.1, for details of the specialist courts.)

The main features of arbitration are that it is expensive, as is litigation, because you must use an expert arbitrator, and it can be fairly long-running as a dispute resolution process. However, your client may have no option but to arbitrate if there is a valid arbitration clause in the contract and, if this is the case, litigation cannot be considered (unless both parties agree). The common practical effect of this is that if a party attempts to litigate a matter where there is a valid contractual arbitration clause, then the opponent can usually apply to the High Court under s. 9 of the Arbitration Act 1996 to stay proceedings whilst the arbitration continues.

5.3.8 ADJUDICATION

If adjudication is pursued, either by virtue of a contractual term, agreement between parties, or pursuant to the Housing Grants Construction and Regeneration Act 1996, a party serves on his opponent a 'notice of intention to proceed to adjudication' and nominates an adjudicator (usually a surveyor, architect, engineer, solicitor, or barrister). The adjudicator will issue directions on paper as to when full written submissions are to be made to him. These submissions are known as the 'referral notice' on the part of the party who commences and the 'response to referral' on the part of the defending party. The adjudicator may require a site inspection or a directions hearing. There are strict time limits imposed under the 1996 Act, which regulates the principles of adjudication.

The most important features of adjudication are that:

- the contract must be a 'construction' contract and must be in, or evidenced in, writing;
- there must be a dispute to refer, not only a difference—that is, a dispute can arise only once the subject matter of a claim, issue, or other matter has been brought to the attention

of the opposing party, and that party has had an opportunity to consider, admit, modify, or reject it;

- the adjudicator must come to his written decision within 28 days of the service of the referral notice;

- the adjudicator has no jurisdiction on costs, therefore each party must bear its own, no matter who is successful; and

- the adjudicator's decision is only binding unless and until it is appealed to the High Court. As such, the losing party must comply with the decision until such times as it may be appealed. If he does not, then an application for a P24 summary judgment can be made.

This process is frequently used in construction and engineering disputes both between contracting parties and professional advisers, such as architects and engineers. There are exclusions as to the type of contract to which this process can apply—notably, domestic building matters and food processing plants, to name but a few.

Figure 5.1 at the end of this chapter offers a summary of some of the advantages and disadvantages of the above types of ADR process to help you to identify which method is most appropriate for your client. The summary is not, however, exhaustive.

The most commonly used process as an alternative to litigation in England and Wales for general civil disputes is **mediation,** and, for this reason, much of this chapter will focus on mediation as a form of dispute resolution.

5.4 **THE BENEFITS OF ADR**

Litigation conducted in an adversarial and combative manner can prove time-consuming and expensive. The process can last many months, or even years, and because the parties are vying to 'win', litigation can end up driving them further apart. The parties become focused on seizing the tactical initiative and undermining each other's case in whatever way they can. In this way, the parties can sometimes forget, if they were in a commercial relationship, why they were in business together in the first place.

Whilst the media hype concerning ADR can sometimes give the mistaken impression that ADR is a panacea, it is true that ADR does have a number of major attractions.

- ADR (save for arbitration)—and mediation in particular—is relatively inexpensive by comparison with litigation.

- Most forms of ADR rarely take more than a day or two.

- Because ADR is not based on 'winners' and 'losers', it tends to encourage the parties to talk more freely. The intention is to provide the parties with a neutral, non-threatening, and totally confidential environment in which they can explore their respective cases, as well as their business relationship.

- ADR is more flexible than litigation. The basis of any settlement arrived at is not limited by the legal remedies available from the courts; rather, settlements can be used to regulate the parties' relationship in the future. For example, a party who has suffered loss arising from a breach of contract may be prepared to forgo the normal legal remedy of damages in return for more preferential trading terms going forward. This may be particularly important if the defendant does not actually have the means in the immediate future to meet an expensive damages claim, in which case, a victory at trial is likely to be a pyrrhic one.

- Many forms of ADR—notably mediations—are conducted in total confidence and on a 'without prejudice' basis. Therefore, the content of the settlement discussions cannot (although there are exceptions) be disclosed to a court or to other third parties. This contrasts with the open arena in which litigation is conducted and the media publicity that is often attendant.

- Many forms of ADR (save for adjudicative forms) are only possible if both parties agree and, unless the parties choose otherwise, settlements cannot be imposed on them. Only once a settlement is reached does it become binding. Before that time, the parties can withdraw or revert to litigation. In litigation, the parties are bound by the rulings of the court however unfair they consider them to be.

- The whole purpose of ADR is to promote early settlement. Even if it does not achieve this aim, it will often provide the parties with a better understanding of the psychology of their opponent and the issues that they see as important. This knowledge may prove useful in any subsequent settlement negotiations.

The key words are therefore speed; flexibility; cost; consensus; confidentiality; and settlement.

5.5 THE ENCOURAGEMENT OF ADR BY PROTOCOL, CPR, AND THE COURTS

Having established that ADR is a 'good thing'—that is, a useful tool in the armoury of dispute resolution—how are the parties and their legal representatives being encouraged to use it? There is now provision and scope for ADR during the Pre-Action Protocol period, and the CPR also give guidance and direction on the use of ADR within proceedings. HM Courts and Tribunals Service has also made strides to help mediation as a form of ADR more accessible to parties.

5.5.1 ADR AND THE PROTOCOLS

A standardized approach has been undertaken for all Pre-Action Protocols, including the Practice Direction on Pre-Action Conduct. They all embody similar paragraphs requiring the parties to consider whether ADR is appropriate and, if so, in what form, warning that the court may, at a subsequent hearing, require evidence that ADR was considered pre-issue. Each Protocol and the Practice Direction on Pre-Action Conduct summarizes the appropriate ADR methods, which are commonly discussion and negotiation, and mediation.

 Practical Considerations

Best practice suggests that a degree of discussion and negotiation with your opponent should be attempted in advance of any other type of ADR, in an effort to save the time and cost of mediation. This could take the form of a 'without prejudice' chat with your opponent's legal representative over the telephone, or a face-to-face discussion and a Part 36 offer.

5.5.2 ADR AND THE CPR

Judicial encouragement of ADR has intensified with the introduction of the CPR. Proceedings can be stayed if the parties wish to attempt ADR and/or the court considers ADR to be appropriate. The CPR encourage the use of ADR in the following ways and at the following prescribed stages of litigation—but remember that the Court Guides for High Court matters also deal with the divisional courts' requirements for ADR.

5.5.2.1 Staying proceedings for ADR after the allocation questionnaire

In all Part 7 claims (for a definition of a Part 7 claim, see Chapter 9, paragraph 9.3), after the defendant has served its defence, the court will issue and send an allocation questionnaire (AQ) to the parties (for the detailed rules, see CPR 26.3 and Chapter 12). This asks the parties specifically about settlement and whether they would like a one-month stay (or such a period as the court deems appropriate) in which to attempt to settle the case by ADR or other means (CPR 26.4(1)).

If all of the parties request a stay, or the court, of its own initiative, considers that such a stay would be appropriate, the court will direct that the proceedings be stayed for at least a month (CPR 26.4(2)). Judicial comments published to date indicate that if one of the parties requests a stay in order to attempt ADR and the party opposing a stay cannot show good reasons why ADR is unlikely to work, the court is likely to order a stay.

Where a stay is ordered, the onus is then on the claimant to notify the court if a settlement is reached. If no notification is given by the end of the period of the stay, the court will go on to make such directions as to the management of the case as it considers appropriate.

5.5.2.2 Case management conferences (CMCs) and pre-trial requirements

Even if ADR is not attempted at the AQ stage of the proceedings, the door remains open to a reference throughout the litigation process.

Intrinsic to the whole new approach to litigation is the concept of 'case management'. It therefore seems likely that the courts will ask parties attending case management conferences (CMCs) whether they have attempted ADR and to justify their position if not.

The point of raising ADR on all of those occasions is to ensure that alternatives to litigation receive proper consideration. It will no longer be sufficient to tick the box in the AQ, indicating that ADR has been considered or rejected as unsuitable. On occasions such as the first CMC and the pre-trial hearing, you should be prepared to explain, in some detail, why your client does not consider ADR to be appropriate or, possibly, why it was tried and failed (without exceeding the realms of confidentiality).

 Practical Considerations

Best practice would suggest that in cases involving many parties, in which the availability of individuals attending a mediation is difficult to coordinate, the court is generally agreeable to granting stays for ADR for periods of three to six months.

 Practical Considerations

ADR in practice is more overarching than the Protocols and CPR actually suggest, because ADR can effectively take place at any time. It is not limited to the Protocol phase, or to points in an action dictated by CMCs or pre-trial matters. Mediation, for example, can take place during lengthy trials. The key point here is that, as a legal representative, you should be constantly considering when and how ADR can be used to avoid trial and/or judgment.

5.5.3 ADR AND HM COURTS AND TRIBUNALS SERVICE

A number of courts in England and Wales have piloted and set up voluntary mediation schemes. These can be found, for example, in the county courts in Birmingham, Manchester, and Stoke-on-Trent, but not all county courts offer these schemes.

The way in which these schemes operate is that, on the filing of a defence to a two-party action, the court writes to the parties asking if they will agree to submit to a fixed three or four-hour mediation at court, usually to take place outside court hours and therefore between 4 p.m. and 8 p.m. for a fixed fee per party.

If both parties agree, the court allows the mediation to take place in the court building, with both parties attending, along with an accredited mediator. The process is wholly independent from the court and, if settlement is reached, a consent order is drawn up there and then, and placed with the court file to be sealed, and the action comes to an end. If settlement is not reached, the court file is returned to the court for consideration by the district judge, with a view to issuing AQs.

5.5.4 **ADR AND COST CONSEQUENCES**

A party who refuses to enter into an ADR process may well now be penalized in costs.

In any case that makes it to trial, the court retains a discretion as to whether costs are payable, and, if so, by whom and when (see CPR 44.3–44.5). The courts' attitude to this is discussed in some detail in Chapter 4, paragraph 4.2.

 Costs

There should be clear documentary evidence (attendance note or letter) on your file of the occasions on which you considered ADR with your client and your opponent. The suggestion of ADR can be very a useful and valuable weapon to use to attempt to defeat an application for costs, even if that party has lost the litigation.

5.5.5 **LORD JACKSON'S PROPOSALS**

Lord Jackson's recommendations suggest a continuation of the current drive to educate legal representatives and clients alike on the benefits of ADR. He suggests an authoritative handbook be prepared explaining clearly what ADR is and providing details of accredited providers of mediation (see paragraph 5.8.2). This approach has been endorsed by the Ministry of Justice whose 2011–2015 business plan is to promote the wider use of ADR. At the time of writing, we are still waiting to hear how!

5.6 **THE SUITABILITY OF ADR IN DISPUTE RESOLUTION**

Following on from some of the discussions in the cases above, ADR may not be appropriate to resolve every dispute. Sometimes, a client's commercial objectives may be best achieved by embarking on litigation. The commencement of proceedings may exert more pressure, at least initially, than a suggestion that the parties attempt ADR. Alternatively, it may be that litigation is necessary because the prime remedy needed is an emergency injunction, which can only be obtained from the courts, or because the parties are looking for a definitive court ruling on a particular issue in order to establish a binding precedent.

Further, there may be little point in delaying litigation if the opposing side is not yet ready to talk settlement in realistic terms, or if a client's case is strong enough to justify an application for summary judgment. In those circumstances, pursuing the litigation route may well result in a quicker settlement than a reference to ADR.

Even if ADR is considered appropriate, there may be a particular type of ADR that is best suited to a client's case or in which the client may achieve a tactical advantage. Likewise, the timing of a reference to ADR may itself be a delicate matter. Whilst there is now a duty imposed on all parties to a dispute to consider ADR pre-issue, sometimes, ADR will be most effective after litigation has progressed to a point at which the issues have been crystallized in the statements of case. These can be difficult decisions that need to be taken on a case-by-case basis. All legal representatives need to be trained to assist clients in making the right decision in line with their personal and commercial objectives.

5.7 **PREPARATION FOR ADR GENERALLY**

As is apparent from this chapter, from the outset of any dispute, the parties should now actively consider whether ADR is likely to be of benefit and if so, how the process is to be handled. This is an exercise that is likely to involve the client and legal representative collaborating closely together, since the issues are likely to be commercial, or personal, as well as legal. Even if a client is intractably opposed to ADR, it can no longer bury its head in the sand and ignore it: if it cannot justify its opposition, it may well find itself penalized in costs, as suggested above.

So what issues need to be considered at the outset?

1. A realistic appraisal of the case is essential, because ADR is likely to be ineffective if the key issues have not been identified and evaluated. As part of this process, the legal representative and client need to consider any commercial and/or personal objectives and whether they might be better achieved by ADR or litigation. The likely costs, timescale, and pressure points may all have a bearing here.

2. Careful consideration needs to be given to any settlement discussions to date, the likely readiness of the opposing side to negotiate realistically, and the timing of any attempt at ADR. Reconsider the points made in paragraph 5.6 above: if ADR is a possibility, the merits of the different types of ADR should be considered. (Figure 5.1 at the end of this chapter may assist.)

3. If some form of intermediary, mediator, expert, or judge is needed, the identity of that person should be discussed. Does the intermediary require expert knowledge of a particular field to grasp the issues, or would a generalist be better suited? Does the legal representative already know a suitably qualified individual, or would it be better to approach one of the leading ADR bodies or courts? Can agreement be reached with the opposition regarding the appointment of the intermediary?

4. The selection of the ADR team to represent a client and/or prepare submissions for the client also requires careful planning. Usually, it will be the client and the legal representative in attendance, but consideration should be given to whether an expert, counsel, or witnesses may be required. (These would only ever be necessary to clarify issues.)

5. Finally, the negotiation strategy needs to be thought through in advance and parties who have not experienced ADR before should be informed about the process, so that they are not caught unawares. Clearly, your strategy and tactics may vary once the process gets underway and depending on how it develops, so it is important to remain flexible and open-minded.

5.8 MEDIATION AS A FORM OF DISPUTE RESOLUTION

Mediation is becoming more predominant in dispute resolution both within our own jurisdiction and in Europe. The Mediation Directive, in this regard, applies to European cross-border disputes (rather than disputes arising within any one member state such as the UK) and must be implemented by May 2011. Many of its regulations are similar in essence to mediation practice in this country.

The remainder of this chapter will concentrate on aspects of mediation in practice within the UK that are important to bear in mind when conducting a piece of litigation and when advising a client.

5.8.1 THE INTERPLAY OF MEDIATION AND LITIGATION

Mediation is a flexible process and can therefore be used at any time: before proceedings are issued; during proceedings; even during a lengthy trial. However, whilst the ethos of the CPR was to encourage the use of ADR and mediation in particular, some thought is required as to the exact timing of the mediation.

It may be the case that there are glaring evidential gaps in relation to liability, causation, and quantum, such as experts' reports to help to assess responsibility and value. Without such a report, it would be pointless to try to compromise any of those issues, because agreement could only ever be 'subject to' its findings. The main focus of mediation is to resolve disputes more quickly and cheaply than litigation. This may not be the case if mediation is entered into too early.

5.8.2 **THE COST OF MEDIATION**

One of the advantages of mediation is that there will be cost savings if resolution is reached. There will also be time savings to the client, whether it is a personal or commercial matter. The cost and time savings will be greater the sooner mediation is entered into (subject to it being an appropriate time to mediate), compared to proceeding through to trial.

However, there is still a cost implication to the client in entering into mediation and, depending on the value of the claim, it could even be seen as disproportionate to mediate. Nevertheless, even if this is the case, it will be wholly disproportionate to litigate. The client must therefore not be misled on the benefits of mediation and, whilst it is considerably cheaper and quicker than litigation, the costs of the mediator are borne jointly and severally between the parties. A party's legal representative's time, the preparation, and any expenses must be met by that party (subject to any agreement reached during the mediation itself).

Mediators are usually either solicitors or barristers, or other professionals, such as architects, surveyors, and engineers who have been specially trained by accredited bodies such as the Centre for Dispute Resolution (CEDR)—http://www.cedr.co.uk—and the ADR Group (ADRg)—http://www.adrgroup.co.uk. (The Civil Mediation Council is looking to establish a regulation and complaints scheme, but this is yet to be implemented.) These accredited bodies can be contacted to find a suitable mediator or, alternatively, individuals can be approached directly. The National Mediation Helpline (0845 603 0809) has also been set up to assist in many aspects of the mediation process.

The mediator's fees are usually based on a fixed fee for a day or half a day and are dependent on experience. The piloted schemes mentioned in paragraph 5.5.3 are subject to a nominal fixed fee payable by the parties to the court, although each party is still bound by its retainer with its own legal representative in respect of the preparation for, and attendance at, the mediation.

5.8.3 **HOW DO YOU 'SELL' MEDIATION TO YOUR CLIENT?**

Despite the fact that the CPR have been in place since April 1999, there are still many legal representatives and clients who have never been involved in the mediation process. Some remain sceptical, but the benefits to the client are significant. The following are some of the major selling points of mediation of which the client should perhaps be made aware at a meeting when the ADR options are being discussed.

- It has been said that mediation leads to a sudden outbreak of common sense, because the aim of mediation is to solve problems, not to find fault—that is, what the client actually wants and can live with, as opposed to what are the issues in the case.

- Mediation provides the forum to 'get things off your chest'. Sitting down face to face with the opponent and telling them what has happened, and the effect that the wrongdoing or breach has had, goes a long way to diffusing the situation and sets the stage for the real work of reaching a settlement.

- Mediation also provides the equivalent for the client of a day in court. Whilst it is an informal and private process with an impartial third party present, the client feels that, within the four walls, he is telling the world that he has been wronged. The presence of the mediator seems to fulfil the client's emotional need in this regard.

- It gives the client the chance to see his case unfold before the mediator and his opponent, and to acknowledge the strengths and weaknesses of both parties' cases. It also gives the client an opportunity to see his legal representative in action, because it is usually the legal representative who conducts the opening statement on behalf of the client. The client has a chance to see his case being presented and feels as though something is finally happening.

- Mediation gives each party an opportunity to hear its opponent's case, facts and issues. The key point here is that all of the parties hear the same information even if they perceive it differently. It is then the mediator's job to define and clarify certain facts and issues.

- Mediation has a way of unearthing the real issues in a case. Sometimes, this requires some digging around by the mediator to get to the root of the problem, because it has been masked by ancillary ones.

5.8.4 WHAT DOES THE CLIENT NEED TO KNOW ABOUT MEDIATION?

The client needs to know full details of the mediation process, including preparation and procedure, how long is required, and what it can achieve in terms of time and cost savings. The length of the mediation will determine the cost and therefore thought should be given to whether a full day is, in fact, necessary, or whether a shorter period—for example, five hours—would suffice. However long the mediation day is anticipated to last, it is always worthwhile blocking out time in your own and your client's diaries in case it should over-run. It would undermine the process if progress were to be made towards settlement during the mediation day, but the parties have to leave for other commitments.

It is often appropriate, when discussing mediation with the client, to provide details of the costs incurred to the date of the prospective mediation and an estimate of costs to trial, whilst also undertaking a risk analysis on the prospects of success and proportionality.

It is, however, very important—especially for those who are new to the mediation process—that the client understands what he will achieve. The client should not be led to have enhanced expectations about a 'victory' at the hands of his opponent. Mediation is not about 'point scoring'; rather, it is about getting on with life and business, and laying the dispute to rest.

As such, it is the legal representative's job to manage those expectations. Mediation is about compromise and it is very unlikely that as matters settle at mediation, either party will be elated with the outcome. It is, however, still a preferable process than proceeding to trial, at which a third party, the judge, decides the case for the parties, and at which there is always a 'winner' and 'loser' on the issues in the case.

5.8.5 PREPARATION FOR THE MEDIATION DAY

5.8.5.1 The appointment of the mediator

The parties may be able to agree on a known individual to act as mediator. Alternatively, they may approach one of the recognized mediation bodies to obtain a list of possible candidates to act as mediator, as set out in paragraph 5.8.2 above. Consideration should be given to whether the mediator needs specialist skills and whether a legal or other professional is required. Sometimes, the appointment of joint mediators may be appropriate. The urgency of the mediation may, of course, determine which mediators are available. Curricula vitae (CVs) are usually requested, along with dates of availability.

Once the parties have agreed on the identity of the mediator, he is informed and contacts both parties simultaneously to confirm his appointment. Most mediators or mediation bodies will require the parties to enter into a mediation agreement. Each party enters into the agreement with the mediator in advance of the mediation day, although it is common that these are left for signing on the morning of the mediation. The agreement will usually cover some basic ground rules, which predominantly include confidentiality and fees. A sample mediation agreement can be seen in the Online Resource Centre.

5.8.5.2 Procedural steps

5.8.5.2.1 *The mediator's requirements*

On the agreed appointment of the mediator, the mediator will write to the parties simultaneously, confirming his understanding as to who they and their legal representatives are, when and where the mediation is to take place, the anticipated duration of the process, and his specific requirements as to documentation. It is very important that a person with authority to settle from each party is present at the mediation. It is frustrating if that person has only a limited authority, although having a client representative at the end of the telephone is a better alternative.

5.8.5.2.2 *The position statement*

The mediator will usually require a position statement as part of the specific documentation from each party. These will be copied to the opposite party and the mediator seven days before the mediation (although this time limit varies in practice). The parties need to consider who will be responsible for the preparation of these submissions and, frequently, this is a role assigned to the legal representative. Generally, mediators will want submissions kept fairly short, giving only a summary of the case and each party's stance in relation to the issues.

 Practical Considerations

The parties should try to agree a core bundle of documents to send to the mediator along with the position statements, because this limits the amount of reading time. The preparation of the core bundle will usually fall to the party who would be the claimant in any litigation.

5.8.5.2.3 *Preliminary discussions with the mediator*

Before the day of the mediation, the mediator may wish to discuss with the parties or their lawyers any difficulties that he has with his understanding of the case, the manner in which the initial presentation of their cases is to be made, and possibly details of any previous failed settlement attempts. These discussions are confidential to each party.

It also gives the mediator a chance to get to know the legal representatives or client ahead of the day, and this will ultimately save time and money. These discussions are usually done over the telephone, but are not always necessary.

5.8.6 THE MEDIATION DAY(S)

The following describes the likely procedure during a mediation day. However, it is important to remember that each mediation day is different and that the discretion lies with the mediator as to how it is conducted. For example, if the relationship between the parties was particularly acrimonious, the mediator may decide to dispense with the opening joint session or to curtail it significantly.

5.8.6.1 The initial joint meeting

The mediation may take place at a neutral venue or at one of the party's legal representative's offices. Once the mediator is ready, the parties will be called into a room, where the mediator will outline the mediation process and establish the ground rules. It is at this stage that the parties or their legal representatives will normally be asked to make short opening statements of their cases. In essence, this will amount to a short summary of the written submissions, again with a view to clarifying the issues in the case. An opening joint session can be seen on the Online Resource Centre video clips.

5.8.6.1.1 *Private 'caucuses' or 'sessions'*

Once the submissions are complete, the mediator may chose to keep the parties together or to invite them into separate rooms, where they can speak privately. These private meetings are called 'caucuses' and nothing said in caucus can be revealed to the other side without the permission of the party in caucus. The caucuses are useful means of exploring the business relationship between the parties, of finding out where they are coming from, flushing out the issues that each side sees as key, and perhaps looking at why previous settlements have failed.

The mediator may well engage in 'shuttle diplomacy', moving between rooms in a series of private sessions, looking for common ground or areas in which the parties feel able to make movement.

5.8.6.1.2 *Joint meetings*

The mediator will not simply wish to act as messenger for the parties. At times during the process, the parties may be brought together for joint meetings so that they can negotiate directly or tackle issues that are proving to be a stumbling block. Likewise, the mediator may wish to meet with the legal representative or the experts separately, or to meet with the parties in the absence of their lawyers. The process is voluntary, however, and the mediator cannot compel a party to do anything with which he does not feel comfortable.

5.8.6.1.3 *The settlement*

If the mediation results in a settlement, the mediator will normally be keen to have the terms written up into a formal agreement there and then. This may be a task delegated to the parties' legal representatives or it may be something that the mediator takes on. It is normally desirable to record the agreement in writing as soon as terms are agreed and whilst there is still an impetus to settle. Once the settlement has been written up and the parties have signed up to it, it becomes binding and can be enforced in the usual way through the courts as examined in Chapter 21. A closing settlement meeting can be seen on the Online Resource Centre video clips.

KEY POINTS SUMMARY

- Consider ADR seriously—if it is not to be tried, have a good reason why not and, even if it gets rejected early on, do not be afraid to reconsider later.

- Change your mindset—aim for resolution, not a judicial determination.

- Understand the different types of ADR and which one may be best suited to the client's case.

- The CPR expects parties to engage with ADR and there can be cost penalties for an unreasonable refusal to consider ADR.

- Consider when is best to mediate. It will be different in every case.

- Make sure that your client understands what he can expect from mediation and curtail those enhanced expectations.

- Be prepared for mediation in terms of written submissions and documents. Whilst mediation is a flexible process, there is no excuse for sloppy or inaccurate presentation.

- If settlement is achieved, ensure that the agreement or order drafted is legally binding and enforceable.

SELF-TEST QUESTIONS

1. What are the available adjudicative methods of ADR?

2. What are the available non-adjudicative methods of ADR?

3. How can mediation in low-value cases be used effectively and proportionately?

online resource centre

Suggested answers to these general questions can be found on the Online Resource Centre.

FIGURE 5.1

TYPE OF ADR PROCESS	POSITIVE FEATURES	NEGATIVE FEATURES	COMMON USE IN
Negotiation/Round table discussions	Voluntary, without prejudice, flexible, legal representation not essential, arranged at short notice and inexpensive	Inequality of parties and parties often become entrenched in their own positions	All types of disputes at any stage
Mediation	Voluntary, confidential, non-binding, proactive intervention of neutral third party, ascertains what your opponent really wants, free to leave at any time, can be arranged quickly and cheaper than proceeding to trial	Both parties must be willing to make it work and there is still a cost implication to the parties	All types of disputes (save for test cases) at any stage even during trial. Can also be used either consecutively or concurrently with adjudication if appropriate.
Conciliation	Voluntary, without prejudice, proactive intervention of independent third party, gain a better understanding of opponent's dispute	Usually no formal written submissions required and this can sometimes hamper the process by clouding issues	Usually a pre-condition in many contracts to arbitration or litigation and is common in employment matters
Executive Tribunal	Voluntary and can be quick and effective. Very low cost implication	The opinion does not have to be followed and the executives can remain entrenched in their respective positions	Commercial matters with reasonably sized commercial entities

TYPE OF ADR PROCESS	POSITIVE FEATURES	NEGATIVE FEATURES	COMMON USE IN
ENE	Voluntary and non binding, usually occurs early on in a dispute, focuses on central issues and relevant law only	If a judge is wanted it may take time to arrange. Still a cost implication as submissions and documentation needs to be prepared	Larger technical building and engineering or commercial cases
Expert Determination	Binding but voluntary process. Decision can be obtained quickly and written submissions are not onerous	Decision cannot be enforced as a court judgment. A fresh action in contract would have to be raised. Selection of agreed expert and the limits of his instruction can be problematic	In ongoing contract where there is an ongoing business relationship to preserve, mostly used in case with technical issues
Arbitration	Specialist arbiter to hear the case, private, can prohibit litigation, finality of award provides commercial certainty	Expensive and time consuming (similar to litigation) but award if unpaid can be easily enforced through the courts	Construction and Engineering claims
Adjudication	Quick, choice of specialist adjudicator, adjudicator has no jurisdiction to award costs (less risk in a difficult case), retains a business relationship or ongoing contract thereby reducing disruption, private	Adjudicator has no jurisdiction to award cost (limits recovery), no automatic right to interest, only binding until appealed, to enforce the decision you must issue fresh proceedings and apply for P24 Summary Judgment, costs implication on enforcement	Construction and Engineering claims, and some professional negligence claims. Can also be used either consecutively or concurrently with litigation if appropriate

6 THE FIRST CLIENT MEETING AND INITIAL CONSIDERATIONS

6.1 INTRODUCTION

As a legal representative new to practice, you will be expected initially to assist in clients' cases and ultimately to handle your own files. New cases for existing and new clients are usually fielded firstly through the firm's receptionist to the litigation (otherwise known as 'dispute resolution') department, where cases are allocated to the various fee earners. In smaller firms, this may mean only one or two fee earners.

In every new matter for every client, two elements should be at the forefront of your mind as a legal representative before you proceed to undertake any work for the client: professional conduct and client care. These are, by their very nature, interrelated and can be addressed to some degree in advance of the first attendance on the client.

The first meeting that you have with a new client is likely to take some time and there will usually be a number of action points that arise as a result of the meeting.

All of these aspects require you, as the legal representative, to spend time with, and incur a cost to, the client.

This chapter will focus on:

- professional conduct issues;
- client care and money laundering requirements;
- the first meeting with the client; and
- initial investigations.

LITIGATION TRAIN: THE FIRST CLIENT INTERVIEW AND INITIAL CONSIDERATIONS

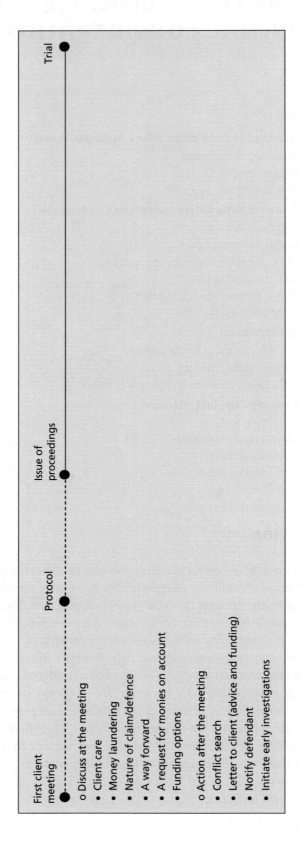

6.2 **WHAT DO YOU NEED TO THINK ABOUT BEFORE DEALING WITH EVERY NEW MATTER?**

6.2.1 **PROFESSIONAL CONDUCT ISSUES**

Your professional conduct duties, as a whole, are, at the time of writing, contained in the Solicitors' Code of Conduct Rules 2007, published on behalf of the Solicitors Regulation Authority (SRA) by the Law Society and also available online at http://www.sra.org.uk/rules/. We felt that it would be beneficial, however, if these were looked at specifically in the context of working in a litigation department so that you have a complete picture of what to look for as a legal representative and what to consider when acting in new matters. You will, however, need to consult the full text of the Code, because, here, we set out only those issues that will appear frequently in litigation. Remember the Code of Conduct is currently being completely revised by the SRA, so keep an eye out for the new Code later in the year. For a summary of the likely new Code see paragraph 1.8 in Chapter 1. Details of the new Code will be included in the Online Resource Centre in the first online update.

online resource centre

At the beginning of every new matter for a client, you need to ensure that you comply with the following current rules, although you should be aware that all of your professional conduct obligations span the lifetime of your retainer with your client and, in some cases, beyond:

- Rule 1—the core duties;
- Rule 2—client relations;
- Rule 3—conflict;
- Rule 4—confidentiality and disclosure; and
- Rule 11—litigation and advocacy.

In the case of a breach of any one of these rules, disciplinary action or even professional indemnity action may follow (see Chapter 3, paragraph 3.2.3, for a discussion of non-compliance with these rules).

In this section, we will look at Rules 1, 3, and 4. These rules are looked at in the context of this chapter and the commencement of your relationship with your client only. Rule 2 is dealt with at paragraph 6.3 below, on a similar basis. Rule 11 features in Chapter 20.

6.2.1.1 **What are the solicitors' core duties? (Rule 1)**

There are six core duties that encapsulate a legal representative's duty to his client, the court, and the public: justice and the rule of law; integrity; independence; the best interests of clients; standard of service; and public confidence.

Therefore, at the outset and throughout every matter that arises with your client, you should bear in mind whether you are the correct level of fee earner to deal with that matter, whether you have the appropriate expertise, and whether you can do the best for your client.

 Professional Conduct

If you feel that you are out of your depth in handling any client matter, discuss this with your supervising partner and the client. It is essential that your client knows your status and experience as a legal representative when you become involved in his case. (We discuss this is more detail in paragraph 6.3 below as part of your client relations.)

6.2.1.2 **Can you act if there is a conflict of interest? (Rule 3)**

The main feature here is that, as a legal representative, you are prohibited from acting for clients in two sets of circumstances:

- where you act for two or more clients in the same or related matters and there is a conflict or a significant risk of conflict between the clients; and

- where you act for a client and there is a conflict or a significant risk of conflict between yourself and your client.

There are, however, exceptions to this rule contained in Rule 3.03, such as the clients consenting to you acting for both. The Guidance Notes to Rule 3 are very full and helpful on conflict generally.

 Example

You are instructed by a husband and wife driver and passenger, respectively, of a vehicle involved in a road traffic accident (RTA) who have sued a motorcyclist for damages for personal injuries that they each sustained. The motorcyclist, however, alleges that the husband was either wholly or partly to blame for the collision.

The potential conflict exists at the outset of the retainer, even before the allegation against the driver has been made, because there is clearly a risk that the innocent passenger may have a claim in negligence against the husband driver.

 Practical Considerations

If you were faced with the example above, then, during your first contact with the clients—whether by telephone or face to face—you would need to explain this potential conflict to them and suggest that either one, or both, seek independent legal advice elsewhere.

6.2.1.3 What is your duty of confidentiality and disclosure? (Rule 4)

You are under a duty to maintain the confidentiality of your client's affairs at all times unless your client (or former client) agrees to the disclosure of confidential information or it is permitted by law. However, your duty goes further than this, because you are not permitted to act if, by acting, you are putting confidentiality at risk at some point in the future.

Again, there are exceptions to this general rule contained in Rule 4.04 and 4.05 allowing you to put confidentiality at risk by acting either with or without your client's consent. The Guidance Notes to Rule 4 give many examples and discuss how to comply with your duty of confidentiality, but with appropriate safeguards.

Perhaps the key point to make here is that the duty of confidentiality will always override the duty of disclosure.

 Professional Conduct

In the example cited above and the corresponding 'Practical considerations' box, it would be very difficult to continue to act for both clients, even with their consent. This is because you would be unable to act in either client's best interests and comply with your duty of confidentiality, given that one client is a potential defendant to a personal injury claim. It is likely that you would be in receipt of material information that would be in either client's adverse interest.

6.2.2 CLIENT CARE OBLIGATIONS

There are a number of client care issues that need to be addressed either before you have that first meeting with your client or at the meeting itself. These are born out of Rule 2 of the Code. You may find it useful to have a 'client care checklist' based on the points raised in this section.

Rule 2 identifies specifically what aspects of your client relations you must consider at the outset of your retainer. Many of these must be explained to your client both right at the start and as the matter progresses. It is best practice both to discuss these with your client and to give this information in writing (where it is not otherwise denoted as mandatory in the Rules).

These important aspects are as follows.

6.2.2.1 Rule 2.02—Client care

(1) You must:

    (a) identify clearly the client's objectives in relation to the work to be done for the client;

    (b) give the client a clear explanation of the issues involved and the options available to the client;

    (c) agree with the client the next steps to be taken; and

    (d) keep the client informed of the progress, unless otherwise agreed.

(2) You must, both at the outset and, as necessary, during the course of the matter:

    (a) agree an appropriate level of service;

    (b) explain your responsibilities;

    (c) explain the client's responsibilities;

    (d) ensure that the client is given, in writing, the name and status of the person dealing with the matter and the name of the person responsible for its overall supervision; and

    (e) explain any limitations or conditions resulting from your relationship with a third party (for example a funder, fee sharer or introducer) which affect the steps you can take on the client's behalf.

 Practical Considerations

When explaining to your client the items in Rule 2.02 above, you should stress that the relationship between the client and yourself as a solicitor is a two-way process. You should therefore highlight to your client that he has to make a time commitment to his own case. It is important to control his expectations early on and to ensure that he appreciates that, with his cooperation, you will endeavour to do your best for him.

(3) If you can demonstrate that it was inappropriate in the circumstances to meet some or all of these requirements, you will not breach 2.02.

6.2.2.2 Rule 2.03—Information about the costs of the retainer

This has been discussed at length in Chapter 3, paragraph 3.2.1, where Rule 2.03 is set out. Rule 2.03 explains the information that you must give to your client on costs. However, it is best practice also to explain to your client the distinction between 'solicitor and client costs'—that is, the sum that the client must pay to his own legal representative—and 'costs between the parties' (otherwise known as *'inter partes* costs')—that is, costs that may be awarded, at the discretion of the court, between the parties once litigation has commenced. This distinction is important, because, as can be seen from Chapter 4, paragraph 4.3, the amount that a client is able to recover from his opponent, should he receive a favourable costs order, is very likely to be less than the client is liable to pay his own legal representative— excluding those clients with conditional fee agreements (CFAs) with success fees. The client will therefore usually be left with 'irrecoverable costs' from litigation. The client must fully understand his liability for those.

6.2.2.3 Rule 2.05—Complaints handling

(1) If you are a recognised body, a manager of a recognised body or a recognised sole practitioner, you must ensure:

    (a) that the firm has a written complaints procedure and that complaints are handled promptly, fairly and effectively in accordance with it;

(b) that the client is told, in writing, at the outset:

   (i) that, in the event of a problem, the client is entitled to complain; and

   (ii) to whom the client should complain;

(c) that the client is given a copy of the complaints procedure on request; and

(d) that once a complaint has been made, the person complaining is told in writing:

   (i) how the complaint will be handled; and

   (ii) within what timescales they will be given an initial and/or substantial response.

(2) If you can demonstrate that it was inappropriate in the circumstances to meet some or all of these requirements, you will not breach 2.05.

(3) You must not charge your client for the cost of handling a complaint.

 Practical Considerations

It is a bizarre concept that, when establishing your client retainer, and setting out the terms for a successful and fruitful relationship, you are obliged to raise the issue of complaints. This must not be overlooked, no matter how awkward you feel about discussing this aspect.

Legal representatives should be aware of the Provision of Services Regulations 2009 that impose new requirements to give information to your client on additional client care issues. Those pertinent to this chapter concern complaint resolution. The Office for Legal Complaints now deals with complaints handling in place of the Legal Complaints Service. The Office has power to consider complaints against all regulated legal service providers. This includes barristers, ILEX fellows, licensed conveyancers and patent agents.

6.2.3 MONEY LAUNDERING REGULATIONS

We thought it appropriate to discuss briefly here how you deal practically with your obligations under the Money Laundering Regulations 2007, SI 2007/2157, as a legal representative in a litigation department. We do not intend to set out your money laundering obligations in detail. A link to further advice from the Law Society can be found on the Online Resource Centre.

online resource centre

When you enter practice, your firm will be required to provide staff with appropriate training on their legal obligations, and information on how to recognize and deal with money laundering and terrorist financing risks (reg. 21). Further, Rule 5 of the Solicitors' Code of Conduct 2007 also requires firms to train staff to a level that is appropriate to their work and level of responsibility, and legal representatives are required, as part of induction requirements, to receive money laundering training.

Money laundering within the litigation and dispute resolution framework is not as prevalent as in other areas of practice, because litigation can probably be classed as fairly low risk. However, you are still required to identify your client's name and address, usually by a passport or driver's licence and a utility bill for an individual or a company search for a limited company, and to report any reasonable suspicions to your money laundering reporting officer.

The Money Laundering Regulations 2007 brought additional burdens to legal representatives in the identification of beneficial owners of client trusts, companies, and partnerships (reg. 5), the customer due diligence measures (reg. 7) to be applied to high-risk (reg. 14) and low-risk (reg. 13) situations, and revised administrative and training requirements.

6.3 **WHAT DO YOU NEED TO DO BEFORE COMMENCING A NEW MATTER?**

Based in part on the theoretical considerations in paragraph 6.2 above, there are some essential tasks that you must undertake before you take substantive instructions from your client, whether a new or an existing client. These items will be mirrored in each new matter that arises, but as you undertake repeat work for an existing client, you will get to know your client and some of these items will become easier to deal with.

6.3.1 **SEND A CLIENT CARE LETTER**

The nature and content of Rules 2.02, 2.03, and 2.05 in paragraph 6.2.2 above are contained in what is known as a 'client care letter', or 'retainer letter'. This letter also sets out the firm's terms and conditions of acting, such as when bills will be rendered, interest provisions for late payments, VAT, storage of client files and documents, dispute resolution and jurisdiction clauses, etc.

The client care letter is best sent out to the client before he has his first meeting with you, although it can be sent out after the first meeting. If it is sent out in advance of the first meeting, then you will not be able to discuss—other than to highlight in a general way—the client's objectives for that particular matter, what the main issues are, the options available, and what steps should be taken. These will have to be set out in a subsequent letter after the first interview. If you elect to send the client care letter after the first interview, you will usually attach it to the initial letter of advice.

Be careful here, in either case, because you will need to have discussed with your client how that first interview is to be paid for. Strictly, there is no legally binding contract between the legal representative and client until the client has agreed to the contents of the client care letter, and you will usually achieve this by sending the letter in duplicate and asking the client to denote his acceptance by signing and returning one copy.

6.3.2 **REQUEST MONIES ON ACCOUNT**

As can be seen from Chapter 3, paragraphs 3.2 and 3.3, the question of how a client is to proceed with or defend a claim needs to be identified right at the beginning of the retainer. However, you are not usually able to help your client to decide how he is able to fund matters until you have attended on him and taken detailed instructions at a first meeting. This first meeting needs to be paid for by the client, unless your firm offers free first interviews or is under a general retainer with a trade union, insurance company, or other association.

It is therefore good practice to ask your client, before attending a first meeting, to give detailed instructions either face to face or by telephone and to provide monies on account to cover the cost of reviewing any documentation or otherwise incurring a fee (see paragraph 6.3.5 below), the cost of the first meeting, and cost of the letter of advice. The amount will depend on the type of matter and your hourly rate.

It is good practice to ask for the monies in cheque or bankers draft form for money laundering reasons. For every new matter that you have for a client, your accounts department, on your instruction, will need to open an account for the client and matter. The account will have a client account and an office account.

The monies on account are client monies. Once you receive the cheque, you should ask your accounts department to place it in the client account. The monies stay there until you render a bill to your client. The monies will then be transferred across to the solicitor's account for that matter and any balance due can be requested from the client. If there is a surplus in the client account, that can remain there until the next bill is rendered.

If monies are to be taken from the client account purely to pay a disbursement (without an interim bill being rendered at the same time), the monies can be used directly from the client account to pay that disbursement.

If disbursements are paid out of the office account (in advance of receiving monies from your client), the appropriate amount in the client account becomes office money and should be transferred to the office account within 14 days. This would only happen where monies on account were received from the client in respect of disbursements and costs (called 'mixed monies'). These must be placed in the client account, then transferred across to the office account.

6.3.3 COMPLY WITH MONEY LAUNDERING REQUIREMENTS

The identification documents for an individual highlighted in paragraph 6.2.3 above are usually dealt with by your firm's receptionist, who will copy them when the client attends the office. Sometimes, the client will bring them with him to your first meeting. If your client is a limited company, then a company search can be done online with Companies House for a nominal fee, which is not charged to the client. In either case, you will need to examine the identification documents to ascertain whether you are satisfied that your money laundering obligations have been complied with.

 Practical Considerations

A common problem arises when you have made a request for the identification documents and they are not forthcoming. The work that your client has instructed you to do may be urgent, such as making an application to set aside default judgment, or going on record as acting and attending a hearing on his behalf. Best practice and compliance with the Money Laundering Regulations 2007 suggest that you are not permitted to act further until you have received such documentation. You may feel that this puts you in difficulties with your professional conduct duties of acting in your client's best interest. However, this frequently occurs in practice and a nominal amount of work can be done whilst the documentation is awaited—but, at some early point, you will need to inform your client that you will be unable to do any further work until the documentation is received.

It is therefore essential that the question of identification is dealt with when you first speak to your client over the telephone.

6.3.4 UNDERTAKE A CONFLICT SEARCH

Your accounts department will usually undertake a conflict search. You will need to inform it of the identity of your client's opponent and it will check to see if anyone in the firm is acting, or has acted, for that opponent. If they have, then you will need to consider, in light of Rule 2.03 above, whether you can, in fact, act for your client in respect of that particular matter. You may need to discuss this with the fee earner who is acting or has acted for the opponent, as well as with your principal and, ultimately, your client.

6.3.5 ASK FOR ANY RELEVANT DOCUMENTATION

In order to enable you to be of more assistance to your client at the first substantive meeting (and ultimately to save time and cost to your client), it is sensible, when arranging the first meeting, to ask for any paperwork that he has in relation to the case itself and in relation to the potential funding of the case, such as insurance policies (see Chapter 3, paragraph 3.3).

For example, if your client has a breach of contract action, contractual documentation should be provided in advance of the first meeting or telephone call to allow you to consider what the relevant terms of the contract are, such as provisions for interest, exclusions, and dispute resolution and jurisdiction clauses. If your client has been injured, any existing insurance policies should be supplied to ascertain whether he has any legal expenses cover for any part of his claim.

With such documentation available to you before you take substantive instructions, you have the opportunity to form preliminary views, devise a list of questions, and consider funding options.

6.3.6 PRE-INTERVIEW QUESTIONNAIRES

Some firms—particularly smaller firms or firms that undertake a lot of personal injury work—send out client questionnaires before the first meeting with the client. These are pro forma questionnaires and are designed to act as an aide-memoire and checklist, particularly for professional conduct, client care, and money laundering requirements.

There are advantages and disadvantages to using these questionnaires. As a legal representative, you will need to recognize your firm's policy on this.

6.4 THE FIRST CLIENT MEETING

Preparation is the key to a good client meeting and we would suggest that you allocate enough time to prepare fully before attending your client. This will include a review of all of the information that you have received and a double check on your professional conduct (especially costs), client care, and money laundering duties. It may also be helpful to prepare your own agenda to form the basic structure for the meeting.

In practice, meetings can be challenging for the legal representative who is new to practice—especially if you are to conduct the meeting on your own. In the early part of your legal career, it is more likely that you will sit in on meetings with other, more experienced, fee earners.

Often, in repeat business with existing commercial clients, there will be no face-to-face meeting, but only an email, fax, or telephone call to provide new instructions. However you receive those first substantive instructions, you must still have regard for paragraphs 6.2 and 6.3 above.

The following sets out some suggestions as to what should and may happen at a first meeting with your client.

6.4.1 CLIENT ETIQUETTE AND PRELIMINARY MATTERS

Client interviewing is a skill that you will develop as you become more confident and experienced in your legal career. If you are having a face-to-face meeting with your client, ensure that you know the date, time, and place of the meeting, because these can take place in the office or at another venue. Wherever the location, of course, you must always be on time.

There are the usual pleasantries in the first few minutes of a client meeting, such as enquiring as to the client's well-being and journey (if he has travelled), offering refreshments, and generally making the client feel at ease. If the meeting is to take place at your offices, either book a conference room or, if the meeting is in your room, make an attempt to tidy and remove from sight any confidential information, and do notify your secretary that you do not want any interruptions.

You may need to deal with any outstanding professional conduct and client care issues, but these can be done either at the outset or the conclusion of the meeting.

6.4.2 THE FORMAT OF THE MEETING

Whether the meeting is undertaken by telephone or in person, there are six main tasks for you to perform during the attendance.

6.4.2.1 Identify what your client wants you to do for him

You need to identify what your client's objectives are, but, at the same time, ensure that your client does not have any enhanced expectations. Your client needs to know the implications of embarking on steps that could involve him in litigation or another form of dispute resolution and all of the financial risks that go with that, but he must be realistic as to the likely cost and the prospects of success.

Your client's goal may be straightforward: for example, in a breach of contract case, this may simply be recovery of losses, or in a personal injury matter, it may be compensation. Your client may, in fact, want something different: for example, in a breach of contract case, it may be rectification of reputation damaged by the breach, or in a personal injury matter, it may be an apology and assurance that the defective piece of equipment has been repaired so as to avoid damage to others.

6.4.2.2 Take full details of your client's version of events

Without wishing to oversimplify any case, there will nearly always be two differing accounts of how the accident happened, how the contract was breached, or why someone was negligent. Your client will need to recount to you his version of events in his own words and it is important that you allow him to do this.

 Practical Considerations

You will spend some time writing this down as your client speaks and therefore do not be afraid to ask your client to clarify anything for you. As your client recounts the facts, you may wish to ask questions—but remember that clients are not always clear on what is relevant to their case, so do not be too keen to interrupt, because they are unlikely to be satisfied that what they have to say on a particular point is not important until they have been given the opportunity to tell you. There is a balance to be struck, because some clients will talk continuously if you allow them to.

This attendance note will, in effect, form your client's proof of evidence and later be used to prepare the particulars of claim (or defence) if proceedings are issued. It may also be useful at this point to ask for any additional documentation in relation to your client's case. For example, if your client has been injured in an RTA, it may be helpful if he draws a sketch plan of the site of the accident, and the direction and position of the vehicles.

6.4.2.3 Explain some basic legal principles

The key to helping your client to resolve his dispute is to identify from the outset the relevant legal issues. These are born out of actions in contract and in tort, in most litigation cases. Every case is made up of legal components, and your client will need to have a basic understanding of these components and how they fit into pursuing or defending his claim.

Any legal action must have a cause of action and can theoretically be divided up into three legal parts, known as 'liability', 'causation', and 'quantum'. Some, or all, of these may be in dispute in a case. For example, if your client were to have a contractual dispute, he would need to prove that there was a contract (cause of action) that the opponent had breached (liability), that the breach caused the losses (causation), and the nature and extent of those losses (quantum). These legal components are discussed in more detail in Chapter 7, paragraph 7.5.

These three legal components are looked at in light of the underlying principle that the claimant has to prove his case against the defendant on a balance of probabilities by way of either original and/or documentary evidence, and lay witness or expert evidence. (See Chapter 18, paragraph 18.2, for a fuller discussion on burdens of proof and evidence.)

In essence, you will need to explain to your client in basic terms, avoiding too much technical legal language, that he may have three hurdles to overcome if he is to be successful in his case—namely, who was responsible, who caused the losses, and what those losses were—and that he will have to prove his case on the basis of what was more likely than not to have occurred. It will also be usual for you to undertake some kind of risk assessment when discussing these fundamentals of his case. (See paragraph 6.4.3.6 below for an outline of how you should approach a risk assessment.)

6.4.2.4 Discuss how his dispute can be resolved

Remember that your client may never have been involved in any type of dispute and its resolution before. If he has, then some of the following suggestions may already be familiar to him.

You will need to explain to him briefly and in simple terms the ethos of dispute resolution, as highlighted in Chapter 2—particularly in relation to the overriding objective, and the principles of proportionality and reasonableness in terms of costs.

He needs to be clear that litigation is a last resort and that his problem may be better resolved by one of the alternatives to litigation. Alternative dispute resolution (ADR) is discussed in detail in Chapter 5, and most commonly includes negotiation and mediation. You should, however, point out to him what he can expect from litigation, if that is the way that his matter is to ultimately proceed, and discuss the necessity and purpose of the Protocol phase (see Chapter 8, paragraph 8.3), as well as outline how a case gets to trial.

ADR considerations

When discussing the possible ADR options, it is important to highlight to your client not only the benefits of ADR but also the potential costs consequences of failing to consider ADR—most notably, costs sanctions.

Tied in with this, as with paragraph 6.4.2.3 above, is your risk assessment and this is discussed in paragraph 6.4.3.6 below.

6.4.2.5 Answer difficult questions

First and foremost, if you are unsure of the correct answer to a client's question, then always inform your client that you will need to check the position—perhaps by undertaking some research or by speaking to a more experienced fee earner—and that you will then get back to him, either in writing or by telephone.

During a first meeting with a client, there will always be a number of questions that he will ask. Most of them can be easily dealt with: for example, 'What can I recover?'. However, there are questions that clients usually always ask and which are very difficult to answer with any degree of certainty at this early stage, as follows.

- **'Have I got a good case?'** The best that you can do is answer the question based on the information that you have at that particular time, and consider making the advice provisional on further investigations and therefore preliminary.

- **'How much will I get?'** You are unlikely to be able to put a precise figure on this, although at a later stage, after further investigations and the collating and exchange of evidence, you will be able to give a bracketed figure.

- **'How long will it take?'** Again the answer to this question will very much depend on the conduct of the opponent and to which method of dispute resolution your client agrees. A bracketed time period can probably be identified.

- **'How much will it cost?'** The costs question is the only question here that must be addressed with some degree of accuracy, as discussed in paragraph 6.2.2 above (see also Chapter 3, paragraph 3.2).

6.4.2.6 Summarize and explain what happens next

Towards the end of the meeting, once both you and your client have discussed the case as described above, it is good practice to summarize your client's case and you can help him. This will enable you to ensure that you have all of the correct material facts and to reassure your client that you fully understand the main issues.

In order for your client to feel that his meeting has been worthwhile, you will need to set out what you will both do following the meeting. All of this should, of course, be followed up by a letter, but it is important that your client feels satisfied that something is being done when he leaves. The problem or dispute still belongs to the client, but a client can feel that he is sharing the burden by feeling satisfied with your understanding and your suggestions as to a way forward. At the end of each meeting with the client, or in a letter following the meeting, the client should be told when he will hear from you again. Good file management practices dictate that you diarize your file to the date upon which you intend to contact the client further. In the interests of good client relations, you must then do so, because he will be expecting to hear from you. Even if there is nothing to report, contact should be made and an explanation for any delay that has occurred provided.

To see how all this gets put into practice, an audiotape of a first client interview appears in the Online Resource Centre with the case study documents.

online
resource
centre

6.4.3 SPECIFIC CONSIDERATIONS ON FIRST TAKING INSTRUCTIONS

Each case that you take on, or in which you assist, will differ to some degree from the last. However, there are certain aspects that can fundamentally shape a case that should also be considered at the first meeting in addition to the six tasks set out above. In many cases, these will not feature heavily, but in others, they may require some detailed consideration, research, or even counsel's advice.

As you start your legal career, it may be helpful to prepare a checklist of these points to which you can refer mentally during the meeting. This may remind you to consider and act upon them, or to consider and dismiss them.

6.4.3.1 Limitation and jurisdiction

Both limitation and jurisdiction are dealt with in some detail in Chapter 7, paragraph 7.2 and 7.4. It is essential, however, in every case and for whichever party you act, that you consider whether there is a limitation issue looming and, if so, what can be done about it to protect your client's interests.

Similarly, if an accident happened abroad, or a contractual dispute involves foreign parties and issues, you will need to turn your mind to any jurisdictional issues.

6.4.3.2 Funding

Unless you are acting frequently for an existing client, you will need to discuss the variety of funding options at the first meeting (see Chapter 3). Remember to make a detailed note of what was discussed and how this is to be followed up.

6.4.3.3 Who is your client?

A legal representative is entitled to act for any person able to instruct him to bring or defend proceedings. There are a variety of different litigants and you will need to ensure, whether you act for the claimant or the defendant, that you know whether your client is one of the following:

- an individual over the age of 18;
- a child or a protected party (CPR 21.1);
- a limited and public limited company, including a limited liability partnership;
- a partnership or sole trader (CPR 7.2A and PD 7.5A–5C);
- the estates of a deceased person (CPR 19.8);

- another incorporated or unincorporated association, including a trade union, a building society, a charity, a local government body, and a club; or
- a trust or a trustee (CPR 19.7A).

There are a number of reasons why you need to know who your client is at this early stage, as follows.

- You will need to consider whether the person from whom you are taking instructions has the authority and capacity to give those instructions. There is a detailed discussion on capacity for children and protected parties in Chapter 7, paragraph 7.3.2, and in Chapter 9, paragraph 9.5.
- The identity of your client is necessary to enable you to identify your client properly for the purposes of money laundering compliance.
- If proceedings do eventually ensue, you will need to know how to describe the parties on the claim form (see Chapter 9, paragraph 9.6 and Figure 9.2).
- You will need to serve those proceedings and there are different rules for service on all of the different types of legal entity listed above. (This is dealt with in Chapter 9, paragraph 9.7 and Figure 9.3.)

For a fuller discussion on legal entities, see Chapter 7, paragraph 7.3.

6.4.3.4 Who do you sue?

In most cases, this will be fairly straightforward. However, in some instances, this may require a little more thought, as follows.

- **Retailer or manufacturer?** For example, if your client purchased a defective portable gas stove, there may be three causes of action to consider: a claim in negligence against any person who puts defective goods in circulation; a consumer claim under the Consumer Protection Act 1987 against a producer of defective goods; or a claim in contract against the seller by the buyer. Under the last two options, there are some strict limitations, so it is as well to know which is your best cause of action and against which defendant, although, wherever possible, proceedings may be taken against both. Clear client instructions will help you to decide which is the most appropriate course of action.

- **Employer and employee?** Where your client was injured by the negligent act of an employee, then the employer will be vicariously liable for the acts of that employee—but only if the employee was acting in the course of his employment. What is deemed to be 'in the course of employment' has, over the years, been extended to include employees not following instructions and even deliberate acts of negligence, but each case will have to be looked at individually (see Chapter 7, paragraph 7.5.1.2).

- **Agent or principal?** This dilemma will feature in commercial cases usually involving contracts. It is best illustrated by way of an example.

 Example

A carpet cleaning company (the principal) appoints a sole trader (the agent) to secure carpet-cleaning contracts for commercial premises. The business relationship is formalized by an agency agreement. The carpet-cleaning services are performed, but damage several carpets at your client's office. The correct opponent in this case would be the carpet company, by virtue of the agency agreement, because the agent concluded the contract on behalf of the principal and not himself. It is essential that the agent acted within his actual or ostensible authority. If he did not, then unless the principal ratified the actions of the agent, the action will lie against the agent if it was clear to the contracting party that the agent was acting for himself.

• **Motorist and insurer?** If your client was injured in an RTA by the negligent driver of an insured vehicle, whilst your client has no common law right to sue the insurer, the insurer has a right to conduct the claim on behalf of the defendant driver. This is usually by way of an express term contained in the contract of insurance entitling the insurer to 'step into the shoes' of the person that it is insuring and to bring or defend an action in the name of the insured—a principle that is known as 'subrogation'. In certain circumstances, it is also possible for a claimant to sue the insurer under the provisions of the European Communities (Rights against Insurers) Regulations 2002, SI 2002/3061 (see Chapter 9, paragraph 9.6.5.1).

 Example

Roger Smith was driving his BMW 3 series and was stationary at a set of traffic lights. A Mondeo, being driven by Peter Anderson, collided with the rear of Roger Smith's car. The car was not owned by Peter, but by his father Simon Anderson, who was fully comprehensively insured with Peter as a named driver with Albatross Insurance Company. Albatross Insurance is entitled to conduct the defence of the claim on behalf of Simon Anderson, but if proceedings are issued, then Roger will need to issue them against Peter Anderson, because he was the negligent driver.

6.4.3.5 Is the opponent worth suing?

At this first client meeting, it is essential that you discuss with your client, once you have identified who the opponent is, whether that opponent is financially capable of satisfying any judgment or order (including costs) made in your favour.

In commercial cases, there are certain limited methods of trying to ascertain the solvency of your client's opponent, which include a bankruptcy search at the Insolvency Register or winding-up search at the RCJ, a company search, a Land Registry search, a search of the Register of Judgments, Orders and Fines or instructing a private investigator to gain a picture of the opponent's ability to pay. Often, your client will have some general information on his opponent from industry rumour. It is important that the question of whether the defendant has the money to satisfy a judgment is kept under review throughout the action.

In personal injury cases, most opponents are insured and so the concern over the opponent's ability to pay is not so troublesome—but see paragraph 6.4.3.7 below for the uninsured position in road traffic cases.

 Professional Conduct

If you do not discuss with your client at the outset of the matter the financial viability and ability of his opponent to pay, and you go on to secure successfully a consent order or judgment in your client's favour, only to find that the opponent is insolvent or does not have the ability to pay, then you are likely to be in breach of your professional conduct obligations to your client under the core duty in Rule 1.04 (acting in your client's best interests) of the Solicitors' Code of Conduct 2007. Your client will have incurred time and, probably, significant expense in pursuing his claim, only to be left with the outstanding debt and additional further costs.

6.4.3.6 Risk assessment

A risk assessment needs to be undertaken periodically throughout a client's case and the first one will be done either at the first meeting or in the follow-up letter of advice.

In order to undertake a thorough risk assessment, you will need to consider and weigh up:

• the substantive legal argument;
• the strength of the three component parts of liability, causation, and quantum, and how you will prove or defend each part evidentially;

- the prospects of success;
- the prospect of losing;
- the cost of proceeding; and
- the likelihood of costs recovery.

Conducting a risk assessment will usually entail a full file review.

Let us consider an example of an RTA in which your client was injured. Acting for the claimant, you will need to include the following in your risk assessment.

1. The cause of the action and who is the opponent—that is, you must acknowledge that this is a negligence action against another road user.

2. What, as a matter of law, your client must establish—that is, that there was a duty of care owed to him, that this was breached by the other driver's negligent driving, that the negligent driving caused the losses, and that the losses were of a specific nature and amount.

3. What facts your client will have to establish—that is, that your client was another road user, details of the other driver's negligent driving, that, by colliding with the claimant, he suffered losses, and the details of those losses.

4. What evidence your client will need to establish these material facts—that is, your client's own evidence in a witness statement (and perhaps other independent witnesses) attesting to his presence on the road, the other driver's negligent driving, the fact of the collision, and the fact that he suffered losses. The losses will need to be proved by documentary and expert evidence.

5. What the strengths and weaknesses of your client's case are—which will depend on any additional information or facts, and these are different in every case. For example, in relation to the liability argument, who was responsible for the accident? If the other driver received a conviction as a result of his driving in relation to the accident and that conviction is relevant to the issues (of liability and quantum) in the case, then this conviction may be used to support your client's case (s. 11 of the Civil Evidence Act 1972 permits you to make use of the conviction by stating it in your particulars of claim). However, in the absence of a relevant conviction, if the opponent had independent witness evidence to support his case, then this would be potentially damaging to your client's case.

6. What the likely value of this case is and the cost of pursuing it—as a legal representative new to legal practice, you will need assistance in both these. Ascertaining these figures requires litigation experience. In respect of the value of the case, you will need to consult practitioner texts such as *Kemp and Kemp on Damages*, Current Law, and the Judicial Studies Board (JSB) Guidelines, or you may even seek counsel's advice. A more senior fee earner will help you to consider the total costing of the matter.

 Practical Considerations

The value of your client's case and its likely costs are difficult figures to assess, but doing so will get easier with experience. If you do find yourself at a meeting with a client on your own at the outset of your legal practice, always inform your client that your views are subject to review by a more senior fee earner and are, as such, preliminary. It may well be the case that, due to the lack of information and evidence, your views would be preliminary in any event at that stage. Do not forget that, in the more complex cases, it may be prudent to seek counsel's advice on any aspect of the substantive case. The dangers of giving robust advice on the merits of a claim without conducting a thorough investigation can be seen from the case of *Levicom International Holdings BV v Linklaters (a firm)* [2010] EWCA Civ 494 where the Court of Appeal held that Linklaters had been negligent when they initially advised the claimant (without all the requisite information available to them) that their chances of success 'were

> not less than 70 per cent'. Based on that advice, the claimant rejected the defendant's offer and commenced arbitration proceedings. Later counsel's advice on behalf of the claimant was much less positive and a less valuable settlement was concluded.

In commercial cases, in addition to the risk assessment, you should also consider the commerciality of pursuing the claim or defence on behalf of your client. Commercial clients often settle cases purely for commercial reasons (cash flow or preservation of a business relationship), but there are also those commercial clients who choose to pursue matters on a point of principle (such as business reputation, industry hierarchy, or just plain stubbornness).

6.4.3.7 The Motor Insurers Bureau (MIB)

This section is particular to RTAs in which your client has been injured in a collision with either an uninsured or untraced driver. The Motor Insurers Bureau (MIB) is an independent body voluntarily set up and financed by motor insurance companies to deal with claims in which injuries were caused by drivers who have no, or no relevant, insurance or in hit-and-run cases.

The MIB has made two main agreements with the government, which can be viewed online at http://www.mib.org.uk. If you are ever consulted by a client in one of these two situations, then it is advisable that you read the agreements in full, because they both contain quite a list of formalities that must be complied with, starting with the pre-issue of proceedings and continuing through to trial. For example, there are notices that you are required to give to the MIB from issue to trial, including proper notice in a specified form before the issue of proceedings (or within days of issue), and when the defence is received. Failure to give notice may mean that the MIB will not be liable for any judgment obtained. (For further information, see Chapter 9, paragraph 9.6.5.)

The claim will otherwise proceed in line with any other RTA personal injury matters with the usual conduct and procedural requirements.

6.4.3.8 The Criminal Injuries Compensation Authority (CICA)

The Criminal Injuries Compensation Authority (CICA) is a statutory body that administers the Criminal Injuries Compensation Scheme (CICS). The Scheme provides compensation payments to victims of violence, such as assault or rape, and covers both physical and psychological injuries valued at a minimum of £1,000. This process is most commonly used where the offender is penniless or not known, and is therefore an alternative to litigation.

Unlike the CPR, the CICS covers injuries sustained in Scotland, but the limitation period for all injuries wherever they were sustained is two years from the date of the incident. The process is by way of an application form to the CICA.

The Scheme will assess the injuries in a similar manner to that used by the courts when assessing damages for personal injuries, but there are some important differences.

If you are ever consulted by a client injured as a result of a criminal offence, you should obtain full details of the Scheme, including the application form and various guides, from http://www.cica.gov.uk. The CICA will obtain medical records and request that the applicant be medically examined.

6.5 ACTION BY YOU AFTER THE FIRST INTERVIEW

There will usually be a number of action points for you to follow up after the first meeting if the case is to be taken forward. Legal representatives should be proactive in their approach to litigation, although what exactly will need to be done will very much depend on the type of case. The following are some basic suggestions of what you might need to do, but remember—whatever the action or steps in a case that you take on behalf of your client, you must have his express instructions to do so.

6.5.1 **WRITE TO THE CLIENT**

A legal representative should always confirm in writing to his client what was discussed at the meeting. This will usually span the following.

- **The funding arrangements.** If a CFA is to be taken out and/or after-the-event (ATE) insurance, the copies of the agreement and policy should be included and explained in the letter. A further meeting may be necessary to go through these two documents with your client before signing him up, in order to comply with best practice and your professional conduct rules (Rule 2.03 of the Solicitors' Code of Conduct 2007). If the client is to pay privately, then you will require further monies on account to cover the work that you are about to do.

- **The return of the signed client care letter and any outstanding money laundering identification documents.**

- **The nature of the client's problem, the advice given (including any risk assessment), and the client instructions.** Often, at first meetings, clients do not give initial instructions on the advice given at the meeting, because they need time to think about it. If this is the case, then the letter will be requesting instructions, usually regarding investigations and moving the claim forward.

- **A costs estimate.** This is mentioned in the client care letter, but an estimated figure needs to be given in this letter to the client to comply with Rule 2.03 of the Code.

- **A request for documentation from your client, such as original documents and photographs.** It is also advisable to remind your client to preserve any relevant documentation as evidence to prove part of his claim: for example, return taxi fares to hospital for out patient appointments in a personal injury claim, or photographs of renovations in a building dispute. Additionally, your client will need to appreciate the nature of the exchange of information and documentation in the Protocol phase and in litigation itself, and that even documents that harm his case may need to be disclosed. This may have been touched on at the first meeting, but is more likely to be dealt with at subsequent early meetings and correspondence in the run-up to, and the duration of, the Protocol. (For details of your client's disclosure duty, see Chapter 8, paragraphs 8.4 and 8.8, and Chapter 17, paragraph 17.4.)

- **Details of when you will next contact your client and what you are doing until you next do so.**

 Practical Considerations

Your client will believe that he is singularly the most important client that you have and, as such, to maintain good client relations, you should provide your client with a time frame within which you will work and report back to him. Even if there is nothing with which to update your client, you should tell him just that. Your client wants to know what you are doing and, if paying privately, how you are spending his money.

6.5.2 **DRAFT YOUR CLIENT'S STATEMENT**

After you have seen your client, the notes of what your client said in the interview can be formulated into the basis of a statement. This should be done as early as possible, especially in personal injury cases. It is even common practice to send the first draft with the letter of advice (see paragraph 6.5.1 above), and to ask for it to be signed and returned. In commercial cases, this is not usually done at this early stage, although a detailed proof of evidence is prepared from which a statement can be formulated later.

6.5.3 NOTIFY YOUR OPPONENT

In most cases, it will be sensible either to call or to write to your opponent or their legal representative (if they have appointed one), to inform them that you have been instructed by your client and that all further correspondence should be directed to you.

This contact also gives you the opportunity to inform your opponent that you intend to comply with Protocol and provides the forum to discuss how you are to proceed in this regard. (See Chapter 8, paragraph 8.2, for a full review of Protocols.)

In some cases, it is appropriate to ask your opponent whether they intend to dispute your client's claim, because this may save a great deal of time and money in the furtherance of the claim by undertaking the investigations detailed below.

6.5.4 INITIATE EARLY INVESTIGATIONS

At this early stage, but subject to funding arrangements being in place, there will usually be a variety of investigations that can be carried out to enable you to give firmer views on how successful you think your client will be. Some of the information necessary for you to give a firmer view on success will come from your client—particularly in commercial cases, in which the client will be in possession of contractual documentation. If not, then your opponent will be, and the securing of such documentation is usually completed through the 'full and frank' exchange of documentation in the Protocol phase (see Chapter 8, paragraph 8.4).

These early investigations can serve a dual purpose, because they can also provide the type of evidence that your client will need to prove his claim at trial. Remember (see paragraph 6.4.2.3 above): your client's claim has three legal components—that is, liability, causation, and quantum—all of which must be proved if your client is the claimant, or disproved if your client is the defendant (unless, of course, your opponent has admitted them).

Before undertaking any investigations, you will need to outline to your client the nature of the investigation and the approximate cost, and receive his express instructions to proceed.

 Practical Considerations

You will need to discuss with your client which investigations are appropriate for his case. If he has a case that is difficult on liability, then it may be more proportionate and reasonable for you to advise that only the liability investigations be done, and the results considered and assessed by you, before proceeding with the causation and quantum investigations. Some investigations, however, provide evidence for more than one of the component parts: for example, a medical report can provide evidence that the type of injury sustained was caused by the negligent act, as well as document the nature and extent of that injury to enable you to assess its value later.

6.5.4.1 Liability investigations

Liability investigations will differ slightly, depending on the type of case that you are preparing.

6.5.4.1.1 *A personal injury matter*

These early investigations are likely to include:

- interviewing witnesses to the accident and preparing draft witness statements (see Chapter 18, paragraph 18.4);
- obtaining a copy of the police accident report book (or an extract if there is a pending prosecution), which should contain any statement taken from the parties, measurements, a sketch plan, and photographs of the site of the road accident;

- attending any proceedings relating to any prosecution;
- obtaining a certificate of conviction if the other driver was convicted as a result of the collision and the conviction is relevant to the issues of the case;
- attending any inquest in a fatal accident case should someone involved have been killed, at which the coroner will try to decide—based on post-mortem evidence, and that of witnesses and police officers (which evidence may be useful for any civil case)—whether the death was accidental or whether there are grounds for a criminal prosecution;
- requesting a copy of the accident report book from your client's employer and a copy of the report of the Health and Safety Executive (HSE) on the incident;
- attending the scene of the accident yourself to inspect the area and take photographs; and
- considering steps that may be needed to preserve evidence.

6.5.4.1.2 *Commercial cases*
These early investigations are likely to include:

- identifying potential parties and causes of action—remembering that commercial cases often have a number of likely parties and/or causes of action, depending on the nature of the dispute (for example, in a building case, if your client instructed an architect and a structural engineer to design and build a commercial warehouse that turned out to be structurally dangerous and therefore unfit for purpose, the cause of action may lie against one or both of the professional parties);
- obtaining copies of all of the relevant contracts and any revisions to those contracts;
- verifying the insurance position of the potential opponents;
- seeking to preserve for inspection any original evidence, such as a defective machine or piece of equipment (for example, a faulty alarm box, which led to the failure of a sensor, which, in turn, led to water-damaged stock);
- requisitioning reports or letters written by third parties (for example, an open letter written by the manufacturer of an inadequate part of a gearbox that was supplied through a chain of contracts to your client, stating that the part manufactured has limitations of use); and
- considering the type of expert that you need and finding one (for example, if your client purchased an unsatisfactory precision piece of engineering for steel cutting, you would need to locate the appropriate type of engineer to prepare a report).

6.5.4.2 Quantum investigations
Again, the nature of quantum investigations will vary.

6.5.4.2.1 *A personal injury matter*
In a personal injury matter, you will need to:

- obtain your client's hospital, GP, and X-ray notes;
- obtain curricula vitae (CVs) from appropriate experts; and
- write to your client's employer for information on loss of earnings and employment details.

6.5.4.2.2 *A commercial matter*
In a commercial matter, you will need to:

- obtain letters or quotations for the replacement cost of goods damaged;
- write to third parties for information (for example, if your client is pursuing a claim alleging that an ex-employee poached customers in breach of a confidentiality and restrictive

covenant clause in the contract of employment, enquiries could be made with those customers regarding the liability issue of poaching and how much business was lost); and

- consider hiring an accountant to quantify your client's business losses.

Once in possession of all relevant information, you will then be able to discuss with your client the implications of the information that you have secured, with a view to moving into the Protocol phase.

KEY POINTS SUMMARY

- Not just with every new client, but with every new matter, you will need to go through your professional conduct obligations, including client care and money laundering, as well as undertaking a conflict search and considering how your client is going to fund the claim.

- Conflicts can arise as litigation progresses, so be alert to the possibility.

- The impressions gained by a client at a first meeting are very important. The key words are: professionalism; competency; empathy; confidence; honesty; and reliability.

- Follow up preliminary views at a first meeting with your further views after you have received further information or undertaken research.

- Keep your client updated with what you are doing.

- Never act without instructions.

Case study *Andrew James Pike and Deep Builders Ltd*

Consider the materials available on the Online Resource Centre in relation to this chapter and answer the following questions.

Question 1

Listen to the audio tape of the first interview with your new client Andrew James Pike and prepare a written attendance note of the meeting, taking care that you record all the key and relevant details of the meeting. Some helpful hints are detailed below:

1. The content of the note should be accurate, precise and succinct.

2. Make use of paragraphs and sub-headings to ensure the attendance note is clear and logical and that the reader is able to follow the content easily.

3. Consider whether this attendance note should form the client's proof of evidence (1st person) or whether it should record what the client said (3rd person). How would you set out the attendance note to record the advice given?

4. This is a document that will be read by a number of people and must be suitably formal and professional in tone.

Question 2

Consider the viability of Andrew Pike's claim at this stage, based on the information contained in the audio tape.

Question 3

How does all pre-CFA work get paid for?

Question 4

Should Mr Pike enter into a CFA with a success fee now?

Question 5

Should he take out ATE insurance? If so, when?

Question 6

If Andrew Pike enters into a CFA with a success fee with your firm, along with ATE insurance, and he wins his case, will he pay any legal costs and/or disbursements?

Question 7

Does the CFA get filed at court and served on the opponent?

Question 8

Draft a letter of advice to Andrew Pike in light of the issues raised in the attendance note.

---

online resource centre

Any documents and the audio tape referred to in these case study questions can be found on the Online Resource Centre—simply click on 'Case study documentation' to access the documents that you need for Chapter 6 and to be reminded of the questions above. Suggested answers to these case study questions can also be accessed on the Online Resource Centre by your lecturer.

7 PRE-ACTION SUBSTANTIVE MATTERS

LITIGATION TRAIN: PRE-ACTION SUBSTANTIVE MATTERS

First client meeting • — — — — — Protocol • — — — — — Issue of proceedings • ———————————— Trial •

o Discuss at the meeting
  • Client care
  • Money laundering
  • Nature of claim/defence
• A way forward – together with instructions to proceed as agreed
  • Request monies on account
  • Funding options
o Action after the meeting
  • Conflict search
  • Letter to client (advice and funding)
  • Notify defendant
  • Initiate early investigations
o Consider the following matters
  • Jurisdiction
  • In which court should the potential action proceed?
  • Does my client/opponent have legal capacity?
  • Limitation
  • Issues on liability, causation and quantum
  • What is my client seeking to recover?

7.1 INTRODUCTION

A student's or a practitioner's role in a litigation department is to assist in the procedural and theoretical aspects of a client's case. These latter aspects can include consideration of matters that can determine where an action proceeds and whether it is capable of proceeding.

The contents of this chapter are purposely substantive in nature and may be considered by you, to varying degrees, either before you see your client on a new matter, at the first meeting, or, more commonly, after you have received detailed instructions and are able to reflect on the overall issues in the case.

In practice, it is crucial that you allow them to become part of your 'checklist' of items that may or may not feature in your client's case.

This chapter will consider:

• jurisdiction and governing law;

• the capacity to sue or be sued;

• limitation;

• the legal components of an action; and

• remedies.

7.2 JURISDICTION AND GOVERNING LAW

7.2.1 IN WHICH COUNTRY SHOULD PROCEEDINGS BE COMMENCED?

7.2.1.1 Jurisdiction

It is important to be sure, firstly, that the courts in England and Wales have jurisdiction to hear a potential action, and secondly, that the courts in England and Wales are the appropriate place in which to hear the dispute. In any action in which the client or opponent is based abroad, or in which the cause of action arose outside of that jurisdiction, questions of jurisdiction must be considered.

There are statutory provisions in the Civil Jurisdiction and Judgments Acts 1982 and 1991 concerning the issue and service of proceedings on parties outside the jurisdiction. The 1982 Act incorporates parts of the 1968 Brussels Convention on Jurisdiction and the Enforcement of Judgments in Civil and Commercial Matters, and the 1991 Act gives effect to the later 1988 Lugano Convention. The Civil Jurisdiction and Judgment Regulations 2009 brought into force the new Lugano Convention on 1 January 2010, which now includes Denmark and Norway. The full detail of these provisions are outside the scope of this book, but any practitioner with issues of jurisdiction will need to study them to ensure which is the correct, as well as the most appropriate, jurisdiction for the proceedings. *Blackstone's Civil Practice* provides a detailed account of jurisdictional matters and is a good source of further reference.

7.2.1.2 Contractual disputes

In addition to the considerations in paragraph 7.2.1.1 above, in breach of contract actions, it will be important to ensure that there are no provisions in the agreement that provide that the parties must arbitrate rather than litigate. Where this is the case, the parties will not be permitted to litigate unless by mutual consent. Parties will therefore be bound by a valid arbitration clause in their agreement. The agreement will usually cover both the 'seat' for the arbitration (that is, where it should take place) and the governing law. These could be either national (that is, specifying that the arbitration should take place in England and Wales, and be subject to the laws of England and Wales) or international clauses.

Often, in commercial agreements, there will be staged alternative dispute resolution (ADR) clauses under which the parties have agreed to try a form (or forms) of ADR, usually culminating in arbitration. These clauses are enforceable, subject to the usual arguments of incorporation and reasonableness, and often include (depending on the nature of the agreement) suggested ADR methods, such as conciliation, followed by mediation, then adjudication, and, finally, arbitration. (See Chapter 5, paragraph 5.3, for a brief discussion on the variety of ADR processes.)

 Practical Considerations

Although a detailed study of the statutes and regulations concerning proceedings outside the jurisdiction of the court is beyond the scope of this book, there are some basic guiding principles that can be used to alert the new legal representative to the need to consider 'jurisdiction' in more detail and to ask the assistance of a supervising partner, as follows.

- Is there a binding agreement that contains a jurisdiction clause to be applied?

- Is there a 'governing law' clause in the agreement?

- Does a party reside or have its business outside the jurisdiction?

- Was the agreement concluded outside the jurisdiction?

- Determine the costs of both your enquiries and the costs of service outside the jurisdiction, and obtain your client's instructions to incur those costs.

- Have you advised your client of the additional time that it may take to issue or serve outside the jurisdiction of England and Wales?

- If your opponent is a limited company registered abroad, does it have a UK division registered in the UK or a UK trading site?

- Might determination of the action outside the jurisdiction be preferable in terms of convenience, cost, or justice?

- Have you checked the provision for the enforcement of any judgment that may be obtained in the proceedings?

7.2.2 IN WHICH COURT SHOULD PROCEEDINGS BE COMMENCED?

The High Court and the county courts have concurrent jurisdiction over most claims. Where there is concurrent jurisdiction between the High Court and the county courts, a claimant generally has freedom to choose in which court to issue his proceedings. However, this general freedom must also take account of those parts of the Civil Procedure Rules (CPR) that exercise restrictions on parties.

In some circumstances, including the following, it can be seen that the complete 'freedom' (of which court to choose) provided by statute is restricted in practice by the CPR.

- CPR Practice Direction (PD) 7A.2.1 states that a claim for a specified sum may only be issued in the High Court where the sum claimed exceeds £25,000.

- PD 7A.2.2 states that a claim for personal injuries may not be issued in the High Court unless the value of the claim is £50,000 or more. In determining the value of the claim, interest, costs, a reduction for contributory negligence against the claimant, the value of any counterclaim or set-off, and the recoupment of benefits under the Social Security (Recovery of Benefits) Act 1997 are all to be disregarded in accordance with art. 9 of the High Court and County Courts Jurisdiction Order 1991, SI 1991/724 (which cross-references CPR 16.3(6)).

- PD 7A.2.3 states that a claim must be issued in the High Court or in a county court where a statute requires it.

- Although PD 7A.2 permits a specified sum claim with a value exceeding £25,000 to be issued in the High Court, PD 29.2.2 restricts a claimant's right to *continue* proceedings issued in the High Court if the claim has a value of £50,000 or less. Unless one of the exceptions set out in that paragraph applies, the claim will usually be transferred to a county court. These exceptions include that:

  - the claim is one that, by statute, should be heard in the High Court;

  - the claim falls within a specialist list, as defined by CPR 2.3(2)—these include claims that would be heard in the Commercial Court, the Mercantile Courts, the Patents Courts, or the Technology and Construction Court (TCC);

  - the claim is one relating to professional negligence, fraud or undue influence, defamation, malicious prosecution or false imprisonment, claims against the police, claims under the Fatal Accidents Act 1976, or contentious probate claims;

  - the claim is otherwise within the criteria of art. 7(5) of the High Court and County Courts Jurisdiction Order 1991, as repealed by the High Court and County Courts Jurisdiction (Amendment) Order 1999, SI 1999/1014. Under these provisions, certain criteria must be applied to determine whether the case issued in the High Court may stay in that court. These criteria are the financial substance of the action, its importance and particularly whether it raises questions of importance to non-parties or the general public, its complexity, and whether a transfer to a county court is likely to result in a more speedy trial of the action (although a transfer cannot be made solely on this final ground).

It is clear that any practitioner wishing to issue a claim in the High Court can seek to justify doing so using any of the above provisions.

 Practical Considerations

The decision of in which court to issue proceedings should never be taken without care or consideration, because the penalties for issuing in the wrong court can be severe. In the worst-case scenario, the wrong decision could result in an action for professional negligence. In most situations, when a genuine mistake has been made and a claim has been commenced in the wrong court, the court will either take the initiative to transfer the action or will do so upon the application of a party. The court will usually effect the transfer, but may impose cost penalties on the claimant representing the costs of the transfer. These penalties can include a continuing penalty as to costs, although the court has the power to reduce the whole costs of the claim by up to 25 per cent (Senior Courts Act 1981, s. 51(8) and (9)). Equally, in cases in which the claimant knew, or ought to have known, that the claim was being commenced in the wrong court, the court has the power to strike out the claim (County Courts Act 1984, ss. 40(1)(b) and 42(1)(b); CPR 3.4).

 Professional Conduct

In any situation in which a mistake has been made, the Solicitors' Code of Conduct 2007 Rules 1.02, 1.04, 1.05, and 2.02 require that the client must be informed of the mistake.

7.2.2.1 Rome II

On 11 January 2009, EC Regulation 864/2007 on the law relating to non-contractual obligations (known as 'Rome II') came into force. This contains provisions that apply to tortious claims in European Union member states. Its application will have most impact in general litigation in personal injury claims in which a party has been injured abroad and in product liability cases. Its provisions will affect questions of liability (and grounds for exemption from liability), and the existence, nature, and assessment of damages in such cases.

The practical significance of the provisions is that a court will now have to hear evidence and consider how damages are assessed in the jurisdiction in which the accident or the harmful physical impact occurred.

The full scope of Rome II is outside the scope of this book, but it is noted for completeness and so that practitioners can be aware that further knowledge should be sought in such cases.

7.3 LEGAL CAPACITIES

7.3.1 INDIVIDUALS OVER THE AGE OF 18

A person who is over the age of 18 and who is not a patient under the provisions of the Mental Health Act 1983 has the capacity to sue and be sued in his own name.

7.3.2 CHILDREN AND PROTECTED PARTIES (CPR 21)

CPR 21 governs the provisions that apply when acting for or against a child or a protected party. CPR 21.1(2) defines a 'child' as 'a person under 18' and a 'protected party' as 'a party, or an intended party, who lacks capacity to conduct the proceedings'—that is, a person who, by reason of mental disorder within the meaning of the Mental Health Act 1983, is incapable of managing and administering his property and affairs.

7.3.3 COMPANIES

Companies are legal 'persons' and therefore can sue or be sued in their own name. A company is one registered under the Companies Act 1985 or an earlier Companies Act. When suing or being sued, it must do so or be so in the full, registered, company name. If the company is in liquidation, then that fact must be added to the name—that is, '(in liquidation)'. A company that is not required to use 'limited' or 'plc' (or the Welsh equivalents) in its name should be referred to by its name, followed by an appropriate description.

7.3.4 LIMITED LIABILITY PARTNERSHIPS (LLPS)

Limited liability partnerships (LLPs) were created by the Limited Liability Partnerships Act 2000. Like a company, an LLP is a legal person separate from its members and, like a company, it must sue or be sued in its own name, which must be the registered name.

7.3.5 PARTNERSHIPS

Partnerships are not legal entities, and the liability of partners is generally joint and several (Partnership Act 1980, ss. 9 and 12). Partners may sue or be sued in their individual names. Alternatively, partners carrying on business within the jurisdiction may sue or be sued in the name of the firm and the words '(a firm)' added to the case title. A party suing or being sued by partners in the name of the firm may serve notice on the firm requiring all of the partners who were partners at the time that the cause of action arose to disclose their names and addresses. Failure to disclose is likely to result in an order for disclosure, with an order that the action be stayed (or the firm be debarred from defending) if disclosure is not made.

7.3.6 SOLE TRADERS

A sole trader may be sued, but may not sue in his trading name. A claimant sole trader should sue in his own name, adding the words 'trading as' (or 't/a') and the trading name.

A defendant sole trader whose real name is not known may be sued in the business name, followed by the words '(a trading name)'.

7.3.7 ASSOCIATIONS

These may include trade unions and employers' associations, building societies, charities, local and central government bodies or departments, and other public bodies. All of these may be sued or sue in their name. Clubs, however, may not; these may sue or be sued in the names of the members of the club, or representative proceedings may be brought. An incorporated club may sue or be sued in its own name.

7.3.8 TRUSTS AND TRUSTEES

A claim by or against a trust is brought by or against all of its trustees. The beneficiaries of the trust need not be parties to the action (CPR 19.7A), but any judgment or order made in the action will bind the beneficiaries unless the court orders otherwise.

7.3.9 ESTATES OF DECEASED PERSONS (CPR 19.8)

Under the Law Reform (Miscellaneous Provisions) Act 1934, s. 1(1), most causes of action subsisting against or vested in an individual survive his or her death. If a party to a claim dies (or is adjudged bankrupt), the court has the power, under CPR 19.5(3), to add or substitute as a party in the action the person to whom the deceased (or bankrupt party's) interest or liability has passed.

7.3.9.1 Where the death of the party is before the claim is issued

The claim must be brought or defended by the personal representatives of the deceased person. If the claim is made against a deceased defendant before there has been a grant of probate or letters of administration, the claim form cannot be served until the court (usually upon the application of the claimant before the expiry of the time limit for service of the claim form) has appointed a person to represent the deceased defendant.

7.3.9.2 Where the death of the party is after the claim has been commenced

The surviving party in the action needs to make an application to the court either to substitute the deceased party for the personal representatives of the estate of the deceased party, or if no personal representatives have been appointed, to direct a person to represent the estate of the deceased party or to order the action to proceed without the deceased party being represented.

Where an action is continued by or against a deceased person, the court has power to order that any interested parties should be served with notice of the action (CPR 19.8A) and, in so doing, that person will be bound by any judgment or order made in the action. If the person so served files an acknowledgement of service, they will become a party to the claim.

These provisions must be distinguished from the restricted circumstances in which a party may voluntarily assign its interest (or liability) in the action to another. Such assignments are, however, outside the scope of this book.

7.4 LIMITATION

7.4.1 THE PURPOSE OF LIMITATION PERIODS

The primary purpose of limitation is to protect a defendant from the potential injustice of having to face a claim that has gone stale and for which reliable, or any, evidence may be difficult to obtain. It also provides an end to the time during which a person has an 'expectation' or concern that an action may be brought against him.

7.4.2 HOW IS 'LIMITATION' APPLIED TO ACTIONS?

7.4.2.1 From the claimant's perspective

Satellite litigation may arise on issues arising to clarify whether a limitation period has expired or not, or from applications in which the claimant seeks to proceed with the action and seeks the court's discretion to permit the action to continue.

Periods of limitation may vary in different jurisdictions; the periods of limitation within the jurisdiction may also vary, depending on the type of claim. The issue of the claim form stops the 'limitation clock' ticking and where the limitation period is nearing its end for the action, there will be a need to issue as a matter of urgency to avoid the claim becoming statute-barred.

 Practical Considerations

Where protective proceedings have to be issued to avoid an action becoming statute-barred, it must be remembered that further investigation can take place before service of the claim form—but care must be taken to serve within the lifespan of the claim form issued. Any application to extend the life of the claim form must be made 'within the period specified by CPR Rule 7.5'—that is, before the expiry of the time for service. Only in exceptional cases can the life of the claim form be extended after the end of the period specified by CPR 7.5 (CPR 7.6(3)—see Chapter 9, paragraph 9.7.1.7).

7.4.2.2 From the defendant's perspective

Limitation is a procedural defence, but it must be specifically stated in the defence itself. It will not arise and apply to the claimant's action automatically. The consequence, therefore, of the expiry of the limitation period for an action is that the defendant, in most cases, where he states the expiry of the limitation periods, acquires an unassailable defence.

7.4.3 LIMITATION PERIODS

Most limitation periods are laid down in the Limitation Act 1980 (LA 1980), as amended. Some procedural rules impose time limits that act rather like limitation periods.

A claim that is outside the provisions of the LA 1980 is not subject to a strict period of limitation. It may, however, be subject to a time limit by analogy to the Act, or it may be subject to the defences of laches and acquiescence. For example, in *Raja and Lloyds TSB Bank plc* (2000) The Times, 16 May 2000, a claim against the mortgagee bank of failing to obtain a proper price on the sale of the mortgaged property was held to be governed by the six-year limitation period, by analogy with LA 1980, s. 2.

Equally, the courts may strike out a claim as an abuse of process, as in *Taylor v Ribby Hall Leisure* [1998] 1 WLR 400, in which an application to commit was delayed by about five years. It was struck out, the court taking into account factors such as the prospects of the court exercising its supervisory powers at the hearing and the public interest in the efficient administration of justice, and compliance with court orders and undertakings.

The main limitation periods are as outlined in Figure 7.1.

7.4.4 WHICH LIMITATION PERIOD APPLIES TO AN ACTION?

It is sometimes difficult to determine into which category a particular case may fall. It is possible that the nature of the claim itself may affect the application of a limitation period. If the action arises from fraudulent behaviour, the court will consider whether it was the fraudulent behaviour of a party or of another. Where the fraud is that of a person who is not a party, then the defendant will normally be able to rely on a limitation period applying. But if the fraudulent behaviour is that of a party, then it is more likely that the court will determine that no limitation period applies. Claims that are a mixture of tort and contract can also cause difficulties.

FIGURE 7.1

CLASS OF CLAIM	LIMITATION PERIOD
Fraudulent breach of trust	None (LA 1980, s. 21(1))
Recovery of land	12 years (LA 1980, s. 15(1))
Recovery of money secured by mortgage	12 years (LA 1980, s. 20(1))
Speciality	12 years (LA 1980, s. 8(1))
Recovery of money due under statute	6 years (LA 1980, s. 9(1))
Enforcement of a judgment	6 years (LA 1980, s. 24(1))
Contract	6 years (LA 1980, s. 5)
Recovery of trust property and breach of trust	6 years (LA 1980, s. 21(3))
Recovery of arrears of rent	6 years (LA 1980, s. 19)
Tort (except those listed below)	6 years (LA 1980, s. 2)
Defective Premises Act 1972 (DFA 1972) claims	6 years (DFA 1972, s. 1(5))
Personal injury claims	3 years (LA 1980, s. 11(4))
Fatal Accident Act 1976 claims	3 years (LA 1980, s. 12(2))
Claims under the Consumer Protection Act 1987	3 years (LA 1980, s. 11A)
Carriage by Air Act 1961 (CAA 1961) claims	2 years (CAA 1961, Sched. 1)
Claims for personal injury or damage to vessel, cargo, or property at sea	2 years (Merchant Shipping Act 1995, s. 190(3) and Sched. 6)
Disqualification of company directors	2 years (Company Directors Disqualification Act 1986, s. 7(2))
Contribution under the Civil Liability (Contribution) Act 1978	2 years (LA 1980, s. 10(1))
Contributions under the Maritime Conventions Act 1911	1 year (Merchant Shipping Act 1995, s. 190(4))
Carriage of Goods by Road Act 1965 (CGRA 1965) claims	1 year (CGRA 1965, Sched., art. 32(1))
Defamation and malicious falsehood	1 year (LA 1980, s. 4A)
Applications for judicial review	3 months (CPR 54.5)
Unfair dismissal under the Employment Rights Act 1996 (ERA 1996)	3 months (ERA 1996, s. 111(2))
Applications for new business tenancies under the Landlord and Tenant Act 1954 (LTA 1954)	Not less than 2 months nor more than 4 months (LTA 1954, s. 29(3))
Actions for an account	Period applicable to claim on which account is based (LA 1980, s. 23)

A full examination of the more complex issues arising from limitation is outside the scope of this book, but any legal representative acting in an action in which 'limitation' is raised will need to examine the law applying in detail (see *Blackstone's Civil Practice* in this regard).

7.4.5 FOREIGN LIMITATION PERIODS

Where the rules of private international law provide that the law of any other country is to be taken into account in any claim in England or Wales, the law of that other country relating to limitation must be applied, under the Foreign Limitation Periods Act 1984.

7.4.6 WHEN DOES THE 'CLOCK' BEGIN TO RUN ON LIMITATION PERIODS?

There are a number of important features that you will need to consider when dealing with a case with an actual or potential limitation problem. These are addressed below, followed by a summary of the practicalities of dealing with cases that are near to the expiry of their limitation period.

7.4.6.1 The time runs from the accrual of the cause of action

Time begins to run from the earliest time at which an action may be brought—that is, time runs from the point at which facts exist establishing all of the essential elements of the cause of action.

A distinction is drawn between mere procedural requirements and substantive elements. This can sometimes be a difficult distinction to draw. The difference between the accrual of a cause of action in contact and tort can be problematic, because for contract, there is no need for damages to have been caused before a claimant is able to sue in contract—the cause of action accrues on the date of the breach and the six-year limitation period runs from this date. For an action brought in tort—for example, in negligence—the limitation period runs from the date on which the damage is suffered (because the 'loss' is an essential component of the tort of negligence). For such actions, therefore, the cause of action accrues when the alleged act of negligence causes loss. Damage may be caused much later than the date of the breach.

 Example

In *Law Society v Sephton & Co (A Firm)* [2006] UKHL 22, the House of Lords clarified (perhaps in anticipation of changes to the law of limitation) the application of the limitation period rules in claims for negligence in which the damage is contingent. It held that the time does not begin to run until the loss becomes actual.

In *Haward v Fawcett* [2006] UKHL 9, the House of Lords considered the three-year limitation period prescribed by LA 1980, s. 14A, and the extent of knowledge required by the claimant to start the period running. It concluded that, for time to start to run, the claimant must have knowledge of the 'factual essence of the act or omission' that caused the loss. It was not necessary for the claimant to know the precise details of the alleged negligence, or for him to identify conclusively that the defendant's acts or omissions were the cause of his loss. It was sufficient that the claimant had enough information to make it reasonable for him to commence investigations into the potential claim against the defendant and s. 14A gives the claimant three years in which to complete those investigations.

 Practical Considerations

Although the cases of *Sephton* and *Fawcett* restate (and clarify) established principles and give excellent guidance to a practitioner towards an understanding of the provisions of LA 1980, s. 14A, the cases also give a clear warning to practitioners that claimants should be advised of the potential difficulties that may arise if investigations are delayed, even in a situation in which the claimant is not certain that the potential defendant caused the loss.

7.4.6.2 Potential parties to an action must exist

There must be a party capable of suing and a party capable of being sued. For example, a company may have been removed from the Register of Companies in the intervening period between the accrual of the cause of action and the issue of proceedings. However, in these circumstances, a company may be restored to the Register for the purposes of making or defending a claim, but the limitation period will run from the date of breach (or whatever the cause of action) and not the date of registration.

7.4.6.3 Persons under disabilities

Where the claimant is a person under a disability, being either a child or a protected party (that is, of unsound mind), the limitation period does not start to run until

- if a child, from the date of the child's 18th birthday;
- if a protected party, if they were of unsound mind at the time of the cause of action (or the unsound mind was caused by the cause of action), from the date on which they are no longer of unsound mind (whenever that may be medically certified). If the person was of sound mind at the time of the cause of action, the limitation period will continue to run.

7.4.6.4 Fraud, concealment, and mistake

In claims based on fraud, the limitation period does not begin to run until the claimant discovers (or could, with reasonable diligence, have discovered) the fraud. The limitation period will also not run whilst the defendant deliberately conceals a relevant fact. Where the claim is for relief from the consequences of a mistake, time does not run until the mistake is discovered, or could have been discovered with reasonable diligence.

7.4.6.5 Latent damage

The Latent Damage Act 1986 created greater fairness in situations in which the limitation period may expire before a party is even aware that a claim exists. In claims in tort (other than for personal injuries), the Latent Damage Act 1986 provides new sections (inserted into the Limitation Act 1980, ss. 14A and 14B). The provisions added to the LA 1980 by the 1986 Act provide two periods of limitation: one that is six years from accrual (the usual period for claims in tort), and another that is three years from the 'starting date'—that is, the earliest date at which the claimant knew that the relevant damage was sufficiently serious to justify proceedings, enabling a claim to subsist, and when it could be attributed to the act of negligence and the identity of the defendant.

To prevent defendants being potentially 'at risk' of a claim indefinitely, s. 14B of the LA 1980 provides a long-stop period for bringing proceedings of 15 years from the act or omission alleged to constitute the negligence causing the claimant's damage.

7.4.6.6 The discretionary extension of limitation periods

Discretionary provisions to extend the statutory limitation period apply in:

- judicial review proceedings (the three-month time limit can be extended if good reasons are shown);
- defamation claims (the one-year limitation period can be extended if it can be shown, on a balance of prejudice between the claimant and the defendant, to be equitable to allow the limitation period to be extended); and
- personal injury claims, in which a wide discretion is provided in s. 33 of the LA 1980 to extend the limitation period. (For recent guidance on the application of s. 33, see *Cain v Francis & McKay v Hamlani* [2008] EWCA 1451.)

7.4.6.7 Practical pointers when calculating the limitation period

As stated above, time 'runs' from the day following the day of accrual of the action. Parts of a day are ignored. Time 'ends' when the action has been issued from a court. The court will not issue a case until all of the necessary documents for issue, and the appropriate fee, have been lodged at court. If the court office is closed on the final day of the limitation period, the action will still be 'in time' if all of the documents and the fee are lodged on the next court business day. If documents and the fee are sent to the court by post, receipt of the documents and fee will be date stamped on receipt and the action will still be 'in time' even if the court does not issue on the day on which it receives the documents. Clearly, in any case in which the limitation period is about to end, it is crucial for the practitioner to ensure that the court receives the documents and fee on time. This is a situation in which the practitioner would make a personal attendance at court to issue the proceedings.

7.4.7 **HOW DO THE PROVISIONS OF AMENDMENT AND SUBSTITUTION AFFECT THE LIMITATION RULES?**

Amendment and substitution are governed by CPR 17.4 and 19.5. These provisions of the CPR are, to a degree, overlapping, in that they both deal with amendments to a statement of case after the expiry of the relevant limitation period. CPR 17.4 deals with applications to allow an amendment to include a new cause of action, or to allow an amendment of the name of a party where there has been a mistake in the name given to a party. CPR 19.5 deals with the provisions applying to add or substitute parties after the expiry of the limitation period.

There is a clear overlap in the provisions and both need to be examined where a new party is to be added after the expiry of the limitation period. Confusion has arisen whether the mistake in naming the wrong party is one concerning the actual identity of the party, rather than a mistake in the name given to the party. In general, the cases seeking to clarify this have upheld the view that a mistake as to name is within the provisions, but not a mistake as to the identity of a party.

In *Sheldon Gary Adelson v Las Vegas Sands Corp v Associated Newspapers Ltd* [2007] EWCA Civ 701, the Court of Appeal sought to clarify some confusion between CPR 17.4 and 19.5(3). The case involved the substitution (after the limitation period had expired) of new parties in existing proceedings in which a party had been named by a mistake. The Court stated that the substitution could not be made, because the applicant had failed to establish that there had been any 'mistake' within the provisions of CPR 19.

In *Finlan and Anor v Eyton Morris Winfield (A Firm)* [2007] EWHC 914 (Ch), the court considered an application to allow an amendment to plead a new cause of action that had arisen after the claim form had been issued. Holding that the new cause of action arose out of the facts and evidence that would already be in issue in the action, the judge permitted the amendment to add the new cause of action. CPR 17.4 implements s. 35(5) of the LA 1980, which allows the addition of a new claim, but only if the new claim arises out of the same facts, or substantially the same facts, as the claim already issued.

7.4.8 **LIMITATION PERIODS APPLYING WHERE THE CLAIM SEEKS A CONTRIBUTION FROM AN ADDITIONAL PARTY**

A claim for a contribution under the Civil Liability (Contribution) Act 1978 must be brought within two years from the date on which the person seeking a contribution is 'held liable . . . by a judgment' (LA 1980, s. 10).

The provision was not clear whether the time ran from the date of judgment or the date on which damages are assessed, and these may often be at different times. In *Aer Lingus v Gildacroft Ltd & Sentinel Lifts Ltd* [2006] EWCA Civ 4, the Court of Appeal clarified that the time runs from the date of assessment of the damages.

Practical Considerations

Limitation is one of a series of 'key dates' that should be logged with any new instructions. On receiving any new instructions, the expiry of the relevant limitation period should always be checked and noted. Equally, in new instructions from a defendant to proceedings, the relevant limitation period should always be checked and noted, because a defendant who takes a step in the action beyond filing his acknowledgement of service and raising limitation in his defence will be unable to raise the issue later in the action.

7.4.9 A DELAY IN POSSIBLE CHANGES TO THE RULES ON LIMITATION

The law on periods of limitation has been subject to consultation and review, and the Law Commission prepared a draft Civil Law Reform Bill in 2001. This bill has now been published but it does not include any of the indicated provision for reform of the law of limitation. There is now no indication when the indicated reforms may be implemented.

7.5 THE LEGAL COMPONENTS OF AN ACTION

In Chapter 6, we looked at the concept of an action having three legal components: liability; causation; and quantum. Here, we aim to focus on these in more detail.

Practical Considerations

Whilst we have divided the legal components into three parts, not every claim will have an issue on all three parts. Part of your role as a legal representative is to ensure that your client understands, in very basic terms, why he has a good, or not so good, case. This will inevitably require an explanation from you on the prospects of success in relation to claim. To help you to provide this advice, we consider that breaking the case down into legal components will allow you to see the case as a whole and advise the client accordingly.

7.5.1 LIABILITY

Liability is the first hurdle that your client will have to get over—unless, of course, the opponent has admitted liability. You will first have to ask yourself, and your client, who was responsible for the breach of contract or accident. In most cases, this will be fairly self-evident. In those cases in which it is not, the most common liability issues that you will come across as a legal representative are as follows.

7.5.1.1 Joint and several liability

Where two or more persons are liable to another, they may be either jointly liable, severally liable, or jointly *and* severally liable. A contract that provides that more than one person will be liable will usually set out the parties' liability. If the contract fails to state the nature of the parties' liability, then determining that liability will be a matter of construction.

7.5.1.1.1 *Joint liability*

Where parties are jointly liable, then either is liable up to the full amount.

7.5.1.1.2 *Several liability*

Where liability is several, then the parties are liable only for their respective shares.

7.5.1.1.3 *Joint and several liability*

Joint and several liability is a mixture of both of the above. The person to whom the parties owe the joint and several liability may elect to pursue the whole claim against either one of those liable (as in joint liability), but as between those liable, the liability is several and thus any party pursued by the recipient of the liability may seek a contribution from his co-obligors in the share of each of their liability (several liability).

7.5.1.1.4 *Who should the claimant sue?*

For joint debts, the general rule is that all of the joint debtors should be made parties to the action. Where the claimant fails to do this, the defendant may make an application for his joint debtor to be added to the action as an additional party. The claimant then has the option of joining in that additional party as a defendant to his action.

For joint and several liability debts, the claimant can choose whether to sue one or more of those who are jointly and severally liable.

7.5.1.2 Vicarious liability

'Vicarious liability' is an employer's liability for the acts of its employees. In common law, an employer is vicariously liable for the tortious acts of its employees if they are carried out 'in the course of employment'. This has, in recent times, had a wide definition, but will not extend to employees acting 'on a frolic of their own'. The court will look at, amongst other factors, the relationship between the employer and the third party, and whether the act of the employee was in sufficiently close connection to his employment.

 Practical Considerations

When considering who is responsible for the wrong done to your client, you will need to turn your mind to whether the person who carried out the breach is the person with legal liability or, indeed, whether there is an additional person or entity that may also be to blame. Be aware that you may need to make some enquiries before you secure a definitive answer.

7.5.2 CAUSATION

Causation is very often either overlooked or simply assumed to be unproblematic in the success of a case. This is a misconception, because causational factors can condemn a case to complete or partial failure.

We have found it helpful to divide causation into two categories: liability causation and quantum causation.

By 'liability causation', we mean whether the negligent acts caused the accident or breach. In many cases, this will be uncomplicated, but you should ask yourself the question in any event.

 Example

Did the negligent driving of the opponent (such as driving through a red light or driving too fast) cause the collision in which your client was injured, or was it the opponent's defective vehicle that caused the accident (the fact that the brakes pads were worn and the tyre tread was bare on the front two tyres, or both)? It is important that you consider this, because it will affect what you say to your opponent, and how you state your client's claim in the letter of claim and in any proceedings that may result. Remember that only facts in issue can be dealt with at trial.

By 'quantum causation', we mean whether the breach caused the loss. At first glance, this may seem unlikely to feature in many cases, but consider the following example.

Example

Did your client's former solicitor's failure to issue proceedings for breach of contract within the limitation period cause the loss that your client is seeking (by depriving him of the opportunity to pursue a claim through the courts), or was his case so poor on liability (your client failed to perform his part of the contract) that it would have failed in any event?

7.5.3 QUANTUM

In paragraph 7.6.3 below, we look at the different types of damages that your client can recover in a civil claim. Here, we will seek to remind you of the theoretical basics that you would have come across in your academic studies in contract and tort.

The general principles that we would like to remind you of are as follows.

- In contract cases, the damages must not be too remote from the breach. What this means is that the losses must have flowed naturally from the breach or have been in the reasonable contemplation of the parties at the time that the contract was made as being the probable result of the breach.

 Practical Considerations

In practice, you are likely to come across this in commercial contract cases, in which you will need to consider whether the losses were consequential losses. Many contracts have incorporated into them purported valid exclusion clauses in this regard excluding any consequential losses. In these cases, you will need to examine the clause carefully (considering whether the clause is, in fact, incorporated into the contract and reasonable), and discuss with your client the circumstances surrounding the making of the contract, as well as the true nature of the losses that occurred and whether they would really fall into the category of consequential losses.

- In cases in tort, the damages must also not be too remote and this is, in part, based on the damages being a reasonably foreseeable consequence of the tort.
- In both contract and tort cases, the claimant has a duty to mitigate his loss. If he fails to do so, then his damages claim may be reduced. The duty only arises at the time of the breach of contract or commission of the tort.

 Example

In a personal injury case, the claimant may fail to attend physiotherapy sessions, consequently prolonging his rehabilitation period. In a breach of contract case, the claimant may fail to secure a replacement machine (for the defective machine supplied by the defendant) and so allow a significant loss of production claim to accrue.

 Practical Considerations

If the defendant wishes to make an allegation that the claimant has failed to take all reasonable steps to mitigate his loss, then he should raise this initially in his response to the letter of claim, then state it in his defence. The burden of proof in this case will lie with the defendant.

7.6 **REMEDIES**

7.6.1 **THE PURPOSE OF A REMEDY**

There are several remedies that may be sought in a civil action. The aim of any action will be to:

- establish, or seek to change, a legal status;
- determine legal rights and duties;
- rectify an infringement or denial of legal rights; and
- seek a declaration of the state between the parties with no further remedy.

In all of these cases, the courts seek to create justice between the parties. The decision, or order, of the court will be based on the law, the evidence, the cogency of the evidence, and the rules of the court.

The remedy that the court decides is called a 'judgment', or an 'order'. In Chapter 9, it will be seen that, in the drafting of a claim form, the remedy that the claimant seeks must be set out. This does not, however, restrict the court in the making of a remedy that it sees to be just and appropriate, although remedies can only be granted in accordance with principles of law. The court does not have an inherent jurisdiction to make any order that appears to be just (but compare this with the outcomes available in ADR when the parties may agree terms that may be far more flexible, pragmatic, or commercial).

Any action commenced in the courts must have a viable cause of action to succeed. The basic outline of the cause of action will be set out in the particulars of claim (the claim will be expanded upon in the witness statements), and to succeed, it must include all of the elements that the action needs. For example, for negligence, there must be a duty of care, a breach of that duty, and, for this part of the allegation, the claimant will need to list all of the aspects of the defendant's conduct that the claimant says fell below the appropriate standard of care. There must be consequential loss or damage, and the claimant must provide details as to how the defendant's conduct caused, or materially contributed towards, his injury (causation) and provide details of the loss or injury (loss).

7.6.2 **WHAT REMEDIES ARE AVAILABLE?**

The principal remedies available in civil proceedings are:

- legal remedies—usually damages, these are legal rights to which the person seeking them is entitled as of right on sufficient proof of the infringement; and
- equitable remedies—usually injunctions or specific performance, the court may award these at its discretion when a legal remedy would be inadequate or is unavailable. Such discretion to award an equitable remedy is exercised by the court in accordance with established principles.

7.6.3 **DAMAGES**

Damages are a monetary payment for an infringement of a legal right. The amount to be paid reflects the sum required to compensate for the loss caused by the defendant's breach or wrongdoing (compensatory damages).

Where the damages arise from a breach of contract, the contract may provide how the damages are to be calculated. Where the infringement of a legal right has caused no loss, the damages may be only nominal.

Damages are categorized in a number of ways: tort and contract; specified and unspecified sums. The most common judgment given is for a sum of money; the money due will either be a debt or damages. Interest may be awarded on a money judgment, but this relief is ancillary to the principal remedy, rather than an independent remedy. Damages in contract aim to put the claimant in the position in which he would have been had the contract been performed satisfactorily. Damages in tort aim to put the claimant in the position in which he would have been but for the commission of the tort. Contributory negligence (that is, when the claimant has contributed to the harm caused to him) will reduce the damages awarded by an appropriate percentage of up to 100 per cent (under the Law Reform (Contributory Negligence) Act 1945).

7.6.3.1 Personal injury damages

Although personal injury damages are tortious cases, the basis for assessment of damages for personal injury cases is a specific field of 'damage assessment'.

Personal injury damages are divided into two categories:

- special damages—all of which are past quantifiable damages that arose from the commission of the tort up to the date of trial; and
- general damages—that is, all other damages, the sum of which is assessed by the court based on the evidence adduced.

7.6.3.2 Contract damages

The aim of damages in contract is to put the claimant in the position in which he would have been but for the breach. The assessment of this principle is made on two different bases:

- to restore the claimant to the position in which he would have been had the contract been properly performed (loss of bargain); or
- to compensate the claimant for expenditure rendered futile by the breach.

When the sum due is known (for example, for the supply of goods that have not been paid for), this would be a 'specified' claim. In contract, however, there may be other losses that are unspecified, which, on the basis of evidence before it, are assessed by the court. These may include damages for loss of profit, distress, or inconvenience. These may relate to 'expectation' loss, 'reliance' loss, or 'restitution'. Where a claim constitutes a claim for a specified sum and unspecified sums, it is called an 'unspecified sum claim'.

7.6.3.3 Nominal damages

Nominal damages may be awarded where there has been an infringement of a legal right, but where there have been no losses arising from the infringement. If actual damage to the claimant is an essential element of a cause of action (for example, for actions in negligence), then a failure to prove any damage will result in the action being dismissed.

7.6.3.4 Aggravated damages

Aggravated damages are defined in the CPR Glossary as 'additional damages', which the court may award as compensation for the defendant's objectionable behaviour. They are intended to compensate for 'injured feelings' (meaning that a company, which has no feelings, may not be awarded aggravated damages). An award is most often made when the defendant's behaviour was designed to injure the claimant's pride or dignity.

The court may increase the sum because of the way in which the defendant may have behaved and because of the additional hurt caused by the objectionable way in which the defendant caused the loss (aggravated damages).

Any claim for aggravated damages must be specifically stated.

7.6.3.5 Exemplary damages

In exceptional circumstances, the court may award enhanced damages as a penalty. These damages are distinct from aggravated damages, but they may be awarded alongside aggravated damages. These damages are defined in the CPR Glossary as 'Damages which go beyond compensating for actual loss and are awarded to show the court's disapproval of the defendant's behaviour'.

Again, as with a claim for aggravated damages, any claim for exemplary damages must be specifically sought in the claim. They will only be made in exceptional circumstances, which include:

- oppressive, arbitrary, or unconstitutional behaviour by government servants;
- where the conduct of the defendant, as well as being objectionable, was designed to make a profit in excess of the compensatory damages that are payable; and
- where exemplary damages are expressly provided by statute.

7.6.3.6 Provisional damages

Provisional damages may be awarded in cases where the claimant *may suffer* a change in his condition, that change being a risk that the injuries he suffered may change in the way identified. For example the injury may cause an early onset of arthritis, arthritis not yet being a part of the claimant's injury. Section 32A of the Senior Courts Act 1981 provides that an award for provisional damages may be made when conditions are satisfied—the claimant has suffered injury—there is a chance or risk of developing a serious disease or deterioration in his condition—and, the court will exercise its discretion when and if to make such an award. The requirements for an award of provisional damages in a personal injury claim were considered and restated (the case did not change the application of s. 32A) in *Chewings v Williams & Abertawe Bro Morgannwyg University NHS Trust* [2009] EWHC 2490 (QB). The 'risk' (of change or deterioration) must be measurable not merely fanciful.

7.6.4 THE DELIVERY UP OF GOODS

A final judgment ordering the delivery up of goods may take one of three forms permitted by the Torts (Interference with Goods) Act 1977, s. 33(2):

- an order for the delivery of the goods and payment of any consequential damages—a discretionary remedy that will generally often only be made when the goods in question are unique or exceptional;
- an order for the delivery up of the goods, but giving the defendant the option of paying a set value for the goods, together with any assessed consequential damages, if any (but any payment of the set value by the defendant extinguishes the claimant's title to the goods); and
- a judgment for damages and not for the return of the goods (but, again, any payment of the set value by the defendant extinguishes the claimant's title to the goods).

7.6.5 INJUNCTIONS

An injunction may be either mandatory (that is, requiring some act to be done) or prohibitory (that is, requiring some conduct to stop or prohibiting threatened conduct). Any injunction is an equitable, and therefore discretionary, remedy and therefore cannot be obtained as of right. The court may award damages in place of an injunction, and will always do so if damages are a suitable and adequate remedy.

7.6.6 SPECIFIC PERFORMANCE

An order for specific performance is an equitable remedy and requires the performance of the obligations of a party. Again, it will be awarded if damages would not be an adequate remedy and the principles of equity are met. Specific performance is sought most often in claims related to land, but it can also be ordered in relation to goods that are rare or unique. Specific performance and damages may be awarded.

7.6.7 RECTIFICATION

Rectification to reflect the parties' true position is also a discretionary remedy. It is not the bargain that is rectified, but the written record of the bargain. An order for rectification is retrospective and the agreement is seen to be in the form rectified from the date on which it was originally made.

7.6.8 ACCOUNTS

A party alleging that an account is inaccurate must give notice of the objections of the account in his claim. The objections must give full particulars and specify the ground on which it is alleged that the account is inaccurate. Accounts are a common remedy between principal and agent, between partners, and in claims involving jointly owned property.

7.6.9 DECLARATIONS

The power to make a final binding declaration is contained in CPR 40.20 and the power to make interim declarations in CPR 25.1(b). The court will consider the justice to both parties in making a declaration and whether the declaration will serve a useful purpose. A declaration may make findings of fact, as well as of legal rights.

7.6.10 RESTITUTION

Claims for restitution can be made in law and in equity, and are based on the principles of unjust enrichment. Restitution deals with the principle of unjust enrichment at another's expense (in contrast to contract, in which the underlying principle is agreement and compensation is for breach of the agreement).

Restitution is used to restore the claimant to his previous position by making good the loss that he has suffered. The claim is for repayment of benefit received by the defendant, not for loss suffered by the claimant. Such a claim can arise when the damages are less than the benefit received by the defendant. The most common claims in restitution are for payment of money had and received, which covers both money paid under a mistake and money paid where there has been a total failure of consideration.

Restitution is viewed as separate and distinct from the laws of contract and tort, although it is, to a large extent, based on remedies and obligations found in contract and tort. The law of restitution does not depend on the existence of a breach of contract, but it may be an alternative action. Enrichment may be either positive (that is, the receipt of money or goods) or negative (that is, the saving of a necessary expenditure).

The remedy to which the claimant is entitled under the law of restitution is generally a personal remedy, which requires the defendant to pay to the claimant the value of the enrichment that the defendant has obtained at the claimant's expense. Alternatively, a claimant may be able to:

- seek a proprietary remedy, such as a declaration that the defendant holds an identifiable asset on trust for the claimant;
- assert a lien over an asset; or
- assert that he should be subrogated to the rights of a third party over the property of the defendant.

The courts have recognized a number of circumstances in which the law of restitution may be utilized—for example, an action for money had and received, or an action for money paid, services rendered, rescission, an account of profits, subrogation, and tracing.

A defendant may seek to defend a claim for restitution where he can show that the benefit was received by him as a valid gift, or as part of a valid agreement, or an equitable or statutory obligation owed by the claimant to the defendant. He may also seek to defend such a claim against him if he can show 'a change of position' as a result of the benefit alleged: for example, if he has donated the money to charity and he is neither a wrongdoer, nor has he acted in bad faith. There are other defences and a practitioner acting for a client making or defending an action in restitution will need to study this area of law in detail.

7.7 YOUR CLIENT'S DISCLOSURE OBLIGATIONS

Full particulars of the disclosure obligations of a party to litigation are contained in Chapter 17, but these obligations are onerous and a client should be made aware of the need to preserve documentary (or real, or electronic) evidence, whether these documents (or things) might assist in any future action or may assist his opponent. For this reason, 'disclosure' and the client's obligations in this respect can be considered to be a pre-action substantive matter.

KEY POINTS SUMMARY

- Identify the type of action that you have, and consider jurisdictional and limitation issues at the outset.

- If acting for a child, diarize any imminent 18th birthday to enable you to deal with the consequential procedural matters.

- Break your case down into the three legal components to help you in risk assessment and evidential issues.

Case study *Andrew James Pike and Deep Builders Ltd*

In the Andrew Pike case study, based on the information contained on the Online Resource Centre (the client's attendance note) consider the following questions.

Question 1

When does the limitation period expire?

Question 2

In which court and area should you issue proceedings, and why?

Question 3

What remedy is Mr Pike seeking? Provide details for your answer.

Any documents referred to in these case study questions can be found on the Online Resource Centre—simply click on 'Case study documentation' to access the documents that you need for Chapter 7 and to be reminded of the questions above. Suggested answers to these case study questions can also be accessed on the Online Resource Centre by your lecturer.

8   PRE-ACTION PROTOCOLS

8.1 INTRODUCTION

In this chapter, we will look at Protocol practice in general, the aims of Protocol, the basic content of all Protocols, and the Practice Direction on Pre-Action Conduct (PDPAC). We will also consider the consequences of non-compliance with Protocol or the PDPAC, and the occasions on which it may be appropriate to issue proceedings without complying with Protocol practice. We also look at some pre-action applications.

The chapter will then continue with a more detailed look at two Pre-Action Protocols—the Personal Injury (PI) Protocol and the Construction and Engineering Protocol. Clearly, for any action covered by a Protocol, it would be essential to look at that Protocol in detail. The aim in looking at two Protocols is to give a flavour of Protocols in practice. Because Protocols are all in a similar (but not the same) format, a closer look at two diverse ones will help the understanding of others.

LITIGATION TRAIN: PRE-ACTION PROTOCOL AND PROTOCOL PRACTICE

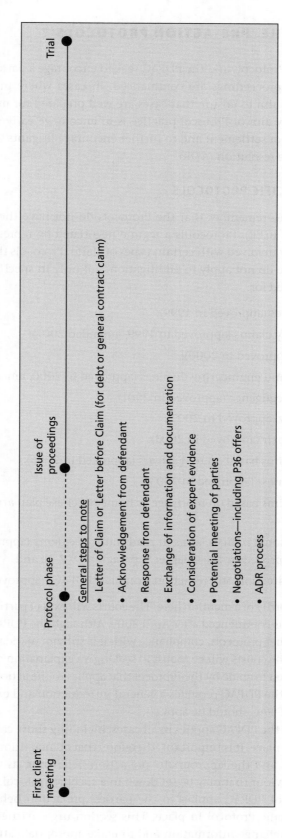

Note: In this context, all references to the 'claimant' or the 'defendant' mean 'potential claimant' or 'potential defendant', because proceedings have not yet been started.

8.2 WHAT ARE THE 'PRE-ACTION PROTOCOLS'?

The Pre-Action Protocols and the PDPAC seek to encourage a pattern of behaviour between litigants before proceedings are commenced. In cases where proceedings are ultimately issued they also aim to ensure that cases are well prepared for management by the court. Another primary aim of Protocol practice is to encourage early settlement in those cases that are capable of settlement and to further encourage litigants to consider methods of alternative dispute resolution (ADR).

8.2.1 THE CASE-SPECIFIC PROTOCOLS

It is important to remember that the Protocols do not have the same status as the Civil Procedure Rules (CPR). Protocol is a regime negotiated by representatives from sectors of society regularly involved with certain types of claim. Protocols that have been drafted and approved to date do not apply to all litigation, but only in specific areas. So far, they have been promulgated for:

- clinical disputes (approved in 1999);
- personal injury claims (approved in 1999, amended 2007);
- defamation (approved in 2000);
- construction and engineering disputes (approved in 2000, amended in 2007);
- professional negligence (approved in 2001);
- judicial review (approved in 2002);
- housing disrepair (approved in 2003);
- possession claims based on rent arrears (approved in 2006);
- disease and illness (approved in 2003);
- possession claims based on mortgage or home purchase plan arrears in respect of residential property;
- low value personal injury claims in road traffic accidents (approved in 2010) (for further detail on this procedure see Chapter 9, paragraph 9.2.7); and
- the Practice Direction on Pre-Action Conduct (PDPAC) (approved in 2009).

The PDPAC is worthy of a mention here. The courts will expect parties to comply with its provisions in all claims commenced after April 2009. Although the PDPAC is classified and appears alongside the other protocols, compliance with it is still not mandatory (see above). In respect of all Protocols the courts will be robust in seeking an explanation of a parties' pre-action conduct if it has failed to abide by the Protocol that applies to the action or to the PDPAC.

Section I of the PDPAC provides a general introduction and explains how the following section of the PDPAC should be applied.

Section II of the PDPAC applies in all cases, including those cases in which there is a specific Protocol in place. It is important, therefore, that all practitioners have a working knowledge of PDPAC and the 'appropriate' pre-action behaviour, as well as the recommended pre-action behaviour that may be set down in a specific Protocol.

Section III of PDPAC applies to the parties' pre-action behaviour in cases in which there is no specific Protocol in place. This section urges parties (see paragraphs 8.5 and 8.6 below) to exchange information and to make appropriate attempts to resolve the matter before commencing proceedings. The parties are expected to act in 'a reasonable and proportionate' manner and 'not use PDPAC as a tactical device to secure unfair advantage or to generate unnecessary costs'.

There are two Annexes to Section III:

- **Annex A**, which sets out recommended procedure and conduct in most cases in which there is no specific Protocol in place, most notably general breach of contract cases; and

- **Annex B**, which sets out specific recommendations for pre-action conduct in debt claims in which the claimant is a business and the defendant an individual. This is helpful, because the Debt Pre-Action Protocol that was drafted in May 1999 has never been adopted as a formal Protocol (although it was adopted by practitioners until 2009).

Section IV sets out recommended procedure in cases whether there is a specific Protocol or not. It contains guidance when an action may be close to the end of its limitation period and the need to issue 'protective proceedings'—including a provision that, where this occurs, the parties should seek to agree a stay of the action for a period to enable PDPAC practice to be embarked on. This section is also supplemented by **Annex C**, which contains guidance for instructing experts. With PDPAC in place, there may not be the need to develop further specific Protocols, but practitioners should be aware of any changes that do occur.

8.2.2 WHAT ABOUT DEBT ACTION WORK?

It is good practice to follow the PDPAC, Section II, Annex A and B as it gives some specific guidance relevant to some debt collection work. The main difference in debt action work is that there is a 'short-form' letter of claim written to identify clearly to the defendant what the claim against him is. In debt action work this modified version of the letter of claim is called a letter before claim. Annex A gives general guidance to any party to an action. Annex B gives guidance to a debt action where the claimant is a business and the defendant is an individual.

The letter before claim is a concise letter requesting payment and usually includes only the following details:

- the identity of the claimant and defendant;
- a copy of the invoice or contract;
- details of the amount sought;
- a statement confirming that an amount is owing;
- an indication of when the amount should have been paid;
- a request for payment by a certain date (usually seven days);
- particulars of how the payment is to be made;
- a warning of costs and interest penalties if payment is not received;
- the basis upon which you are claiming interest (usually contractual or by statute); and
- your contact details.

These points are the basic points to be included subject to any additional information required by Annex A and B.

The time limit for replying here is very short, up to 14 days, but typical of debt collection work. If no payment is made, it is, however, good practice to attempt to contact the debtor by telephone—but if this fails, then you are entitled to commence proceedings immediately without any sanction from the court.

 Professional Conduct

Many clients in commercial work—particularly debt collection work—want to take immediate action and issue proceedings without a letter of claim or letter before claim. This is usually because of their wish to safeguard, as far as they can, their cash flow position. Often they may have taken steps to try and secure payment of the debt before instructing a lawyer and feel the 'the debtor has had enough time to pay'. However as his legal representative, you are obliged to act in your client's best interest (under Rule 1.04 of the Solicitors' Code of Conduct 2007), and this means advising him to comply with the spirit of Protocol and best practice. You will need to explain to your client the potential consequences of failing to comply (as detailed in paragraph 8.6 below). If he continues to choose not to comply, then you must ensure that you have a detailed note on your file and a letter to your client pointing out those consequences of non-compliance. You are entitled to continue to act, however.

8.3 THE AIM OF THE PROTOCOLS OR PROTOCOL PRACTICE

Each of the current Protocols in place and the PDPAC state their purpose to be:

- to focus minds on resolving the dispute, not litigating it;
- to enable a party to obtain sufficient information to make a sensible and informed settlement offer, and to attach the appropriate costs risks to that offer if it is not accepted; and
- if settlement is not possible, to lay the ground for the efficient conduct of the proceedings.

In the same way that costs penalties may follow for a litigant who unreasonably refuses to participate in a form of ADR or who refuses a reasonable pre-action offer, costs penalties may also follow for litigants who unreasonably do not comply with protocol (see Chapter 4, paragraph 4.2.3.1, for further examples).

The concept of Protocol practice is relevant to a range of initiatives for good litigation and pre-litigation practice—especially:

- the predictability of the time needed for steps that should reasonably be taken pre-proceedings; and
- a standardization of relevant information, including documents to be disclosed.

8.4 WHAT ARE THE COMMON FEATURES OF THE PROTOCOL PHASE?

There is a pattern to all of the Protocols in place. Each contains:

- a template for the recommended contents of a letter of claim, so that appropriate enquiries can be commenced upon receipt;
- guidelines for the contents of a letter of response;
- guidelines for parties to provide pre-action information to each other, using standard forms and questionnaires;
- guidelines for parties to give pre-action disclosure;
- guidelines to encourage parties to instruct a single, common, expert—instead of each party having its own expert witness;
- guidelines to encourage the parties to try to settle their dispute without resorting to litigation—for example, by mediation, or another form of ADR; and
- a suggested bar on starting proceedings until a certain period has elapsed from the sending of the initial letter of claim.

8.5 HOW DOES THE COURT ENCOURAGE COMPLIANCE WITH PROTOCOL PRACTICE?

The need to undertake pre-action work within the spirit of the Protocols cannot be overemphasized.

Section II, paragraph 4 of the PDPAC states that 'the court will expect the parties to have complied with this [PDPAC] or any relevant protocol' and that it 'may ask the parties to explain what steps were taken to comply'. This effectively means that parties should comply wherever practically possible. Any infringements are likely to have to be explained or justified, and any failure on one party's part to comply will not justify the other party no longer seeking to comply within the spirit of the Protocol. When the court is considering any non-compliance with Protocol, it will be concerned whether the parties have complied 'in substance'. This means that the court is unlikely to be concerned with minor infringements (these are not defined—but see Chapter 4, paragraph 4.2.3.1, for cases on this). The court will also take account of issues of proportionality and situations in which 'urgency' had been a factor: 'urgency' might include not only short time caused by the ending of a limitation period, but also perhaps where an injunction was needed (see paragraph 8.7 below).

Both CPR 3 and 44 make provision for the court to be able to take account of a party's pre-action behaviour either when making directions for the management of the case or in making costs orders between the parties. So whilst the Protocols themselves are not part of the CPR, the possible 'sanctions' and 'encouragements' put in place by Protocol often make it difficult for any party to be able to justify any non-compliance.

The court will exercise its powers to sanction the defaulting party with the object of placing the non-defaulting party in the position they would have been had Protocol practice been complied with.

8.6 WHAT ORDERS CAN THE COURT MAKE IF PROTOCOL IS NOT COMPLIED WITH?

An important consequence of the Protocols not forming part of the CPR is that a party who fails to conduct his pre-action work within the actual aims—or the spirit—of the Protocols cannot be ordered to comply. Instead, the court uses a combination of **post-action** sanctions and orders, but only once the litigation has been commenced. These include:

* costs orders—these may include costs orders in whole or in part, on the indemnity basis, or for payment immediately; and

* 'penalties'—for example, depriving a party at fault of interest or ordering additional interest to be paid.

The aim of the court is to place the ('innocent') party in no worse a position than that in which he would have been had the Protocol been complied with.

The following cases are illustrative of the way in which the courts will exercise these powers.

* *Daejan Investments v Park West Club* **[2003] EWHC 2872** In this case, the successful additional party (then called a 'Part 20 defendant') was able to recover all of its costs, the court finding that, due to the claimant not complying with Protocol practice and not clarifying its case until (in this case) eleven months after proceedings had been commenced, the defendant was deprived of the opportunity of settling the claim.

* *Phoenix Finance Ltd v FIA* **[2002] EWHC 1028** In this case, the court awarded indemnity costs against the claimant where it had pursued a claim without first writing a letter of claim.

There are some pre-action applications that a party can make over which the court does have jurisdiction to make orders for compliance, but the jurisdiction for these (for example in an application for pre-action disclosure) is contained in the CPR, not the Protocol (see paragraph 8.8 below).

Practical Considerations

The following are useful guidelines to which to adhere in practice to ensure that Protocol practice is followed.

- Always engage with the opposing party at the earliest opportunity.

- Always write a full letter of claim and give a reasonable time in which the potential defendant can respond.

- If proceedings have to be issued before Protocol steps (for example, because of the limitation period), always give a clear indication of the reasons for issuing at this stage and suggest that directions are sought to provide a stay for Protocol practice to run its course, or give full reasons why the Protocol cannot be followed.

- Protocols are not inflexible and where it is not possible to adhere to the 'letter' of a Protocol, it should be possible nonetheless to adhere to its 'spirit'. For example, where time limits can justifiably and reasonably be varied, they should be varied to take account of the particular characteristics of the dispute.

- Reasonable early exchange of documents is essential, as is the move towards attempting to use agreed experts. Consider exchanging experts' reports early or seeking to engage an agreed expert.

- Take care not to overstate the case or to fail to mention issues that were known at the time, but which 'tactically' have not been mentioned at an early stage.

- If an opponent is failing to engage with Protocol, make this clear as soon as possible, in open correspondence. Where necessary (or at every occasion on which there has been non-compliance), state that a claim for costs or indemnity costs will be sought in any subsequent action for the non-compliance (see Chapter 4, paragraph 4.3, for a definition of indemnity costs).

- Do not reject the opponent's proposals without giving your considered (and reasonable) reasons.

- Remember that Protocol does *not* mean that you have to bend and concur with every request made. Protocol is essentially an exchange of letters, detail of the claim, and a settlement meeting. Once those obligations are concluded, you are at liberty to refuse to continue corresponding with the opponent until proceedings have been issued.

8.7 WHEN WOULD IT BE APPROPRIATE TO ISSUE PROCEEDINGS WITHOUT REFERENCE TO PROTOCOL PRACTICE?

There are essentially three situations in which it may be appropriate to take steps in the action without the cooperative communication with the opponent anticipated in any Protocol practice or when proceedings should be issued without reference to Protocol, as follows.

8.7.1 WHEN THE END OF THE LIMITATION PERIOD FOR THE ACTION IS CLOSE

When the end of the limitation period for the action is close, the claimant should issue 'protective' proceedings to avoid the action becoming statute-barred. To comply with Protocol practice and the overriding objective, the claimant should inform the defendant of the reason for his early issue. The claimant then needs either to:

- serve the proceedings and suggest to the opponent that the court be asked to give directions for the conduct of the action to include a stay for Protocol practice to be observed; or

- diarize the time by which the claim form must be served (to be within four months—or six months, if the defendant resides outside the jurisdiction of the court) and suggest that the parties continue to conduct their exchanges in accordance with Protocol practice in the intervening time.

8.7.2 WHEN AN INTERIM REMEDY IS REQUIRED TO PROTECT OR PRESERVE EVIDENCE OR THE ASSETS OF THE PROPOSED DEFENDANT

When an interim remedy is required for the protection or preservation of evidence, or of the assets of the proposed defendant, once the interim application has been heard, the claimant should consider seeking directions to enable Protocol practice to be engaged with and conducted. An interim application that could be required before engaging in Protocol might be that for a search order or freezing injunction.

8.7.3 WHEN THE PROPOSED DEFENDANT MAY ATTEMPT TO ISSUE PROCEEDINGS OUTSIDE THE JURISDICTION OF THE COURT TO AVOID THE COURTS OF ENGLAND AND WALES ASSUMING JURISDICTION OF THE ACTION

Some actions may have a choice of jurisdiction and if it is felt that a party may issue proceedings to avoid the jurisdiction of the courts of England and Wales, it may be reasonable and justifiable to issue proceedings quickly. Again, once the proceedings have been issued, the claimant should seek directions of the court to consider how best to incorporate Protocol practice.

8.8 PRE-ACTION DISCLOSURE APPLICATIONS

An application for pre-action disclosure is a step that can be taken pre-action—that is, probably in the Protocol phase of an action—but it is not part of Protocol. Where the circumstances are met under the provisions of CPR 31.16, such an application is one made under the CPR. It is one of the instances in which a party can seek an order of the court for compliance with a pre-action step.

In order to investigate a potential claim fully, pre-action disclosure may be required. A court order can only be made in limited circumstances—usually where:

- the respondent is likely to be a party to the proceedings;
- the applicant is likely to be a party to the proceedings;
- the documents, or classes of document, requested would be disclosed under standard disclosure rules; and
- disclosure now would fairly assist in disposing of the claim without the need to issue proceedings and save costs.

(For more details on applications for pre-action disclosure, see Chapter 17, paragraph 17.10.)

An order made will specify the documents, or classes of document, which must be disclosed. The respondent must specify any documents that he no longer has or which he claims the right or duty to withhold from inspection.

Orders can be made against a person who is a non-party, but only where the document sought will support the applicant's case (or adversely affect the other party's case) and disclosure is necessary to dispose of the claim fairly or save costs. (For further details, see Chapter 17, paragraph 17.10.3.)

Both potential parties to a claim should fully identify if there are any other potential parties, and their names, addresses, and details of insurers (if known). A delay in notifying such information could lead to a delay in progress and such delay could be construed as a failure to abide by the Protocol practice.

8.9 PRE-ACTION APPLICATIONS TO INSPECT PROPERTY

These applications are also contained within the CPR, not the Protocols, although the application is made in the Protocol phase.

CPR 25.5 deals with the ability to inspect property before the commencement of proceedings against a potential party to the action or against a non-party. This may be required when dealing with an accident at work claim. If the injury was caused by machinery, it may be prudent to inspect this machine before it is altered, adjusted, repaired, or removed. To obtain such an order, it must be shown that the property:

- is, or may become, the subject matter of the proceedings; or
- is relevant to the issues that will arise in relation to those proceedings.

 Practical Considerations

The template letter of claim supplied in the Protocol does not include a request that evidence should be preserved intact. This may be due to CPR 25.5, but it may be worth considering including this request in either the letter of claim or in the first letter to the proposed defendant.

8.10 PART 36 OFFERS TO SETTLE

An offer can be made before proceedings are commenced and provided that it is not withdrawn, it will have the same impact and cost consequences as a Part 36 offer made after the issue of proceedings if rejected. (For further detail on offers to settle, see Chapter 16.)

8.11 THE JACKSON REVIEW AND PROTOCOL

FIGURE 8.1

CURRENT POSITION	LORD JACKSON'S PROPOSALS
1. There are eleven pre-action protocols in existence.	The eleven protocols should be retained subject to minor amendments.
2. The Practice Direction on Pre Action Conduct exists where there is no protocol in places for a particular dispute.	(a) The general protocol in Sections III and IV should be repealed. Instead there should be an obligation for appropriate pre-action correspondence and exchange of information with costs sanctions; (b) Annex B should be incorporated into a new Debt Protocol.
3. There is currently no legislation to permit pre-action applications for breach of protocol.	The enactments of primary legislation to permit pre-action applications for breach of protocol.

8.12 THE PERSONAL INJURY (PI) PROTOCOL

In this section, we will take a closer look at the Protocol that is in place for personal injury (PI) cases. The aim, as with all Protocols, is to encourage better and more standardized pre-action work.

8.12.1 FOR WHICH CASES IS THE PI PROTOCOL DESIGNED?

The PI Protocol is designed for use in road traffic cases, tripping and slipping cases, and employers' liability cases in the fast track with a value of up to £25,000.

However, if your client's claim is worth no more than £10,000 and arises from a road traffic accident, then you will need to follow the new protocol for low value personal injury claims in road traffic accidents.

Because the PDPAC expects litigants to conduct their pre-action work in accordance with an appropriate Protocol or in the 'spirit of' Protocol practice, multi-track PI claims could also be conducted within the spirit of this Protocol, with appropriate adaptations being made to time limits or procedure to take account of the higher value and/or more complex PI actions in the multi-track. Any adaptations made should be capable of being justified in accordance with the overriding objective and the aims of Protocol practice.

 Practical Considerations

It is essential to come to a conclusion as soon as possible about to which track a potential case would be likely to be allocated. The court makes a final determination of 'which track' on allocation, but legal representatives should undertake all of the relevant Protocol steps before such an allocation is made. It is therefore important to know where the case may fall, because a failure to abide by the Protocol in a case in the fast track may have significant cost consequences for you or your client. Even for a case falling within the multi-track, you will have to justify any steps taken that diverge from Protocol.

8.12.2 WHAT PRE-ACTION STEPS ARE RECOMMENDED BY THE PI PROTOCOL?

8.12.2.1 Early contact

The claimant is encouraged to contact the prospective defendant as soon as practicable to advise that investigations are underway, giving as much detail as possible at that stage. It may be some weeks before the claimant is in a position to prepare a full letter of claim (see below), but any early contact apart from putting the prospective defendant on notice may enable useful questions to be asked about the selection of experts, the availability of documents, or the intention to abide by the Protocol. Such a letter could also usefully make enquiries about the prospective defendant's views on seeking to mediate or resolve the potential dispute by way of another form of ADR. The letter should say how long it is likely to be before a formal letter of claim might be sent.

An early letter of this kind will not start the timetable of time limits proposed in the Protocol.

8.12.2.2 The letter of claim

The time limits of Protocol-compliant steps are started once the formal letter of claim is sent to the proposed defendant.

The letter should contain enough information to enable the defendant to investigate the proposed claim and to put a broad valuation on the claim. It therefore needs to contain:

- a clear summary of the facts on which the claim is based;
- an indication of the nature of all injuries that have been sustained;
- the name and address of the hospital at which the claimant was treated;
- where available, the claimant's hospital reference number; and
- an indication of other financial losses.

The letter also needs to contain:

- confirmation of for whom you are acting and sufficient details of the claim to enable the potential defendant to identify the action;

- a request to identify the name of the proposed defendant's insurers;

- in road traffic accident (RTA) cases, a statement of whether a police accident report is or has been obtained (and, at the same time, an attempt to seek agreement that the fee for this should be shared);

- the documents that the prospective claimant proposes to disclose (if any) and seeks from the prospective defendant;

- whether a conditional fee agreement (CFA), with a success fee, has been entered into (see paragraph 8.12.2.3 below);

- a spare copy (or copies) of the letter that the prospective defendant can pass on to his insurers and/or his legal representatives; and

- the date on which the letter must be acknowledged (under the Protocol, this is within 21 days).

The letter needs to be phrased in such a way that the defendant (possibly an individual) can easily understand it. It also needs to stress the requirement that this should be passed to the defendant's insurer (if there is one) immediately. If the details of the insurer are known, then a copy should be sent to the insurer at the same time. The letter should also state when a reply is expected—usually within 21 days. It should state clearly on the letter that it is the letter of claim for the proposed action.

The PI Protocol has a template letter of claim annexed to it as Appendix A.

 Practical Considerations

Although the PI Protocol has a template letter of claim, it should not be thought that the letter of claim should contain only those matters set out in the template. Each particular case will be different, and there will be other matters that can usefully, and effectively, be raised and added to the template letter. It is therefore useful to see the template letter as a template for the bare minimum that the letter should contain. For example, where no earlier attempt has been made to agree a medical expert, the letter of claim could include proposals to set in motion the process for agreeing a medical expert. The letter of claim could also set out any proposed alterations to the Protocol timetable, as well as the reasons for the suggested alterations. Similarly, if earlier correspondence had not made any reference to the claimant's willingness to embark on a form of ADR, this could be a useful time to do this and, at the same time, to set out the suggested ADR timescale. Paragraph 2.8 of the PI Protocol states that, in RTA claims, the letter of claim should also include the name and address of the hospital at which the claimant was treated, together with the claimant's hospital reference number, as indicated above.

8.12.2.3 Details of any conditional fee agreement or insurance

If the claimant has a CFA, with a success fee, and/or after-the-event (ATE) insurance, then, if the claimant seeks to recover the costs of any success fee or ATE premium, notice of the CFA should be given at this stage. Paragraph 3.2 of the revised Protocol states:

Where the case is funded by a CFA (or collective CFA), notification should be given of the existence of the agreement and where appropriate, that there is a success fee and/or insurance premium, although not the level of the success fee or premium.

It is therefore apparent that there is no duty to disclose the precise amount of the success fee or premium, because it is only the existence of these agreements or conditions that is relevant.

8.12.2.4 Sufficient detail of the value of the claim

The priority at the letter of claim stage is for the claimant to provide sufficient information for the defendant to assess liability *and* sufficient information for the defendant to assess the likely value of the claim.

8.12.2.5 Rehabilitation

Paragraph 4 and Annex D of the Protocol incorporate the Code of Best Practice on Rehabilitation, Early Intervention and Medical Treatment in Personal Injury Claims (the Rehabilitation Code). There is a duty on both the claimant and defendant to consider, at a very early stage, any reasonable needs on behalf of the claimant for rehabilitation and/or medical treatment.

The Protocol reads:

> The claimant or the defendant or both shall consider as early as possible whether the claimant has reasonable needs that could be met by early rehabilitation treatment or other measures.

The parties should therefore consider at an early stage (even before liability is resolved) how those needs might be met. The provision of any report obtained for the purposes of assessment of provision of a party's rehabilitation needs shall not be used in any litigation arising out of the accident, the subject of the claim, save by consent.

The Code applies regardless of the severity of the claimant's injury. Both parties and the insurer have duties to consider rehabilitation (and the insurer will pay the costs of any rehabilitation report). (For further detail of the Code, see Chapter 19, paragraph 19.8.3.)

8.12.2.6 The promotion of early settlement

To further the promotion of early settlements, the Protocol suggests full and early disclosure. It also states that the claimant must wait 21 days before issuing proceedings where:

- the defendant has admitted liability (either wholly or in part); and
- there has been full disclosure of medical reports on which the parties rely; and
- after admission of liability, the claimant sends to the defendant schedules of loss and damage (if not already sent).

8.12.2.7 The defendant's response

Note: There is further detail of the defendant's pre-action responses in Chapter 10, paragraph 10.3.

The defendant (or his insurer) needs to reply by acknowledging the letter within the time limit (for example, 21 days). If there is no response within the 21 days, then proceedings can be started. It can be sensible to try to make direct contact with the defendant (or his insurer) to find out the reason for any delay. This may not be caused by the defendant (or his insurer) trying to avoid the issue; it is more likely to be the tardy process of the letter of claim being passed from the defendant to his broker, then to the insurer, and ultimately being allocated to a case handler, which can often take more than 21 days.

Once a response has been made, the defendant (or his insurer) has three months in which to investigate the claim. The reply must deal with liability, either admitting or denying it. If the defendant wants to admit the claim, then the defendant is bound by any admission (up to £25,000). If the defendant denies the claim, then his reasons for denial must be given.

8.12.2.8 The early disclosure of documents

Disclosure of the defendant's documents can clarify the issues that are in dispute. The claimant can send a list requesting documents that are considered relevant, and which are believed to be in the defendant's possession and should be disclosed. Where there is a denial of liability, the reply should include a list of all documents material to the issues and likely to be ordered to be disclosed by court.

If the defendant admits liability, but alleges contributory negligence, the defendant should disclose the documents that are relevant to his allegations.

Annex B of the PI Protocol sets out tables of the expected documents for disclosure in different PI actions.

8.12.2.9 The selection of experts

Whilst the use of experts in the Protocol phase is not governed by the CPR (Part 35, in particular), it is still intended that a joint expert is used by the parties either pre or post the issue of proceedings. (For further details on joint experts, see Chapter 19, paragraph 19.8.4.)

However, the treatment of joint experts during the Protocol stage is fundamentally different from the treatment of experts during the course of litigation. This is because the PI Protocol suggests that the expert is jointly selected by the agreement of both parties, although there is nothing stopping the parties from agreeing to the joint instruction of a medical expert pursuant to CPR 35.

Joint selection under the Protocol, however, is effected by the claimant or defendant (usually the claimant) putting forward a list of suggested joint experts. If, within 14 days, no objections are raised by the opponent, then one of the mutually acceptable experts can be approached to examine the claimant medically and he will be an 'agreed' expert.

Once a jointly selected report has been prepared, it is only sent to the claimant. If the claimant decides to rely on the report, then he must disclose it to the defendant. Both parties can ask the expert written questions on relevant issues, such questions usually being copied to the opponent. Answers to the questions will be sent to both parties.

If a defendant has agreed to the joint expert, but then wishes to instruct his own expert witness in any subsequent proceedings, he is not entitled to rely on such a report unless:

• the claimant agrees that he may do so; or

• the court so directs; or

• the claimant's expert's report has been amended and the claimant is not prepared to disclose the original report.

Under Protocol, however, if the parties cannot agree on the identity of a jointly selected expert, then the parties may instruct experts of their own choice. If proceedings are subsequently issued, the court will decide whether either party has acted unreasonably and, if so, the court will consider whether any expert evidence is required (and, if so, in what fields and how many), and will consider whether costs penalties should be imposed.

The key features, therefore, of joint selection are that there is likely to be a letter agreed by the parties instructing the medical expert to prepare a report, but that the report belongs to the claimant and is paid for by the claimant. It is therefore the claimant's decision whether he wishes to rely on it and subsequently to disclose it to the defendant. The agreement by the defendant to agree a particular medical expert gives him no entitlement to see the report unless the claimant discloses it. Any report prepared by a joint expert selected in the Protocol phase is therefore not a joint report for the purposes of CPR 35.

Annex C of the PI Protocol contains a template letter of instruction to a medical expert.

The Court of Appeal has recently given further guidance on the selection and use of an agreed medical expert in the pre-action stage. In the case of *Edwards-Tubbs v J D Wetherspoon*, CA, 25 February 2011 the claimant had selected an expert's report from one of the nominated experts. The defendant, in response to the list of experts, had not objected to any. When proceedings were issued, settlement not being achieved in the Protocol stage, the claimant issued proceedings and served a report from a different expert. The Court of Appeal held that the first 'agreed' expert's report should be disclosed before permission would be given for the claimant to use a different expert. The court further stated that such a condition would be the 'usual' order that would be made. Hughes LJ said 'Expert shopping is undesirable and, wherever possible, the court will use its powers to prevent it.'

Practical Considerations

It should be noted that the template letter in Annex C is a letter to a party's own expert, not to a jointly agreed expert. Care should be taken to amend the detail of this template letter if an expert has been jointly agreed. For example, the letter would say that both parties have agreed to the use of the named expert i.e. joint selection and the expert should be given instructions whom he should contact if he needs to do so. In the absence of agreement, the expert will report to the claimant. The letter also implies that the time by which the expert will provide the report is not yet determined. In practice—and given the timescales proposed by the PI Protocol—this detail would have been obtained before instructing the expert and the letter will then merely confirm the timescale for production of the report that has been agreed.

8.12.2.10 ADR

There are no rules regarding which methods of ADR to adopt. Discussion and negotiation are usually considered first, then perhaps early neutral evaluation (ENE) and mediation. However with any of these options, it will not be easy to proceed fully before receiving expert evidence—especially the medical report—because full awareness of the injuries is needed to assist in quantifying the claim (see further Chapter 5, paragraphs 5.6 and 5.7).

8.12.2.11 If settlement fails, what next?

If the PI Protocol fails to secure settlement, then the claimant can proceed to issue his claim, although, in practice, the parties usually reflect on what has been achieved during the Protocol phase rather than rush to issue. This may involve seeking counsel's opinion.

8.13 THE CONSTRUCTION AND ENGINEERING PROTOCOL

8.13.1 GENERAL OBSERVATIONS

The Construction and Engineering Protocol was revised in 2007 with the aim of making it less expensive and cumbersome to comply with in practice. As a result, it is now one of the shorter Protocols. As a legal representative, you should be aware that this Protocol applies to all construction and engineering disputes, including professional negligence claims against architects, engineers, and quantity surveyors. The Professional Negligence Protocol would therefore be inappropriate to use in such negligence cases for these professions.

As with all Protocols, it expressly states in its introduction its aims and objectives. It also specifically highlights how the court should deal with compliance with this Protocol and suggests that 'it will be concerned with substantial compliance and not minor departures' in so far as sanctions are concerned. This Protocol also indicates that the overriding objective applies to the pre-action period, but that whilst the Protocol should be entered into in 'good faith' and not to secure a 'tactical advantage', with building cases generating a plethora of documentation, it will not be necessary for the parties to collate and disclose 'all supporting details and evidence that may be ultimately required for litigation'.

8.13.2 THE LETTER OF CLAIM

Like the majority of the Protocols, the commencement of the Protocol is signified by a letter of claim containing enough basic information to enable the defendant to investigate the claim further. The Protocol suggests that the following information should be included:

- the parties' full names and addresses;
- a clear summary of the facts upon which each claim is made;

- the principal contractual or statutory provisions relied on;
- the nature of the relief sought—in building cases, this may be damages (for which calculations must be provided), an extension of time, or even specific performance;
- details of why the claimant believes that the defendant has wrongly rejected his claim (if the parties had been in prior correspondence); and
- the name of any expert instructed by the claimant and the issues to which that evidence will be directed.

 Practical Considerations

The upfront costs of litigation, when adhering to the Protocol, can often involve costly experts right from the very start. Consequently, the whole exercise can become very expensive. Moving towards the use of a joint expert in these kinds of dispute is likely to be more cost-efficient, as well as proportionate, for both parties.

8.13.3 THE DEFENDANT'S RESPONSE

The defendant has 14 days in which to acknowledge the letter of claim and has a total of 28 days from the date on which he received the letter of claim in which to send a full response to the claimant.

The response will indicate the following:

- which are agreed and which are not agreed facts, with reasons;
- claims that are accepted or rejected, with reasons;
- if any claims are accepted, either in whole or in part, whether the relief claimed is accepted or rejected—again, with reasons;
- details of any allegation of contributory negligence on the part of the claimant;
- details of any proposed counterclaim (on a similar basis as that which is required by a letter of claim); and
- the name of any expert instructed by the defendant and the issues to which that evidence will be directed.

If the defendant either fails to acknowledge within the 14 days or to provide a full response within the 28-day period (or any other period agreed up to a maximum of three months), then the claimant is able to commence proceedings without fear of sanctions. Clearly, if a counterclaim has been raised, then the claimant will be required to respond to that within the same time limit and to the same degree of detail as the defendant's response.

 Practical Considerations

There is still a great deal of reluctance in practice about this Protocol, with the result that you may have to bring this to the attention of your opponent. With these types of case generating a lot of paperwork, there is also a reluctance to photocopy files on large projects. Remember, copying charges can be mutually requested from the opponent, but be mindful of becoming embroiled in protracted discussions regarding who should pay for the copies. Realistically, there is a practical limit to what the opponent will supply you with in terms of documents that should accompany a letter of claim or response.

8.13.4 THE PRE-ACTION MEETING

The pre-action meeting is the main feature of this particular Protocol and can often incur the greatest expense. However, the Protocol requires that, within a time period of a further

28 days after receipt of the defendant's response (or after the claimant's response to a counterclaim), the parties are to meet.

 Practical Considerations

Construction and engineering disputes often involve many parties. In order to meet the strict timetable of the Protocol, the parties may, for example, need to fix a date for an all-parties meeting in advance of the final exchanges of correspondence on the issues to ensure availability and that the meeting takes place within 28 days of the end of that exchange. In practice, it may take more than 28 days for the meeting to take place, but as long as the parties are cooperating and acting reasonably, it is unlikely that either party will be penalized.

It is envisaged that more than one meeting may be necessary as the purpose of the meeting is to narrow issues and identify how the issues can best be resolved. Obviously, ADR is strongly suggested in the Protocol, but it is acknowledged that if the parties see litigation as the only way forward, then the Protocol contains provisions for the parties to agree:

- whether expert evidence is required, on what issues, and whether this should be joint;
- the extent of disclosure; and
- the conduct of any potential litigation, having regard to minimizing delay and cost.

It is also worth noting that the Protocol permits any party who attended the pre-action meeting to disclose the following facts to the court if proceedings ultimately ensue:

- where and when the meeting took place;
- who attended, who did not and why, and any agreement reached; and
- whether ADR was discussed.

This is notwithstanding the fact that the court recognizes that these pre-action meetings are without prejudice.

 Practical Considerations

As a legal representative, you will need to be careful in disclosing the facts of the meeting to the court. Legal representatives may be expected to supply information to the court that meets the above requirements whilst at the same time protecting the 'without prejudice' status of the meeting.

8.14 THE LOW VALUE RTA CLAIMS PROCEDURE

For details of this procedure, see chapter 9 paragraph 9.2.7.

KEY POINTS SUMMARY

- Be familiar with which Protocols apply to which types of case, and deal with their compliance reasonably and proportionately.
- Be familiar with the guidance laid down in the Practice Direction on Pre-Action Conduct (PDPAC), because this guidance applies both to cases that have a specific Protocol and those that do not.

- Do not be afraid to request amendments to any of the Protocols to suit your case. As long as you act reasonably and within the spirit of the Protocol generally, you cannot not be criticized.

- Ensure that your client understands what the Protocol phase is all about.

- Understand the interplay of the CPR in some pre-action matters in the Protocol phase.

Case study *Bollingtons Ltd and Mrs Elizabeth Lynch t/a The Honest Lawyer*

Consider the following questions.

Question 1

What information would go in your letter before claim to Mrs Lynch?

Question 2

What points would you cover in your first letter to your new client Bollingtons Ltd? Consider whether you should justify and explain the step that you have taken, and what professional conduct points could arise at this stage in this case study.

Case study *Andrew James Pike and Deep Builders Ltd*

Consider the following questions.

Question 1

Is there a Protocol in place for this action? If so, which is it?

Question 2

What work would you suggest is undertaken in this matter in the Protocol phase?

---

online resource centre

Any documents referred to in these case study questions can be found on the Online Resource Centre—simply click on 'Case study documentation' to access the documents that you need for Chapter 8 and to be reminded of the questions above. Suggested answers to these case study questions can also be accessed on the Online Resource Centre by your lecturer.

9 STARTING YOUR COURT ACTION AND SERVING IT ON THE DEFENDANT

Relevant court forms relating to this chapter:

- N1 Claim Form
- N251 Notice of Funding
- N208 Part 8 Claim Form
- RTA1 and RTA3 if the claim is under the low value RTA procedure

9.1 INTRODUCTION

No resolution has been found to your client's dispute. This, despite all of the steps taken in the Protocol phase, or the failure of any attempts that have been made to settle with alternative dispute resolution (ADR), or perhaps because your client is faced with an intransigent opponent. If your client wishes to proceed to seek justice, litigation is now your last option. This is exactly what Lord Woolf had in mind when he talked of the courts being 'a forum of dispute resolution of last resort'.

Clearly, when we consider the emphasis that there is for pre-action preparation of a case to create every possible chance for a resolution to be found it will be clear that it is only those more difficult, less black-and-white cases that *will* proceed to litigation. Obviously, there will be those cases that proceed because the opponent has no intention of cooperating in finding a settlement or because he does not have the funds to settle. But, in general, the cases that proceed to litigation will be those in which both parties feel they have a good case—to win or to defend.

 Practical Considerations

This very generalized overview of the nature of the cases that do proceed to litigation is worth bearing in mind. It is rare that a party will want to proceed to litigation and face the heavy burden and uncertainty of it without feeling, in his own mind, that he has a good case. As the legal representative for such a client, you need to manage his expectations very carefully. A client may have a very firm conviction that he has a good case or that he has the moral high ground, but this does not necessarily mean that there is a good case in law. It is these 'certain' clients who nonetheless have a difficult case to prove who are perhaps the most difficult to manage. It is also these clients who will look to complain if things do not go as they expected, so all advice and risk assessment analysis needs to be carefully explained, and supported with a file note and correspondence. There is a balance to be struck between positive support and risk assessment: you may be doubtful, but do not overlook the fact that your client may win.

This chapter will deal with the procedural steps, considerations, and issues that need to be considered when commencing proceedings. It will include:

- the 'tracks' created by the CPR—the 'small claims track', the 'fast track', and the 'multi-track';
- the documents needed to issue proceedings;
- parties and joinder; and
- service provisions;

Once a defence has been filed, the court's proactive case management processes will begin with the issuing of the allocation questionnaire (AQ) to the parties. Thereafter, the management of the case will begin by the court. But that is the continuing story (see Chapter 12); for now, we are assuming that the decision to commence proceedings has been taken by your client and that you have your client's instructions to proceed. This chapter will tell you how you will take the necessary steps towards the process of litigation.

LITIGATION TRAIN: STARTING YOUR CLAIM AND SERVING IT ON THE DEFENDANT

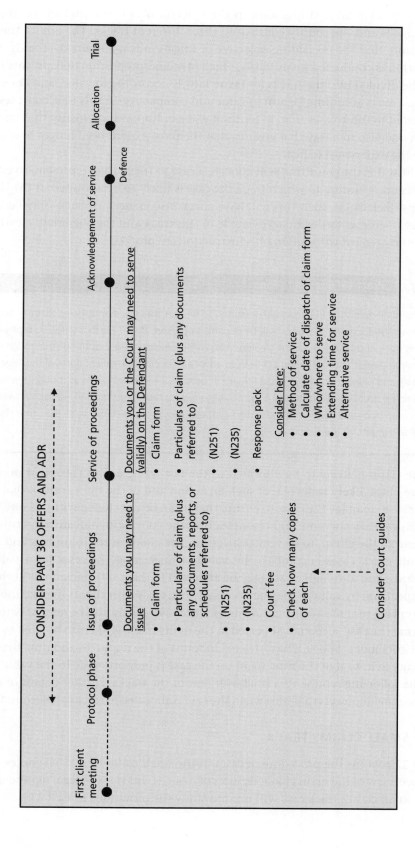

9.2 THE TRACKS

The CPR have divided litigation in the Queen's Bench Division of the High Court into two tracks and the county courts into three different tracks. The aim of these divisions is to ensure that the overriding objective of litigation is maintained—that is, to ensure that litigation is conducted justly, fairly, efficiently, and proportionately. In this way, an action will be divided into the tracks for **issue** largely according to value, and cases will be **tried** by the courts according (again) to value and complexity. In this way, court resources will be allocated to those cases that, in terms of value or importance, justify the time employed on them and also in a way that ensures that the most experienced judges hear cases that they have the experience to hear.

Whilst it is the court that will allocate a case to track, legal representatives need to make a decision regarding to which track the case is likely to be allocated. If the claim is a small claims track claim, then this will have cost consequences, because only very limited costs for legal representation are recoverable in this track and the client will clearly need to take this into account when giving his instructions to proceed.

 Practical Considerations

The small claims track is designed ultimately to be user-friendly. It anticipates that the majority of cases being conducted in this track will be litigants in person. If you are instructed to represent a client in this track and face a litigant in person, it is worth remembering that the district judge may adopt an interventionist approach, and act both as advocate (to elicit the salient parts of the litigant in person's case) and judge. He will assist the litigant in person. It will often seem as though the district judge is bending over backwards to assist the other party who represents himself—and that will often be true. Be prepared to engage with the district judge in this, be cooperative with the other party, and assist in gently getting the case in order.

If the claim is likely to be allocated to the fast track, again, the client needs to be made aware of the likely timescale of such an action and of the tight control that the judge will exercise to manage the case, to ensure that it can be concluded within a one-day trial time. To ensure this, the time and resources that the court will allocate to a fast-track case may appear, to the client, to be very restricting. The client needs to understand the reasons.

Multi-track cases encompass, by value, a huge range of cases (of a value of £25,000 upwards) and although a case may be allocated to the multi-track if it is at the lower end of the spectrum by value, it may be necessary to discuss with clients the likelihood or merits of attempting to agree a fast-track regime for the case. It may also be necessary to advise the client that the case, although allocated to the multi-track, is likely to be tried by a circuit judge or district judge, and will be restricted in terms of the resources and time that the court will allocate to it, so that the time spent on the case is proportionate to the value claimed.

The following represents a brief overview of the tracks. Further details of the courts case management powers that start when the case is allocated to track can be found in Chapter 12.

9.2.1 THE SMALL CLAIMS TRACK

CPR 27 governs the procedure of cases in the small claims track. The notes that follow are an overview of the main characteristics of cases in this track. A legal representative involved in a small claims track case will need to study the provisions in CPR 27.

9.2.1.1 What cases are likely to be allocated to the small claims track?

Cases in this track will be those cases that:

- have a value up to £5,000—except in the following cases:
- personal injury cases, in which the upper financial limit in this track is £1,000 in value of damages for pain, suffering, and loss of amenity;
- claims by a residential tenant against his landlord for repairs or other work to the premises, with an upper limit of £1,000 in value of those repairs and an upper limit of damages;
- cases involving claims against landlords for harassment or unlawful eviction;
- disputes involving an allegation of dishonesty;
- under CPR 26.6 and CPR 27.1:
- have a value exceeding the financial limits above if the parties consent and the court agrees that it is appropriate to place the case in this track;
- exceed the financial values above, but in which the defendant files an admission before allocation of part of the claimant's claim and the net sum then in dispute is within the financial limits of this track.

 Practical Considerations

In cases that fall below the financial limits of the small claims track by an admission of part of the claim by the defendant, the claimant should consider making an application for judgment on the admission under CPR 14.1(4) in order to recover costs, because these may amount to more than will be permitted in the small claims track. CPR 44.11(2) states that a case that has been in another track before transfer to the small claims track will have those costs provisions applying in its previous track. This provision will not apply, however, in the circumstances of a part admission, because the case will not have been 'previously allocated'.

9.2.1.2 What are the main features of cases in the small claims track?

The main characteristics of small claims track cases are as follows.

- Hearings will be less informal. The court has the power (under CPR 27.8) to conduct the hearing in a way that it considers is fair. Evidence will often not be taken on oath and the court may limit cross-examination. The judge may act as 'advocate' and may ask questions of witnesses, and he may limit or exclude cross-examination. The hearing will be tape-recorded and a party may obtain a transcript upon payment of the fee. CPR 27.10 permits the court, at the request of the parties, to hear the case without the parties being present—that is, as a 'paper' hearing.
- Lay representation is permitted and it is common for parties to represent themselves. Lay representatives or lawyers may represent companies.
- Costs are restricted and, in general, will be fixed costs, any court fees paid, and the reasonable expenses of the successful party in attending the hearing, including a sum, not exceeding £50, for lost earnings or loss of leave. Experts' fees (if, indeed, expert evidence has been permitted) will be restricted to £200 per expert. The court may also award such other costs as it thinks reasonable if it thinks that a party has behaved unreasonably.

Costs

Although the court has a wide discretion to award costs in the small claims track, it will rarely do so outside the fixed costs listed. The power to award additional costs in the face of 'unreasonable behaviour' could include making a wholly false claim, paying the whole sum just before the hearing, or deliberate delay. Where the party seeking these discretionary costs is legally represented and the party against whom these costs are sought is not, the court will look very carefully before making any additional discretionary order for costs. Clients instructing a lawyer to represent them in cases in this track need to be aware of this even in the face of what appears to be 'unreasonable behaviour'.

- Some procedural rules do not apply—these include CPR 25 (except those parts relating to interim injunctions) and CPR 31 (disclosure and inspection in this track is governed more informally). Appendix A of Practice Direction (PD) 27 sets out the documents that will normally be required. CPR 32, 33, 35, 36, 39, and 18 also do not apply to this track. These, in general, deal with evidence, offers to settle, and requests for further information.

- The path a small claims track case will take to a hearing is short-circuited and the district judge may well set a final hearing date when he sets down the directions for the case. The hearing itself will usually be before a district judge or deputy district judge.

9.2.1.3 Can small claims track judgments be set aside or appealed?

9.2.1.3.1 *Setting aside*

A party in a small claims track case who was neither present nor represented at the hearing, and who had not given notice to the court and the other party that he would not be attending under the provisions of CPR 27.9(1), may apply to have any decision made at the hearing set aside and the claim reheard. To do this, the party will need to make his application to set aside not more than 14 days after the order has been served on him (CPR 27.11(2)) and he will need to establish that:

- he had a good reason for not attending or not being represented, or that he had not given notice to the court to proceed in his absence; and

- he has a reasonable prospect of success.

Therefore, a party, no matter how good his case, will have no right to have the order set aside if he was deliberately absent from the hearing. If the court does make an order to set aside, it may continue to rehear the case immediately after its decision on the application to set aside or it may list an alternative date and give such further directions as it sees fit.

Any other party who is 'unhappy' with the judgment of a small claims track hearing will need to consider whether he has grounds to appeal.

9.2.1.3.2 *Appealing*

The provisions for appeal in the small claims track are similar to those in the fast track and multi-track, but simplified. Any appeal can only be with the permission of the court that decided the case or the appellate court.

9.2.2 A 'EUROPE-WIDE' SMALL CLAIMS PROCEDURE

In 2006 and 2007, the European Parliament and the Council of the European Union created two new Regulations to simplify the procedure for cross-border civil and commercial debt collection and small claims procedures. These are known as the European Order for Payment (EOP) and the European Small Claims Procedure (ESCP). They are both paper-based processes, using the standard forms and procedures set out in CPR 78.

9.2.2.1 The European Order for Payment (EOP)

The EOP was adopted under EC Regulation 1896/2006 and came into force in stages between June and December 2008. The purpose of the EOP is to speed up and reduce the cost of debt collection in cross-border uncontested money claims. This is achieved essentially by creating a payment procedure between member states that obviates the requirement for prior recognition of the resultant EOP by member states before enforcement.

The procedure serves as an option to claimants. In the UK, should a claimant not wish to proceed with an EOP, he is free to proceed with his own debt collection under the CPR.

9.2.2.2 The European Small Claims Procedure (ESCP)

The ESCP was adopted under EC Regulation 861/2007 and came into force in January 2009. The purpose of the ESCP is to simplify and speed up small claims litigation in cross-border cases, with the ultimate aim of reducing costs. As with the EOP, this is achieved by means of a procedure that eliminates the need for the issue of further proceedings to recognize and enforce the eventual judgment.

Again, as with the EOP, it is an optional process for claimants to take. It can, however, only be used where the value of the claim does not exceed €2,000.

9.2.3 THE FAST TRACK

CPR 28 governs the procedure of cases in the fast track. The notes that follow are an overview of the main characteristics of cases in this track. A practitioner involved in a fast-track case will need to study the provisions in CPR 28. The stages of a fast-track action will also be considered in greater detail later in the book.

9.2.3.1 What cases are likely to be in the fast track?

Cases in this track will be those cases that:

- have a monetary value of between £5,000 (£1,000 in the personal injury, landlord and tenant, and other claims detailed in paragraph 9.2.1.1 above) and £25,000;

- have no monetary value (these could include a claim for an injunction, specific performance, or a declaration), which the court considers suitable for this track (and which do not require the more complex treatment that may be given in the multi-track);

- any other case, irrespective of its monetary value, which the court considers is suited to this track; and

- cases that the parties elect to be in this track (and where the court agrees that it is appropriate to manage the case in this track).

9.2.3.2 What are the main features of cases in the fast track?

The main characteristics of fast-track cases are as follows.

- There will be tight court control with strict time limits. When a case is allocated to the fast track, the court will set a programme for the case that enables the trial to take place within 30 weeks of allocation. The trial 'window' (a period of time—usually three weeks—within which the trial date will ultimately be set) will be set at allocation.

- Costs will be strongly linked to 'proportionality'. Increasingly, the CPR are looking to impose (and increase the scope of) fixed costs in this track. The fast track provides a 'no frills' procedure for medium-sized cases that do not justify detailed or extensive preparation. In effect, there will no more than seven months available in which to make the case ready for trial.

- Allocation and directions (usually standard directions) will usually be made by the court without a case management conference (CMC) and based on the responses that the parties have given in their AQs (see Chapter 12). Parties are encouraged to agree directions, and where these agreed directions enable the case to proceed within fast-track principles, the parties have every expectation that they will secure those agreed directions within the directions order.

- The court will restrict expert evidence, and if expert evidence is permitted, the emphasis will be on joint experts and written, but not oral, evidence from the expert(s) at the trial.

- Evidence of fact will also be restricted so as to enable the case to be heard within the short trial time of one day that will be allocated to it. A witness's statement will invariably be ordered to stand as his evidence-in-chief.

- Requests for further information (usually to clarify another party's case) will be controlled and time limits imposed to respond will be tight—usually within 14 days of the order.

- The filing of pre-trial checklists will be standard. As a further incentive to settle, the fee paid on the filing of pre-trial checklists will be refunded if a settlement is reached at least 14 days before the trial date.

- Trial timetables will often be set. Simple trial timetables will set a limit for the time that each party will have in which to submit its evidence and give its closing submissions. More complex trial timetables will set the time allowed and the order of each stage of the trial—the whole providing for a five-hour trial period, to include judgment and summary assessment of costs.

- Trial bundles will be standard and a direction may be made for a case summary to be lodged.

- The parties will submit costs schedules before the trial and the judge will be expected to deal with costs at the end of the trial by way of summary assessment. The court's power to award costs in fast-track trials is limited by CPR 28.2(5), which sets fixed amounts for the costs of the trial depending on the amount recovered.

- Trials will be heard by circuit judges or district judges.

 Costs

The emphasis for fast-track trials is to provide an efficient, speedy resolution to disputes that have not been settled by other means. Costs are restricted and clients need to be kept fully informed of the amount of time that their legal representative can justifiably spend on the case. Where a client has not been kept fully informed of this and a high legal bill is incurred, even where the client may have won the action, the courts are unlikely either to impose a full costs recovery order against the losing party, and in circumstances in which the legal representative cannot show that the client has been kept fully informed of what is a 'reasonable level of time spent', the courts are unlikely to allow those costs to be recovered from the client either.

9.2.3.3 Can fast-track judgments be set aside or appealed?

The provisions for setting aside default judgments in the fast track are those set out in CPR 12 and 13, and these are dealt with in Chapter 14, paragraph 14.2. Appeals procedure against judgments is contained within CPR 52 and is dealt with in Chapter 20, paragraph 20.7.3.

9.2.4 THE MULTI-TRACK

CPR 29 governs the procedure of cases in this track. The notes that follow are an overview of the main characteristics of cases in this track. A legal representative involved in a multi-track case will need to study the provisions in CPR 29. The stages of a multi-track action will also be considered in greater detail in the relevant sections of this book.

9.2.4.1 What cases are likely to be in the multi-track?

Cases in the multi-track will be those cases that:

* have a value over £25,000;

* have a value of less than £25,000, but in which the trial will last for more than one day; and

* complex or important cases of any, or no, value, in which it is appropriate for them to be dealt with in this track.

The financial value of cases in the multi-track will not be the only criterion to be applied when considering its suitability for this track, and CPR 26.8 sets out additional criteria that will be applied to the allocation of cases to this track. These include:

* the nature of the remedy sought;

* the likely complexity of the facts, law, or evidence;

* the number of parties or likely parties;

* the value of any counterclaim or other CPR Part 20 claim (additional claim) and the complexity of any matters relating to it;

* the amount of oral evidence that may be required;

* the importance of the claim to persons who may not be parties to the proceedings; and

* the views expressed by the parties (although the court is not bound by these views).

The court has the power to take any other factors into account when considering whether to allocate a case to this track. Cases within the financial criteria of the track may still find that they are transferred for trial to the equivalent of a fast-track judge, because the case does not require the experience of judges hearing the multi-track trials. In general, cases with a value of £50,000 or less will be transferred to a county court for trial.

Cases that are likely to stay and be tried in the Royal Courts of Justice (RCJ) or a district registry in this track will be:

* cases of a high financial value (exceeding £50,000);

* cases involving issues of public importance;

* test cases;

* clinical negligence cases; and

* cases in which there is a right to trial by jury, including deceit cases.

9.2.4.2 What are the main features of cases in the multi-track?

The main features of cases in the multi-track include the following.

* Judicial management is tight, but in this track, the courts will employ a greater range of management decisions, because the value of cases in this track is so broad. The case management decisions in this track will be designed to reflect this range. The more complex cases may have several CMCs and a pre-trial hearing. The lower value, simpler cases will have directions applied to them that are the same as, or not very dissimilar to fast-track directions. Directions that are tailored to the requirements of each case are more likely to be made in this track if it is proportionate to do so.

* Statements of case are still intended not to be technical. Simplicity and clear English is the key with all documents drafted for trials under the CPR, and the multi-track is not excluded from these aims.

* The will be a focus on precise issues. As with all tracks, the courts will expect parties to narrow the issues in dispute.

- Stays for the purpose of ADR will be encouraged. In this track, the procedural judge, who will have experience of these cases, may use CMCs as mediation-style hearings to promote settlement, and will attempt to restrict and identify the issues to be tried.

- If a multi-track case is being dealt with in the Commercial Court or the Technology and Construction Court a judge will be assigned to that case, and he will handle all CMCs and pre-trial reviews. The RCJ also encourage this and judges can reserve future CMCs or pre-trial reviews, or hearings, for a case to themselves. As with any CMC in this track or the fast track, it should be a legal representative (or counsel) who has knowledge of the case who attends and, when attending, he should ensure, so far as possible, that he has authority to act on the matters likely to arise at the CMC. Where the person attending does not have this knowledge and authority, and this causes an adjournment of the hearing, the courts will be more ready to impose a wasted costs order in this track.

- The court will exercise greater flexibility with expert evidence in this track and will more commonly allow parties to have their own experts or experts in more than one field. However, the principles of the overriding objective will still apply—notably, that of proportionality.

- Case summaries and skeleton arguments are commonly ordered in the directions in this track for CMCs, interim and final hearings.

9.2.4.3 Can multi-track judgments be set aside or appealed?

The provisions for setting aside judgments in the multi-track are those set out in CPR 12 and 13, and these are dealt with in Chapter 14, paragraph 14.2, for default judgments. Appeals against judgments procedure is contained within CPR 52 and is dealt with in Chapter 20, paragraph 20.7.3.

9.2.5 A 'MASS' ISSUE OF CLAIMS

Claim forms may be issued in bulk in debt recovery claims—for example, claims being brought by credit card companies or mobile phone companies—and may be issued electronically at the claim production centre. The provisions are set down in PD 7C. Claims issued from this centre are restricted to county court claims for specified sum claims not exceeding £100,000. There are further restrictions for claims issued here: for example, there must be no more than two defendants to any action and service cannot be effected on any party outside the jurisdiction. If a defence is filed and the claimant indicates that he wishes the claim to proceed, the action will be transferred to the defendant's home court if the defendant is an individual otherwise to the claimant's home court. Cases will also be transferred to the defendant's home court for many types of enforcement proceedings (enforcement by warrant of execution, third-party debt order, or charging order are excluded) or if an application is made for an information hearing.

9.2.6 MONEY CLAIM ONLINE

A claimant may start an action electronically via Money Claim Online—http://www. moneyclaim.gov.uk. A claim issued here enables a party to view the progress of an action electronically. If a defence, or part-admission, is filed, the action will be transferred as in 9.2.5 above. Again, claims issued here are restricted to specified sum claims not exceeding £100,000 and the further restrictions detailed in PD 7E.

9.2.7 A NEW CLAIMS PROCESS FOR LOW-VALUE ROAD TRAFFIC CLAIMS

A new claims process for personal injury road traffic claims with a value up to £10,000 has now been implemented. The new process is intended to speed up matters that are relatively straightforward up to this value. 'Straightforward' in this context would not include, for example, claims in which contributory negligence is alleged or those in which issues of causation are raised.

9.2.7.1 Low value RTA claims procedure

A brief resume of this procedure is detailed below.

- This procedure came into force on 30 April 2010.

- It applies in road traffic accident (RTA) cases (injury arising out of the use of a vehicle), with a value of damages between £1,000–10,000 (with the claim for personal injuries of at least £1,000, excluding vehicle damage).

- The following claims are excluded from the procedure: MIB claims, deceased party (claimant or defendant) claims, claims where the claimant is bankrupt, or where the claimant or the defendant is a protected party.

9.2.7.1.1 *Commencement procedure Stage 1*

- Form RTA1 is completed—this is called a Claims Notification Form (CNF).

- The procedure is dealt with online and RTA 1 is completed and submitted online.

- The CNF is also submitted electronically to the insurer and by 1st class post to the defendant. The insurer must acknowledge receipt of the CNF the next day but has 15 days to respond in full.

- If the claim is admitted, costs of £400 are payable within ten days (if the claim had been taken on under a CFA the uplift will be at 12.5 per cent).

9.2.7.1.2 *The procedure in cases where the CNF procedure does not settle the action*

The case re-enters pre-action protocol if:

- the insurer had failed to respond to the CNF;

- liability has been admitted but subject to an allegation of contributory negligence (other than on the issue of the wearing—or not—of a seat belt);

- liability is denied;

- it is alleged that the CNF is incomplete;

- it is alleged that the claim is overvalued;

- if the fixed costs on an admission have not been paid within ten days.

9.2.7.1.3 *CNF procedure Stage 2*

This will occur when liability has been admitted on the CNF and fixed costs paid. In this situation:

- The claimant completes the Medical Report Form—sends to an appropriate expert who completes the form, dealing with injury (diagnosis), opinion and prognosis. The expert also deals with any seat belt issues if raised.

- The claimant confirms the content of the Medical Report Form.

- The claimant's legal representative completes the Settlement Pack Form (SPF)—this will include the agreed Medical Report Form and sets out calculations and a settlement figure the claimant feels is justified.

- The insurer has 15 days in which to accept or make a counter-offer. If a counter-offer is made, the claimant has 20 days within which to consider it.

- If the action is concluded, the agreed sum is paid plus an additional sum of £800 costs for this stage (note: £400 costs will already have been paid for Stage 1 above). Again, if a CFA is in place, this sum will be uplifted.

9.2.7.1.4 *CNF procedure Stage 3*

This stage will be implemented where there has been a settlement on liability but not on quantum. In this situation:

- The claimant's legal representative sends the insurer a Court Proceedings Pack (CPP).

- Proceedings are commenced by a modified Part 8 procedure.

- The final assessment hearing can be a paper or oral hearing.
- The fixed costs for this stage are £250 (if a 'paper' hearing) plus an additional £250 advocate's fee (if the matter is listed for a hearing).

9.3 THE DOCUMENTS NEEDED TO COMMENCE AN ACTION

The most common way in which to start civil proceedings is by issuing a claim form (Form N1), although there are still several different ways in which an action may be commenced depending on the type of action, as follows.

1. A claim form under CPR Part 7—Form N1—is the standard (and by far the most common) method under the CPR. There are specialist versions of Form N1 for use in Admiralty claims and in the Commercial Court.

2. A claim form under CPR Part 8—Form N208—can be used in proceedings in which there are no substantial factual disputes (for example, in a claim by or against a child or patient that has been settled before the commencement of proceedings and the sole purpose of which is to seek approval of the court to the settlement), or where a Practice Direction directs the use of a Part 8 claim form (for example, in actions seeking a company director's disqualification).

3. A CPR Part 20 claim form—Form N211—can be used for additional claims and other subsidiary claims.

4. An arbitration claim form—Form N8—is available for use in applications under the Arbitration Act 1996.

5. Special claim forms—Forms N5, N5A, and N5B—are available for starting a claim in possession cases and for actions seeking relief from forfeiture.

6. A specialist claim form—Form N2—is available for use in probate proceedings.

7. A 'petition', rather than a claim form, is used in family proceedings, the winding up of a company, or administration proceedings and bankruptcy actions.

8. An originating application form can be used in actions under the Insolvency Act 1986.

9. An interpleader notice is to be used in some county court interpleader proceedings.

10. 'Informal' applications may be available under a specific statutory authority (for example, an application under the Deeds of Arrangements Act 1914, s. 7).

Although each of these forms of initiating proceedings is quite common, a legal representative new in the litigation department is unlikely to have much experience of many different methods of initiating proceedings outside the use of Form N1 procedure. However, one of the other proceedings that may more commonly be used is the Part 8 proceeding. We will therefore look at the Form N1 procedure in some detail for Part 7 claims and highlight the main features of Form N208 for a Part 8 procedure.

9.3.1 THE CLAIM FORM N1 FOR PART 7 PROCEDURE

Unless, under the CPR, another method of commencing proceedings is required or permitted, an action will be commenced using the Claim Form in Form N1. The definition of 'starting proceedings' is when the court issues, at the request of the claimant, a claim form prepared by, or on behalf of, the claimant. Issuing a claim involves the court sealing the claim form with its official seal. This is important because it:

- **stops** time running for limitation purposes (it is 'issue', not service, that is the relevant date for limitation purposes); and
- **starts** time running for service.

CPR 7 and 16.2 govern the claim form requirements. The front page of the claim form is essentially an administrative document. It assists the court office to see 'at a glance' for which court the claim is intended, the names of the parties, the nature of the action (for example, contract or tort), the value of the action, the addresses of all of the parties to be served, and the fee paid.

See the Online Resource Centre for a completed and annotated Form N1.

> ### ✔ Practical Considerations
>
> It is always worth remembering these basic facts about the front page of the claim form. Those new to litigation, commonly and consistently tend to put far too much detail on the front page of the claim form—especially at the section headed 'Brief details of claim'. The judges, who will be managing the case and hearing the trial of the action, will rarely, if ever, read the front page of the claim form. The detail of the claim should be reserved for the particulars of claim.

9.3.2 WHAT INFORMATION SHOULD BE INCLUDED ON FORM N1?

CPR 16.2 states that the claim form must include all of the following.

1. It must set out the names and addresses of the respective parties, including the parties' titles and postcodes. (The postcode can be obtained from Royal Mail, online at http://www.royalmail.com.)

2. It must concisely state the nature of the claim, and whether the PDPAC has been complied with.

3. It must specify the remedy sought.

4. Where possible, it must state the value of the claim by stating that the claimant expects to recover:

   - not more than £5,000 (but note the exceptions to this—in a claim for personal injuries or in a claim by a tenant against his landlord for repairs where the figure is stated as 'not more than £1,000'—see paragraph 9.2.1 above), which will indicate a case that is likely to be allocated to the small claims track; or

   - more than £5,000 (or £1,000, as above), but not more than £25,000, which will indicate a case that is likely to be allocated to the fast track; or

   - more than £25,000, which will indicate a case that is likely to be allocated to the multi-track.

   The statement of value on the claim form does not limit the court to award a judgment in that sum.

   In computing the value to place on the claim form, the following are disregarded:

   - interest (for unspecified sum claims);

   - costs;

   - any potential finding of contributory negligence (unless admitted);

   - any potential counterclaim or set-off (unless admitted); and

   - any amounts to be recovered from state benefits under the Compensation Recovery Rules contained under the Social Security (Recovery of Benefits) Act 1997, s. 6.

   If the claim is for a sum set out in a foreign currency, then the claim form must specify the sterling equivalent and the source of the conversion rate used.

5. On the back page of the claim form, the claimant has the option of stating his case in full in accordance with the drafting requirements for the particulars of claim (see Chapter 11, paragraph 11.4) if there is room to do so. Where the particulars of claim

are included in this section, the claim form is called an 'indorsed' claim form. In these circumstances, the statement of truth must also be completed. If, as is often the case, there is insufficient room to set out the claimant's case fully, the claim form will merely indicate whether the particulars of claim are 'attached' or 'to follow'. The options available for the claimant are:

- to serve the indorsed claim form, together with the documents detailed in paragraph 9.3.5 below;
- to serve the 'unindorsed' claim form—in which case, the particulars of claim must be served within14 days of service of the claim form (see paragraph 9.3.5 below); or
- to serve the unindorsed claim form with the accompanying particulars of claim, together with the other documents set out in paragraph 9.3.5 below.

The claimant will also need to indicate whether a Human Rights Act 1998 issue is being raised in the claim on this reverse side of the claim form (and, if so, the human rights issue being raised must be specifically stated in the particulars of claim).

9.3.3 IN WHICH COURT SHOULD THE CLAIMANT CHOOSE TO ISSUE?

There is an apparent 'conflict' between the law and the CPR in the choice of court. The provisions relating to jurisdiction need to be considered when completing the claim form. As stated in Chapter 7, the High Court and county courts have, in general, jurisdiction for all cases, whatever the value in contract and tort. To this extent, therefore, a party may issue his claim in the High Court or a county court. However, the CPR provide that a case should not be issued out of the High Court unless the value exceeds £25,000, and if the claim is for personal injuries, should not issue out of the High Court unless the value of the damages claimed exceeds £50,000.

 Practical Considerations

As long as you can justify your decision (in terms of the overriding objective) to issue in the chosen court, the court will not penalize you. The prime point to note is to act reasonably.

9.3.3.1 Summary

For the practitioner undertaking less specialist litigation, the important rules can be summarized as in Figure 9.1.

FIGURE 9.1

TYPE OF CLAIM	JURISDICTION
A money claim	May be commenced in the High Court only if the claimant expects to recover more than £25,000 (PD 7A.2.1)
A money claim issued in the Royal Courts of Justice	May be commenced in the RCJ, but the claim will usually be transferred to the county court if the claim is worth less than £50,000, unless one of the exceptions stated in PD 29.2.2 applies
A claim for personal injuries	May be commenced in the High Court only if the value of the claim is £50,000 or more (PD 7A.2.2)

Practical Considerations

If a claim is issued in the High Court when it should have been issued in the county court, the court will often exercise its powers of management contained in CPR Part 3 and, specifically, the powers for transfer contained within CPR Part 30. The powers under these provisions include a power to rectify such an error (and order a transfer), as well as a power to strike out. A practitioner cannot be certain which of these powers the court will decide to exercise. The court will consider whether the error was deliberate or a bona fide mistake. It is important that the court is informed if an error is noted as soon as practicable. Care must always be exercised when deciding in which court to issue, because the consequences could be significant. If a mistake is made very close to the end of the limitation period, an order to strike out the claim issued in error could be a grave mistake. Even if the order to strike out were well within the limitation period, the issue fees would have to be paid again. If an order to transfer is made that rectifies the error, then the party at fault will usually be ordered to pay the costs involved in the transfer.

It should be noted that the court officials who deal with issue will generally accept the papers for issue even if they believe that the case has been issued in the wrong court, because these court officials have no power to make judicial decisions.

Professional Conduct

Where a mistake has been made by a legal representative, it should be noted that certain professional conduct rules may apply and require the legal representative to inform the client of the mistake. The core duties contained in the Solicitors' Code of Conduct 2007, Rule 1, provide that a solicitor must act with integrity towards the client and act in the client's best interests. Additionally, Rule 4.21 provides that a solicitor has a duty to disclose all information that is material to the client's matter. For those new to practice, Rule 5 is also important—this rule provides that a firm must have in place a suitable system of supervision. Also consider CPR 44.2: where a costs order has been made against a legally represented party, that legal representative must inform the client of this within seven days of receipt of the order. Consider also CPR 48.7.5 in a situation in which the court considers making a 'wasted costs order' and the information that should be given to the client concerning this.

9.3.4 DOES INTEREST NEED TO BE SPECIFIED ON THE CLAIM FORM?

In specified sum claims, only the sum of interest accrued needs to be stated on the claim form, but the sum of interest will not be part of the 'value' of the case for tracking purposes.

9.3.5 WHAT OTHER DOCUMENTS ARE NEEDED TO START THE ACTION?

Although the claim can be issued by sending (or taking) to the court the completed Form N1, the court will not issue the claim until the following steps are taken and the further documents are lodged:

- the court fee—the fee to be paid will vary according to the sum claimed and can be found in the Civil Proceedings Fees (Amendment) Order 2009, and on HM Courts and Tribunals Service website (http://www.hmcourts-service.gov.uk);
- sufficient copies of the claim form for service on each of the defendants, together with a copy for the court file. Where there is more than one defendant, each copy of the claim form will have the relevant address of the defendant (including his postcode) on the front of the form in the bottom left-hand box. The address needs to be an appropriate address for service on that defendant (see the service provisions in paragraph 9.7 below);

- where there is a party acting through a litigation friend, the litigation friend's certificate of suitability (Form N235); and

- where there is a conditional fee agreement (CFA), with a success fee, and/or ATE, a notice of funding must also be lodged (Form N251).

Once the relevant documents have been received, the court issues the claim by sealing the claim form and enters details of the claim in the court 'issue book'. It enters a claim number against these details in the issue book and stamps the number on each claim form. The court will then send a notice of issue to the claimant. Form N205A will be used for a specified sum claim, Form N205B will be used for a non-specified sum claim, and Form N205C will be used in a non-monetary claim.

The court may then effect service of the claim form on the defendant(s) or return the documents to the claimant for service (see paragraph 9.7.2 below).

The claimant has the option of filing with the above documents the particulars of claim, in which case, the response pack (Form N9) will be included in the documents served on the defendant. The court will supply Form N9 for this purpose. If the claim form is served on the defendant(s) without the particulars of claim, the defendant need take no action in response.

The claimant must serve the particulars of claim within 14 days of service of the claim form. Service of the particulars of claim must be accompanied by the response pack (and if it is not, there has not been effective service).

Once he has been served with the particulars of claim and response pack, the defendant must now take steps to respond to the action (see Chapters 10 and 11 for detail of the particulars of claim and see the court forms available on the Online Resource Centre).

online
resource
centre

9.3.6 **THE FORM N208 PART 8 PROCEDURE**

Part 8 procedure is intended for cases in which the nature of the relief or remedy sought, or the lack of factual dispute, makes using standard Part 7 Form N1 procedure unnecessarily cumbersome: for example, Part 8 will be used if a case concerning a child litigant is 'settled' in the Protocol phase of the action. Such a settlement will not give a sufficient discharge to the paying party unless the court has approved the settlement. To do this, an application will be made in Part 8 proceedings using Form N208. Similarly, a CPR 8 application may commonly be made when your client is seeking a declaration, for example, that a contractual term is incorporated into an agreement. Part 8 proceedings are also used in 'costs only' applications and in the new low value personal injury cases arising out of road traffic accidents. (see paragraph 9.2.7 above).

This procedure does not require particulars of claim, a defence, or an AQ (because all Part 8 claims are 'treated' as allocated to the multi-track). Judgment in default is not available. It cannot be used, however, as a means of avoiding Part 7 Form N1 procedure and can be used only when:

- the claimant seeks the court's decision on a question that is unlikely to involve a substantial dispute of fact; or

- when a Practice Direction, or rule, requires that Part 8 procedure be used and the ruling or Practice Direction has modified or disapplied parts of the procedure for the action to enable this procedure to be used. Sections A, B, and C of the CPR PD 8 sets out general provisions about claims and applications to which Part 8 applies.

9.3.6.1 What forms are needed for a Part 8 application?
Form N208 must be used for Part 8 claims and applications. Form N208 must state on it:

- that Part 8 applies;

- the question that the claimant wants the court to decide, or the remedy sought and the legal basis for the claim to that remedy;

- details of the claim if being made under an enactment; and
- the capacity of the representative if the claim is being made in a representative capacity.

Any evidence supporting the claim must be served with Form N208 and this must contain a statement of truth.

Additionally:

- if there is a funding arrangement, notice of it must be given, as for Part 7 procedure; and
- the service requirements are the same as those set out for Part 7 claims—except in the situations in which a defendant is not being named in the Part 8 claim and permission has been granted to issue without naming a defendant.

9.3.6.2 Responding in Part 8 claims

CPR 8.3 sets out the procedure for responding to a Part 8 claim. The defendant must acknowledge service in Form N210. If he objects to the use of the Part 8 procedure, he needs to set down his reasons. If a defendant wishes to rely on written evidence, he must file this with his Form N210. If the defendant fails to return Form N210, he may attend the hearing of the claim, but may not take part in it unless the court gives permission.

9.3.6.3 The hearing of Part 8 claims

Any evidence at the hearing is usually written evidence that has been served as set out in paragraphs 9.3.6.1 and 9.3.6.2 above. The court has power to permit oral evidence, but it will be rare that this will be required (because when it is, the Part 8 procedure is probably not appropriate for the claim).

9.4 CAN MORE THAN ONE CLAIM, OR MORE THAN ONE PARTY, BE INCLUDED IN ONE CLAIM?

9.4.1 JOINDER

CPR 7.3 reflects the statutory requirement of s. 49(2) of the Senior Courts Act 1981 that 'as far as possible, all matters in dispute between the parties are completely and finally determined, and all multiplicity of legal proceedings with respect to any those matters is avoided'.

Generally, it is for the claimant to decide which causes of action he wishes to pursue against which parties. Where he has more than one claim against the same party, he has the right to issue separate claims for each (and to pay separate fees in respect of the issue of each). However, CPR 7.3 permits more than one cause of action to be claimed on one claim form and therefore, in terms of economy and the provisions of s. 49(2) of the Senior Courts Act 1981, he would be best advised to issue all claims that he has against the defendant in the one action unless it would be inconvenient to do so.

Where there is more than one defendant, the claimant will usually issue against all defendants that he alleges are liable to him in the claim in the one action. His decision to do this will depend on a number of factors, including the nature of the liability of the defendants (whether they are jointly liable, or severally liable, or jointly and severally liable—see Chapter 7, paragraph 7.5.1), and whether all of his potential defendants are worth suing and his claim can be more easily satisfied against one. CPR 19.1 provides that 'any number of claimants or defendants may be joined as parties to a claim'. No guidance is given about which claims it might be considered convenient to dispose of in the same action. The court will take into account the overriding objective—in particular the objectives of saving expense, and ensuring that cases are dealt with justly, expeditiously, and fairly. Thus, in general, claims involving common questions of law or fact between different parties, or different causes of action involving the same parties, should be dealt with in the same proceedings.

Where there are joint claimants, they must have the same legal representative (and have no conflicting interests between them). Co-defendants may choose whom they wish to represent them.

Even though a party may issue a multiple of claims in the one action, and/or multiple parties may be joined in the action, the court has a discretionary power in CPR 3.1(2)(i) to order separate trials and it will do so if, in separating the claims or the parties, the cases will proceed more efficiently.

Further, parts of CPR 19 need to be considered if it seems convenient to allow 'representative' actions. These provisions allow a single action to proceed that would bind all parties into an identified group. CPR 19.7 also deals with situations in which the persons that may be the subject of the action are unascertained or as yet unknown—this may apply in actions in an estate of a deceased person and persons unknown or not yet born, who may have an interest in the estate.

The Civil Justice Council has submitted recommendations to the Lord Chancellor that would have the effect of improving access to justice by widening the scope of collective actions. At the time of writing, there is no date yet set for the implementation of those proposals, although a draft Collective Action Bill and draft new CPR have been prepared. News of these developments is awaited.

CPR 19.4 also contains the rules that relate to a person who wishes to intervene in an action and be added as a party. This may arise when the party who wishes to 'intervene' would be affected by any judgment that may be made in the action.

9.5 PROCEEDINGS BY AND AGAINST CHILDREN OR PROTECTED PARTIES

9.5.1 HOW DOES A CHILD OR PROTECTED PARTY EITHER MAKE OR DEFEND A CLAIM AGAINST HIM?

With the exception set out in CPR 21.2(3), a child or a protected party must sue and be sued by a litigation friend. Under the provisions of CPR 21.2(3), the court may grant permission for a child to conduct proceedings without a litigation friend. In practice, this is only likely to arise if the child is very close to becoming of age, and can show that he has the skill, knowledge, and understanding to conduct those proceedings. Any defendant faced with an application by a child to conduct proceedings himself will wish to be assured that any costs payable are secured in some way.

9.5.2 WHO MAY BE A LITIGATION FRIEND?

A child's litigation friend is normally a relative with no interest in the litigation adverse to that of the child. A protected party's litigation friend is usually a receiver appointed by the Court of Protection.

Unless the court appoints a litigation friend, the person who is to act as the litigation friend must follow the procedure set out in CPR 21.5. These provisions include:

- filing of an official copy of his authority to act if his authority to act has been given under Pt VII of the Mental Health Act 1983; or

- filing a certificate of suitability, which certifies that the person seeking to be the litigation friend satisfies the conditions set out in CPR 21.4(3); and

- serving the certificate of suitability on each party and filing a certificate of service when the certificate of suitability has been served.

The court may appoint the litigation friend upon the application of the person wishing to be the litigation friend or upon the application of a party. The claimant will need to make the application if the defendant in his action requires a litigation friend and no appointment has been made.

9.5.3 WHEN DOES THE APPOINTMENT OF A LITIGATION FRIEND TERMINATE?

When a child (who is not otherwise a protected party) attains the age of 18, the litigation friend's appointment ceases. When a protected party ceases to be such, the appointment of his litigation friend continues until it is ended by a court order—the application to do this may be made by the former protected party, the litigation friend, or a party.

Once the appointment of the litigation friend has terminated, the new party (being the former child who is now of age or a former protected party) must:

- serve notice on the other parties, stating that the appointment of his litigation friend has ceased;
- state his address for service; and
- state whether he intends to carry on the proceedings.

He must do so within 28 days of the date on which the appointment of his litigation friend ceased. If he fails to do this, then the court, or another party, may seek to strike out his claim or defence.

On his appointment as litigation friend, the litigation friend undertakes to pay any costs that the child or protected party may be ordered to pay in relation to the proceedings (subject to any right that he may have to be repaid from the assets of the child or protected party) (CPR 21.4(3)(c)). The liability for the costs continues until either the former child or protected party has served his notice above, or when the litigation friend serves notice that his appointment has ceased.

 Practical Considerations

Once a child attains the age of 18 or a former protected party is no longer a protected party, then he becomes a new client for the purposes of client care and any CFA entered into with the litigation friend. The new client must then receive the standard retainer and client care correspondence that all new clients receive. If a funding arrangement is to be entered into with the new client, then notice of this must be given to the court and the other parties to the action in the normal way.

9.5.4 WHAT IS THE POSITION WITH REGARD TO EXPENSES INCURRED BY THE LITIGATION FRIEND IN CONDUCTING THE ACTION?

A litigation friend is entitled to recover money paid and expenses incurred from any monies secured by the action provided that they have been reasonably incurred and are reasonable in amount (CPR 21.12(1)). The criteria that the court will use to determine the reasonableness of their expenses are those set out in CPR 44.5(3). The litigation friend may not receive more than 25 per cent (of the sum awarded) if the claim is concluded by settlement or judgment in a sum not exceeding £5,000, unless the court directs otherwise.

9.5.5 SERVICE WHERE A PARTY IS A CHILD

Service of proceedings where that party is a child must be in accordance with CPR 6.13 (for service of the claim form) and CPR 6.25 (for service of an application for an order appointing a litigation friend and service of documents other than the claim form).

9.6 HOW ARE THE PARTIES IN AN ACTION DESCRIBED?

9.6.1 THEIR TITLES

The words that should be used to describe the parties in an action are set out in CPR PD 16.2.6.

- Under the CPR, the party who makes a claim is known as 'the Claimant'.
- The party against whom proceedings are brought is 'the Defendant' (CPR.2.3(1)).

- Parties to applications are referred to as 'Applicant' and 'Respondent' (CPR 23.1).
- Parties to petitions are referred to as 'Petitioner' and 'Respondent'.

Parties to Part 20 counterclaims and other additional claims are known by their names in the main statement of case (if they were a party), but if they have been brought in under CPR 20, they are known as 'third party', or 'fourth party', etc.

Figure 9.2 details the description to be given to parties in an action depending on their form of 'identity'.

FIGURE 9.2 PARTIES AND THEIR DESCRIPTIONS IN STATEMENTS OF CASE

CLASS OF PARTY	FORM OF DESCRIPTION
An individual	The full name if known and the title by which he or she is known
A child or, a protected party within the Mental Health Act 1983	The child's (or protected party's) full name followed by the full name of the litigation friend, ie Jane Bloggs (a child by Joe Bloggs her litigation friend or if a protected party: by Joe Bloggs her litigation friend)
A child conducting the proceedings himself (where the court has permitted this under CPR 21.2(3))	Master Thomas Green
A child once he has adopted the proceedings on attaining 18 years of age	Miss Hilary Green (formerly a child but now of full age)
An individual who is trading under another name	Joe Bloggs t/a Blogg's Store
An individual who is suing or being sued in a representative capacity	Joe Bloggs as the representative of Jane Bloggs (deceased)
An individual who is being sued in the name of a club or other unincorporated organisation	Joe Bloggs, suing/being sued on behalf of the Browntown Tennis Club
A firm (other than an LLP)	Bloggs and Co. (a firm) or the full name of each partner
A corporation (other than a company)	The full name of the Corporation
A company	The full name of the company with an indication of its legal form (i.e Ltd, LLP, plc) and if registered outside the jurisdiction the place of registration

For further clarification of the identity of a party, see Chapter 7, paragraph 7.3.

9.6.2 WHAT HAPPENS IF A MISTAKE IS MADE IN THE NAME GIVEN TO A PARTY?

The court may substitute a new party for an existing party. Remedying the name of a party may even occur after the limitation period has expired, but this is limited to situations in which the mistake is in the name, not the identity of the party (CPR 19.5, and see Chapter 7, paragraph 7.4). The provisions for substitution of a party to rectify such a mistake apply when the mistake was genuine. In situations in which there has been a mistake as to the identity of the person, the proper course of action will be to reissue proceedings.

9.6.3 WHAT HAPPENS IF A PARTY DIES?

Under the Law Reform (Miscellaneous Provisions) Act 1934, s. 1(1), most causes of action subsisting against or vested in an individual survive his or her death. If a party to a claim dies (or is adjudged bankrupt), the court has the power under CPR 19.5(3) to add or substitute as a party in the action the person to whom the deceased (or bankrupt party's) interest or liability has passed.

Further details of the effect that the death of a party may have either before proceedings are commenced or during proceedings is set out in Chapter 7, paragraph 7.3.9.

9.6.4 CAN A CLAIM BE MADE AGAINST A PERSON WHO IS NOT KNOWN?

There are limited circumstances in which a claimant can avoid the requirements set out in PD 7A.4.1, which provides that the claim form should include the full name of each party. When a claimant does not know the identity of the defendant, but can identify him by a description that is sufficiently clear to determine who would be within that description, then he may seek permission to commence the claim by the description of the defendant (as yet unknown). This is useful in some intellectual property claims and is outside the scope of this book.

9.6.5 PARTIES IN CLAIMS FOR LOSS AND DAMAGE ARISING FROM A ROAD TRAFFIC ACCIDENT (RTA)

In a road traffic accident (RTA) claim, the usual procedure will be for the claimant to issue proceedings against the person(s) whom he alleges owed the claimant a duty of care and who has breached that duty of care, as a result of which breach the claimant has suffered loss. These are the normal provisions for a claim in tort. However, there are further provisions that may need to be considered concerning a claim arising from an RTA, as follows.

9.6.5.1 A claim against the insurer of a vehicle

Under the European Communities (Rights against Insurers) Regulations 2002, SI 2002/3061, a claimant who is resident in the European Economic Area (EEA)—that is, any member state of the European Union, but also Iceland, Liechtenstein, Norway, and Switzerland—bringing proceedings in tort arising out of an RTA may issue proceedings against the insurer of the vehicle alleged to be responsible for the accident. This right is in addition to the right to issue proceedings against the driver of the vehicle. In most circumstances, the claim will be made against the driver, not the insurer, but it will be the insurer who will meet any judgment in the claim. The judgment may be enforced directly against the insurer, provided that notice has been given to the insurer either before or within seven days of proceedings being commenced (Road Traffic Act 1988, s. 152).

 Practical Considerations

The notice under s. 152 of the Road Traffic Act 1988 is a vital part of any claims arising from an RTA and should part of the aide-memoire or list of 'key dates' that will be created for any new claim of this nature. The letter of claim written in the Protocol phase of such an action is not sufficient notice by itself unless the notice specifies that it is 'notice under the provisions of s. 152 of the Road Traffic Act', and the letter of claim is written directly to the insurers and not simply 'handed to the insurers' by the insured. If notice has not been given and the insurer takes the point—that it has not been served—the claimant is left with no alternative but to discontinue the defective claim and issue fresh proceedings, giving proper notice under s. 152.

9.7 **SERVICE OF THE PROCEEDINGS**

9.7.1 **WHAT (AND WHEN) IS 'SERVICE'?**

9.7.1.1 What is 'service' of the claim form?

'Service' involves formally notifying the defendant(s) of the action against them. It is worth noting here to avoid confusion that CPR Part 6 distinguishes the requirements for service of the claim form from 'other documents'. Section II of Part 6 sets out the rules for service of the claim form and Section III sets out the detail for service of 'other documents'. 'Other documents' are defined as all those documents that require service that are *not* the claim form. In this regard 'claim form' includes other documents that can be used to commence an action, for example petitions.

Valid service of the claim form, in the manner specified by the court rules (and as it has been interpreted by case law), is a precondition to the exercise of the court's jurisdiction. In certain circumstances, the need to 'serve' the claim form may be dispensed with. It is also worth noting that what is sometimes described as the fiction of service is preserved—that is, the fact that a person has (or has not) *received* a document does not necessarily mean that the person has (or has not) been *served* with the document. The rules provide for a 'deemed service' rule, although the 'deemed' date of service may vary depending on the *method* of service that has been used. The 'deemed' date of service of the claim form is less important than it used to be because it is the date of 'dispatch' that is necessary to determine whether a claim form has been served 'on time' (that is within the limitation period). See paragraph 9.7.2 below. But the deemed date of service, by the method chosen by the claimant, is needed for the defendant to determine when the acknowledgement of service and/or defence is due.

The table below sets out the deemed date of service of the claim form by each method of service.

FIGURE 9.3

METHOD OF SERVICE	DEEMED DATE OF SERVICE
1. First class post (or other service which provides for delivery on the next business day)	The second day after it was posted, left with, delivered to or collected by the relevant service provider provided that day is a business day; or if not, the next business day after that day.
2. Document exchange	The second day after it was left with, delivered to or collected by the relevant service provider provided that day is a business day; or if not, the next business day after that day.
3. Delivering the document to or leaving it at a permitted address	If it is delivered to or left at the permitted address on a business day before 4.30p.m., on that day; or in any other case, on the next business day after that day.
4. Fax	If the transmission of the fax is completed on a business day before 4.30p.m., on that day; or in any other case, on the next business day after the day on which it was transmitted.
5. Other electronic method	If the e-mail or other electronic transmission is sent on a business day before 4.30p.m., on that day; or in any other case, on the next business day after the day on which it was sent.

6. Personal service		If the document is served personally before 4.30p.m. on a business day, on that day; or in any other case, on the next business day after that day.

Parties in an action must give an address for service when responding to a claim (CPR 6.23).

9.7.1.2 When does service take place?

9.7.1.2.1 *Time periods for serving the claim form*

The rules relating to the service of a claim form are as follows.

- A claim form issued for service within the jurisdiction must be served within four months after the date of issue (CPR 7.5(2)).

- A claim form issued for service outside the jurisdiction must be served within six months after the date of issue (CPR 7.5(3)).

9.7.1.3 Can the parties extend the period of service of the claim form?

The parties can agree between themselves to extend the time for service of the claim form (CPR 2.11). This was extensively considered in *Thomas v Home Office* [2006] All ER (D) 243 (Oct).

In order to extend the time for service, the parties may:

- agree to the extension in writing (CPR 2.11)—and this must be more than an oral agreement to extend the time recorded by a written note on each legal representative's file. A specific exchange of letters is recommended, which includes a precise deadline; or

- create a single document—that is, an agreement, signed by both parties, which sets out the determination to extend to a precise deadline.

When such an extension is agreed, it will be the claimant who will bear the risk of the court subsequently concluding that the agreement to extend was not valid.

 Practical Considerations

The safest procedure for the claimant is to serve the claim form within the period of its validity (four or six months—see paragraph 9.7.1.2. above). Although the Court of Appeal has confirmed that the parties may agree an extension of the four- or six-month period, it is almost certainly better—and safer (for your client)—to serve the claim form on the defendant and then make a joint application to the court for a stay of the proceedings for the period of the extension that had been agreed.

9.7.1.4 Extending the time of validity for service of the claim form and/or seeking an order for alternative service

The courts have traditionally not shown much sympathy for a claimant or legal representative who has issued his claim form and then waited until the end of the period of validity of that claim form to serve it, but then encountered difficulties. Although the new (October 2008) CPR 6 does, to some extent, make it easier to avoid difficulties, there is no reason to suppose that this attitude will change. It is therefore vital to understand the rules of service and to adhere to them strictly, so that good service is achieved—especially when service has been left late and is very near to, or at, the end of the period of validity of the claim form.

9.7.1.5 Extending the period of validity of the claim form

CPR 7.6 states that an application to extend the period of validity of the claim form must be made 'within the period specified by rule 7.5' (that is, within the period of validity of the claim form). Only in exceptional cases can the life of the claim form be extended after the end of the period specified by CPR 7.5 (see CPR 7.6(3)). The case of *Cecil & Others v Bayat* [2011] EWCA Civ 135 is a recent case that emphasizes the fact that applications to extend the life of the claim form should not be used where the reasons for non-service are practical, and where an application is being made it should be made before the time of validity has expired.

9.7.1.6 Is it sensible to wait to serve a claim form?

Once the claim form has been issued, whether pre-emptively to avoid an issue arising from expiry of the limitation period or on occasions on which it has been issued, but the particulars of claim are not yet drafted, it is still usually better to serve promptly. The claim form could be served with an explanation, and where the parties can agree an extension of the time for the claimant to serve his particulars of claim, this may be achieved, by consent, under CPR 2.11 (see paragraph 9.7.1.3 above).

9.7.1.7 Seeking an order for 'alternative service'

In certain circumstances in which service may not have been effectively achieved within the period of validity of the claim form, it may be possible (including retrospectively) to seek an order that service has, in fact, been successfully effected by 'an alternative method'. CPR 6.15 enables the court, for good reason, to make an order permitting service by an alternative method or at an alternative place. This was the position under the old (pre-October 2008) CPR Part 6. What is new, however, is the courts' power to order this *retrospectively*. By CPR 6.15(2), the court may order that steps *already* taken to bring the claim to the attention of the defendant by an alternative method or at an alternative place have the effect of being 'good service'. How the courts will deal with applications seeking, in effect, to rectify a situation in which service has not otherwise been achieved is yet to be known. There is every reason to believe that the courts will entertain such applications sympathetically when it is quite clear that the defendant has had notice of the proceedings and that the failure of good service may have been by some *understandable or reasonable* mis-understanding. It is doubtful, however, that the courts will agree to rectify a position in which the claimant (or his legal representative) has failed to serve properly by a basic misunderstanding of the CPR.

 Example

In a personal injury claim in which the claimant's legal representative has been corresponding with the defendant's insurer, it may be that the legal representative has had many cases with this particular insurer and that, in previous cases, this insurer has nominated its in-house lawyer to accept service. However, in this particular instance, the insurer has not expressly done this, although the claimant had sent the documents to the in-house lawyer in the 'normal' way, and the insurer had taken no issue on the point and continued to correspond on the claim with the claimant's legal representative. However, after the four-month period of validity has expired, the insurer takes the point, and declares that purported service is bad and that service has not been effected. It is thought that, in these circumstances, the courts *may* grant an order under CPR 6.15(2) allowing the 'service' on the insurers' in-house lawyer to be declared 'good [alternative] service'.

If and when the court makes an order under CPR 6.15(2) that service has been effected (by an alternative method), it must specify the date on which the claim form is deemed to have been served (by the 'alternative method'). This is contained in CPR 6.15(4)(b).

9.7.2 **THE METHODS OF SERVICE**

The methods of service that may be used are set out in CPR 6.3. Where the Claim Form is served within the jurisdiction, the claimant must complete the step required by the following table [see Figure 9.4] in relation to the particular method of service chosen, before 12.00 midnight on the calendar day four months after the date of issue of the claim form.

It is clear that it is the taking of the 'step required' that is the relevant time in which to determine whether service has been effected in time (that is, within the period of validity of the claim form), not the date on which the document is deemed served by the method chosen. Therefore, the deemed date of service for a claim form is only relevant when calculating the date on which the defence or acknowledgement of service is due. If the claim form is posted or dispatched by midnight on any day within its validity period (four months within the jurisdiction), then it will be deemed served on the second business day after the 'step required' and it will not matter that that the deemed date of service is outside the four-month validity period of the claim form.

FIGURE 9.4

METHOD OF SERVICE	STEP REQUIRED
First-class post, document exchange, or other service that provides for delivery on the next business day	Posting, leaving with, delivering to, or collection by the relevant service provider
Delivery of the document to, or leaving it at, the relevant place	Delivering to, or leaving the document at, the relevant place
Personal service under CPR 6.5	Completing the relevant step required by CPR 6.5(3)
Fax	Completing the transmission of the fax
Other electronic method	Sending the email or other electronic transmission

9.7.2.1 The 'default' position of service—by the court

In the High Court (but not the specialist divisions) and the county courts, the court will serve the claim form and accompanying documents unless the party lodging the document *expressly* indicates that it wishes to effect service. When a party is legally represented, his legal representative will usually arrange service. If the court is to serve, it will decide the method of service and this will usually be by first-class post. After service, the court will issue to the claimant (or his legal representatives) a certificate of service, and if the documents are returned by the post, notice will be given to the claimant (or his legal representatives).

 Practical Considerations

Before issuing proceedings, it will be necessary to obtain specific instructions from the client regarding the method of service that he wishes to employ, so that monies on account for service can be obtained—for example, for the costs of engaging a process server—and so that the express request can be made to the court for 'documents to be returned (to the legal representatives acting) for service'.

Where the claimant elects to serve the documents, he must file at court a certificate of service in Form N215 within 21 days of service.

9.7.2.2 A clarification of 'personal service' under CPR 6

The new CPR 6.5 clarifies 'personal service' under CPR 6.5(3). The claim form must be served personally if a court order, a Practice Direction, or another enactment provides that it must be personally served. In all other cases, a claim form may be served personally unless service is to be effected on a party's legal representative or upon the Crown.

Under CPR 6.5(3), personal service is effected on:

(a) *an individual by leaving it with that individual;*

(b) *a company or other corporation by leaving it with a person holding a senior position* [defined in PD 6A.6.2] *within the company or corporation* [for example, a person in a 'senior position' of an incorporated company is defined as a treasurer, the secretary of the company (or corporation), the chief executive, a manager, or other officer—and the definition of a person in 'a senior position' of an unincorporated association is also defined in PD 6A.2(2)]; *or*

(c) *a partnership (where partners are being sued in the name of their firm) by leaving it with—*

(i) *a partner; or*

(ii) *a person who, at the time of service, has the control or management of the partnership business at its principal place of business.*

 Practical Considerations

Personal service will often be completed by a process server. The person serving the document(s) should hand the document(s) to the individual and inform the individual of the contents of the document(s) in general, not specific, terms. When instructing a process server or agent to effect service for the first time, ensure that he has the experience and knowledge to effect service according to the rules.

9.7.2.3 What happens if the document(s) being served are handed back to the process server by the person who is to be served?

This happens quite commonly in practice: quite often, the person against whom proceedings have been brought is not entirely happy about the event and he may simply, once he is told the general nature of the documents being served on him, hand them back (or throw them on the ground). There is no post-CPR authority on the point, but in *Nottingham Building Society v Peter Bennett and Co* (1977) The Times, 26 February, the Court of Appeal held that once the document was handed over and the person had been told of the general nature of the document, it had been duly served. There is no reason to suppose that the courts would make any different finding on the point under the provisions of the CPR.

9.7.2.4 Service by or on partnerships

Where the claim is by or against two or more persons who were partners and who had carried on business within the jurisdiction (at the time that the cause of action accrued), under the provisions of PD 7A.5A.2, the term 'partners' includes both those claiming to be entitled as partners and those alleged to be partners.

Further, under the provisions of PD 7A.5A.3, where a claim is commenced by a partnership, it should be in the name of the partnership that was in existence when the cause of action accrued.

When acting in a claim against a partnership, it may be necessary to obtain details of the names and last-known addresses of each of the partners at the time that the cause of action arose. This is known as a 'partnership membership statement' and the partnership has 14 days in which to provide such a statement when requested to do so (PD 7A.5B).

This is required because CPR 6.9 provides that where partners are sued in the name of a partnership, service should be at the principal or last-known place of business of the partnership or at the partners' 'last known residence'.

However, where service is being made on an individual as a partner of the firm being sued, a notice must also be given specifying whether the person being served, is being served as:

• a partner;

• a person with control or management of the partnership business; or

• both of the above.

This information is contained in Form N218. It is advisable to include this notice with the document(s) being served.

Practical Considerations

Where service is being effected on a person who may not be a partner, but who is stated to have 'control or management', it would be prudent to include Form N218 with the documents for service on every occasion and also whenever a partner is being served at his home or 'last known residence'.

9.7.2.5 Companies and limited liability partnerships (LLPs)

The Civil Courts (Amendment) Order 2009 came into force on 1 October 2009. It includes provisions for service on companies that are in line with parts of the Companies Act 2006 and Limited Liability Partnerships Act 2000 and permits the courts to exclude a county court from having jurisdiction to deal with matters under the Companies Act 2006. It also specifies the rules for service of documents on companies will be in accordance with s. 1139(1) of the Companies Act 2006. This provides that 'a document may be served on a company by leaving it at, or sending it by post to, the company's registered office'.

Where service is to be to an overseas branch of a company registered in England and Wales or on an overseas registered company's. 1139(2) will continue to permit a document to be served at the UK branch or a person who is authorized to accept service or at any place of business in England and Wales.

Section 725(1) of the Companies Act 1985 also applies to a limited liability partnership (LLP). Therefore, an LLP can be served at its registered office. Service under the provisions of s. 725(1) is an additional place of service on a company or LLP and is effective even if the company or LLP has legal representatives acting, who have signified that they have instructions to accept service of proceedings.

Practical Considerations

Where service is to be effected under s. 725(1) rather than the CPR, note that the 'deemed date of service' (see paragraph 9.7.6 below) does not apply. The wording in the statute is 'in the ordinary course of post' and service is assumed to have occurred 'unless the contrary is proved'. Because this is a rebuttable presumption, it is again different from the 'deemed date of service' rule in the CPR. Also, under the Companies Act 1985, service by second-class post is permitted, whereas it is not under the CPR.

CPR 6.5(3) provides that a document is served personally on a company or other corporation by leaving it with a 'person who holds a senior position'. A list of who is such a person is set out in PD 6A.6.2 (with regard to a registered company), and appear above in paragraph 9.7.2.2.

For an unregistered company or corporation, such a person might include:

• the mayor;

• the chairman;

- the president;
- the town clerk; or
- a similar officer.

 Practical Considerations

When instructing a process server to effect service on such a body, it would be prudent to provide the process server with a list of the people who are eligible to accept service.

9.7.2.6 Service on the Crown
Personal service cannot be made on the Crown.

9.7.2.7 What steps must be taken to ensure that the address for service is the correct one?
Where a claimant has reason to believe that the address of the defendant—whether he is being served as an individual, or as a partner in an (unincorporated) partnership or in the name of a business—is an address at which the defendant no longer resides or carries on business, the claimant must take 'reasonable steps' (and make 'reasonable enquiries') to ascertain the defendant's current address (CPR 6.9(3)).

In *Smith v Hughes*, sub nom *Cranfield v Bridgegrove Ltd* [2003] EWCA Civ 656, [2003] 3 All ER 129, the Court of Appeal held that the words 'last known address' were plain and unqualified. It did not matter that the defendant was no longer there.

Since that case, however, it must be borne in mind that CPR 6.9 now states that where the claimant has reason to believe that the address is an address at which the defendant no longer resides, he must now make 'reasonable steps to ascertain the defendant's current address' (see paragraph 9.7.6.1 below).

 Practical Considerations

The practical effect of this is that, where the claimant does have reason to believe that the defendant no longer resides at the address that he has, it appears that it would be safer to make an application for an order for 'alternative service' under CPR 6.15 than to rely on the court's interpretation of the 'reasonable steps' that have been made under CPR 6.9(3). An application under CPR 6.15 could seek, for example, an order for service at an alternative place (such as place of work) or by an alternative method (for example, care of a relative).

9.7.2.8 Service by first-class post (or an alternative service that provides for delivery on the next working day)
By this provision, a courier service or any 'next day delivery service' can be used. But it would be prudent to obtain a 'proof of posting' receipt in order to establish the fact of deemed service by the method.

9.7.2.9 Leaving the document at a specified place
The provisions for this must be distinguished from personal service: personal service requires the document(s) to be handed to an individual, while leaving document(s) at a specified place requires that it be placed through the letterbox or left at reception. Confusing the two can result in ineffective service, as in *Cherney v Deripaska* [2007] EWHC 965 (Comm). In this case, the claim form was 'served' on a security guard at an address that was not 'the last known residence' of the defendant, nor was the security guard an agent for the defendant for personal service to be effective, nor was it effective service by being left at a specified place.

9.7.2.10 Service through the document exchange (DX) system

Service through the document exchange (DX) system may only take place when:

- the party's address for service includes a DX number;
- the DX number is on the party's writing paper; and
- neither party nor his representative has indicated that he will *not* accept service by this method.

9.7.2.11 Service by fax or other electronic means of communication

Under the provisions of PD 6A.4, service by fax or other electronic means may only take place when:

- a party or his legal representative has expressly (in writing) indicated that he is willing to accept service by this means; and
- a party has given the fax number or email address to which documents should be transmitted;
- a fax number on the legal representative's writing paper or on a statement of case is 'express notice', unless a contrary intention is given; and
- service on the party 'express notice' is satisfied by express prior written consent or by the number appearing on a statement of case or in a response to a claim that has been filed at court.

Thorne v Lass Salt Garvin [2009] EWHC 10 (QB) considered the requirement to obtain a party's express consent to serve by fax. The court held that service was invalid because the claimant had not first obtained the defendant's agreement, in writing, to accept service by fax. Although the defendant was a firm of solicitors, at the time of alleged service, it was not acting as its own legal representative, therefore the existence of the firm's fax number on the notepaper did not (in these circumstances) indicate its agreement to accept service by fax. The judgment emphasizes the importance of strict compliance with the provisions relating to service.

There is no requirement to send a hard copy of a document served by fax, but if a hard copy does follow, it would be prudent to confirm which method of service is being employed, so that there can be no confusion as to the date of dispatch of the claim form for limitation purposes, or the 'deemed date of service' from which the defendant can calculate when his defence is due.

It is also worth remembering, in preparing to serve document(s) by fax or other electronic means of communication, that the fax number must be 'in the jurisdiction'.

 Practical Considerations

Previous correspondence by fax or email in a claim will not constitute 'express consent' (see *Kuenyehia v International Hospitals Group Ltd* [2006] EWCA Civ 21 and *Hart Investments Limited v Fidler* [2006] EWHC 2857, TCC). In the former case, the Court of Appeal confirmed that a failure to obtain express written consent could not 'happen' in this way, and in the latter case, service by fax on the second defendant's liquidator was held to be equally ineffective through lack of express consent. The detail of these cases goes to show quite how easily a mistake can be made, through a failure to abide by the strict letter of the procedural rules for service requirements.

9.7.2.12 Service by email

The appearance of an email address on notepaper is not deemed to be 'express consent', as it can be in some circumstances for service by fax. For this to be implied, the email address will need to appear on a statement of case filed at court.

For any situation in which service is proposed to be effected by email, it is good practice to check whether there are any limitations of format or size of document to be sent. It is also good practice to confirm whether incoming emails are checked on a daily basis and who checks them—it could be that the email does not reach its intended recipient as quickly as other methods of service.

Considering the potential for error in email transmission and the fact that the deemed time for service is the same day if a business day and sent before 4.30 p.m. or the next business day, many firms will not accept service by email. Despite the fact that express notice is strictly required where email addresses appear on a firm's notepaper, it will often be accompanied by a notice 'not to be used for service'.

As with faxes, there is no requirement to send a hard copy of a document served by email, but if a hard copy does follow, it would be prudent to confirm which method of service is being employed, so that there can be no confusion of the 'deemed date of service'.

9.7.2.13 Contractually agreed methods of service

CPR 6.11 provides that a claim form may be served by a contractually agreed method where:

- the contract provides that if a claim form is issued in relation to the contract, it may be served by a method specified in the contract; and

- the claim form contains only a claim in respect of the contract.

 Practical Considerations

A contractual method of service is commonly used in contracts in which the transaction is based outside the jurisdiction, and in which it would save time and expense to serve in the agreed way (for example, on a nominated firm of solicitors). In using a contractually agreed method, it is prudent to check and take care that the claim arises out of the contract.

9.7.2.14 Service on a European lawyer

The 55th amendments to the CPR have included an amendment to CPR 6.7 and 6.8 to allow as an address for service the address of a European lawyer in a European Economic Area (EEA) state or, for a litigant in person, the litigant's normal residence or place of business in the UK or failing that any EEA state.

9.7.3 EXAMPLES OF THE EFFECT OF THESE SERVICE RULES

To help you understand these examples, remember that the date of dispatch is the key date for limitation and the deemed date of service is the key date from which the defendant calculates when his defence is due.

 Example 1

A claim form expires on Friday 31 October. On that day, it is placed in a post box at 11.30 p.m., addressed to the defendant at his usual address. The defendant is deemed served on Tuesday 4 November (the second business day after completion of the relevant step—see CPR 6.14 and 7.5). The claim form has been served 'in time'—that is, within its validity period—because the 'step required' was undertaken before the end of the period of validity of the claim form.

 Example 2

A claim form expires on Saturday 1 November and is handed to the defendant personally on that day. The defendant is deemed served on Tuesday 4 November (see CPR 6.14 and 7.5). Again, the claim form has been served 'in time'—that is, within its validity period.

Example 3

A claim form expires on Friday 31 October. It is transmitted by fax that afternoon at 4.15 p.m. Provided that the transmission of the fax is completed, the claim form has been served 'in time'—that is, within its validity period—because the time given in which to complete the transmisson of the fax is until midnight on Friday 31 October. The deemed date of service will be on the second business day after dispatch—that is, Tuesday 4 November.

Note: Under PD 6A.10, it is quite clear that the deemed date of service of 'other documents' by fax, email, and personal service must be completed before 4.30 p.m. This is not noted in any part of the CPR or the Practice Direction in relation to service of the claim form. The author is therefore interpreting the rules in relation to the dispatch of a claim form to cover any method of service set out in Figure 9.4 and that the step to effect service by the method chosen should be before midnight. There are no provisions in the new rules that indicate that the date when the 'step required' is made can ever count as the first business day, even when that step is effected before 4.30 p.m.

 Example 4

A claim form expires on Friday 31 October. At 3 p.m. that afternoon, the claim form is given to the accounts clerk at the defendant company's registered office in purported performance of effecting personal service. Here, there has not been valid service of the claim form, because the method chosen has not been done correctly—the accounts clerk not being within the definition of 'a senior person'.

Note: In this situation, CPR 6.15(2) may act to 'save' the situation.

 Example 5

In an action, the defendant has indicated that service may be on his nominated solicitor, but there has been no confirmation of this by the legal representatives. Service is duly effected on the firm within the time of validity of the claim form. Here, again, valid service has been effected, because for service on nominated solicitors where the nomination has been given by the defendant, there is no need to obtain the express consent of the legal representative for service on it to be good service (CPR 6.7). There has to be express consent for service on nominated solicitors, but that consent may be given by the defendant or the legal representatives.

 Example 6

Service has been effected personally on the defendant within the time of validity of the claim form, but, in this case, the legal representatives of the defendant had indicated that they have authority to accept service on their client's behalf. In this situation, there has not been good service as consent to service on nominated legal representatives now excludes personal service on the defendant and service must be effected on the nominated solicitors (CPR 6.7).

9.7.4 SERVICE OF DOCUMENTS OTHER THAN THE CLAIM FORM

CPR 6.20–6.29 provide separate rules for service of 'other' documents. These rules cover service of all other documents created in the action that require service *other than* documents used to initiate the proceedings (this therefore includes not only claim forms but also petitions) other than the claim form. Essentially, many of the provisions for service of 'other' documents are repeated in these sections of CPR 6.

9.7.5 **WHEN MAY A PARTY SERVE DOCUMENTS ON A PARTY'S LEGAL REPRESENTATIVE?**

It is important to know when service is required on a party or whether it may be effected on its legal representative. It is often more convenient to serve on an opponent's legal representative, because it will be with that representative that you will probably have had all of your correspondence. Usually, when service can be effected on the legal representative, no other form of service will be valid. Where the legal representative works from within the European Economic Area (EEA) service must still take place on the legal representative where service on the legal representative has been notified to the serving party as the means of service on their client.

9.7.5.1 Are there any occasions on which service cannot be effected on the legal representative of a party?

The general rule is that any document may be served personally (CPR 6.5(2)). However, when a solicitor has been properly authorized to accept service, this will override the general rule and service *must* be made on the firm of solicitors authorized to act unless:

- the document is one that must be served personally—this is when a court order requires it, or when the document or order contains a penal notice. In these situations, service on the person to be served is the only effective method of service;
- the contractual provision relating to the action provides for a method of service that excludes service on solicitors authorized to act; or
- under the provisions of s. 725(1) of the Companies Act 1985, the defendant is a company, and even where the defendant has provided an address for service (which may be those of the legal representative who is acting), the claimant has the additional option of serving at the company's registered office either by post or by leaving the documents there.

9.7.5.2 When does a legal representative have 'authority' to accept service?

CPR 6.7 operates to prevent any other method of service being effective where the legal representative, who is acting, is authorized to accept service except in the circumstances noted in CPR 6.5(1). The important point to note is that the legal representative must have the necessary express authority. Notice of this authority can be given:

- by the legal representative;
- by the party; or
- by the party's insurer when the action is subrogated to the insurer.

 Practical Considerations

Where notice has been given by the party to be served or his insurer, it is usual to seek confirmation from the legal representative in writing that he has that authority and will accept service, despite the implication from the CPR that notice may be given by the person to be served or his insurer.

An 'assumption' should never be made that a legal firm has the authority and instructions from its client to accept service on its client's behalf. Instructions authorizing a legal representative to accept service on his client's behalf must always be expressly given by the client (preferably in writing) and be expressly confirmed to the opponent wishing to serve documents. When a legal representative is acting in such a matter, and has been so acting during the course of all pre-action work and negotiations, it could be easy for an 'assumption' to be made that they will accept service on their client's behalf. But despite the fact that all correspondence on the matter has been directed to the legal representative, this does *not* mean that they have authority to, or will, accept service of proceedings—specific confirmation is required.

Professional Conduct

The Solicitors' Code of Conduct 2007, Rule 11.06, provides that you, as a legal representative, may not act as an advocate at trial or act in litigation if 'it is clear that you, or anyone within your firm, will be called as a witness, unless you are satisfied that this will not prejudice your independence as an advocate, or the interests of your client or the interests of justice'.

Where deciding the appropriate method of service to employ for your client's proceedings, as a legal representative, you need to consider whether you could be 'called as a witness' in the action—if, for example, issues arise relating to service. If you, or someone in your firm, has been engaged in effecting personal service of the proceedings, the concern that you, or someone in the firm, may be called as a witness must be 'clear'. The Guidance Notes to this rule—especially Guidance Notes 25 and 26—need to be considered in detail. These considerations will not arise when postal service is being effected, but where personal service is being effected, the implications of this rule should be considered and the likelihood of issues arising in relation to that service. It is often difficult to determine whether issues might arise in relation to service—but in a case in which service has been problematical and perhaps when the defendant appears to be taking steps to evade service, it would be prudent to engage a third party or process server to effect service. Many firms do this as a matter of course.

9.7.6 WHEN SERVICE ON A PARTY'S LEGAL REPRESENTATIVE IS NOT AVAILABLE, WHO MUST BE SERVED AND WHERE CAN THEY BE SERVED?

Save where service is to be on a person's (or firm's) legal representative who has been authorized to accept service on their behalf, service will be on the party, as set out in Figure 9.4 above.

9.7.6.1 What steps must a party take to ensure that the address that they will use is a suitable place at which to serve?

The claimant must make 'reasonable enquiries' to ascertain the defendant's current address. 'Reasonable' enquires is not specifically defined and will be given its natural meaning. The consequences of getting methods of service muddled or not taking enough care with ensuring proper service can be severe. In *Cherney v Deripaska* [2007] EWHC 965 (Comm), some problems arising with service were highlighted. In this case, among other things discussed, a defendant's 'occasional' residence did not fall within the definition 'usual or last known residence'. In *Cranfield v Bridgegrove appeals* [2003] EWCA Civ 656, the Court of Appeal held that where the party had not provided an address for service, the meaning of 'last known address' could include a place at which the defendant used to live, even though it was known that he had left there (provided that 'reasonable' enquiries had been made to discover his current whereabouts).

In *Marshall v Maggs* [2006] EWCA Civ 20 (one of the *Collier v Williams* appeals), it was held that an address at which the defendant had never lived (although he was known to have visited that address) could not come within the definition of 'last known address'.

In the case of *Relfo Ltd (in liquidation) v Varsani* [2009] EWHC 2297 (Ch) the court noted that it was possible for an individual to have more than one residence and that a party wishing to serve should look at the 'quality' of usage of the property not simply how much time the defendant spent there.

If the defendant is in prison, he should be served in prison, not at his 'last known address'.

In effect, whenever the defendant's whereabouts is known and service on him could therefore be effected, it must be.

Practical Considerations

If the defendant is thought not to be at his 'last known address', it may be more prudent to apply under CPR 6.15(2) for alternative service than to risk a conclusion that service has not been effective because the 'reasonable enquiries' were not sufficient. See examples in paragraph 9.7.3.

9.7.6.2 What happens if the documents are returned before the claimant has entered judgment?

If the document(s) served are returned undelivered before the claimant has obtained judgment, service will not be effective. In that situation, the claimant will have actual knowledge that the defendant has not received the document(s) and a valid certificate of service could not be completed.

Where this happens, the claimant will either have to try another method of service or apply to the court under the provisions of CPR 6.15 for an order for service by an alternative method.

However, if the document(s) are not returned before judgment is entered, service will be deemed to have taken place (provided that the provision as to 'reasonable enquiries' is met) even if, in fact, the defendant had never received them.

9.7.7 WHAT IS THE DEEMED DATE OF SERVICE BY EACH OF THE METHODS OF SERVICE?

Provided that the 'step required' to effect service by the correct chosen method is achieved before the expiry of the period of validity of the claim form, it does not matter that the deemed date of service may be outside this period of validity. It is necessary to calculate the deemed date of service of the method chosen, because that is the date from which a party can calculate the appropriate period for taking a step in the action—for example, to seek a default judgment should the defendant fail to respond.

Remember, where service is by a method outside the CPR, the date of service may not have the benefit of the 'deemed service' rule.

The key to service is:

- do it on time; and

- do it properly.

KEY POINTS SUMMARY

- Understand the criteria that will be applied to cases to place them into one of the three tracks.

- Look out for Europe-wide procedures.

- Make sure that all documents required to start an action are in place and correctly completed. Decide who the parties are and describe them correctly.

- Understand and apply the rules for joining parties or causes of action together in the one claim.

- In relation to service—decide on the appropriate method of service, and ensure it is carried out properly and on time.

Case study *Bollingtons Ltd and Mrs Elizabeth Lynch t/a The Honest Lawyer*

Question 1

Having prepared your letter before claim to Mrs Lynch (see Chapter 8), write to your client, taking care to justify and explain the step that you have taken. Assume that you have received instructions from Bollingtons Ltd to proceed. Be aware of any professional conduct implications.

Question 2

Assume that it is now 7 October 201?. There has been no response to the letter before claim. Locate a blank claim form and complete it. A debt action such as this is relatively straightforward and this is the kind of case in which it would be appropriate to include the particulars of claim on the reverse side of the claim form itself—that is, an indorsed claim form. You will need to consider, and deal with, the claim for interest. You do not need to complete any calculations for interest, but make any provision in your draft for what you would have done.

Case study *Andrew James Pike and Deep Builders Ltd*

Question

Look at the draft particulars of claim available on the Online Resource Centre. Consider this draft document and consider how it needs to be improved to meet with the requirements of the CPR.

---

online resource centre

Any documents referred to in these case study questions can be found on the Online Resource Centre—simply click on 'Case study documentation' to access the documents that you need for Chapter 9 and to be reminded of the questions above. Suggested answers to these case study questions can also be accessed on the Online Resource Centre by your lecturer.

10.1   INTRODUCTION

It would be wrong to believe that the defendant will take a reactive role in the action, seeking only to fend off the claimant's case, sitting back and waiting to see if the claimant can establish his case. In modern litigation, the defendant will take a more proactive role. In any event, the Civil Procedure Rules (CPR) deny the defendant the right, in his defence, simply to deny the allegations against him. A defendant is now charged with the duties of explaining any defence that he files and setting down why he submits that the claimant's allegations are false or cannot be substantiated.

Where the defendant makes an additional claim (which may be a counterclaim) in his defence (see paragraph 10.6.2 below), whether that be against the claimant or against another person not yet a party, he will be in the position of 'claimant' in that action, so will have the burden of proof for that claim.

Notwithstanding this more proactive role of the defendant, there are distinct differences and similarities in the way in which both the claimant and the defendant are 'involved' in the action.

LITIGATION TRAIN: ACTING FOR A DEFENDANT, RESPONDING TO THE CLAIM, THE CONSEQUENCES OF FAILING TO RESPOND

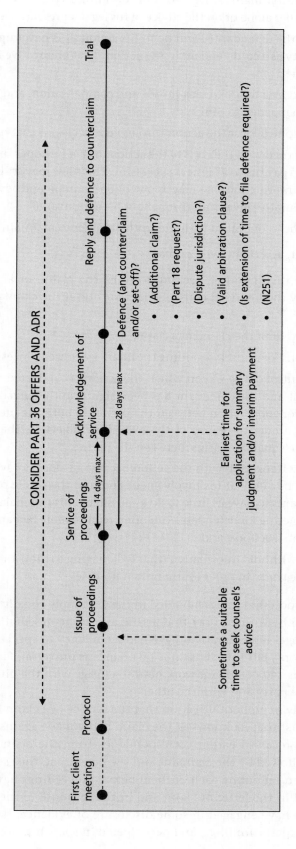

The claimant, as a client, will, or may:

- take an active role in initiating the action, deciding on the cause(s) of action that he intends to pursue either alone or on the advice of his legal representative;
- decide who the defendant(s) will be in his action. It is never up to the defendant to join another party as a co-defendant in the action. That prerogative is the claimant's and only the claimant's;
- be motivated by a desire to seek justice and compensation, and to 'right a wrong' that he alleges has happened to him;
- exert some control over the action through the decisions that he takes;
- be less concerned with the costs of the action in that he hopes that the court will order the defendant to pay his costs if he is successful. This view may still manifest itself despite all of the costs information that may apply to the claimant and advice on costs risks that the legal representative gives him throughout his action; and
- potentially be 'economical with the truth' in order to maintain the strengths of his case.

The defendant, as a client, will, or may:

- have a defensive mindset, seeking to resist the claim, or at the very least to reduce significantly the financial consequences for him if the claimant should succeed in his claim;
- be seeking to limit the claimant's claim;
- have concerns for himself regarding the financial consequences of the action against him;
- have less control of the way in which the action is conducted. This 'difference' between the claimant and the defendant has been significantly reduced by the CPR and the requirement for cooperation between the parties in both the pre-action and the litigation stages. Also, under the terms of the overriding objective, the court will be looking to maintain an 'equality of arms' between the parties;
- simply be less 'engaged' with the action because he does not want to be involved in it at all. He may be angry at his involvement and find the whole procedure something with which he wants to have as little to do as possible. This can make the legal representative's job harder. Acting for defendants can often require more tact and perseverance in obtaining timely instructions; and
- potentially withhold information (that is damaging to him) and he may also be 'economical with the truth' in order to strengthen his case.

Whilst the procedural rules embodied in the CPR apply equally to claimants and defendants, it would be wrong to say that acting as legal representative for either is the same. In practice, legal representatives have had a tendency to specialize in 'claimant work' or 'defendant work', but this division is by no means universal. Firms that regularly handle both claimant and defendant work need to engage with the differing skills that apply to acting for one party and with the other.

It is unlikely in modern litigation that the service of a claim form upon the defendant will be the first that he knows of the claim being made against him. It is probable that he will have received earlier correspondence from the claimant and, if protocol has been fully followed by the claimant and the defendant, the essence of each party's case will have been set out by each of them before proceedings have been started. This will be contained in the letter of claim and in the response to the letter of claim. The parties may also have engaged in some disclosure of evidence, had meetings, disclosed or exchanged experts' findings, and participated in some form of alternative dispute resolution (ADR).

This chapter, in considering the options open to a defendant faced with a claim against him, will cover:

- the emotional responses of the defendant;
- the defendant's pre-action position;
- the way in which a defendant may fund the litigation;
- the essential steps needed to respond to a claim;
- the substantive responses to the action; and
- tactical responses to the claim.

10.2 THE EMOTIONAL RESPONSE OF THE DEFENDANT

There is a wide spectrum of emotional responses that the defendant, as your client, may take to the action issued against him.

- He may **deny liability**—that is, he may entirely refute the liability allegations made against him. In order to do this, he will need to be able to proffer an alternate version of the story that the claimant has put forward. He will need to be able to give a version that satisfies the court that the claimant's case is not made. He may seek to achieve this by challenging the evidence of the claimant or by adducing evidence of his own that supports his version of how the 'event' (the allegations of the claimant) happened.

- He may **deny causation**—that is, he may accept some involvement in the events set out by the claimant, but deny that his actions either caused the breach or accident, or that the breach or event caused the damages and losses that the claimant alleges. To do this, he will need either to refute and challenge the claimant's case on causation, or to adduce evidence of his own that substantiates his denial.

- He may **deny quantum**, either by:
  - stating that he denies the nature and extent of the injuries or damage, and seek to suggest that the claimant contributed to his injuries; or
  - both admitting and denying—that is, by admitting parts of the claimant's case, but denying other parts of it.

- He may **seek a settlement**—in which case, he will be motivated to bring the action to an end as quickly as possible.

Clearly, in acting for a defendant, 'what' the defendant seeks to do will affect 'how' he will achieve it. A defendant can alter or affect the way in which the claim continues by the way in which he responds to it, and thus it is extremely important that the legal representative has clear instructions from the defendant and that the defendant fully understands the steps that will be taken on his behalf by the legal representative.

10.3 THE DEFENDANT'S PRE-ACTION BEHAVIOUR

10.3.1 WHAT IS A DEFENDANT'S LEVEL OF ENGAGEMENT IN PROTOCOL?

Chapter 8 deals with much of the pre-action work to be undertaken by the parties if they abide by Protocol. This section concentrates on, and will act as a reminder of, Protocol practice—but from the defendant's perspective.

Within Protocol, the defendant will need to ensure that he acknowledges the claimant's letter of claim (or letter before claim), because, under most Protocol practice, a failure to acknowledge the letter of claim will enable the claimant to proceed to issue proceedings. In those circumstances, it is highly likely that the defendant's failure to abide by Protocol practice will come back to haunt him in an unfavourable costs order within the litigation, especially if the court regards the failure to have significantly increased the costs or been the main reason why the action was started, when, had he cooperated, there may not have been a need for the action to have been started at all.

Having acknowledged the claimant's letter of claim, the defendant will then have a period of time in which to investigate the claimant's claim so that he can respond to the allegations. The period of time that the defendant should have to undertake these investigations will vary, but will be suggested in a Protocol applying to the action, or in the Practice Direction on Pre-Action Conduct (PDPAC). The courts will expect the parties to act 'reasonably' and in accordance with the spirit of Protocol practice, and in accordance with the aims of the overriding objective.

Once the defendant has investigated the claimant's allegation, he should reply fully to the letter of claim with a letter of response.

10.3.2 THE CONTENTS OF A LETTER OF RESPONSE

The letter of response should:

- say whether the claim is accepted in whole or in part, and make proposals for settlement; or
- state that the claim is not accepted.

In either of these two situations, the defendant needs to define which parts he accepts (if any) and which he refutes. Where he refutes the allegations, he needs to give detailed reasons for his conclusions.

- Where the claimant's allegations are being refuted, in addition to giving detailed reasons, the defendant should enclose documents for which the claimant has asked. If any documents requested by the claimant are not being sent, the defendant will need to give his reasons why they are not being supplied.
- The defendant may also request documents from the claimant (and the claimant should respond to this request within a reasonable time, and if the documents requested are not being sent, give reasons why not).
- The defendant should also state whether he is prepared to enter into a form of ADR, which might include
  - discussion and negotiation;
  - early neutral evaluation (ENE) by an agreed third party; or
  - mediation.
- Although a party cannot be compelled to enter into a form of ADR, we have seen in Chapter 5 that the courts will take account of a party's response to the possibility of settling the dispute by a form of ADR when considering the appropriate costs order that may be made in the action (see also Chapter 16, which contains details of the powerful use that a defendant may make of CPR Part 36 offers to settle).
- The parties should also take steps to consider any expert evidence that may be required and seek to agree on the use of an independent expert. Any steps that the parties make towards agreeing the use of experts does not, however, preclude the court from making any order as to expert evidence that it feels is appropriate. Both claimants and defendants in litigation should be advised by their legal representatives that any expert engaged in Protocol may not be permitted in the litigation, and that the costs of engaging that expert may not be recoverable.
- The defendant should also notify the claimant if he has entered into a funding arrangement that falls within the meaning of CPR 43.2(1)(k).

10.3.3 **IS THE DEFENDANT BOUND BY THE MATTERS THAT HE RAISES IN HIS LETTER OF RESPONSE IN ANY SUBSEQUENT LITIGATION?**

In the Protocol phase, neither party is restricted to the matters and allegations that they raised in their letter of claim or letter of response. However, if the changes or additions to a party's case arise from an intent to mislead the other party during the Protocol phase, the court is likely to impose cost sanctions against the misleading party.

 Practical Considerations

Notwithstanding the professional conduct implications of inconsistencies between the defendant's letter of response and his subsequent defence, a significant departure from the defendant's original position contained in the letter of response can reduce his credibility. This may also encourage a claimant's application for summary judgment or strike-out (see Chapter 14, paragraph 14.3, and see paragraphs 10.7.1 and 10.7.2 below).

10.3.4 **WHAT IS THE POSITION IF THE DEFENDANT MAKES AN ADMISSION DURING PROTOCOL?**

Where the defendant makes an admission of liability during Protocol, he will be bound by any admission up to a value of £25,000. The CPR encourage admissions, because they narrow the issues between the parties, usually save costs, and they will perhaps aid settlement being achieved. However, legal representatives should be aware of the importance of admissions and the consequences of them.

10.3.4.1 What constitutes an admission?

An admission may be made of the truth of an allegation or of the facts stated, and it may be express or implied. It may be found in correspondence, or in oral discussions between the parties and their legal representatives, or between a party and a third party. An admission can also be inferred by conduct.

10.3.4.2 What are the consequences of a pre-action admission?

The consequence of a formal admission (for example, made in response to a notice to admit, in writing in open correspondence) will be that neither party will need to adduce evidence at trial of the issue or fact admitted. Informal admissions, such as an implicit acknowledgement of a state of affairs, are treated as pieces of evidence and further evidence may be adduced to disprove the informal admission or to explain away its apparent result. Equally, an admission made without knowledge of a material fact will have little evidential value.

10.3.4.3 Is a potential party always bound by a pre-action admission?

A party will not be bound by a previously made admission in the following circumstances:

• an admission made in previous proceedings that have not been placed before the current court as adopted and true;

• an informal admission that is not proved;

• an admission made by a person not authorized to make it unless there existed ostensible or apparent authority (of the agent), in which case, the admission may bind (the principal), but he may have a right to claim an indemnity from the person who made the unauthorized admission; and

• an admission that is not clear and unambiguous.

10.3.4.4 Can admissions be withdrawn?

A formal admission may be withdrawn in certain circumstances, as follows.

- It may be withdrawn with the permission of the court. The court will consider the over-riding objective when considering such an application and will consider such issues as prejudice to a party, the reasons why the admission was made, the stress that a party was under when the admission was made, the interests of the public in permitting the withdrawal of the formal admission, and the time at which the application to withdraw from the admission is made.

- Three important cases have considered the effect of formal admissions: *Sowerby v Charlton* [2005] EWCA Civ 1610; *The Governing Body of Charterhouse School v Hannaford Upright* [2007] EWHC 2718; and *Stoke on Trent City Council v John Walley* [2006] EWCA Civ 1137. These cases have held that:

  - permission may not be granted if it is made late (and close to the trial);

  - permission may be granted when the admission was made by mistake; and

  - permission will depend upon whether the admission was made pre-action or not.

- Following the outcome of the cases above and further consultation, CPR 14.1A states that a person may withdraw a pre-action admission:

  - with the consent of the person to whom the admission was made; and

  - after commencement of proceedings with the permission of the court.

  These conditions apply when:

  - the admission was made in proceedings listed under the rule—that is, personal injury, clinical disputes, and disease and illness claims; and

  - the admission was made after a letter of claim has been sent, or if before, the admission states that it has been made under the provisions of CPR 14.

The rule also makes provision for these pre-action admissions to be dealt with in subsequent litigation as follows:

- that any party may apply for judgment on a pre-action admission that is covered under the rule; and

- the party who made the admission can apply to the court to withdraw it (and the court will apply the criteria noted above when considering the application).

10.3.5 WHAT IS THE POSITION OF AN EXPERT ENGAGED BY A PARTY IN PROTOCOL?

It will be for the claimant to decide whether any expert report that he has obtained in Protocol will be disclosed to the defendant (see also Chapter 8, paragraph 8.12.2.9, and Chapter 19, paragraph 19.12.1). A favourable report may increase the chances of achieving a settlement, but it will also give the defendant plenty of time to 'pick holes' in the claimant's expert report. Although there is encouragement in Protocol to seek to agree the use of a jointly selected expert, this does not mean that the claimant is forced to do so and, in any event, he may have engaged an 'advisory expert' (see Chapter 19, paragraph 19.8.1) to help him to formulate his case. The defendant also may wish to engage the assistance of his own expert. The claimant should not unreasonably refuse to be examined by the defendant's nominated expert.

Where the claimant has proffered the names of experts in Protocol, and where the defendant has not rejected an expert from that list and the claimant so instructs that expert, the defendant will not be permitted to engage his own expert within proceedings unless the court permits.

10.4 HOW MAY A DEFENDANT FUND THE COSTS INCURRED IN DEFENDING THE CASE AGAINST HIM?

A defendant has the same methods of funding his action available to him as those that are available to the claimant and he may agree or negotiate any of these with his legal representative. Essentially, these include:

- a private retainer with his legal representative; or

- a conditional fee agreement (CFA)—the definition of what would be deemed a 'success' in such an arrangement (where a success fee is included in the agreement) will be specifically set down in the CFA contract with his legal representative. It may vary from succeeding in resisting the claim to attaining a reduction in the sum of the claim. Notice of such a funding arrangement must be given to the claimant and notified to the court by the filing of Form N251.

Further details of these funding arrangements are outlined in Chapter 3, paragraph 3.3.

Defendants are under the same obligations to abide by the principles of the overriding objective to ensure that the litigation is conducted with 'a view to controlling expenses' and in conducting the action 'proportionately'.

A defendant who is engaged in litigation, but feels that the claimant may be unable to satisfy any costs order made against him may, in certain circumstances, apply to the court for an order for security for costs within the provisions of CPR 25.12 (see paragraph 10.7.3 below).

10.5 THE STEPS AND TIME LIMITS FOR RESPONDING TO A CLAIM

The defendant need not take any action in response to the claim issued against him until the particulars of claim have been served on him. Remember that the claimant is not obliged to serve the particulars of claim at the same time as the claim form, but if he does serve the claim form without the particulars of claim, he must serve the particulars of claim within 14 days of serving the claim form (see Chapter 9, paragraph 9.3.5). When the claimant has served the particulars of claim, it will be accompanied with the response pack in Form N9A or Form N9C, which are supplied by the court. Form N9A will be used when the claimant's action is for a specified sum; Form N9C will be used when the claim is for an unspecified sum.

Time begins to run from the deemed date of service of the particulars of claim on the defendant (CPR 9.2). The defendant has 14 days from that date in which to:

- file or serve an admission; or

- file a defence (which may be combined with a counterclaim); or

- file an acknowledgement of service.

Each of these options is considered below.

10.5.1 ADMITTING THE CLAIM AND REQUESTING TIME TO PAY

Forms N9A and N9C make provision for admissions to be made. Admissions may be made of the whole claim or a part of it. Where only part is being admitted, the defendant will need to file a defence to that part of the claim that is not admitted, otherwise the claimant will be able to apply for judgment in default of that part. In either case, the forms also make provision for the defendant to make provision to pay the sum admitted or to ask for time to pay.

Where the defendant seeks time to pay the sum admitted, he must also complete those parts of the form that require details of his assets, income, and outgoings. The completed form will be sent to the claimant, who may raise objections to the defendant's instalment payment offer that he will include in the form. Where the claimant raises objections to the offer, the court will either set the level of instalments or set the matter down for a disposal hearing. The specific detail and order of instalment offers and terms are set down in CPR 14.

Where the defendant admits the whole claim within 14 days of service of the particulars of claim, he will be liable for the fixed costs of the action. Details of the sum of these fixed costs will be contained in the bottom right-hand box on the front page of the Form N1 claim form. Where the defendant admits the whole claim, the admission in one of the Forms N9 will be sent directly to the claimant rather than filed at court and the claimant will be able to obtain judgment on the claim by filing a request for judgment in either Form N225 or Form N227.

Where the defendant has requested time to pay, the claimant will have to respond to the offer and either accept it or raise objections. If the admission is of the whole claim, or the claimant accepts the instalment offer, the court will proceed to issue the judgment order in Form N30. The judgment will include accrued interest and the fixed costs. The judgment is also registered in the Register of Judgments. Because registration of a judgment debt may affect a defendant's creditworthiness, it is worth noting that a defendant may avoid registration of the debt if he has admitted the whole claim and paid the sum due and fixed costs within 14 days of service of the particulars of claim.

If the defendant's admission is for part of the claim, but as an offer to satisfy the whole claim, the claimant has the option of accepting the sum offered. If he does accept the sum offered, the matter will proceed as above and the court will proceed to make the judgment order. If the offer is rejected, the case will proceed as a disputed claim.

In unspecified sum claims in which the defendant has filed an admission of the claim, the matter will be stayed and set down for a disposal hearing for the court to determine the sum of the claim. Directions will be given as to the evidence to be filed and exchanged in advance of the disposal hearing.

Where the claimant is a child or protected party, the court must approve any admission, or part-admission, or offer to pay by an instalment option. (For further details of child or protected party applications, see Chapter 9, paragraph 9.5.)

10.5.2 FILING A DEFENCE

If the defendant intends to defend the action against him, he will need to file and serve his defence. CPR 15 contains the rules for the filing of the defence and service upon every other party in the action. These rules include provisions that:

- a defendant who wishes to file a defence should do so within 14 days after service upon him of the particulars of claim;

- a defendant who files an acknowledgement of service within 14 days (after service upon him of the particulars of claim) must serve his defence within 28 days after service upon him of the particulars of claim; and

- the time limits of 14 days and 28 days above do not apply when the defendant resides outside the jurisdiction (the alternative time limits are set down in CPR 6.23), or when the defendant is disputing jurisdiction, he need not file a defence (CPR 11), or when the defendant makes an application for summary judgment, he need not file a defence before the hearing of his application (CPR 24.4).

Forms N9A, N9C, and N9D provide space for a defence to the claim to be made. Where a party is legally represented, the defence will usually be separately drafted in the form and structure detailed in Chapter 11, paragraph 11.5.

Practical Considerations

Acting for a defendant will require as many, if not more, matters to be discussed with the client than may be discussed with a claimant to establish whether he has a claim. Although the claimant will have formulated the substance of the claim, a defendant has a variety of options that may be available to him to respond and defend the claim (see further paragraph 10.6 below). A defendant should admit what should be admitted. Costs penalties and professional conduct rules—particularly the duty not to mislead the court under the Solicitors' Code of Conduct 2007, Rule 11.01—arise if a defendant is reluctant to admit those parts of claim that clearly should be admitted. Ambiguous claims can be amended or put right, and it is important that you, as the legal representative, seek to balance the interests of the overriding objective and the need to be 'cooperative' in litigation with what may be in the 'best interests' of the client. Where a claim is being 'denied', the legal representative will be mindful of establishing whether there is evidence that is credible and admissible to support the defence. It is not simply a case of waiting to see if the claimant can establish his case.

Further, clients may not always understand the intricacies of their actions—for example, in claims for misrepresentation. Misrepresentation arises where something is said with the *intention* of inducing a contract and *does* induce a contract. Clients will not always understand the difference between pre-contractual enquiry and true misrepresentation. These misunderstandings have to be managed by the legal representative. These and many other matters may arise in acting for a defendant in even the simplest of actions.

10.5.2.1 Extending the time for service of the defence

The time limits for filing a defence may be extended by agreement between the parties. The parties can agree an extension up to a maximum of a further 28 days. When such an agreement is made, the defendant must inform the court of the period of the extension (CPR 15.5). If any greater extension of time is required, whether the claimant consents or not, an application must be made to the court. The application must be justified in terms of the overriding objective.

 Practical Considerations

In any dispute resolution department, any legal representative has to be more than simply able to undertake the procedural requirements of litigation—he must also be commercially aware. In commercial matters, one or both sides to the claim may be in business and an awareness of the implications of this are important if the legal representative is to 'serve' his client's best interests. The action may have a significant cash flow impact on the business; the parties to the action may need to, or wish to, continue their business relationship. These, and other, business-related issues need to be understood and 'managed' within the action.

Once the defence is filed, the court's case management role is started with the issuing of Form N150 (the allocation questionnaire) to all parties. Chapter 12 sets out the detail and consequences for the parties of this step.

10.5.2.2 If no defence is filed and served

If the defendant fails to file a defence within the period specified, in most actions, the claimant will be able to obtain default judgment. This precludes the defendant from defending the claim further (see Chapter 14, paragraph 14.2 for details of how the claimant can secure default judgment and what the defendant can do to have it set aside). Default judgment is not permitted if the claim is for delivery of goods that are subject to an agreement regulated by the Consumer Credit Act 1974, or in CPR Part 8 proceedings, or in any other case in which a Practice Direction provides.

If a defence is not filed and the claimant fails to seek default judgment, six months after the date on which the defence should have been filed, the claim will be stayed (CPR 15.11).

10.5.3 FILING AN ACKNOWLEDGEMENT OF SERVICE

The form of acknowledgement of service is used by a defendant for two reasons, both of which can be relied upon in the same action, if appropriate. The defendant will file and serve the acknowledgement of service when he is unable to file his defence within 14 days of the service upon him of the particulars of claim, but intends to defend some or all of the claim, or when he intends to use it to signify (and take no other step in the action) that he disputes the jurisdiction of the court to hear the action.

In either case, the form is included in the Form N9 (A, B, C, or D) and must be filed at the court out of which the claim is issued. It will ask for the following information:

- the defendant's full name—if the defendant's name has been incorrectly stated in the claim, the defendant will set out his correct name in the acknowledgement of service; and

- the defendant's full address for service, including postcode—this may be a personal or a business address, and if the defendant is legally represented, his legal representative will state the firm's address for service. Service of the claim on a partnership may be acknowledged by any of the partners served or someone authorized to acknowledge on behalf of the partnership, and if served on a company, the form of acknowledgement may be signed by a director or a person holding a senior position in the company (the person signing also indicating his position in the company).

A copy of the acknowledgement can be found in the Appendices at the back of this handbook.

10.5.3.1 Disputing all or part of the claim

The defendant must tick one of two boxes on the form confirming whether he intends to defend all or part of the claim. He must then file his defence within the time limit now available to him by having filed the acknowledgement of service (see paragraph 10.5.2 above). The filing of the acknowledgement of service is also the trigger point for some interim applications—for example, either party may make an application for summary judgment, or the claimant may make an application for an interim payment.

10.5.3.2 Contesting jurisdiction

If the defendant intends to contest the jurisdiction of the claim against him, he must tick the box confirming this. If a defendant intends to do this, he must take care not to take steps in the action beyond acknowledging service of the claim form (CPR 11). He must then, within 14 days, make an application, supported with written evidence, disputing the jurisdiction of the court (CPR 11(4)). The defendant need not—in fact, should not—file his defence until after the court has heard his application. A defence will be required from him if his application disputing jurisdiction has failed, usually within 14 days of the court's decision declaring that the action is correctly being dealt with within the jurisdiction. Sometimes, the application is clear: for example, there may be a valid agreement for the matter to be submitted to arbitration. Sometimes, the application disputing the jurisdiction of the court may be made because there is a choice, in which case, the court will exercise its discretion in accordance with the principles of the overriding objective.

If the defendant does not make an application to the court under the provisions of CPR 11(4), he will be treated as if he has accepted that the court does have jurisdiction to hear the claim.

10.6 **THE DEFENCE OF A CLAIM**

10.6.1 **COMMON DEFENCES**

A defence is required when a defendant wishes to defend all or part of a claim. Once filed, a copy of the defence must be served on every other party. The time limits for the filing of a defence are set out at CPR 15.4 and in paragraph 10.5 above.

'Defences' can be broadly subdivided into the following categories, which can be used exclusively or concurrently if appropriate.

- **Procedural defences** These could include, for example:
  - a submission that the court does not have jurisdiction; or
  - a submission that the claim is outside the limitation period.
- **Defences to the cause of action** These could include submissions that state:
  - that the claim does not disclose a cause of action; or
  - that, on the evidence, the cause of action is not established on the balance of probabilities, or
  - that, on the grounds of the defence, the defendant is absolved from liability.
- **Defences to the claim for damages** These could include submissions that:
  - the claim does note set out all of the required elements for a claim for damages; or
  - on the evidence, the elements of the remedy sought are not, on the balance of probabilities, substantiated; or
  - on the facts, the loss was not caused by the breach (causation); or
  - on the facts, the loss was not foreseeable; or
  - on the facts, the claimant has failed to mitigate his loss; or further
  - in a negligence or breach of contract action, the claimant was also negligent or in breach, and contributed to his loss and damage.

It can be seen that some of these defences will act as defences to the claim itself, while others will seek to reduce (or eliminate) the liability that the claimant alleges has arisen, but 'liability' itself is accepted. We refer to the latter case as an admission of 'primary liability' coupled with an allegation of contributory negligence against the claimant. (See Chapter 11, paragraph 11.5, for details on how to draft some of these defences.)

One of the options that may be part of the defendant's case may be to seek to pass the blame or liability of the claimant's action to another. This is dealt with next.

10.6.2 **PART 20 CLAIMS**

A defendant faced with an action against him may have:

- no issue with the fact that the claimant has suffered a loss, but he may feel that responsibility for some or all of those losses does not lie with him, but with somebody else;
- a claim of his own that he would like to bring that arises out of the same set of circumstances.

In these circumstances, a defendant can use the provisions set out in CPR 20. CPR 20 has, however, been drafted poorly and many new to practice find its categorization of claims unhelpful. CPR 20 essentially enables the defendant to make four types of additional claim, the nature of each of which is examined below. The correct terminology for this type of claim is an 'additional claim', but you will often see it referred to as a 'Part 20 claim'.

By way of definition, an 'additional claim' is any claim other than that initiated by the claimant against the defendant. This could also be called the 'main action'. Although CPR Part 20 claims are procedurally connected with the main action, they can be entirely separate claims. A settlement or action terminating the main action will not usually terminate an additional claim unless it is included in the agreement or order terminating the main action. It will depend on the nature of the additional claim and whether it is worth pursuing it after the settlement or termination of the main action. For example, if the defendant has sought a contribution or indemnity, the dismissal or striking out of the main action will render it pointless continuing with the claim for a contribution or indemnity, because there will be no sum to which to contribute or to indemnify.

10.6.2.1 A counterclaim brought by the defendant against the claimant (CPR 20.4)

A counterclaim is a claim in its own right that lies against the claimant in the action. It could form the basis of a separate claim by the defendant against the claimant in separate proceedings, but in these circumstances, the defendant does not have the choice of issuing his own proceedings against the claimant, because when there is already litigation existing between the parties (because of the main action started by the claimant), the defendant must—apart from for reasons of convenience, efficiency, and cost-effectiveness—bring his counterclaim in the same set of proceedings where the counterclaim arises from the same— or substantially the same—set of facts as the claimant's claim.

The subject matter of the counterclaim need not be precisely the same as the proceedings started by the claimant against the defendant, but the claimant and the defendant must sue and be sued in the same capacity.

Determining whether the defence has a true counterclaim requires careful legal and factual analysis, as follows.

- A defendant's case that amounts to a simple dispute of the facts set down by the claimant in the action is not a counterclaim. An example of this could be where the defendant disputes the terms of the contract that form the basis of the claimant's case.

- If the defendant's case against the claimant amounts to a simple defence to the allegations against him, these are matters that would be raised in the defence, not in any counterclaim. An example of this situation would be where the defendant alleges contributory negligence on the part of the claimant. This also is not an 'additional claim' under CPR Part 20. In this situation, the defendant should set out his allegations in the defence, stating what duty or act the claimant failed to discharge or undertake that contributed to the losses that he sustained.

- Any situation in which the defendant has a separate claim that has all of the requirements of a true action against the claimant (where related to the facts of the main action), would be a counterclaim within the provisions of CPR Part 20.

- Where the defendant blames someone else and claims to have no personal responsibility for the claimant's loss or damage, such a claim would be included in the defendant's defence and would not be a counterclaim. An example of such a situation would be if, in a road traffic accident (RTA), the defendant were to claim that the RTA was **wholly** caused by the claimant or someone else, or in a breach of contract action, if the defendant were to claim that he acted as agent rather than principal, or where the defendant claims to be absolved from the claim by an exclusion clause. These are defences, not counterclaims.

 Example

A claimant issues proceedings against a defendant for non-payment on an information technology (IT) service and maintenance contract. The defendant denies the allegations, stating that the IT works had not been effected correctly and that, as a result, his company has suffered loss of production.

The defence here is the allegation that the claimant had not performed his part of the contract properly and the counterclaim is the monetary losses to the defendant, which he incurred as a result of those breaches by the claimant. The flowchart in Figure 10.1 at the end of this chapter illustrates this.

Therefore, the key features of a counterclaim are as follows.

• It is brought by an existing defendant in an action against the claimant.

• It arises out of the same, or substantially the same, facts as the claimant's claim against the defendant.

• It is a monetary claim in its own right.

• It is not a defence.

• The court heading identifying the parties will not change. It will be identical to the court heading on the particulars of claim.

A 'simple' counterclaim by the defendant against the claimant (such as that described in the example above) is a situation in which it can be seen quite clearly that the party's claims against each other should be heard in the same action, avoiding the potential situation of two courts reaching different conclusions based on the same facts. However, if the claims are so different from one another that there is no overlap of evidence or facts, and the combining of the actions is unlikely to result in a saving of costs or time, it may indicate that the claims should be independently processed.

See Chapter 11, paragraph 11.6.1, for an example of a drafted counterclaim.

10.6.2.2 A counterclaim brought by the defendant against a person other than the claimant (CPR 20.5)

This type of additional claim is against a person who is not already a party to the action, but against whom the defendant has a monetary claim that arises out of the same set of facts. Therefore, much of paragraph 10.6.2.1 will apply in terms of identifying a true counterclaim as opposed to a defence, but, of course, the additional party will not be the claimant, because it must be a person who is not already involved in the proceedings.

The easiest way to explain this is by way of an example.

 Example

The claimant, Pearl Fisher, is injured in an RTA whilst driving in the course of her employment with Purcell Logistics Ltd and issues proceedings against the defendant, Scott Butler. The defendant denies negligence and alleges contributory negligence against the claimant. The defendant wants to make a counterclaim, because his truck was badly damaged, as were the materials in the truck. The counterclaim technically lies against the claimant's employer, due to the principle of vicarious liability, but the employer is not a party to the action. If the defendant wants to pursue a counterclaim formally, then he will need to issue a Part 20 claim against the claimant's employer under CPR 20.5. The flowchart in Figure 10.2 at the end of this chapter illustrates this.

 Practical Considerations

In practice, as would have been identified during Protocol correspondence between the claimant and defendant, what, in fact, would happen in the example above is that the claimant's legal representative would have passed details of the counterclaim on to her employer's insurer, which would subrogate the counterclaim. It would confirm that the claimant was driving in the course of her employment and, in order to deal with the defence of the counterclaim proportionately and reasonably in this case, it would agree with the claimant's and defendant's legal representatives that it would allow the claimant's legal representative to conduct the defence to the counterclaim, indemnify them in respect of any costs, and abide by any judgment and costs orders made in respect of the counterclaim.

In such actions, the title of the action will change. The heading of a claim with a CPR Part 20 claim could look like that detailed below. (Note that the defendant refers to the Part 20 defendant as a 'third party'.)

PEARL FISHER   Claimant

    and

SCOTT BUTLER   Defendant

    and

PURCELL LOGISTICS LTD   Third party

These additional claims do not operate as a defence to the action either.

10.6.2.3 An additional claim brought by the defendant seeking a contribution or an indemnity (CPR 20.6)

A defendant may make such a claim for a contribution, or an indemnity or other remedy, from an existing party, usually another defendant, in which case, the claim will be called a 'Contribution Notice'. Such a claim may arise between joint tortfeasors, joint contractors, joint sureties, joint debtors, or joint trustees. The sum of the 'contribution' will be based either on the facts of the joint responsibility, or on the basis of the degree of blame for the claimant's loss and damage. A claim for a contribution will usually seek to share the liability. A claim for an indemnity, however, seeks to pass on the entire liability to the indemnifier; an indemnity may arise under a contract, under statute, or by virtue of the relationship between the defendant and additional party. A party can also seek to claim both a contribution and an indemnity from its co-defendant.

 Example

Claims for contribution are frequently found in road traffic actions, as follows.

The claimant had emerged from a set of traffic lights at a crossroads and was waiting to turn right in the junction. He was stationary. Two vehicles travelling in the opposite direction collided with him. The claimant issued proceedings against both defendants. The first defendant served a contribution notice, requesting that the second defendant agree to a 60:40 liability split in favour of the first defendant, in accordance with CPR 20.6.

Claims for indemnity are frequently found in commercial claims, as follows.

The claimant contracted with an architect to design a home for him. He also engaged a building company to construct the property. The property was defective, and the claimant issued proceedings against both the architect and the building company. In the architect's defence, he denied the claimant's claim and blamed his co-defendant for all of the claimant's losses. The architect in this situation served an additional claim for an indemnity against the building company. The flowchart in Figure 10.3 at the end of this chapter illustrates this.

In such actions, the court headings identifying the parties will not change. These additional claims do, however, operate as a type of defence to the claimant's claim.

10.6.2.4 An additional claim brought against other persons (CPR 20.7)

Such a claim is made in the first instance by a defendant to the action who wishes to blame someone other than the claimant for the claimant's losses. The new additional party will be called a 'third party'. If that third party then wishes to blame someone else, whether that 'someone else' is a party to the action or not, then that 'someone else' is called a 'fourth party'—and so on. These allegations and counter-allegations can become complex in, for example, large building and construction contracts—although the numbers of additional parties continues with the allegations and counter-allegations, it remains 'convenient' to hear all of the claims together (or as managed by the court), because all relate to the same facts (that is, the subject of the construction contract).

Example

> A garden centre contracted with a greenhouse supplier to supply and install two large warehouse green-houses for indoor plants. The heating system did not work, to the extent that it overheated and killed the plants. The garden centre issued proceedings against the greenhouse supplier for loss of revenue. The greenhouse supplier defended the claim, blaming the electrical contractor that it had engaged to install the heating system. The electrical contractor denied liability and blamed its subcontractor—an individual who had actually undertaken the works. The flowchart in Figure 10.4 at the end of this chapter illustrates this.

When this occurs, the heading of the action will continue to 'evolve' as new parties are added and additional claims are made, and it might look like this:

DALE GARDEN CENTRE LTD	Claimant
and	
WIRRAL GREENHOUSES LTD	Defendant
and	
S & S ELECTRICAL SOLUTIONS (A FIRM)	Third party
and	
BERNARD TALBOT T/A TALBOT ELECTRICIANS	Fourth party

See Chapter 11, paragraph 11.6.2.1, for a drafted third-party claim.

These additional claims do operate as a defence to the claimant's claim.

10.6.2.5 How to issue an additional claim

10.6.2.5.1 *A counterclaim against the claimant*

Where the counterclaim is a 'simple' one, being a counterclaim made by the defendant in the main action against the claimant, the defendant may raise the counterclaim:

- without the permission of the court, provided that he files it with, or at the same time as, his defence (CPR 20.4.2(a)). Practically, the counterclaim is drafted so that it follows directly on from the defence. This can sometimes be confusing for those new to practice as the counterclaim has the appearance of being part of the defence. It is however a sep-arate legal document with its own cause of action and loss claimed. Again, see paragraph 11.6.1.1 in Chapter 11 for a draft counterclaim attached to a defence; or

- at any other time with the court's permission (CPR 20.4.2(b)). Here the counterclaim will more obviously stand alone as a separate legal statement of case. The only difference to the example given in paragraph 11.6.1.1 is that the full title of the action and the heading will need to be inserted at the top of the document.

In either of these cases above a fee is payable for the counterclaim that is equivalent to the fee for issuing a fresh claim, although there is no claim form to complete.

10.6.2.5.2 *A counterclaim against a person other than the claimant*

Where the defendant wishes to seek an additional claim by way of a counterclaim against a person who is not a party to the proceedings, he must apply to the court for permission to do so (CPR 20.5). When he makes an application, it must be accompanied by a statement of case (of the additional claim), and will set out details of the stage that the main proceedings have reached, the nature of that claim, and details of the nature of the claim against the new party. The statement of case will be headed 'Defendant's Counterclaim against a Third Party'.

If the court makes an order permitting the addition of the new party, it will also give directions for managing the case. These directions are likely to include provision for service of all statements of case on the new party, together with a response pack and an order stat-ing the time allowed for responding to the additional claim, together with directions of the role that the new party will take in the action (if any). Further case management directions will also be given for disclosure, exchange of witness statements, etc.

A fee is also payable here and, again, there is no claim form.

10.6.2.5.3 *An additional claim for a contribution or indemnity*

Where the defendant seeks a contribution or indemnity from someone who is already a party to the action, he may file a Contribution Notice setting out the grounds of the additional claim, and serve that on the claimant and the additional party without the permission of the court, provided that he files the notice and claim at the same time as filing his defence (CPR 20.6). He may also serve notice of an additional claim for a contribution or an indemnity against a person who later becomes a party to the proceedings, provided that he serves the notice within 28 days of the new party being added to the claim. In any other circumstances, the defendant must seek the court's permission, by way of an application, to seek a contribution or indemnity.

No fee is payable and no claim form is issued.

10.6.2.5.4 *An additional claim against persons not party to the proceedings*

Where an additional claim is made against someone who is not yet a party to proceedings, the defendant can make this additional claim without the court's permission if the additional claim is issued before or at the same time as he files his defence, or at any other time with the court's permission on a without-notice application (CPR 20.7). The statement of case could be headed 'Defendant's Additional Claim against a Third Party'. Again example of how to draft this document can be found at paragraph 11.6.2.1 in Chapter 11.

A fixed fee is payable though the sum differs in the High Court and the county courts. There is also an additional (Part 20) claim form to complete.

Please see the appendix for a copy of a Part 20 Claim Form.

10.6.2.6 The service of additional claims

When permission of the court is not required, a counterclaim made in the situations above in which the permission of the court is not required must be filed at court with the defence and served on each party. Any additional claim issued by the court at a later date must be served on the person against whom it is made within 14 days of issue by the court.

When permission of the court is required, the court will make directions for the service of the additional claim when it gives permission for the additional claim to be made within the main action.

In either case, service of the additional claim will be accompanied with:

- a form for defending the claim;
- a form for admitting the claim;
- a form for acknowledging service; and
- a copy of every statement of case already served in the main action and any other documents that the court has directed should also be served (CPR 20.12).

10.6.2.7 What response does a claimant or other person give to the counterclaim (CPR 20.4 and 20.5)?

Save where CPR Part 20 states to the contrary, the provisions of the CPR apply to counterclaims as if they were claims. In this way, a 'defence to the counterclaim' must be served. Failure to do this will enable the defendant to seek judgment in default on the counterclaim.

Whilst defending the counterclaim, a reply to the defendant's defence can be raised. The statement of case is known as a 'reply and defence to counterclaim' and forms one document. The reply is optional and is only usually prepared where something has been raised in the defence (and counterclaim) that requires a response, so that the issues between the parties are defined. When there is no counterclaim, the usual time for service of the reply is on the filing of allocation questionnaires with the court.

See Chapter 11, paragraph 11.7, for a drafted reply.

10.6.2.8 What action must an additional party take in an additional claim (CPR 20.6 and 20.7)?

For additional claims brought by the defendant, the additional party must serve a defence (if already a party to the action), or an acknowledgement and defence if not already a party to the action.

If the additional party fails to acknowledge or defend the additional claim, he will be deemed to admit the main action and be bound by the outcome of it so far as it relates to him by the additional claim made against him by the defendant.

See Chapter 11, paragraph 11.6.2, for a drafted additional claim.

10.6.2.9 CPR Part 20 claims and costs

The general rule is that the loser should pay the winner's costs. As we have seen in Chapter 4, there are many factors that influence the order for costs that the court will make. Where an action has included additional claims, then the issue of costs demands special attention. In some situations, with additional claims, the defendant may be in the unenviable position of incurring costs in defending the main action, but also incurring costs in pursuing his additional claim. The issue of who has 'won' an action in which there are multiple claims may make it difficult to deal with the issue of costs orders between the parties, as well as the sum of those costs orders. These types of costs order are outside the scope of this book, but are 'flagged' up here as an area in which careful study and attention must be paid in any dealings with an action that includes an additional claim.

10.6.3 THE DEFENCE OF 'SET-OFF'

The law relating to set-off is complex, because it is based on legal doctrines (legal set-off and equitable set-off) and case law. Here, we set out only the basic principles in relation to the simplest and most common type of set-off: the legal set-off.

A legal 'set-off' is a money claim that a defendant has against the claimant. It is for an ascertainable amount and is usually used as a defence with a view to reducing significantly, or even extinguishing, the claimant's claim against the defendant. Another feature of a set-off is that it is 'separate' to the cause of action that the claimant has brought against the defendant in his particulars of claim.

 Example

Sole Trader A supplies goods totalling £20,000 to Limited Company B in July. In August, Limited Company B supplies goods to the value of £30,000 to Sole Trader A. Neither company pays for the goods. Both transactions had a separate written contract. If A were to sue B, it is likely that B would raise a defence of set-off that, in this case, would completely extinguish A's claim if successful. B would then counterclaim, seeking the remaining £10,000. Therefore, in this example, B has both a defence of set-off and a counterclaim.

Here, the court could award the claimant judgment on his claim, but order a stay of execution pending the determination of the counterclaim.

 Practical Considerations

In practice, you may come across contracts that stipulate that the debtor has no right of set-off against the creditor. You will need to consider the clause carefully, taking into account whether it may be held to be unreasonable and rendered ineffective under the Unfair Contract Terms Act 1977. The purpose of these clauses is to cover the situations in which contracting parties undertake reciprocal business.

A defendant who has an unquantified set-off against the claimant that is not connected with the claimant's claim is not usually entitled to a set-off, although the doctrine of equitable set-off would need to be examined. This is outside the scope of this handbook.

Legal set-offs are therefore most successfully used by defendants in mutual debt-type claims as in the example above—but compare the following example.

 Example

> A building contractor undertakes building works for a homeowner. The homeowner alleges that the works are of unsatisfactory quality and refuses to pay. The contractor issues proceedings for the amount owed, and the homeowner defends on the basis of poor workmanship and seeks to set off, by way of a counterclaim, the value of the remedial works to rectify the job against what he owes the contractor.

This second example can be distinguished for two reasons: firstly, the second example concerns a set-off for an unquantified amount, because the value of the remedial works would need to be ascertained; and secondly, the counterclaim operates as a set-off within the claimant's action. Although the situation of the homeowner in this second example is not strictly a set-off, these types of scenario can also be treated as set-offs in practice.

10.7 COMMON TACTICS AVAILABLE IN DEFENDING A CLAIM

In addition to defending a claim, a defendant has a selection of tactics to employ where appropriate and proportionate to do so. The tactics listed below are not exhaustive, however, and all are also available to a claimants, save for the security for costs application (unless the claimant is defending a counterclaim), which rests exclusively with the defendant.

10.7.1 MAKING AN APPLICATION FOR SUMMARY JUDGMENT

An application for summary judgment may be made by the defendant under the provisions of CPR 24 when he believes that he can show that the claimant's case is so weak on the facts that it has no real prospect of succeeding. (See Chapter 14, paragraph 14.3, which deals with applications for summary judgment.)

An application for summary judgment can also be made for part of a claim, and in this way, the issues between the parties can be narrowed and be used by a defendant who wishes to restrict the claim being made against him. The requirements for summary judgment for part of a claim are the same as an application for summary judgment on the whole.

A defendant's application for summary judgment can be made at any time after he has filed his acknowledgement of service indicating an intention to defend the action (in whole or in part).

10.7.2 MAKING AN APPLICATION TO DISMISS THE CLAIM

A defendant may make an application to dismiss the claim under the provisions of CPR 3 (to strike out the claim or to dismiss the claim as a sanction). This could arise if the claim raises no proper cause of action, or is an abuse of process, or on the basis that there has been a failure to abide by an order of the court.

Examples of each of these could include:

• that the claim sets out no known 'cause of action' in law;

• that withdrawing, in bad faith, an admission previously made could be construed as an 'abuse of process';

- that attempting to relitigate a cause of action previously tried could also be an example of an 'abuse of process'; and
- a failure to abide by a court order or inordinate delay on the part of a party.

The court has the power to make orders under the provisions of CPR 3 on its own initiative, but the provisions can be used upon the application of a party. On occasion, an application under CPR 3 will be made in conjunction with an application for summary judgment under CPR 24—but note the distinction between the two applications set out in Chapter 14, paragraph 14.3.2.

 Practical Considerations

The provisions in CPR 3 will be exercised sparingly. In situations in which CPR 3 may apply, the court may determine that it would be more 'just' or appropriate to use the provisions of CPR 18 (see paragraph 10.7.4 below) to clarify the inadequate case. Alternatively, in the interests of 'justice', a court may also allow a party to amend its case rather than impose an order to strike out the claim.

10.7.3 MAKING AN APPLICATION FOR SECURITY FOR COSTS

A defendant has often not chosen to be embroiled in the litigation (although his behaviour may have been deliberately such that the claimant had no other option but to commence proceedings). Defending his position against the claim will cost him money. These costs can be considerable. Equally, a defendant will be at risk of an order for damages being made against him.

A defendant's armoury to protect against a judgment for damages against him will be in the steps that he can take to:

- prove his version of the 'story' that gives rise to the claim and absolve himself from any liability;
- show that a head of damage or a part of the loss is not recoverable so as to limit the claim against him; and
- show that the sum claimed should be as low as possible—that is, by showing a failure to mitigate by the claimant.

A defendant's armoury to protect him from the legal costs that he may incur in defending his claim includes:

- making a carefully pitched CPR Part 36 offer to transfer some of the risks of the costs of the action to the claimant (offers to settle and the consequences of such offers are detailed in Chapter 16);
- making an application for security for costs under the provisions of CPR 25.12. An application for security for costs is an interim application that a defendant (who may include the claimant in an action if the defendant has lodged a counterclaim against him—see *Nicholas G Jones Envircom Ltd and Ors* [2009] EWHC 16) can make in the circumstances set down in CPR 25.12. A successful application for security for costs will result in the claimant being ordered to pay a sum of money into court. The sum so held by the court office can then be used to meet all or some of any costs order that the claimant is ordered to pay to the defendant in the conclusion of the action. The overarching condition that needs to be satisfied is that the court will only make the order if it is just to do so. It could be argued that it would therefore be unjust to make an order when to do so would stifle the claimant's claim: for example, by restricting his financial viability or flexibility such that he is no longer able to fund and pursue his claim. In these situations, the court will have to balance the interests of the claimant and the defendant in any order it makes.

10.7.4 **MAKING A PART 18 REQUEST FOR FURTHER INFORMATION**

CPR Part 18 covers a situation in which a party's case may not have been made clear or explained in sufficient detail in his statement of case. One way in which to remedy this is to make a request for further information. The rule, subject to any rule of law or procedure to the contrary, enables a party to make a request of another party for:

- clarification of any matter that is in dispute in the proceedings; and/or
- additional information in relation to any such matter.

A defendant who wishes to make an application for further information is not thereby given additional time to file his defence unless the opponent agrees or an application is successfully made for additional time. Where a claimant's case is so badly drafted as to make filing a defence to it difficult, the defendant may often be better advised to make an application to strike out the case or to seek summary judgment than to use the provisions under CPR Part 18.

10.7.4.1 Procedure

Before making an application to the court for an order under Part 18, the party seeking clarification should first make a written request for the clarification that it seeks. It is generally good practice to create this request in formal form, so that it can be used as the application to the court if there is no, or a negative, response to the written request. The written request should allow the other party a reasonable time in which to respond (PD 18.1). The Practice Direction also gives guidance on the content of the formal request (PD 18.1.2–7).

Any response to the request should be in writing and should respond only to the matters raised in the request. In this way, the request and the response will clearly set out the issues arising from the Part 18 procedure. The response should contain a statement of truth.

If the respondent to the request objects to complying with the request, he should respond and say so with his reasons (PD 18.4).

If the respondent does not comply with the written request, and the party raising the request is not satisfied with the reasons and decides to proceed, he should file the application at court, and consider whether and what evidence should be filed. He must serve the other party with the application unless that party has made no response to the written request, in which case, the court can hear the application without a hearing. If the other party has responded to the request, but has objected to answering, the court will list the matter for a hearing.

The criteria that the court will apply in considering the matter will be whether the requests are reasonably necessary and proportionate to enable the requesting party to prepare his case or to understand the other party's case.

Details of the drafting of a request for further information are found in Chapter 11, paragraph 11.8.

KEY POINTS SUMMARY

- There are a variety of 'tactics' available to a defendant that may have the outcome of dismissing the claim (summary judgment) or securing him against the risks of the costs of defending the action (security for costs).

- A defendant need not take any action in response to the claim until he has been served with the particulars of claim.

- A defendant must take some step in response to the particulars of claim within 14 days—either by filing his defence or returning the form of acknowledgement of service.

- If a defendant intends to dispute the jurisdiction of the court, he must file the acknowledgement of service indicating that intention, but he must not take any other step in the proceedings.

- Be aware of the different types of additional claim and the defence of set-off.

- There are occasions on which more than one step may be taken and care needs to be taken to determine which is the most appropriate.

- Understand the position of admissions made by a party.

- Note the position when a case may be transferred to another court and when it will be automatically transferred.

SELF-TEST QUESTIONS

1. What are the elements of an action and in what way might a defendant seek to respond to them?

2. If a defendant makes a pre-action admission, how will the admission be treated in any subsequent litigation?

3. Which applications may be made by a defendant who believes that the claimant's case is very weak or does not (as it has been set down) reveal any substantive cause of action?

4. When will an application for security for costs *not* be successful?

5. When *must* a defendant respond to a claim made against him? What are the steps that he can take and when must he take those steps?

Suggested answers to these general questions can be accessed on the Online Resource Centre by your lecturer.

Case study *Bollingtons Ltd v Mrs Elizabeth Lynch t/a The Honest Lawyer*

The claim form indorsed with the particulars of claim has been correctly served in accordance with the CPR. The date upon which the defendant should have filed her acknowledgement of service and defence has passed. Default judgment has now been entered by the claimant's solicitors, although your client does not know that this has happened.

Acting for the defendant, you have today been telephoned by Mrs Lynch, a new client to the practice. You made a detailed note of your conversation, which appears as the attendance contained in the Online Resource Centre.

Question 1

What are the initial steps that you would take regarding the claim form and particulars of claim?

Question 2

Consider what issues you will need to cover in your first letter to your client.

Any documents referred to in these case study questions can be found on the Online Resource Centre—simply click on 'Case study documentation' to access the documents that you need for Chapter 10 and to be reminded of the questions above. Suggested answers to these case study questions can also be accessed on the Online Resource Centre.

FIGURE 10.1 COUNTERCLAIM BY DEFENDANT AGAINST CLAIMANT IN BREACH OF
CONTRACT ACTION. SEE EXAMPLE IN 10.6.2.1

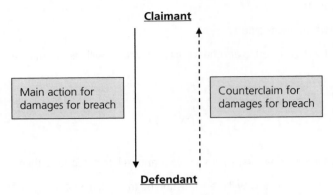

Note here that the title of the action remains the same.

FIGURE 10.2 COUNTERCLAIM BY DEFENDANT AGAINST SOMEONE OTHER THAN THE
CLAIMANT IN PERSONAL INJURY CLAIM WHEN CLAIMANT DRIVING IN THE COURSE OF HIS
EMPLOYMENT. SEE EXAMPLE IN 10.6.2.2

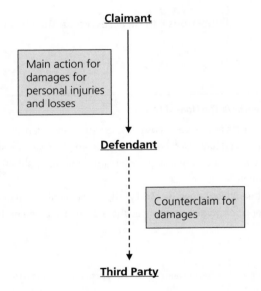

Note here that title of action changes but no court fees for
additional claim, i.e. the counterclaim.

FIGURE 10.3 ADDITIONAL CLAIM BY DEFENDANT SEEKING A CONTRIBUTION OR INDEMNITY IN BUILDING DISPUTE. SEE EXAMPLE IN 10.6.2.3

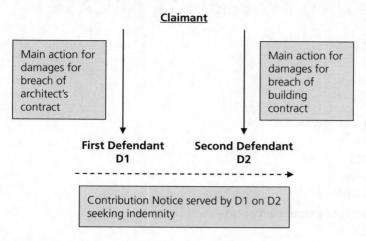

Note here that the title of the action remains the same.

FIGURE 10.4 ADDITIONAL CLAIM BY DEFENDANT AGAINST SOMEONE NOT YET A PARTY TO THE PROCEEDINGS IN BREACH OF CONTRACT ACTION. SEE EXAMPLE IN 10.6.2.4

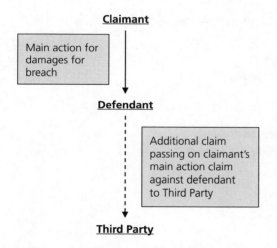

Note here that title of action changes and a court fee is required to move Third Party claim, i.e. the additional claim.

11 DRAFTING STATEMENTS OF CASE

11.1 INTRODUCTION

Drafting statements of case requires a logical and clear mind. Legal representatives will draft many statements of case, with the aim of producing accurate, relevant, and compelling formal court documents. This chapter provides key formulae to help those new to practice produce competent statements of case.

Whilst a claim form is a statement of case, how to complete this standard form has been dealt with in Chapter 9, paragraph 9.3.2. The Online Resource Centre features the claim form N1, accompanied by drafting tips on the form itself.

Below, we examine some statements of case. This list is not exhaustive, but represents those statements of case that you will come across most frequently in practice:

- particulars of claim;
- defences;
- additional claims;
- replies; and
- Part 18 requests.

11.2 THE PURPOSE OF A STATEMENT OF CASE

Whenever preparing a statement of case, there are a number of cardinal rules to remember in relation to the purpose of the statement of case, as follows.

11.2.1 PROVIDE AN OUTLINE

The court requires only an outline of a party's case on liability, causation, and quantum. In essence, this means the statement of case needs to set out the cause of action, the exact nature of the allegation(s) being made, and the financial consequences. The temptation is to provide each and every detail that you have in relation to each of these points, but these are to be left to form the basis of the main witness statements in the action.

11.2.2 PROVIDE CLARIFICATION

The purpose of the statement of case is to clarify matters in dispute so that the issues can be clearly identified by the court and the parties to the action.

11.2.3 SET OUT FACTUAL DETAILS

All matters being alleged are stated so that all parties in an action know in advance what is being alleged by each party against them. Generally, it is only the facts of a case that are 'stated'—that is, facts relating to the nature or background to a case, the issues, the allegations, and losses.

However, because the Civil Procedure Rules (CPR) encourage considerable pre-action work being undertaken, the parties will normally be in a position to refer to some evidence in the statement of case and, on occasions, to exhibit it. This makes the art of drafting considerably simpler. It will also have the benefit of adding weight to a case for the party who can refer to or exhibit strong evidence in favour of his case. It may, however, be a question of reasonableness, judgment, or a mandatory requirement as to the relevancy or the inclusion of the evidence to be included or annexed.

11.2.4 IDENTIFY LEGAL REQUIREMENTS

Every piece of litigation must have a legal basis upon which a claim can be founded: for example, a claim in tort must be considered to exist before a negligence claim can proceed. However, generally, the law is not to be stated in the statement of case, because the judge is presumed to know it. Nevertheless, there is no prohibition against doing so and the law, in terms of a statute or regulation, may be stated where it is thought necessary. For example, if there is a particularly unusual point of law to be taken, or a little-known piece of legislation or a statutory defence, then the relevant law can be stated. This is particularly prevalent in accident at work claims (see the example in paragraph 11.4.1.3 below).

11.3 THE STANDARD REQUIREMENTS OF A STATEMENT OF CASE

In paragraph 11.4 below, we have set out a series of 'formulae for drafting' specific to different types of civil action. Here, it is the intention to highlight some general practical, but important, drafting hints that are particular to all statements of case, as follows.

- The statement of case should import the court heading of the action and state what type of statement of case it is directly below the court heading.
- The statement of case should always be in the third person: 'the claimant', 'the defendant', etc.
- Numbered paragraphs should always be used, frequently with subparagraphs or even subheadings if a paragraph is long. The judge, opposing lawyers, and any expert witnesses in the case do not want to lose the 'thread' and have to reread the statement of case. This may only irritate those who read it. Paragraph numbers also make reference to specific parts of a statement of case much simpler.
- The statement of case is the draftsman's opportunity to be articulate and clear on paper. When reading older statements of case, take care not to pick up on and replicate antiquated language such as 'hereinbefore' and 'bequeath'.
- There is a requirement to include a statement of truth on every statement of case. The statement of truth is said to add weight to a statement of case and should act to restrict the action to legitimate issues rather than statements of 'hopeful' allegations, which may have little chance of succeeding at trial. Increasingly, the judges are making costs orders (CPR Part 44) that reflect the numbers of issues with which a party may have proceeded to trial, and considering whether this was a sensible, proportionate, fair, and just thing to do (CPR Part 1).

11.3.1 THE STATEMENT OF TRUTH

All statements of case, witness statements, experts' reports, applications in support of interim matters, or reply to CPR 18 requests must contain a statement of truth. CPR 22.1 provides additional occasions when a statement of truth must be provided. Disclosure must also be accompanied by a statement that the party making disclosure understands his duties to disclose and that he has carried out the search for documents to the best of his ability (CPR 31.10(6)(b) and (c)).

A failure to provide a statement of truth on a document where one is required will mean that although the document will remain effective unless it is subsequently struck out, the party may not rely on the statement as evidence of any matter set out in it (CPR 22.2). Where a witness statement does not contain a statement of truth, the court may direct that it may not be admissible as evidence (CPR 22.3).

The form of the statement of truth is set out in Practice Direction (PD) 22.2.1 and 22.2.2 as follows.

- For a statement of case:

    [I believe] [the (claimant or as may be) believes] that the facts stated in this [name the document being verified] are true.

- For a witness statement:

    I believe the facts stated in this witness statement are true.

11.3.2 WHO SHOULD SIGN THE STATEMENT OF TRUTH?

Practice Direction 22.3 sets out who should sign the statement of truth. In general, it should be the party or his legal representative, but best practice indicates that, for all statements of case, the party itself should sign the statement of truth. PD 22.3 will need to be looked at where the party is a company, a partnership, or an insurer.

11.3.3 WHAT ARE THE CONSEQUENCES OF MAKING A STATEMENT OF TRUTH WHEN THE CONTENTS OF THE DOCUMENT, OR ANY PART OF IT, ARE KNOWN TO BE FALSE?

Proceedings for contempt may be brought against a person if he makes, or causes to be made, a false statement of truth. Proceedings for contempt may only be brought by the Attorney-General or with the permission of the court (CPR 32.14 and PD 32.28).

11.4 THE PARTICULARS OF CLAIM

The principal rules surrounding the drafting of a particulars of claim can be found in CPR 16 and its Practice Direction. On the reverse side of Form N1 can be found a space in which to draft the particulars. It is not mandatory and usually not sensible or appropriate to draft the particulars of claim in that section of the claim form in every case; rather, it will be a question of common sense in terms of how much you have to say and whether there is enough room to set out your case clearly. It will usually only be a fairly straightforward claim, such as a debt claim, that can be fitted on the reverse side of the claim form.

Drafting can get quite technical, but it is important to remember a guiding principle—that is, 'tell the story'. The story is told to the defendant from the claimant's point of view, and is essentially very simple, as follows.

1. 'This is who we are ...'
2. 'This is who you are ...'
3. 'This is what happened ...'
4. 'It is your fault/breach ...'
5. 'This was the result of what happened ...'
6. 'And so this is what I want from you ...'

Remember, the claim must set out those facts and allegations that, if proved, would give the claimant the right to the remedy sought as a matter of law.

Against this simplistic theory of drafting a particulars of claim, the drafting formulae can now be brought into play. These will assist in the drafting of each of the most common statements of case and, if followed, can provide a good basic structure for even the most complex of cases, whether of high or low value.

11.4.1 THE FORMULAE

11.4.1.1 A claim for a breach of contract

A claim for a breach of contract should deal with the following matters in the following order.

1. The parties (and, if appropriate, the name of the parties' representatives) to, and the date (if written) or approximate date (if oral) of, the agreement.
2. The nature and purpose of the agreement and the consideration.
3. Any relevant express or implied terms of the contract that the claimant alleges have been breached by the defendant, generally stating any express terms first and then any implied terms.

4. The facts concerning each breach alleged (with sufficient details to identify what is the alleged breach).

5. Losses that flow from the alleged breach (with particulars of the losses).

6. Interest (see the worked example in paragraph 11.10 below for a fuller consideration).

7. The 'prayer'—that is, a brief summary of what is being claimed. It does not add anything new to the document. For example:

AND THE CLAIMANT CLAIMS—

1. The sum of £ . . . . . . ;

2. Interest.

8. A statement of truth and relevant authorization paragraph, if appropriate.

9. The date of the document and the 'author' (which may be the firm acting).

A detailed discussion of a worked example of a breach of contract claim is examined in paragraph 11.10 below.

11.4.1.1.1 *Example of breach of contract claim*

IN THE HIGH COURT OF JUSTICE   201?- L- 6776

QUEEN'S BENCH DIVISION

LEEDS DISTRICT REGISTRY

BETWEEN

           DALE AND CO LTD   **CLAIMANT**

                     AND

           MPR LTD   **DEFENDANT**

PARTICULARS OF CLAIM

1. The Claimant is a private limited company carrying on business as a manufacturer of wood products.

2. The Defendant is a private limited company supplying woodworking machinery.

3. By a written Purchase Order dated 10 . . . . , the Defendant agreed to supply and the Claimant agreed to purchase an MPR X20 woodcutting machine ('the X20') for the total cash price of £45,000 plus VAT payable by an initial deposit of 20% on the placement of the order and the balance due on delivery of the X20. The Claimant made the deposit payment on 25 . . . . in the sum of £9,000 plus VAT and paid the balance plus VAT on 1 . . . . Payment was therefore made in full by the Claimant.

4. There were implied terms of the agreement that the X20 would be of satisfactory quality and fit for the purpose for which it was provided—namely, as a specialist woodcutting machine capable of achieving a high degree of accuracy and speed.

5. The X20 was delivered on the due date, and installation and commissioning of the X20 was completed on or about 17 . . . .

6. In breach of the implied terms, the X20 was neither of satisfactory quality nor fit for the purpose for which it was supplied.

PARTICULARS OF BREACH

6.1. The X20 seized up within five hours of installation.

6.2. The speed of the X20 was much slower than the more inferior model (the X18) in the range.

6.3. The operating cycle had been jarring, which caused the head synchronization and changing process to become significantly slower than the X18.

6.4. The X20 was supplied as a precision piece of machinery with four adjustable heads, but two of those adjustable heads regularly fell out of alignment by 0.3 mm during the production process, with the result that the X20 was rendered unsuitable for the production of products that required precision woodcutting.

The Claimant will seek to rely on the engineer's service reports for the period January . . . . , October . . . . , and the evidence of a jointly instructed expert at the trial of the matter.

7. By reason of the breach of the implied terms, the Claimant has suffered loss and damage.

PARTICULARS OF LOSS AND DAMAGE

The purchase price plus VAT	£52,875
Loss of production costs resulting from 125 hours of down time due to the failure of the X20	£10,000
Loss of business and goodwill	To be quantified

8. Further, the Claimant claims interest pursuant to s. 35A of the Senior Courts Act 1981 on the amount to be found due to the Claimant at such a rate and for such a period as the court thinks fit.

AND THE CLAIMANT CLAIMS—

(1) Damages pursuant to paragraph 7 above;
(2) Interest pursuant to s. 35A of the Senior Courts Act 1981.

STATEMENT OF TRUTH

I believe the facts stated in these Particulars of Claim are true. I am duly authorized by the Claimant to sign this statement on its behalf.

Signed . . . .

Managing Director

Dated this . . . .

11.4.1.2 An action in negligence—a road traffic accident (RTA)

An action in negligence relating to a road traffic accident (RTA) should deal with the following and usually in this order.

1. Sufficient details to identify the incident should be set out, including a simple description that a collision occurred, on a particular date, at a particular time and place, and between the parties. Where an existing duty of care applies by implication, there is no need to state this: for example, where the RTA occurred on the public highway, then

there arises a clear duty of care by all road users to other road users and pedestrians. Where the existence of the duty of care is less obvious, it may be necessary to state it in the document.

2. A statement, with details of the negligence of the defendant, including specific examples of his negligence.

3. Any **relevant** previous convictions. When a conviction of an offence is relevant to the issues of the case, it may be pleaded. When this occurs, details of the conviction, its date, the court in which it was made, and the relevance to the cause of action in which that conviction is stated should be stated.

4. The fact that the claimant suffered injury as a result of the negligence, along with brief details of those injuries, referring to the appended medical report(s).

5. That losses have been sustained as referred to in a schedule of losses containing full details of those losses.

6. Interest pursuant to the relevant statute.

7. The 'prayer' for the relief sought, as above: damages and interest.

8. A statement of truth and authorization (if appropriate), as above.

9. The date of the document and the 'author' (which may be the firm acting).

11.4.1.2.1 *Example of a particulars of claim*

IN THE CREWE COUNTY COURT   Case No.CR345267

BETWEEN

Miss Chloe Whitfield   Claimant

and

Mr Stephen Broad   Defendant

PARTICULARS OF CLAIM

1. The Claimant was the driver of an Audi A4 motor car, registration number GH51 OLM. The Defendant was the owner and driver of a Ford Focus, registration number VG52 BLU.

2. On 16 July 201?, in the vicinity of the Cloversmead Shopping Centre, the Claimant was driving down Hayhurst Avenue and turned left into Warrington Way, when a collision occurred with the Defendant's car. The position of impact is indicated on the attached map.

3. The collision was caused by the negligence of the Defendant.

PARTICULARS OF NEGLIGENCE

(1) The Defendant failed to keep any or any proper lookout.

(2) The Defendant failed to stop, or slow down, or swerve, or in any other way to control his motor car so as to avoid the accident.

(3) The Defendant was driving at a speed that was excessive in the circumstances.

(4) The Defendant drove through a red light on Warrington Way.

(5) The Defendant was speaking on his mobile phone.

4. As a result, the Claimant has sustained injuries and suffered loss and damage.

PARTICULARS OF LOSS AND DAMAGE

The Claimant's date of birth is 20 November 1983. The Claimant suffered a whiplash injury and fractured her sternum. She suffers from headaches, pain in the neck and chest, and numbness in the outer upper arms. The Claimant held twice-weekly yoga classes at the local community centre, but has been unable to resume these classes since the accident. The injuries and symptoms are fully described in the attached medical report, prepared by Mr Christopher Kartby, consultant orthopaedic surgeon, dated . . . . . .

The Claimant refers to the attached Schedule of Losses for details of her special damages.

5. The Claimant claims interest pursuant to s. 69 of the County Courts Act 1984 at such rate and for such period as the court thinks fit.

AND THE CLAIMANT CLAIMS—

(1) Damages;
(2) Interest pursuant to s. 69 of the County Courts Act 1984.

STATEMENT OF TRUTH

I believe that the facts stated in these Particulars of Claim are true.

Dated this . . . .

11.4.1.3 An action in negligence—a factory accident

An action in negligence relating to a factory accident should deal with the following matters and usually in this order.

1. The relationship of the employer and employee should be established (or that of the factory owner and the visitor), and the application of any relevant statutory provisions (for example, the Factories Act 1961) should be set out.
2. Details of the accident at the premises, with brief particulars as to how it happened.
3. An allegation that the accident was caused by the negligence or breach of statutory duty of the owner, or employer, or employee, with particulars and any specific statutory provisions.
4. That, as a result of the alleged negligence/breach of statutory duty the claimant suffered injury and loss, with particulars of both and annexed medical report(s) and schedule of losses.
5. Interest.
6. The 'prayer' for relief—damages and interest (as above).
7. A statement of truth and authority (if appropriate).
8. The date of the document and the 'author' (which may be the firm acting).

 Professional Conduct

Often, accidents at work are caused by the incompetence of a fellow employee. Consider the situation in which, acting for a claimant employee, you enter into Protocol with a potential employer defendant claiming damages for personal injuries. The employer fails to confirm that the fellow employee was acting in the course of his employment. If it is necessary for you to commence proceedings, you will need to issue against both the fellow employee and the employer until such time as the employer confirms vicarious liability either in correspondence or on the filing of his defence, at which point you can amend your particulars of claim to remove the fellow employee. This course of action is necessary to ensure that you have a cause of action against an appropriate party.

11.4.1.3.1 *Example of a particulars of claim*

IN THE HIGH COURT OF JUSTICE   201?-D-8976

QUEEN'S BENCH DIVISION

STOKE ON TRENT DISTRICT REGISTRY

BETWEEN

MR SIMON HERBERT   Claimant

and

ARISTA LOGISTICS LIMITED   Defendant

PARTICULARS OF CLAIM

1. The Claimant was employed by the Defendant as a forklift truck driver at Gladstone Lock warehouse, Regent Road, Stoke on Trent. The nature of the Claimant's work is regulated by the Provision and Use of Work Equipment Regulations 1992, SI 1992/2932, and the Manual Handling Operations Regulations 1992, SI 1992/2793.

2. On 29 May 201?, in the course of his employment, the Claimant was loading a steel rod of approximately 3.5 metres in length and weighing just over 100 kilos onto his forklift truck. By reason of the weight of the rod, it had to be loaded mechanically, and by reason of its length, it had to be placed on the forklift truck lengthways. Accordingly, it could not be placed across the forklift truck, but had to be positioned on the forks pointing away from the mast of the forklift. By reason of its length and despite using long forks, it would not stay on the forks unless strapped on. The Claimant and his colleague were attempting to strap the steel rod onto the forks of the forklift truck in order to secure it for transportation to the back of a lorry when it rolled off the forks and dropped directly onto the arch of the Claimant's left foot.

3. The accident was caused by the negligence and/or breach of statutory duty of the Defendant or its employees.

PARTICULARS OF NEGLIGENCE/BREACH OF STATUTORY DUTY

The Defendant was negligent in that it—

(i) Failed to devise and implement for the Claimant a safe system of work;

(ii) Failed to ensure that the Claimant had received adequate training and/or health and safety information, negligently and/or in breach of its statutory duty under regs 8 and/or 9 of the Provision and Use of Work Equipment Regulations 1992;

(iii) Failed to provide competent staff (the Claimant's case is that an overhead crane ought to have been used in order to load the metal rods onto the lorry);

(iv) Failed to exercise any or any adequate care for the safety of the Claimant;

(v) Failed, so far as was reasonably practicable, to avoid the need for the Claimant to undertake the said manual loading operation, in particular by not providing any, or any suitable, mechanical lifting equipment, negligently and/or in breach of its statutory duty under reg. 4(1)(a) of the Manual Handling Operations Regulations 1992;

(vi) Failed, so far as was reasonably practicable, to make a suitable and sufficient assessment of such manual handling operation, negligently and/or in breach

---

of its statutory duty under reg. 4(1)(b) of the Manual Handling Operations Regulations 1992;

(vii) Failed to ensure that lifting equipment—namely, the forklift truck—was suitable for the purpose for which it was used, negligently and/or in breach of its statutory duty under reg. 5 of the Provision and Use of Work Equipment Regulations 1992;

(viii) Failed to ensure that the said forklift truck was used only for operations, and under conditions, for which it was suitable, negligently and/or in breach of its statutory duty under reg. 5 of the Provision and Use of Work Equipment Regulations 1992.

4. By reason of the above, the Claimant has suffered personal injury, loss, and damage.

PARTICULARS OF LOSS AND INJURY

The Claimant, who was born on 26 January 1950, sustained two broken bones in his left foot. Full details of the Claimant's orthopaedic injuries are contained in the medical report of Mr Mark O'Brien, dated 15 September 201?, annexed. The Claimant also now suffers from post-traumatic stress disorder as a result of the crush injury to his left foot. A psychiatric report of Dr Nichola Davies, dated 29 October 201?, is also attached.

The Claimant sustained a variety of financial losses and these are detailed in the attached Schedule of Losses.

AND THE CLAIMANT CLAIMS—

(1) Damages;
(2) Interest at such rates and for such periods as the court deems fit.

Dated this . . . .

STATEMENT OF TRUTH

I believe that the facts in these Particulars of Claim are true.

11.4.1.4 A debt action for goods sold and delivered, but not paid for

A claim for goods sold and delivered, but not paid for, should deal with the following matters and usually in this order.

1. The nature of the goods sold and delivered, the date of the delivery, any invoice details (with attached copy), and the price.

2. The fact that the goods have not been paid for, and that payment is still due and owing.

3. Interest pursuant to statute or under the terms of the contract.

4. The 'prayer' for relief—the price of the goods and interest.

5. A statement of truth with relevant authorization (if appropriate).

6. The date of the document and the 'author' (which may be the firm acting).

The particulars for debt claims are usually very short and appear on the reverse of the claim form.

The following example shows the particulars as seen on the reverse of a claim form in a straightforward debt action. A claim form that contains the particulars of claim in this way is known as an 'indorsed claim form'.

11.4.1.4.1 *Example of an indorsed claim form*

---

1. The Claimant claims the sum of £5,000 plus VAT in respect of electrical components supplied and delivered to the Defendant in accordance with the terms of a written contract made between the parties dated 25 April 201?.

2. The Claimant delivered the goods on the agreed delivery date of 1 February, but the Defendant has failed to pay the invoice, a copy of which is attached.

3. The total sum of £5,000 remains due and owing.

4. The Claimant claims interest at the contractual rate of 8% per annum from the due date of payment to judgment or sooner payment in the sum of £xxx and continuing at a daily rate of £x.

AND THE CLAIMANT CLAIMS—

(1) The sum of £5,000;

(2) Interest in the sum of £xxx and continuing at a daily rate of £x, pursuant to the contractual interest rate.

I believe the facts stated in these Particulars of Claim are true. I am duly authorized by the Claimant to sign this statement on its behalf.

. . . .

Dated . . . .

11.5 THE DEFENCE

The principal rules concerning the drafting of the defence can be found in CPR Parts 15 and 16, and their associated Practice Directions. The use of Forms N9B (a claim for a specified sum) or N9D (a claim for an unspecified claim or a non-money claim), included in the response pack and served with the particulars of claim, may be used to file a defence.

The use of these forms is not mandatory and often there is insufficient space in any but the simplest claim to prepare a fully pleaded defence on the forms. These forms are usually only ever completed by litigants in person—that is, those without legal representation. In practice, the defence will be prepared as a separate document.

A defence is required when a defendant wishes to defend all or part of a claim. Once filed, a copy of the defence must be served on every other party. The time limits for the filing of a defence are set out at CPR 15.4 (see also Chapter 10, paragraph 10.5).

Under CPR 15.5, the defendant and the claimant may agree that the time for filing a defence be extended for a period up to a maximum of an extra 28 days. Where the claimant consents to the requested extension, the defendant must notify the court in writing of the agreement to extend time. Any need for further time must be made by application to the court under CPR 3.1, because the CPR do not afford any authority to the claimant to agree to any further extensions of time (see also Chapter 10, paragraph 10.5.2.1).

11.5.1 THE FORMULA

The defence should deal with every material allegation contained in the particulars of claim. The simplest way in which to do this is to respond to each paragraph of the statement of case in the order in which it appears, and to deal with each allegation in each paragraph.

For each response, the defendant has four options:

- he may **admit** the allegation;
- he may **deny** the allegation;
- he may **refuse to admit** or **make no admissions** to the allegation; or
- he may seek to shift the blame.

11.5.1.1 Admissions

Allegations that can be admitted *should* be admitted: for example, if there was a collision or a contract, in accordance with your client's instructions, you should be able to admit that fact. However, care should be taken not to admit that which should not be admitted (see the 'Professional Conduct' box below). Conversely, a failure to admit statements that should have been admitted may have costs consequences for the defendant (see Chapter 10, paragraph 10.3.4.2).

 Professional Conduct

If, in drafting a defence, you admit an allegation that should not have been admitted, then, depending on the nature and extent of that which has been admitted, this may have a profound effect on the ability to continue to defend either part or all of the case on liability, causation, and quantum. It may be possible to amend the defence under CPR 17, but this, again, will depend on the nature of erroneous admission made. Needless to say, you may need to cease acting for your client, because a conflict is likely to arise under Solicitors' Code of Conduct 2007, Rule 1.05, on the basis of not being able to provide a good standard of service to your client.

11.5.1.1.1 *Example of an admission in an RTA claim*

'Paragraph 1 of the Particulars of Claim is admitted.'

11.5.1.2 Denials

Where an allegation is denied, in accordance with your client's instructions, the defendant needs to put his side of the story forward. A bare denial is not acceptable under the CPR. It is therefore important to remember, when drafting the defendant's version of events, that he needs to give an explanation of *how* and, in some cases, *why* the event happened, not simply to justify his own position. This will often involve allegations that the accident or breach and the resultant losses were caused by the negligence or breach of either the claimant or somebody else.

For example, in an action for damages arising from an RTA, it is likely that the *fact* of the collision can be admitted. The defendant, in his defence, may be saying that the collision was not his fault (that is, he may be denying the allegation), but if he has admitted that a collision occurred, his defence needs to explain how the accident happened. Simply denying the allegations of the claimant does not do this; rather, the defendant needs to explain by blaming someone else or by some other event *how* the accident did happen. This explanation in this example will need to set out clearly allegations of contributory negligence.

 Practical Considerations

This is an aspect of drafting that those new to practice find difficult, because there is a tendency to try to justify why the defendant was not doing what the claimant is alleging he did in its particulars of negligence, or breach of contract, or statutory duty. When planning out what you are going to say, do not attempt to justify his position by saying 'it was not the defendant who was driving negligently because he did not drive too fast, he did keep a proper lookout, etc . . . .', but instead put the ball back into the claimant's court by saying 'it was not the defendant who was driving negligently, it was the claimant, and this is what the claimant did to show that he drove negligently: he drove too fast; he did not keep a proper lookout, etc . . . .'

The theoretical reason why we do not recite why the defendant personally did not drive negligently relates to burdens of proof, which is discussed in Chapter 18, paragraph 18.2.1.

A defendant can also deny a claim if the limitation period for the action has expired: for example, in a breach of contract action, proceedings must be issued within six years of the date of the breach. For the defendant to take advantage of this defence, he must state limitation as an issue in the defence. If he fails to do so, then he will not be able to rely on it unless he seeks to amend his defence.

For further discussion on limitation periods generally, see Chapter 7, paragraph 7.4.

11.5.1.2.1 *Example of a personal injury RTA claim (as in paragraph 11.4.1.2)*

'3. It is denied that the Defendant drove negligently as stated in paragraph X. The collision was caused or contributed to by the Claimant.'

11.5.1.2.2 *Example of a breach of contract claim (as in paragraph 11.4.1.1)*

'4. Paragraph 5 of the Particulars of Claim is admitted, save for the fact that it is denied that the X20 was delivered on time, and that the installation and commissioning processes were completed satisfactorily, or at all.'

11.5.1.3 Refusing to admit, or making no admissions

The defendant may refuse to admit allegations that he can neither deny nor admit usually because he has no knowledge of those elements. For example, in a claimant's claim for personal injuries, this will include both general and special damages, and the defendant will have to consider what he has to say in relation to the cause, and the nature and extent, of the losses.

In relation to the claim for general damages, at this early stage of the litigation, the defendant is usually unlikely to be in a position to deny that the claimant has been injured. Remember that the purpose of the defence is to deny liability for them. By the time of the preparation of the defence, the defendant will have seen the claimant's evidence of its general damages—namely, the medical report. If the defendant has not either agreed the claimant's medical report or obtained its own medical report, or a joint report, then he is not in a position either to admit or deny either the causation, or the nature and extent, of those injuries until such time as he has his own evidence or has agreed that of the opponent.

In these circumstances, it is usual for the defendant to make no admissions as to the cause, or nature or extent, of the injuries, because he simply has no knowledge of these. By making no admissions, the defendant is effectively refusing to admit a statement by the claimant, the effect of which is to leave the claimant with the burden of proving his allegation or fact. Thus the claimant will have the burden of providing evidence for his losses.

In relation to the special damages claim, in straightforward cases, the defendant will probably try to agree only the amount with the claimant (either part of or all the claim for special damages) at some stage in the action before trial because the evidence has been seen and is usually not wholly contentious. The defendant's assertion that he is not liable for them remains and therefore he is said 'to admit special damages subject to liability'.

In theory, therefore, it would be perfectly acceptable to admit the claimant's financial losses if, for example, the pre-action work had enabled the defendant to see evidence of the claimant's claim for special damages. The defence will make it quite clear that the defendant denies being the cause of those losses.

11.5.1.3.1 *Example of 'no admission' in the RTA personal injury claim (as in paragraph 11.4.1.2)*

'4. No admissions are made as to any of the Claimant's injuries as set out in paragraph 4 of the Particulars of Claim and in the medical report of Mr Kartby, dated . . . The Claimant is put to strict proof of the nature and extent of the those injuries.'

11.5.1.4 Shifting the blame

The 'option' for the defendant in drafting his defence of 'shifting the blame' is a hybrid and is usually linked to the option to deny outlined in paragraph 11.5.1.2 above. The defendant, in giving his explanation as to 'how' the events described by the claimant happened, may seek to attack the claimant's statement of case by alleging, in his own version of events, that the blame lay elsewhere. If this is to be done, then, again, the defendant's version of events needs to be set out.

For example, in an RTA claim, the defendant may seek to assert in his defence that the collision did not occur through the defendant's negligence, but rather as a result of the claimant's own negligence. The statement of case would then need to particularize the allegations of negligence of the claimant.

When someone other than a party in the proceedings is alleged to have been negligent, then that third party will have to be made aware of the allegations being made against them, as set out in CPR Part 20, and separate proceedings will need to be concurrently issued. This is known as an 'additional claim' and is discussed in Chapter 10, paragraph 10.6.2.

11.5.1.4.1 *Example of an RTA personal injury claim (as in paragraph 11.4.1.2)*

PARTICULARS OF NEGLIGENCE

The Claimant was negligent in that she:

(a) failed to keep any or any proper lookout;

(b) drove too fast in the circumstances;

(c) drove into a collision with the Defendant's vehicle;

(d) failed by means of the brakes, steering, gears, or otherwise to manage and control her car so as to avoid the collision.

11.5.1.4.2 *Example of a breach of contract claim (as in paragraph 11.4.1.1)*

'5. It is denied that the X20 was neither of satisfactory quality nor fit for purpose, as alleged in paragraph 6 of the Particulars of Claim. The Defendant states as follows:

(i) in relation to 6.1 of the Particulars of Claim, the Defendant contends that the Claimant's operative, Timothy Grave, failed to follow the operator's manual steps 1–3, causing the X20 to seize;

(ii) . . . .'

11.5.1.5 A 'traverse'

The part of a defence often called a 'traverse' contains a 'general denial' clause. This has the intended effect of dealing with any matter with which the defendant has failed to deal in the main body of his defence. It is a safety precaution, but must not be used to protect against poor drafting.

11.5.1.5.1 *Example of a standard traverse*

'In the circumstances, it is denied that the Claimant is entitled to the losses claimed or any losses for the reasons alleged or at all.' *or*

'Save where expressly admitted or not admitted, each and every allegation set out in the Particulars of Claim is denied.'

11.5.2 **WHAT IF THE PARTICULARS OF CLAIM HAS BEEN POORLY DRAFTED?**

The structure illustrated in paragraph 11.5.1 has set a framework for drafting a defence to a well-articulated particulars of claim. In practice, many are not so well set out—especially those that are drafted by litigants in person. Rather than trying to respond to each and every paragraph, no matter how long or confusing the particulars of claim may be (which will only create an unintelligible defence), a more effective way to deal with the inadequate statement of case would be to draft the defence as if it were a particulars of claim, with an introductory paragraph informing the court and your opponent what you are doing. To give you the added protection of not failing to respond to any allegation, make use of the traverse clause and use it as your comfort zone. (Here, you would not be using it to cover up poor drafting.)

11.5.2.1 Example of an extract of a poorly drafted particulars of claim

1. I bought a Ford KA from Andersons in July for £3,750. When I took it back I told Mr Sharpe that it vibrated. He said it was nothing to worry about so I went home. Three weeks later the car broke down on the motorway. The RAC man said the cambelt had gone. I asked Mr Sharpe for my money back but he refused.

2. I felt that I have been duped and that I should be entitled to my money back as I only had the car for 4 months.

I believe that the contents of the Particulars of Claim are true.

11.5.2.2 Example of an extract of a properly drafted defence

The Defendant responds to the entirety of the Particulars of Claim as follows:

1. The Defendant is a sole trader carrying on business as a retailer of new and used cars.

2. By a written agreement dated . . . , the Defendant sold the Claimant a used Ford KA for £3,750. At the time of the sale the Claimant was aware that the sale price had been reduced to reflect the fact that the car had not had its 30,000-mile service.

3. There were the following relevant terms of the agreement:

(i) That in consideration of the Defendant having reduced the purchase price to £3,750, the Claimant would have the car serviced by a third party;

(ii) that the Defendant gave the Claimant a 3-month warranty in respect of faults developing in the Ford KA.

4. In or about July 201?, after expiry of the warranty period, the Claimant returned the Ford KA and complained that it was vibrating. The Defendant inspected the car and identified that the wheels needed tracking. Thus was done without charge to the Claimant.

5. At the end of November 201?, the Claimant complained that the cambelt had broken and demanded a refund of the purchase price. Her request was refused for the reasons stated above.

6. No admissions are made to any of the breakdown allegations or the causes of those breakdown allegations. If, which is not admitted the cambelt did break, it did so after the expiry of the 3-month warranty.

7. It is therefore denied that the Claimant is entitled to a refund of the purchase price or to any losses for the reason set out in this defence.

I believe the contents of this Defence are true.

11.6 ADDITIONAL CLAIMS

Here, we are going to look at two of the four possible additional claims identified in Chapter 10: the counterclaim against the claimant (CPR 20.4), and the additional claim against another person (CPR 20.7).

11.6.1 A COUNTERCLAIM AGAINST THE CLAIMANT

The nature of this counterclaim is covered in Chapter 10, paragraph 10.6.2.1. This is the situation in which the defendant alleges that he has (usually) a monetary claim against the claimant that may arise from the same set of facts as appear in the particulars of claim and defence, or it may be an entirely separate matter. A counterclaim is capable of standing alone as an action in its own right, but it is raised as a counterclaim for convenience, and to save time and money. The rules, therefore, for drafting a counterclaim are the same as those for drafting an initial statement of case—that is, the particulars of claim.

11.6.1.1 Example of a counterclaim in an RTA personal injury claim (as in paragraph 11.4.1.2)

COUNTERCLAIM

1. The Defendant repeats paragraphs . . . to . . . of its defence.
2. By reason of the matters raised in the defence, the Defendant has suffered the following loss and damage:

PARTICULARS OF SPECIAL DAMAGE

Repair costs to car   £2,000

3. The Defendant further claims interest at such a rate and for such a period as the court deems fit.

AND THE DEFENDANT COUNTERCLAIMS—

(1) Damages in the sum of £2,000;
(2) Interest as above.

I believe the contents of this counterclaim are true.

. . . .

Dated . . . .

11.6.2 AN ADDITIONAL CLAIM AGAINST ANOTHER PERSON

The nature of this type of additional claim is covered in Chapter 10, paragraph 10.6.2.4. Here, there are two sets of documents that you will need to prepare: the 'Part 20 claim form', and the 'defendant's additional claim against the third party'.

The drafting of the Part 20 claim form follows the same principles as those set out in Chapter 9, paragraph 9.3.2, for the main action claim form. In this chapter, we will therefore focus on the defendant's additional claim against the third party. This statement of case can be adapted for further derivatives of additional claims under CPR 20.7: for example, a third party's claim against a fourth party, and so on.

The key to drafting these additional claims is set out as follows.

1. The opening paragraph of this statement of case should summarize the original and existing statements of case already served—that is, the particulars of claim against the defendant and the defence (and counterclaim).

2. The additional claim should also state and annex to it copies of all of these statements of case.

3. The additional claim should expressly deny the claim being made against the defendant.

4. The additional claim should then go on to make allegations against the third party and explain why the defendant is blaming him.

5. The additional claim should state the losses the defendant is seeking. These cannot be particularised at the time of drafting the additional claim. As such, all the defendant can do is to state that he seeks to recover the amount which the claimant may recover against him in the main action. This is done by way of an indemnity or contribution in the prayer, or by a request for damages generally.

11.6.2.1 Example of a defendant's additional claim against a third party

---

IN THE HIGH COURT OF JUSTICE   201?- R-2456

QUEEN'S BENCH DIVISION

MANCHESTER DISTRICT REGISTRY

BETWEEN

MILLARD AND CO LTD   CLAIMANT

AND

SMT LTD   DEFENDANT

AND

COLVILLE CONTRACTORS (A FIRM) THIRD PARTY

DEFENDANT'S ADDITIONAL CLAIM AGAINST THIRD PARTY

1. This action has been brought by the Claimant against the Defendant. The Claimant claims from the Defendant damages and interest for an alleged breach of contract for the manufacture and supply of stainless steel cladding ('the Cladding'), as appears from the Particulars of Claim, a copy of which is served with this Additional Claim, along with the written contract, dated 17 September 201?.

2. The Defendant denies that it is liable to the Claimant on the grounds set out in its Defence, a copy of which is also served with this Additional Claim. These Particulars of Additional Claim set out the Defendant's Additional Claim against the Third Party on which the Defendant will rely if it is found liable to the Claimant.

3. By a written purchase order no. 55648 dated 1 October 201?, a copy of which is annexed to this Additional Claim made between the Defendant and the Third Party, the Third Party agreed to manufacture and deliver the Cladding for a price agreed at £32,500.

4. It was an implied term of the agreement that the Cladding would be of satisfactory quality and fit for its purpose.

5. On 5 January 201?, the Third Party, pursuant to the purchase order, manufactured and delivered the Cladding to the premises of the Claimant at Runcorn Works.

6. In breach of the above implied term, the Cladding was neither of satisfactory quality nor fit for purpose.

<u>**PARTICULARS OF BREACH**</u>

6.1. The Cladding buckled when fixed to the rear elevation of the claimant's commercial unit at Runcorn Works.

6.2. The Cladding rusted and detached from the entrance area to the said commercial unit.

6.3. Over the entire unit, the Cladding has discoloured and deteriorated to the extent that water ingress has occurred.

7. As a result of the matters set out above, the Defendant has suffered loss and damage to the extent of its liability (if any) to the Claimant, any costs that it may be ordered to pay to the Claimant, and its costs incurred in defending the Claimant's claim.

AND THE DEFENDANT ADDITIONALLY CLAIMS—

(i) An indemnity or contribution in respect of the Claimant's claim;

(ii) Alternatively, damages.

STATEMENT OF TRUTH

I believe that the facts stated in these Particulars are true. I am duly authorized by the Defendant to sign this statement.

Signed . . . .

Dated. . . . .

11.7 THE REPLY

11.7.1 WHAT IS A REPLY?

A 'reply' is a statement of case that responds to a defence, as discussed in CPR 15 and 16 and in Chapter 10, paragraph 10.6.2.7. It deals in essence with any matters raised in the defence to which the claimant feels that he should respond and which were not covered in the particulars of claim. There is no obligation on the claimant to serve a reply and, as such, no admissions are to be implied from the absence of one.

As with the drafting of a defence, the reply can respond to each, but not necessarily all, of the paragraphs of the defence in a structured and clear manner, explaining and clarifying (both by way of additional factual information) and taking issue with its contents.

 Example

In a simple debt action for the supply of flour to a commercial bakery, in which the formula described in paragraph 11.4.1.4 has been followed correctly, no details of any contract terms other than type of goods, delivery date, and price are relevant to the pleaded claim at this stage. The defendant defends the claim and refuses to pay the amount due, on the basis that the flour supplied and delivered was not of satisfactory quality, and he particularizes the problems—in this case, mite infestation.

Whilst there is no counterclaim raised in this scenario, the claimant may wish to respond by way of a reply and set out any relevant facts that could be brought to the attention of the court that might have a bearing on the success of his action, such as a contract term that the quality of the flour be maintained by storage in airtight containers and, in his reply, asserting the fact that the defendant kept the flour in open sacks.

A reply is not, however, an opportunity for the claimant to rectify any mistakes made in the particulars of claim; that is something that is left to the formal process of amendment (see paragraph 11.9 below).

11.7.1.1 *Example of a reply based on the 'Example' box above*

1. Save as is expressly admitted or not admitted below, the Claimant joins issue with the Defendant on its Defence.

2. As to paragraph . . . of the Defence, the Claimant avers that a term of the said agreement, at clause . . . , between the parties was that the quality of the flour was to be maintained by storage in airtight containers.

3. As to paragraph . . . of the Defence, the Defendant refers to a report from a Mr . . . , an independent quality assurance inspector, who examined the flour for contamination. At paragraph 7 of the report dated . . . ., Mr . . . states that 'the flour was contained in open sacks . . . .'.

I believe the contents of this Reply are true. I am duly authorized to make this statement on behalf of the Claimant.

. . . .

Dated . . . .

11.8 THE PART 18 REQUEST FOR FURTHER INFORMATION

For a reminder of what a Part 18 request is, see Chapter 10, paragraph 10.7.4.

The doctrine of proportionality and the greater burden under the CPR for parties to state their cases in detail should mean that requests for further information are needed less frequently. They should be used with some caution.

 Example

A particulars of claim alleges that an agreement was made whereby the defendant agreed to supply the claimant with a quantity of mixed Mediterranean vegetables at a price of £10 per box and that, despite numerous requests by the claimant, the defendant has refused to supply any of the vegetables. The defendant therefore had to buy them elsewhere at a greater cost. The particulars are vague and incomplete in relation to the date of the agreement, whether it was written or oral, who made it, the amount of the order in terms of number of boxes and overall price, and the delivery date.

11.8.1 WHAT IS THE FORM AND CONTENT OF THE PART 18 REQUEST?

There is no requirement that the Part 18 request should be in a particular form, although guidance is given in PD 18 1.2–1.7. It should be expressed to be a request under the provisions of CPR 18.

It may be in a letter form, as suggested above, or drafted as a stand-alone formal document with a court heading. It is often thought helpful to make the request in formal form, so that if there is no response to the request, it can form the basis of the application to the court for an order for the information sought.

In formal form, the document can also allow space for the recipient's reply (this is a different document from the reply discussed in paragraph 11.7 above) and therefore be prepared in tabular form. The reply to a CPR 18 request must contain a statement of truth, because it is a statement of case in its own right.

Whether made by letter or in formal form, the request must:

(a) be headed with the action title and number;

(b) state that it is a request made under CPR Part 18;

(c) identify the party making the request and the party to whom the request is made;

(d) set out, in numbered paragraphs, each request and identify which part (by repeating the words) of the other party's statement of case is either unclear or upon which clarification is sought; and

(e) state the date by which a response is expected and state that an application will be made to court if there is a failure to respond.

11.8.1.1 Example of a Part 18 request in respect of the 'Example' box above

---

IN THE CARDIFF COUNTY COURT **CASE NO. CA443576**

BETWEEN

MR CAMERON STUART

AND

MR WILLIAM STODDARD

DEFENDANT'S PART 18 REQUEST FOR FURTHER INFORMATION OF THE PARTICULARS OF CLAIM

<u>Under paragraph 1</u>—'By an agreement made in or about March 201?, the Defendant agreed to supply the Claimant with a quantity of mixed Mediterranean vegetables at a price of £10 per box.'

Please state:

1. The alleged date of the agreement;

2. Whether it is alleged that the agreement was oral or written;

3(a) If the agreement was oral, who made the agreement and what was said;

3(b) If the agreement was written, the terms of the agreement, along with a copy of the contract or documentation relied on in support thereof;

4. The date on which it is alleged that the Defendant agreed to supply the boxes of mixed Mediterranean vegetables;

5. The quantity of the said vegetables to be supplied.

<u>Under paragraph 3</u>—'notwithstanding several requests to do so . . . . . .'

Please give full particulars of:

6. The date/s of every such request;

7. Whether such requests were made orally or in writing;

8(a) If orally, by and to whom the requests were made, the content of the request/s and the answer/s;

8(b) If in writing, the details of the request/s and any documentation in support thereof.

<u>Under paragraph 6</u>—'.... the Claimant had to purchase the same elsewhere at a greater cost'

Please state:

9. From where is it alleged that the Claimant purchased the mixed Mediterranean vegetables;

10. The quantity and price of the mixed Mediterranean vegetables.

Dated . . . .

11.9 AMENDMENTS TO STATEMENTS OF CASE

CPR 17 generally sets out the position on amendments to statements of case. A party may amend a statement of case at any time before it has been served on any other party. Once served, a statement of case may only be amended with the consent of all parties or the permission of the court, unless the amendment relates to the removal, addition, or substitution of a party, in which case, the procedure set out in CPR 19.4 must be followed.

An amended statement of case must be marked as amended and set out as under PD 17.2.1. The original text need only be shown if the court considers it appropriate and desirable. If the substance of the statement of case is changed by the amendment, it should be re-verified by a statement of truth.

The judge is not permitted to give judgment on the basis of a claim not set out in the statement of case. If this is done, a retrial will be ordered.

For the purposes of the Limitation Act 1980, an amendment to add or substitute a new party or to add a new cause of action is deemed to be a separate claim and to have been commenced on the same date as the original claim.

 Costs

The party applying to amend its statement of case will usually be responsible for its own costs, as well as any costs of the opponent, especially if the opponent then needs to amend his statement of case as a result of the amendment. Again, it is good practice to ask your opponent to agree to the proposed amendment before making an application to the court for permission. If your opponent unreasonably refuses, then it will be incumbent on you to raise this at the hearing on the question of costs, because the time and cost incurred by you and your client may have been unnecessarily incurred.

11.10 A DETAILED WORKED EXAMPLE

To demonstrate the thought processes behind drafting a statement of case, a detailed worked example of what should be considered when drafting an effective breach of contract claim is set out below. There are eight important stages.

11.10.1 **THE ESSENTIAL INGREDIENTS**

The essential ingredients of a successful claim for damages for breach of contract, leading to full recovery, are as follows.

1. That there was a contract, which involved:
   - an agreement;
   - between C and D;
   - a promise;
   - consideration; and
   - an intention (to create legal relations).

2. That there was, in the contract, a material term—that is, one that D is alleged to have breached, or one that entitles C to the relief sought.

3. That C has performed any obligation that was a precondition to the performance of D's obligation, or to his entitlement to relief.

4. That D was in breach of his obligation.

5. That C has suffered loss and damage.

6. That such loss and damage was caused by D's breach.

7. That the loss is not too remote—that is, that it was reasonably within the contemplation of the parties at the time that they entered into the contract as a likely consequence of the breach, in the light of their knowledge at that time.

8. That the claim is not statute-barred.

11.10.2 **THE PARTIES**

This stage is partly a matter of setting out essential ingredients to do with the parties and partly a matter of story-telling. If either party has a business or is a company, then you will almost always state what that party's business is. This may be an essential ingredient if you have to establish any of the following—for example:

- that a party entered into the contract in the course of his business;
- that a party was dealing as a consumer;
- that a term should be implied into the contract; or
- that a party held himself out as having a particular skill or expertise.

If the terms of a contract are to be inferred from the previous course of dealing between the parties, then this will need to be established. If there have been significant pre-contract negotiations, then these will have to be set out. If the claimant is making a claim for the loss of or damage to his property, then he needs to state his ownership of the property.

11.10.3 **THE CONTRACT**

To set out the contract properly, you must:

- state that there was a contract (or agreement);
- state the date (or the approximate date) of the contract;
- identify the parties to the contract;
- state whether either party acted through employees and, if so, identify them;
- confirm the form of the contract, whether written or oral, or partly both, or implied from a number of circumstances;

- attach any documents evidencing the contract;
- if the contract is oral, state how it was made (for example, by phone), between whom, and when and where;
- confirm the subject matter of the contract—that is, what it sought to do or what was promised; and
- identify the consideration.

11.10.4 THE DEFENDANT'S KNOWLEDGE

Where you are relying on the defendant's knowledge of certain facts to show that the loss and damage that you seek was within the contemplation of the defendant and so is not too remote, you need to state those facts and allege that he had that knowledge. The material time is at the time at which the contract was made, so it is usual to confirm the date of the contract.

11.10.5 THE TERMS

At this stage, you should set out any material terms that have not already been covered when setting out the contract (see paragraph 11.10.3 above). It is a matter of judgment whether a term is really part of the basic subject matter of the contract (in which case, it belongs in the setting out of the contract) or whether it is a separate term. You should state whether the term is an express or implied term, and then set out its effect. The best practice is to paraphrase concisely, rather than to copy out the exact words of the term—but this is pointless if it will not make the term any more clear or concise. Do not set out terms that are not relevant.

If relying on an implied term, you should state the basis on which it is implied, unless it is obvious, or is implied by statute.

Where relying on express terms and implied terms, it is usual to set out the express terms first.

11.10.6 PERFORMANCE OF THE CONTRACT

It may be that the defendant was only obliged to carry out his obligations under the contract if the claimant had first performed his part of the bargain. If this is the case, then these obligations need to be set out.

11.10.7 THE BREACH

Breach of contract must be expressly alleged and particularized. You should start by alleging that the defendant was in breach of contract and then set out in full what it is that constitutes the breach. It may be an act or an omission, or a state of affairs, or the fact that some representation was untrue. If the defendant's breach brought the contract to an end, then this must be expressly stated by using the word 'repudiated'. If the defendant has repudiated the contract, thereby giving the claimant the right to treat the contract as at an end and the claimant has done so, it will be necessary to state that the claimant accepted the repudiation.

Where the breach consists of an act, omission. or event, you should state the date on which it occurred.

It may also, at this stage, be necessary to state any additional facts that entitle the claimant to the relief sought.

11.10.8 THE LOSS AND DAMAGE

It is essential to allege causation, as well as damage. This may take a considerable amount of explanation. It is sometimes not obvious why the breach alleged should have led to the loss claimed.

Particulars of the loss and damage must be given. You should state the nature of the loss and the basis on which the claimant wants damages to be assessed, set out the financial losses in an itemized schedule (if there are many), and quantify each item as far as possible.

11.10.9 INTEREST

Interest must always be stated in the particulars of claim. If it is not, the court is unlikely to award interest.

The sum of interest accrued in a specified sum claim only must be stated on Form N1, as well as in the particulars of claim.

Interest may be pleaded as follows:

- under the terms of the contract, if there was a contractual provision;
- under s. 35A of the Senior Courts Act 1981 (if the action is a High Court action)—that is, at 8 per cent;
- under s. 69 of the County Courts Act 1984 (if the action is in the county court)—that is, at 8 per cent; or
- under the Late Payments of Commercial Debts (Interest) Act 1998—that is, at 8 per cent above base rate.

If there is a contractual provision for interest, then there is a choice as to whether interest is stated under the contract or the Court Acts above. It is not, however, permitted to state the Late Payments of Commercial Debts (Interest) Act 1998 as an alternative to a contractual term for interest. If there is no contractual provision, then any one of the applicable statutes above can be applied.

If interest is stated on the terms of a contract, then express reference to the term in the contract needs to be made. Also, the rates of interest set out in the contract must be stated and the calculations given (both the total interest that has arisen and the continuing daily rate).

If interest is claimed under one of the above statutes, then the claim must be for a specified sum. The statement for interest must state the authority (the relevant statute) and must also calculate the amount of interest that has accrued since the accrual of the cause of action (that is, the date of the breach) to the date on which the proceedings are issued, and thereafter a daily rate is calculated so that the court can readily calculate the sum due when judgment is given (if that is the outcome).

If the claim is for an unspecified sum (for the court to award), then interest is simply pleaded generally, requesting the court to award an appropriate amount.

KEY POINTS SUMMARY

- Remember that all statements of case are designed to provide an outline. Do not be tempted to include all of the details of your case.

- Even in the more complex cases, if you stick to the 'formulae', they will serve as a good basic structure for your case.

- Be ready to acknowledge that some drafting may be very complicated and best left to counsel. This is not 'passing the buck', but rather acting in your client's best interests by avoiding unnecessary amendments and adverse costs orders.

- Well-drafted statements of case will reflect well on you in the eyes of the judge if the matter ever gets to trial and should help to clarify the main issues in the case.

- In practice, it is common for practitioners to rely on precedent statements of case. Be aware of antiquated language and ensure that every paragraph used has a purpose for your own statement of case—such reliance must be undertaken intelligently.

- Do not forget the strategic use of a Part 18 request when acting for either the claimant or the defendant on service of their particulars of claim or defence.

Case study *Andrew James Pike and Deep Builders Ltd*

Question 1

Refer to the draft particulars of claim attached to the case study questions in Chapter 9 on the Online Resource Centre. A medical report by Edgar Higgins is provided on the Online Resource Centre.

Draft your particulars of claim in this matter. (Please note that the medical report of Edgar Higgins is also defective, but you are not being asked to comment on this at this stage in these case study questions—although you may wish to refer to the report in your draft particulars of claim.)

Question 2

The insurer of Deep Builders Ltd has indicated that it accepts that Mr Deep was acting in the course of his employment, but denies negligence, alleging that Andrew Pike was responsible for the accident. Andrew Pike's solicitors have obtained a medical report prepared by a consultant orthopaedic surgeon. You undertake research and the information provided by the client leads you to believe that total damages on a full liability basis would be in the region of £40,000–£55,000. Settlement was not achieved in the Protocol.

The claim form has already been drafted. You will also have drafted the particulars of claim (see Question 1 above).

Now, **acting for the defendant**, consider the points that you believe the defendant needs to raise to defend this case and how it can deal with its own losses. Then draft the defence and any other statement of case that you feel is appropriate.

Any documents referred to in these case study questions can be found on the Online Resource Centre—simply click on 'Case study documentation' to access the documents that you need for Chapter 11 and to be reminded of the questions above. Suggested answers to these case study questions can also be accessed on the Online Resource Centre by your lecturer.

12 CASE MANAGEMENT

12.1 INTRODUCTION

This chapter considers the way in which the court 'actively manages' cases. All disputed cases will be subject to a level of court management.

The chapter aims to give you an understanding of the time at which active case management commonly occurs and will address:

• the ethos of case management;

• allocation; and

• case management directions through the tracks.

In the online resources there is a short podcast on case management and directions that will help your understanding of this part of the litigation process.

LITIGATION TRAIN: CASE MANAGEMENT OVERVIEW

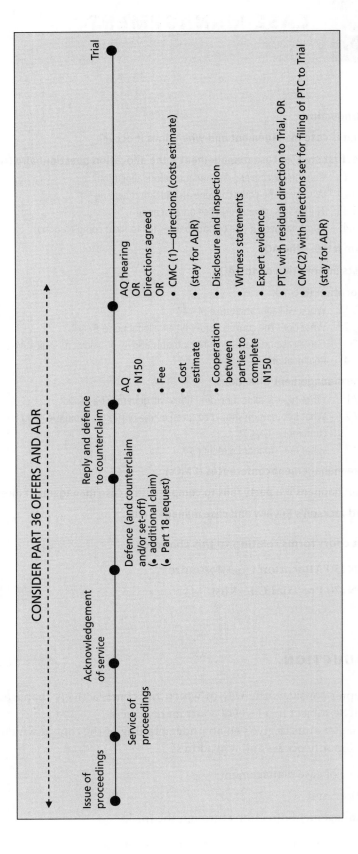

12.2 **WHAT IS CASE MANAGEMENT AND WHEN DOES IT OCCUR?**

'Case management' includes all of the ways in which the court will control the progress and disposal of actions. The bulk of the rules relating to these processes are contained in Civil Procedure Rules (CPR) Parts 3 and 26–29, and the Practice Directions that accompany them. Case management can be exercised at any time in an action's process through to trial but there are times in the litigation process when it most commonly occurs—at allocation, at further CMCs or whenever a party makes an interim application. However 'case management' does mean that once a case is issued the court will 'manage' the action throughout—this will include management decisions made after trial where continued directions may be needed to resolve remaining issues concerning costs or enforcement. It is important to understand that case management is management *by* the court. This management will be exercised by the district judges, Masters, and circuit judges. Whilst parties (and their legal representatives) may have a voice in these case management decisions, it is ultimately the court that controls how a case will progress.

The range of ways in which the courts will monitor and control cases can include:

- identifying disputed issues at an early stage, and how those issues are to be presented and proved;
- giving directions to ensure that the progress of the case is efficient;
- fixing timetables (essentially these comprise the directions order that sets out the steps that each party must take and the date when that step must be done by);
- combining several aspects of management in one stage;
- controlling costs;
- disposing of cases summarily where they disclose no case or defence;
- expecting the parties to cooperate with each other on a number of fronts (see Chapters 3–6 and 17);
- dealing with matters without the parties having to attend court; and
- ordering a stay to encourage the parties to settle.

 Practical Considerations

The provision to seek a stay of the action for the purposes of attempting alternative dispute resolution (ADR) cannot be used as a way of generally 'buying' additional time to prepare a case, or of creating delaying tactics to put pressure on a party. Although the court will readily grant a stay of the action for the purposes of ADR, the stay will not be open-ended (often, it will be for a month), and if a longer stay is requested or granted, it will usually be on terms that the parties report to the court on a regular basis in respect of their negotiations.

The aim of 'case management' is included within the ethos and the aims of the overriding objective—that is, ensuring that cases are dealt with justly, fairly, expeditiously, and proportionately. To accommodate these objectives, fixed or standardized management directions and timetables are used as much as possible. In both the fast track and the multi-track, it will be for the parties to seek directions and management decisions that better suit their cases if these fall outside the 'standard directions' to be normally applied in the case. Any requests for management decisions that fall outside the standardized directions and timetables will need to be justified, again within the provisions of the overriding objective. Requests for 'tailor-made' directions will usually be set out in, or accompany, the allocation question-naire, Form N150 (see paragraph 12.3 below). The courts can, however, entertain requests for specific directions at any time but if an application is made late, the justification for it will have to be strong and very persuasive—especially if it adversely affects the opponent or the timescale that the court wishes to impose for the action.

The court has powers to encourage (and ultimately to compel) parties to comply with court decisions. A failure to meet the directions and orders set can result in a variety of costs penalties. Apart from simple orders for an intransigent or uncooperative party to pay the other party's costs of a hearing or application, the costs orders can include 'wasted costs' orders against the legal representatives (see Chapter 4, paragraph 4.8). The court can also make 'unless' orders in which a party can be penalized for failing to meet the requirements of a court order—this may mean that a party is prevented from pursuing a part of its case or defence, but it can also ultimately include an order to strike out that party's case or defence.

 Professional Conduct

Rule 11.01 of the Solicitors' Code of Conduct 2007 provides that a solicitor (or a registered European or foreign lawyer) must never 'deceive or knowingly mislead the court'. This professional obligation runs alongside the duty to 'act in the best interests of their client'. CPR 1.3 requires parties to help the court to further the overriding objective. As yet, it is unclear if the duty under Rule 11 of the Code would mean that the solicitor must withdraw from the action if the client's instructions are contrary to the overrid-ing objective. However, if the client's instructions would involve the solicitor in knowingly deceiving the court, then the solicitor must stop acting. Section 27 of the Courts and Legal Services Act 1990 provides that any person exercising a right of audience before a court has 'a duty to the court to act with independ-ence in the interests of *justice*' [emphasis added] and that this duty shall 'override' any other obligation.

12.3 THE 'FIRST STEP' OF CASE MANAGEMENT—THE ALLOCATION QUESTIONNAIRE (AQ) (FORM N150)

The first step in case management by the court will usually be taken once a defence is filed and allocation questionnaires (AQs) are sent out by the court to the parties. Thinking about this logically, though the case 'belongs' to the court in terms of the management of it from the moment the case is issued there is little point in the court engaging with active case management until a defence is filed. If a defence is not filed the case is likely to end peremptorily (with a default judgment) with no need for any further management decisions.

12.3.1 CAN THE COURT EVER CASE MANAGE BEFORE ALLOCATION?

In some circumstances, steps will be taken on a case *before* the AQs are sent out to the par-ties. These provisions are listed in CPR 26 and predominantly include the occasions on which a case may be *automatically* transferred to the defendant's home court (CPR 26.2).

CPR 26.2 provides that the following claims will be automatically transferred to the defendant's 'home' court once a defence is filed:

• those that are defended;

• those that are for a specified sum; and

• those that are against individuals.

If there is more than one defendant, then the transfer will be to the home court of which-ever of the defendants is an individual, or if there is more than one defendant who is an individual, the transfer will be to the home court of the first defendant to file his defence.

The definition of the defendant's 'home court' includes:

- for the High Court, the district registry for the district in which the defendant resides or carries on business, or where there is no such district registry, the Royal Courts of Justice; and

- for the county court, the county court in the jurisdiction in which the defendant resides or carries on business.

Other than the provisions above that deal with an automatic transfer to another court, the procedure for and transfer between courts of other claims is dealt with in CPR 30. These provisions provide that a case may be transferred to another court when it has been commenced in the wrong court, or it may be struck out. Having regard to the provisions of the overriding objective, the court will not lightly strike a case out if it has been commenced in the wrong court, but it will probably impose costs sanctions (of the costs of transfer and any other costs incurred incidentally) against the claimant for the error.

Where the court orders a transfer, the court from which the claim is to be transferred must give notice of the transfer to all parties.

12.3.2 WHEN WILL THE COURT CONVENE AN ALLOCATION HEARING?

In most cases, where there is no need for an allocation hearing to take place, the court will deal with case management and make the directions orders without a hearing and based on the responses the parties have given in their AQs. However, the court will convene an allocation hearing if it thinks that it is necessary to do so (CPR 26.5(4)). Where, for example, the appropriate track for a case is not clear, the court may convene an allocation hearing, or it may seek further information about a party's case (CPR 26.5(3)). This is unusual in practice, but it could happen if the information contained in the completed AQs was not sufficient to enable the court to make a decision on the appropriate track for the case. It could also treat any hearing that has occurred *before* it has sent out AQs *as* an allocation hearing, and thus dispense with the sending out and filing of AQs. In this way, the court will use some of the time of the hearing that is being heard to make an order for allocation and give directions for case management. This might happen if, for example, a party has made an application to the court for an interim injunction or for summary judgment (see Chapter 14): such applications can be made before a defence has been filed and so could be heard before the 'trigger' for the court to send out AQs to the parties.

An allocation hearing may also be ordered by the procedural judge if the requests for specific, tailor-made directions are either not agreed, or where the request does not seem sufficiently justified.

12.3.3 THE COURT'S GENERAL PRACTICE ON ALLOCATION

After a defence is filed (or in a case in which there are multiple defendants, when the time limit for the filing of defences by all defendants has expired), the court will send each of the parties a blank AQ in Form N150. A modified form of the AQ (in Form N149) will be used where it appears to the court that the case is likely to be allocated to the small claims track. (See a blank copy N150 in the Court Forms' Appendix.)

The claimant is required to pay the allocation fee. The fee is payable on the filing of his completed AQ. The fee is also payable even if the court has dispensed with the filing of AQs and will become payable usually within 14 days of the allocation order or directions made by the court. Practitioners will obtain details of the current fee for the filing of the AQs from the court office or online at the HM Courts Service website—http://www.hmcourts-service. gov.uk. They are contained in the Civil Proceedings Fees (Amendment) Order 2009, which sets out details of the fees payable in both the High Court and the county court.

CPR 3.7 deals with the provisions applying when the allocation fee is not paid after due warning.

Usually, the parties will be given 14 days in which to complete and return the AQ. Parties may not, of their own accord or by agreement between themselves, vary the time permitted for the completion and filing of the form (CPR 26.3(6A)). Parties are expected to complete AQs, because the information sought from the parties on this form will enable and assist the court to make the best use of the available resources, including the amount of 'judicial time' that should be spent on the case. In this way, the procedural judges will be able to make decisions and directions for the future conduct of the case that are 'proportionate', 'fair', and 'expeditious'. Normally, if the form has been completed well and properly, it will provide the court with additional information about the progress (if any) that the parties have made towards resolving the dispute through alternative methods, and the progress that has been made in preparing evidence and settling the identity of any expert that may be needed.

12.3.4 WHAT HAPPENS IF ONE OR BOTH PARTIES FAIL TO FILE A COMPLETED AQ?

In practical terms, it is unlikely that the claimant will fail to complete his AQ. There are many rules and safeguards within the CPR that are intended to prevent parties from filing cases in court as 'threats' to their opponent, but with which they have, in reality, no real intention of proceeding. These include the need to sign statements of truth, and the costs penalties of unreasonably starting a case or raising issues that are not, or should not, be proceeded with. These sanctions and safeguards should mean that the number of cases in which the claimant intentionally fails to complete and file the AQ is few. It could happen that the claimant has simply failed to diarize the date on which the completed AQ should be filed at court, but even in these circumstances, the provision requiring parties to consult with one another and to cooperate in completing their AQs (PD 26.2.3) should mean that where one party may have forgotten the deadline date, they are likely to be reminded of the need to complete and file it by the other party. It is important to note that even though the CPR seek to ensure that the parties consult and cooperate in the filing of the AQs, this consultation process cannot be used to delay the filing of the completed forms. In genuine cases in which there is a good reason for the delay in completing and filing the forms, and more time is needed (and can be justified), then the party (or parties) may apply to the court for further time.

12.3.4.1 If completed AQs are not returned by the parties

If completed AQs are not returned by the parties, the court will order that unless an AQ is filed by a certain date (usually with seven days from the date of service of the order), the claim, defence, and any counterclaim will be struck out (PD 26.2.15(1)).

12.3.4.2 If completed AQs are filed by one (or some) of the parties, but not the other(s)

If the completed AQs are filed by only one (or some) of the parties, but not all involved, the case will be referred to the procedural judge and he may:

* allocate the case to a track should he feel that there is enough information supplied within any AQs that have been returned; or

* order that the parties attend an allocation hearing. These are now automatically conducted by telephone (PD 23.6(2))—see below). The court may also order that the costs of the parties attending the allocation hearing be paid by the party that failed to file its AQ.

In reality, if it is the claimant who has failed to file his AQ, the more likely order will be along the lines of that in paragraph 12.3.4.1 above, because the court is unlikely to see any benefit in progressing a case with which the claimant does not seem to wish to pursue. Where the defendant has included a counterclaim in his defence and he has filed his completed AQ, then the court may, if it is appropriate to do so, either order an allocation hearing that all parties must attend, or make an order that will enable the defendant's counterclaim to proceed.

AQs will not normally be sent out to parties in cases that will be automatically allocated to the multi-track, such as cases likely to be allocated to a specialist court (for example, the Technology and Construction Court, or TCC). Those cases that will be dealt with by one of the specialist courts will have directions tailor-made concerning the management of these cases under the provisions of that court's specialist court guide.

12.4 FORM N150—THE AQ

Please see both the blank AQ in the Court Forms' section in the Appendix in the 'Case study documentation' section of the Online Resource Centre and the 'Annotated forms' section, in which there are some practical notes to aid completion of the form. A completed version of the Case study AQ is available to lecturers.

12.5 COSTS INFORMATION ON THE AQ

The Online Resource Centre chapter on 'Costs Assessment', paragraph 4.6.7, notes that a legal representative's costs estimate made, for example, in section G of the AQ may be binding. CPR 6.5A states that if there is a difference of 20 per cent or more between the estimate given and the final costs being claimed (although there are conflicting cases cited in the online chapter which both support and challenge this 20 per cent), that party may be asked to provide a statement of the reasons for the difference. It will also be very pertinent to any costs recovery that the client had been made aware of the difference and had authorized it.

A costs estimate made in the AQ should therefore be as accurate as possible and must be served on the client. If steps are taken on the case that would increase this estimate, a full file note should be made, the client informed, and his instructions to incur the additional costs obtained. The 51st amendment to the CPR which came into force on 6 April 2010 has now removed the need for an AQ in a fast track case to have a costs estimate filed and served with it.

12.6 ALLOCATION TO TRACK

Once a defence has been filed, the court must allocate the action to one of the three tracks (see Chapter 9, paragraph 9.2, and paragraph 12.6.2 below). The procedural judge will carry out the allocation of the case. A 'procedural judge' may include a Master (for cases proceeding in the Royal Courts of Justice), or a district judge and circuit judge in the district registries and county courts. The parties have the opportunity in their replies to the questions in the AQ, or in the additional information that they have supplied to the court with their completed AQs or at a subsequent allocation or directions hearing, to influence the orders that the judge will make to manage the case. Any request for tailor-made orders for the particular case will need to be justified by the party requesting it. The ultimate power to make case management decisions rests with the procedural judge.

The court will now automatically hear allocation hearings over the phone wherever possible (PD 23.6(2)). Chapter 15, paragraph 15.5, deals with how to set up and conduct a telephone hearing.

There are provisions to allow an allocation hearing to be listed. This will only happen if the court considers that it is necessary to do so. This could happen if the application was without notice or if none of the parties are represented, in which case, the court will give the parties at least seven days' notice of the hearing using Form N153. This will include a brief statement of the reasons for calling an allocation hearing. If the hearing of another application is *treated* as an allocation hearing, then clearly, the requirement to give parties seven days' notice is not applicable. Parties should always attend any pre-allocation hearing fully prepared to discuss with the judge issues of allocation and the appropriate directions to be made for the future management of the case. Where an allocation hearing is listed, a legal representative who attends the hearing should, wherever possible, be the person who is responsible for the case (or at least part of the legal team responsible for the case). In any event, he must be familiar with the case, and have sufficient authority to deal with issues that may arise so as to be able to provide the court with any information that it might seek in order to make its decision on matters of allocation and directions.

To ensure that case management is proportionate, the court only actively intervenes (as against issuing standard orders and directions) in cases that require that level of intervention, either in terms of value and/or complexity. 'Basic' management, with a fixed timetable and standard procedure and directions, is used wherever possible—notably, in the fast track, but also in the multi-track. The majority of cases therefore proceed between the filing of the defence and trial with directions in a more or less standard form, but, when **necessary**, tailored to the needs of the particular case.

12.6.1 WHEN WILL ALLOCATION TAKE PLACE?

Generally, the allocation order—which includes both the allocation to track and any directions—will be made once the procedural judge has considered the AQs returned, or when the time limit for the filing of AQs has expired (see paragraphs 12.3.4.1 and 12.3.4.2 above).

If one or more of the parties have requested it, or if one of the parties has requested, or if the court decides that it is appropriate to do so, the action can be 'stayed' for a period of time (in the fast track, often for a period of one month) to enable ADR to be tried. In these circumstances, the allocation order will not be made until after the period of stay ordered.

In cases in which the case is to be transferred to another court or to a specialist court, allocation decisions will be taken after the transfer by the procedural judge in the court to which the case is transferred—although note CPR 26.3(3), under which the court in which the claim was started will issue AQs to the parties before transferring the case and order that the completed AQs be returned to the court to which the case is transferred.

12.6.2 WHAT DOES THE COURT CONSIDER WHEN ALLOCATING TO TRACK?

There are nine basic principles that the court will consider when allocating a case to the appropriate track. These are set out in CPR 26.8(1) and they include:

- the financial value of the claim—that is, the sum that represents the 'financial value' of the case for tracking purposes, disregarding any amount not in dispute, any claim for interest or costs, and any claim of contributory negligence. This principle is important to bear in mind in practice at all times. Both the Protocol phase of litigation, the rules of litigation and drafting statements of case, are designed to encourage parties to narrow the issues between them and, in doing so, the value of the claim may well be reduced. Narrowing the issues, admitting or agreeing what can be agreed, or being realistic in terms of the sum claimed in the Protocol phase can have significant impact on the 'value' of the claim for tracking purposes. Where the court believes that the amount being claimed by the claimant (or the defendant in any counterclaim) exceeds what that party may reasonably be expected to recover, it can make an order directing that the party justify the amount being claimed (CPR 26.5(3));

- the remedy sought;

- the complexity of the claim—which may include complexities of law, fact, and/or evidence; and

- where there is no financial value, the court will allocate the case to the most appropriate track, having regard to matters such as complexity, numbers of witnesses, the importance of the claim to persons who are not parties (in effect, those matters listed in CPR 26.8(1)).

12.6.3 **CAN A CASE BE PLACED IN A TRACK THAT IS ABOVE, OR BELOW, ITS INDICATIVE TRACK?**

If all parties and the court agree, a case can be placed in a different track. The criteria for cases to be heard in the small claims track should not be seen only as a question of value, although 'value' is the guiding principle that sets a case in that track. The small claims track is intended to provide a proportionate procedure for the most straightforward claims. Although a claim may exceed the small claims track financial limit, parties should consider whether it would, in fact, be more proportionate, more just, and more efficient for the case to be heard in the small claims track rather than the track that its value would indicate. If this occurs, the parties could still also agree that the costs provisions that apply in the fast track should apply to the claim so 'down-tracked' to the small claims track (CPR 27.14(5)), so a party is not prejudiced by the more restricted costs rules applicable in the small claims track. This applies equally to claims with a financial limit above £25,000 that, for similar reasons, might be better placed in the fast track rather than the multi-track. This 'down-tracking' of a case can only take place where all of the parties agree.

The court may also place a case in a track higher than its financial value would indicate if it is appropriate to do so (having regard to the matters listed in CPR 26.8(1)). However, the judgment in *Peakman v Lindbrooke Services Ltd* [2008] EWCA Civ 1239 provides a cautionary reminder of the potential sanctions that can be imposed against a party who pursues exaggerated or unfounded claims, with the result that the case is allocated to an inappropriate track.

In practice, there may be cogent reasons why a party may wish to have his claim allocated to the 'highest' track, because it may mean that:

- the matter will be determined by a more senior judge;
- there may be more flexibility to recover more costs; and
- there may be more flexibility in the directions orders that can be made, and more flexibility in the amount of oral evidence to be given and the amount of expert evidence that may be permitted.

Once the procedural judge has made its decision on the track that is most appropriate for the case, it will send out to all parties a 'notice of allocation'. In the fast track (and sometimes in the multi-track), the notice will be accompanied with a copy of each party's completed AQ—although the contents of these should generally not be a surprise to any parties if proper consultation has taken place between the parties before their filing. The 'Notice of Allocation' will usually be accompanied with the directions orders (see paragraph 12.7) if the parties had agreed the directions beforehand.

12.6.4 **REALLOCATION**

The court has discretion to reallocate a claim to a different track (CPR 26.10). This may happen if there has been a change in the circumstances, or nature, or value of the claim.

If a party is unhappy with the allocation order that has been made, he may appeal the order if he (or his legal representative) had been present at the allocation hearing (if such took place), or apply to the court to reallocate. In either case, the party should have clear reasons for asking the court to reallocate. An appeal would be with permission to a circuit judge, or if by application, either by letter or Form N244, usually to the district judge who made the original order.

If a reallocation order is made, it is also likely to result in a change of the directions made for the future management of the case. Any appeal or application by a party for reallocation should therefore also take account of, and suggest where appropriate, the changes that may be needed in the case management directions.

12.7 **CASE MANAGEMENT DIRECTIONS**

Upon allocation, the case management directions that the court will make will set down all of the steps which the parties need to comply with and when they must comply in order to make the case ready for hearing. The directions order that will be made may indicate the steps which the parties need to comply with all the way to trial, or (more commonly) will set directions orders up to the point of the issuing of pre-trial checklists (Form N170—see paragraph 12.7.3.3 below), at which time the court will undertake a similar review of the action and set further directions orders of the steps that are required to manage the case on to trial.

12.7.1 **WHAT TYPE OF ALLOCATION DIRECTIONS WILL GENERALLY BE MADE?**

Details of the most likely directions that may be made in an action will be contained in the CPR applicable to the track in which the case is likely to be placed (CPR Parts 27–29).

When making directions, the court will be seeking to apply the principles of the overriding objective. The aim of the directions made will be to ensure that the case proceeds on its path to trial properly, efficiently, and proportionately. Accordingly, every attempt will be made to clarify the issues in dispute (and encouragement is evident for the parties to seek to narrow the issues in dispute) and to control the evidence.

In the AQ, parties may set out agreed directions and/or either party may propose directions. The court may seek more information (see Forms N155 and N156). Where inadequate information has been given in the AQs, the court is more likely to set down standard directions and timescales arbitrarily. This may put parties under enormous pressure unless one (or both) applies promptly (within 14 days) for more tailored directions. If any later application is made, the court is likely to take the view that the directions were right when they were made. Because promptness and effective case management are key provisions of the CPR, any application to tailor the directions ordered or to extend time limits would have to be fully justified.

12.7.2 **WHAT INFORMATION SHOULD BE GIVEN BY THE PARTIES TO AVOID THE NEED FOR A CASE MANAGEMENT CONFERENCE (CMC)?**

If the parties have cooperated with each other in the preparation of their AQs or in the provision of additional information needed (for example, to narrow the issues in dispute, or in agreeing the number of, or requirement for, expert evidence), and, further, they have agreed the directions that they feel are needed for the management of the case either to trial or to the next case management conference (CMC) (which will probably be a pre-trial review), the procedural judge may simply endorse their proposals and make the directions order proposed.

In order to obtain the court's approval in this way, any proposals should:

- if appropriate, deal with the filing of a reply to a defence;
- if appropriate, deal with any amendments to a statement of case;
- make provisions for disclosure and inspection—its extent, as well as the time allowed;
- propose directions concerning the exchange of evidence of fact and expert evidence (if any). If there is expert evidence, the proposals should include a direction concerning the type of expert permitted, the timing of exchange of reports (if more than one), questions to the expert, and any meeting between experts (again if more than one expert has been permitted). In the fast track, the normal order for any expert evidence will be for a single joint expert;
- include dates on which any requests for further information may be made and complied with;
- state when the trial period should be set and the date for the sending out of pre-trial checklists (PTCs) and the pre-trial review or hearing;
- if appropriate, set a date for a further CMC; and

- consider a stay for ADR.

The court may accept or reject the proposals, but, in making its directions order, will have regard to the proposals put forward by the parties. The ultimate responsibility for case management directions remains with the court.

Normally, the order will be for 'standard directions'.

12.7.3 WHAT ARE 'STANDARD DIRECTIONS'?

'Standard directions' are established under the CPR for each of the tracks. They represent the case management directions that apply generally to the average claim in that track. They seek to ensure that the claim will progress efficiently, proportionately, and justly.

12.7.3.1 In the small claims track

Standard directions in the small claims track are set out in CPR 27.4(3) and PD 27, Appendix B. These include:

- the requirement to exchange copies of all documents on which a party will rely usually at least 14 days before the hearing;
- a requirement that the parties should bring originals of the documents to the hearing;
- a notice of the date and time of, and time allowed for, the final hearing;
- a note encouraging parties to communicate with each other, with a view to settling the dispute, coupled with a requirement that they should notify the court in writing if they do settle; and
- a note that no expert report will be permitted unless express permission has been granted.

PD 27, Appendix C, sets out the special directions that may be made or requested in this track. The purpose of special directions is to enable the case management of these low-value claims to be more effective, just, and proportionate. They may include directions regarding the issues on which the court requires evidence, the nature of the evidence required, and the way in which the evidence will be presented. (This is not a definitive list of special directions that could be made, but it gives useful guidance to any practitioner who is assisting a party who is conducting or defending a claim in this track, or a party who is acting in person.)

Because some of the CPR on matters relating to expert evidence, witnesses of fact, disclosure, and inspection do not apply to the small claims track, it may be necessary for the court to specify, or for the parties to seek, special directions because of the particular needs of the case, although it must be borne in mind that the overriding objective applies to the small claims track and that any request for special directions must meet with this objective. If the number of special directions needed, or some other reason, means that it is appropriate to do so, the court may, of its own initiative or upon the application of a party, reallocate a case from the small claims track to the fast track. It may also add, vary or revoke any special directions made.

One of the most common special directions that may be sought may be a special direction that the parties exchange witness statements before the final hearing (this being a standard direction in both the fast track and the multi-track). Before making any such order, the court will have regard to the matters set out in the PD 27.2.5. These considerations include:

- whether either or both parties are represented;
- the amount in dispute;
- the nature of the matters in dispute;
- whether it would be better for a party to be asked to clarify his case better before the hearing;
- the need to provide for 'justice' without undue formality, cost, or delay.

12.7.3.2 In the fast track

Case management directions in cases allocated to the fast track will generally (but not always) be given in two stages:

(a) at allocation; and

(b) on the filing of PTCs (formerly known as 'listing questionnaires') (Form N170—see paragraph 12.7.3.3 below).

On both occasions, the court will expect a degree of cooperation between the parties and will make directions wherever possible without a hearing. Where a hearing does have to take place, this will be by telephone (PD 23.6.2). The court will also readily impose costs sanctions if the requirement for a hearing has been necessitated by either a lack of cooperation of a party or the default of a party. Also, if a hearing for directions has to take place, the parties have a duty to attend that hearing, having considered what directions it is that they wish the court to make.

The court will take account of the steps that the parties have already taken in the Protocol period to make the case ready for trial.

The Appendix in PD 28 contains the form of fast-track standard directions and, wherever possible, the court will base its directions on those set out in the Appendix.

One of the principles that guide the decisions that the court will make for fast-track directions will be the court's duty under CPR 28.2(2) to set a case management timetable and to fix a trial date (or trial period). This trial date or trial period shall not be longer than 30 weeks from the date of the directions order made at allocation. Where parties recommend agreed directions to the court, they must equally ensure that these agreed directions give specific dates for steps to be completed, include a trial period (that must not be longer than 30 weeks from the date of the directions order), and must include provisions about disclosure of documents and the management of both fact and expert evidence.

A typical timetable for the preparation of a fast-track case to trial would be directions that provided for:

- disclosure within four weeks (from the date of the directions order);
- an exchange of witness statements within ten weeks (from the date of the directions order);
- an exchange of expert reports within 14 weeks (from the date of the directions order), together with any additional directions that may be needed—for example, concerning questions to the expert, or who is to pay the expert's fees;
- the date on which PTCs will be sent out by the court—typically, 20 weeks (from the date of the directions order);
- the date on which the PTCs must be returned—typically, 22 weeks (from the date of the directions order); and
- the date of the trial or trial period—typically, 30 weeks (from the date of the directions order).

If a party is dissatisfied with the directions order, or the parties have agreed that there should be changes to the order made, or if, for other reasons, changes are appropriate, an application for the change should be made at the earliest opportunity. This would be by notice of application to the court on Form N244, with reasons. Such an application will usually be heard by the Master or district judge who made the original order. If an application is made later than 14 days from the date of the order, the court will assume that the directions made were appropriate at the time and therefore any changes will need to be justified. If the original directions order was made at a hearing at which the party was present or represented (or at which the party had had due notice of the hearing), he must appeal the order if he seeks changes. In any other circumstance, the party may apply to the court to reconsider the order made. In these circumstances, the application will usually be heard by the judge (or at least a judge of the same level) who made the original directions order.

Practical Considerations

Some directions set by the court can only be changed by order of the court—that is, the date for the filing of AQs, PTCs, and the actual trial date. All other directions can be varied by agreement between the parties, as they encounter the directions in the timescale set, or failing that, by application to the court. In practice, most solicitors are amenable to requests, for example, for further time in which to exchange witness statements.

Three things need to be borne in mind when requests by an opponent are made for further time to comply with a direction order, as follows.

- You may need such a concession yourself at some point.

- Any extension agreed must not affect the key dates set by the court—most notably, the trial date. Any extension of time to comply with a court direction that would affect the trial date must be referred to the court. The court will not readily change the dates set.

- You must always obtain your client's instructions for any agreement or request.

 Practical Considerations

If a case requires special directions, it will be essential in practice to be prepared to state, and justify (within the provisions of the overriding objective), what special directions you think your case needs and make a request to the court for the special directions at the earliest opportunity. This will probably be in the AQ in section I, 'Additional information'. Where the additional information being filed with the AQ is lengthy, a supplemental sheet will be filed.

12.7.3.3 The pre-trial checklists (PTCs) Form N170

Where case management directions for a case allocated to the fast track have been given in two stages, the initial directions order will usually give directions up to the point at which the court sends out PTCs to the parties. This form has a similar function to the AQ—that is, it seeks information from the parties that enables the court to determine the appropriate directions that should be made guiding the case to trial and enables the parties to seek specific tailor-made directions if justified. Again, the parties should cooperate with one another in the completion of the PTC.

There is a fee for the filing of the PTC, which is payable by the claimant. Even when the court has not made two-stage directions to trial, the pre-trial fee will be payable by the claimant within 14 days of the notice of the trial date. If the case is proceeding on a defendant's counterclaim alone, he will need to pay this fee. The fee is refundable if the party who paid it gives written notice to the court at least seven days before the trial date (or before the trial date has been fixed) that the case has been settled or discontinued. If the fee is not paid, the court will issue a reminder to the party, but CPR 3.7 enables the court to strike out the claim for non-payment after the reminder.

The purpose of the PTC is to:

- check that orders and directions to date have been complied with; and

- provide more detailed information about the trial requirements so that it can make trial directions.

The completed PTCs will be placed before the procedural judge, who will decide whether to make trial directions from the completed lists or to call a pre-trial review (or pre-trial directions) hearing. This could include directions to limit issues or evidence. The court will also again consider whether there should be a stay for any further attempt at settlement by a method of ADR.

The typical directions that may be made on receipt of the completed PTCs include:

- confirming or fixing the trial date;
- directions concerning evidence, the number of witnesses, expert evidence (if permission has been granted at allocation directions or subsequently), or for expert evidence to be adduced;
- indicating whether a trial timetable and trial estimate are required;
- provisions concerning the preparation of the trial bundle; and
- any other relevant directions (for example, the provision of an interpreter, specific IT facility, etc.).

The trial judge can be pragmatic in his requirements for individual trials and such 'hands on' directions were given in the *Wembley* litigation in 2008, in which the TCC trial judge ordered that each party were to share the time allocated for the trial equally, that parts of the evidence were to be left to the trial judge's private reading, and that post-trial hearings were to take place to provide the parties with parts of his judgment and to discuss issues in the case. This style of case management is becoming more prevalent in the specialist courts.

12.7.3.4 In the multi-track

The CPR defines the multi-track as the track for all cases that are not suitable for allocation to either of the other tracks. There is a financial criterion that, in general, guides the allocation of a case to this track, but other considerations apply. In practice, therefore, this means that multi-track is the appropriate track for any case:

- that is worth more than £25,000;
- in which the trial is estimated to last for more than a day; and
- in which each party will need to adduce expert oral evidence either in more than one field of expertise, or from more than one expert in a particular field.

Multi-track claims can be heard in either the county court of the High Court, but unless there are particular factors of the case (complexity, legal principle), any case that is worth less than £50,000 will invariably be listed *for trial* in the county court. Cases on the multi-track will generally be dealt with either in the Royal Courts of Justice or other trial centres in district registries.

12.7.3.4.1 *Case management directions in the multi-track*

Cases on this track are typically more complex and higher value than the cases in the small claims track or the fast track; accordingly, case management decisions for these cases are more flexible and more likely to be tailored to meet the specific requirements of the case. The degree of flexibility available for actions within this track will reflect the wide variety of actions—from complex, but quite low-value claims, to claims involving great sums of money, or claims that raise matters of public importance. The emphasis is again on 'efficiency', 'fairness', and 'proportionality', and in claims that are less complex, the court will seek to make standard directions without the need for hearings. In this way, these claims will be given directions with tight timetables that are similar to the standard directions in the fast track. As in the fast track, parties are under a duty to be well prepared for hearings and to give consideration to the directions orders that they may require. Again, parties are expected to cooperate with one another in agreeing the directions that they seek.

At the time that the case is allocated to the multi-track, the procedural judge will decide whether to give directions or to fix a CMC. The procedural judge will also consider whether to order a stay (whether sought by one or more parties in the action or not) while ADR procedures are attempted to settle the case or to narrow the issues.

In cases in which the court decides that it needs to call a CMC, it may also order a party (or parties) to provide more information. If the CMC has been called due to a failure of a party to provide adequate information and if its provision would have enabled the court to make case management directions without the need for a hearing, the defaulting party may be ordered to pay the costs of the hearing. Alternatively, in cases in which parties have failed to cooperate with each other in providing information (either on the AQ or otherwise), the court may decide to make tight case management directions. These could put the parties under enormous pressure to comply or to apply promptly for tailored directions. The rule that applies in the fast track concerning an order for directions applies equally in the multi-track—that is, that the court will assume that the directions made are correct for the circumstances of the case unless a prompt application to vary is made (within 14 days, under PD 29.6.2(2)).

12.7.3.4.2 *What are the 'usual directions' in a multi-track case?*

Case management directions in cases allocated to the multi-track will also generally (but not always) be given in two stages:

(a) at allocation; and

(b) on the filing of PTCs (Form N170—see paragraph 12.7.3.3 above).

As in the small claims track and the fast track, the court aims to set an efficient path for the action to trial. The court will usually consider:

- whether there is a need for an order to clarify the points in issue. This may be undertaken either by making orders for further information to be filed (CPR 18), or for amended statements of case to be prepared and filed and served;
- whether there should be an order for a stay to enable the parties to engage in a form of ADR;
- what should be the scope of any disclosure and inspection;
- the number of witnesses of fact that are required and provision for the exchange of witness statements. Orders can be made to restrict the issues on which evidence will be given;
- whether there is a requirement for expert evidence. The court will further consider whether this should be by single joint experts, or by each party having their own expert, and consider in which fields of expertise expert evidence is required. The court will consider what provisions need be made concerning expert evidence (for example, 'questions to an expert', or 'meetings between experts') and whether there needs to be a provision for oral evidence by the expert(s) at trial. As with witnesses of fact, orders can be made to restrict the issues on which expert evidence will be given;
- whether it is appropriate, on grounds of costs, efficiency, fairness, or proportionality, for there to be an order for a 'split trial' (between matters of liability and quantum), or whether there should be a trial of one or more preliminary issues (see Chapter 17, paragraph 17.2.2);
- whether there should be another CMC or pre-trial review hearing and when;
- whether it is possible to fix a trial period; and
- at which court, or before which calibre of judge, the matter should be listed for trial.

As with the fast track, any party, or the court at its own instigation, may seek any additional directions or orders. In each case, these additional directions orders should be justified within the provisions of the overriding objective. Please have a look at the Andrew Pike case study on the Online Resource Centre to see how directions are dealt with in a multi-track case both in the anwers to the case study questions and in a video clip of a CMC.

 online resource centre

12.8 CASE MANAGEMENT CONFERENCES (CMCS)

CMCs may be held immediately after allocation to the multi-track or at any time thereafter when either the court or a party seeks a hearing. If listed after allocation, they will be used to set down the directions for the future management of the case (where the court feels that the directions proposed in the AQs require discussion before a final decision is made), or to assess progress of the case to trial, or to determine particular issues raised. Often, the parties will be prompted to try (or to try again) some form of ADR procedure to settle the case. In any event, the procedural judge will seek to use the hearing to progress matters more efficiently—for example, by encouraging parties to narrow the issues in dispute, or to order that certain issues shall not be proceeded with.

Practical Considerations

It is important to remember that no mention must be made by the parties at the CMC of any CPR Part 36 offers that have been made in the action, or the details of any attempts at ADR.

Attendance at CMCs should be by a legal representative who is familiar with the issues of the case and who has the appropriate authority to deal with matters arising at it.

Practical Considerations

If the person attending the CMC does not have sufficient knowledge, or experience, or authority to deal with matters arising at the hearing, and the hearing has to be adjourned because of that lack of knowledge or authority, then a wasted costs order will usually be made.

If parties have been ordered to attend and the party is a company, it should be someone from the company who has knowledge of the history of the case.

At the CMC, the court will:

• make a review of the steps taken by the parties to progress the action;

• review how far the parties have complied with any previous directions or orders;

• decide on further directions or orders (that are within the spirit of the overriding objective);

• seek to encourage consensus, wherever possible, on issues, directions, orders, or future conduct; and

• record any agreements.

If the court feels that it will assist the efficiency of the CMC or the progress of the action, an order may be made in advance of the CMC or before the hearing of any next CMC for a case summary to be prepared by the parties and lodged at court. The 51st amendment to the CPR now requires a case summary to be prepared for all multi-track interim hearings and CMCs. The court may equally order that certain documents (in a 'case management bundle') be prepared and lodged for the hearing. The Court Guides for High Court matters may also specify certain requirements for CMCs.

12.9 WHAT HAPPENS IF A PARTY FAILS TO COMPLY WITH A CASE MANAGEMENT DIRECTION?

The court retains control of actions, and has powers of coercion and sanctions to ensure that, so far as possible, parties comply with the orders made. These include the following provisions and powers:

• to strike out a party's case—that is, the most draconian measure that is used in only the most serious cases of default or breach;

• an 'unless order'—that is, the court will make an order against the defaulting party to compel compliance, but if they fail to do so, the 'unless' provision will apply. This 'unless' provision could be an order to strike out all or part of that party's case. In either track.

where directions for trial have been set and the times allowed are 'tight'. the court will be prepared to impose an 'unless' order on a party even after only one breach (see Chapter 13, paragraph 13.9);

- adverse costs orders—the court may also provide that those costs orders be payable immediately;

- an order for indemnity costs or increased interest on damages or costs;

- an order that a defaulting party pay money into court;

- debarring a party from proceeding with an issue, or from amending its statement of case, or from filing additional evidence;

- restricting the numbers of witnesses that may be called (including an expert witness); and

- refusing to grant any application for further time.

In respect of any of the above orders and sanctions, the court will consider wasted costs orders against the legal representative if the reason for the party's default rests with the legal representative.

If both parties, or more than one party, in an action are in default, the court will consider a sanction order against either or both parties in default.

 Practical Considerations

Legal representatives have a duty to help to further the overriding objective (CPR 1.3). It is therefore inappropriate to 'sit back' and let an action stagnate: delay by one party does not justify any delay by any other party.

12.10 LORD JACKSON'S REVIEW AND CASE MANAGEMENT

Lord Jackson has made some workable and sensible suggestions in relation to case management as can be seen below.

FIGURE 12.1

CURRENT POSITION	LORD JACKSON'S PROPOSALS
1. Non-specialist court judges can hear any type of matter whether this be personal injury, mortgage repossessions etc.	The assignment of cases to designated judges with relevant expertise.
2. Generic directions are contained in the PD to CPR 27, 28 and 29 for the three tracks.	A menu of standard paragraphs for case management directions for each type of case of common occurrence. These should be available both in hard copy and electronically.
3. Either CMCs and/or PTRs are fairly common occurrences in fast track and multi-track cases.	CMCs and PTRs should either be replaced with directions on paper or be used more selectively.
4. Many multi-track cases do not receive directions from the court that take them all the way to trial. There are frequently one or more CMCs.	In multi-track cases the entire timetable for the action to trial should be drawn up as early as possible.

KEY POINTS SUMMARY

- Often, the court's first step in 'active case management' will occur in allocating a case to track and proceeding to make case management directions to provide a timetable of the steps to trial.

- Parties are expected to cooperate in assisting the court in the preparation of case management directions.

- The court will look to impose 'standard directions' wherever possible.

- Details of the standard directions applicable to each track can be found in the CPR and accompanying Practice Directions pertaining to the track (CPR 27–29).

- Any directions outside standard directions will need to be justified within the provisions of the overriding objective.

- Parties must be prompt in applying to the court for tailored directions orders and prompt in seeking to vary any direction order that has been made.

- The court will impose sanctions if a party fails to comply with the directions set down.

Case studies *Andrew James Pike and Deep Builders Ltd/Bollingtons Ltd* and *Mrs Elizabeth Lynch t/a The Honest Lawyer*

Question 1

Complete the AQ for each of the two case studies.

Question 2

Prepare a list of suitable directions that you feel should be sought from the court for each of the two case studies.

---

online resource centre

Any documents referred to in these case study questions can be found on the Online Resource Centre—simply click on 'Case study documentation' to access the documents that you need for Chapter 12 and to be reminded of the questions above. Suggested answers to these case study questions can also be accessed on the Online Resource Centre by your lecturer.

13 INTERIM APPLICATIONS—GENERAL CONSIDERATIONS

It may also be appropriate to access and read the additional chapter 'Injunctions—other Equitable Remedies' contained in the Online Resource Centre when reading parts of this chapter.

 online resource centre

Relevant court forms relating to this chapter:

• N244 Notice of Interim Application

• N260 Statement of Costs

13.1 INTRODUCTION

This chapter will consider the following (but it would be useful to read Chapter 15 alongside this chapter):

• the nature of interim applications.

• interim applications made with and without notice, and those made with and without a hearing;

• common procedure; and

• time estimates.

See Chapter 4 for details of the likely costs orders that may be made in an interim application.

An interim application is any application made to the court that requires a judicial decision. This is usually in the time between a case being issued and the final trial or determination of the action. Because litigants now have little freedom to manage or control the path that an action takes to trial (see Chapter 12), many steps that a party may wish to take, both significant and less significant, will require a 'judicial decision' before those steps can happen. These 'steps' are known as 'interim applications'.

13.2 WHY DO WE MAKE INTERIM APPLICATIONS?

Interim applications are often made in the following circumstances:

- applications of a minor procedural nature—for example, for more time in which to do something;
- applications for more significant case management decisions—for example, applications relating to disclosure, exchange of evidence, or directions; or
- applications for specific remedies—for example, for specific disclosure, interim injunctions, and interim payments.

Interim applications can be used for a variety of purposes:

- they may enable an action to progress to trial more quickly;
- they may preserve evidence; or
- they may be used to exert pressure on an opponent.

The more significant interim applications may, by their very nature, have a direct impact on the outcome of the action and may, in themselves, result in a determination of the action or a settlement being reached. Apart from the numerous encouragements and incentives contained in the Protocols and in the CPR for litigants to resolve their disputes without recourse to the courts, many of the more significant interim applications can be seen as part of the armoury with which a party—often the stronger party—can force its opponent to the negotiating table and to settle on terms that are favourable to that stronger party. In this way, interim applications can be used tactically to gain the upper hand. The court will always consider the aims of the overriding objective so it is also important for any party making such an interim application to be prepared to give his reasons and justify the application to the court within the terms of the overriding objective—that is, that making the application is 'just', 'fair', and 'proportionate'.

Because of the significance of the outcome of some interim applications, the process of making them and the evidence supplied to support them needs to be considered every bit as carefully as the trial itself.

13.3 THE NATURE AND PURPOSE OF SUPPORTING EVIDENCE IN INTERIM APPLICATIONS

Interim applications can be included in the generic definition that we have given them—that is, 'any application that requires a judicial decision in the time between commencement and trial'—but there are many different kinds of application that can be made. The procedure for each interim application is not generic, and although there are common traits, it is very important for any legal representative making or responding to an interim application to have sought out and considered the CPR that applies, so as to be sure what the procedure and requirements are for that particular interim application.

Another very important matter to understand in relation to interim applications is that although the evidence or arguments that need to be made to support or oppose the application will always have to be carefully thought out and be properly prepared, the quality of the evidence, in terms of the 'weight' attached to it, can often be quite 'light'.

Legal representatives commonly put forward many persuasive arguments in support of their client's interim application or to oppose the other party's application, but it is very important to remember that these arguments are often little more than assertions (however powerfully or persuasively made) as they do not comprise 'evidence' with any credible weight attached to it (see chapter 18 paragraphs 18.4.3 and 18.5).

Oral evidence by witnesses is rarely permitted in interim applications. Care must always be taken, therefore, with the more relaxed rules of evidence that are often permitted in the making of interim applications that the party making the application is aware of the distinction between an 'assertion' and 'evidence supported by fact'. Equally, any party who seeks to oppose an interim application can often make very good use of the distinction in trying to persuade the Master or district judge that the application should not be granted when it is based merely on an 'assertion', rather than evidence supported by fact, or evidence that can be more carefully tested at trial by cross-examination. It is very important, therefore, to consider the inclusion of material evidence in an interim application so as to add 'weight' to the persuasive assertions that the legal representative may make at the hearing of the application. An assertion that is supported by contemporaneous material evidence can be, and often is, sufficiently persuasive to meet the criteria of the interim application, and is sufficient to address the Master's or district judge's discretion and his decision whether or not to make the order.

Apart from appreciating the need to be persuasive in seeking or opposing any interim application (but at the same time understanding the limitations of that persuasiveness described above), it also has to be remembered that all interim applications are 'procedural' in nature. An interim application can only be made if it is provided for in the CPR. Therefore, for any interim application to succeed, the rule providing for it must be complied with in full.

Making or responding to interim applications is where the practitioner can reveal his real understanding both of the issues affecting his client's case, as well as his powers of persuasiveness. Preparing the written evidence for the application is the practitioner's chance to demonstrate his skills of 'advocacy on paper'. Similarly making or responding to the application before the Master or district judge is the practitioner's chance to practise skills of advocacy in a 'real' environment.

13.4 THE NATURE OF INTERIM APPLICATIONS

There is no single CPR that applies to all interim applications.

CPR 23 and the accompanying Practice Direction provide the general rules for interim applications. The court's general power to make interim orders is contained in CPR 3.1(2). The court's power to grant interim remedies is contained in CPR 25.1. However, the power to make orders is not restricted to these sections and other parts of the CPR will apply. It will often be necessary to consider the Court Guides (if you are dealing with a High Court matter) applying to the court in which the action lies for further specific procedural guidance for the application that is to be made.

 Practical Considerations

The fact that there is no all-encompassing part of the CPR that covers the procedure for all interim applications may create a difficulty for any practitioner new to litigation. For some applications, whilst the procedure for making the application is neatly contained in a section of the CPR designed specifically for the application, others will be contained within the 'ethos' of the overriding objective and they may also be a minor part of a particular CPR's application. Ensuring, therefore, that the application covers all that is required for it to succeed is not always so certain. Often, both identifying a possible application that can be made, and knowing what procedure and weight of evidence is required to make it successfully, will be a question of experience. The applications, where a specific CPR designed for the application does not cover them, often seem innocuous. However, a failure to appreciate the chances of success of the application or a failure to abide by the procedural practice for it (and thus failing to gain the order sought) can knock a young practitioner's confidence significantly, as well as leave him with the unpleasant task of having to admit that failure to the client and his supervising partner.

Practical Considerations

A young practitioner (perhaps straight from an LPC course) will be fully aware of the need to conduct litigation in accordance with the overriding objective, and will be similarly aware that compliance with the CPR is essential. It is what he will have been taught to do and it is clearly 'best practice'. However, real life is often not so 'black and white' or so clear-cut, and the same is true even of litigation in practice. For example, a young practitioner, fresh from the idealism of taught (as against experienced) CPR in practice may feel confident that an opponent who has failed to comply with a direction order will be left without the benefit of the order. The young practitioner may find, however, that the court is less rigid in its application of the rule and allows the breach to pass with little or no penalty. Knowing when this may happen, knowing how to conduct litigation within the rules, and knowing when to make or respond to interim applications that arise are all important parts of the 'experience' that is acquired with increased practice. A young practitioner lacking this experience must not hesitate to seek guidance and confirmation from the supervising partner.

The young practitioner must also always remember to ensure that the client is aware of the consequences of any step taken or responded to, and has given specific instructions to take the step that has been identified as necessary and in the client's best interests.

13.5 COMMON PROCEDURE

It is important to note that the specific CPR that contains the power or the procedure to follow in some interim applications will take precedence over any general rule. However, the generic rules of procedure that will apply where there are no specific rules are contained in CPR 23 and are as follows.

- Any interim application should be made as soon as it is apparent that it is necessary or desirable to make it (PD 23.2.7).

- Wherever possible, an interim application should be made and heard at any hearing that has already been listed (PD 23.2.8). Most commonly, this will be at a case management conference (CMC—see Chapter 12).

- The interim application should generally be made to the court in which the action is proceeding (CPR 23.2). If a trial has been fixed, the interim application should be made to the trial court. If the application relates to enforcement, it should be made to the court dealing with enforcement. If the application is being made pre-action, it should be made to the court in which the action is likely to be commenced.

- The application notice states the intention of the party applying. This notice should always be prepared (CPR 23.1) and, save in very exceptional circumstances, this notice should be filed at court even if the application is being made without notice (CPR 23.3). The formal requirements for application notices are set out in PD 23.2.1—this refers to Form N244, which may be used to make the application. (See the Online Resource Centre for a description of Form N244 and annotated notes for its completion.)

online resource centre

- Generally, an interim application should be an 'on notice' application unless there is good reason for it to be 'without notice' (CPR 23.4(2)).

- If there is a time limit for making an interim application, the application is treated as being made on the day on which the application notice and fee are received by the court (CPR 23.5).

- All of the evidence being relied on for the interim application should be filed at court, ideally at the same time as filing the application notice (PD 23.9.4). If the evidence is already with the court, then further copies need not be filed.

- The application notice, evidence, and order should be served at least three clear days before the hearing (CPR 23.7(1)(b)). If the matter is to be heard by way of a telephone conference hearing then these documents should be served within five days of the hearing date.

- A draft order (of the application sought) should be filed at court, and if it is long or complex, it should also be supplied on disk (PD 23.12.1). If the matter is a multi-track case, then a case summary must also be served. Both the draft order and a case summary must be filed and served no later than 4pm at least two clear days before the hearing.

- Supporting evidence is not always required for case management directions, although reasons should normally be given that seek to justify the application.

- The court may allow urgent applications to be dealt with on short notice (PD 23.3 and 23.4).

- Most interim applications are dealt with by the Master and district judges, although some applications may be referred to a judge for hearing (CPR 23.1). If a particular Master, or district judge, or judge has heard an earlier interim application, the matter can be referred to that Master, district judge, or judge if it would be helpful to do so. The Master or district judge may also refer the matter to a judge (PD 2 and PD 23.1).

- A fee is payable unless the applicant can obtain exemption on grounds of financial hardship.

- If the court is to serve the respondent, the applicant must file sufficient copies of the application notice, supporting evidence, and draft order for it to do so. The court will then serve these documents, together with notice of the hearing date and time.

- If the respondent wishes to rely on evidence to respond to the interim application, such evidence should be filed at court at least two days before the hearing. This would include a case summary if the case is a multi-track case as stated above.

- If an application for costs is being made in the application, the party's cost schedule (Form N260) must be lodged at court and served on the other party at least 24 hours before the hearing.

Note: Reference should be made to Chapter 4 for detail of the most common costs orders and cost procedure in interim applications, along with the 'Costs' box in Chapter 2, paragraph 2.4.8.

 Practical Considerations

In many courts, it is possible to liaise with the court listing officer of the court regarding obtaining a hearing date or telephone conference call appointment.

13.6 TIME ESTIMATES

The court will expect the applicant to give an assessment of the likely time that the hearing of the interim application will take. Where the application is to be on notice, the court also expects the parties, wherever possible, to cooperate in agreeing a time estimate for the hearing.

Practical Considerations

The time estimate should include not only the time for both parties to make their representations, but should also include time for the judge to make a decision and time for any applications for costs to be considered. In more complex matters, the estimate should also include time for the judge to read the papers.

13.7 NOTICE AND HEARING PROVISIONS FOR INTERIM APPLICATIONS

13.7.1 APPLICATIONS WITH NOTICE

Applications on notice may occur with a hearing. They may also occur without a hearing when, for example, the parties have agreed that the order sought should be made or the court considers that a hearing is not appropriate (CPR 23.8). Many of the applications for which a hearing is listed will be heard by telephone, or by video conferencing (see Chapter 15, paragraph 15.5).

The above general rules apply, but remember that the procedure set out in a CPR specific to the interim application being made will take precedence over the general rules in CPR 23.

 Practical Considerations

The CPR state that the notice of the interim application, the supporting evidence, notice of the hearing date, and the draft order should be served on the respondent 'at least three days before the hearing' (note five days if the matter is being heard by way of a telephone conference hearing). However, it is important also to note the words 'as soon as practicable' that are contained in PD 23.4.1. If, as the legal representative for the applicant in an interim application, you have filed your application at court in good time, and have received back from the court the date and time of the hearing, you could be severely criticized by the court for holding back serving the application and notice of hearing on your opponent until much nearer the time of the hearing or telephone appointment (the aim being to gain the tactical advantage of time and giving the respondent limited time in which to respond). It would be wrong to choose to comply with that part of the rule for service that requires service 'at least three clear days before the hearing' and not that part which expects service 'as soon as practicable' in order to gain a perceived advantage of surprise. The criticism by the court could mean that the application is dismissed, adjourned, or if the Master or district judge does hear the application in these circumstances, he may make adverse costs orders against the applicant for the failure to serve 'as soon as practicable'.

13.7.2 APPLICATIONS WITHOUT NOTICE

Applications without notice can occur either with or without a hearing.

The basic principle of litigation is that an order should not be made against a party without him having an opportunity to be heard. However, there will be occasions on which it is necessary to do so, such as:

- when giving notice may defeat the purpose of the application, or could create an injustice through delay or action that the respondent may take to defeat the application—examples include search orders and freezing injunctions; (for further details of these, and other, injunctions see the online additional chapter 'Injunctions—other Equitable Remedies' on the Online Resource Centre);

 online resource centre

- when the opponent is not yet on the court record—an example of which might be when the claimant seeks more time in which to serve the claim form, or when a defendant seeks permission of the court to issue an additional claim (CPR 20) (on the occasions on which permission is needed); or

- when the defendant can only be identified by description and not by name—an example may occur in intellectual property claims.

PD 23.3 sets out a list of occasions on which an interim application may be made without notice. These include when:

- there is exceptional urgency;
- the overriding objective is best furthered by the application being made without notice;
- the parties consent;
- the court grants permission;
- a date for a hearing has been fixed and a party wishes to make an application at that hearing, but does not have sufficient time to serve an application notice; and
- where a rule, Practice Direction, or court order permits.

The evidence in support of an application without notice must include the reasons why notice was not given (CPR 25.3(3)).

 Practical Considerations

Except where secrecy is essential, an applicant who does not have time to give proper notice of the application should give as much informal notice as possible (PD 23.4.2 and 23.2.10, and PD 25). This informal notice could include phoning the respondent and giving him details of the application. This may enable the respondent to attend and participate in the hearing. Such an application will be called an application 'opposed but without notice'. Giving informal notice may result in delays, because the respondent who attends the hearing after informal notice may well succeed in obtaining an adjournment while he prepares evidence to oppose the application. This possibility does not give the applicant good reason for not giving informal notice when it is felt that such notice would ordinarily be given but for the shortage of time.

An applicant and his solicitors each have special obligations when making a without-notice application to the court. This reflects the fact that they are asking the court to make an order without hearing any evidence or opposing arguments from the respondent. These obligations include a 'high duty to make a full, fair and accurate disclosure of material information to the court and to draw the court's attention to significant factual, legal and procedural aspects of the case' (*per* Mummery LJ in *Memory Corporation plc v Sidhu (No 2)* [2000] EWCA Civ 9). The applicant must carry out proper enquiries to ensure that this duty is met. The applicant is also often required to give an undertaking as to damages to protect the respondent from any losses that he may incur as a result of the order being made against him unjustly.

The most common without-notice applications are freezing injunctions, search orders, and intellectual property claims, all of which are outside the scope of this book (but see the online additional chapter 'Injunctions—other Equitable Remedies').

online resource centre

13.7.2.1 What happens if an application is made without notice when it is not appropriate to do so?

If an application is made without notice in circumstances under which the court concludes that it was not appropriate to have done so, the application will be dismissed or adjourned until proper notice is given.

13.7.2.2 When does the respondent hear of the order made?

CPR 23.9 states that when an order has been made on a without-notice application, unless the court orders otherwise, it must be served on the respondent. This service will include the application notice, the evidence that supported the application, and the order that has been made. Usually, the court will effect service—but see CPR 6.3 and CPR 40.4 for details of these service provisions, and the option that the applicant has of effecting service himself.

The notice to the respondent will include a statement setting out the respondent's right to make an application to set aside or vary the order that has been made (CPR 23.10), but such application by the respondent must be made within seven days after the date of service.

13.7.3 APPLICATIONS WITHOUT A HEARING

Applications without a hearing are otherwise known as 'paper applications' and are discussed in some detail in Chapter 15, paragraph 15.3.

13.8 'CARELESS' NEGOTIATIONS—THE STATUS OF THINGS SAID IN THE PRE-HEARING DISCUSSIONS

online
resource
centre

It is important to make a careful file note of any discussions between the legal representatives that takes place either on the telephone before the hearing, or if an attendance at court is required, whilst waiting. It is important to note that no form of privilege will cover the pre-hearing discussions unless they are stated to be 'without prejudice'. Care needs to be taken, in any pre-hearing discussions, not to make careless concessions or unsubstantiated assertions of fact, because these could come back to haunt you as informal admissions and may bind the client, or be used to challenge your client's or another witness's testimony at the trial. Please see the Bollington Beer case study on the Online Resource Centre as this demonstrates how pre-hearing discussions can be misconstrued.

  Practical Considerations

It is important to remember that the 'without prejudice' rule only covers discussions that take place 'with a view to settlement' and that this will not, therefore, cover general case management discussions. This is important to remember so as to avoid making an 'informal admission', or an acknowledgement of a state of affairs in an 'open', not 'without prejudice', forum—a reminder that was reinforced in *Stax Claimants v Bank of Nova Scotia Channel Islands Ltd* [2007] EWHC 1153.

13.9 AN UNLESS ORDER

13.9.1 WHAT IS AN 'UNLESS ORDER'?

If the court concludes that the opponent in an interim application has failed adequately to comply with the obligations of a previous order or within the general ethos of litigation practice (he may have failed to respond to an early request to comply), or if the court doubts the bona fides of the opponent, it will often make an order and, at the same time, specify a sanction to be imposed if the order is not complied with. Any order that imposes a sanction for non-compliance must specify the date and time by which the steps of the order must be complied with (CPR 2.9). The sanction part of the order may take the form of an 'unless' provision. PD 40B.8.2 lays down formulae for drafting unless orders. Compliance with the time limits set in court orders is regarded as fundamental to litigation practice under the CPR, and the courts will not shirk from making unless orders within the terms of a first order so as to ensure that the strict timetable for the action can be met. However, the court will generally only make such an order if there has been, or there is, evidence that there will be a deliberate failure to comply with earlier orders of the court, or where any default would make a fair trial of the action impossible.

Example

Your opponent has failed to serve his list of documents in accordance with the direction of the court for standard disclosure made at a recent CMC. You have requested the list and warned that an application will be made to the court if it is not forthcoming. The list still does not materialize and you are forced to apply to the court, requesting an order that your opponent be compelled to serve his list of documents within 14 days, failing which he should be deprived of the opportunity to defend the action.

If your application is successful, the order might be drafted as follows:

- 'The defendant is to serve its list of documents by 4 p.m. on 25 May 201?, failing which he shall be debarred from defending the claim further …'; or
- 'Unless the defendant serves its list of documents by 4 p.m. on 25 May 201?, its defence will be struck out …'.

£ Costs

If, in your warning letter, you had also said that if you had to make an application to the court for an order compelling your opponent to comply, you would seek an order for costs on the 'indemnity' basis, the court may also consider making a costs recovery order on the application on this enhanced basis.

13.9.2 RELIEF FROM SANCTIONS

If an unless order is made against a party and the order is not complied with, the sanction will automatically be imposed, even if, at a later date, the party complies with the order. Consider the example above: if the defendant did not serve his list by 25 May, but served it on 29 May, his defence would still be struck out by virtue of the breach of the unless order.

To try to remedy the situation, the defendant and his legal representative should consider making an application under CPR 3.9 for relief from sanctions—that is, ask the court to consider CPR 3.9(1) and not to strike out the case, nor to make the adverse costs order. The application must be made as soon as practicable and be supported by evidence.

KEY POINTS SUMMARY

- An interim application is a step in the action between issue and trial that requires a judicial decision.
- There are some interim applications that can be made pre-action.
- Interim applications require strict adherence to the requirements set down in the CPR.
- The key rules are CPR 1, 3, 23, and 25.
- Applications are usually made in Form N244.
- Applications may be applications with notice, application without notice, with a hearing, or without a hearing.

SELF-TEST QUESTIONS

1. What is the general purpose of interim applications?

2. The evidence submitted in support of an interim application is usually written evidence. What is the effect of this?

3. In terms of any interim application, what two most important matters must the person applying ensure that he can do or has done?

4. When would an interim application be made without notice?

5. What is the purpose of an 'unless order' and when might one be made in connection with interim applications?

online resource centre

Suggested answers to these general questions can be accessed on the Online Resource Centre.

Relevant court forms relating to this chapter:

- N244 Notice of Interim Application
- N260 Statement of Costs

14.1 INTRODUCTION

This chapter will consider the interim applications that a legal representative may most commonly come across in practice. We will consider both the procedure for the specific interim application, as well as the form of the evidence needed to make or oppose it.

The interim applications that will be considered in this detail will be:

- an application to set aside default judgment;
- summary judgment;

- interim payment; and

- an application for specific disclosure.

It should be noted that the number of interim applications that can be made is far greater than those listed above (see Chapter 13 paragraph 13.2). Some will follow the generic procedure detailed in Chapter 13; others may have a specific CPR covering the procedure and criteria for the application. It is important to remember that in nearly all interim applications (except, for example, those that require secrecy), a legal representative will be expected to ask his opponent to concede voluntarily to the relief or order being sought before proceeding with an application to the court. A failure to do this will usually result in an adverse costs order being made.

You may also wish to refer to the additional chapter 'Injunctions—other Equitable Remedies' contained in the Online Resource Centre for further details on injunctions.

14.2 SETTING ASIDE DEFAULT JUDGMENT

14.2.1 WHAT IS 'DEFAULT JUDGMENT' AND HOW IS IT OBTAINED?

Default judgment enables the claimant to obtain an early determination of his action, without a trial and where a defendant fails to file an acknowledgement of service or a defence within the time limits prescribed by the court rules. It is judgment by an administrative, rather than a judicial, act.

Any application or request for default judgment will need to have careful regard for the relevant time limits within which the defendant should have either lodged his acknowledgement of service or filed his defence. The following should also be noted and CPR Part 12 considered in detail in relation to the following circumstances.

- Default judgment does not apply, for example, when there is an application pending to strike out the claim, or when an application for summary judgment is pending (CPR 12.3), or when the situations set down in CPR 12.2 arise.

- The procedure is modified for certain claims—for example, where the claim includes a claim for 'any other remedy'.

- A defendant cannot obtain a default judgment on a counterclaim against a claimant on the basis of failure to acknowledge service, because CPR 10 does not apply to counterclaims, but default judgment may be obtained on a counterclaim once the time for filing the defence to the counterclaim has expired (CPR 12.2.2(b)).

- Special rules apply if a defendant is a child, patient, or state. In these situations, an application for default judgment must be supported by evidence (CPR 12.11.3).

- If a claimant, rather than the court, had served the claim form, default judgment cannot be entered until a certificate of service is filed.

- There is also special provision in the rules for obtaining default judgment against defendants sued in the alternative, and those sued jointly, or jointly and severally. These provisions will either deal with the disposal of the whole claim, or enable default judgment to be obtained against one defendant and the action to proceed against the remaining defendants (CPR 12.8).

14.2.1.1 The procedure for securing default judgment

Depending on the type of claim, default judgment is sought either by:

- filing a request (CPR 12.4 (1) or (3)); or

- an application to the court (CPR 12.4(2), 12.9 *and* 12.10).

14.2.1.1.1 *By request*

If default judgment is sought by filing a request:

- Form N225 will be filed if the claim is for a specific amount of money or for delivery up, in which case the defendant is given the alternative of paying a specific amount;
- Form N227 will be filed if the claim is for a sum of money to be determined by the court;
- the relevant completed form will be lodged at the court and no fee will be required;
- the request will be dealt with by the court administratively (rather than judicially); and
- if the requirements are made out, judgment will be entered.

14.2.1.1.2 *By application*

If default judgment is sought by application to the court:

- Form N244 will be completed, with supporting evidence;
- a fee will be payable;
- notice of the application must be given to the defendant (as soon as practicable after it is filed, or at least three clear days before the hearing) unless the defendant has failed to lodge an acknowledgement of service or an exception under CPR 12.11(4) applies; and
- at the court hearing, if the requirements are made out, judgment will be entered.

14.2.2 WHEN MAY AN APPLICATION BE MADE TO SET ASIDE A DEFAULT JUDGMENT?

CPR 13 sets out the rules and procedure for applications to set aside a default judgment. It makes a distinction between the two sorts of default judgment that may be sought under CPR 12—that is, those that the court *must* set aside (CPR 13.2) and those that the court *may* set aside (CPR 13.3).

The court *must* set aside a default judgment when a ground listed in CPR 13.2 has been established—that is, when the defendant can show that the default judgment was wrongly entered by the claimant in that:

- it may have been entered too early;
- it was made after the defendant had made an application to strike out the claim or had applied to dismiss the claim summarily, but where the application by the defendant has not yet been concluded;
- it may have been entered even though the whole claim (including interest and costs) had already been paid or settled; or
- it was entered after the defendant had filed an admission, but had made a request for time to pay, and that request has not yet been dealt with.

In each of the above situations, the defendant's request to set aside the default judgment need only establish one of the grounds listed and the default judgment will be set aside.

In the case of *Rajval Construction Ltd v Bestville Properties Ltd* [2010] EWCA Civ 1621 the Court of Appeal declared that where the claimant had failed to serve the Response Pack with the Particulars of Claim (as required by CPR 7.8) the claimant's default judgment would be set aside.

The court *may* set aside a default judgment that has been entered by the claimant in all other situations. CPR 13.3 provides that the court has discretion to set aside the default judgment entered. A defendant who wishes to seek an order to set aside a default judgment will need to act promptly and satisfy the two grounds set out in CPR 13.3.1—that is, he must:

- show that he has a real prospect of successfully defending the claim; or
- establish some other good reason why the judgment should be set aside and the defendant be permitted to defend the claim.

and under CPR13.3.2:

- In considering whether to set aside or vary a judgment entered under CPR 12, the matters to which the court *must* have regard include whether the person seeking to set aside the judgment made an application to do so promptly. (author's italics)

The case of *Mullock v Price t/a the Elms Hotel Restaurant* [2009] EWCA 1222 is a recent illustration of the importance of 'acting promptly' (CPR 13.3(2)) in an application to set aside a default judgment. In this case both the party seeking to set aside and his legal representative were considered 'blameless' for the delay; the court felt that unravelling the judgment two years after the judgment was not justified. The case is also a reminder that parties themselves owe a duty to 'act promptly' and they cannot hide behind the delay of another. This point has again been emphasized in the case of *Standard Bank plc v Agrinvest International Inc1* 14 January 2011, CA, where Lord Justice Moore-Bick set out some important observations on the necessity of timeliness in making applications to set aside default judgment. He confirmed that where there had been a lack of timeliness, even when a potentially successful defence had been put forward, the application may still be rejected.

14.2.3 WHAT EVIDENCE IS REQUIRED TO SET ASIDE A DEFAULT JUDGMENT?

14.2.3.1 Where the court must set aside the default judgment

An application need only submit the chronology or the facts that bring the application under the provisions of CPR 13.2. These facts may include copies of supporting evidence and, usually, there is sufficient space within Part C of the application notice (Form N244) in which to set out this detail. The court may be prepared to consider the application as a 'paper hearing' without notice (see Chapter 15, paragraph 15.3). In any application to set aside default judgment under the provisions of CPR 13.2, the consent of the other party should be sought, and if it is obtained, the application can be submitted as an agreed application. The court will then almost certainly consider the application as a paper application and no hearing will be listed. In all cases in which it is clear that the defendant can establish a ground under CPR 13.2, the claimant would be well advised to consent to the application, because he may otherwise incur penalty costs for his failure to cooperate in such an application.

14.2.3.2 Where the court has discretion to set aside a default judgment

For applications to set aside under CPR 13.3, evidence must be submitted. The evidence that the defendant needs to produce to succeed in the application will need to address the court's discretion that will be used to consider whether to make the order. The supporting evidence will therefore need to address the following.

- The prospects of success of the defence—this could be achieved by presenting a witness statement that sets out the basis of the intended defence. One of the most persuasive ways of doing this would be to exhibit a draft of the intended defence to the witness statement (provided that the legal representative has the client's approval to incur the additional costs of drafting the defence).
- If the ground set out in CPR 13.3.1(b) is being relied on, the witness statement needs to address the 'other good reasons' why the defendant should be permitted to proceed and defend.

- The defendant will also need to set out in what way he has acted 'promptly' in making the application, or any valid and excusable reasons that he may have for any delay.

14.2.4 THE PROCEDURE FOR MAKING AN APPLICATION TO SET ASIDE A DEFAULT JUDGMENT

An application to set aside a judgment in default is made in the normal way in Form N244. Under CPR 13.4, the application will be transferred automatically to the defendant's home court if not already issued from that court when:

- the claim is for a specified sum; and
- the defendant is an individual.

If the defendant does not fall within the criteria of CPR 13.4, he could apply for a transfer to his home court as part of his application to set aside, but the application will be heard in the court in which the claim was issued, and if a set aside order is made, the court will then consider the request to transfer on the criteria set down in CPR 30.3. These include the financial value of the claim and convenience.

Supporting evidence may be contained in Part C of Form N244 or in a separate witness statement. It is unlikely that the evidence will be contained in a statement of case available in the case, because at this stage, the only statement of case is likely to be the claimant's particulars of claim. The application must be submitted promptly and will, in nearly every case, be 'on notice' with the requisite current fee.

14.2.5 ORDERS THAT MAY BE MADE IN AN APPLICATION TO SET ASIDE DEFAULT JUDGMENT

Where the application is made in a case in which the court must set aside, any order made for payment to the claimant will also be set aside.

In applications in which the court has a discretion to set aside, the court will consider the evidence supporting the application, and may make such orders and directions as it thinks are appropriate. This can include dismissing the application, or granting the application, either conditionally or unconditionally. (See the video clips on the Online Resource Centre for an example of an application to set aside default judgment.)

online resource centre

14.3 SUMMARY JUDGMENT

14.3.1 SUMMARY JUDGMENT AND THE EUROPEAN CONVENTION ON HUMAN RIGHTS (ECHR)

Summary judgment is available both to claimants and to defendants. It seeks to avoid the occasions on which an opponent's case shows no reasonable prospects of success. It provides a quick and efficient solution to the case. It is therefore clearly distinguished from a default judgment, which relies on a 'default' on the part of the defendant.

Of course, because an order for summary judgment will prevent the opponent from having 'his day in court' and would therefore potentially be a breach of Art. 6 of the European Convention on Human Rights (ECHR), the court will only make the order when the criteria for it are precisely met. It can be seen that when the strict criteria have not been met, the court cannot make an order for summary judgment. In these situations, the court does however have the power to make lesser orders (see paragraph 14.3.5.2).

Any judgment or order made in the absence of a party contravenes the basic core principle of domestic law and human rights that the party against whom the order or judgment has been made should have the right to have the judgment or order set aside. But this right is not an absolute one: the courts will frequently require the party who wishes to set aside the judgment or order made in their absence to show that they have a defence with 'real prospects'—that is, that there is 'no other compelling reason' why the matter should be heard at a trial. Article 6 of the ECHR does not say that every piece of evidence must be tested at trial. The fact remains, however, that in any situation in which an injustice may occur, the court must be careful to ensure that due regard is given to these points before refusing a party a right to a 'fair hearing'. The CPR seek to embrace these issues. But, the courts have limited scope to make an order that could breach this basic human right. This arises most clearly in applications for summary judgment. There will be occasions in applications for summary judgment on which the court can only make an order that is, in reality, a compromise—a balancing act, ensuring that cases are dealt with efficiently, but also fairly.

There is an advantage in a successful application for summary judgment in that it secures a quick determination of the action. But the disadvantages of a failed application must also be borne in mind. An application for summary judgment that has failed may, in addition to the likelihood of bearing an adverse costs order (these can be substantial and will be payable promptly), also result in delays, because until the application has been heard, further progress of the action is suspended.

14.3.2 WHEN IS SUMMARY JUDGMENT USED?

CPR 24 sets out a procedure whereby the court may make a decision on a claim or a particular issue without the delay and expense of trial. This has the benefit of precluding a claim that has no real merit proceeding to trial. It may apply at the same time as an application to strike out under CPR 3.4. It is worth making a note of the differences between CPR 3.4 (applications to strike out a claim) and CPR 24.2 (applications for summary judgment).

CPR 3.4 provides that a claim, or part of a claim, may be struck out when:

- the statement of case discloses no reasonable grounds for bringing or defending the claim; or
- the statement of case is an abuse of the court's processes; or
- where there has been a failure to comply with a rule, Practice Direction, or order.

CPR 24.2 provides that the court may grant summary judgment against a claimant or a defendant (for all or part of a claim) when:

- the claimant has no real prospect of succeeding on the claim or issue; or
- the defendant has no real prospect of successfully defending the claim or issue; and
- in respect of either of the grounds above, there is no other compelling reason why the case should be disposed of at trial.

In an application for summary judgment, the court may strike out the claim or defence if it is so weak on the facts that it will not succeed.

There is clearly an overlap between the two provisions, but the substance for each is not identical. Although there will be situations in which a combined application can be made, this will not always be the case and the practitioner must not assume that an application for summary judgment should always be conjoined with an application to strike out, or vice versa.

 Practical Considerations

It would not be appropriate to combine every application for summary judgment with an application to strike out the claim or issue. But if a combined application is being made, then the general requirements for any interim application set out in Chapter 13, paragraph 13.4, will apply, and the exact wording of each provision will have to be stated and the evidence being used for each should be applied. The witness statement supporting a combined application will need to show, for example, both that a statement of case discloses no reasonable grounds for bringing or defending the claim, and also that there is no real prospect of successfully defending the claim or issue and that there is no other compelling reason why the case should be disposed of at trial. A failure to address the exact requirements of both CPR 3 and 24 will result in a failure of that part of the application not complied with. (See also the 'Practical Considerations' box in Chapter 2, paragraph 2.3.2.)

14.3.3 THE PROCEDURE FOR SUMMARY JUDGMENT

An application for summary judgment is one of the interim applications the procedure of which is neatly contained in a part of the CPR designed specifically for that interim application. In this case, procedure is set out in CPR 24.4, which includes provisions that:

- either party can make the application, although it may not be made until the claimant has served his particulars of claim, and the defendant has served either his acknowledgement of service or his defence;

- if the claimant has failed to comply with any Pre-Action Protocol, an application for summary judgment by the claimant will not usually be entertained by the court until after the defence has been filed or the time for doing so has expired (in the latter situation, the application will often be an application for default judgment rather than summary judgment);

- if the application is made on the defendant lodging his acknowledgement of service and before the defence is filed, then the defendant need not file his defence until after the hearing of the summary judgment application;

 Practical Considerations

Although the defendant need not file his defence before a claimant's application for summary judgment is heard, any defendant who intends to oppose the claimant's application for summary judgment would often be well advised to give specific details of the nature of the defence that they intend to raise, or indeed to attach a draft of their intended defence to the evidence that they lodge to oppose the application, because this will give the court the clearest possible opportunity of seeing the defence that is intended and showing that the claimant has not met the criteria required to be successful in the application.

- a defendant may make an application for summary judgment against the claimant's claim at any time after issue;

 Practical Considerations

The ideal time for a defendant to make an application for summary judgment against the claimant's claim would be at, or immediately before, allocation. This would delay allocation until after the application has been heard. In practice, however, the court will often move on to matters of allocation at the summary judgment hearing, if the application for summary judgment has failed. The application for summary judgment will be heard first. This power is provided for within the court's general powers of management, but is also specifically referred to in CPR 24.6. An application for summary judgment by the defendant that is filed before he has filed his acknowledgement of service or defence also has the effect of preventing the claimant seeking default judgment until after the summary judgment application has been heard.

- the application will usually be supported by written evidence and this written evidence must be served on the other party at least 14 days before the hearing;

- if the application is being opposed, that written evidence must be served on the other party at least seven days before the hearing;

- any evidence in reply needs to be filed and served at least three days before the hearing;

- the application notice (usually in Form N244) must precisely identify and specify the application being made, and should state when any evidence to oppose the application should be filed and served;

- any written evidence to be relied on that is already filed at court and on the other party need not be served again, although reference to that evidence will need to be made in the application notice;

- if the defendant does not attend the hearing, any order made may be set aside on just terms;

- skeleton arguments and court bundles should be prepared in all but the most straightforward applications; and

- a draft order should be prepared and filed with the application.

14.3.4 THE EVIDENCE FOR A SUMMARY JUDGMENT APPLICATION

The essence of any evidence supporting an application for summary judgment will need to establish the two grounds set down under CPR 24.2. It must cover both elements—that is, the 'no reasonable prospects' test, as well as the 'no other compelling reason' test.

The burden of proof is on the applicant. There is no trial of the issues in a summary judgment hearing, and the applicant needs to satisfy the court that the claim or the defence has 'no reasonable prospect of success'. Accordingly, where assertions are made in the written evidence, the court will not be able to make an order for summary judgment if any issues arise that make it clear that a proper investigation should be made of the facts asserted—that proper investigation being at trial, where there can be a testing of the evidence by oral examination and cross-examination. The case of *Lexi Holdings v Pannone and Partners* [2009] EWHC 2590 (Ch) clearly illustrates the requirement to show 'real prospect' and it was not enough to argue that 'something might turn up' to prove the point being made to establish the application.

The evidence must also satisfy the second arm—that is, that there is 'no other compelling reason why the matter should go to trial'—and an application may fail under this part of the criterion even where it may have succeeded under the first: for example, where the applicant has behaved in a way that is not in keeping with the ethos of litigation or within the guidelines of the overriding objective, especially when that behaviour may have prevented the other party obtaining evidence that would reveal 'real prospects of success'. Another example of this second element arising (and causing the application to fail) may be when the defendant needs more time to investigate, and there is reason to believe that time and investigation may provide 'real prospects', although they are not evident at the time of the application.

 Practical Considerations

The fine distinction between facts that should be tested at trial and those that the court can accept as supporting the application for summary judgment is one that is best learnt and understood by experience. For a practitioner new to litigation, much can be learnt from reading the judgments of important cases that have considered such applications. Cases such as *Swain v Hillman* [2001] 1 All ER 91 and *Three Rivers District Council v Bank of England (No 3)* [2001] 2 All ER 513 are good examples. However, a reasonable electronic search with the key words 'summary judgment' will produce an array of cases to learn and understand the distinction better. The Court of Appeal set out some useful guidelines for making successful applications for summary judgment in *S v Gloucestershire County Council* [2000] 3 All ER 346.

14.3.5 **ORDERS THAT MAY BE MADE IN AN APPLICATION FOR SUMMARY JUDGMENT**

14.3.5.1 Successful applications

Where the application is successful, the court will order (for the claimant) summary judgment on the claim or issue, and that will be the end of the claim or issue, or it will order (for the defendant) that the claim or issue be struck out. Once summary judgment has been obtained, enforcement can proceed in the usual way (see Chapter 21 for details of enforcement options).

14.3.5.2 Partially successful applications

If the application has failed to establish the criteria for summary judgment, the application must fail. But this does not necessarily mean that the application will have had no benefit for the applicant. In a situation in which, for example, the defendant has raised a defence that has 'prospects', but which the court believes may not succeed, or if the motives of the defendant in raising the defence are in question, the court can make a conditional order instead of dismissing the application. This conditional order may include an order to pay part of the claim into court or to take a step in the action within a specified time (for example, for the defendant to 'file his defence'). The consequence of not complying with the condition may be that his right to defend will be struck out.

In this way, lesser orders may have the effect of ending the case.

 Practical Considerations

It is wise to specify, in any advance letter to your opponent, the intended application for summary judgment and to state further that an application for a conditional order will be made if the application should fail. The court will not usually make such an order if the party is unable to comply with the condition. The burden will be on the party subject to the condition imposed to show that he cannot comply.

14.3.5.3 Unsuccessful applications

If the application has failed or failed in part, as described in paragraph 14.3.5.2 above, the court will proceed to make an order for the progress of the action. The order may include directions for the time to file the defence, for allocation, or for substantive directions for the future management of the case. In effect, at the conclusion of the hearing, the court may treat the hearing as a case management conference (CMC—see Chapter 12).

14.4 INTERIM PAYMENTS

14.4.1 WHAT IS AN 'INTERIM PAYMENT'?

An interim payment made to a party in an action—usually the claimant—is one of the more significant interim applications that can be made. CPR 25 deals with interim remedies in general; CPR 25.6–25.9 deal with the grounds and procedure specific to an application for an interim payment. The remedy can alleviate hardship for a claimant caused by the delays of the litigation process. It is always discretionary, because there is no right to an order. Once the court has concluded that a ground has been established, it will first exercise its discretion whether to make an order at all and then will consider what the sum of the order should be.

 Practical Considerations

This remedy may be used to secure an advance payment of damages to a claimant in a personal injury claim (the early payment may assist in his treatment or recovery), or it may be used to secure an early payment for a commercial client who is experiencing cash flow problems whilst awaiting the process of his case claiming a large debt from the defendant against whom the interim payment application is made.

The rules set out several grounds on which an application may be made. The guiding principle for any award of an interim payment is to ensure that any award made does not cause an injustice. An early payment to the claimant who does not succeed in his case at the final determination of the case at trial has the potential to create a grave injustice to the defendant. Equally, an award that is higher than the sum finally secured by the claimant at trial can also cause an injustice to the defendant.

CPR 25.9 provides that any interim payment that has been made, whether it is by agreement or by order, should not be disclosed to the trial judge until after judgment of both liability and quantum has been made, unless the defendant consents.

See the Online Resource Centre for a video clip of an interim payment application, combined with a CMC.

14.4.2 THE GROUNDS ON WHICH AN INTERIM PAYMENT APPLICATION CAN BE MADE

CPR 25.7 contains five 'grounds' on which an order can be made and the burden for the claimant to persuade the court to make the award will increase in line with the potential for risk of injustice. Each of the grounds sets out clearly the remit and discretion that the district judge has when considering an application. It goes without saying that in the making of any interim application, or in opposing an application, the persuasive arguments needed to persuade the district judge to make the order or not make the order must directly address the criteria set in the relevant CPR. Any application for an interim payment must be supported with evidence.

The five grounds set out are as follows.

- Where the defendant has admitted liability (CPR 25.7.1(a)).

- Where the claimant has obtained judgment, but the sum to be paid is not yet assessed (CPR 25.7.1(b)).

- When the court is satisfied that if the action were to go to trial, the claimant would obtain judgment for a substantial sum (CPR 25.7.1(c)).

- In a claim in which there are two or more defendants and an order is sought against any one or more of the defendants, the court must be satisfied that if the action were to go to trial, the claimant would obtain judgment for a substantial sum against at least one of the defendants (but the court does not need to be sure which one), and in these circumstances, each of the defendants must be insured in respect of the claim (whether directly, or under s. 151 of the Road Traffic Act 1988, or the Motor Insurers Bureau), or be a public body (CPR 25.7.1(e)). The court has powers to make orders between defendants as to reimbursement of the award, provided that the defendant seeking reimbursement or contribution has made a claim against the other defendant for a contribution, indemnity, or other remedy.

- The other ground relates to an action for the possession of land, which is outside the scope of this book (CPR 25.7.1(d)).

> ### ✓ Practical Considerations
>
> CPR 25.7.1(c) is distinctly different from the grounds set down in CPR 25.7.1(a) and (b), because in this ground, there is the potential that any order granting an interim payment to the claimant *could* create an injustice to the defendant—the claimant may lose at trial. The words 'would obtain judgment' and 'substantial' are not defined by the rules. They will be given their 'natural' meaning. 'Would' means that, on the balance of probabilities, the claimant will probably win; it does not mean that he will definitely win, but the region of doubt should be narrow. Again, 'substantial' does not necessarily mean a large sum; rather, it will be a figure that, to *this* claimant, would be substantial.

14.4.3 **THE PROCEDURE FOR MAKING AN APPLICATION FOR AN INTERIM PAYMENT**

Before an application is made and filed at court, the defendant should be invited, by written request, to agree to make an interim payment.

The CPR provide that an application cannot be made before the end of the period for the filing, by the defendant, of the acknowledgement of service. A claimant may make more than one application for an interim payment in an action, but, clearly, each application would need to be made with the overriding objective in mind, and be proportionate, fair, and just (CPR 25.6).

There is a specific CPR designed for this interim application and the rules of procedure set out in the specific CPR must be followed. These are set out in CPR 25.6 and PD 25B.

The application must be supported by evidence, which must be filed and served at the same time as the application notice.

The time limits set out in CPR 25.6.3–25.6.6 and PD 25B are as follows.

- The application notice and evidence in support must be served 'as soon as practicable' (see the 'Practical considerations' box in Chapter 13, paragraph 13.7.1), but this must not be less than 14 days before the hearing date.
- If the defendant wishes to rely on written evidence at the hearing, he must file the written evidence at court and serve the claimant at least seven days before the hearing.
- If the claimant wishes to respond to the written representations served by the defendant, he must file his written representations at court and serve them on the defendant at least three days before the hearing.

The written evidence supporting the application must comply with PD 25B.2.1 and include details of:

- the sum of money sought;
- the items or matters in respect of which the payment is sought;
- an estimate of the likely sum of any final judgment (and reports that support that estimate, such as medical reports, should be exhibited);
- the reasons why the application meets the requirements of CPR 25.7;
- any other relevant matters; and
- in claims for personal injury, details of the special damages, and past and future loss, and in a claim under the Fatal Accidents Act 1976, details of the person(s) on whose behalf the claim is made and the nature of the claim.

 Practical Considerations

Applications for an interim payment may, when it is appropriate to do so, be combined with an application for summary judgment. For example, where a claimant has sought, and obtained, summary judgment in a claim for personal injuries and for damages to be assessed at a later hearing, it would be an advantage to the claimant to seek an interim payment pending the assessment hearing. The application for an interim payment would then proceed immediately after a successful (or partially successful) application for summary judgment. Where this is done, care should be taken when indicating the time estimate for the hearing to allow sufficient time for the application to deal with both interim applications.

As this section has stated, the evidence supporting an application for an interim payment will usually be in the form of a witness statement. For applications that are made under the grounds set out at CPR 25.7.1(a) and (b), the main emphasis of the witness statement will be to set out how the particular ground being relied on applies (that is, to state the admission or judgment) and then continue with the most up-to-date evidence to support the damages claim, so that the district judge can consider the sum of the award that he wishes to make and ensure that he does not award too much.

For applications made under the grounds set out at CPR 25.7.1(c) and (e), there is a risk that the claimant may fail in his case, so in these circumstances, the witness statement will need to state arguments that directly address the district judge's concern not to make an award when failure by the claimant is a real possibility, as well as contain detail and evidence of the damages claim.

Chapter 18, paragraph 18.4, sets out further guidance on the form of witness statements.

14.4.4 ORDERS THAT MAY BE MADE IN AN APPLICATION FOR AN INTERIM PAYMENT

14.4.4.1 How much can be awarded?

The court must not make an award of an interim payment that is more than a reasonable proportion of the likely amount of the final judgment (CPR 25.7.4). In assessing the sum to award, the court must take account of contributory negligence, as well as any set-off or counterclaim (CPR 25.7.5).

In *Fiona Jordan and Philippe Jordan v Dean Greason (No 2)* [2007] EWHC 2270, the Technology and Construction Court (TCC) set out some relevant guidelines to consider the amount of an interim payment award. These include:

- a consideration of a sum that was just and would not exceed a reasonable proportion of the estimated final judgment award (in this case, the TCC awarded an interim payment approximately 15 per cent below the sum sought by the claimant);
- the claimant's ability to repay the sum, as well as the financial position of the defendant to make a payment (a provision that is only likely to have any real significance in interim payments made under CPR 25.7.1(c)); and
- that the court should not be overly (or at all) concerned with the claimant's 'need' for the money, nor should it be concerned with what the claimant intends to do with the money.

 Practical Considerations

Again, it would be a very brave applicant, making his application under CPR 25.7.1(c), who did not seek to add weight to his application by setting out what the money was needed for and how it might ultimately benefit the claimant. Equally, if it can be shown that an interim payment now might have the outcome of assisting the claimant's recovery and might help to reduce the sum of the final award, it would be prudent to include such evidence.

14.4.4.2 Can payments by instalment be ordered?

The court has the power to make an interim payment award payable by instalment under CPR 25.6.7, and where such an order is made, the order should contain:

- details of the total sum awarded;
- the amount of each instalment;
- the number of instalments; and
- to whom the payments should be made.

14.4.4.3 Social Security benefit payments

In the making of an interim payment award in a personal injury claim, the defendant should notify the court of any sum that is to be deducted under the Social Security (Recovery of

Benefits) Act 1997. These are amounts that the claimant has received in respect of certain benefits, such as statutory sick pay. Any amount of an interim payment will be net of those (relevant) benefits that the claimant has received and with the relevant sum so deducted being repaid. The defendant will do this by obtaining a 'certificate of recoverable benefits' and filing this at court before or at the hearing of the application.

14.5 AN APPLICATION FOR SPECIFIC DISCLOSURE

Note: This section should be read in conjunction with Chapter 17.

14.5.1 WHAT IS 'SPECIFIC DISCLOSURE'?

The purpose of disclosure generally is to make available documents that either support or undermine the respective parties' cases. It is designed to maintain the 'all the cards on the table' approach to litigation. As part of its management role, the court will usually make an order for standard disclosure (see Chapter 17, paragraph 17.4.1). The court can also order that certain specific documents, or classes of document, are disclosed, or it may order that further specific searches are conducted where there is evidence that a party is in breach of its disclosure obligations. The underlying purpose of specific disclosure is to ensure that justice is done between the parties and to avoid a situation in which a party may have, or obtain, an unfair advantage, or suffer an unfair disadvantage as a result of a document not being produced for inspection under standard disclosure.

Under Practice Direction (PD) 31.5.5(1)(b), the court can make a specific disclosure order requiring a party to disclose, or to search for and disclose, documents that:

- 'it is reasonable to suppose may contain information' that will assist the applicant's case or damage the respondent's case; or

- 'which may lead to a train of enquiry which has either of those consequences'.

Where a party believes that another party's disclosure is inadequate, he can apply to the court for an order for specific disclosure under CPR 31.12(1).

14.5.2 WHEN CAN AN APPLICATION FOR SPECIFIC DISCLOSURE BE MADE?

An application for specific disclosure is usually made after standard disclosure under CPR 31.5 has taken place. However, it may be made before service of the list of documents (CPR 31.12—see *Dayman v Canyon Holdings* (unreported, 11 January 2006, Ch D)). This will be subject to the specific procedural requirements in each track and any specific requirements in each of the divisions of the High Court.

14.5.3 APPLICATIONS AT A LATE STAGE OF PROCEEDINGS

There is no reason why the court will not order specific disclosure even a couple of weeks before trial, or even at trial, provided that it can be shown that the likely significance of the specific disclosure sought is substantial, the cost of complying is not disproportionate, and compliance with the order is within the capabilities of the respondent to the application even at a late stage in the proceedings (*Legal & General Assurance Society Ltd v Taulke-Johnson* [2002] EWHC 120).

14.5.4 IN WHAT CIRCUMSTANCES IS THE COURT LIKELY TO MAKE AN ORDER?

Under CPR 31.12, the court will make an order for specific disclosure if standard disclosure is inadequate (PD 31.5.1). 'Inadequate' has not been precisely defined, but it may arise when:

- it is clear on the face of the opponent's list of documents that it is inadequate—for example, if there are gaps in dates in a list of chronological documents;

- important documents that are known to exist, or to have existed, have not been disclosed;
- it is apparent that the search undertaken by the opponent was inadequate—for example, if there are documents that fall into a specific category, or which were created before or after a certain date that were not searched for, but which you believe support your case or adversely affect your opponent;
- documents are referred to in a statement of case, but not provided following a request under CPR 31.14;
- documents are referred to in correspondence, but are not included;
- documents to which your client or your potential witnesses have referred as existing, but which do not appear in the list;
- the disclosure statement is limited in a way that would mean that relevant documents would not be disclosed—for example, where your opponent objects to you inspecting on the grounds of proportionality and you believe that inspection would be proportionate; or
- there appear to be documents set out in your opponent's list in the section withheld from inspection on the grounds of privilege, but which you believe may not be privileged (see Chapter 17, paragraph 17.9).

 Practical Considerations

Was the opponent's search unreasonably limited? Look carefully at the disclosure statement. Was it unreasonable to exclude documents pre or post a certain date, or in a certain category?

Remember also that the disclosure obligation is a continuing one. Documents that may have come to light after your opponent has served his list of documents still need to be disclosed. In practice, the list of documents is amended mutually. If the documents are not forthcoming on inspection, then an application for specific disclosure may follow.

14.5.5 WHAT WILL THE COURT ORDER?

Under CPR 31.12(2), if an order for specific disclosure is granted, the court may order a party to do one or more of the following:

- to disclose documents or classes of documents specified in the order;
- to carry out a search to the extent specified in the order;
- to disclose any documents located as a result of that search.

However, in deciding whether to grant an order, the court will (under PD 31.5.4):

Take into account all the circumstances of the case and, in particular, the overriding objectives. But if the court concludes that the party from whom specific disclosure is sought has failed adequately to comply with the obligations imposed by an order for disclosure (whether by failing to make a sufficient search for documents or otherwise) the court will usually make such order as is necessary to ensure that those obligations are properly complied with.

14.5.6 THE FORM OF AN ORDER FOR SPECIFIC DISCLOSURE

Under CPR 31.12, the court may order specific disclosure by ordering a party to:

- prepare a supplemental list of documents, specifying the documents available for inspection;

- give disclosure of specific documents, or a specific class of documents;
- carry out a new specified search and disclose documents revealed by that search.

14.5.7 'FISHING EXPEDITIONS'

When you have a belief that documents exist, but have no substantive evidence, your application for specific disclosure may be more akin to a 'fishing expedition' (that is, a search undertaken only in the hope that the documents will show up). This is known as the 'Peruvian Guano test' (after *Compagnie Financière du Pacifique v Peruvian Guano Co* (1882) 11 QBD 55).

PD 31.5.5(1) provides that, in appropriate cases, the court may direct a party to carry out a search for documents that may:

(a) enable the party applying for disclosure either to advance his own case or to damage that of the party giving disclosure; or

(b) lead to a train of enquiry which has either of those consequences.

Under the CPR and the definition applied to 'standard disclosure', the ability to insist on a search that could lead to relevant, but as yet unknown, documents being discovered was effectively removed. However, because of the grounds set out in PD 31.5, the ability to seek 'train of enquiry' disclosure can be made in an application for specific disclosure. As always, such an application would need to be justified under the principles of the overriding objective, and be 'fair', 'just', and 'proportionate'.

Documents that need not be disclosed on a standard basis may well be disclosable on a specific disclosure order, which can extend the duty to 'a train of enquiry'.

 Example

Document A may be a letter referring to bank statements of a party. Whilst Document A, in itself, may not fall within the scope of standard disclosure (CPR 31.6), the underlying bank documents referred to may contain information that could assist the other party's case. On an order for specific disclosure, it may be possible to obtain an order for the disclosure of the letter and the bank statements, because such disclosure may lead to 'a train of enquiry' if the applicant has established that they may assist his case.

14.5.8 STEPS TO TAKE BEFORE MAKING AN APPLICATION

To avoid the unnecessary cost penalties that may be incurred by making a premature application, the party seeking disclosure should make a written request to its opponent before making an application for specific disclosure.

- This request should explain what is wanted and why—that is, it should explain in detail what part of the opponent's list is inadequate and why. If documents are required that would lead to a 'train of enquiry', evidence will need to show that it is reasonable to ask for these and why.

- If the applicant believes that the search was inadequate, it would be appropriate to seek full particulars of the search that has been made. The application can ask more directly whether a search was made for a particular type of document, or it could directly ask why there are no documents in a particular category.

- The written request should give the opponent sufficient time in which to respond, but it should also impose a deadline (usually 14 days, depending on urgency). The letter can say that an application for costs (including indemnity costs) will be made if the application has to proceed. The deadline should be noted and an application made if there has been no, or an inadequate, response.

14.5.9 THE APPLICATION

The procedure for making a specific disclosure application is set out in PD 31.5.2–31.5.5.

The evidence in support of the application must include a statement of belief that the disclosure of documents by the disclosing party is inadequate. The grounds for the order may be set out in either the application notice (Form N244, Part C), or in a supporting witness statement. It may include some, or all, of the following points:

- a description of the document, or classes of document, and the extent of the search sought;
- an explanation of why it is reasonable and proportionate for each class or category of documents to be disclosed, having regard to the overriding objective;
- an explanation of how the requested documents are relevant to the matters in issue;
- a statement of the source (if relevant) and the grounds for believing that such documents are, or have been, in the control of the opponent; and
- if the application might raise concerns from the other party as to trade secrets or other confidential matter, an offer of a safeguard—such as agreeing to a limit on the numbers of copies of the document(s) sought, and the number of people entitled to view the documents—and provision for their return to the other party at the end of the litigation. The court will also seek to balance the interests of a party seeking disclosure and a party whose trade secrets may be put at risk. In such cases, the court will consider what safeguards should be put in place to provide adequate protection of any trade secrets.

The only guidance given in the CPR as to the factors that the court will take into account in deciding whether to make the order are as set out in PD 31.5.4. Further guidance can be found in the Court Guides, which will give an idea of the way in which the High Court may approach the application.

 Practical Considerations

Take care when drafting the class of documents or the extent of the search sought: if defined too broadly, the court may refuse disclosure of the whole class.

In the High Court (QBD Guide, paragraph 7.8.5), additional guidance is given as follows.

- Specific disclosure must be 'necessary'.
- The cost must be proportionate.
- A party's ability to continue the litigation must not be impaired by the order. For example, if the request for specific disclosure places very onerous costs demands on a party, with the result that he could not continue to bring the claim or defend the proceedings if the order were to be made, it is unlikely that the order will be made.
- Any specific disclosure ordered must be appropriate to the particular case, taking into account the financial position of the parties, the importance of the case, and the complexity of the issues.
- The court will also consider whether the provisions of CPR 18 (requests for further information) might eliminate the need for a specific disclosure order.

Practical Considerations

Make sure that you have identified the factual issues that are to be determined at trial by scrutinizing the statements of case and explain in your evidence how the documents that you are seeking by way of specific disclosure are relevant to these issues.

If you fail to do so, the court is unlikely to grant your application (see *Paul Sayers v Smithkline Beecham plc* [2003] EWHC 104 (QB)).

14.5.10 THE EXERCISE OF THE COURT'S DISCRETION

There is very little guidance in the CPR as to the circumstances in which the court will grant an order for specific disclosure, other than as set out in PD 31.5.4—that is, taking into account all of the circumstances of the case and, in particular, the overriding objective. In practice, it seems likely that the court will consider the following matters.

- Is standard disclosure inadequate? For example, is the search or categories of document listed inadequate?

- What is the importance of the documents sought to the case as a whole?

- Are there gaps in the list?

- Whilst relevance on its own may no longer be sufficient to obtain an order, the court will still want to be satisfied that the documents are relevant to the issues in the case.

- What is the complexity and nature of the issues?

- What are the costs and burden to the disclosing party of complying with the order?

- What is the amount at stake in the litigation and what is the financial position of the parties?

The court will seek to balance the ECHR, Art. 6(1) right to a fair hearing with the opponent's Art. 8 right to respect for private life.

The court must be satisfied that:

- there is *prima facie* evidence that the documents are (or have been) in the control of the party; and

- although relevance is no longer a sufficient test upon which the court will grant the order, the court will still want to be certain that the documents sought are relevant.

The court may inspect documents for relevance (although it is only likely to do so where there is a disputed claim to privilege).

Where an application is based on mere probability arising from the surrounding circumstances, the court will take into account all of the circumstances of the case and, in particular, the overriding objective.

14.5.11 WHAT GROUNDS TO OBJECT TO AN ORDER FOR SPECIFIC DISCLOSURE COULD AN OPPONENT CONSIDER?

14.5.11.1 Before an application has been made

On receipt of correspondence from the other party requesting specific disclosure, an opponent should consider if the request is reasonable, bearing in mind CPR 31 and the overriding objective.

Particular points that the opponent to the application may consider are as follows.

- Are there issues of confidentiality? If so, can these be overcome by agreeing to disclosure in a limited way?

- Have the documents in question already been referred to in the defence? If so, the claimant may have a right to inspect under CPR 31.14.
- Can specific disclosure be avoided by agreeing to provision of information under CPR 18 or staged disclosure?
- Have duties regarding electronic disclosure, if appropriate, been complied with?

If specific disclosure is not appropriate, give a reasoned explanation why in correspondence. Remember that this correspondence will be shown to the court and may be relevant on the question of costs.

14.5.11.2 Once an application has been made

On receipt of an application for specific disclosure, it will almost always be sensible to file evidence in response. When preparing this evidence, consideration should be given to the following matters.

- Has a proper search been made for the documents requested?
- Have any issues of confidentiality been sufficiently dealt with?
- Should you obtain a witness statement from any third party who may be affected by an order for specific disclosure? Remember that the court will seek to balance the right to a fair trial with the right to respect for private life.
- Is your opponent seeking specific disclosure at an early stage in the proceedings? If so, has he provided adequate reasons why this is necessary and are there valid reasons for objection?

14.5.12 COSTS

The usual order is that the costs will be awarded to the successful party in the application. However, bear in mind that costs are always in the discretion of the court and that a party's conduct may be drawn to the court's attention on the question of costs, if relevant. (See Chapter 4 for further detail of the likely costs orders that may be made.)

Specifically, in applications for specific disclosure and the issues that the court will consider when deciding the appropriate costs order, the following points should be considered.

- As an applicant, have you set out the grounds for your application in correspondence before making an application and given sufficient time for a response?
- As a respondent, have you responded to any correspondence in a timely way and set out in full any reasons for refusing to give specific disclosure?
- Have you considered fully:
  - staged disclosure?
  - the provision of further information?
  - the requirements of the Court Guide relating to the division of the High Court in which your action is proceeding?

KEY POINTS SUMMARY

- An interim application must comply precisely with the rule providing for it.
- The evidence supporting an interim application should, wherever possible, be given added 'weight' by the inclusion of material evidence.
- All interim applications must be justified within the terms of the overriding objective.
- Nearly all interim applications should be preceded with an informal request.

- Most interim applications that are listed for less than one hour will be heard by way of a telephone conference call.

- Interim applications, such as setting aside, default judgment, and summary judgment, are significant and important applications, because they can bring an end to proceedings if successfully defended or made. Make sure that your evidence is accurate, articulate, and persuasive.

- Always discuss the purpose of making or defending an application with your client, as well as the prospect of success, and costs incurred and/or recoverable.

- Ensure that you have specific instructions to proceed to make or oppose the application.

Case study *Andrew James Pike and Deep Builders Ltd*

Question 1

You have a witness statement of Andrew Pike dated 17 November 201? and an application notice dated 20 November 201?. You have also received a draft order. Assume that it is now 20 November 201?, and that the partner supervising the case has instructed you to attend to service of and preparation for this application. Consider the following:

- the purpose of this application and witness statement;

- the formalities relating to the making of the application, such as when and how you will serve the application;

- whether the statement is either necessary or adequate in terms of its compliance with any formalities and its substantive contents;

- determine whether the application complies with the requirements of the CPR and PD;

- what other preparations you would make for the hearing and what you would expect to be the outcome of the hearing.

Question 2

Assume that you are acting for the defendant in this matter. For the purposes of this stage, you are a legal representative with Rasputin & Co, and you have just received the application and witness statement. Your instructions from the insurer of the defendant are to resist the application with a view to ensuring that the claimant's application is refused or that any payment ordered is as small as possible. John Deep has told you that, at the time of the accident, he may have had 'a pint or two at lunchtime', and that he may possibly have been in a hurry to get to an appointment and so 'a little over the speed limit'. However, he is adamant that he was not over the centre line and points out that he passed a breathalyser test. The accident was, in his view, the fault of the claimant, who was over the centre lines.

Draft a short witness statement to resist the application.

Question 3

What would happen at the hearing—for example, who would be present, in what order would things happen, and what matters may be discussed, apart from simply whether or not an order for a payment would be made? If you were to be present, what would you need to do at the end of the hearing and following the hearing?

What document will have been lodged at court (and served on your opponent) at least 24 hours before the hearing? What is the purpose of this document?

---

online resource centre

Please refer to the Online Resource Centre video clip of this interim payment application.

Case study *Bollingtons Ltd and Mrs Elizabeth Lynch t/a The Honest Lawyer*

Question 1

You now have instructions to pursue the matter privately for Mrs Lynch. You have informed her that the judgment was entered correctly, but have advised that it will be necessary to apply to have judgment set aside if she wishes to defend the claim. What documentation will you need to prepare? Prepare the documents that you believe are appropriate for this type of application. If you believe that a defence is necessary, then, for the purposes of this exercise, you do not need to draft a defence, but you may wish to refer to one if you think that, in making the application, you would have prepared one.

Question 2

Consider the prospects of success of the defendant's application and the likely costs orders.

online resource centre

Any documents referred to in these case study questions can be found on the Online Resource Centre—simply click on 'Case study documentation' to access the documents that you need for Chapter 14 and to be reminded of the questions above. Suggested answers to these case study questions can also be accessed on the Online Resource Centre by your lecturer.

15 A PRACTICAL GUIDE TO COURT HEARINGS

15.1 INTRODUCTION

As a dispute resolution practitioner, you will almost certainly be involved in the preparation of, and attendance at, hearings before the district judge or Master. This chapter provides a practical guide outlining the mechanics of preparing for an application, and the format and etiquette of attending the hearing itself. The hearings that are described in this chapter are 'run of the mill' applications that those new to legal practice are likely to encounter. The focus is therefore on county court and High Court Queen's Bench non-specialist matters, such as the two case studies that run through this book. Specialist courts can handle interim applications in a different manner and this falls outside the scope of this book.

The substantive issues in relation to the different types of interim hearing are dealt with in Chapters 12–14. This chapter considers:

- paper applications;
- face-to-face hearings;
- telephone hearings;
- attending court with counsel; and
- instructing agents to attend court.

15.2 THE DIFFERENT TYPES OF INTERIM HEARING

The most common types of interim hearing that those new to legal practice will come across are included in the following non-exhaustive list:

- the setting aside of default judgments (see paragraph 14.2);
- Part 24 summary judgments (see paragraph 14.3);
- strike-out applications pursuant to Civil Procedure Rule (CPR) 3.4;
- interim payment applications (see paragraph 14.4);
- security for costs hearings;

- injunctions (see the Online Resource Centre—'Additional chapters—Injunctions and other Equitable Remedies');
- allocation hearings (see Chapter 12);
- case management conferences (CMCs) (see paragraph 12.8);
- pre-trial review or hearings, including listing hearings;
- applications to vary directions;
- applications to compel a party to comply with a direction; and
- applications in which permission is required pursuant to a part of the CPR.

These types of hearing prominently feature within the scope of Parts 7 and 8 claims. However, legal representatives are frequently required to deal with enforcement applications after judgment has been secured. The same principles apply to those applications in relation to pre-application preparation.

There are three different methods of undertaking interim hearings: on paper without attending court, at a face-to-face hearing at court, or by telephone. Some types of interim application are more suited (or are subject to mandatory requirement) to one of these methods.

15.3 PAPER APPLICATIONS

15.3.1 WHAT ARE 'PAPER APPLICATIONS'?

'Paper applications' are otherwise known as applications without a hearing. This means that the intention before making the application is that no hearing, whether face to face or by telephone, is necessary, but notice of the application is still given to your opponent. These applications simply require the submission of documents to the court for consideration, with the expectation that an order will be made without oral submission by either party. Many of these types of application are submitted with the consent of the opponent, or where the court considers a hearing is not necessary. However, as can be seen below, not all 'on paper' applications fall within these categories (CPR 23.8).

 Practical Considerations

The court will usually make agreed orders without a hearing in either situation, provided that it feels that the general timetable for the action as a whole, or the standard directions that have been made or would apply to the action, would not be affected by the terms of the order that the parties have agreed. If the directions orders would be affected, or if the court timetable is affected, the court is likely to insist that these matters be considered at a hearing. It is part of the overall objective of the CPR for the parties to cooperate more fully in the preparation and conduct of cases, as well as to settle interim applications. This is generally seen as good practice. However, the court will always retain overall control and management of cases, and will insist on a hearing if it feels the need to do so. The court will apply the criteria set out in CPR 3.9(1) if the interim application has been made due to a failure on the part of the respondent to comply with an order or time limit previously set.

The legal representative has to decide whether it is appropriate to make a paper application. Consideration may be given to the obvious costs savings or mandatory requirements of the CPR in respect of obligatory hearings, but it is essentially a judgment call on the part of the legal representative, and discussion with a more experienced fee earner may be appropriate.

15.3.2 WHAT IS THE USUAL FORM OF A PAPER APPLICATION?

It will come as no surprise that the conventional application is on Form N244, with supporting evidence. The supporting evidence may be completed on Part C of the form, or in a separate witness statement. The paper application, together with the usual draft order and court fee, are sent to the court. Details of court fees are contained in the Civil Proceedings Fees (Amendment) Order 2009.

The general rule is that, when making a paper application, it must be served on your opponent, because it is, in essence, an on-notice application (CPR 23.4). Your opponent may wish to object to the application being dealt with on paper and this will give him the opportunity to do so. He can do this by a letter to the court requesting a face-to-face or telephone hearing, and the court will consider the request.

The court will refer all paper applications to a Master or district judge for a decision as to whether it is appropriate to proceed without a hearing. If this is the case, the court will inform all parties to the action. The court may give directions about further evidence to be filed. If an order is made in this way, your opponent can apply to have it varied or set aside, but to do so, he must apply within seven days after service of the order (CPR 3.3(5)(a) and (b)).

If the court does not believe it is appropriate to proceed without a hearing, it will issue to both parties a notice of hearing with a time, time estimate, and date for the hearing, along with directions for the filing of further evidence if necessary (PD 23A.2.3–23A.2.5).

 Practical Considerations

Whilst the CPR state that paper applications must be made using the traditional Form N244, frequently, in practice, where the parties consent, a letter confirming both parties' agreement, along with a consent order and a court fee, will suffice. This will usually occur when the parties are agreeing to the re-timetabling of directions.

15.3.3 EXAMPLES OF PAPER APPLICATIONS

Paper applications are often appropriate in the following types of application:

- a change of firm of solicitors (CPR 42.3);
- service outside the jurisdiction (CPR 6.36–6.38)—there is also no notice required here;
- payment out of funds in court (PD 21.13.1);
- where the parties agree to the terms of the order sought—for example, an application by the parties to grant an extension of time for the filing of the defence; or
- where the parties agree that the court should dispose of the application without a hearing—for example, when an interim application has been served and a hearing date or telephone appointment fixed, but the parties have subsequently settled the application

and have agreed the order that should be made. In those circumstances, the parties will write in to the court, inviting it to make the order that is agreed and to vacate the hearing date.

15.4 FACE-TO-FACE HEARINGS BEFORE THE COURT

Attending court on an interim hearing can be as a result of an application made on notice to your opponent or as a result of an application made without notice to your opponent (see Chapter 13, paragraph 13.5 and 13.7). A legal representative needs to appreciate when to prepare an application with notice and one without notice, and how the courts will deal with the attendance on each. Additionally, the way in which the court system deals with face-to-face applications differs in cases heard outside London and those in the Royal Courts of Justice in London.

This section will deal with both on-notice and without-notice applications, both outside London and in the Royal Courts of Justice.

15.4.1 ON-NOTICE APPLICATIONS

15.4.1.1 When do these occur?

On-notice applications are probably the most frequently occurring applications and involve the usual Form N244, plus supporting evidence, draft order, and court fee, being sent to the court. Many of the applications listed in paragraph 15.2 above can proceed in this way. On-notice hearings are particularly suited to non-urgent matters that require discussion and argument before the court in relation to substantive legal, procedural, and factual issues not agreed upon by the parties to the action.

15.4.1.2 General preparation points

In advance of any application, legal representatives should undertake the following.

- Inform your opponent that you intend to make the application and ask for his consent.
- Check Court Guides in High Court matters for any special provisions relating to hearings, such as the provision of a case summary and core bundle of documents.
- Check the service requirements for the application.
- Request a payment on account from the client in respect of the court fee and hearing itself.
- Serve the application notice at least three clear days before the hearing and ensure all documents in respect of the application, including the case summary if a multi-track case, are served by 4 p.m. at least two clear days before the hearing
- Serve a Form N260 summary assessment of costs 24 hours in advance of the hearing.
- Review the file, making sure that you have read and understood the rules and Practice Directions. Take the full file of papers to the hearing.
- Liaise with your opponent on the issues arising on the application.
- Allow adequate travelling time and keep all receipts.

15.4.1.3 What will the court do when it receives an application outside London?

On receipt of the application, the court will consider the time estimate box at point 6 on the front page of the Form N244 and list the case in one of the district judges' lists for the time required. A notice of hearing is sent to both parties. A specific time is given for the hearing—for example, 10.15 a.m.—and only one matter is listed at a time for that time slot. Both parties must attend in good time to commence the hearing at the given time. In the county court, it is up to the party making the application to specify to the court whether he wants the court to serve the other party with the application formally, or whether he wants to do it himself. In the High Court, the applicant usually serves the opponent, not the court. In many courts, it is possible to speak to the listing officer to determine, and agree, a date and time for your application to be heard.

 Practical Considerations

If the application is contested, it is good practice to speak with your opponent over the telephone in advance of the hearing, to try to clarify outstanding issues and gauge your opponent's stance. When making your way to the court, make sure that you arrive in good time, because further discussions can also be conducted whilst waiting for the hearing to commence. Some care should be taken, however, with these 'pre-hearing' discussions, because they will probably not (unless the discussions are with a view to settlement of the action) be covered by any privilege unless the discussions are stated to be 'without prejudice'.

Once you arrive at court, you should make your way to the district judges' hearing rooms section of the court. The list of cases to be heard will be displayed on the walls, and these will confirm the time of the application and the district judge before whom it is to be heard. The district judges' hearing rooms have an appointed usher with whom you must register, and to whom you must provide your name and status (solicitor, legal representative, legal executive, paralegal, or counsel), along with the names of the parties to the action, noting for which party you act. The usher will provide one of the legal representatives—usually the first one to arrive at court—with an attendance sheet to be completed with the information given to the usher. This record will include the name of both parties' legal representatives, and is handed to the district judge at the start of the hearing and placed on the court file.

The usher will call the name of the case when the district judge is ready and the parties will be directed to the appropriate hearing room, in which the allotted district judge will be waiting. Alternatively, some courts operate a 'traffic light' system whereby the district judge makes use of a light code system that is displayed outside his room, as well as in the waiting area. There are usually two or three lights on display: a red light denoting that the district judge is engaged; amber indicating that he is preparing for the next appointment; and a green light indicating that he is free to receive the parties.

15.4.1.4 The format of, and etiquette at, the hearing

Hearing room appointments for interim hearings in the High Court and county court usually follow a similar format. However, the legal representative should ascertain, if it is a High Court interim hearing, whether this is, in fact, a private hearing room appointment or whether it is an open court hearing listed in a hearing room. This is important, because the term of address will change, depending on what type of judge is hearing the matter.

In terms of dress, different court dress is required for different divisions of the High Court. Generally, in the Queen's Bench Division or in the county court, robing is not required by either solicitors or counsel in any hearing room appointment on an interim matter. All parties attending, however, must be respectably dressed. Business suits are therefore required to be worn at all other times.

Once called by the usher or once the green light is switched on, the legal representatives of the parties should proceed to the hearing room together. The district judge will call you in when he is ready. On entering, the parties should both address the district judge—'Good morning/afternoon, Sir/Madam'—and proceed to sit at the desk in front of the district judge. In many courts, the tables are arranged so that both the parties face the district judge, sitting side by side, not facing each other. The parties remain seated throughout the hearing.

The attendance record needs then to be handed to the district judge and the hearing formally commences. All interim hearings should be recorded and it is incumbent on the district judge to commence the recording. Both parties will be asked to confirm their names and the party for whom they act, along with an explanation of who the applicant is. The applicant is usually asked to make his oral submissions first. If the hearing has been convened at the request of the court, then the usual procedure is for the district judge to deal with the claimant to the action first.

The district judge will usually have read the application notice, supporting documents and case summary if a multi-track case in advance of the hearing (in these types of hearing, the district judge works from the court file and unless there is any additional documentation to give to the court, there is no requirement by the parties to prepare a bundle of documents for the hearing unless specifically ordered by the court, or if the Court Guide denotes otherwise, which tends to be the case in the specialist courts). This is not always possible due to previous applications overrunning and, as such, it is good practice for the party submitting first to enquire whether the district judge has had the opportunity to read the application. If he has, then the party can proceed to make his additional submissions as discussed below. If the district judge has not had the chance to look at the papers, then it will be necessary to take the district judge through the application notice and supporting evidence for the applicant.

A party's written and oral submissions are his chance to be persuasive. This is looked at in some detail in Chapter 13, paragraph 13.3. It should be noted that, when a party is making submissions, it is good etiquette for the opposing party not to interrupt, although the district judge is at liberty to ask either party questions during submissions.

Your submissions may be structured as follows.

1. Outline the nature of the application, stating whether it is opposed.

2. Explain the facts giving rise to the application.

3. Direct the district judge to any relevant statements of case and/or documents—in particular, any written submissions in witness statements.

4. Direct the district judge to any relevant law.

5. If appropriate, state the power of the court to make the order.

If the application is to proceed by consent, then it will only be necessary to outline the nature of the application and confirm the parties' agreement to the draft order annexed to the application notice, or to any amended version of the same.

If the application is opposed, then the opposing party may then present his case in the same way. The district judge may then invite either party to address him for a second time on the merits or difficulties of the application, although practice does vary on this. The district judge may again ask further specific questions to either or both parties.

After all submissions and questions, the district judge will then proceed to make the order straightaway. The district judge may grant or refuse the application, and he may give a short judgment in a contested case and/or give further directions. He will speak slowly whilst giving his judgment, to give the parties the opportunity to write down, word for word, the terms of the order being made. As he does so, he will also indorse the court file with a written version of the order. If you have not secured a full written note of any part of the order, then, for the sake of clarity, you should ask the district judge to repeat any paragraph of the order that you have not taken down fully. The reason for this is that if it is a county court hearing, then the court drafts and serves the order (although it is good practice in appropriate cases for one of the parties to draft the order). You will need to check the terms of the order when you receive it from the court. If the matter is a High Court matter, then the duty is on the applicant (or the claimant, if it is a hearing convened at the court's request) to draft the order. To do this, you will need an accurate note and may wish to confirm it with your opponent before submitting it to the court for sealing.

Once the substance of the order has been made, submissions must then be made in relation to the costs of the application. Remember that both parties are required by PD 43–48.13.5(2) to file a Form N260 24 hours in advance of the hearing. These should be on the court file for the district judge to consider. The successful party will address the court on his entitlement to costs and the amount claimed, and the losing party will usually try to oppose both. The district judge will then make his decision and this will then be indorsed on the court file.

On leaving, the parties will thank the district judge and bid him 'Good morning/ afternoon'.

The Online Resource Centre features a face-to-face hearing of an interim payment application and a CMC. You will see how the hearing proceeds in terms of etiquette and submissions, and hear from the advocates and the district judge on their 'top tips' for advocacy, and a successful and well-prepared hearing.

online resource centre

15.4.1.5 The format of hearings in the Royal Courts of Justice

The format of hearings conducted in the Royal Courts of Justice (RCJ) varies to quite some degree. On the issue of a claim, the claim is assigned to a Master, as the procedural judge responsible for managing the claim.

An interim application can be made on Form N244, but can also be made on Form PF 244 in the RCJ only. Interim hearings of an administrative and relatively straightforward nature are dealt with by the Master's Support Unit, in Room E16.

 Practical Considerations

More substantial interim applications either in respect of time or complexity (or specific provision under the CPR) are dealt with by the Clerk of the Lists in Room WG3, and referred to an interim applications judge. These fall outside the scope of this book, because these are usually the types of hearing that are dealt with by more experienced legal practitioners or counsel.

On receipt of the application notice, the Master's Support Unit will consider the time estimate and decide which method of listing is appropriate, as follows.

15.4.1.5.1 *The Bear Garden list*

If the time estimate is for between five and ten minutes (the 'short application' list), the Master's Support Unit will bulk-list matters at half-hour intervals from 10.30 a.m., 11 a.m., 11.30 a.m., until 12 p.m. If the time estimate is for 10–20 minutes (the '12 noon' list), the appointment will usually take place after 12 p.m. and the Master's Support Unit will also bulk-list these matters. These lists are known as the 'Bear Garden' list, and the hearings take place in Rooms E102 and E103. The Master's Support Unit will indorse the application notice with the name of the next available Master to hear the matter and the room number. As such, the parties are aware in advance which Master will hear the application and where it is to take place.

In so far as practice in the short application list is concerned, the parties should report to the usher for the appropriate room, providing a copy of the indorsed application notice. These applications are dealt with on a 'first come, first served' basis. If the case is listed at 10.30 a.m., for example, the usher will allow all of the parties in that list to go and sit at the back of the room in silence. If the case is listed in the 12 noon list, the parties will wait outside the room until the case is called.

When the Master calls the case on for both lists, the parties should stand at the Master's desk. The party making the application should hand to the Master the application notice, witness statement, and draft order. The practice is then followed as in paragraph 15.4.1.4 above in relation to the format and etiquette relating to the conduct of the hearing.

When the Master has made his order, he will hand back the application notice and draft order, indorsed with his shorthand, but he may keep the witness statement(s).

15.4.1.5.2 *The Master's private room*

Where the time estimate indicates an appointment of longer than 20 minutes, even up to several hours, then the applicant must request a private room appointment with the assigned Master, and to do so, must complete a standard private room appointment form and submit this with the application notice to the Master's Support Unit. This form gives details of the parties' availability. This is then passed directly to the assigned Master, who personally lists the matter before him, based on the available dates given.

When attending the hearing, the parties should attend the Master's private room early, because much can be negotiated whilst waiting in the corridor. The parties enter the room when they are called in and ask permission to sit down. Permission is always given, and the party who is making the application should hand to the Master the application notice, witness statement, and draft order. The practice is then followed as in paragraph 15.4.1.4 above in relation to the format and etiquette relating to the conduct of the hearing.

When the Master has made his order, he will hand back the application notice and draft order, indorsed with his shorthand, but he may keep the witness statement(s).

On attending any on-notice application before a Master at the RCJ, the parties are to complete the court record sheet (PF 48), which is used to record details of the claim, representation, and the nature of the application, and this will be used by the Master for his notes.

15.4.1.6 Types of on-notice interim application heard before district judges and Masters

Certainly outside London, all of the interim applications listed in paragraph 15.2 above would fall to be heard by the district judge. In the RCJ, most of the applications listed would also fall within the remit of the Master, although particularly long and complex strike-out (CPR 3.4) and Part 24 summary judgment applications, injunctions, and appeals may fall to a judge in the 'interim hearings' list. Permission from the Master is required before the interim applications judge can hear the application.

15.4.2 WITHOUT-NOTICE HEARINGS

15.4.2.1 What are 'without-notice hearings'?

Without-notice hearings are made by a party without giving notice to the other party (or parties) to the action. The following applications are usually made without notice and are described in Chapter 13, paragraph 13.7.2. (See also the Online Resource Centre chapter on 'Injunctions and other Equitable Remedies'.)

15.4.2.2 How are they made?

The actual procedure and format of the hearing is similar outside London and in the RCJ. The usual application notice and evidence, draft order, and court fee are either sent or taken by hand to the court. In very urgent applications, a CD-ROM or memory stick containing the draft order is also sent to the court.

Postal applications are less urgent and the hearing will be listed on the first available date either before a district judge, Master, or a judge, depending on the nature of the application.

More urgent applications delivered by hand are dealt with on the day if there is a practice district judge or Master sitting. They sit purely to hear without-notice applications and sit most days in most district registries. Once the court office has issued and sealed the application, the applicant should proceed to the appropriate usher and wait to be called.

15.4.2.3 The conduct of a without-notice hearing

The format and etiquette of the hearing is very much in line with that outlined in paragraph 15.4.1.4 above, apart from the fact that there will be no opposing party, and that you will need to explain fully the nature and purpose of the application. The district judge or Master may also require some reading time.

15.5 TELEPHONE HEARINGS

15.5.1 WHAT ARE 'TELEPHONE HEARINGS' AND HOW DID THEY COME ABOUT?

Telephone hearings are, in essence, hearings that take place between the parties and the district judge by telephone conference call, rather than by all parties attending court, even if the court in which the action is proceeding is your local court and only a short walk or drive away.

In order to try to reduce the cost and time burden that face-to-face hearings produce, many hearings now take place by telephone. The governing part of the CPR is PD 23.6.

15.5.2 WHEN CAN A HEARING BE CONDUCTED BY TELEPHONE?

Telephone hearings can take place in any court except the RCJ. Therefore, no Master appointments take place by telephone, but many hearings outside London before a district judge do.

Certain types of hearing are now automatically conducted by telephone and these are listed below (PD 23A.6.2):

- allocation hearings;
- listing hearings; and
- interim applications, CMCs, and pre-trial reviews with a time estimate of less than one hour.

This covers the majority of interim applications with a relatively short time estimate and raises the question as to when the legal representative will ever get the opportunity to attend court. Since the CPR came into force, the number of interim and final hearings has dropped considerably, and the implementation of these rules on telephone hearings will further reduce time taken at court on interim matters. This is however, financially advantageous for the client.

However, there are a number of exceptions to this rule also contained in PD 23A.6.2 and the following hearings will not take place by telephone:

- a without-notice hearing;
- a hearing at which either one or both parties are not represented; and
- a hearing at which there are more than four separately legally represented parties.

Whilst PD 23A.6.2 refers to an automatic right to a telephone hearing, this is not a mandatory provision. As such, should you not wish your hearing to take place by telephone where it appears in the automatic entitlement list, or conversely, should you wish your hearing to proceed by way of a telephone conference call where it is either excluded or simply does not appear in the list for automatic entitlement, then PD 23A.3–23A.8 deals with how this can be practically achieved and the court's discretion in such matters.

15.5.3 CONSIDERATIONS IN ADVANCE OF A TELEPHONE HEARING

PD 23A.6.10 sets out directions for the telephone conference. This specifies how to set up the hearing, which party is responsible for setting it up, and that the telephone charges will be treated as part of the overall costs. It is usually the applicant's legal representative who will set up the telephone hearing.

15.5.4 **SETTING UP THE TELEPHONE HEARING**

The following is a checklist of steps that you should take to arrange a telephone hearing effectively.

- Ascertain from all of the parties the identity of the fee earner conducting the hearing, whether this be a legal representative or even counsel, and obtain their direct dial telephone numbers.
- Ascertain from the court the identity of the district judge, if not already known, and a direct dial telephone number.
- Contact a suitable telecommunications provider, such as BT Conferencing (http://www.conferencing.bt.com) or Legal Connect (http://www.legalconnect.co.uk).
- The information that needs to be given to the telephone operator will include the time, time estimate, and date of the hearing (it is sensible to arrange for the call to be connected at least five-ten minutes before the start of the hearing, even if this means waiting on the telephone for the district judge to join the call), the direct dial telephone numbers of the parties and district judge, and the sequence in which they are to be called. The usual sequence is: (1) applicant's legal representative; (2) the other party's (or parties') legal representative; then (3) the district judge.

 Practical Considerations

Whilst waiting for the judge to join the call, it is sensible to avoid informal 'chit chat', because this will give an unprofessional impression to the court. It is far better to follow the guidance below in paragraph 15.5.5 and avoid the court overhearing any potentially embarrassing information.

15.5.5 **THE CONDUCT OF THE TELEPHONE HEARING**

Once the district judge joins the call, he will introduce himself and ask each party to do the same, asking each legal representative to confirm his name and on whose behalf he acts, as well as to identify who has made the application. The district judge usually begins with the claimant.

Once the introductions have been made, the application will proceed very much in line with an on-notice face-to-face hearing, as has been described in paragraph 15.4.1.4 above.

In order to make the telephone hearing flow as smoothly as possible, the following considerations should be borne in mind.

- Give realistic time estimates that allow time for the order to be made and any costs arguments. Whilst the conference provider will not cut you off if you overrun (calls are charged per minute), the court is likely to have other face-to-face or telephone hearings to attend.
- Remember that the time for serving the application notice for a telephone hearing is five clear days before the hearing.
- Ensure that all documents in respect of the hearing are lodged on time as with your face to face hearing, i.e. by 4 p.m. at least two clear days before the hearing and clearly marked with the date and time of the hearing. This would include the case summary if a multi-track case. (You are not able to hand anything to the district judge.) The Form N260 summary assessment of costs can however be filed no later than 24 hours before the hearing.
- There is usually a split-second time delay when speaking on a conference call. This needs to be taken into account, otherwise, when one party has finished speaking, you may end up speaking over them. Because there is no body language or eye contact on the

telephone, it is also difficult to gauge in the hearing when to speak, particularly if there are more than two parties on the call. The district judge will usually indicate to whom he wishes to speak next, and should ensure that all parties have had adequate opportunity to make submissions and respond as they wish. It may be helpful to remind the district judge who you are and for whom you act at appropriate points during the hearing.

- Ensure that those in the surrounding offices and your secretary are aware that you are conducting a conference call. There needs to be as little noise as possible and no interruptions during the call. It is advisable to use a conference room, or to put a sign on your door to avoid anyone walking in and disturbing you.

The Online Resource Centre contains a telephone hearing relating to a setting aside of a default judgment application in the Bollington Beer case study.

15.6 ATTENDING COURT WITH COUNSEL

Attending court with counsel has always been one of the main and most enjoyable tasks of those new to legal practice. The CPR have significantly reduced the number of court hearings, both interim and final. This, coupled with the onset of more telephone hearings, has further reduced the legal representative's exposure to advocacy at court.

However, whilst attending court with counsel—otherwise known as 'sitting behind counsel' (because, traditionally, many interim hearings were conducted in open court and the legal representative always sat in the row behind counsel)—does not involve any advocacy for the legal representatives, it still provides an invaluable experience on how interim applications are conducted in terms of format and etiquette. It also gives those new to legal practice a chance to see how effective or ineffective oral submissions can be.

15.6.1 WHEN DOES THE LEGAL REPRESENTATIVE SIT BEHIND COUNSEL?

Counsel is usually instructed to attend court on longer and more complex interim applications, such as a CPR Part 24 summary judgment, or a strike-out pursuant to CPR 3.4. These types of hearing can be listed for several hours.

 Professional Conduct

When deciding whether to brief counsel to attend an interim hearing, consideration needs to be given to the cost of doing so and whether this is recoverable from your opponent if successful. However, perhaps the first thought should be to the importance of the application and the Solicitors' Code of Conduct 2007, Rule 1.03. Are you acting in the best interests of your client by attending the hearing yourself, or would it be reasonable and appropriate to brief counsel? You may feel out of your depth as a legal representative in conducting a long and complicated application, and this should be discussed with your supervising fee earner. You will obviously need to seek your client's instructions and monies on account.

Once the decision has been made with your client to brief counsel to attend a hearing, it is professionally courteous to notify your opponent that you will be 'appearing by counsel' at the hearing of the application.

15.6.2 WHAT IS EXPECTED OF A LEGAL REPRESENTATIVE WHEN SITTING BEHIND COUNSEL?

The duty imposed on a legal representative when attending court with counsel is quite considerable and is not to be underestimated. The following outlines the role of the legal representative.

- Primarily, the role of the legal representative is to take detailed and coherent notes of the hearing, and the ability to do so requires significant concentration and quick writing, or shorthand, skills.

- In order to produce an intelligible note, a good knowledge of the file is required, but legal representatives are often asked to sit behind counsel on a file in which they may have had no involvement. Time will therefore need to be spent in perusing the file and possibly discussing it with the appropriate fee earner.

- The entire file should be taken to the court appointment should counsel require any additional documentation. Ensure that files are carried in a suitable briefcase to prevent any loss of papers.

- Both the legal representative and counsel should arrive at court in advance of the start time of the hearing in order to discuss any outstanding matters. This also gives both the opportunity to liaise with the opponent, who may also be appearing by counsel.

- Once the hearing commences, counsel will make all submissions on behalf of a party. It is therefore not appropriate to speak to the court unless through counsel or asked a specific question by the district judge or Master. If you feel that counsel has made an omission or an error in his submissions, then it is incumbent on the legal representative to bring this to the attention of counsel effectively. This may be done either by passing a short, handwritten note to counsel, or by seeking his attention at an appropriate moment.

15.7 INSTRUCTING AGENTS TO ATTEND HEARINGS

15.7.1 WHEN WOULD THIS OCCUR?

Where a hearing proceeds in a court that is not local to you, there is the option, rather than travelling to the court, of instructing an agent—usually a legal representative local to the court—to attend on your behalf. The instruction is made with a view to saving time and cost, but consideration must be given to the nature of the hearing itself, in terms of whether it is appropriate and in your client's best interest to do so. Some hearings are best attended by a fee earner who has an in-depth knowledge of the file. An agent is likely not to have this and, as such, their appointment is usually for less complicated hearings.

The requirement to instruct agents to attend hearings has diminished due to the ability to conduct hearings by telephone. If the application is important or substantial and some way away, you would probably be instructing counsel to attend on the application. There is, of course, still the option of instructing a legal representative to sit behind counsel, but usual practice is that a legal representative from your own firm would attend, taking the full file of papers with them, as highlighted above.

15.7.2 HOW DO YOU INSTRUCT AN AGENT?

An agent is usually instructed initially by telephone to ensure that a legal representative is available to attend and is not 'conflicted out' from acting, and to confirm the charges. Your client will also need to be informed of the arrangement and the fees.

A letter of instruction is sent to the agent enclosing the notice of application, plus supporting documents, the notice of hearing, and any relevant statements of case, experts' reports, witness statements, or correspondence between yourself and your opponent. The Form N260 (costs statement) can be sent nearer the hearing (and must be filed and served on the opponent at least 24 hours before the hearing).

It is courteous to inform your opponent that you will be attending by an agent and to provide those details to your opponent. It is also good practice to liaise with your agent on the morning of the hearing to verify that they have all of the requisite papers and to clarify any outstanding queries.

15.7.3 ATTENDING COURT AS AN AGENT

There is no difference in attending a hearing as an agent in terms of format and etiquette, although when introducing yourself to the district judge or Master, it is again good practice to inform them that you 'act as agent for the claimant . . .'.

Once the hearing has taken place, it is good practice to telephone your instructing so-licitor to inform them of the outcome, and then to prepare a written report, enclosing your invoice for the work undertaken.

KEY POINTS SUMMARY

- Have regard to express court directions and Court Guides to confirm what documentation is required for the hearing.

- Always attend court with a full file of papers, and a well-founded knowledge of the key facts and issues of the case.

- Contact your opponent in advance of the hearing and, in accordance with CPR practice, use your best endeavours to create an amicable relationship with him.

- Take clear and detailed notes at all hearings, and do not forget to make representations on costs.

- Remember the type of judge whom you are before, and ensure correct dress code and forms of address.

SELF-TEST QUESTIONS

1. Can you request a face-to-face hearing before a district judge where a telephone hearing has been automatically listed?

2. Would your answer be any different if the application were to be before a Master?

3. Who arranges a telephone hearing?

online resource centre

Suggested answers to these general questions can be accessed by adopting lecturers on the Online Resource Centre. Your lecturer can provide these to you.

16 PART 36 OFFERS

Within the online resource there is a short podcast that will help you understand the nature and application of Part 36 Offers.

16.1 INTRODUCTION

Offers to settle pervade the practice of dispute resolution and litigation. Whilst this chapter is self-contained, the proactive legal representative should constantly be aware that it may be appropriate to make an offer to settle at any time.

ADR considerations

You should read Chapter 5 in conjunction with this chapter, on the basis that offers to settle may form part of the negotiation spectrum—usually as the first step in attempting to settle a claim.

It is extremely rare that a dispute is resolved or proceeds to trial without some type of offer being made. There does not, however, appear to be a limit on the number of offers that can be made, although credibility and common sense would indicate that offers to settle should be made purposefully, but not irrationally.

LITIGATION TRAIN: PART 36 OFFERS AND CONCLUDING A CLAIM

First client meeting

Protocol

Issue of proceedings

Service of Proceedings

Acknowledgement of service

Defence (and counterclaim)

Reply and defence to counterclaim

AQ

AQ hearing
OR
Directions agreed
OR
CMC (1)—directions
(• cost estimate
• case summary)

Disclosure and inspection

Exchange of evidence

Trial

These are potential key points when P36 offers and/or ADR should be considered in an action that has proceeded to allocation.

This chapter considers:

- the main features of Part 36 of the Civil Procedure Rules (CPR) and its Practice Direction;
- practical suggestions on dealing with Part 36 offers; and
- advising the client.

16.2 WHAT ARE 'PART 36 OFFERS'?

The ethos of a Part 36 offer is as follows.

- It is a formal offer to settle an action or part of an action. Part 36 offers have significant cost and interest consequences if they are rejected, and, as such, have been designed as a tactical tool to put pressure on an opponent to compromise the dispute.
- They are made on a 'without prejudice save as to costs' basis, which means that they cannot be disclosed to any third party. The significance of this is that only the party who has made the offer—that is, the offeror—and the party who has received the offer—that is, the offeree—are entitled to know the content of the offer to the exclusion of any other party to the action and the trial judge (CPR 36.13(1) and (2)). This is the case even where there has been a split trial on liability and quantum although it does raise a real issue as it is often desirable to deal with costs at the conclusion of the liability hearing.
- They are open for acceptance indefinitely unless expressly withdrawn or amended by the offer.
- The acceptance of a Part 36 offer, provided it has not previously been expressly withdrawn or amended, and is being accepted within the 'relevant period' (which must be not less than 21 days), implicitly signifies that the offeror (or the party who is to pay) is agreeing to pay the offeree's (or the party who is to accept) costs of the proceedings on the standard basis (see Chapter 4 for a definition of 'standard'), up until the date of acceptance was served by the offeree. This will invoke the deemed service rules set out in CPR 6.26 for service of 'Documents other than the claim form' (CPR 36.10(1)).

 Costs

If you are acting for a claimant offeror who has had his offer accepted, it is important to stress to your client that the defendant offeree's liability for his costs ceases on the day that he accepts the offer (or in a case where one of the parties is a protected party, when the court has approved the settlement). However, the claimant will undoubtedly continue to incur costs in negotiating a cost settlement, which he may have to bear himself.

- Part 36 offers are inclusive of interest until the expiry of the time period, after which time interest will continue to accrue in addition to the offer.

 Practical Considerations

In relation to the implicit nature of interest within a Part 36 offer up to the end of the relevant period, the settlement figure put forward includes interest calculated to the end of the relevant period (that is, an advance interest calculation). It is also good drafting practice to make provision for interest to run in the wording of your Part 36 offer after the expiry of the relevant period.

16.3 THE FORM AND CONTENT OF A PART 36 OFFER

For the offer to be CPR 36-compliant and take advantage of the cost consequences detailed in paragraphs 16.7 and 16.8 below, there are five mandatory requirements under CPR 36.2. The Part 36 offer must:

- be made in writing—usually in letter format or Form N242A;
- state clearly—usually in bold in the heading—that it is a Part 36 offer;
- specify a period of not less than 21 days (the relevant period) within which the paying party will be automatically liable for the receiving party's costs if the offer is accepted within the relevant period (unless it is less than 21 days before the start of a trial), in accordance with CPR 36.10;
- state whether the offer is made in respect of the whole or part of the claim, or to the whole or part of an issue; and
- state whether the offer takes into account any counterclaim.

Careful drafting of Part 36 offers is crucial. Should the requirements of Part 36 not be adhered to, the purported Part 36 offer may lose those vital costs consequences sought. For example, a settlement offer cannot be a Part 36 offer if it is time limited. Take care therefore not to express your offer to be open for acceptance for a period of time, for example 21 days. This issue was brought to light recently in the case of *C v D and D2* [2010] EWHC 2940 (Ch).

These requirements are the bare minimum and additional information can be included in a CPR 36 offer. For example, if the claim is for personal injuries, then there is specific information that needs to be included in the offer, which is set out in CPR 36.5 (a claim for future pecuniary loss), CPR 36.6 (a claim including provisional damages), and CPR 36.15 (deduction of Social Security benefits and lump-sum payments).

Figure 16.6 at the end of this chapter is a template claimant Part 36 offer letter, which can be used as a basis for Part 36 offers in individual cases (this can be amended for a defendant offer in accordance with the specific provisions of Part 36). If the offer is not made in accordance with CPR 36.2, the offer is not likely to have the cost consequences set out in this chapter.

16.4 WHEN CAN PART 36 OFFERS BE MADE?

Part 36 offers can be made in any type of dispute or proceedings, including both Part 7 and Part 8 claims, but are not applicable to cases allocated to the small claims track (CPR 27.2). They do, however, apply to proceedings with additional claims (CPR 20.3). If the offeree is a 'protected party'—that is, a child or patient—then whilst the offeree can indicate a willingness to accept, acceptance is not, in fact, valid unless the court approves the settlement (CPR 21.10).

Part 36 offers can be made at any time during proceedings (including trial) and also before proceedings are issued (CPR 36.3(2)(a)). They can even be made in appeal proceedings (CPR 36.3(2)(b)).

By definition, the time at which a CPR 36 offer is actually made is when it is served on the offeree (CPR 36.7). CPR 6.20–6.26 deal with permitted methods of service and deemed service that apply in calculating when Part 36 offers are made.

16.4.1 PRACTICALLY

The timing of Part 36 offers can be important from both a tactical and a costs point of view.

Generally, a Part 36 offer, or any 'without prejudice save as to costs' offer, should be considered being made with your client as soon as a firm view can be given on liability and quantum. As can be seen from the 'Litigation train' diagram that features in this book, there are key times at which Part 36 offers should be considered to be made: for example, after disclosure and inspection of documents. However, Part 36 offers can be made for more tactical reasons, as highlighted below.

> **Example**
>
> Your client has not yet been minded to make a Part 36 offer in a dispute. Proceedings have not been issued and little information has been exchanged. He instructs you to make a low Part 36 offer directly before a mediation—that is, less than 21 days beforehand—to put pressure on the opponent and to 'test the water'.
>
> What is the impact of this offer? One school of thought is that this could speed up the process on the day of the mediation, and that the offeree can consider the cost consequences of not accepting it in light of the further work to be done on the case and make a balanced and informed decision. However, the whole purpose of mediation is to understand and explore the strengths and weakness of your own and your opponent's case with a view to considering settlement options. A derisory pre-mediation Part 36 offer may hamper this process. In practice, it would be better to make any first-time or renewed Part 36 offers during the mediation itself (rather than immediately before), because they are likely to be taken more seriously, having then been made on a full appraisal of your opponent's case.

Part 36 offers can also be made on purely commercial grounds to dispose of a time-consuming and expensive litigation.

16.4.2 COSTS ON PRE-ACTION PART 36 OFFERS

We can see from paragraphs 16.4.1 above that pre-action Part 36 offers can be made. If the offer is not accepted and proceedings are issued, it is possible to recover the costs of any pre-action work, as well as the costs of the litigation itself. However, the position is different if the pre-action offer is accepted before proceedings are issued.

In this case, it is not possible to seek Part 36 costs (see paragraphs 16.7.1.2 and 16.8.2.2 below) because CPR 36.10(1) states that 'the claimant is entitled to the costs of the proceedings': there have been no proceedings, because the acceptance of the Part 36 offer ended the dispute without litigation. This does seem potentially unfair and contrary to the whole ethos of modern litigation: on the one hand, parties are being encouraged to avoid litigation and negotiate; on the other, they are being expected to do so without costs recovery in this situation.

The way around this is to follow one of the following courses of action.

- At the time of making the pre-action Part 36 offer, you might make the terms as to costs explicit, but state that they do not form part of the Part 36 offer itself (a Part 36 offer is not permitted to include provisions as to costs—see below). In this way, if the offeree accepts the Part 36 offer, he is implicitly accepting to pay the offeror's costs.

- Instead of making a pre-action Part 36 offer, you might make a 'without prejudice save as to costs' offer—that is, a non-Part 36 offer. This can include terms as to costs, but if it is not accepted and proceedings are issued, the offeror will obviously not be entitled to the costs consequences under Part 36 (see below). The court, however, will exercise its discretion on costs under its more general powers under CPR 44.3.

16.5 CLARIFICATION OF PART 36 OFFERS

Once a Part 36 offer has been made, the offeree has seven days within which to request clarification of the offer (CPR 36.8). Requests for clarification are usually made where the offeree is seeking a breakdown of the overall settlement figure to enable him to consider how much the offeror has allocated for different issues or heads of damage. Although there are no stipulations that the request should be in writing, it is good practice to make it in letter form. Under the provisions of CPR 36.8, an offeree who has not received any, or adequate, clarification requested within seven days of the offeror receiving its request may apply to the court for an order that he do so. If the court makes an order, it must also specify the date on which the offer is deemed to have been made. This provision does not, however, apply if the trial has started (CPR 36.8(2)).

Responses to clarification requests should also be in writing and should be done on a 'without prejudice' basis, because you are explaining the basis of a Part 36 offer. It should also be noted that a failure to provide the offeree with the clarification information to enable him to decide whether to accept the offer or not, does not invalidate the offer although the conduct of the offeror in this regard may be taken into account when the court is considering whether to make the usual Part 36 costs order.

 Practical Considerations

It should be borne in mind that, often, claimant legal representatives will make a request for clarification and use this as an excuse for not properly assessing their own case. Defendants frequently make offers based on commercial grounds to promote settlement and apply a global figure for damages—especially when there are numerous heads of damages. Figures are often not arrived at by way of scientific calculation. Some defendants, in practice, are reluctant to reveal exact figures, because this may, in turn, reveal their strategy or tactics. These requests for clarification are therefore designed to force a defendant to provide a breakdown of its assessment of an opponent's case where it may be impracticable or unreasonable.

16.6 HOW AND WHEN CAN PART 36 OFFERS BE ACCEPTED?

16.6.1 HOW?

As with the making of a Part 36 offer, the mode of its acceptance is also in writing. There is no guidance in CPR 36 or its Practice Direction as to the form that the notice of acceptance should take, but it should probably be by letter, making specific reference to the CPR 36 offer made and sent to the offeror (CPR 36.9).

16.6.2 WHEN?

A Part 36 offer can be accepted at any time, even outside the relevant period, by the offeree without seeking the court's permission. There is, however, a proviso to this concerning withdrawal or amendment of the offer, as follows.

- The offeror may withdraw or amend the offer within the relevant period, but only with the permission of the court (CPR 36.3(5)). If permission is granted, then the offeree is not able to accept the offer.
- The offeror can withdraw or amend the offer in writing outside the relevant period without the court's permission, provided, of course, that the offeree has not accepted it in writing (CPR 36.3(6)).
- If the offer is withdrawn, then it will not have the usual Part 36 cost consequences (CPR 36.14(6)).

If you seek to merely amend your own Part 36 offer, then be clear if you are withdrawing any or all of the previous Part 36 offer(s). See paragraph 16.9 below.

Practical Considerations

In practice, it appears that few legal representatives—especially when acting for the defendant—are actually withdrawing offers. The reason for this is the impact of a significant Court of Appeal case, *Lisa Carver v BAA* [2008] EWCA Civ 412 (see paragraph 16.9 below).

There are, however, provisions set out in CPR 36.9(3)–(5) in which, in specific circumstances, a Part 36 offer can only be accepted with the permission of the court. Perhaps the most significant one is where the trial has started (CPR 36.9(3)(d)).

 Professional Conduct

When making a Part 36 offer, make a diary note of when the relevant period expires. Consider with each offer made—both at this stage and periodically through to trial—whether the offer should be withdrawn to avoid the situation in which CPR 36.9(2) applies.

By way of example, consider the situation in which you have been instructed to make, and have made, an offer on behalf of the claimant in a personal injury claim based on a medical report. The relevant period elapses and the offer is not accepted. You do not withdraw or amend it. The litigation continues and, shortly before trial, you seek a supplemental report from your expert, which indicates that the claim for pain and suffering is more extensive than originally thought in the first report. The supplemental report is disclosed and, tactically, you make an increased Part 36 offer to reflect the greater damages potential recovery. The defendant accepts by letter the first offer, because it had not been withdrawn. This places you in potential conflict with your client.

It is in these circumstances that we see an interesting apparent conflict between the common law and the procedural code. The operation of common law would mean that a counter-offer would have the effect of a rejection of an existing offer and, under common law, this would mean that the previous offer could not subsequently be accepted. This would not assist negotiation and settlement. CPR 36.9(2) seems to be an attempt to modify the common law in this regard.

The application of the costs consequences of a Part 36 offer has always been complex and this very complexity accounts for the vast amount of case law that has arisen on this point since 1999. Since April 2007, there are now two levels of application of any adverse costs consequences on offers:

- for a proper compliant Part 36 offer to be enforced automatically, unless the court considered it unjust;

- for any other offer, the residual discretion of CPR 44.3 could be applied.

16.7 CLAIMANT OFFERS

This section discusses what happens when a defendant receives a Part 36 offer made by a claimant.

16.7.1 THE PROCEDURE AND COST IMPLICATIONS OF ACCEPTING THE CLAIMANT'S OFFER

16.7.1.1 Procedure

Once the decision had been made by the defendant to accept the Part 36 offer, as stated above, in paragraph 16.6.1, this is simply done by letter. If proceedings have not yet been issued, then the defendant notifies the claimant in writing and the parties proceed to comply with the terms of the Part 36 offer. If proceedings have been issued, then the defendant sends a notice of acceptance to the claimant and files a copy with the court. The claim is then automatically stayed (CPR 36.11(1)).

The Part 36 offer and subsequent acceptance may not have been in respect of the whole claim, and any subsequent stay would therefore only affect the part of proceedings to which the Part 36 offer related (CPR 36.11(3)).

16.7.1.2 Cost implications

By accepting the Part 36 offer within the relevant period, the defendant is liable to pay the claimant's costs up until the date on which the letter accepting the Part 36 offer is served on the claimant (CPR 36.10(1)). The claimant has an automatic entitlement to these costs, which are assessed on the standard basis (CPR 44.4(2) explains what this means).

So what happens if the defendant decides that he wants to accept the Part 36 offer, but outside the relevant period? CPR 36.10(4)(b) and (5) provide that the parties can try to agree liability for costs, but in the absence of agreement, the court is likely to order that the defendant pays the claimant's costs up until the end of the relevant period and the offeree—in this case, the defendant—will be liable for the claimant's costs incurred thereafter on the standard basis. Ultimately, the claimant is likely to get an overall costs order in his favour. Despite attempts by claimants to seek indemnity costs (on their own offers accepted out of time under CPR 36.10), from the end of the relevant period to the later date of acceptance, this part of the CPR makes no such provision. Standard costs are all that the claimant is likely to recover here on the basis that Part 36 permits an offeree to accept out of time if the offer has not been withdrawn or amended. This does not, of course, mean that the claimant could not try to seek indemnity costs elsewhere under the CPR (such as under CPR 44.3).

16.7.2 THE PROCEDURE AND COST IMPLICATIONS OF REJECTING THE CLAIMANT'S OFFER

16.7.2.1 Procedure

If the defendant decides that he does not wish to accept the claimant's offer, he merely notifies the claimant in writing. The rejection of the offer by the defendant does not have the effect of withdrawing the offer. This can only be done by the claimant and must be done expressly by letter or notice. If this is not done, the offer will remain open for acceptance indefinitely (see *Gibbon v Manchester City Council* [2010] EWCA Civ 726 (25 June 2010) in paragraph 16.9 below).

 Practical Considerations

There is no requirement to give reasons for the rejection, although practically, to encourage further negotiation, there is no reason why the claimant cannot be informed of the reason for the rejection. It is in circumstances such as these that a without-prejudice chat over the telephone with the claimant's legal representative may be worthwhile. However, any proactive practitioner should be considering a Part 36 counter-offer and alternative dispute resolution (ADR) when an offer is not acceptable.

16.7.2.2 Cost implications

The cost consequences to a defendant of rejecting a claimant's Part 36 offer are more cumbersome than those of a claimant rejecting a defendant's Part 36 offer.

The current position is outlined at CPR 36.14(3), as follows. Where the defendant rejects the claimant's offer made more than 21 days before trial and the matter eventually proceeds to trial, if the claimant is successful and is awarded a sum that is the same or greater than his Part 36 offer, then the claimant is entitled to:

- interest on damages, awarded at an enhanced rate of 10 per cent above base rate from the date upon which the Part 36 offer's relevant period expired to the end of the trial;

- his costs to be assessed on the indemnity basis rather than the standard basis; and
- interest on those costs at an enhanced rate of 10 per cent.

If the claimant failed to equal or beat his own offer at trial, the costs will be decided in the usual way, in accordance with CPR 44.3. This would therefore make a claimant offer 'non-effective', save for being taken into account in a party's general conduct in an action.

16.8 DEFENDANT OFFERS

This section discusses what happens when a claimant receives a Part 36 offer made by a defendant.

16.8.1 THE PROCEDURE AND COST IMPLICATIONS OF ACCEPTING THE DEFENDANT'S OFFER

16.8.1.1 Procedure

Generally, where a claimant decides that he wants to accept a Part 36 offer made by a defendant, the procedure is the same as that set out in paragraph 16.7.1.1 above.

Where the Part 36 offer made by the defendant includes an offer to pay a single sum of money, in addition to there being a stay of proceedings, on acceptance of the lump sum, the defendant is obliged to pay the sum accepted directly to the claimant within 14 days of the date of acceptance (CPR 36.11(6)).

The parties can agree—usually in writing—an alternative time limit for payment of the monies, but the significant feature of this arrangement is that if the lump sum is not paid over to the claimant within the stipulated time frame, the claimant may enter judgment for the unpaid sum (CPR 36.11(7)).

Where there are multiple defendants to an action and the claimant wishes to accept a Part 36 offer from one of them, the claimant needs to seek the court's permission to accept. CPR 36.12 sets out the criteria that the court will consider in granting permission, based on the nature of the liability of each defendant (joint and several, or just several) to the claimant.

16.8.1.2 Cost implications

The cost implications of a claimant accepting a defendant's offer are, for the most part, the same as those of a defendant accepting a claimant's Part 36 offer, as set out at paragraph 16.7.1.2 above. The only difference is in relation to the acceptance of the offer outside the relevant period. Therefore, a point of note is that because it is the defendant here who is the offeror and the wording of CPR 36.10(5)(b) refers to the situation in which a Part 36 offer is accepted outside the relevant period, then unless the parties agree otherwise, it will be the claimant who will be liable for the defendant's costs from the expiry of the relevant period to the actual date of acceptance.

 Practical Considerations

There is some merit when acting for a claimant, in terms of adverse cost consequences, to accepting a Part 36 offer within the relevant period if at all possible. The information given to any claimant client when a Part 36 offer is made should include the possibility of adverse cost consequences if the offer is accepted after the relevant period.

16.8.1.3 The creation of a legally binding contract

The Part 36 offer of both a claimant and defendant and the letter of acceptance create a contractually binding arrangement between the parties. Consequently, should the receiving party not abide by the agreement, then it can be enforced within the same set of proceedings without having to go to the time and expense of issuing fresh proceedings on the breach of that agreement. The procedure is even simpler where there is a defendant offering a lump sum, as has been highlighted in paragraph 16.8.1.1 above.

16.8.2 THE PROCEDURE AND COST IMPLICATIONS OF REJECTING THE DEFENDANT'S OFFER

16.8.2.1 Procedure
As with paragraph 16.7.2.1 above, if the claimant wishes to reject the defendant's Part 36 offer, this is simply done in writing. and unless the defendant expressly withdraws the offer, it is open for acceptance at any time.

16.8.2.2 Cost implications
If the claimant makes the decision to reject the defendant's offer and proceed to trial, but fails to secure a judgment that is more advantageous than the defendant's Part 36 offer—that is, if the judgment is for an amount less than or equal to the Part 36 offer—then the court has a discretion to make the following orders unless it is unjust to do so (CPR 36.14(2)):

- award the defendant his costs on the standard basis from the date upon which the relevant period has expired; and

- award interest on those costs.

It is important to note here that the claimant has to do better then the Part 36 offer. What this means is that if the defendant offered £20,000 and the claimant rejected this, but at trial was only awarded £20,000, then the court may invoke the costs and interest penalties. Compare this to the situation in paragraph 16.7.2.2 above, in which the defendant rejects the claimant's Part 36 offer: in that case, the claimant only has to achieve a sum that is the same or greater. So if it was the claimant who had offered £20,000 and the defendant who rejected the same, and at trial the judgment of £20,000 was still made, the court has the discretion to award the costs penalties set out in CPR 36.14(3).

If the claimant beats the defendant's offer, however, then his costs will be decided in the usual way, in accordance with CPR 44.3. This would therefore mean that the defendant's offer has been 'non-effective', save for being taken into account in a party's general conduct in an action.

16.8.2.3 How can the court decide if a Part 36 offer has been beaten?
In many cases, due to the difference in the amount offered and the amount recovered at trial, the fact that a Part 36 offer has been beaten will be apparent. However, in cases in which it is a closer call—usually in unspecified sum claims—it may not be so easily ascertainable whether an offer has been truly beaten. This is usually either because the amount recovered in comparison to the offer is negligible (see paragraph 16.9 for a further discussion on this), or because of the interest awarded.

Remember that Part 36 offers are inclusive of interest and this is where the difficulty can sometimes lie. If this is the case, you may need to calculate the interest that would have accrued on the sum awarded at trial from the date on which the interest became payable up until the last date for acceptance of the Part 36 offer. Once calculated, you will need to add this to the amount of judgment and assess whether the sum awarded at trial is more or less than the amount of the Part 36 offer.

16.8.2.4 Part 36 and conditional fee agreements (CFAs)
Consider the situation in which your claimant client, operating under a conditional fee agreement (CFA) with a success fee and after-the-event (ATE) insurance, rejects a defendant's Part 36 offer and, at trial, is awarded less than the offer. In accordance with CPR 36.14(2), the

claimant will probably be ordered to pay the defendant's costs from the end of the relevant period to trial. It would follow that the claimant would pay his own costs for that period too.

Two issues arise here: firstly, because the claimant has ATE in respect of an adverse cost order, he will not be required to find the funds to pay the defendant, because his ATE insurers will pay—but, secondly, who will pay the claimant's own costs for that period? Unless the claimant purchased ATE to protect against him paying his own costs in this situation (which is unusual and expensive), the claimant will be responsible for payment of these to his legal representative in accordance with the terms of the CFA. This is because the CFA only stipulates 'no win, no fee' if the claimant fails to recover damages, but in this case, he has done so: he has just failed to beat a Part 36 offer.

But what of the level of the success fee if the claimant did not beat a defendant's Part 36 offer? The case of *Tony Lamont v James Burton* [2007] EWCA Civ 429 has raised the issue of the interrelation between the success fee and CPR 36. Despite the fact that the case dealt with the old CPR 36 provisions, it offers some practical guidance on whether a claimant who has not beaten a defendant's offer at trial should be entitled to a 100 per cent success fee in a personal injury claim. Whilst it was argued for the defendant that, had the claimant accepted the Part 36 offer, the success fee would have been limited to 12.5 per cent, the Court of Appeal held that there was nothing in CPR 44 or 45 that permitted it to vary the success fee where a party had not bettered a Part 36 offer.

For a full discussion on CFAs with success fees, see Chapter 3, paragraph 3.3.5.

 Practical Considerations

As a practitioner, you will need to discuss this with your client, because the usual terms of CFAs allow the legal representative to use his discretion as to whether to claim back these costs, which include the base costs and success fee, from his client.

16.9 HOW THE COURT EXERCISES ITS DISCRETION ON COSTS IN 'UNBEATEN' PART 36 OFFERS AT TRIAL

It is important to remember that all costs awards made by the court, not only those in respect of Part 36 offers, are discretionary and that whilst CPR Part 36 may stipulate cost consequences for rejection of offers, it is for the court to decide whether it wishes to implement those sanctions or not.

Specifically in relation to CPR Part 36, the court will only award the penalties set out in CPR 36.14(2) and (3) if it is 'just' to do so, based on considerations set out in CPR 36.14(4)—that is:

- the terms of the Part 36 offer;
- when the offer was made;
- the information available to the parties when the offer was made; and
- the conduct of the parties in relation to providing information to enable the offeree to give proper consideration to the offer.

The courts, in accordance with CPR 36.14, will decide whether to award the costs consequences where a claimant fails to obtain a judgment that is more advantageous than a defendant's Part 36 offer, or where judgment against a defendant is at least as advantageous to the claimant as the defendant's Part 36 offer. Sometimes, it is not obvious when a Part 36 offer has been beaten, or if it has, by how much. Consequently, there has been a plethora of case law on how the court deals with awarding the costs sanctions in CPR Part 36 and the most noteworthy cases are as follows.

- The first Court of Appeal case to deal with Part 36 offers since April 2007 was *Lisa Carver v BAA* [2008] EWCA Civ 412, in which the claimant had, in fact, beaten the defendant's Part 36 offer (which had never been withdrawn). The claimant beat the offer by £51 and the Court decided that it would need to look at all of the circumstances of the case in deciding whether she had obtained a judgment that was 'more advantageous' than the defendant's Part 36 offer. It was held that the gain of £51 was simply 'not worth the fight' and proceeded to make a costs order that reflected the fact that the litigation to trial had been unnecessary. Therefore, the Court imposed costs sanctions against the claimant as if she had not beaten the Part 36 offer.

- *Fitzpatrick Contractors Ltd v Tyco Fire and Integrated Solutions (UK) Ltd (No 3)* [2009] EWHC 274 (TCC) considered whether the claimant was entitled to indemnity costs following the defendant's acceptance of its Part 36 offer more than a year after it had been made. It was held that whilst this was an attractive submission made by the claimant, the rules, particularly CPR 36.10, were silent on this point and such inference should not be encouraged.

- *Mary Gray Ritchie decd, Ritchie and Ors v Joslin and Ors* [2009] EWHC B7 (Ch) held that the erroneous calculation of the 21-day time limit (to make the offer effectively less than 21 days) did not in fact invalidate the offer. This is an example of the court exercising its discretion when the wording and ethos of Part 36 seemed to indicate that the courts would adhere to a narrow interpretation.

- Until *AF v BG* [2009] EWCA Civ 757, it had been unclear whether a defendant with a counterclaim could take advantage of the provisions of CPR 36.14 for claimants despite the fact it was a defendant in the litigation. It was held here that a defendant could make a claimant Part 36 offer relating to its counterclaim and taking into account the original claim so that the more favourable costs consequences of a claimant offer applied. However, this would only ever apply to counterclaims that significantly exceeded the claim and where it was obvious that the flow of monies was from the claimant to the defendant. Otherwise it could just be characterized as a defendant offer. There may be more to be heard on this subject-matter in years to come.

- One of the most notable cases is the conjoined appeal of *Gibbon v Manchester City Council* [2010] EWCA Civ 726 (25 June 2010), which included the case of *Blower v Reeves* (same citation) where the Court of Appeal had to consider two Part 36 issues. In *Gibbon*, the court reinforced the fact that a Part 36 offer can be accepted at any time unless it has been withdrawn and any withdrawal must be done expressly by a letter or notice. There can be no implied withdrawal even if the offeree had rejected the Part 36 offer or made a counter-offer. As a result of the CA decision in *Gibbon*, there can be no discretion on this point. Advice to legal practitioners is to proceed with caution and be watchful of Part 36 offers made. In *Blower,* the CA had to deal with the *Carver* point: whether the judgment in question had been more advantageous than the relevant Part 36 offer. Here the claimant had beaten the defendant's offer by some £660 on an offer figure of £7,700. In so doing the CA recognized that it was bound by the decision in *Carver*, but it went on to emphasize that, in most cases, success in financial terms should be the governing factor. The authors' view is that in most cases obtaining judgment for an amount greater than the Part 36 offer is likely to outweigh all other factors. The *Blower* case is trying to weaken the impact of *Carver* and narrow the court's discretion only to make the costs' order under Part 36 if it is 'just to do so'.

- In *Midland Packaging Ltd & Ors v HW Chartered Accountants (a firm)* [2010] EWHC B16 (Mercantile) the court had further opportunity to consider the appropriate costs orders after two Part 36 offers had been made during the litigation by the defendant and one counter-offer by the claimant, taking account of the *Carver* decision and the Jackson proposals. Though heard after the *Gibbon/Blower* case above, the judge's attention was not drawn to it. In this case the judge tackled the question of costs on an issue-by-issue basis and in stages at the times the various offers were made. The judge considered in his stage 1 the general rule that the unsuccessful party pays the costs (CPR 44.3(2)). He then went on to consider analysing the Part 36 offers in his stage 2. Finally in his stage 3, he considered whether a party had been partially successful, the conduct of the parties and their offers to settle (CPR 44.3(4)). It was held that the claimant was entitled to all its costs on the standard basis until the date of its Part 36 counter-offer. When stage 3 became a factor, he awarded the defendant 75 per cent of its costs thereafter. The case is interesting in the judge's approach to determining 'success'; he also redefined 'success' in the case again after the counter-offer by the claimant.

- In *Moira Walsh v Mark Buddah Singh* [2011] EWCA 80, the defendant submitted that he had substantially won and should therefore have his costs awarded in accordance with Part 36 as he had made an offer that the claimant had rejected. The Court of Appeal agreed that the claimant had not beaten the defendant's offer and therefore went on to consider whether it would be 'just' to invoke the costs consequences of Part 36 against her. The court took into account all the circumstances including the conduct of the parties. The Court of Appeal upheld the first instance decision and said it would be 'unjust' to order the claimant to pay the defendant's costs and interest for the date of the expiry of the defendant's Part 36 offer as the defendant had behaved 'disgracefully' throughout. It was clear from the judge's determinations that he applied both the discretion contained in CPR 44.3(4) and CPR 36.14 before reaching his conclusions on the appropriate costs order.

- In *James Pankhurst v Lee White* [2010] EWHC 311 (QB) the court considered the implication of a rejected Part 36 offer on the costs order the court should make. The claimant in this case had made a Part 36 offer that was rejected by the defendant. On the hearing on liability (a split trial had been ordered) the claimant had succeeded on the issue of liability. Even though the defendant had rejected the Part 36 offer the claimant wrote to the defendant to inform them that he would no longer be prepared to accept their Part 36 offer but intended to rely on it on the question of costs. The costs judge held that the offer continued to be relevant, as an historical fact, for costs assessment. The decision, though probably fair and sensible on the facts, adds complexity to the effect of withdrawing Part 36 offers.

- *AB v CD and Ors* [2011] EWHC 602 (Ch) held that the claimant's purported Part 36 offer was not valid because the offer merely replicated the entirety of the claimant's claim and as such there had been no concession made by the claimant. If the offer were allowed to stand as a Part 36 offer then every claimant could obtain favourable costs consequences simply by making an offer to settle requiring total capitulation by the defendant.

It should perhaps be mentioned here that if either the claimant or defendant to an action make an offer and they do not beat their own offer at trial, then it is of no consequence as far as cost sanctions are concerned.

16.10 ISSUES TO DISCUSS WITH YOUR CLIENT ON MAKING OR RECEIVING A PART 36 OFFER

Having now discussed the substantive requirements of CPR 36, as a legal representative, there are a number of matters that you will need to consider and discuss with your client when either making or receiving a Part 36 offer, as follows.

- Consider what type of offer should be made: a Part 36 offer, or a non-Part 36 offer—that is, a 'without prejudice save as to costs' offer? You will need to explain to your client what a Part 36 offer and a 'without prejudice save as to costs' offer are, because he is unlikely to understand this unless he has been involved in dispute resolution before. There are several tactical reasons why your client may wish to make one or the other, as follows, and you will need to discuss these with him.

- He may wish to make a global non-Part 36 offer to settle, incorporating a provision for costs in addition to damages and interest (remember that Part 36 offers are not valid Part 36 offers if they include provisions for costs) either for a tactical or commercial reasons. You must therefore advise your client—preferably in writing—that any global offer if not beaten at trial will attract the court's discretion on costs under CPR 44.3 and not CPR 36.10.

- He may wish to make sequential Part 36 offers—that is, to make an optimistic Part 36 offer early on that, if rejected or once the relevant period expires, is withdrawn and a lower offer is made—to encourage negotiation and settlement.

- More often in personal injury claims, it may be a prudent step in most cases to make an early Part 36 offer on liability alone—for example, at 99 per cent—which need not be withdrawn.

- Check compliance with CPR 36.2—you will need to check the wording of the Part 36 offer, whether making or receiving it, especially if there are special requirements in addition to the basic points set out in paragraph 16.3 above.

- Seek clarification—if a Part 36 offer is unclear, then do not make assumptions about what it may or may not include. You have the benefit of CPR 36.8, which allows you to seek clarification of the offer, as discussed in paragraph 16.5 above.

- Advise on the procedural and cost consequences of accepting or rejecting the Part 36 offer-as soon as a Part 36 offer is made to your client, it is incumbent on you as a legal representative to act quickly if there is to be acceptance within the relevant period. You will need to advise your client, both in writing and then verbally either over the telephone or at a face-to-face meeting. (See the Online Resource Centre for extracts of a meeting with a legal representative and a client at which a Part 36 offer is discussed.) The key point here is that the advice that you are seeking to give is not whether your client should accept or reject the offer (despite the fact that this is probably the first question that your client will ask you), but how well or not he may do at trial—that is, whether your client will beat the offer. Also ensure that you have discussed with him all of the relevant information to enable him to make his *own* decision on the offer. In essence, he needs to understand the risks of accepting or not accepting the offer in light of the fact that the costs of an action dramatically increase as the action proceeds to trial.

online resource centre

To provide such information to your client and discuss matters with him takes experience and professional judgment, neither of which a legal representative new to litigation is able to acquire at the outset. However, there are a number of important considerations, as follows, through which you can take your client to demonstrate as a starting point whether the Part 36 offer is well pitched or not, or whether it might be construed to be derisory. This exercise will then assist your client in coming to his decision.

1. You will need to undertake a risk assessment of your case and explain to your client the risk on liability (including contributory negligence, set-offs, and counterclaims), any causational difficulties (both in respect of liability and quantum), and the risk on quantum, considering the likely level of interest that may be awarded.

2. In some cases, prospects of success can turn on what evidence might be allowed or disallowed, or how well your witnesses perform in the witness box. These are matters that will also need to be taken into account.

3. Your client is entitled to know the reasons for your advice and, as such, you may need to review the file in its entirety to ensure you have all of the requisite information to hand when conducting your overall risk assessment.

4. If your client is under a CFA, review the terms in relation to Part 36 offers. Additionally, consider whether a staged success fee is now appropriate (see Chapter 3, paragraph 3.3.5).

 Professional Conduct

Practitioners have a duty under the Solicitors' Code of Conduct 2007 to act in their client's best interests (Rule 1.03). If you find yourself in the position in which you are unsure as to the litigation risk or what the client may recover at trial, discuss the case with a senior fee earner and/or seek counsel's opinion in writing or in conference. In your early days as a legal representative, you will benefit from the use of counsel to enable you to approach the CPR Part 36 issue with greater confidence. You may advise your client that a conference would be appropriate, because this will give counsel the opportunity to assess your client as a witness. (Counsel's opinion may also, however, be reasonable.) You will need your client's instructions and probably a payment in respect of counsel's fees (this will depend on the terms of the CFA if there is one, because some CFAs state that the solicitor will pay the disbursement). This course of action will ensure that you are fulfilling your professional conduct obligations and avoid any reproaches from your client at a later stage if the matter proceeds to a trial in which he is unsuccessful, resulting in an adverse costs order.

 Costs

When undertaking your risk assessment, it may be appropriate to provide your client with a costs estimate for costs already incurred and costs to be incurred to trial. This will deal with the proportionality aspect and focus your client's mind on a realistic settlement.

---

5. Consider any tactics with your client on the receipt of a Part 36 offer—these should generally have the effect of moving the dispute resolution process forward and may include the following.

(i) It may be genuinely difficult for your client to decide whether he should accept the offer within the relevant period: for example, because the case is large and complex, or because the case is at such an early stage that a true valuation of the case is problematic. In this situation, you can try to agree an extension of the relevant period with your opponent. The advantage of this is that the offer cannot be withdrawn during any extended period without the court's permission.

(ii) Do not formally reject the offer because there is no CPR requirement to do so, because Part 36 offers remain open for acceptance until withdrawn or amended.

(iii) Make a counter-offer. This should be CPR 36-compliant and may be a useful and effective tactic depending on how much it is for and when exactly it is made.

(iv) Suggest ADR.

16.11 **LORD JACKSON'S PROPOSALS FOR PART 36**

It would appear that Lord Jackson does not propose tampering too much with Part 36 but rather wishes to ensure that his recommendations elsewhere are reflected consistently with this part of the CPR.

FIGURE 16.1

CURRENT POSITION	LORD JACKSON'S PROPOSALS
1. The Court of Appeal case of *Carver* (see above) has created some uncertainty (perhaps unintended) within Part 36. It has not yet been either appealed or overruled.	The effect of *Carver* should be reversed.
2. Where a defendant rejects a claimant's offer and fails to do better at trial the costs consequences are set out in CPR 36.14.	CPR 36.14 should be amended to permit if 'just' to do so, an enhancement on the claimant's damages recovered of 10 per cent. This would be in addition to the indemnity costs and enhanced interest provisions.
3. The basis for the recovery of costs is that the payment of costs by one party to another is discretionary but that the starting point is that the loser generally pays the winner's costs.	If qualified costs shifting is introduced as proposed (Chapter 4 at paragraph 4.9), no amendment will be required to CPR 36 in order to provide incentives to claimants to accept adequate Part 36 offers.

KEY POINTS SUMMARY

- Part 36 offers represent one of the most important tactical steps that a party to a dispute can take.

- If you are acting for a party who is offering to pay a sum of money in settlement and this is formulated in a Part 36 offer, you must explain to the client that the payment of damages is not the end of his liability to his opponent, because there is an implicit duty to pay the opponent's costs up to the date of acceptance, if within the relevant period, on the standard basis.

- It is the client's decision to decide whether to accept or reject a Part 36 offer. The role of the legal representative is to ensure that the client has all of the requisite information before him to enable him to make that decision on an informed basis.

- Control your client's expectations on costs awards. Remind your client that costs are in the discretion of the court, and that the cost sanctions that are a feature of CPR 36 may not be awarded even if offers are equalled or beaten at trial.

- Because Part 36 offers can be accepted at any time as long as they have not been withdrawn or amended, it is important that you keep your own client's offers under review and withdraw them if appropriate. Therefore, it is important to consider at all key stages whether these offers should be made, accepted, withdrawn, or revised, and if withdrawn, to ensure your client understands that the offer then loses the cost implications of a Part 36 offer.

- Watch out for the development of Lord Jackson's proposals on *Carver* and CPR 36.14.

Case study *Andrew James Pike and Deep Builders Ltd*

Andrew Pike has now been medically examined by Mr Higgins, but the report was not wholly conclusive, because further investigations need undertaking. Proceedings have now been issued, and a defence and counterclaim filed by Deep Builders Ltd. The case has been allocated to the multi-track and directions set for the action. At the time of allocation, the claimant's legal representative made an application for an interim payment. Neither party has yet complied with the directions, because the timetable set by the court has not yet started.

Shortly after the interim payment application, the defendant made a valid Part 36 offer of £20,000. A copy of the letter appears in the Online Resource Centre. You have telephoned your client to inform him of the offer and that you will be contacting him by letter.

Question 1

At this particular stage in the action, consider what advice you would give to Andrew Pike on the timing of the offer. Consult the 'Litigation train' both in the book and online to help you to contextualize where we are in the process of litigation.

Question 2

Andrew Pike is being funded by way of a CFA. What advice do you need to give him in relation to the Part 36 offer?

Question 3

Please consider the contents of the defendant's Part 36 offer letter and draft a letter to Andrew Pike about the offer made by the defendant.

Helpful hints to consider for the letter include:

- note the type of letter that this will be in terms of style, length, formality, and content—and gauge the intellect of your client;

- note where we are in the litigation—that is, what has happened and what will happen;

- consider the impact of the timing of the offer on your advice;

- consider whether there is any additional information needed to help you to advise Andrew Pike;

- take into account Andrew Pike's funding arrangements—that is, whether CFA and ATE; and

- consider how you can move the action along proactively.

Case study *Bollingtons Ltd and Mrs Elizabeth Lynch t/a The Honest Lawyer*

A defence and counterclaim has been filed and served by Mrs Lynch. Acting for Bollingtons Ltd, you are completing the allocation questionnaire and have prepared a cost estimate to the client, which shows that costs to date are £500, but anticipated costs to trial in light of the disputed nature of the debt are likely to be an additional £6,500. Mrs Lynch has now made a Part 36 offer of £2,000.

Question 1

Consider the proportionality issues in this case and the discussions that you will need to have with Mr Green of Bollingtons Ltd.

Question 2

How will this impact on your advice to him?

Any documents referred to in these case study questions can be found on the Online Resource Centre—simply click on 'Case study documentation' to access the documents that you need for Chapter 16 and to be reminded of the questions above. Suggested answers to these case study questions can also be accessed on the Online Resource Centre by your lecturer.

FIGURE 16.2 FLOW CHART SHOWING WITHDRAWAL AND ACCEPTANCE OF A PART CPR 36 OFFER

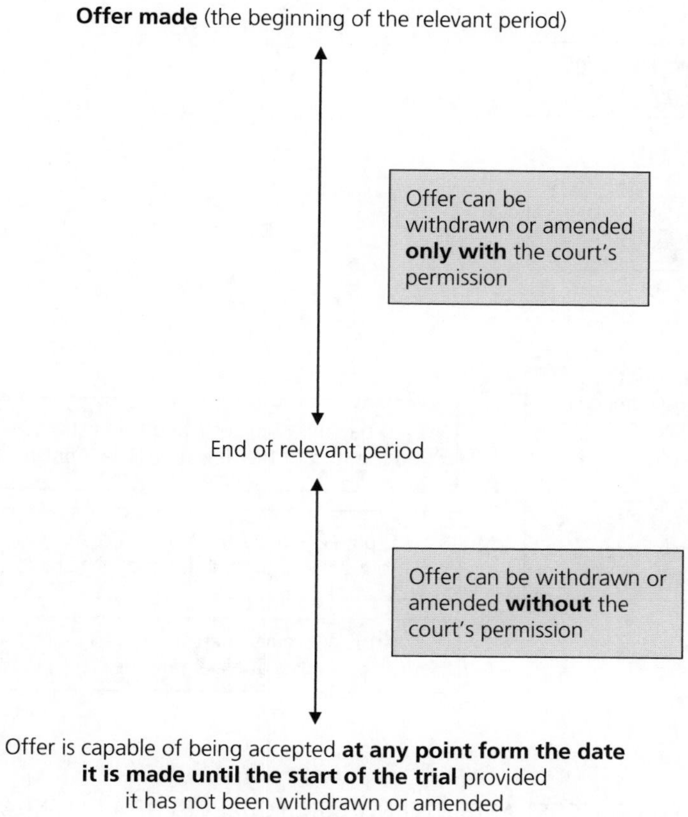

Offer made (the beginning of the relevant period)

Offer can be withdrawn or amended **only with** the court's permission

End of relevant period

Offer can be withdrawn or amended **without** the court's permission

Offer is capable of being accepted **at any point form the date it is made until the start of the trial** provided it has not been withdrawn or amended

FIGURE 16.3 FLOW CHART FOR THE CLAIMANT'S ACCEPTANCE OF A DEFENDANT'S PART 36 MONEY OFFER FOR THE WHOLE CLAIM

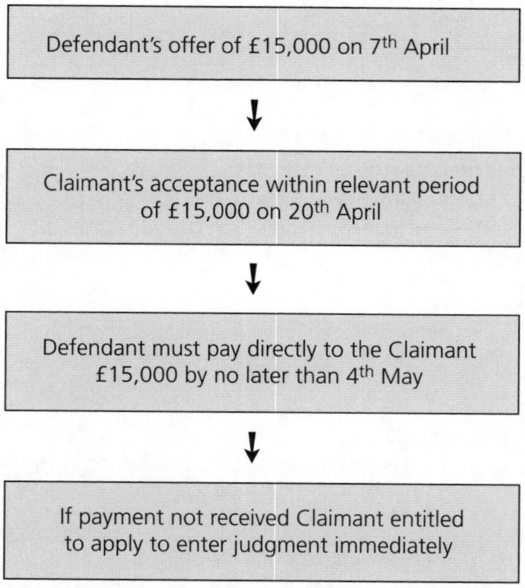

Defendant's offer of £15,000 on 7th April

Claimant's acceptance within relevant period of £15,000 on 20th April

Defendant must pay directly to the Claimant £15,000 by no later than 4th May

If payment not received Claimant entitled to apply to enter judgment immediately

FIGURE 16.4 FLOW CHART FOR THE COST AND INTEREST CONSEQUENCES OF A CLAIMANT NOT 'BEATING' A DEFENDANT'S OFFER

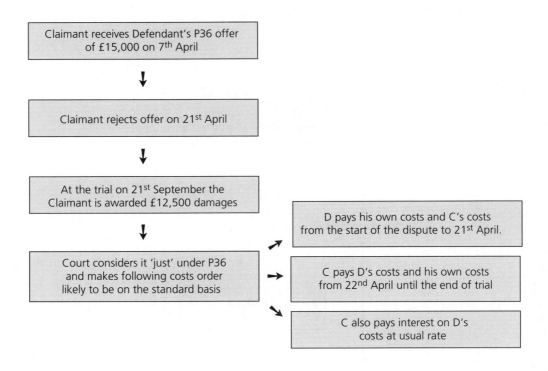

FIGURE 16.5 FLOW CHART FOR THE COST AND INTEREST CONSEQUENCES OF A DEFENDANT NOT 'BEATING' A CLAIMANT'S OFFER

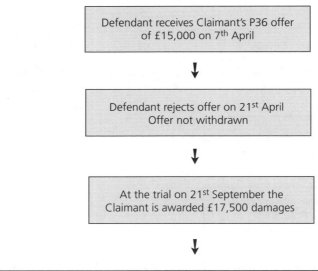

FIGURE 16.6 A TEMPLATE CLAIMANT PART 36 OFFER LETTER

Dear Sirs,

Without prejudice save as to costs—Offer to settle under Part 36

(Heading of matter)

We refer to the above matter in which we act for . . . . Our client is confident that it has a strong case against your client, ..., and is entitled to substantial damages, [as set out in its particulars of claim OR as set out in correspondence OR for the reasons set out below]. Nevertheless, our client is [keen to resolve this matter amicably OR mindful that under the Civil Procedure Rules litigants are expected to try to resolve their disputes whenever possible]. We are, therefore, authorised by our client to make the following offer to settle under Part 36.

This Offer is intended to have the consequences set out in Part 36 of the Civil Procedure Rules. In particular, your client will be liable for our client's costs up to the date of notice of acceptance which must be in writing in accordance with CPR 36.10, if the offer is accepted within . . . . (the relevant period).

TERMS OF THE OFFER

Our client is willing to settle [the whole of the claim referred to above OR specify which part of the claim or issue the client is willing to settle] on the following terms:

- Your client to pay our client, within [14 or such other number as client is willing to accept] days of accepting this Offer, the sum of £ . . . . by [means of payment—eg. electronic transfer] into [give account details] or [set out precise terms of offer in a non-money claim].

- This Offer [takes OR does not take] account of your client's counterclaim [or/and any other claims your client may have against ours] in this matter.

- The settlement sum does not include costs and, as mentioned above, your client will be liable to pay our client's costs on the standard basis, to be assessed if not agreed, up to the date of service of notice of acceptance if this Offer is accepted within the relevant period.

- The settlement sum is inclusive of interest until the relevant period has expired. Thereafter, interest at a rate of . . . .% p.a. will be added.

FAILURE TO ACCEPT THIS OFFER

If your client does not accept this Offer, and our client obtains a judgment which is equal to or more advantageous than this Offer, our client intends to rely on CPR 36.14. In other words, our client will be seeking an order in the following terms:

- Your client to pay our client's costs up to the expiry of the relevant period.

- Your client to pay our client's costs on the indemnity basis from the date on which the relevant period expired, with interest on those costs of up to 10% above base rate and interest on the whole or part of any sum awarded at up to 10% above base rate for some or all of the period starting from the same date.

If you think that this offer is in any way defective or non-compliant with Part 36, please let us know.

We look forward to hearing from you.

Yours faithfully,

17 DISCLOSURE AND INSPECTION

Relevant court forms relating to this chapter:

- **N265 List of Documents**

- **N244 Interim Application (for pre-action disclosure applications dealt with in this chapter)**

LITIGATION TRAIN DISCLOSURE AND INSPECTION

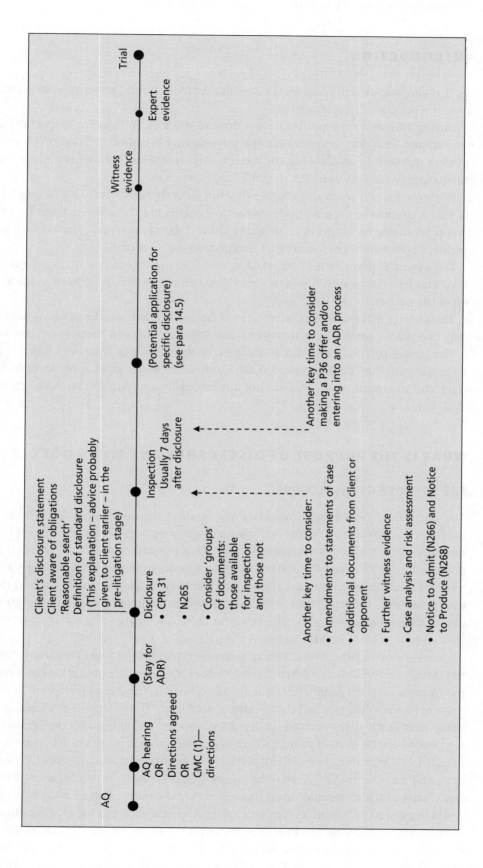

Within the online resource there is a short video clip that will help you understand the nature and purpose of the 'directions' order (or orders).

17.1 INTRODUCTION

In this chapter, we will consider the definition of 'disclosure', its *purpose*, its *extent*, and the *process* whereby it is implemented.

During litigation, the parties have a duty to disclose and permit inspection of certain documents. This duty accords with the premise that litigation is based on all of the information that will be available to the court at trial will already have been made available to the parties—that is, a 'cards on the table' approach.

However, we will see in this chapter that not all of the 'cards' need be 'face-up' at the time at which disclosure must be made. Some documents may be disclosed, but be 'face-down' and unavailable for inspection. Whether these documents remain 'face-down' will be dependent on a number of factors that this chapter will consider.

The essential point to note in relation to disclosure is that any document that is to be used and referred to at trial will, at some time before the trial, have been made available to all of the parties.

This chapter will also look at other types of disclosure and the times at which such disclosure may take place—some of which may be *before* litigation has been commenced (see 14.5).

The formal provisions for disclosure are contained in Civil Procedure Rule (CPR) 31 and its accompanying Practice Direction. The formal disclosure rules apply to cases in the fast track and the multi-track. They do not automatically apply to the small claims track (CPR 27.2(1)(b)).

17.2 WHAT IS THE PURPOSE OF DISCLOSURE AND WHEN DOES IT OCCUR?

17.2.1 THE PURPOSE OF DISCLOSURE

The purpose of disclosure is to make a list of all of the documents (and the word 'documents' is not restricted to paper documents—see paragraph 17.3 below) that either support **or** undermine the respective parties' cases. This purpose is a general one that applies to both parties. In this way, the obligation to disclose documents that either party has that are relevant to the issues of the case applies whether they support or do not support that party's case. The aim of the obligation to disclose those documents that might undermine a party's case or support its opponent's case, as well as those documents that a party has that support its own case, is to do **justice** between the parties.

One of the main aims of the CPR was to seek to restrict the amount of disclosure between parties. Although the CPR have restricted the scale of the disclosure obligations in some respects, the increase, in sheer numbers, of documents created in the digital revolution now threatens to increase vastly the size and complexity of disclosure. The process of disclosure is often one of the most costly parts of an action. It is also, however, one of the most important stages, and is a time when the relative strengths and weaknesses of each party's case may be more clearly revealed. It is after disclosure and inspection that both parties will probably fully review their case, and consider making, repeating, increasing, decreasing, or withdrawing Part 36 offers (see Chapter 16) and consider again the options for alternative dispute resolution (ADR).

It is important to remember that 'disclosure' means identifying the existence of all of these documents. This identification process notes every document that should, under the terms of the court order to disclose or as agreed by the parties, be disclosed. This process does *not* make all of the documents available to be seen or 'inspected'. Later in this chapter, we will define the process of 'disclosure' and, from that process, it can be seen quite clearly that there are some documents that are listed or 'disclosed' that may not be inspected by the other party.

17.2.2 WHEN DOES DISCLOSURE OCCUR?

Disclosure is a stage in the process of an action to trial. This can be seen in the 'Litigation train' diagram at the beginning of this chapter. The timing, and extent, of the disclosure obligations of either party are within the court's discretion. In most cases, however, an order for disclosure will be defined and made immediately after allocation of the case to track or at the first case management conference (CMC—see Chapter 12 generally). Either event is usually the first opportunity that the court will take to manage the case actively and to set down a timetable for the progress of the case to trial.

The order for disclosure will be contained in the general directions that the court makes which set out the timetable of the action towards trial. It is often the first direction with which the parties must comply. In the fast track, it will often be ordered to take place within four weeks of allocation to that track. In the multi-track, where directions for the progress of a case towards trial may be more specific to the factors of the case, the direction to give disclosure will still often be one of the first stages with which the parties will comply, although the time within which it should be undertaken may be (but not necessarily is) longer.

The parties may agree, or the court may order, that disclosure takes place in stages (CPR 31.13). This might happen if a decision has been made for a 'split trial' (see Chapter 12, paragraph 12.7.3.4.2). For example, a case that proceeds on issues of liability, firstly, an order for disclosure on the issues relating to liability will be made, and only after the liability issue has been determined, and if necessary, will an order for disclosure on issues of quantum be made. In hotly contested actions that may have complex and costly evidence to produce for issues of quantum, it can have significant costs savings for the parties to have disclosure (and, in part, evidence gathering) in stages.

Sometimes, an action can have a clear division of the issues and the court may seek to restrict the issues to be tried within its case management powers (to ensure that the action proceeds within the aims of the overriding objective), or the parties may agree to restrict the number of issues. Where such a restriction occurs, there will be an equal restriction on the scope of the parties' disclosure obligations.

It is important to note that the obligation to disclose documents may, and commonly does, arise at other times. The provisions of CPR 31.16 provide the circumstances under which an application for *pre*-action disclosure may be sought (see paragraph 17.10). In compliance with a Pre-Action Protocol or the Practice Direction on Pre-Action Conduct (PDPAC), the parties are required to exchange documents that will help to clarify issues. Where parties have conducted their pre-action behaviour in accordance with Protocol, it is likely that some disclosure will have already taken place between the parties before the court orders them to give standard disclosure within the order for directions that it makes (see Chapter 8). It is also important to note, however, that if a party has failed to abide by the Protocol and has not given any disclosure before commencement of proceedings, the sanctions for this non-compliance will be in an adverse costs order within the action. The courts do not have the power to order compliance with a Protocol, and thus unless an order for pre-action disclosure is appropriate under the provisions of CPR 31.16, the courts will only 'take note' of the non-compliance of a party in the pre-action phase and, if it is appropriate to do so, will make a costs sanction against that party.

It is also important to note that the obligation to give disclosure continues until the conclusion of the proceedings. Accordingly, if a relevant document comes to light after the parties have complied with the direction to give disclosure, it must be disclosed to the other side immediately.

17.3 **WHAT IS A 'DOCUMENT'?**

A definition of 'document' is contained in CPR 31.4. It is not restricted to paper or only to originals. It extends to anything upon which information of any description is recorded and will include electronically held information, such as databases, emails (including deleted emails), electronic personal organizers, file servers, back-up tapes, and hard drives, as well as hard-copy correspondence, faxes, memoranda, reports, photographs, plans, maps, diaries, and board minutes, as well as objects. This definition includes therefore several possibly different versions of a document when one has been amended or annotated, and the dates of those amendments or annotations may be an important part of the document.

The rules dealing with the disclosure of real evidence, such as plans, maps, models, and photographs, are contained in CPR 33.6.

17.4 **THE EXTENT OF A PARTY'S DISCLOSURE OBLIGATION**

The obligation to make disclosure will arise from either a court order or the parties' agreement. The usual court order is a direction that the parties give 'standard disclosure', but the court may order, or the parties may agree, to limit this. In some circumstances in which the issues of the case demand it, and where it is *proportionate, fair, and just* to do so, the obligation to give disclosure may be greater than 'standard disclosure'.

17.4.1 **WHAT DOES 'STANDARD DISCLOSURE' REQUIRE A PARTY TO DISCLOSE?**

'Standard disclosure' requires a party to disclose:

- documents on which it relies; and
- documents that:
  - affect its own case adversely;
  - affect the other party's case adversely;
  - support the other party's case; and
- documents that, in particular types of claim, are specified by the court.

This relates to all documents within a party's 'control'.

The question of whether a document should be disclosed is determined by reference to the issues raised in the parties' statements of case. Only those documents that have reference to the issues between the parties are to be disclosed. It is important, therefore, that where parties (or the court) limit the number of issues between them, the disclosure obligation will be reduced to meet only those issues remaining. In order to meet with the overriding objective—that is, the requirements of proportionality, fairness, and justice—parties are encouraged to be both realistic and reasonable in determining with which issues to proceed. It is often at the stage of disclosure—or later, at the stage at which witness statements of fact and expert reports are exchanged—that a party is able to determine more clearly the strengths and weaknesses of parts of (or the whole of) its case. Where a part of the case seems unlikely to succeed, it may be sensible for that party to seek to agree those parts, and in this way further restrict the amount of disclosure and documents to be referred to at trial. Obviously, if the reappraisal process determines that that party's whole case has been seriously undermined, then settlement of the whole should be sought.

Further examination of the definition of 'standard disclosure' reveals that:

- the obligation is a wide-ranging one and that clients will usually need specific guidance on the extent of their obligation;

- it does not include documents, or classes of document, that are, in effect, documents that may simply lead a party on a 'train of inquiry'.

 Professional Conduct

A legal representative is under a professional duty to advise clients of their disclosure obligations. This advice should be given at the earliest opportunity to avoid clients removing documents from their possession that they consider to be harmful to their position. Where a client does deliberately remove or destroy harmful documents in their possession, the legal representative has further duties to the court (a duty 'not to mislead the court', under Rule 11.01 of the Solicitors' Code of Conduct 2007) that require him to advise the court and the other party in the disclosure process of the existence of the document so removed or destroyed, together with the circumstances of its removal or destruction, and the court is entitled to draw adverse inferences from the client's behaviour. If a client will not give instructions to give that information, the legal representative must not continue acting for the client (Rule 11.01). The professional duties relating to disclosure are onerous.

17.4.2 THE MEANING OF 'CONTROL'

The obligation to disclose documents includes those that are within a party's control. 'Control' extends to documents of which a party:

- has physical possession;
- has a right to possession, or to inspection, or to take copies;
- had, but no longer has.

This definition will mean, therefore, that a party has an obligation to give disclosure not only of documents that it has, but also of documents that it does not have, but which it has the right to reclaim or of which it has the right to obtain copies. This could include, for example, documents that are held by a party's accountants, or documents held by a subsidiary company in an action in which the parent company is a party.

It also includes the obligation to disclose documents that it did have, but does not have anymore. At one end of the spectrum, this will include letters that have been sent, and at the other end of the spectrum, it can include documents that have been deliberately destroyed (see the 'Professional Conduct' box above). In the case of 'letters sent', it is likely that a duplicate of that original letter is still retained by the party and that, also, is a document that must be disclosed. With the degree of electronically created documents and the extent to which these can be 'retrieved', the preparation of a party's list of documents in order to comply with its disclosure obligation can be very onerous indeed. However, some restriction on the potential scope of this obligation is provided by CPR 31.9(1)—that is, that 'A party need not disclose more than one copy of a document'. This rule would not apply, however, if any amendments or annotations were to have been made to the document in its exchanges to and fro, and the amendments on it met the definition of 'standard disclosure'.

17.5 THE OBLIGATION TO MAKE A REASONABLE SEARCH FOR RELEVANT DOCUMENTS

17.5.1 THE OBLIGATIONS AND DUTIES OF THE PARTIES AND THEIR LEGAL REPRESENTATIVES

Each party that has an obligation to give disclosure is required to make a reasonable and proportionate search for documents. The duty of a party in an action to disclose is qualified by the principle of 'reasonableness'.

Determining what is a 'reasonable and proportionate' search includes a review of the nature, the importance, and the value of the case. It also includes a consideration of the costs and the ease of retrieval of the documents.

Clients will need guidance on the extent of the search that the client should make so that he can make an honest and true 'disclosure statement'. A solicitor has an obligation to the court to ensure that his client makes full disclosure.

When the client declares, when he makes disclosure, that he has conducted a 'reasonable search' for documents, he is saying that he *understands* the duty to disclose and that, to the best of his knowledge and belief, *he has discharged* that duty. This declaration has a profound influence on the way in which parties should approach their obligations of disclosure. The client will therefore need to have a clear understanding of the issues of the case in order to carry out the search effectively. It will be for the solicitor to ensure that the client has this level of understanding. The case of *CMCS Common Market Commercial Services AVV v Taylor* [2011] EWHC 324 (Ch) confirms the risks for a legal representative who fails to undertake his disclosure obligations. In this case the court ordered a wasted costs order against the legal representative for their failure to supervise the client in undertaking their disclosure obligations.

 Professional Conduct

As an 'officer of the court', a solicitor owes a duty to the court to have gone through his client's disclosure list carefully in order to make sure, so far as is possible, that no relevant documents have been omitted.

It is therefore good practice to give clients timely advice, both orally and in writing, about the types of document that are to be disclosed and the appropriate person in the client's organization to make the search, as well as advice concerning the retention, storage, and filing of documentation. The burden on the solicitor to ensure that he meets all of the professional obligations relating to disclosure is a heavy one.

17.5.2 THE IMPACT OF 'E'-DISCLOSURE

PD 31(6) contains guidance for all e-disclosure.
    'Document' under the CPR includes

- emails and other electronic communications;
- word-processed documents;
- databases;
- documents readily accessible from computer systems, and other electronic devices and media, such as memory sticks, CDs, and mobile phones;
- documents stored on servers and back-up systems;
- electronic documents that have been deleted; and
- metadata.

 Practical Considerations

Any legal representative engaged in the process of disclosure must think carefully about the range and extent of e-disclosure required of the client. There is a misconception that deleted files can very easily be retrieved; they can be retrieved—but not always that easily. Files often become fragmented when placed in the 'deleted files bin'. Does an isolated fragment found in an unallocated fragment or cluster on a disk constitute, for the purposes of disclosure, the document that is relevant to disclose? Advising a client of their disclosure obligations and blithely stating that this includes 'deleted electronic materials' is likely to cause great consternation in the client's IT department, or for a smaller company client, great concern because of the man hours, and expense, of complying with the advice given. Any early advice to a client about its obligations of disclosure in any action in progress or that might affect it in a possible future action should include advice that might result in its reviewing the way in which the company processes, stores, retains, or deletes data.

There are additional questions that must be asked of the client that will assist them in complying with an order for e-disclosure. There are also further questions that will be asked in a review of a list of documents provided by an opponent. These might include the following.

- Has all equipment holding electronic data been searched?
- Are individuals (within the client's or opponent's workplace) able to store documents on their local hard drives, and have they been doing so?
- Is material on local hard drives routinely backed up onto the client's central server?
- What type of, and how many, servers are used? If they are web-based, does the client have 'control' of documents backed up this way?
- Do individuals have documents on their personal computers at home?
- Does the company operate a 'hot-desk' system, whereby employees may use more than one computer?
- How are documents backed up? (A full, detailed explanation is needed.)
- How is data stored? (A detailed explanation of the methods used is required.)
- Are mobile phones used to store documents and data?
- Do individuals use memory sticks, flash cards, external hard drives, CD-Rs or DVD-Rs?
- What is the client's (or opponent's) email policy (particularly in relation to storage and deletion)?

In *Digicel (St Lucia) Ltd v Cable and Wireless plc* [2008] EWHC 2522 (Ch), Morgan J stressed that the parties should meet early on in the litigation to discuss potential issues regarding electronic disclosure and that, where used, keyword searches should be agreed as far as possible. Where the extent of the search for e-documents is challenged, there is also useful guidance supplied by this case, in which it was held that the proper interim application that may need to be made is not one for specific disclosure, but instead an interim application for specific inspection.

Further useful guidance on the view that the court may take in matters relating to e-disclosure is contained in *Abela v Hammonds Suddards (a firm)* [2008] EWHC 3153 (Ch). The judge in this case, Paul Girolami QC, sought to apply principles from the *Digicel* case (above) and took three elements from that decision:

- the potential value of appropriate electronic searches to identify important documents that might otherwise be missed;
- but that the rules do not require that 'no stone should be left unturned'; and
- that it is the court who ultimately decides what the scope of the e-search and e-disclosure should be.

The case of *Earles v Barclays Bank plc* [2009] EWHC 2500 (QB) raises some interesting issues for e-disclosure. In this case the judge was unimpressed with the defendant's e-disclosure efforts (as in the *Digicel* case above) and felt that the claimant had missed an opportunity to (*perhaps*) gain sight of documents that *may* have been supportive of their claim and which would have enabled the matter to be resolved earlier—their costs of the action were significantly reduced because of this conclusion. However the interesting point here, for disclosure, is that the judge was not referring to documents that were known to exist but to those that 'might have' existed—this seems to revert back to the concept of 'fishing' expeditions in the disclosure obligations. This case is also a clear illustration of the courts' use of costs sanctions when it feels a party has failed to engage with its disclosure obligations sufficiently.

17.6 FORM N265 AND THE 'DISCLOSURE STATEMENT'

When a party complies with his obligation to give disclosure within the directions order made by the court, he will usually do so on Form N265. The document is known as the 'list of documents'. The front page of this document includes the disclosure statement, which complies with CPR 31.10(5). If disclosure is not being made using Form N265, then the party should make his disclosure and accompany it with a declaration in the form set out in CPR 31.10(5).

17.6.1 WHAT THE STATEMENT MUST INCLUDE

The disclosure statement must:

(a) detail the extent of the search that has been made to locate documents that are required to be disclosed;

(b) certify that the person signing the statement understands the duty to give disclosure;

(c) certify that, to the best of his knowledge, that person has carried out that duty;

(d) declare that he believes that the extent of the search made is a reasonable one, in all of the circumstances; and

(e) if a particular search has not been carried out, specify the search that has not been carried out and give reasons for not carrying it out, or declare, if any searches made were limited in any way, what those limitations were and why the limitation was imposed.

17.6.1.1 In relation to (d) above

In 'all of the circumstances' means what it is reasonable to have done having regard to the value and/or importance of the case. 'Importance' here means important in terms of either a legal principle or issue. All cases are important to the parties, but a low-value case, albeit one of great importance to the party, will not have a higher degree of the duty to 'search for documents' than it is proportionate, in terms of the value of the case, to carry out. This may not be the position if the case is one of relatively low value, but which may have a significant contribution to make in terms of legal principle or legal clarification.

17.6.1.2 In relation to (e) above

The usual reason that will be given for any restriction in terms of time or extent of the search will be that it is 'not proportionate' to make that search. In a relatively simple road traffic accident (RTA), this could be a restriction of the search for documents 'from the date of the accident and not before it'. It is open to a party to challenge any restriction declared. For example, if the claim being made is one against the local authority and concerning its duties to maintain the highway, it may be appropriate to challenge the extent of the search and to seek to widen it to include statistics on accidents that may have occurred at the spot before the accident that is the subject of the claim, in order to establish that the place at which the accident occurred was an 'accident black spot'.

Very frequently, limitations or restrictions will be placed on the extent of any electronic search for documents. An example might be that the search has been restricted to 'existing emails'. Again, it will be open to the opposing party to seek to challenge whether it would be reasonable to make a search that included 'deleted emails' and the extent of that further search. A further example could be a restriction on the search for electronic documents to have been by defined 'keywords'. Again, any such restriction may be open to challenge by the opposing party.

17.6.2 WHO WILL SIGN THE DISCLOSURE STATEMENT?

Under CPR 31.10(6), a disclosure statement is defined as 'a statement made by the party disclosing the documents'.

In the great majority of cases, it will be the client, or a representative of the client, who signs the statement. It will not usually be the legal representative, because it is the client who will declare his understanding of his disclosure obligations and who will have carried out a reasonable search for the documents. Under CPR 31(6) it *may* be most appropriate for another person to make the disclosure statement. The legal representative's duty is to ensure that the client understands the obligations and carries out the obligations accordingly (PD 31.4.4).

 Practical Considerations

When considering who will sign the disclosure statement, ensure that the appropriate person is available to sign the list before exchange. This is of particular relevance when the client is a company and the person signing the statement is away on business or on holiday. It is good practice to check the availability of the person to sign to avoid being in breach of the direction for disclosure by the date set by the court.

In certain circumstances, a person other than the client or a representative of the client may sign the disclosure statement and this is provided for in CPR 31.10(9)—that is, 'A disclosure statement may be made by a person who is not a party where this is permitted by a relevant practice direction'. PD 31.4.7 sets out circumstances in which an insurer or the Motor Insurers' Bureau (MIB) may sign the disclosure statement on behalf of a party.

Where the party making disclosure is a company, firm, association, or other organization, CPR 31.10(7) provides that the party signing the disclosure statement must also:

- identify the person making the statement; and
- explain why or certify that he is the appropriate person to make the statement; and
- give his name, address, and position in the organization.

17.6.3 HOW ARE DOCUMENTS SORTED AND LISTED ON FORM N265?

CPR 31.10, PD 31 and PD 31(6) set out the detailed instructions for compiling the list in Form N265. There are three sections in Form N265 and documents to be disclosed need to be placed in one of the three sections. A blank N265 can be found in the Appendix at the end of the handbook.

In the 'top' section on the list, the party making disclosure lists and numbers all of those documents that it does not object to the opponent inspecting. As stated in paragraph 17.8 below, this inspection process includes physically inspecting the documents listed and/or seeking copies of them.

In the 'middle' section on the list, the party making disclosure lists and numbers all of those documents that it does object to the other party being able to inspect. In this section, the disclosing party also needs to give the reason for withholding the documents from inspection. There is usually standard wording for this section.

In the 'bottom' section on the list, the party making disclosure lists and numbers all of those documents that it no longer has in its control, and goes on to state when they were last in its control and where the documents are now. There is also usually standard wording for this section.

17.6.4 GUIDANCE FROM THE COMMERCIAL COURT

Many innovations of High Court practice filter into other divisions, including the ordinary Queen's Bench Division. At times, therefore, it may be useful to know what innovative processes the Commercial Court is operating. Where there are a great number of documents to be disclosed in an action, it might be worth considering how the Commercial Court handles disclosure, because that court will frequently handle cases with a large volume of documents being disclosed. The new *Commercial Court Guide* (May 2009) requires parties to produce disclosure schedules. The schedules must state by reference to categories of documents, the location of documents and the period of time covered by the documents, state what the party believes to comprise 'standard disclosure' and state any limits which that party intends to place upon their search and their reason for any limitation. The court will then invite observations of the other party(ies) of the disclosure schedule. These schedules will then be discussed at the ensuing CMC and a tailored disclosure order will be made. These provisions envisage disclosure in a two-stage process—the proposal for disclosure by a party (in the schedule) and then an order for disclosure.

These provisions may be worth following in any high value, high volume (of documents for disclosure) case even if outside the Commercial Court.

17.7 THE PROCESS OF DISCLOSURE

17.7.1 THE EXCHANGE OR SERVICE OF LISTS OF DOCUMENTS

The order for disclosure will usually be made on allocation or at the first CMC. The order will include a date by which the parties' lists of documents are to be made available to each other. The order will usually provide for either exchange of lists (where both parties are to give disclosure), or service of lists where only one party may have disclosure obligations, or that the service of the lists is to be sequential. Generally, the order will provide that the lists should be contained within Form N265. The order will provide a date for the exchange of the lists and the date may provide for simultaneous exchange or for sequential exchange. CPR 31.10 assumes 'service' of lists. This, it could be argued, does not assume 'exchange' of lists. In most cases, it would be sensible to agree—or, in the absence of agreement, to ask for—a direction for 'exchange'.

 Practical Considerations

Solicitors should consider the form of the order for disclosure for which they intend to ask before completing the allocation questionnaire (Form N150), or before attending the allocation hearing or first CMC. Consideration should be given not only to the dates by which parties should serve their lists of documents, and whether these should be simultaneous or sequential, but also what the scope of the disclosure obligation should be and the dates, or period, in which the search for documents should be made. Requests for disclosure that is outside the scope of 'standard disclosure' can be made, but should be justified (within the provisions of the overriding objective).

When listing is complete, the parties will:

- confirm to each other that they are ready to exchange or serve their lists;
- exchange or serve their lists;
- in the case of the party in receipt of an opponent's list of documents, consider the list served and give notice to exercise its rights of inspection; and
- carry out inspection.

There may also be either requests or applications for specific disclosure, or a challenge to the list supplied by a party. These matters are considered further below.

17.7.2 DISCLOSURE IS AN ONGOING OBLIGATION

The duty of disclosure continues until proceedings are concluded and this probably means after judgment, but before the judgment has been handed down (*Vernon v Bosley (No 2)* [1997] 3 WLR 683).

Often, the list of documents prepared and served or exchanged may be incomplete. This may be because investigations are ongoing. Where this occurs, the fact that further documents will be disclosed should be stated in the disclosure statement. It may be because documents come to light later. If the reason for prior or timely disclosure is because the client felt the document to be damaging, then this reason and the client's reluctance will need to be explained. A legal representative who is not given instructions to explain the delay will have to cease acting.

Practical Considerations

It is important to remind clients of the ongoing duties of disclosure, as well as of the disclosure obligations referred to in previous 'Practical Considerations' boxes. Clients should be reminded not only of the ongoing duty, but also of the possible consequences of a breach. Any costs implications of late disclosure should also be raised.

If additional material does come to light after the list of documents has been served, CPR 31.11(2) provides that the other party must be notified immediately. A supplemental list should be prepared and served. If there are only a small number of additional documents, these can be simply added to the original list. There is no prescribed form of the supplemental list, although Form N265 could be adapted for this purpose.

Practical Considerations

If new material arises, it may be necessary to review your client's case again in the light of the new documents and then to update any advice to the client in the light of the new information. A further review of the documents listed should also be made to ensure that no further documents have slipped though the net of the 'reasonable search'.

17.7.3 THE ROLE OF THE LEGAL REPRESENTATIVE IN THE PROCESS OF DISCLOSURE

Part of the legal representative's role in the process of disclosure will be to ensure that disclosure has been properly made and then to ensure that the organization of the documents is appropriate, so that the documents being disclosed are placed in the right part of Form N265.

17.7.3.1 Considerations of the legal representative when compiling a list of documents

In relation to each document being considered, the following will need to be considered.

- Is the document, in principle, one that is to be disclosed?

- Does the client have the right (or a duty) to withhold inspection?

Thus, in the first part of the process, the documents that have been revealed by the 'reasonable search' may be sorted into five categories, as follows.

- **Documents that are to be disclosed, but disclosure of which is being withheld** There will not usually be many documents, if any, in this category. If a document is to be disclosed, then few grounds will justify it *not* being contained within the list of documents being disclosed. One such reason might be a claim for 'public interest immunity'. This may happen, for example, in proceedings involving sensitive political or state information.

- **Documents that are to be disclosed, but inspection of which is being withheld** These will most often be privileged documents. A full discussion of 'privilege' arises in paragraph 17.9 below. These documents will be listed in the middle section of Form N265.

Some of the documents listed here may be withheld from inspection at the time that parties are ordered to 'disclose by an exchange of lists of documents' because they are, for example, privileged. However, the client may waive the privilege at a later stage and make the document available to the opponent. Thus draft (or final) witness statements may be withheld from inspection, but will ultimately be made available to the opponents at the time at which the parties have been ordered to 'exchange witness statements' in the court's directions order made after allocation. This direction will usually be after the order for 'disclosure by list' (see Chapter 12).

- **Documents that are to be disclosed, and which will be disclosed and inspection of which will be permitted** These are the documents that the opponent will be entitled to see once they exercise their rights of inspection. These documents may make up the bulk of the list and will be listed in the first section of the list. How the parties exercise the rights of inspection is detailed below.

- **Documents that are partly to be disclosed** Part of such documents will be redacted. Privileged or irrelevant commercially sensitive material can be 'blanked out' of (that is, redacted from) a document that otherwise needs to be disclosed. The description of the document in the list should make it clear that it has been redacted (see also the case of *CMCS Common Market Commercial Services AVV v Taylor* [2011] EWHC 234 referred to above at paragraph 17.5.1, a case concerning the redaction of documents).

- **Documents that are not to be disclosed** The search for documents in an action may reveal documents that are either not relevant to the issues of the case and/or do not fall within the ambit of order to disclose. Most likely, it will be that they do not fall within the definition of 'standard disclosure', because that is the most likely definition of a party's duty to give disclosure (see paragraph 17.4 above).

 Practical Considerations

When documents are being sorted for disclosure, a file note should be made in respect of each document (or class of documents) of the reason for the category in which it has been placed. The transparency of the disclosure process in this way both shows that a proper consideration has been given to the process and will record the time spent on the process (and thus justify the charges applied to the process). A proper recording will also ensure that the whole team involved on the case is able to see the work done on the process, as well as the reasons for the categories into which the documents have been placed. The recording in this way will also be a starting point for dealing with any challenges that may be made to that party's disclosure or in responding to any application for specific disclosure.

When the documents have been categorized, sorted, and listed in Form N265, the client will be asked to sign off the prepared list and make the disclosure statement on the front page of the form. At this stage, the legal representative will indicate to his opponent that he is ready to effect exchange. This may include a letter, email, or fax that states, for example:

> In accordance with the Order of [example: 'Mr District Judge'] made on the [date of the order] at paragraph [relevant paragraph of the order], we confirm that we are ready to effect exchange of our client's list of documents. Please confirm that you are ready to exchange your client's list.

17.7.3.2 Considerations of the legal representative when receiving a list of documents
When a party receives the opponent's list, he will undertake the following.

- The legal representative should review the list. This review will initially compare each party's list to ascertain what documents both parties have and do not have. The revision will also need to consider whether there are any obvious omissions from the documents being inspected: perhaps a reference to another document is made in a document that has been disclosed for inspection, but which is not itself in the list. A review could reveal whether there are any surprises in the documents: for example, where a copy has been made available, but not the original. It could equally show up any queries of the scope of the search that has been made for documents or the extent of the documents that are held back from inspection (whether the claim for privilege can be justified, and whether it should be challenged). The review should include a review of the disclosure statement and whether any restrictions in the search for documents are reasonable. Has an appropriate person signed the disclosure statement?

- As a result of the review undertaken, that party's legal representative will prepare correspondence setting out any concerns and, at the same time, decide how they wish to exercise 'inspection', giving notice of same.

- The legal representative will serve a notice to inspect the documents available for inspection. The procedure for inspection is set out in CPR 31.15—that is, that a request to inspect should be given in writing and that the party disclosing the documents must permit inspection within seven days after receiving notice to inspect. The request to inspect may specify that the party requires copies and it is provided in the rules that they are also agreeing to pay the reasonable photocopying charges. It is good practice to seek to agree these charges.

- It is open to the inspecting party to inspect the originals either before or after receiving photocopies. There is no prescribed form of the 'notice to inspect'. Typically, the notice to inspect takes the form of a letter specifying the documents, or categories of document, inspection of which is sought—specifying whether this is by the provision of photocopies (or on disk) or by physical inspection.

 Practical Considerations

The process of inspection is often a paper exercise, with each party requesting certain documents from its opponent's list and agreeing to pay reasonable photocopying charges. It is therefore unusual for legal representatives and/or clients to attend inspection of the documents personally. But it should be remembered that it is the client's right to 'inspect' and that his legal representative is carrying out that right on the client's behalf. There may be situations in which it would be appropriate for the client to attend the inspection. Personal inspection will happen, however, when the numbers of documents to inspect are great and/or in a complex action, or where the list has been compiled in such a way as to make identification of specific documents difficult and unreliable.

If the list of documents for inspection is a lengthy list, it is important to ensure that the documents are made available to you to inspect in the order in which they appear in the list. If they are not, it can make inspection more time-consuming and therefore more costly for your client. Given the work that can take place in a review of a party's list of documents, the time limits are tight and should be diarized as a 'key date'.

17.8 INSPECTION

The time period for inspection of documents is invariably set out in the directions order and, as indicated above, is usually seven days after disclosure. If the time for inspection has not been fixed in the directions order, reference should be made to CPR 31.15, which contains default provisions on the timing of the provision of copies and inspection.

The place at which inspection should take place will often be at the offices of the disclosing party's legal representatives, but the court may order, or the parties may seek an order, that inspection should take place at another (more convenient) location.

When a party formally discloses a document in civil proceedings by stating that it exists, his opponent will have the right to inspect the document unless the disclosing party claims a right or duty to withhold inspection. Inspection means physically looking at the document, calling for a copy of it, or calling for a copy then physically inspecting it. Specific provision should be made regarding inspection of electronic materials.

If the disclosing party is claiming a duty or a right to withhold inspection, the basis of that claim must be set out on the Form N265. If the disclosing party is claiming that it would be 'disproportionate' to make the document available for inspection, this reason should also be given. Any claim to withhold inspection may be challenged by the opponent.

Unless the list of the documents available for inspection states that they are 'copies', the assumption will be that the document available is the original. A document that has been amended in any way from the original is treated as a separate document.

 Practical Considerations

If there is any doubt about the authenticity of a document, it will be important to inspect originals. Important information can be observed by inspecting original documents, because they can reveal differing ink colours, the use of highlighters, pencil annotations, or other information that shows a transition in the form of the document. These additions to a document can provide valuable evidence when reviewing the documents.

CPR 32.19 provides that 'A party shall be deemed to admit the authenticity of a document disclosed to him under CPR Part 31 unless he serves notice that he wishes the document to be proved at trial'. Any notice under this provision must be served by the latest date for serving witness statements, or *within seven days of disclosure of the document*, whichever is later.

17.8.1 GROUNDS FOR WITHHOLDING INSPECTION

Under CPR 31.3, a party to whom a document has been disclosed has a right to inspect that document unless:

- the document is no longer in the control of the party disclosing it—in which case, the disclosing party is simply stating a fact that inspection of the document with them is not possible. In this situation, the opponent will need to consider the meaning of the word 'control' and determine whether examination of the document should be sought in the hands of another person, who may not be a party in the action (see paragraph 17.4 above). It may also involve consideration of an application for non-party disclosure under the provisions of CPR 31.17 (see paragraph 17.10.3 below);

- the party disclosing it has a right or a duty to withhold inspection of it—where a party claims a right to withhold inspection, it is usually on the basis (or ground) that the disclosed documents are 'privileged'. There are a number of different types of privilege, including:
  - legal advice privilege;
  - litigation privilege;
  - common interest privilege; and
  - without-prejudice privilege.

  A detailed examination of 'privilege' is contained in paragraph 17.9 below;

- the party disclosing it considers that it would be disproportionate to the issues in the case to permit inspection of it. This is in keeping with the overriding objective. Whether or not this claim will withstand a challenge from the opponent will depend on the facts of the case. A claim might be made to withhold inspection, for example, when there are large numbers of documents held abroad, and it would be 'disproportionate' and little assist the court's ability to deal with the issues of the case 'fairly', 'justly', or 'expeditiously', to enforce inspection of these documents.

17.8.2 CHALLENGING THE EXTENT OF THE SEARCH AND CHALLENGING THE ALLOCATION OF DOCUMENTS TO THAT PART OF THE LIST THAT IS NOT 'AVAILABLE TO INSPECT'

Any party in receipt of another party's list of documents needs to undertake a careful review of the documents listed. The existence of the disclosure statement of the listing party does not mean that the receiving party has to take at face value the accuracy or the completeness of the list provided. Where you have identified concerns about the list provided, there are several steps that can be taken to ensure that an accurate or complete list is provided.

CPR 31.23 provides that proceedings for contempt of court can be brought against a party who makes, or 'causes to be made', a false disclosure statement without an honest belief in its truth. Such proceedings are quite rare and other options will usually be taken before contempt proceedings are considered. These 'other options' include the following.

- You might choose to set out your specific concerns by letter to your opponent's legal representative. This should include a full explanation of the reasons for your concerns, as well as, if possible, details of the documents that you feel are not included in the lists. The letter could have included in it advance warning that if an application has to be made to the court, then indemnity costs for the application will be sought.

- You might consider making a specific disclosure application (see Chapter 14, paragraph 14.5). Under CPR 31.12(2), the court may order a party to:
  - disclose documents, or classes of document, specified;
  - carry out a search as specified; and/or
  - disclose any further documents revealed by the search or as ordered.

- Any application for specific disclosure will need to consider the overriding objective: is the further disclosure *necessary* to do *justice* between the parties? Is it *proportionate* to the issues of the case? Is it *economic* to make the order for further disclosure?

- Consider whether it is appropriate to serve a 'notice to admit facts' (see Chapter 18, paragraph 18.6.1). Under CPR 32.18(1), a party may serve another party with a notice requiring him to admit the facts or the part of the case that the party serving the notice states in the notice. The aim of the notice is to seek admissions on evidence or stated issues of the case, thereby avoiding the serving party from having to prove the stated facts or issues set out in the notice. The provisions have the benefit of both narrowing issues and saving costs, both of which are important aspects of the CPR. The notice to admit facts can be used effectively to put pressure (usually costs pressure) on an opponent.

- In either of the above applications, you should consider asking the court to include an 'unless order' that is intended to ensure that a party complies (see Chapter 13, paragraph 13.9). An 'unless order' is one that provides for a further step to be taken—usually to debar a party from proceedings with a step, or more critically, their action, if they do not comply with the initial part of the order. It would always be appropriate to seek an 'unless order' where the opponent has repeatedly failed to comply, or has unreasonably failed to respond to an early request, or when his good faith in not responding to the order is in doubt in some other way.

17.8.3 CHALLENGES MAY BE RAISED FROM A REVIEW OF AN OPPONENT'S LIST OF DOCUMENTS AND THE INSPECTION PROCESS

The following is a non-exhaustive list of the grounds on which challenges may be made to an opponent's list of documents:

- a failure to disclose a document referred to in documents that are disclosed and that have been inspected;

- that there are documents that, as a matter of common sense, should be in the list;
- in relation to documents that may be in the 'middle' section of the list and unavailable for inspection, but the claim for privilege of which can be challenged;
- that the disclosure statement has not been signed by an 'appropriate person';
- that the parameters of the search for documents are too narrow or otherwise too restricted either as to the search made or the period in which the search is made;
- in relation to e-disclosure (see paragraph 17.5.2 above), that the keyword search is too narrow, or the search has not been wide enough; or
- that the listing is too vague and is inadequate, and/or it is not possible to have a clear enough idea of the documents being listed.

In any request or challenge to a party's list of documents, consideration must be given to 'relevance', as well as to the aims of the overriding objective. The request and, especially, any application to the court should be supported with details of the likely cost (to the party) of complying with the application, so that the court can apply the concept of proportionality to the application, as well as the need for the further disclosure or verification in terms of fairness, justice, or expedition. Consideration can also be given to any alternative means of achieving the aim: for example, by CPR Part 18 requests if they would achieve a more efficient and cheaper, as well as fairer, outcome.

The CPR do not specify the format of most applications that may be made to challenge a party's list of documents. Most applications would include a written request first, then an application, either by letter or on Form N244, with supporting evidence.

 Costs

The process of scrutinizing your opponent's list of documents and inspecting the copies of documents that you request can be time-consuming, and therefore costly to your client. The time spent on this is regularly challenged at costs assessments (both summary assessment and detailed assessment). Make a careful note of the time spent and, with that note, your notes justifying the time spent. Inform your client before the cost is incurred in the larger 'document dense' cases, so that he is aware of the impact on proportionality and his overall costs, which he may not fully recover even if he is ultimately successful and secures a costs order in his favour.

17.9 PRIVILEGE

'Privilege' entitles a party to withhold evidence from production to a third party, an opponent in proceedings, or the court. Once privilege has been established, an absolute right to withhold the document in question arises. In litigation, 'privilege' entitles a party to withhold the 'inspection' of the privileged document; it does not provide a right not to 'disclose' the document. So privileged documents must still be contained within the list of documents, but they will be contained in the middle section of that part of Form N265 that lists the documents being disclosed.

Where privilege is claimed, neither the court nor the opponent can ask the court to draw adverse inferences by the exclusion of the document from the proceedings.

In paragraph 17.8.1 above, the types of privilege were identified as:

- legal advice privilege;
- litigation privilege;
- common interest privilege; and
- without-prejudice privilege.

The exclusion of privileged documents from the litigation process is highly important—not least because the documents that are being withheld may be highly relevant to the issues of the case. In only four areas will documents be excluded from the court irrespective of the court's attitude to them:

(a) documents that are irrelevant;

(b) documents containing opinion evidence (save where expressed by an expert appointed for that purpose);

(c) where the document is privileged; and

(d) where public immunity interest applies.

Irrelevant documents—that is, area (a)—and opinion evidence that is not authorized by it being given by an appointed expert—that is, area (b)—are often included in a party's case, sometimes through mistake or, more commonly, because of a lack of good preparation by the legal representative. The courts do not exclude this type of evidence; they instead usually adopt the response of 'attaching very little or no weight' to such evidence.

However, in the case of evidence that is covered by privilege—that is, area (c)—or public interest immunity—that is, area (d)—the rights attaching to them for individuals amount, in practice, to an important personal constitutional right. These rights are underwritten by Arts 6 and 8 of the European Convention on Human Rights (ECHR). Accordingly, a person who has a (possibly highly relevant) document to which privilege or public interest immunity attaches may:

• refuse to give oral evidence or to produce the document to the court at any trial or hearing;

• refuse to disclose the information under any Pre-Action Protocol;

• refuse to answer a witness summons to answer questions or to produce documents relating to the privileged information;

• refuse to permit inspection of the document either pre-action or during the action or at trial;

• refuse to give any access to the documents to any person with a search warrant or search order; and

• refuse to answer any questions relating to the privileged materials from a police officer or other investigator.

The importance of these rights cannot be overemphasized—especially because it is also to be noted that these rights may apply regardless of how relevant or otherwise admissible the materials might be, and, further, no adverse inferences can be drawn by the court from the exclusion of the material.

17.9.1 LEGAL PROFESSIONAL PRIVILEGE

Legal professional privilege includes 'legal advice privilege' and 'litigation privilege'. Privilege cannot be claimed unless the evidence in question is confidential, so where the information or the document has ceased to be confidential, the document containing it can no longer be subject to a claim for privilege. For the same reason, no privilege can attach to communications between opposing parties (unless they are subject to 'without prejudice' privilege). Equally, and for the same reason, when it is no longer 'confidential to one party', there can be no privilege in:

• transcripts of proceedings in chambers, in open court, or before arbitrators;

• attendance notes of meetings at which both parties were present; and

- telephone attendance notes of conversations between legal representatives of both sides. (The exception to this is if the notes contain additional notes by one party's legal representative that detail strategy, advice, or the merits of a party's case.)

The underlying purpose of legal professional privilege is to allow a party access to legal advice, to the lawyer's professional skill and judgment, without compromising his position with the opponent. In this context, 'lawyer' includes all members of the legal profession: solicitors; barristers; in-house lawyers, in part of their work; and foreign lawyers. It also covers supervised legal executives and trainees. The narrow definition of 'legal adviser' would probably exclude legal advice given by lay advisers at advice centres.

The position of in-house lawyers is more complex. Some of what they do is covered by legal professional privilege, but that part of their work that deals with business advice or administration will not be privileged. In-house lawyers should distinguish in their work between the giving of legal advice and work that, for example, ensures compliance with regulations for the business for which they work or which relates to their executive functions.

Legal professional privilege belongs to the client and it is therefore only the client, or an agent of the client with ostensible authority, who can waive the privilege applying.

17.9.2 WHAT IS THE DISTINCTION BETWEEN 'LEGAL ADVICE PRIVILEGE' AND 'LITIGATION PRIVILEGE'?

Legal advice privilege and litigation privilege are distinct types of legal professional privilege. See also Figure 17.2 at the end of this chapter.

17.9.2.1 Legal advice privilege

Legal advice privilege can apply whether or not litigation is pending or contemplated, whereas litigation privilege can apply only when litigation is pending or contemplated. 'Pending' or 'contemplated' means a real likelihood, rather than a mere possibility. A distinct possibility that sooner or later someone might make a claim, or a general apprehension of future litigation, is not enough.

Legal advice privilege protects against compulsory disclosure of all types of communication made between a client and his lawyer in which advice is sought or given within a relevant legal context. The subject matter of the advice sought or given is irrelevant, so long as it is in a legal context. Therefore, legal advice privilege protects advice sought by, or given to, a client in relation to both contentious and non-contentious matters. The key test of what constitutes 'legal advice' was considered in *NRG v Bacon and Woodrow* [1995] 1 All ER 976, in which Colman J stated that the advice must be 'directly related to the performance by the solicitor of his professional duties as legal advisor'. This position, although threatened in the Court of Appeal decision in *Three Rivers District Council v Governor and Company of the Bank of England (No 5)* [2002] EWHC 2730, was restored by the House of Lords in *Three Rivers District Council v Bank of England (No 6)* [2004] 3 WLR 1274, where it was confirmed that:

- legal advice privilege covers advice relating to public rights, liabilities, and obligations; and hence

- includes presentational advice given by lawyers to a party whose conduct might be the subject of public criticism; and

- would extend to advice and assistance given with reference to a range of inquiries, including coroners' inquests, statutory and ad hoc inquiries; but

- if the lawyer became the client's 'man of business' advising across a wide range on non-legal topics, such as investments and other business matters, the advice might lack the relevant legal context to uphold the privilege; and

- there does not appear to be a 'dominant purpose' test as there is in litigation privilege.

The privilege does not apply in other types of 'confidential' discussion that a person may have with another person who is not their lawyer: for example, their doctor or priest. This applies even if the discussions with that person relate to legal matters. However, the court will consider the position carefully before compelling such persons to divulge the confidential information. This ability to include otherwise confidential information in proceedings has been held to apply in many situations in which the client may find it hard to understand, in the light of the absolute privilege that arises with legal advice privilege: for example, information held by personnel consultants (*New Victoria Hospital v Ryan* [1993] ICR 201) and industrial relations consultants (*M and W Grazebrook Ltd v Wallens* [1973] 2 All ER 868).

17.9.2.2 Litigation privilege

Legal advice privilege does not, however, protect third-party communications—that is, a communication between either a client or his lawyer and a third party, such as a factual or expert witness. The latter privilege can only be protected within litigation privilege, and for that to arise, litigation must be pending or contemplated. A further distinction is that, where litigation privilege is being claimed, but the document had more than one purpose, the courts will look at the dominant purpose of the document to determine whether litigation privilege applies. The 'dominant' purpose of the document must be to prepare for the litigation in progress or in contemplation.

Provided that the communication is made with one of the following as its sole or dominant purpose in relation to the actual litigation in process or in contemplation, the document will be privileged:

- giving advice; or
- obtaining evidence; or
- collecting evidence.

Once established as this, litigation privilege will attach to the communications themselves (for example, the letter of instruction to the expert, although this will be lost if that party intends to use that expert to give evidence at the trial of the action), the documents or materials used to provide the advice (unless those documents are already out in the open and no longer confidential), and the documents generated from the communications—that is, the reports that are prepared.

The 'dominant purpose' test is one of dominance and not exclusivity. Documents are frequently brought into existence for more than one purpose and close scrutiny of the purpose of the existence of the document will be made by the court to determine its 'dominant purpose'. The actual wording in the document may not be conclusive so, for example, if the document states on it that it was for the particular purpose of enabling litigation advice to be given, or was for another unrelated main purpose, the courts will look beyond the stated purpose of the document to determine its 'dominant' purpose. This could mean that the courts will conclude the dominant purpose to be other than its stated intention (see *National Westminster Bank plc v Rabobank Nederland* [2006] EWHC 218 (Comm) for further discussions on this subject).

The leading decision in seeking to define the 'dominant purpose' test is still *Waugh v British Railways Board* [1980] AC 521. The case involved the preparation of statements after a fatal rail accident. The courts decided that in order for litigation privilege to attach to a document, it must satisfy the 'sole dominant purpose' test. If the purposes for which the document were of equal weight, then the privilege would not attach. This decision has had significant repercussions for all compliance investigations, because as a result of the conclusions of this case, much of the collected material from inquiries and investigations will not attract litigation privilege. And it may not attract legal advice privilege as a result of the decision in *Three Rivers (No 5)* (above). In *Axa Seguros S.A. De C.V. v Allianz Insurance plc & Ors* [2011] EWHC 268 (Comm) the court has again considered the extent and impact of the 'dominant purpose' test—and here concluded that the engineering reports in question had two purposes, one of which was to determine whether the highways in question had been constructed to internationally accepted standards. They concluded that the 'dominant purpose' test was not satisfied sufficiently to secure a finding of privilege.

 Practical Considerations

Advising clients in this area is fraught with uncertainties and difficulties. It is important to give advice concerning the existence or not of 'privilege' to a document only after careful thought and research. Problems tend to arise in relation to documents not privileged in themselves and collected from the client or third parties, or copied during the course of preparing for litigation. The 'start point' for your considerations will be that all documents that are within the definition of standard disclosure or within the definition of any specific disclosure order that has been made, and that have, at any time, been within the client's control are to be disclosed and available for inspection *unless* privilege is available (or there is some other reason why it would be wrong to make it available—for example, that it is disproportionate to do so). The mere fact that the client seeks legal advice or that the document has been assembled for litigation does not cloak all otherwise unprivileged documents with privilege.

'Litigation' in this context means proceedings before the courts, but also before arbitrators and tribunals when exercising judicial functions. Thus it will probably not apply in forums that are designed to be 'fact-finding', or those that are not 'adversarial'. Litigation privilege can normally be claimed in proceedings in which a judicial function is being exercised, but if the proceedings are merely fact-finding (for example, an inquiry under the Banking Acts—see the *Three Rivers* case again) or the tribunal has an administrative function, it is unlikely that litigation privilege can arise. The distinction is a fine one, because often an inquiry or inquest will result in litigation once the inquiry or tribunal has reached its conclusions.

It is important to understand that litigation privilege relates to 'communications' and therefore documents arising that are not actually communicated may not attract the privilege. However, it was accepted in the *Three Rivers* litigation that a lawyer's own drafts of documents and memoranda were privileged even if not transmitted to the client. This was restated in *USP Strategies plc v London General Holdings Ltd* [2004] EWHC 373 (Ch). However, it is clear the transmission or 'communication' will always be needed for the privilege to apply to documents going **from** a client **to** his lawyer. Consequently, notes and memoranda prepared by the client as a preparatory step to obtaining legal advice are unlikely to be privileged. In each respect of the need (or not) of 'communication' between the client, the lawyer and the third party each may use agents, provided that the agent is acting as the conduit for the information and not in any other capacity.

Accordingly, the main difference between the two types of legal professional privilege is that litigation privilege enables the client or the lawyer to communicate under the protection of privilege with a third party, but is confined to situations in which litigation is in process (or contemplated). Legal advice privilege does not. On the other hand, legal advice privilege applies to communications between client and lawyer that may relate to both contentious and non-contentious matters.

Because legal professional privilege is a substantive right, it can be asserted in any situation and regardless of how old the document is (see *Calcraft v Guest* [1898] 1 QB 759, in which documents that were a hundred years old were still privileged).

Practical Considerations

When advising clients of their disclosure obligations and the existence of legal professional privilege, it is important that both you and the client have an understanding of the consequences of actions taken. Being over-efficient can sometimes have unexpected and unwanted consequences, so, for example, take care in gathering evidence too early. If evidence is gathered before there is any reasonable prospect of litigation, then only 'legal advice' will be protected by privilege. Conversely, sending off a 'letter before action' or an early notice letter too early can equally have the effect of covering all of your opponent's 'fact-finding' steps as 'evidence gathering' covered by litigation privilege.

17.9.3 WHAT HAPPENS IF DOCUMENTS ARE 'COMMUNICATED' BY A PARTY WITHIN ITS ORGANIZATION?

So what happens if documents are communicated by a party within its own organization? Will this result in the document no longer being 'confidential' and no longer capable of attracting privilege?

The *Three Rivers* litigation has placed important practical limitations on the scope and availability of legal advice privilege where the client instructing the legal representative is a corporate entity (or similar). In *Three Rivers (No 5)*, the Court of Appeal decided that, in such circumstances, the client is not the corporate entity itself, but a narrow group of individuals employed by the entity charged with seeking and receiving legal advice on its behalf. Others outside this group of individuals who make communications related to the legal advice run the risk of exposing those communications, because they will not attract legal advice privilege (and they may not fit the criteria of litigation privilege either). This position applies even in relation to documents generated by employees (who are outside the group of employees defined as 'the client') that are necessary to provide information to the lawyers to advise (although here litigation privilege may apply).

 Practical Considerations

Because of the practical effects of *Three Rivers*, there is a view that dissemination of advice given by the legal representative to others within the corporate entity should be made subject to appropriate confidentiality obligations. Consider whether your clients should be asked to exercise caution and accompany such notes disseminating legal advice with words such as 'privileged' or 'this communication does not amount to a waiver of privilege', and ask for an acknowledgement that the information will be held in confidence.

Designating the whole workforce of the organization as 'the client' is very unlikely to work; nor does it seem to be an answer to channel all communications through the in-house lawyer. Equally, it is impractical to construct an 'inner client' for every single legal issue that confronts any large entity. These very real problems, only very briefly highlighted here and the in-depth study of which is outside the scope of this book, are set out to alert any practising legal representative of the extent of the knowledge that they must have to advise clients about the complex issues of disclosure and privilege.

17.9.4 OTHER TYPES OF RELEVANT PRIVILEGE

17.9.4.1 Common interest privilege

Common interest privilege is a relatively new variant of legal advice privilege. It operates to preserve privilege in documents that are disclosed to third parties. It may occur in group actions, or in cases in which there is more than one claimant or defendant—that is, situations in which the group (who may not be parties to the action) or co-litigants have the same self interest. All of these parties may collect information for the purposes of the litigation, and all may take copies of documents and relevant information.

The privilege is applied as follows. If party A has a sufficiently common interest in communications that are held by party B, then party A can obtain disclosure of those communications from party B even though, as against third parties, the communications would be privileged from production. In *Buttes Gas and Oil Co v Hammer (No 3)* [1981] QB 223, Lord Denning MR concluded that, for the purposes of disclosure, the court should treat all of the persons interested as if they were partners in a single firm. Each can avail himself of the privilege. Where common interest privilege applies, the document remains privileged in the hands of the recipient. The recipient can assert the disclosing party's privilege as against the world. For common interest privilege to be asserted, the common interest between the communicators must have existed at the time of disclosure between them. The principle of common interest privilege can apply in both arms of legal professional privilege: legal advice privilege and litigation privilege. Guidance as to when common interest privilege arises was given more recently in *Winterthur Swiss Insurance Company and Anor v AG (Manchester) Ltd and Ors* [2006] EWHC 839 (Comm).

Common interest privilege could be used as a 'sword' (to obtain disclosure), as well as a 'shield' (to prevent disclosure). It has been held to apply between companies in a group, insurer and insured, and agent and principal. However, the case law remains uncertain and each situation needs to be considered on its own merits.

 Practical Considerations

Because the case law is relatively uncertain in this quite modern form of privilege, it is best to be cautious when considering or advising clients about the disclosure of documents to third parties who could be considered to have a 'common interest'. If in doubt, consider disclosure only on the basis of express contractual undertakings that privilege in the document is not being waived.

17.9.4.2 Joint interest

Where a third party can establish a joint interest with another, then even though there is no confidentiality between them, each can assert joint privilege if they should subsequently fall out. That joint privilege enables each to assert the privilege against the 'rest of the world' and, importantly, the privilege arising can only be jointly, not severally, waived. In situations in which joint privilege arises, documents can be shared between the parties without the risk that they have waived privilege by making the documents no longer 'confidential' by their exchanges. It also means that neither party can assert privilege against the other in respect of the communications between them (before they fell out). It also means that neither will be able to deny the other the right to access to the documents held by the other. As stated above, both can assert the privilege to prevent disclosure to others.

Examples of joint privilege have been held to arise in a subsequent conflict of interest arising between beneficiaries and trustees, a company and its shareholders, partners, and a parent company and its subsidiaries.

17.9.4.3 The privilege against self-incrimination

A person is entitled to refuse to give evidence or disclose information if the revelation of the information would have the effect of increasing the likelihood of his being prosecuted for a criminal offence or being subjected to a penalty. This privilege, or right, can be asserted at any stage, including within the process of disclosure. It is an important facet of Art. 6 of the ECHR and the 'right to silence'.

It does not arise commonly, but may arise, for example, in a claim based on fraud or corruption. It could be assumed that it could commonly arise in many RTA claims when criminal proceedings (against a driver) often ensue, or in employer liability cases, but in these cases, the civil claim will usually get going after the conclusion of any criminal proceedings. It should be noted that any *relevant* criminal prosecutions that have been made may be stated in a party's case under the provision of s. 11 of the Civil Evidence Act 1968.

The right to withhold information that may have a tendency to incriminate is based on s. 14(1) of the 1968 Act. There are several exceptions to this right: under s. 31 of the Theft Act 1968; under s. 72 of the Senior Courts Act 1981; under s. 291 of the Insolvency Act 1986; and under s. 434 of the Companies Act 1985.

17.9.4.4 Without-prejudice negotiations

It is within the spirit of the Woolf reforms for civil litigation and the ensuing CPR that every encouragement should be given to parties to settle their disputes. Any genuine attempt to settle proceedings will be regarded as 'without prejudice' and parties may not make any reference to those offers or concessions made in the action. The principles established play an important role in the concept of protective offers on costs made within the provisions of CPR Part 36 (see Chapter 16).

The protection conferred by the 'without prejudice' principle means that neither party to the 'without prejudice' negotiations may put in evidence the content or detail, or the fact that an offer or concession has been made at all. This is provided that it was made:

- as part of attempts made in good faith to negotiate a settlement of the case or some of the issues; and

- expressly or impliedly 'without prejudice'.

This is also unless:

- all parties consent to revealing the existence of or detail of the negotiations;

- a concluded settlement is reached (that is, a new agreement is formed);

- it has been made 'save as to costs' (this applies whether or not it complies with CPR Part 36); and

- disclosure is sought by an individual who is not a party to the proceedings in which the negotiations took place.

The case of *Shepherd Construction Ltd v Berners (BVI) Ltd & Anr* [2010] EWHC 763 (TCC) is very useful reading for a review of the without prejudice rule.

17.9.4.5 Public interest immunity

Under CPR 31.19, a party is entitled to 'withhold disclosure of a document on the ground that disclosure would damage the public interest'. This right is a form of privilege and it is a right to withhold a document from disclosure itself, not just from withholding 'inspection' of a disclosed document. Its aim is to prevent disclosure of material that would harm the nation or the administration of justice.

Claims to withhold disclosure on this ground are relatively rare, and to apply it, a without-notice application must be made. Courts may adopt a more active role in monitoring the assertion of this right than they used to do and the court is required to carry out a balancing exercise to determine whether the 'public interest' identified by the party resisting disclosure outweighs the potential value that it may have for the party who would otherwise have access to it.

Public interest immunity differs from 'privilege' in that, once the public interest is established, the court has no choice and the document must not be disclosed.

17.9.5 LOSS OF PRIVILEGE, WAIVER OF PRIVILEGE, AND REFERENCE TO PRIVILEGED DOCUMENTS

There are no definitive rules setting out the circumstances in which privilege may be lost. Usually, for privilege in a document to be lost, some act must have occurred that results in an implied or actual loss of the right. Thus, enabling inspection of a previously privileged and 'withheld from inspection' document will usually result in the right of privilege being lost. This can happen because of a deliberate intention to waive privilege, or it may happen because of an accident: for example, if the document is inadvertently referred to in a statement of case, or inadvertently made available for inspection. Privilege may also be lost if the document becomes no longer 'confidential'. Privilege may be lost if it is necessary to refer to the privileged document in order to establish a claim or defence.

Whenever a document is referred to in a statement of case, witness statement, or affidavit, any privilege attached to it may be lost. However, this may not happen if only a short reference to the privileged document is made. Generally, a court will not permit a party to put in evidence part only of a privileged document and a limited waiver (of privilege) is treated as a waiver in respect of the entire document. However, if the 'separate subject matter' test (as defined in *Great Atlantic Insurance Co v Home Insurance Co* [1981] 1 WLR 529) applies, then the court may permit a partial waiver of privilege being applied to the document. It must also be borne in mind that the court will permit redacting from a document being disclosed that contains privileged material in part of it. However, if the document is referred to at trial, then the whole may have to be revealed unless the 'separate subject matter test' is applied. If a document is inadvertently included or referred to, it will usually be possible to retain the privilege, provided that the party ceases to rely on the document.

Service of an expert report waives privilege in the report and in documents referred to in it. Experts' reports are not disclosed subject to any confidentiality. Therefore privilege cannot be claimed in any subsequent action against a third party.

 Practical Considerations

The whole arena of 'experts' and the 'instructions given to an expert' within the context of disclosure and privilege is complex. Often, litigation requires both expert guidance (for the party preparing his case) and expert opinion for the court. In exceptional cases at trial, two experts could be retained: one to provide advice, and one to provide the expert evidence for the court. However, where this is not economic or practicable, consideration needs to be given to the issues surrounding disclosure and privilege. For the expert's report, as a CPR Part 35 expert, the content of the instructions to that expert will form part of the documentation that is to be disclosed; so too will the information on which the expert has relied to prepare his report, which may include information, instructions, and discussions that he had *before* he was retained as the CPR Part 35 expert and when he was only giving 'advice' to the party in the preparation of his case. Guidance has been given by the Court of Appeal in *Lucas v Barking, Havering & Redbridge Hospitals NHS Trust* [2003] EWCA Civ 1102.

17.9.6 **THE INADVERTENT DISCLOSURE OF PRIVILEGED MATERIAL**

CPR 31.20 provides the court with discretion to consider the position of privileged documentation being inadvertently revealed to an opposing party. In general, it provides that the court will consider the nature of the material inadvertently disclosed and decide whether to grant permission for it to be used by the party who has seen it. A full discussion of the factors that the court will take into account in deciding whether to grant permission or not is set out in the Court of Appeal's judgment in *Al Fayed v Commissioner of Police of the Metropolis* [2002] EWCA Civ 780.

ADR considerations

In large commercial cases, the whole process of disclosure and inspection can be challenging, time-consuming, and expensive. After inspection of documents, it is often a good time to take stock of where you are in the litigation and consider what you are trying to achieve for your client. It is all too easy to become embroiled in expensive arguments over privilege and lose sight of your client's goals (which may change as the case progresses), but you must remain in 'tune' with the overriding objectives. Consideration should therefore be given to whether it is an appropriate time to enter into an ADR process (see the 'Litigation train' diagram at the beginning of this chapter).

17.10 PRE-ACTION DISCLOSURE

17.10.1 PROTOCOL DISCLOSURE

Early disclosure of relevant documents is an important feature of civil procedure. In any dispute, parties are expected to comply with either a specific Pre-Action Protocol, or if the dispute is not one that is governed by a specific Pre-Action Protocol, then within the Practice Direction on Pre-Action Conduct in general.

Pre-Action Protocols are designed to:

- encourage the exchange of early and full information about the prospective legal claim;
- enable parties to avoid litigation by reaching a settlement before proceedings are commenced; and
- support the efficient management of proceedings where litigation is not avoided.

Further detail of pre-action work including disclosure is contained in Chapter 8.

The general expectation is that parties to an action will be expected to disclose any **relevant** and **essential** documentation at the pre-action stage. Prospective claimants can, and usually do, set out a list of the documents that they wish to see and there is the expectation that the responding party will either comply, or say why they will not, or why they believe the requested documents not to be relevant.

Failure to comply with the Pre-Action Protocols can, and generally will, be penalized in costs if the action is commenced.

17.10.2 APPLICATION FOR PRE-ACTION DISCLOSURE

A party who is dissatisfied with the response to their request of documents pre-action can apply to the court before proceedings are issued for an order for disclosure, provided that their request meets the requirements of CPR 31.16. It should be noted that the provisions under CPR 31.16 are the exception to the general principle that a party who is dissatisfied with the pre-action behaviour of a party does not have the right to apply to the court for an order that the uncooperating party cooperate. This is because the Pre-Action Protocols are not part of the CPR and, therefore, the courts do not have jurisdiction to order compliance with the Protocol **in general**.

17.10.2.1 What are the provisions of CPR 31.16?

An application for pre-action disclosure can be made under the provisions of CPR 31.16, provided that:

- the application is by, and sought against, parties who are 'likely to be parties in a subsequent action'. In this context, 'likely' does not mean 'probable', it means 'no more than "may well" ' (*Herbert Black and Ors v Sumitomo Corp* [2002] 1 WLR 1562, [71], *per* Rix LJ). The jurisdictional threshold is not 'intended to be a high one' (ibid, [73], *per* Rix LJ). However, an order will not be made 'routinely'—and it must be justified;
- the application relates to documents that fall within the definition of 'standard disclosure'; and
- the advance disclosure is necessary to:
- dispose fairly of the anticipated proceedings; and/or

- save costs; and/or
- assist resolution of the dispute without the need to commence proceedings.

In the *Sumitomo* case, the judge addressed himself to four questions in turn in determining whether to order pre-action disclosure:

1. Are proceedings (between the parties) likely?
2. Do the documents sought fall within the scope of standard disclosure?
3. Is pre-action disclosure desirable for any of the three reasons set out in CPR 31.16?
4. Should the court order disclosure in the exercise of its discretion?

In *Total E & P Soudan SA v Edmonds and Ors* [2007] EWCA Civ 50, the Court of Appeal also seems to be adding to this guidance by stating that an application for pre-action disclosure may be granted if the applicant can show that such early disclosure would 'enable the prospective claimant to plead their case in a more focused way'. The case of *Moduleco v Carillion* [2009] EWHC 250 (TCC) also suggests that a party who unreasonably refuses an application for pre-action disclosure may be penalised in costs.

 Practical Considerations

The judgment delivered by Rix LJ in the *Sumitomo* case is useful and essential reading before preparing any application for pre-action disclosure. The four questions set out above would be followed (and 'answered') in any supporting evidence for an application. It guides any application beyond the words of CPR 31.16. The more focused the application and the more limited the disclosure sought, the more likely that the court will exercise its discretion in the applicant's favour.

17.10.2.2 The availability of other types of pre-action disclosure

Other types of pre-action disclosure may be available in applications for:

- a freezing injunction under the provisions of CPR 25.1 and PD 25.6;
- a search order under CPR 25.1, which may have the effect of providing information early;
- an application for the preservation of property under CPR 25.5, which can be made pre-action; and
- *Norwich Pharmacal* orders.

These substantive applications are outside the scope of this book. Further reading can be undertaken in the additional online chapter 'Injunctions'.

17.10.3 DISCLOSURE AGAINST NON-PARTIES

It must be noted that an application for pre-action disclosure under the provisions of CPR 31.16 is only available against a person who is likely to become a party to proceedings. An order to disclose may be available against persons who are not parties to the proceedings under the provisions of CPR 31.17 in:

- *Norwich Pharmacal* orders;
- freezing injunctions;
- search orders;
- applications for the preservation of property;
- *Bankers Trust* orders; and
- requests for further information under the provisions of CPR 18.

Again, this substantive application is outside the scope of this book.

17.11 **LORD JACKSON'S REPORT AND DISCLOSURE**

Lord Jackson's review mainly concerned improving costs and disclosure in the larger commercial cases.

FIGURE 17.1

CURRENT POSITION	LORD JACKSON'S PROPOSALS
1. Little emphasis on specific training for e-disclosure.	The topic of e-disclosure should form a substantial part of the professional training for legal representatives.
2. The process of disclosure is currently limited to standard disclosure in CPR 31.5.	CPR 31.5 should be supplemented (perhaps by a new CPR 31.5A) for large commercial claims. This could be achieved by a 'menu option approach'. This approach could also be used for cases where standard disclosure is likely to be disproportionate.

KEY POINTS SUMMARY

- Not disclosing a document means not listing it. A failure to do this can be serious, because the 'cards on the table' approach to litigation is entrenched within the CPR.

- Not permitting inspection means listing a document and putting your opponent on notice that it exists, but for the reason claimed, withholding it.

- Ensure that the 'appropriate person' in the client's organization signs the disclosure statement.

- Carry out 'inspection', and make a thorough and careful review of the opponent's list.

- Challenge grounds to withhold from inspection or challenge the substance of an opponent's list when it is proportionate, fair, and just to do so.

- The legal representative's duties in relation to disclosure are onerous—ensure that early advice is given to the client of his disclosure obligations.

- Ensure that the client is told, and understands, what disclosure means and that the client understands the key message not to destroy documents that might be relevant to the matters in issue, not to create new documents without consideration of the disclosure obligations, and not to ask third parties to send you documents or to send documents out to others without consideration of the disclosure obligations.

- Treat the use of privilege with respect. It is a complex area of litigation, and if in any doubt on any aspect of privilege, then seek advice from a more experienced colleague.

Case study *Andrew James Pike and Deep Builders Ltd*

Acting for the defendant, assume that it is 16 December 201? and that you are a trainee with the defendant's solicitors. You have just received the letter dated 14 December 201? from LPC & Co, enclosing the claimant's list of documents.

Question 1

Consider how directions, including disclosure, are dealt with in the High Court. What are the main directions? When do they come into effect? When is there a duty to give disclosure? Which documents do you have to disclose, but withhold from inspection?

Question 2

Draft a letter replying to the letter dated 14 December 201?. You will, of course, need to consider whether there are any documents that you would wish to see and for which you would want to ask the other side.

---

online resource centre Any documents referred to in these case study questions can be found on the Online Resource Centre—simply click on 'Case study documentation' to access the documents that you need for Chapter 17 and to be reminded of the questions above. Suggested answers to these case study questions can also be accessed on the Online Resource Centre by your lecturer

FIGURE 17.2 LITIGATION PRIVILEGE AND ADVICE PRIVILEGE FLOW CHART

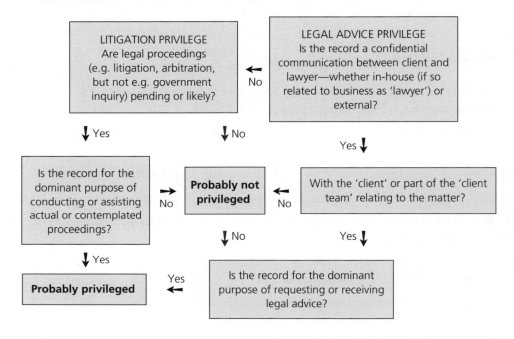

18 WITNESS STATEMENTS AND DOCUMENTARY EVIDENCE

18.1 INTRODUCTION

A case can readily be won or lost on the strength of witness evidence at trial. Similarly, important applications may fail if a witness statement does not adequately deal with all of the issues. A legal representative must therefore understand both the underlying theory behind the use of witness evidence and documentation during the course of litigation, including the rules on hearsay, as well as the practical requirements and challenges encountered in the preparation of witness statements.

The relevant parts of the Civil Procedure Rules (CPR) are Parts 32 and 33. The governing statute is the Civil Evidence Act 1995.

This chapter covers:

- the use of evidence at trial;

- the preparation of witness statements for interim applications and at trial;

- the use of hearsay in civil cases; and

- evidential tools.

LITIGATION TRAIN: WITNESS STATEMENTS AND DOCUMENTARY EVIDENCE

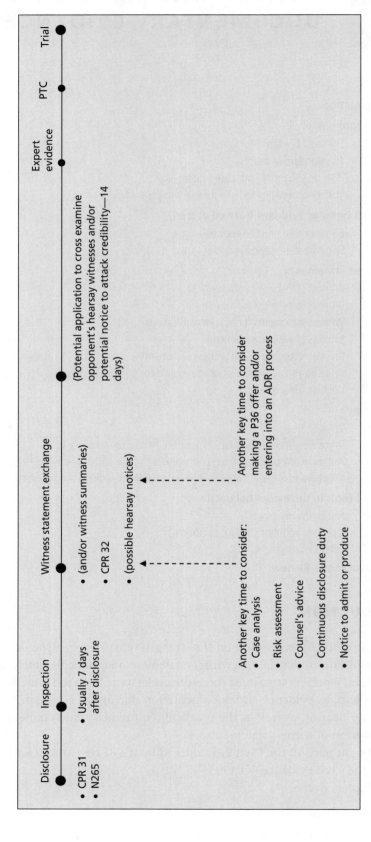

18.2 THE PROOF GAME

As a reminder of the general background to this, see Chapter 6, paragraphs 6.4.2.3 and 6.4.3.6.

18.2.1 THE LEGAL BURDEN

The general rule is that the claimant has to prove every element of his case. In most claims, this will include proving liability, causation, and quantum. If he fails to prove any part of his case, that will mean that he has lost the issue in question. However, what part does the defendant play in the proof game?

Sometimes, the burden of proof will shift from the claimant to the defendant, and this will depend on the type of case and defence raised.

For example, in road traffic accidents (RTAs), defendants often raise allegations of contributory negligence against the claimant. If this happens, then the claimant will initially have to prove that the accident was caused by the defendant's negligence (primary liability). If the claimant fails to do so, then the case is lost, because the claimant's burden has not been discharged. If he succeeds, the burden would then pass to the defendant to prove contributory negligence. Another common instance in which the burden of proof may 'shift' from the claimant to the defendant is in cases in which a breach of statutory duty is alleged: for example, under s. 40 of the Health and Safety at Work Act 1974, the burden of showing that the defendant has taken all 'reasonably practicable' steps is on the defendant, not the claimant.

18.2.2 THE STANDARD OF PROOF

In terms of the standard of proof, the party with the burden of proof has to prove his claim on a balance of probabilities. Taking the example of the RTA again, the claimant, when proving his case against the defendant, will need to persuade the judge at trial that it was more likely than not that:

- the defendant drove negligently in the way(s) particularized by the claimant;
- those negligent actions caused the collision to occur;
- the injuries were caused as a direct result of the collision; and
- the injuries were of a particular type and severity.

18.2.3 HOW DO YOU PROVE YOUR CASE EVIDENTIALLY?

When preparing your client's case, because your allegations are being formulated in your statements of case, thought needs to be given simultaneously to how each of those allegations are going to be proved or refuted. There are three methods of proving a case evidentially, as follows, and these can be used individually or cumulatively in respect of each allegation made:

- by oral evidence at trial—that is, lay witness evidence, based on written witness statements, or expert evidence, based on experts' reports;
- by the provision of documentary evidence at trial—that is, a contract, expert's report, or hospital notes; and/or
- by real evidence being available at trial—for example, a faulty machine or defective car.

However, as can be seen from paragraph 18.3 below, the court can control whether or not you are allowed to use a type of evidence at trial. This chapter concentrates on lay witness evidence and documentary evidence. (For a discussion of the use of expert evidence, see Chapter 19.)

18.2.4 THE CONCEPT OF PROPORTIONALITY AND WITNESS EVIDENCE

The concept of proportionality may influence the decisions that you make concerning the collection of witness evidence. The lower the 'value' of the action, the more likely it will be that you will have to undertake some considered 'pruning' of the numbers of witnesses that you wish to use.

18.3 CAN ALL TYPES OF EVIDENCE BE USED AT TRIAL?

A party to litigation is at liberty to obtain any type of evidence to prove or disprove the case against him. However, whether that party will be permitted to use and rely on that evidence at trial will depend on mandatory requirements and the court's discretion.

18.3.1 EVIDENCE THAT MUST BE EXCLUDED

In your early practice as a legal representative, it is unlikely that any of these exclusionary rules will be problematic. However, you are required to know that the following categories of evidence cannot be used or relied upon at trial:

• irrelevant evidence, such as similar fact evidence and previous judgments or convictions;

• opinion evidence, except from that of an expert in his field;

• privileged evidence;

• without prejudice communications; and

• evidence protected by public interest immunity.

(See Chapter 17 for a fuller discussion on privileged evidence, without prejudice communications, and public interest immunity.)

18.3.2 EVIDENCE THAT MAY BE EXCLUDED

The court has a discretion to exclude evidence that is ordinarily admissible and its powers to do so are derived from the CPR. The most common areas are as follows.

• The court's discretionary powers under CPR 32.10, CPR 32.12 and CPR 35.13, regarding lay and expert witness evidence, respectively, permit the court to exclude the use of oral witness evidence at trial, and to rely on experts' reports and oral testimony at trial. Therefore, where the party wanting to use the evidence has failed to disclose it in accordance with directions set by the court, the court can exclude it altogether.

• The court's powers under CPR 32.1 are general and far-reaching, to the extent that the court can exclude evidence that would otherwise be admissible—for example, a second witness statement attesting to the same facts as appear in another witness statement obtained by you.

• The court's case management powers specifically under CPR 3.1(2)(m) mean that the court can take any other step or make any other order for the purpose of managing the case and furthering the overriding objective.

 Practical Considerations

In practice, you are far more likely to have material evidence excluded as a result of the court exercising its discretion under any one of the above parts of the CPR. It is therefore advisable to raise the admissibility issue with your client before you incur the fee or cost of obtaining the evidence, so that he is aware that there is a possibility that the court may disallow it.

18.4 WITNESS STATEMENTS

This section deals with some early considerations of which a legal representative should be aware in order to ensure that witness statements are well prepared and presented in the correct format, whether the statements are for use at an interim hearing, at which the witness is not generally required to attend, or for use at trial, at which the witness is obliged to attend.

18.4.1 WITNESS STATEMENT OR AFFIDAVIT?

In most aspects of High Court and county court litigation, evidence at interim hearings and at trial is given by way of witness statements. However, Practice Direction (PD) 32.1.4 sets out the occasions on which an affidavit must be used—most notably, in applications for search and freezing orders, parts of insolvency proceedings, and in applications for contempt of court. These applications fall outside the scope of this book (but see the additional chapter 'Injunctions' on the Online Resource Centre).

online resource centre

18.4.2 WITNESS STATEMENTS FOR TRIAL

18.4.2.1 First steps

The preparatory work that is needed to prepare an effective witness statement of fact for trial starts well in advance of the issue of proceedings. For example, if you act for the claimant, you will want to obtain a proof of evidence (a 'warts and all' record of what was first said by your client or witness, including a full commentary on any documents) to help you to draft your letter of claim and statement of case. Conversely, if you act for the defendant, you will require your client's proof of evidence to assist in the response to the letter of claim and the preparation of the defence.

18.4.2.2 Preparing the witness statement

With this in mind, once you are in a position to commence the preparation of the witness statements for trial, which may be many months after you have taken the proof, there a number of important points to note, as follows.

- You only need to refer to facts that are in issue. Therefore, review the statements of case, and assess which facts are agreed and which are not agreed.

- Decide which party has the burden of proving those facts.

- Assess which witness(es) can prove which facts, and if there is more than one, assess which witness is in the best position to prove the fact in issue.

- If you have not already made contact with a witness, do so, explaining who you are, who you represent, and why you would like to speak to them.

- Arrange a meeting and send any key documents in advance.

- At the meeting, let the witness tell his story and take him through the relevant documents, ensuring that you ask questions to clarify his evidence.

- After the meeting, prepare the witness statement as soon as possible. This must be in the witness's own words, not yours. The statement may take some careful drafting to achieve this. Remember that the witness can be cross-examined on any part of his witness statement and so be sure how the witness would respond on cross-examination.

• Send the statement in draft to the witness, with a covering letter inviting him to make any amendments, approve, and sign the statement of truth. This may need to be explained to the witness.

 Practical Considerations

The witness statement may need to be passed between the witness and yourself many times before it is finalized. Once a final draft has been signed, create a witness statement section in your file. Any witness who is not your client may have no interest in the outcome of the trial, and so treat them with respect and keep them fully informed of their impending attendance at trial.

 Professional Conduct

There is no 'property' in a witness, therefore you may approach any witness who has already been approached by your opponent, asking them to talk to you and to provide a witness statement. Whilst interviewing the witness, it would therefore not be sensible to give the witness a view of the merits of the case or details of your tactics. However, you must never try to persuade the witness to change his evidence (Solicitors' Code of Conduct 2007, Rule 11, Guidance Note 13(e)). There maybe a risk, if you do decide to interview your opponent's witness, that such allegations will be made. Therefore, to avoid this, either record the interview or ask the other side to attend.

 Practical Considerations

Discuss with your client, at the outset of the claim or defence of the claim, which facts need to be proved and how. If your client is to give evidence in the form of a witness statement, then he should be aware of the fact that his statement will contain a statement of truth. Remember that a list of witnesses and the facts/issues to which they will be attesting is to be inserted in section D of the allocation questionnaire, although, in practice, it is often too early to have the identity of all of your witnesses at the allocation stage. The more up-to-date list of witnesses will go in section B of the pre-trial checklist.

18.4.2.3 Formatting the witness statement

Every witness statement must contain certain information to make it compliant with CPR 32 and its Practice Direction. If it is not in the required form, then, in accordance with PD 32.25.1, the court may disallow the use of the evidence and the costs arising from it. It is therefore important that you are aware of these basic formalities that appear in PD 32.12– 20, starting from the beginning of the statement as follows:

1. The top right-hand corner of the witness statement must include five points and these are usually numbered for ease:

    (i) the party on whose behalf the statement is made;

    (ii) the initials and surname of the actual witness;

    (iii) the number of the statement for that particular witness in the litigation—that is, is it the first statement, second statement, etc.;

    (iv) the initials of the witness and the number of exhibits attached to the statement; and

    (v) the date on which the statement was made.

2. The statement must be headed with the title of the action. This can be obtained from an indorsed claim form or the particulars of claim. The heading stays the same even if, for example, it is the defendant who makes the interim application.

3. The statement should set out in heading form, usually in bold, the full name of the witness. This is helpful to the parties to the action and the court when sifting through large numbers of statements, because it makes it easily identifiable.

4. The maker of the statement must then set out his name (again), address, occupation, and whether he is a party to the proceedings or employed by a party to the proceedings.

5. Numbered paragraphs must also be used throughout.

6. The statement will be in the first person.

7. A standard introductory paragraph must be used for all witness statements for trial and includes the following:

   (i) who the maker of the statement is in relation to the claimant or defendant, if not a party to the action;

   (ii) that the witness, if not a party to the action, has authority to make the statement on behalf of that party—remembering that, if a party is a limited company, it will always need a representative to speak for it and so 'the authority point' will need to be dealt with;

   (iii) the witness must declare that the information he will give in the statement is either from his own knowledge and are matters of information of belief, or from the source stated (and then, when appropriate, to say in the statement the source of a particular fact—that is, 'I am informed by xxx that …').

8. A statement of truth must conclude the witness statement as required by CPR PD22.2: 'I believe that the facts stated in this witness statement are true …'

18.4.3 WITNESS STATEMENTS FOR INTERIM APPLICATIONS

In order to be successful at an interim hearing, you will need to prepare evidence to prove your case. This very often takes the form of a witness statement. The party making the application is called the 'applicant' and the party opposing the application is known as the 'respondent' (but they may also be referred to as if 'claimant' or 'defendant' is their title in the action). Many of the points in paragraph 18.4.2.3 above also apply to witness statements prepared for interim applications. However, there are a number of additional considerations that are dealt with below. It may also be helpful to refer to Chapters 13 and 14 when considering the drafting of witness statements for interim applications.

18.4.3.1 Preparing the witness statement

18.4.3.1.1 *Fact or submissions*

Whatever type of interim application you are preparing for or opposing, it is very likely that you will be outlining facts to the court at the hearing, having regard to the order that you are asking the court to make or oppose. You will also be making written submissions in relation to your legal arguments to be put to the court to persuade the district judge or Master to grant or dismiss the order.

For example, if you act for a defendant who has had default judgment entered correctly against him in an alleged debt action, an application to have that judgment set aside under CPR 13.3 can be made on his behalf. A factual background will need to be set out in the witness statement to highlight the fact that the defendant does not believe it to be an undisputed debt case, but a contested dispute. Those facts can then be drawn upon when the written submissions are made in relation to the requirements of CPR 13.3.1 being 'a real prospect of successfully defending the claim', or 'another good reason why the defendant should be allowed to defend the claim'. In essence, there must be a marrying up of the facts to the legal submissions (see Chapter 14 for further discussion).

18.4.3.1.2 *Who should make the statement?*

In light of the fact that an interim application is likely to contain both facts and submissions, you will need to give some thought as to in whose name the witness statement should be: you as the legal representative, the client, or another witness? This will depend on who is best placed to give first-hand evidence on the information that you intend to place before the court.

Where detailed legal submissions are to be made, it is more usual for the legal representative to make the witness statement, but this still leaves the problem of the factual submissions in relation to which the client or another witness may have first-hand knowledge. If this is the case, there are two options: either prepare two witness statements for the application, one being a factual statement for the client or witness, or a carefully worded statement from the legal representative covering both facts and submissions. The latter is the most common way of dealing with this problem and how to achieve this is highlighted below.

18.4.3.1.3 *Where the legal representative makes the statement*

The following important features will also need to be included where a solicitor makes the witness statement.

- In relation to the point made in paragraph 18.4.2.3 above, rather than state whether you are a party to the proceedings, it is more usual to state that you are the solicitor for the claimant or defendant, and include your firm's address.

- In addition to the points raised in paragraph 18.4.2.3 above, as a new legal practitioner, you are required to state that you 'have the care and conduct of the matter on behalf of the claimant (or defendant), subject to the supervision of [your] principal'. Obviously, on qualification, the supervision point can be relinquished.

- It is important to remember that where you, as the legal practitioner, are making reference to the factual background to the case, you must use the words 'I am informed by . . .', or 'the claimant/defendant has informed me that . . .', to ensure that you are relaying the source of your knowledge to the court.

18.4.3.2 Formatting the witness statement

Much of paragraph 18.4.2.3 above applies to witness statements for interim applications, but the following additional features should be noted.

- The second paragraph of the statement should inform the court of the purpose of your witness statement. As with the earlier example of the application to set aside default judgment, an appropriate sentence to achieve this would be: 'I make this statement in support of the defendant's application to have default judgment set aside.'

- In terms of formatting the structure to the statement, subheadings may be useful—especially to identify any relevant factual background and any legal submissions. Alternatively, when opposing an application, your witness statement in response may flow better if you respond to the witness statement in support, and, where appropriate, make additional relevant factual and legal arguments.

- It is helpful, when you come to making the written submissions in the statement, to state the part of the CPR (if there is a relevant part to your application) under which you are seeking the order, such as CPR 13.3.

- After the introductory statements and declaration of what the witness statement seeks to achieve (to make or oppose an application), it is usual for the applicant to set out a brief chronology of the relevant facts or the progress of the case. This should, in effect, make it clear that the application has been made at the correct time. Unless this is contested by the respondent to the application, the respondent will be able to agree this brief chronology.

- Once you have completed your submissions, conclude by repeating what it is that you are requesting: 'I therefore respectfully ask this honourable court to set aside default judgment in accordance with the terms of the draft order annexed to this application.'

- Finally, the statement of truth is as in paragraph 18.4.2.3 above, but because you are not a party to the action, this statement must be qualified with an authority sentence as follows: 'I am duly authorized to make this statement on behalf of the claimant/defendant ...'

 Practical Considerations

When setting out the persuasive elements of your client's case, you can be as articulate as you like, making reference to parts of the CPR. Here, you are seeking to persuade the district judge that he should make the order sought. The degree of persuasion needed may vary with the particular interim application or ground under the CPR on which the case relies. Another way to look at how these 'persuasive' elements of the witness statement should be drafted is to consider the discretion that the district judge or Master has in relation to the application and, in effect, draft arguments that enable the district judge or Master to make the order that you seek within the remit of his discretion.

Figure 18.1 at the end of this chapter is a template for a witness statement for an interim hearing.

18.4.4 EXHIBITS TO WITNESS STATEMENTS

A witness statement for trial or for an interim application can refer to documents. If this is the case, the documents must be exhibited to the witness statement. Reference to the number of exhibits is made at point (4) in the information given in the top right of the front page of the statement itself.

When referring to an exhibit in the body of the witness statement, the witness should state, 'I refer to [description of the document including a date] marked "TS 1/2/3 etc" '. Detailed provisions relating to exhibits can be found in PD 32.11–15. Each exhibit, or bundle of exhibits, should have a covering sheet featuring (or should have expressly written upon it) the court heading, the name of the witness, and that 'this is the exhibit marked "TS1/2/3 etc" referred to in the statement of . . . '.

18.4.5 DISCLOSURE AND SERVICE OF WITNESS STATEMENTS

18.4.5.1 Witness evidence for trial

Witness statements for use at trial must be disclosed to your opponent (CPR 32.4). The terminology for this is 'exchange of witness evidence'. This must be done in accordance with the directions laid down by the court at allocation or at a CMC. As can be seen from Chapter 12, the usual order is for exchange of lay witness evidence, which should be mutual and simultaneous among all parties to an action, to be effected by 4 p.m. on a specified date.

Practical Considerations

Once you are ready to exchange witness statements, it is good practice to telephone or write to your opponent to confirm that you are in a position to exchange in accordance with the order of the court. If your opponent is also ready, then exchange can proceed, and both parties usually confirm during the telephone call or in the reciprocal letters when and how they will serve their witness statements: for example, by putting the statements in first-class post on a particular date.

Professional Conduct

If your opponent is not ready to exchange witness statements in accordance with the order given, with your client's instructions, you may wish to give him an extension of time in which to do so. If you do agree to an extension, ensure that the revised date does not conflict with any other direction laid down by the court. Do not serve your witness statements on your opponent, but hold them back if you are not prepared to grant an extension. If you were to serve your statements unilaterally, then your opponent would be given an unfair advantage in the final preparation of its own evidence by tailoring the same or seeking additional statements to deal with issues raised in your statements. This may not be in your client's best interests. If you do not agree to an extension, then your opponent will be forced to make an application to the court for an extension of time.

18.4.5.2 Witness evidence for interim applications

Witness evidence in respect of interim applications is usually required to be unilaterally served either in accordance with the specific provisions of a part of the CPR, such as CPR 24, or if the CPR are silent on this, then the evidence should be served as soon as possible, but in any event at least three days before the hearing (CPR 23.7(1), (4) and (5)).

18.4.6 WHAT DO YOU DO ON RECEIPT OF YOUR OPPONENT'S WITNESS EVIDENCE?

18.4.6.1 Witness evidence for trial

This is probably one of the key points in litigation at which to reassess your client's claim by undertaking a file review and conducting a risk assessment. You should specifically look at:

- a review of the prospects of success;
- costs to witness exchange and to trial;
- any additional evidence (lay, expert, or documentary), or investigations to deal with any issues raised on exchange of witness statements;
- dealing with any hearsay issues (see paragraph 18.5 below);
- making a Part 36 offer or revised Part 36 offer;
- requesting a stay for alternative dispute resolution (ADR);
- seeking counsel's opinion in writing or in conference; and
- strategy and tactics in moving forward to trial.

Because this is an important stage, a detailed letter to your client will be necessary, enclosing your opponent's statements, highlighting the salient points, and underlining any issues that have arisen. A meeting may also be necessary.

The 'Litigation train' diagram at the beginning of this chapter illustrates how this fits in, in practice.

ADR considerations

As can be seen from the 'Litigation train' diagram with which this chapter opens, at a time after exchange of witness statements, ADR should be reconsidered by you and discussed with your client to decide whether it is, indeed, appropriate to try to resolve the dispute by other means.

18.4.6.2 Witness evidence for interim applications

On receipt of your opponent's witness statement either in support of or in opposition to the application, it may be appropriate to:

- check their grounds for the application;
- prepare a witness statement in response, if permitted by the CPR or if appropriate;
- in larger, more complex applications, send a copy to your client and request further information or clarification if required;
- reassess the prospects of success of the application in light of the evidence; and
- consider whether it is in your client's best interests to brief counsel to attend or whether you are, in fact, capable of undertaking the advocacy at the hearing.

18.4.7 WITNESS SUMMARIES

If a witness is unwilling or unable to provide a statement for trial voluntarily, then you will be unable to rely on what the witness has to say at trial: for example, where you have spoken to a witness and have sent them the statement to sign, but they do not want to sign it, or are out of the country. The absence of their evidence may be potentially damaging to the success of your client's case.

If you find yourself in this situation, consider the use of a witness summary. A witness summary identifies the witness and summarizes the factual issues that his evidence will cover. In order for you to take advantage of a witness summary, you will need the permission of the court. The application is without notice (see Chapter 15). The witness summary must contain the witness's name and address, and must be served by the date set for exchange of witness statements. You will therefore need to decide some time in advance of the date set for exchange whether you wish to rely on a witness summary.

 Practical Considerations

The purpose of the witness summary is to enable you to call the witness to trial to give evidence. Witness summaries can also be used where you have not interviewed the witness and do not know what they are going to say. Caution should be exercised if you wish to call such a witness to trial and when the content of their evidence is unknown, because this could be particularly damaging to your client's case.

 Costs

As with the disclosure and inspection process, preparing and scrutinizing witness statements for trial can be an expensive and time-consuming process. Remember that costs are usually awarded on the standard basis, and that therefore, even if your client is successful and secures an order for costs in his favour at trial, those costs must be reasonable in amount, reasonably incurred, and proportionate. Be mindful of the time taken by you in the preparation and exchange of witness statements, and remind your client that, even if successful, he is unlikely to recover all of his legal costs.

18.5 HEARSAY

Hearsay evidence is now classed as admissible evidence in civil proceedings by virtue of the Civil Evidence Act 1995 and is defined by s. 1(2) of that Act as a statement made otherwise than by a person while giving oral evidence in the proceedings, which is tendered as evidence of the matters stated. The use of hearsay evidence is regulated by the Act in terms of how and when it can be used at trial, and the weight attached to it by the trial judge.

18.5.1 WHAT IS 'HEARSAY'?

You will come across hearsay most commonly in the following situations.

18.5.1.1 When calling another witness to testify as to what the eyewitness saw

When you are interviewing your witness for the purposes of, firstly, preparing a proof, and eventually, preparing a witness statement for trial, the 1995 Act permits you to include his hearsay comments—that is, his comments in relation to what someone else told him about an issue in the claim. The witness's evidence of what he said or saw is first-hand evidence, but the evidence of what someone else told him is second-hand evidence and thus 'hearsay'. If there is more than one person removed from the original statement, then this is known as 'multiple hearsay'.

 Example

An RTA occurred on a country lane between a van and a red car, and was observed by a hill walker in the adjoining field. He proceeded to the next village and went into the local shop, where he informed the shopkeeper that he had seen an accident. He told her that he had seen the driver of the van speaking on his mobile phone immediately before the accident. Later that week, the driver of the red car came into the shop, asking if anyone in the village had seen the accident. The shopkeeper informed him of what the hill walker had told her.

The witness statement of the red car driver could potentially contain multiple hearsay, as follows: 'The shopkeeper told me that she had been told by a hill walker that the driver of the van had been speaking on his mobile phone immediately before the accident.'

18.5.1.2 Adducing the eyewitness's written statement to prove what was seen

Hearsay evidence will also arise when your witness has signed a witness statement, but is unable to attend trial. Even though you have no difficulty in proving the statement as a document, tendering his written statement in place of the witness giving oral evidence in the witness box at trial constitutes reliance on hearsay evidence.

 Example

In the above example, if the shopkeeper were to have provided a written witness statement, but then disappeared, the witness statement would still be admissible evidence and can still be relied upon at trial, subject to the requirements detailed in paragraph 18.5.3 below.

18.5.2 WHAT WEIGHT DOES THE TRIAL JUDGE ATTACH TO HEARSAY EVIDENCE?

The most persuasive evidence that can be put before the court is first-hand evidence, as highlighted in paragraph 18.2.3—namely, oral evidence at trial by the eyewitness, or an original document or object.

In terms of witness evidence, if the maker of the statement does not attend the trial to give oral evidence, or a witness's recollection whilst in the witness box of what happened refers to what somebody else told him about a fact in issue, the court is unlikely to place as much weight on either forms of the evidence as it would if the original witness were there in court.

The question is exactly how much weight will the court give to the evidence in these circumstances? Section 4(2) of the 1995 Act confers a duty on the court to have regard to six factors, as follows.

(a) *whether it would have been reasonable and practicable for the party by whom the evidence was adduced to have produced the maker of the original statement as a witness;*

(b) *whether the original statement was made contemporaneously with the occurrence or existence of the matters stated;*

(c) *whether the evidence involves multiple hearsay;*

(d) *whether any person involved had any motive to conceal or misrepresent matters;*

(e) *whether the original statement was an edited account, or was made in collaboration with another or for a particular purpose;*

(f) *whether the circumstances in which the evidence is adduced as hearsay are such as to suggest an attempt to prevent proper evaluation of its weight.*

The trial judge will usually explain in his judgment the weight that he has attached to hearsay evidence.

18.5.3 ARE THERE ANY PROCEDURAL REQUIREMENTS FOR THE USE OF HEARSAY EVIDENCE?

Section 2(1) of the 1995 Act requires any party wishing to adduce hearsay evidence to serve notice on his opponent. CPR 33.2 sets out the court's requirements where the hearsay evidence is to be given either by a witness giving oral evidence at trial, or where the hearsay evidence is contained in a witness statement of a witness who is not being called to give oral evidence.

18.5.3.1 Where hearsay evidence is to be given by a witness who is attending court to give oral evidence

Let us look at the driver of the red car in the example given in paragraph 18.5.1.1 above. The notice formalities are complied with by the service of the witness statement itself. Therefore, because the red car driver's witness statement for trial contains hearsay evidence from the shopkeeper and the hill walker, the service of the witness statement, in accordance with the directions set by the court for witness statement, exchange will suffice as formal notice.

18.5.3.2 Where the evidence is contained in a witness statement of a person who is not giving oral evidence

Remember from paragraph 18.5.1.2 that a written statement from someone who will not be attending trial is also classed as hearsay evidence. If this is the case, then a separate formal notice should be served with the witness statement, identifying the hearsay evidence, confirming that hearsay evidence will be relied upon at trial, and giving reasons why the witness will not be called.

There is no guidance given in the CPR as to the exact format of the notice. We would suggest that the template found in Figure 18.2 at the end of this chapter be used as a starting point for a hearsay notice.

Practical Considerations

In practice, very few legal representatives serve a notice, and even fewer will ever raise the point. Failure to serve the notice does not affect the admissibility of the hearsay evidence, but the court may exercise its discretion on the question of costs.

18.5.4 WHAT ARE YOUR CLIENT'S OPTIONS IF HEARSAY EVIDENCE IS BEING USED AGAINST HIM?

If, in the course of litigation, you receive a hearsay notice, you will need to consider the effect that the weight of the hearsay evidence will have on your case and whether there is anything constructive that you can do about it.

In terms of the effect of the weight of the hearsay evidence, this will very much depend on the strength of your own evidence, the type of hearsay evidence against you, the strength and type of any other evidence against you, and the six factors listed in paragraph 18.5.2 above.

Constructively, the best that you can hope to do, where you believe the hearsay evidence to be effective for your opponent, is to try to reduce any weight that the trial judge may attach to it. This can be done in one of two ways: either by calling the maker of the hearsay statement to court to be cross-examined, or by attacking the credibility of the maker of the hearsay statement in his absence.

18.5.4.1 Cross-examination

Section 3 of the 1995 Act allows a party who has been served with a hearsay notice to apply to the court for an order to call the maker of the hearsay statement to court to be cross-examined. The application is effected in the usual way, with a Form N244 plus witness evidence in support of the application. CPR 33.4 requires that the application be made no later than 14 days after service of the hearsay notice.

 Practical Considerations

Applications of this nature would only be used in cases in which the whereabouts of the witness is known, because the court is unlikely to make the order if the witness has disappeared. In practice, consideration should be given to cross-examination orders where your opponent has obtained and served a witness statement, but decides not to call the witness to give oral evidence at trial, relying on the statement of the absent witness as hearsay. You are permitted to apply to cross-examine. If you do succeed and cross-examine your opponent's witness, there is a risk that the witness may be uncooperative and this may damage your client's case.

18.5.4.2 Attacking credibility

Section 5(2) of the 1995 Act permits a party who has been served with a hearsay notice to attack the credibility of the maker of that hearsay evidence. This is done by serving a 'notice to attack credibility' on your opponent within 14 days after service of the hearsay notice under CPR 33.5. There is no guidance on the form of the notice in the CPR, but it usually follows the format of the hearsay notice and will include an outline of the reasons why you seek to attack the witness's credibility

 Practical Considerations

When trying to identify the reasons for attacking a hearsay witness's credibility, try imagining that the witness is, in fact, in the witness box at trial and consider what questions you would put to him to discredit him. Go on, then, to consider what trait it is about the hearsay witness's character that you are trying to highlight to the judge: is he biased, untrustworthy, or unreliable? It is these character defects that need to be included in the notice to attack credibility, not the questions that you would have put to the witness had they attended court.

In practice, trial judges place limited weight on hearsay evidence.

 Practical Considerations

You may wish to consider taking both of the steps in paragraphs 18.5.4.1 or 18.5.4.2, because they both operate under the same time limits—particularly if you are trying concurrently to trace the hearsay witness. If you are unable to locate them by the time that your application comes to a hearing, you have the option of withdrawing the application—but be mindful of any costs consequences. Alternatively, you may not wish to take either step. This would probably only be the case if you were to feel you have a sufficiently strong case, but care should be taken, because if you do choose to do nothing on receipt of the hearsay notice, then, at the trial, you will not be permitted to make any representations to the judge on the character or credibility of the hearsay witness.

18.6 USEFUL TOOLS IN THE EVIDENTIAL BATTLE

Usually, at a point after disclosure and exchange of witness statements, when reviewing your client's case generally and conducting your risk assessment, as illustrated in the 'Litigation train' diagram at the start of this chapter and that at the start of Chapter 17, there may be facts or parts of the case that could usefully be admitted by your opponent with a view to putting some pressure on your opponent and saving costs. There are two methods available to you, as follows.

18.6.1 NOTICE TO ADMIT FACTS

In order to ensure that the court's time at trial is not wasted in having to determine facts and issues that could be reasonably admitted, consideration should be given to serving a 'notice to admit facts' in Form N266, in accordance with CPR 32.18. This can be served at any time, but no later than 21 days before trial. (See the Online Resource Centre for a copy of the form.)

 online resource centre

If an admission in relation the fact or issue sought is not forthcoming from your opponent, then you have the burden of proving or disproving the fact at issue at trial. If you are successful on that issue, then your opponent may be asked to pay your costs of proving or disproving those particular facts or issues, irrespective of the overall outcome of the case.

The use of the notice to admit facts is, perhaps, best explained by way of an example.

 Example

A defendant serves a defence denying liability in a personal injury claim. However, the real issue is quantum. The defendant makes a Part 36 offer to put pressure on the claimant. The claimant could serve a notice to admit facts on the defendant to put him at risk on the costs of defending the liability issue, where the costs would be significant.

18.6.2 NOTICE TO ADMIT OR PRODUCE DOCUMENTS

CPR 32.19 is concerned with the position in which a document is deemed to be authentic, unless you serve a 'notice to prove a document at trial' in Form N268 (a copy of which can be found on the Online Resource Centre). This must specify the document being challenged

 online resource centre

and must be served by the latest date for exchange of witness statements, or within seven days of disclosure of the document, whichever is the later.

These notices are not as commonly used as notices to admit, but feature in cases in which the signature or date on a contract is being challenged. If such a notice is served and your opponent successfully proves the authenticity of the document, the court has a discretion to make an adverse costs order against you.

18.6.3 LETTERS OF REQUEST

Letters of request are essentially a request by a court in one jurisdiction to a court in another jurisdiction to take evidence on its behalf where there is an unwilling witness in another jurisdiction. The letters can request oral evidence or documents. There are three different scenarios:

• letters of request from courts within the European Union (other than Denmark) are governed by EC Regulation No. 1206/2001 on cooperation between the courts of the member states in the taking of evidence in civil and commercial matters;

• where a domestic court receives a letter of request from a non-EU court, the governing legislation is the Evidence (Proceedings in Other Jurisdictions) Act 1975, which applies to the domestic court's handling of the request;

• if a party is seeking a letter of request to be issued to a non-EU court in proceedings in this country, an application must be made to the High Court (even if a county court matter) under CPR 34.

Within each of the above, there are different rules to be followed and, as such, you will need to consult the appropriate authority.

Letters of request usually feature in international commercial cases.

18.7 LORD JACKSON'S REVIEW

Lord Jackson's main concern was that witness statements for trial should not be unnecessarily lengthy. Having conducted his review he concluded that no rule changes were required, simply a more effective use of the existing rules in CPR 32, 33 and 34. You may therefore see no more than express references to these already existing powers in the Court Guides.

KEY POINTS SUMMARY

• Key witnesses need to be identified pre-action or immediately after statements of case.

• Non-essential witness statements should not be exchanged.

• Be aware of the court's discretionary power to control evidence for trial.

• Take greater care than ever to ensure that witnesses' own words are used in witness statements—in particular, that the language of any contemporaneous notes is carried through into the final statement.

• Ensure the correct format of witness statements.

• Note the differences between witness statements for trial and those for interim hearings.

• Hearsay may be written or oral, and may be first-hand, second-hand, etc.

- Hearsay notices should be served at the same time as witness statements if hearsay evidence is to be relied upon at trial.

- Try to reduce the weight that the trial judge will attach to the hearsay evidence by making an application to cross-examine or by serving a notice to attack credibility.

Case study *Andrew James Pike v Deep Builders Ltd*

Disclosure and inspection have now taken place. The only documents of which you have received disclosure and inspection from the defendant are the costs of repairs to the truck and the cost of the damaged materials. You have disclosed all of Andrew Pike's receipts in relation to his special damages claim, along with his hospital and doctor's notes. The defendant is still denying liability, causation, and quantum.

Question 1

Consider what points you will have to prove at trial.

Question 2

If the defendant's legal representatives refuse to accept any of your points, how will you prove those points and what steps will you have to take prior to trial?

Exchange of witness statements has taken place. You act for Andrew Pike and exchange only one witness statement—that of Andrew Pike based on his original proof of evidence. The defendant exchanged a witness statement of John Deep, denying that he was responsible for the accident. They also disclosed a witness statement of Raquel Hake, along with a hearsay notice. (See Raquel Hake's statement and the hearsay notice that appear in the Online Resource Centre.)

online
resource
centre

Question 3

Consider how you would respond to this notice and consider the weight of Raquel Hake's evidence at trial. What are the possible lines of attack on her evidence?

Question 4

What options do you have? Prepare any documentation that you think may be necessary to carry out the step(s) that you have set out.

Case study *Bollingtons Ltd v Mrs Elizabeth Lynch t/a The Honest Lawyer*

Question

In Mrs Lynch's witness statement prepared for trial, she mentions the fact that many of the guests at the party had tasted the beer and had commented to her on how disgusting it was. Is this hearsay evidence? Would it be necessary to obtain statements from the guests, and if you were to do so, would the court allow you to rely on them at trial?

---

online
resource
centre

Any documents referred to in these case study questions can be found on the Online Resource Centre—simply click on 'Case study documentation' to access the documents that you need for Chapter 18 and to be reminded of the questions above. Suggested answers to these case study questions can also be accessed on the Online Resource Centre by your lecturer.

FIGURE 18.1 TEMPLATE FOR A WITNESS STATEMENT FOR AN INTERIM HEARING

1. Claimant/Defendant

2. T. Solicitor

3. 1st/2nd etc

4. TS 1/2/3 etc

5. Date

IN THE   COUNTY COURT   CASE NO

BETWEEN

MR   CLAIMANT

AND

MR   DEFENDANT

WITNESS STATEMENT OF TRAINEE SOLICITOR

Witness name: insert name of trainee solicitor

Witness address: insert firm's address

Witness occupation: insert the fact that you are a trainee solicitor and that you act on behalf of either the Claimant or the Defendant

1. I am a trainee solicitor and have the care and conduct of this matter subject to the supervision of my principal. I am duly authorized to make this statement on behalf of the Claimant/Defendant. I make this statement from my own knowledge, belief and from the information given to me by the Claimant/ Defendant/someone else.

2. I make this statement in support of the Claimant/Defendant's application for . . . .

Chronology/facts/procedural events
Insert any relevant background here in numbered paragraphs 3-?

Submissions
Insert your legal arguments here repeating the wording of a relevant part of a CPR part if appropriate in consecutive number paragraphs.
   Conclude your submissions with 'I therefore respectfully ask this honourable court to make the order as asked in accordance with the terms of the draft order annexed to this application'

Statement of truth and authority
I believe that the facts stated in this witness statement are true. I am duly authorized to make this statement on behalf of the Claimant/Defendant

FIGURE 18.2 TEMPLATE FOR A HEARSAY NOTICE

IN THE	COUNTY COURT	CASE NO

BETWEEN

Claimant

and

Defendant

NOTICE OF INTENTION TO ADDUCE HEARSAY EVIDENCE

Take Notice that at the trial of this action the Claimant/Defendant intends to give in evidence the statement made in the following document, namely the statement of . . . . dated . . . . a copy of which is annexed hereto.

And further take notice that the particulars relating to the said statement are as follows:

1. It was made by . . . .

2. It was made to . . . . of the Claimant/Defendant's solicitor.

3. The said statement was made on . . . . at . . . .

4. It was made in the following circumstances, namely that the Claimant/Defendant's Solicitor obtained the witness name from . . . . and attended . . . . for the purpose of obtaining a statement from him/her.

And Further Take Notice that the said . . . . cannot be called as a witness at the trial because . . . .

To: The Claimant/Defendant

Dated . . . .

LITIGATION TRAIN: EXPERTS AND EXPERT EVIDENCE

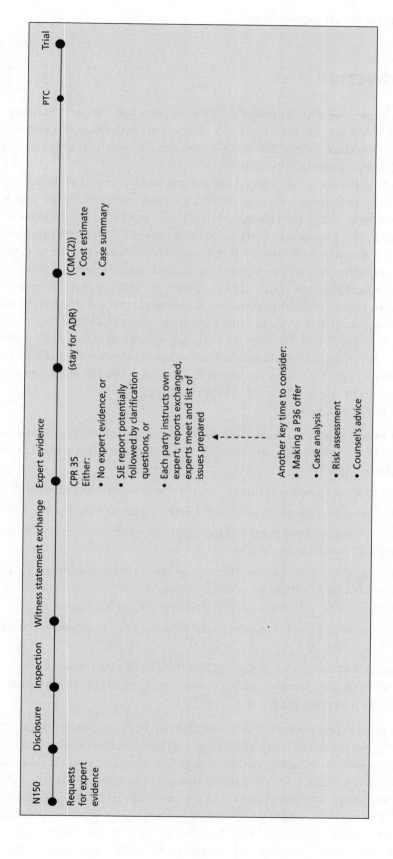

19.1 INTRODUCTION

In this chapter, we will consider the role of experts and the part that they may play in an action that ensures that their input to a case accords with the overriding objective set out in the Civil Procedure Rules (CPR) Part 1—most notably, for the court to ensure that 'justice' is done between parties in an action.

The role and use of oral expert evidence and written expert evidence in civil (and criminal) court proceedings has come under increasing critical scrutiny, and legal representatives need to be fully conversant with the times at which expert evidence is *needed* in an action and, in engaging an expert, to be fully clear of the *role* that expert will take.

The CPR provide very firm guiding principles to make the role of experts in litigation consistently effective and fair. We will see that the use of expert evidence in actions will be strictly controlled by the court, not the parties. We will see that the experts themselves are required to make declarations that they understand their duties (to the court). It will be for the legal representative to ensure that the expert understands his role, irrespective of who is paying the expert's fees. The expert's job is to give a full appraisal of the views (opinion) that he puts forward and he should also seek to evaluate these views in the light of other scientific (or technical) opinion, outcomes, or views. The judge should, at all times, be *assisted* in his deliberations by the involvement of expert evidence.

This chapter will consider:

- when expert support is *needed*—whether that is as part of the *evidence submitted* in the action, or as part of the *advice sought* to prepare the client's case, or perhaps for both situations;

- the *role* that the expert will take in both of the situations identified above;

- when *permission* of the court is needed to engage and submit expert evidence in the action;

- the *costs consequences* for the client in engaging expert evidence for advice or as part of the evidence submitted to the court;

- the management and suitable direction of steps taken in advising your client and proceeding with an action, so as to meet the *court's overall discretion* to control the evidence in relation to the inclusion of expert evidence (or not to include it);

- the important matters to consider in the *engagement* of an expert and in managing several experts in a case; and

- the important matters of procedure that need to be considered when experts are used to support an action, together with a consideration of the directions orders that the courts may make for expert evidence.

Where a party is permitted to use its 'own' expert, CPR 35 clearly imposes significant duties and obligations upon that expert. And we will see from this chapter that no expert who will be giving evidence (whether oral or written) to the court, even if appointed by a party to give evidence for that party, is actually that party's expert. Under the CPR, the expert has to take responsibility for ensuring that his own objectivity is both demonstrated and preserved. This very objectivity of the expert is often the very area in which an attack on that expert's evidence may be made by the other party in cross-examination at the trial. These duties of objectivity, integrity, and independence of the expert from the parties make a legal representative's job of working alongside an expert more difficult. This manifests itself in relation to difficulties over issues such as retaining privilege in instructions and materials given to an expert, and, so far as is possible, ensuring that the expert is, ultimately, on the client's side, but without being tainted with the client's or his legal representative's views. Apart from the technical rules concerning expert evidence, these other matters must be fully understood by any practitioner. They will also be considered in this chapter.

At the time of writing, the Civil Justice Council has indicated that it is considering proposals for a complete review of CPR 35. Matters that it highlights for review include:

- the accreditation of experts; and
- the degree of inconsistency in the way in which different courts direct the appointment of single joint experts.

The outcome of this review is awaited. Similarly, the Law Reform Commission has embarked on a consultation process for expert evidence. The criteria that the Commission sets out for this consultation process gives a valuable insight into the use of experts in litigation, and the areas in which reform and changes to the CPR can, perhaps, be expected. The Lord Jackson review also made suggestions for the reform of the use of experts in litigation, some of these are now part of pilot studies, and judges have already taken on board some of the issues he has raised and these are being reflected in recent decisions.

19.2 THE USE OF EXPERT EVIDENCE IN CIVIL ACTIONS CONSTITUTES AN EXCEPTION TO THE RULE AGAINST OPINION EVIDENCE

Experts are permitted to give opinion evidence. As a general rule, opinion evidence is inadmissible because it is the role of the court to form its opinion of the evidence presented to it. However, in providing this exclusion to this rule and permitting an expert to give opinion evidence, the court is acknowledging that, in some areas, it requires guidance and assistance on matters that are outside the expertise of the judge to determine. Often, the opinion evidence of an expert in an action is peripheral to the main liability issues that the judge must determine. The evidence from the expert may do any one or more of the following whenever the judge needs the expert's assistance to decide the key issues and make a judgment on the issues before him:

- deal with the valuation of an asset;
- explain a physical or mechanical process;
- clarify technical jargon;
- make an assessment of 'risk' or likelihood (of an event happening);
- give evidence on standard or benchmark behaviour or practices; or
- give an assessment of 'blame'.

Section 3 of the Civil Evidence Act 1972 sets out the test for calling an expert witness in civil proceedings:

(a) *The expert may give his opinion on any relevant matter and,*

(b) *The expert must be qualified to give the opinion.*

We shall see that both 'relevance' and 'qualified to give' are important matters to consider whenever seeking leave of the court to adduce expert evidence.

19.3 WHO OR WHAT IS AN 'EXPERT'?

19.3.1 A DEFINITION

A basic law dictionary (*Black's*) sweepingly defines 'experts' as 'men of science educated in the art, or persons possessing special or peculiar knowledge, acquired from practical experience'.

The CPR defines an 'expert' as a person who has been 'instructed to give or prepare expert evidence for the purpose of proceedings'. Further the rules define a 'single joint expert' as an expert instructed to prepare a report for the court on behalf of two or more of the parties to the proceedings. The reality of these definitions is that an 'expert' can be anyone with knowledge or experience of a particular field or discipline beyond that to be expected of a layperson. The expert witness is allowed to give an opinion to the court on matters that they may not have seen directly, but in which matters they are an 'expert'. Anyone who can convince a judge of their knowledge, skills, or training in an area of knowledge that the court needs to understand to try the case fairly can act as an expert. A professional qualification is not necessarily required. The expertise of the 'expert' is gauged from their professional training, but also their employment or experience in other ways.

19.3.2 THE WEIGHT OF EXPERT EVIDENCE

There are a number of factors that will determine the weight that the judge will attribute to the expert witness's evidence, including the extent to which he backs up his opinions with current scientific thinking, and the degree to which he accepts and analyses alternative views and conclusions. The expert's opinion evidence will also be 'weighed' against the evidence of fact of lay witnesses who have seen, or had direct involvement in, the issues of the case.

In civil litigation, an ordinary witness is called to tell the judge, and is only allowed to tell, what he himself actually perceived. An expert witness may, however, draw an inference from his conclusions of the facts. It is always for the judge to decide if the alleged facts are true; he will do this by balancing the evidence that he hears or reads from both types of witness. The expert witness differs fundamentally from the ordinary witness: he did not see or hear the incident in dispute; he gives evidence of scientific fact; and he gives his opinion based on professional knowledge and experience. Although the expert witness may subsequently see the injured person, the damaged equipment, the accounts, or the scene, his evidence of the 'facts' of the event are his 'opinion' of it.

For example, a lay witness may not say that a vehicle was being driven recklessly; only that it ended up in the ditch. It is the function of the court to decide the cause of the accident, based on the evidence placed before it. It is the task of the expert witness (say, in this example, an accident investigator) to assist the court in reaching its decision, with technical analysis and opinion inferred from the factual evidence: for example, by an expert determination of skid marks on the road.

An expert witness can give evidence based on opinion, or his conclusions, if four basic conditions are met, as follows.

1. The opinion, inferences, or conclusions must depend on special knowledge, skill, or training that is not within the ordinary experience of the judge.

2. The expert must be shown to be qualified as a true expert in the particular field of expertise.

3. The expert must give evidence to a reasonable degree of certainty regarding his opinion, inferences, or conclusions.

4. The expert must be able to demonstrate, or persuade from scientific fact, the basis of his opinion, inference, or conclusions.

The 'weight' to be attached to the expert's evidence is a matter for the judge to determine. Critical matters will be his status, qualifications, interests, experience, reputation, bearing, and response.

It is essential that the expert's report and evidence is a frank statement by the expert of the limits of the accuracy of his opinion, inferences, or conclusions. He must be prepared to indicate, whether asked to do or not (but the legal representative instructing the expert also has a duty to ensure that the expert fully understands the extent of his duties and obligations), what his evidence suggests as likely. Just as litigants are obliged under the rules of disclosure (see Chapter 17, paragraph 17.4.1) to disclose documents that are against his case or support the other party's case, the expert is under an obligation to make sure that the court does not, unwittingly, use his evidence without realizing its scientific limitations.

The three 'i's of an expert are: independence; integrity; and impartiality. All of these are vital if an expert's opinion is to carry weight. An interest in the outcome of the case, rather than seeking to discover the truth, will produce unhelpful evidence for the court. Any expert who is more concerned in the outcome of the case will find himself the subject of sustained attack in cross-examination—he will be asked to comment, in the witness box, on contradicting authoritative materials or publications, or to comment on the effect of his hypotheses on a differing statement of facts. Any expert witness who has not fully appraised the conclusions that he makes without proper regard to alternative conclusions will find his evidence discredited in this way. The same can be said of written experts' reports prepared by experts who are 'interested in the outcome of the case' more than it is proper to be, so the opposing party's will raise questions on the content of the report setting out contradicting conclusions and evidence. In paragraph 19.8.1 below, there is a discussion of circumstances in which an expert may be used to assist a party in the preparation of his case—that is, the 'behind the scenes' expert. These experts will assist a party to prepare a trial strategy plan. This may include questions to ask the opposing party's expert witness in cross-examination and prepare written questions to that expert on the contents of his report.

It is the aim of a good expert to ensure that the judge not only understands the words, terms, and expressions that the expert uses, but also to ensure that the judge is able to do so without too much effort. The expert must build this bridge between science and knowledge to every conclusion that he states. Some experts, when faced with a difficulty, will 'dig in their heels' and refuse to budge. These are unhelpful experts. There are those who show an over-enthusiasm in expressing their opinions—and these, too, are unhelpful. Finally, there are the experts who, when faced with something new, consider it, and then fairly and properly, if they think it right to do so, modify their opinions or do not modify their opinions, but in either case, give a full explanation of their reasons. Sometimes, 'more is less' in the realm of expert evidence.

A useful recent judicial overview of the duties and responsibilities of expert witnesses is contained in the Technology and Construction Court case *London Fire and Emergency Planning Authority v Halcrow Gilbert Associates Ltd* [2007] EWHC 2546.

19.3.3 DOES THE EVIDENCE OF THE EXPERT WITNESS CARRY MORE OR LESS WEIGHT THAN THE EVIDENCE OF THE EYEWITNESS?

The court is not required to accept the evidence of the expert over the evidence of witnesses of fact (who are giving evidence of what they have actually perceived). Two cases illustrate this clearly: *Armstrong & O'Connor v First York* [2005] EWCA Civ 277; and *Breeze v Ahmad* [2005] EWCA Civ 233.

In the *Armstrong* case, two claimants claimed that, whilst waiting at traffic lights in the centre of York, one of the defendant's buses collided with their car and that they sustained back injuries as a result. The single joint expert in the matter, a forensic motor vehicle engineer, gave evidence to the effect that the damage sustained to the claimants' car was so minimal as to suggest that the collision had not caused the car to move at all, let alone jolt sufficiently to cause back injury. The claimants called no technical evidence to challenge the expert's view, and simply relied on their own evidence that the collision had happened and had caused them injury.

In effect, the expert's view meant that the judge at first instance was faced with, on the one hand, accepting the claimants' evidence—thereby undermining the expert's conclusion—and, on the other hand, finding that the claimants were lying. The judge at first instance found for the claimants. He found the claimants to be honest and thus necessarily decided to reject the expert's view as containing a 'possible error'—although he could not identify what, if anything, was specifically wrong with it.

The Court of Appeal upheld the judge's approach, holding that there was no principle of law that required an expert's view on a matter such as this to be preferred to the evidence of eyewitnesses.

It is clear that the Court of Appeal will, when necessary, uphold decisions that prefer the evidence of an eyewitness to that of an expert. This makes logical sense, because the expert is giving his *opinion* and, in doing just that, is not giving a guarantee or assurance that every view that he expresses is necessarily 100 per cent correct.

The *Breeze* case concerned Mrs Breeze's partner, who had suffered sudden cardiac death following a negligent examination by the defendant general practitioner (GP). The GP had diagnosed muscular skeletal pain and had not referred Mr Breeze to hospital urgently following his presentation with chest pains. Less than a month later, Mr Breeze had died. It was contended that, had the GP examined him properly, his death could have been avoided.

There was an expert on each side at the trial and the judge preferred the evidence of the defendant's expert, which was to the effect that even if the defendant had carried out a competent examination, there had been an admittance to hospital, and subsequent medical intervention, none of this could be said, in all likelihood, to have averted Mr Breeze's death. The judge preferred the defendant's expert's evidence on the basis that it was 'supported by recent literature', which the expert had told the judge about in the course of his evidence, but, crucially, had failed to produce. The trial judge found for the claimant on the question of liability for negligence, but, importantly, for the defendant in respect of causation. The claimant appealed on the question of causation.

At the appeal, the sole issue concerned causation and the non-production of two pieces of medical literature relied upon by the defendant's expert. It was clear that the trial judge had materially relied upon the reference by the defendant's expert to those documents as supporting what he was saying, but that the judge had not actually seen the literature, because it was not produced by the defendant's expert at the trial. The claimant contended that the defendant's expert had not accurately reported the contents of the literature to which he referred, and that, in not producing it, the claimant had lost the chance to show that it said something other than what the defendant's expert reported.

The Court of Appeal agreed, concluding that there had been a 'serious procedural or other, error' (CPR 52.11(3)) and that the matter needed to be retried. Given that the literature had been relied on, but had not been produced, and that the judge had not read it, he had attached more weight to it than he should have done.

 Practical Considerations

Clearly, the moral of these cases is that all experts should, where their evidence contradicts that of a witness of fact, seek to qualify how and why this may arise, and all expert witnesses should be further advised that where they refer to current scientific or other reports to support their view (and they should be encouraged to do this), they should produce the literature with their report (see paragraph 19.10.1 below).

19.3.4 IS IT POSSIBLE TO USE AN EXPERT WHO HAS A CLOSE CONNECTION WITH A PARTY?

It has previously been thought that it would be inappropriate to use an expert who has a close connection with a party. The requirement to be 'independent' is crucial for an expert to assist in the litigation process. The Civil Justice Council has stated that experts should 'provide opinions which are independent, regardless of the pressures of litigation. In this context a useful test of "independence" is that the expert would express the same opinion if given the same instructions by an opposing party. Experts should not take upon themselves to promote the point of view of the party instructing them or engage in the role of advocate.' Provided this very 'independence' can be shown the courts have concluded that, in certain circumstances, using an expert who has a close connection to a party, may not always be a bar to instructing the expert. In *Gallagher International Ltd v Tlais Enterprises Ltd* [2007] EWHC 464 (Comm), the judge permitted the use of an expert who was employed by the claimant. The defendants in this case had applied that the claimant's employee should be debarred from giving expert evidence. Aitkens J agreed with and adopted the reasoning set down in an earlier case (*Armchair Passenger Transport Ltd v Helical Barr plc* [2003] EWHC 367 (QB)) of the circumstances in which it may be appropriate to permit a person to give expert evidence despite a close connection with a party.

The reasons given in the *Gallagher* case were as follows.

- The fact (of the expert's employment with the claimant) was openly declared.
- The terms of engagement of the expert have been clearly defined within the provisions of the CPR, and the claimant had done as much as it could to 'isolate and separate' the expert from the affairs of the company in the litigation and his duties as an expert in the proceedings.
- The expert had relevant experience and was wholly aware of his duties to the court.
- Experts in the field were scarce—and further, the timescale before trial indicated that it would be unfair for the claimant to have to try to seek another expert in the field at the late stage of the proceedings.
- The expert would be open to cross-examination.
- The claimant bore the risks that the weight of the expert's evidence may be reduced by the judge at trial because of the connection to the party calling him.

Clearly, these reasons would not apply in many situations and the principle remains that an independent expert should be sought whenever possible.

The case of *Smolen v Solon Co-operative Housing Services* [2003] EWCA Civ 1240 can be distinguished from the *Armchair* and *Gallagher* cases above because it was not clear, in that case, that steps had been taken to ensure the impartiality of the expert (who had previously worked for a party), and experts in that field were not so difficult to find. It is also clear, though, that, in the circumstances listed above, 'a close connection with a party' will not automatically render the evidence of that expert as inadmissible.

The case of *Edwards v Bruce & Hyslop (Brucast) Ltd* [2009] EWHC 2970 (QB) is a recent timely reminder of the need for the expert to maintain his impartiality. In this case communications between the appointed SJE and the defendant (that had not been revealed to the claimant) had 'tainted' the expert's impartiality and his position as SJE was untenable.

19.4 WHAT RULES NEED TO BE CONSIDERED TO UNDERSTAND THE USE AND APPLICATION OF AN EXPERT IN AN ACTION?

CPR Part 35, its supporting Practice Direction (PD), and the Protocol for the Instruction of Experts that now appears as an annex to PD 35 are the rules that govern the use of experts once litigation has commenced.

However, CPR 32 also needs to be considered, because this provides the power for the court to control the evidence before it and this will include the control of expert evidence.

19.5 HOW DOES A PARTY SEEK TO USE EXPERT EVIDENCE IN HIS ACTION?

19.5.1 PRE-ACTION

A party can decide himself when and how to use an expert in the pre-action stage. This may be to help him to formulate his case, or to add strength and weight to his arguments. Expert evidence at this stage may be required to support the claim if proceedings are instigated (for example, in personal injury litigation).

Protocol—whether it is one specifically designed for the action or within the Practice Direction on Pre-Action Conduct (PDPAC)—sets down guidelines for the use of expert evidence. The aim in Protocol is that parties should seek to agree how to use an expert. However, the ultimate decision will lie with the claimant. The legal representative's role will be to ensure that the client has given instructions to engage the expert and that he understands the costs implications of engaging the expert. Unless Protocol has been followed, there is no certainty that the courts will allow any costs recovery of the fees of retaining the services of an expert in the pre-action stage.

19.5.2 DURING LITIGATION

If the action does not settle in the Protocol stage and proceedings are issued, any future use of evidence will be strictly controlled by the court under CPR 35 and parties may only use expert evidence at trial if given permission to do so. The court will also define the way in which expert evidence will be used (see paragraph 19.6 below).

Where a party has defined a need to use expert evidence in his action, he should make a request for that evidence as soon as practicable. The arguments for permission to adduce expert evidence will usually be set down in the allocation questionnaire and at a later stage regarding oral evidence of the expert, in the pre-trial checklist (see Chapter 12). Any further requests for the permission of the court to define the use of expert evidence by the parties further, or for permission for additional expert evidence, must be made by an interim application or at a subsequent case management conference (CMC).

It is expected that the Civil Procedure Rules Committee will shortly provide some minor amendments to PD 35.6 by adding some non-exhaustive considerations that courts should take into account when deciding whether to give permission for the evidence of a single joint expert or separate experts. The aim of the amendment will be to reduce the number of inconsistencies between decisions made by different judges and different regions.

19.6 WHAT FACTORS WILL THE COURT AND THE PARTIES TAKE INTO ACCOUNT CONCERNING THE USE OF EXPERT EVIDENCE?

The court will consider at the first opportunity—usually on receipt of the completed allocation questionnaires—whether expert evidence will be required. Both parties' legal representative should have considered their requirement for expert evidence in the action and should be prepared to address the court on this, having raised the issue in the completed Form N150 or at a subsequent CMC. No expert evidence may be adduced without the permission of the court (CPR 35.4(1)), so any perceived need for it must be fully set out as 'necessary' within the aims of the overriding objective. CPR 35.1 provides that expert evidence should be restricted to that which is reasonably required to resolve the proceedings.

Where the opinion evidence of an expert is peripheral, the court tends to take a robust view of its necessity. This is particularly so in low-value cases, in which the issues of proportionality come sharply into focus. If not ruling out the need for expert evidence altogether, the court may decide to allow only the engagement of a single joint expert (see paragraph 19.7 below).

Expert evidence may be central to issues of liability and causation, and/or quantum. Although parties are expected to cooperate in the preparation of their cases, the need for expert evidence is often one area in which the parties are unable to agree. The disagreement may concern:

- whether expert evidence is needed at all;
- whether expert evidence is needed in a particular field; and
- whether a single joint expert should be used.

 Practical Considerations

Where the parties are unable to agree on the need for, or form of, expert evidence in the action, it would be prudent to submit 'additional information' with Form N150 that supports the application that you are making for expert evidence. If, for example, you are seeking for your client permission from the court for leave to adduce expert evidence in a particular field and you are aware that this is being opposed by your opponent, it may be necessary to obtain a short report from the expert that you have identified, setting out the background of the evidence that the expert is able to cover. You will then, within your representations to the court at a CMC, also need to seek to justify the relevance and need for that evidence within the aims of the overriding objective, paying particular regard to the principles of proportionality, as well as relevance and justice.

19.7 LIKELY DIRECTIONS ORDERS ON EXPERT EVIDENCE

If the court concludes that expert evidence may be adduced at trial, the following directions orders may be made.

19.7.1 NO EXPERT EVIDENCE

No expert evidence being necessary, no party has permission to rely on expert evidence.

19.7.2 A DIRECTION FOR A SINGLE JOINT EXPERT (SJE)

In the small claims track or fast track, any permission for expert evidence to be adduced will **normally** only be given to call expert evidence on a particular issue from one expert (CPR 35.4(3A)). This is intended to provide consistency and directly refers the courts to PD 35.7, which sets out the criteria to apply when the court considers whether to direct the use of expert evidence in a matter.

Any direction order for a single joint expert must use the term 'single joint expert'. A direction for a single joint expert (SJE) could include some or all of the following directions.

- 'Permission is given to the parties to rely on the written evidence of an SJE in the field of [specify field], instructed jointly by the parties on the issue of [specify issue], and the parties have agreed to use [name expert].'
- 'If the parties cannot agree who the SJE should be, any party may apply to the court to obtain further directions.'
- 'In the event that the parties cannot agree the identity of the SJE by [date], the parties shall, on or before [date], apply to [specify who—for example, the President of the Royal Institute of Chartered Surveyors] to nominate a suitable SJE.'
- 'The claimant shall inform the court, in writing, when the SJE has been appointed.'
- 'Instructions are to be provided to the SJE by [date], and the report is to be simultaneously served by [date] on both parties.'

- 'The parties are to serve any written questions on the SJE and the other party by [specify timescale—for example, within 28 days of receipt of the expert's report], and the SJE shall file and serve the answers to any such questions on both parties by [time—for example, 28 days thereafter].'

- 'Unless the parties agree in writing or the court orders otherwise, the SJE's fees and expenses shall be paid by the parties [equally or in the proportions agreed or ordered], and the total amount of the SJE's fees and expenses shall be limited to £x [amount].'

- 'The evidence of the SJE shall be given at trial by [written report **or** oral evidence of the SJE].'

19.7.3 A DIRECTION THAT EACH PARTY MAY INSTRUCT ITS OWN EXPERT

A direction that each party may instruct its own expert might include the following options.

- 'Where the parties have not decided whether they want to call experts by the time of allocation or the first CMC, this will be considered at the CMC, and permission to apply for and adduce expert evidence may be given, or a direction may be made that consideration of the issue will be reserved to a later CMC.'

- 'Where, at the first CMC, the parties have decided in principle that they will want experts, but have not yet decided on the area of expertise [for example, whether it should be expert evidence of a quantity surveyor or a chartered surveyor], a further CMC can be held to deal with expert evidence [and any other outstanding matters], to be fixed for the first available date after [date], and to be reserved to [specify Master or district judge], if possible.'

- Where the parties have decided that they each want to rely on their own expert:
  - 'permission is given to each party to rely upon the written evidence of [specify number of] in the field of [specify field] expert(s) addressing the following issues [list issues]. [Specify which party] intends to use [name expert] and [specify other party] intends to use [name expert]';
  - 'the parties shall exchange their lists [of issues] and the experts of both parties shall consider both parties' issues in their reports';
  - 'the experts' reports shall be exchanged simultaneously by [date]', **or** 'there shall be sequential exchange of experts' reports, the claimant's [specify field] expert's report to be served by [date] and the defendant's [specify field] expert's report to be served by [date]';
  - 'written questions may be put to the experts on their reports within [number of days—usually 28 days] of the report being served. The experts are to respond to the questions in writing within [number of days] of being served the questions';
  - 'the reports are to be agreed if possible';
  - 'if not agreed, the experts shall hold a without prejudice meeting for the purpose of identifying the issues, if any, between them and, where possible, reaching agreement on those issues. The experts shall be [specify date] prepare and file [at court] and serve a statement showing:
    - those issues on which agreement has been reached; and
    - those issues on which they have not agreed, with a summary of the reasons why they disagreed'.

- 'All supplemental experts' reports shall be limited to [specify number of] pages, excluding supporting documentation and appendices, and shall be served by [date].'

- 'No party shall recover from any other party more than £[amount] for the fees and expenses of an expert.'

- 'The parties have permission to rely upon the oral evidence of [specify the experts] at trial'**; or**

- 'Each party has permission to use in evidence their [name expert] reports and the court will consider when the claim is listed for trial whether expert oral evidence will be allowed'; **or**

- 'If the experts' reports cannot be agreed, the parties are at liberty to rely on and call expert witnesses to give oral evidence at trial, limited to those experts whose reports have been served pursuant to paragraph [number] above.'

ADR considerations

As can be seen from the 'Litigation train' diagram at the beginning of this chapter, in addition to disclosure and inspection, and exchange of witness statements, expert evidence is another key stage in the litigation at which the case needs to be reassessed, another risk assessment needs to be carried out, and consideration given to whether an alternative dispute resolution (ADR) process would be appropriate. Once expert evidence has been dealt with, this often signifies the end of the 'information gathering' in an action and the matter now moves towards trial preparation, which is another costly part of the litigation. The courts expect parties to embrace resolving their dispute by an ADR process and will question them on their attempts at this in any forthcoming pre-trial hearing or review, and questions are asked concerning this in the pre-trial checklist (Form N170).

19.8 IN WHAT WAYS MAY AN EXPERT BE USED IN LITIGATION?

19.8.1 IN AN ADVISORY ROLE

An expert witness is different from an 'expert adviser', sometimes also known as an 'independent expert'. The expert adviser is a person who advises a party on a specialist or technical matter within his expertise at any stage of a problem, dispute, or claim. He may also assist with the formulation of the case, and thus be employed in the pre-action phase, or he may assist in the drafting of a witness statement (this could be pre-action). There may be considerable advantages, or certainly some justification in a high-value case (in which the additional costs of instructing an expert adviser can be justified), of instructing an expert early on in an action, because his expertise may assist the client (and his legal representatives) to assess the strengths and weaknesses of their case so as to decide whether to pursue or defend it. Using an expert adviser later on, during the course of the action, may also assist the client (and his legal representatives) to assess the strengths and weaknesses of any evidence that has been disclosed and revealed either by inspection, or at the exchange of witness statements and expert's report stage. The disadvantages of their use is that the costs of the expert advisers are not likely to be recoverable and, if used pre-action, that expert may not be acceptable as an expert witness in the action, because he may no longer be considered sufficiently independent. The differences between the different 'experts' who have had involvement in the action or with the party are important when considering the duties of the expert, the communications that the legal adviser or client may have with him, the expert's immunity from suit, and in several other respects.

 Practical Considerations

It is always essential, when considering using an expert to advise on a case to assist you to understand the technically difficult matters or facts arising, or to assist you to formulate your case, to think first whether you might wish to seek the court's permission to use your instructed expert adviser to act as your expert witness in the action (as an SJE or as your client's expert). If you have previously used the expert as an adviser, he may no longer be considered sufficiently independent to be used as an expert witness. Even if the court does permit his use, the court is likely to order that all of your communications with that expert, even during the time that he acted as your expert adviser, be disclosed. Care must always be taken in any communications with an expert at any stage and for whatever purpose.

 Costs

It is important, whenever considering the use of an expert in litigation, at whatever stage of the action, that the legal representative informs the client of the cost consequences of instructing the expert and gives appropriate advice concerning the likely recoverability (or not) of those costs. At all times, the client's specific instructions should be obtained to retain an expert in the action. It may also be necessary to obtain from the client the expert's fees in advance.

19.8.2 THE 'TREATING' EXPERT

Understanding the fundamental differences of 'role' between the litigation expert and the treating expert is vital.

A litigation expert (no matter who instructed him) owes primary duty to the court over and above any duty to any party (CPR 35.3). CPR 35 controls his participation in the proceedings. His very existence as an expert is subject to the court's permission (CPR 35.4). His evidence is to be 'objective, unbiased opinion'.

The treating expert owes primary duties to the party or client. That relationship is governed not by the court, but by the ethical requirements of the treating expert's profession for providing such treatment. That relationship will usually have arisen pre-action. The records of such a treating expert are, *prima facie*, documents that are to be disclosed within the proceedings. Additionally, if he becomes a witness in the proceedings, he is a witness of fact, not an expert.

 Practical Considerations

All too often in low-value cases and in an attempt by the parties to consider the sum of costs being expended, a claimant's legal representative will seek to put forward the claimant's 'treating expert' as the litigation expert in the action. Rarely will this be appropriate, but it occurs usually because the legal representatives have lost sight of the roles and duties of the expert in the role that he has had compared with the one that he will have if he becomes the litigation expert. The treating expert will immediately have a conflict of interests—a conflict between his professional obligations to the claimant as a patient and the duties that he owes to the court as a litigation expert. Often, the clarification of these 'roles' will not become apparent until long into the action (the judge is unlikely to know from the allocation questionnaire that the proposed 'selected joint expert' was the claimant's treating expert). By that stage, time and expense will have been lost and incurred, as well as significant embarrassment for the legal representatives of both parties. Also, because of the mistake, the court could readily impose 'wasted costs' orders against the lawyers' firms involved.

19.8.3 THE OPERATION OF THE REHABILITATION CODE

An anomaly to what should be a clear division between the types of expert that can become involved in an action is raised by the Code of Best Practice on Rehabilitation, Early Intervention and Medical Treatment in Personal Injury Claims (known as the Rehabilitation

Code), now incorporated into the CPR by being annexed to the Pre-Action Protocol on Personal Injury.

The Code is predicated on the idea that it is in everyone's interests to get the claimant into as recovered a state as possible. The purpose of the Code is to encourage claimants' lawyers and insurance companies to cooperate as soon as possible after the claimant's injury to procure appropriate treatments, without either side feeling that this will disadvantage them in the future conduct of the litigation. The Code has, to a limited extent, achieved this, although many claimants' representatives remain wary of giving too much away at an early stage.

The Code primarily provides for an 'independent assessment', either by a treating physician or surgeon, or (more usually in practice) an agency that is suitably qualified and/or experienced in such matters, which is financially and managerially independent of the claimant's solicitor's firm and the insurers. The assessment is carried out on a joint instruction basis and the report should cover:

- the claimant's injuries and present condition;
- the claimant's domestic circumstances;
- for what injuries intervention or rehabilitation is suggested; and
- what is the intervention, its cost, and its likely benefit.

The report does not deal with diagnosis, causation, or long-term care requirements. It is an 'immediate needs' report only.

In some ways, the rehabilitation assessor is treated like an SJE because the report is disclosed simultaneously and each party can raise questions, but must disclose those questions and any answers to the other party. However, the report is explicitly and specifically produced outside the litigation process, and is described as 'covered by legal privilege', although it is hard to see exactly what is meant by this in the Code, because the document is disclosed to both parties, but the report, all notes, and all correspondence is not referred to in any legal proceedings. But it is important to remember that this only applies to the report and ancillary documents. Any treatment or therapy that the claimant receives as a result of the report is subject to the same general principles as relate to any other 'treating expert', because the relationship is that between a patient and doctor (or therapist), and the treating expert, if he gives evidence, is giving evidence of fact, not opinion.

The confusions that can arise to identify the expert's role (even with experienced legal representatives) are clearly revealed by Brooke LJ in *Wright v Sullivan* [2005] EWCA Civ 656, [13]. The role of the legal representatives to ensure that confusion does not arise is an onerous one.

However, once the distinction between a treating expert and a litigation expert is clear, the next matter about which you must be clear are the distinctions between, and appropriate times to use, a 'single' joint expert, when each party may instruct and use the evidence of their own expert, and when an 'agreed' expert is used.

19.8.4 AS AN SJE

CPR 35.7.1 states that where two or more parties wish to submit expert evidence on a particular issue, the court may direct that the evidence on that issue is to be given by one expert only. The court will consider the overriding objective when deciding whether to allow the parties to have their own experts or insist on an SJE. CPR 35.7.3 provides that where the parties cannot agree who should be the SJE, the court may select an expert from a list prepared by the parties, or it may direct that the expert be selected in such manner as the court directs.

Under the provisions of the overriding objective and the drafting of the CPR, the court is clearly under a duty to consider, where expert evidence is identified and justified as necessary to the case, directing SJEs when giving case management directions (see Chapter 12).

Equally, the parties have a duty to conduct their cases within the spirit of the overriding objective and therefore should themselves have already considered whether the appointment of an SJE is the appropriate way forward. In the fast track, the court must 'give directions for an SJE unless there is good reason not to' (PD 28.3.9(4)). Similar provisions apply in the multi-track, where the court is urged to 'give directions for the appointment of an SJE on any appropriate issue unless there is good reason not to do so' (PD 29.4.10(4)). The emphasis therefore is on the use of SJEs. However, limiting the use of expert evidence in this way (to an SJE) will often not be possible in cases in which the expert evidence is central to liability. This is especially so in high-value cases and clinical negligence cases.

In view of the wording of PD 28.3.9(4) (above), SJEs are most commonly appointed in cases allocated to the fast track, where it will often be difficult to justify the cost of two experts in the claim. Also, in the multi-track, because the value band for actions in this track can start at a figure 'exceeding £25,000', it would be equally difficult to justify the cost of two experts for actions at the lower end of the spectrum of cases, in value terms. In the Technology and Construction Court (TCC), *Quarmby Electrical Ltd v John Trant t/a Trant Construction* [2005] EWHC 608, at [53], Jackson J stated:

> … in the smaller (construction) cases … if expert assistance is required, it is difficult to see any alternative to the use of a SJE in respect of the technical issue. If adversarial experts had been instructed to prepare reports and then give oral evidence in the present case, I do not see how there could have been a trial at all. The respective experts' fees and the trial costs would have become prohibitive. In lower value cases such as this one, I commend the use of a SJE.

Also, even in higher value multi-track cases, it would be difficult to justify or persuade a judge that more than one expert was necessary if the issue on which the expert is needed to report is not the central issue, or is relatively uncontroversial. Even in the Commercial Court, where, in general, the minimum value of actions is £50,000 (and usually considerably more than that), parties are encouraged by the Commercial Court Guide, paragraph H2.2, to consider the use of an SJE.

The use of an SJE necessarily means that only one view is being expressed. Paragraph 19.9.4 below sets out the safeguards that are in place within the CPR to ensure that the SJE's views are not partisan. Because of this, the opinion of the SJE is often determinative, and once the report of the SJE is produced, settlement will often be achieved. This is particularly so in fast-track cases, in which the costs of challenging an SJE, whether by application to the court for permission for another expert or by an order for his attendance at trial for the purpose of cross-examination, are likely to be disproportionate to the amount at stake. However, the court must have proper regard to the evidence of the SJE when looking at the evidence as a whole and does not have to accept everything that the expert says (see paragraph 19.3.2).

19.8.4.1 The advantages and disadvantages of using an SJE

19.8.4.1.1 *Advantages that can be identified*

- It is usually cheaper—but not always: for example, when the parties have already each appointed experts in the pre-action phase.
- It is usually quicker, because there is no need to meet to address the opposing issues of another expert.
- It is less likely that the expert will attend trial to give oral evidence, and this also will usually produce a cost and time saving.
- The use of an SJE often helps to encourage settlement negotiations.

19.8.4.1.2 *Disadvantages that may arise*

- It is not possible to have discussions or a conference with counsel on the more difficult parts of the report, or where a party wishes to challenge some parts of the report, without also involving the other party.

- It may be difficult to dispute the evidence of the SJE if it does not support the client's case.

- A party will not have had unfettered choice as to which expert should be appointed, and if agreement cannot be reached as to the identity of the expert, the court may choose the expert or direct a default mechanism for the appointment of the expert, which would leave the parties with no control of the identity of the expert to be appointed.

- It may still be necessary for a party to have its own expert to comment and advise (the advisory expert) on the report of the SJE, and the costs of this advisory expert are usually not recoverable.

- The courts are often reluctant to order the SJE to attend trial for questioning.

19.8.4.2 Instructing an SJE

Once an SJE has been selected, CPR 35.8 and sections 8 and 17 of the Experts Protocol give guidance on the instructions to the expert. It is clear that both parties are at liberty to send separate instructions to the expert, although they must send a copy of their instructions (and of any other communications that they may have with the expert) to the other party in the action. Ideally, the letter of instruction to the expert should be agreed, because this is more likely to create a clearer list of the issues on which the expert is being asked to report. If any instructions are given by telephone or in person, then the content of the instructions should be confirmed in writing. All communications from the SJE should be addressed to all parties. The case of *Edwards v Bruce & Hyslop (Brucast) Ltd* [2009] EWHC 2970 (QB) is a reminder of the importance of openness in all communications with the SJE.

The instructing parties are jointly and severally liable for the SJE's fees unless the court directs otherwise. The court will often also direct that the sum of the SJE's fees shall not exceed a certain figure (that the court will set) and further direct the proportion of those fees that each party should pay. This is often an equal division. The court also has the power to order either or both parties to pay that sum into court (see also *Smolen v Solon Co-operative Housing Services Ltd* [2003] EWCA Civ 1240).

Costs

The direction by the court as to how the SJE's fees should be divided between the parties does not decide the issue of which party will ultimately bear the costs of the expert—this will depend on the ultimate order for costs that the court makes. The earlier direction indicating the share each party should pay of the SJE's fees merely ensures that the expert gets paid.

When sending instructions for a report, it is necessary to ensure that the expert is aware of all of the issues in the case, where the burden of proof lies, and what the relevant standards of proof are. This will ensure that the expert produces the right kind of report.

19.8.5 EACH PARTY ENGAGING ITS OWN EXPERT

For each party to be able to adduce its own expert evidence at the trial of an action, a direction for each party to have its own expert must be made.

Given that there is so much emphasis on the use of SJEs in actions, when would it be appropriate to oppose the appointment of an SJE and seek instead an order that each party may instruct 'its own' expert?

The use of more than one expert may be justified if:

- there are several tenable schools of thought on the relevant issue;

- the issues on which the expert will be advising are very complex.

- the issues on which the expert will be advising are so important to the likely outcome of the case that the parties should be allowed to instruct their own expert;

- the value of the claim is sufficiently high that the appointment of separate experts would not be disproportionate;

- the parties have already appointed their own experts before proceedings began and it will be more cost-effective to continue using them, and to try to resolve the expert evidence issues through written questions and experts' discussions, rather than to appoint a new SJE; or

- the expert is being asked to report on difficult issues of liability and causation. It is more difficult to persuade the court of the need for separate experts where the issue to be addressed is quantum only, unless those issues are particularly complex and substantial.

Where the court has made an order that each party should have its own expert, it will normally wish to state the purpose or field of expertise required.

 Practical Considerations

If a specific expert is named in the order for directions, it will not be possible to use a different expert in that field without seeking the court's permission. If only the *field of expertise, not a named expert in that field*, is referred to, it will not be necessary to obtain permission to use a different expert. However, if more than one expert's report is obtained in the field directed and a party decides to rely on the later report, that party is likely to have to disclose the original expert's report—especially as the instructions are very likely to have referred to the first expert's conclusions.

19.8.6 AS AN 'AGREED' EXPERT

The distinction of what is an 'agreed' expert is not an easy one to define and the word is perhaps used by legal representatives without clearly defining what they mean by it, and where in reality what is being referred to is an SJE.

For clarity, an 'agreed' expert (otherwise referred to as a 'jointly selected expert' or a 'mutually accepted expert') is one proposed by the Personal Injury Protocol and is an expert retained in the pre-action phase. Under the Protocol, an expert (or a list of experts) is proposed by one party (usually, but not always, the claimant) to his opponent. If an expert is 'agreed' from that list, the expert remains that party's own, solely instructed expert, but the other party has the right to raise questions. If the expert is not 'agreed', the parties may instruct experts of their own choice.

19.8.7 THE EXPERT'S ROLE IN ADR

An expert may have a relevant and positive role to play in any ADR process—particularly in any mediation into which the parties enter. The parties may agree, or the mediator may require, that some areas of expertise be one of the areas that require examination in the mediation. If both parties have retained experts, they can be asked to explain their differences in a joint session in the mediation, so that all participants can get a better understanding of the different points of view. The expert's role in a mediation may be helpful in assisting the decision-making processes. Any legal representative in the process should be also aware of the difficulties that can arise in the use of experts in mediation: they could create further divisions; they may make admissions or concessions that may damage the strength of a party's negotiating position; costs will be increased; and issues of privilege may arise if the mediation does not result in a settlement and litigation proceeds. It is also worth noting, however, that using experts in ADR may have consequences in any subsequent proceedings on the issue of privilege. In *Aird v Prime Meridian Ltd* [2006] EWCA Civ 1866, the Court of Appeal held that a joint statement by experts used in a mediation could be disclosed and could be ordered to be produced within the proceedings, and concluded that it was not privileged just because it was used in the mediation.

19.9 CHOOSING AN APPROPRIATE EXPERT

It is important to choose an expert wisely, but equally it is important to select an expert who is available in the timescale that the court directions have allowed. A failure to find the right expert and instructing one who proves to be unable to deliver his report in time can be disastrous, and the court will not readily permit extensions of time for the preparation of a report, or to attend to questions, or to attend a meeting between experts without regard to the overriding objective.

19.9.1 THE EXPERT'S RETAINER

The Practice Direction on Experts and Assessors contains useful advice on appointing an expert in paragraphs 7.2 and 7.4. The terms of the retainer with an expert are suggested to include:

- the capacity in which the expert is to be appointed (that is, as an SJE, an expert adviser, or an expert for one party);
- the services required (that is, to prepare a report, answer questions, have a meeting with any other expert appointed, participate in the preparation of an expert's schedule of issues, attend court, etc.);
- the time for the delivery of the report; and
- the basis of the expert's fees, and how disbursements will be dealt with and whether any cancellation charges have been agreed. How and when the expert will be paid and whether his fees will be subject to assessment by a costs officer.

 Practical Considerations

It may be helpful to set out the terms of the retainer with the expert separately from the letter of instruction to that expert. If this is done, the expert should be asked to acknowledge the retainer letter and confirm that he accepts the terms of appointment. A sample letter of retainer is available to lecturers in the Online Resource Centre.

 online resource centre

19.9.2 DEALING WITH AN UNFAVOURABLE EXPERT

Because of the need for impartiality of the expert evidence, it can be difficult to deal with the expert who proves to be unfavourable, whether this is an SJE or an expert for one party only. Where this happens, any application to the court for permission to obtain an alternative expert report or for leave to appoint a new expert is likely to be met either with an order refusing permission (because it would not be within the provisions of the overriding objective to give permission), or where permission is being granted, an order that the earlier report also be disclosed with the alternative expert's report. On the basis that any subsequent expert is likely to have had sight of the earlier report and have been asked to comment on it, any privilege attaching to the earlier report will be lost. The recent decision of *Edwards-Tubb v J D Wetherspoon plc* [2011] EWCA Civ 136 highlights the court's view when a further expert is being sought by a party—here the courts concluded that it should be 'the usual' order to make any permission for a further expert to be used to be conditional on the first expert's report being disclosed.

Practical Considerations

How can you deal with an unhelpful SJE?

If the report of the SJE is adverse to your client's case, it can be very difficult to remedy the damage caused. If the case is substantial and the expert evidence is crucial, or at least very important, then an application for permission to adduce further expert evidence should be made, and in those circumstances (crucial or very important), permission will often be granted. The application will be on Form N244, with supporting reasons. Sometimes, an advisory expert's report will assist. However, the concept of proportionality is also a factor the court will take into account, and if the amount at stake in the action is small, the court may decide that further questions to the expert may be the way forward rather than an order for another report from another expert. Before any application for a further expert is made, the chances of the success of the application should be discussed with the client, including the costs consequences of the application and of the additional expert (or further questions to the expert). Before making such an application, cases such as *Smolen v Solon Co-Operative Housing Services Ltd* [2003] EWCA Civ 1240 and *Daniels v Walker* [2000] 1 WLR 1382 (at 1387) need to be considered.

19.9.3 **WHERE DO YOU FIND AN EXPERT?**

One of the most effective ways of selecting an expert will be by recommendation, and in this, your client (possibly with the exception of personal injury claims) may be an obvious starting point. They will have a feel for who is rated in their industry. However, whenever taking the client's views, it is important to ensure that there is no possibility of a conflict arising for the expert or a finding that the expert is not sufficiently impartial (but note the special circumstances referred to in paragraph 19.9.2 above).

However, a search for an appropriate expert may also be made by:

• reviewing any lists of experts previously used that your client may hold—usually with an assessment of that expert and whether it is worth using them or not;

• consulting Judicial Studies Board publications;

• consulting the Expert Witness Institute; or

• consulting the Academy of Experts—which advances the role of expert evidence in the following ways:

  • it keeps and provides a directory of members, categorized according to discipline and experience;

  • it develops and maintains the standards of excellence—vetting all applicants for practising membership; and

  • it is cooperating with, and making representations to, judicial and legal authorities, government departments, official enquiries, and tribunals to ensure that the best use is made of experts' advice;

• following the recommendation of other lawyers working in that field, colleagues, opponents, the Association of Personal Injury Lawyers (APIL), counsel, and other experts.

Clearly, the 'type' of expert needed will be indicated by the nature of the case and the issues on which the expert will be expected to comment: for example, in a case needing technical expertise in manufacturing, an engineer may be what is required; on accounting matters, an accountant. It is necessary to be clear of exactly what the expert is needed for and this may not necessarily be directly related to the subject matter of the cause of action.

It is also important that the retained expert is well respected in his field. Notoriety, or a person who has a reputation for novel and untested theories, is not what is needed.

Additionally, the expert will ideally be a person who has some experience of being an expert witness—that is, a person who will not be undermined or intimidated by the judicial process or by cross-examination. Although it is perfectly proper to advise your expert of the *form* of their report and thereby assist them with the judicial process, it is not in any way acceptable to make any attempt to guide or influence the expert as to his *findings and conclusions*.

19.9.4 WHAT ENQUIRIES NEED TO BE MADE OF YOUR CHOSEN EXPERT?

You chosen expert will need to provide you with a curriculum vitae (CV) and references before they are engaged.

You will also need to assess whether they have the required experience for your case. One way in which you can do this is to give brief details of the case in which they will be expected to act as expert and to ask directly whether they think they have the requisite experience. Alternatively, you can make enquiries of them regarding details of:

- in which courts they have previously appeared;
- the nature of the cases in which they have previously been engaged; and
- their previous court experiences—for example, whether they have been cross-examined.

You will also need to ensure that there is no conflict of interest with engaging your chosen expert. To ensure this, you will need to advise the expert of the names of the other parties in the action, any other experts that have been engaged, and the names of the other party's legal representative, asking the expert to confirm that he has no conflict of interest. It has also been suggested that an expert should be required to make an additional statement at the end of his report in relation to conflicts of interest, although there is no formal requirement for this (see *Toth v Jarman* [2006] EWCA Civ 1028 for detail of the Court of Appeal's recommendation on this point).

Despite the fact that it is, in certain circumstances, acceptable to utilize an expert who is connected to a party (see paragraph 19.9.2 above), it is generally best to avoid any connection with the instructing party and care should, wherever possible, be taken to ensure that:

- the recommendation does not come from colleagues or friends of the expert;
- the expert does not have any out-of-court contact with judges, or the parties, or their legal representatives, on their cases.

19.9.5 CHECKING THE AVAILABILITY OF AN EXPERT

With the timetable of an action being strictly controlled by the court and because, particularly in the fast track, the timetable of the time to trial is short (within 30 weeks from allocation), the availability of the expert to be able make his enquiries, deliver his report, deal with any questions, and take any further steps directed by the court, as well as be available at trial if he is required to give oral evidence, is vital. The courts will not readily adjourn the proceedings to fit in with the availability of expert evidence. It is the responsibility of the legal representative to ensure that the chosen expert will be available within the timescale set down by the court.

19.10 HANDLING EXPERT EVIDENCE AND PREPARING A LETTER OF INSTRUCTION TO AN EXPERT

A copy of any order concerning expert evidence must be served on the expert by the party instructing him. If the expert is an SJE, then the claimant must serve the expert (PD 35.6A).

The duties of an expert are clearly set down in CPR 35.3:

(1) It is the duty of an expert to help the court on matters within his expertise.

(2) This duty overrides any obligation to the person from whom he has received instructions or by whom he is paid.

It will be for the legal representative to ensure that the expert understands his duties. A good letter of instruction will be well structured and, it is suggested, should include (at least) the following:

- basic information, such as names, addresses, and contact details of those instructing the expert;
- notice that the report should be addressed to the court, be in the first person, and should set out the expert's qualifications;
- other contact details—for example, those of the client;
- guidance on whom to contact in the first instance if queries or instructions need amending or clarifying;
- advice that there should be no formal or informal unrecorded discussions;
- a summary of the case and the purpose of the report, or of the issues that it should cover, including specific questions to address;
- a chronology, which should include a programme of the key dates of which the expert should be aware;
- reference to, and a list attached of, all documents and/or relevant evidence (that is, relevant to the expert);
- general points that the expert should address and advice on the 'form' of the report (but not, of course, its content). This may include the guidance set down in CPR PD35 paragraph 2.4, which states the form of the expert's statement of truth and declaration of awareness.
- suggested training in report-writing skills or courtroom skills—these may be tax-deductible and will provide continuing professional development (CPD) points for the expert;
- an emphasis of the overriding duty to the court;
- a request that the report be signed and contain a statement of truth; and
- many practitioners will also send a copy of CPR Part 35 or the Expert Protocol, with particular reference to guidelines for the expert.

The obligations of an expert witness were summarized and clarified (by Cresswell J in the Court of Appeal) in the *Ikarian Reefer* case (*National Justice Compania Naviera SA v Prudential Assurance Co Ltd (No 1)* [1993] 1 Lloyd's Reports 455, [2000] 1 WLR 603, [2001] WL 753347:

(a) Expert evidence presented to the court should be seen to be the independent product of the expert uninfluenced as to form or content by the exigencies of litigation.

(b) An expert witness should provide independent assistance to the court by way of objective unbiased opinion in relation to matters within his expertise. An expert witness in the court should never assume the role of advocate.

(c) An expert witness should state the facts or assumptions on which his opinion is based. He should not omit to consider material facts which detract from his concluded opinions.

(d) An expert should make it clear when a particular question or issue falls outside his expertise.

(e) If an expert's opinion is not properly researched because he considers that insufficient data is available then this must be stated with an indication that the opinion is no more than a provisional one.

(f) If, after exchange of reports (if there is more than one expert), or at any other time, an expert witness changes his view on a matter, such change of view should be communicated to the parties (or party) instructing him without delay and, when appropriate, to the court.

Further guidance of what should be included in an expert's report is contained in the case of *Bowman v Fels* [2005] EWCA Civ 226:

(a) Details of the expert's academic and professional qualifications, experience and accreditation relevant to the opinions expressed in the report and the range and extent of the expertise and any limitations upon his expertise.

(b) A statement setting out the substance of all the instructions received (written and oral), questions asked, the materials provided and considered, and the documents, statements, evidence, information or assumptions which are material to the opinions expressed or upon which the opinions are based.

(c) Information relating to who has carried out measurements, examinations, tests, etc. and the methodology used, and whether or not such measurements etc were carried out under the expert's supervision.

(d) Where there is a range of opinion in the matters dealt with in the report a summary of the range of opinion and the reasons for the opinion given. In this connection any material facts or matters which detract from the expert's opinions and any points which should fairly be made against any opinions expressed should be set out.

(e) Relevant extracts of literature or other material which might assist the court should be referred to and may be attached.

(f) A statement to the effect that the expert has complied with his duty to the court to provide independent assistance by way of objective unbiased opinion in relation to matters within his expertise. An acknowledgement that the expert will inform all parties, and where appropriate, the court, in the event that his opinion changes on any material issues.

(g) Where, on exchange of experts' reports (where there is more than one expert) matters arise which require a further, or supplemental, report the above guidelines should be complied with.

A synopsis of this is contained in CPR 35.10, PD 35.2, and the Experts Protocol at sections 7, 8, and 13.

A sample letter of instruction is available to lecturers on the Online Resource Centre.

online resource centre

19.10.1 COPING WITH EXPERTS' REPORTS

To be effective, the expert's report needs to be comprehensible to the parties, the legal representative, and any other professional employed to assist in the case, as well as the court.

When an expert's report has been received, not only will the report need to be carefully read, but the implications of it will also need to be understood. Additionally, there will be more peripheral matters to consider. These include a need to check whether:

- there has been full disclosure regarding all documents upon which the expert relies;

- the chronology schedule to the particulars of claim accords with the expert's chronology;

- there are any discrepancies or inconsistencies in the lay evidence that is being adduced. If there are, have all discrepancies or inconsistencies been identified and explained? Alternatively, check that the expert evidence dovetails with the witness statements and pleadings in the case; and

- the evidence covers all of the issues.

 Practical Considerations

The following represents a template 'checklist' that might be used when receiving any expert report.
Content A legal representative cannot influence the content and conclusions of the expert, but the following is a list of the matters that should be considered when an expert's report is received.

- Can you understand it?

- Is it in layperson's language? Are technical terms explained?

- Is it independent?

- Does it have the 'declaration' (understanding expert's role and duty)?

- Is it authoritative?

- Is it persuasive?

- Does the expert avoid going outside his area of expertise?

- Have opinions been qualified where they are outside the area of expertise?

- Are 'facts', 'assumptions', and 'opinions' clearly defined?

- Is it signed?

Form Under the provisions of CPR 35, the report should be in proper form. Has the expert:

- given his name?

- given his address?

- identified his specialist area?

- included his qualifications and experience?

- confirmed his instructions?

- added a summary?

- inserted paragraph numbers and/or headings?

- inserted page numbers? (Is an index necessary?)

- included a glossary?

- dealt with the issues to be addressed?

- dealt with the facts (research, experiments, investigation)?

- given his opinion?

- stated the range of opinions in the field and commented on the reasons for this?

- concluded his report?

- included any necessary appendices for his investigations, references. or exhibits, etc?

 Practical Considerations

When instructing an expert, whether as your own expert or an SJE it is important that the expert is asked to cover all the 'lifestyle' aspects of your client's case so that the expert can comment on the way the claimant's injuries have affected his pre-accident lifestyle. In this way, where the expert agrees, the claimant's own witness statement will be supported by the medical report. This will give considerable evidential weight to the claimant's claim under the heads of damage. The expert should be asked to allow sufficient time in his appointment with the claimant to discuss these aspects of his lifestyle changes.

19.10.2 DEALING WITH QUESTIONS TO AN SJE OR THE OPPOSING PARTY'S EXPERT

The written questions to experts should be 'proportionate'. This is intended to avoid instances when the questions put to an expert go beyond the issues identified in the case.

CPR 35.6 contains the provisions that permit either party to put questions to an SJE or to the opposing party's own expert. It includes provisions that:

- questions may be put to that expert once;
- questions be put to the expert within 28 days of receipt of the report; and
- questions must be for the purpose of clarifying the report.

The court may, however, modify these provisions either on its own initiative or upon the application of a party.

The expert will be required to answer the questions put to him as directed and in the time ordered by the court. His answers will be treated as part of his report. If the expert fails to answer questions put to him, the court may direct that the expert's evidence cannot be relied on and/or provide that the costs of that expert shall not be recoverable by the party who has engaged him. A party raising questions should serve a copy of the questions on the other parties in the action. The party asking the questions must initially bear the costs of the expert in answering the questions, but this does not affect any decision that the court may make concerning the costs orders that it may make at the conclusion of the case.

The CPR state that the questions to an expert should only be 'for the purpose of clarifying the report'. This is not defined by the rules. In *Mutch v Allen* [2001] EWCA Civ 76, the Court of Appeal considered the meaning of 'clarification' and concluded that it did enable a party to put a question to the expert that would have the effect of extending his report—that is, a question may be put on a matter not covered in the report. However, if the questions put to the expert are oppressive, in number or content, the court will not hesitate to disallow or restrict the questions asked.

19.10.3 DISCUSSIONS BETWEEN EXPERTS

Experts' discussions may take place at any time by arrangement between the parties, but they are usually ordered by the court in a direction made at a CMC (see paragraph 19.7 above) (CPR 35.12). The court may also direct that the experts produce a statement after their discussions, setting out those areas on which they agree and those on which they do not. In the areas in which they disagree, they should give reasons.

 Practical Considerations

The CPR do not specify exactly how meetings of experts should be set up. The Practice Direction on Experts and Assessors, at paragraph 18, sets out guidelines on how the parties and their legal representatives should cooperate in preparing an agenda, and making all of the necessary arrangements. The Practice Direction specifically states that instructing solicitors must not seek to restrict these discussions in such a way to 'avoid reaching areas of agreement on areas within their competence', but they can be reminded not to disclose certain confidential information of their client's. Equally, the legal representative must not instruct the expert to submit any schedule of agreed issues for 'approval' before it is finalized.

The Practice Direction on Experts and Assessors states, at paragraph 18.8, that legal representatives should not be present at the meeting of experts unless all parties and their experts have agreed, or the court orders the presence of legal representatives. In practice, many meetings of experts take place over the telephone for convenience and costs reasons.

Practical Considerations

A practical compromise to the probable exclusion of legal representatives at the meeting between experts is to provide that both parties' legal representatives will be available on the telephone at the time of the meeting, so that they may be available if and when the experts determine that they need to speak to them.

19.10.4 THE EXPERT'S RIGHT TO ASK THE COURT FOR DIRECTIONS

Experts are entitled to ask the court for directions to assist them in carrying out their responsibilities and duties to the court, and where they feel that they need assistance. If the expert does ask the court for directions in this way, he is required to let his instructing party have a copy of his request to the court at least seven days before filing it at court, and all other parties, at least four days before his request is filed (these times can be varied by the court in the directions order that it makes concerning expert evidence).

 Practical Considerations

It may be a good idea to include in your terms of engagement with the expert a provision concerning the notification of any request to the court for directions. This will give the legal representative the chance to explore with the expert whether it is possible to resolve the difficulties that the expert has identified, and if it is not possible to resolve the issue that the expert has identified, to assist him in formulating the request to the court.

19.10.5 THE EXPERT AT COURT

Oral evidence at trial can only be given with the court's permission and this includes expert oral evidence. In the fast track, the court is more likely to order that expert evidence be adduced in writing and that there is no oral expert evidence. Where oral expert evidence is provided for, the order will probably not be given until after the pre-trial checklist, which will be after the conclusion of experts' meetings and the preparation of the schedule of issues between the experts. If a party seeks an order for expert oral evidence, he will be expected to establish all, or one, or some, of the following:

- that the expert oral evidence is likely to have an impact on the outcome of the case;
- that the expert oral evidence will assist the judge;
- that there is a risk of injustice if the expert evidence is not tested at trial; or
- that the costs of expert oral evidence are not disproportionate.

 Practical Considerations

If your expert is giving oral evidence at trial, it is important that you make the necessary arrangements concerning the expert's availability (that is, serve a witness summons—see Chapter 20, paragraph 20.4.1), and that he is aware what to expect and of the likelihood of cross-examination. If the trial is listed for several days, consideration should have given in the trial timetable to provide on which day(s) the expert should be available. It is important, though, that the expert is in court not only for the time of his own oral evidence, but also for the time during which other evidence is being given that is within his area of expertise, so that he is able to comment on it and explain its significance. A single expert may assist his instructing party in the cross-examination of a witness or expert of the opponent. If the expert is not giving oral evidence or is not in court when judgment is given, as a matter of courtesy, make sure you that inform the expert of the outcome of the case.

19.10.6 PRACTICAL MATTERS—THE EXPERT'S ORAL EVIDENCE

Prior to attending court to give evidence, you need to ensure that the expert being called as a witness is aware that he will be expected:

- to speak clearly, briefly, and in simple, non-technical terms, where possible;
- to look at the judge, rather than the legal representative;
- not to be evasive, obstructive, hostile, or obstinate when his opinion is shown to be wrong—particularly if the point is not detrimental to the client;
- to be detached and concerned for the truth at all times, and not to be perceived as always allied with only one side;
- to be positive and assured about having his experience tested under cross-examination and not be resentful or antagonistic;
- not to become emotionally involved with the client;
- to stay within the boundaries of his own expertise and experience;
- to come up to proof;
- to be well prepared and as knowledgeable about the case as possible, including his opinion on prognosis; and
- not to be mislead by omissions—you need to ensure that he has, and has considered, all of the material facts.

19.10.7 PRACTICAL MATTERS—THE EXPERT'S WRITTEN EVIDENCE

If experts look for and report on factors that tend to support a particular proposition, the report should still:

- provide a straightforward, not misleading, written opinion that the court will readily understand;
- be objective and not omit factors that do not support the expert's opinion—remembering that you may find that the expert has to give an opinion that is adverse to your client, and if this occurs, you need to consider how to inform the client;
- be properly researched—if the expert considers that insufficient data is available, then he should say so and indicate that his opinion is no more than a provisional one.

19.11 THE EXPERT AND HIS IMMUNITY FROM SUIT

The common law concept of witness immunity is that all witnesses, including expert witnesses, are immune from civil suit, in that 'no action lies against parties or witnesses for anything said or done, although falsely and maliciously and without any reasonable or probable cause, in the ordinary course of any proceedings in a court of justice' (*Dawkins v Lord Rokeby* (1873) LR 8 QB 255, 264). However the justification for giving immunity from suit has been questioned in recent cases. In the recently handed down judgment of *Jones v Kaney* [2011] UKSC 13 the Supreme Court, by a majority decision, has concluded that the immunity from suit that experts have had in the work they undertake in legal proceedings should be abolished. This was probably an inevitable decision as a barrister's previously enjoyed immunity was abolished several years ago (*Arthur JS Hall & Co v Simons* [2002] 1 AC

615, 740). There were dissenting judgments (Lord Hope and Lady Hale, who felt there was not justification, on the facts, to remove the immunity from suit) so we cannot be sure that the case is the final word on this.

19.12 EXPERTS AND PRIVILEGE

An expert's report, which is prepared for the purpose of contemplated or pending civil actions for obtaining or giving legal advice, is privileged. There is no obligation to disclose a report on which the party does not intend to rely at trial. Provided that a report is not used as a source of evidence, it may be used in cross-examination of the other side's expert—to test the strength of his opinion. However, once a report has been disclosed by a party, notwithstanding any later decision not to adduce it as evidence at trial, the opponent is permitted to rely on it if he so wishes. This is because once a report has been disclosed, it loses its privilege.

Disclosure of a privileged report cannot be ordered in a subsequent claim. However, this rule may not apply if, as the result of a second accident, the claimant sustains an injury to a part of his body that has already been injured at an earlier accident, so that it is material to know what his state was before the second accident occurred. If, in these circumstances, the legal representative who acted for the defendant in respect of the earlier accident has in his possession a medical report that bears upon the issue that is material to decide in the subsequent claim, he may be ordered to disclose that report (*Earle v Medhurst* [1985] CLY 2650).

Any advice given by an expert acting in an advisory role for a party will be privileged (*Carlson v Townsend* [2001] EWCA 511).

In *Aird v Prime Meridian Ltd* [2006] EWCA Civ 1866 (see also paragraph 19.8.7 above), the Court of Appeal concluded that the joint experts' statement produced as a result of their meeting and ordered by the court as part of its general directions order under CPR 35.12(3) was not privileged, even though it was prepared in advance of a mediation. The court concluded that it was not appropriate to 'look behind' the case management order. The court reasoned that, viewed objectively, the order had been made as part of its standard case management directions concerning the use of expert evidence and that, on that basis, it would not be privileged. It concluded that the statement did not become privileged because the statement was used in the 'without prejudice' forum of mediation.

19.12.1 WHEN WILL EXPERTS' REPORTS BE DISCLOSED?

In personal injury claims, the claimant must disclose a report when issuing proceedings. Any further use of expert evidence in personal injury actions will be controlled by the court in the normal way (see paragraph 19.3 above).

In all other cases, the courts will usually make orders detailing the exchange of experts' reports as part of its case management directions. Usually, reports will be ordered to be exchanged after an appropriate period of time, but usually after disclosure and exchange of witness statements. Generally, disclosure of expert evidence should be simultaneous. PD 29.4.11 provides that if it appears that expert evidence will be required both on issues of liability and on the amount of damages, the court may direct that the exchange of those reports that relate to liability will be exchanged simultaneously, but that those relating to the amount of damages will be exchanged sequentially.

19.13 EXPERTS AND THE JACKSON REPORT

Lord Jackson has made some far-reaching suggestions on experts but acknowledged that CPR 35 now deals with the issue of experts adequately.

FIGURE 19.1

CURRENT POSITION	LORD JACKSON'S PROPOSALS
1. Whilst the court has powers under CPR 35 to control expert evidence, they are not being used regularly to control the costs of an expert.	Judges should make appropriate use of CPR 35.4(4) to restrict recoverable costs.
2. The Practice Direction on Pre Action Conduct contains provisions on expert evidence (Annex C).	Annex C may be repealed if his recommendations concerning protocols are adhered to. He felt that Annex C was flawed as it could not fit all types of cases, particularly complex actions.
3. CPR 35 makes no reference to the provision of a costs estimate (or the cost of that evidence) to the court as a prerequisite for an order permitting the use of expert evidence at trial.	CPR 35 or its PD should be amended to require that a person seeking permission to adduce expert evidence furnish an estimate of the cost of that evidence to the court.
4. Oral expert evidence at trial is given consecutively, i.e. the claimant's case including any expert evidence and then the defendant's case including his expert evidence, both with the opportunity to cross-examine.	The hot-tubbing of experts in the witness box: both experts give evidence concurrently in court and are asked to respond to each other 'on the spot'. This is currently being piloted in some specialist courts.

KEY POINTS SUMMARY

- The key provisions of CPR Part 35 are:
  - CPR 35.1—there may be no experts at all;
  - CPR 35.2—expert evidence defined;
  - CPR 35.3—expert's duty to court prevails;
  - CPR 35.4—court control;
  - CPR 35.6—questions to experts;
  - CPR 35.7—single joint experts;
  - CPR 35.9—sharing unilateral expertise;
  - CPR 35.12—experts' discussions;
  - CPR 35.14—experts applying to the court.
- Experts have a variety of roles (and uses) in litigation—be sure to understand the distinctions.
- Expert evidence can only be adduced in litigation with the permission of the court. Essentially, it will only be permitted if it can be shown to be probative, useful, and cogent, and the cost of obtaining it must be proportionate.
- The duties and obligations of the expert to the court take precedence over any obligations that he may feel to the party who engages or is paying him. Remember the 3 'i's of an expert: integrity; independence; and impartiality.
- A legal representative may influence and guide the expert of the *form* of his report, but not its *content* or the *conclusions* reached by the expert. There must be complete transparency of communication between expert and legal representative.
- The trial judge is ultimately the person who decides on which of two conflicting opinions he will rely and he can reject expert opinion in favour of the evidence of witnesses of fact.
- Handling experts and expert evidence takes considerable care and skill.

Case study *Andrew James Pike and Deep Builders Ltd*

Question 1

In this case, you have now received, from the court, the allocation questionnaire (Form N150). Do you feel that you should ask for a direction that each party may instruct, and rely on, their own expert? If so, what are your reasons for this and what directions do you think you should ask the court to make? If you think the appropriate order should be for an SJE, give your reasons for this and suggest the directions order that you will seek.

Question 2

Prepare a letter instructing an SJE in this matter.

online resource centre

Any documents referred to in these case study questions can be found on the Online Resource Centre—simply click on 'Case study documentation' to access the documents that you need for Chapter 19 and to be reminded of the questions above. Suggested answers to these case study questions can also be accessed on the Online Resource Centre by your lecturer.

Relevant court forms relating to this chapter:

- **N20 Witness Summons**
- **N260 Statement of Costs for Fast Track Trials**
- **N292 Draft Consent Order (Children's Claims)**
- **N320 Court Funds Form (Children's Claims)**

Within the online resource there is a short podcast that will help you understand the nature and purpose of Tomlin orders.

online resource centre

20.1 INTRODUCTION

Despite the fact that the whole philosophy of litigation today is to avoid trial by engaging in and complying with Protocol, alternative dispute resolution (ADR), and case management, all legal representatives need to know how to run a case up to trial and through the trial day itself. A high percentage of civil cases settle well in advance of trial, but it is still important for you to look to the possibility of running a case to trial, because this is, in essence, the benchmark of the basis of your advice to your client—the benefit to your client of settling at an earlier stage, or continuing to fight or defend a case, is measured against what is likely to happen on the day of the trial.

This chapter will therefore focus on:

- fast-track and multi-track cases that proceed to trial;

- professional conduct issues;

- procedural and administrative preparation for trial;

- the day of the trial;

- judgment and appeals; and

- settlement without trial.

20.2 **RULE 11 OF THE SOLICITORS' CODE OF CONDUCT 2007**

Throughout your retainer with your client, right up to and including the trial, you must be mindful of your professional conduct obligations. In particular, at this stage of the action, you need to acknowledge that the Solicitors' Code of Conduct 2007, Rule 11, deals with your litigation and advocacy obligations. For the sake of clarity, we set out the relevant paragraphs of Rule 11, as follows.

11.01 Deceiving or misleading the court

(1) You must never deceive or knowingly or recklessly mislead the court.

(2) You must draw to the court's attention:

    (a) relevant cases and statutory provisions;

    (b) the contents of any document that has been filed in the proceedings where failure to draw it to the court's attention might result in the court being misled; and

    (c) any procedural irregularity.

(3) You must not construct facts supporting your client's case or draft any documents relating to any proceedings containing:

    (a) any contention which you do not consider to be properly arguable; or

    (b) any allegation of fraud unless you are instructed to do so and you have material which you reasonably believe establishes, on the face of it, a case of fraud.

...

11.05 Appearing as an advocate

If you are appearing as an advocate:

(a) you must not say anything which is merely scandalous or intended only to insult a witness or any other person;

(b) you must avoid naming in open court any third party whose character would thereby be called into question, unless it is necessary for the proper conduct of the case;

(c) you must not call into question the character of a witness you have cross-examined unless the witness has had the opportunity to answer the allegations during cross-examination; and

(d) you must not suggest that any person is guilty of a crime, fraud or misconduct unless such allegations:

    (i) go to a matter in issue which is material to your client's case; and

    (ii) appear to you to be supported by reasonable grounds.

As a new legal representative in practice, Rule 11.01 will feature more heavily in the work that you do than Rule 11.05, by virtue of the fact that you will not be conducting your own advocacy (unless in small claims cases). Nevertheless, you need to be aware of the whole picture and the Guidance Notes to Rule 11 are helpful, giving examples of what is considered to be deceiving or misleading the court, and when you should attend court to sit behind counsel.

20.3 AN ADVOCATE'S LIMITED IMMUNITY FROM SUIT

A solicitor-advocate or counsel will only be liable in negligence in respect of his work as an advocate when it can be shown that 'the error was one that no reasonably competent member of the profession would have made' (*Arthur J S Hall & Co v Simons* [2000] UKHL 38). Mere 'error of judgment' on the part of the advocate will not make him liable in negligence. In practice, this means that an action against a solicitor-advocate or counsel who acts honestly and carefully is unlikely to succeed. More recent case law has further defined this level of competence to one that is also related to the advocate's level of expertise (or seniority) (*William v Leatherdale & Francis* [2008] EWHC 2574 (QB)). This test was also applied in the Technology and Construction Court (TCC) case of *McFaddens (a firm) v Platford* [2009] EWHC 126. It cannot be finally concluded from the judgments of these cases that the 'seniority' test can be relied on in all situations in which a solicitor-advocate or barrister is in court.

20.4 IMMEDIATE ACTION ON RECEIPT OF THE TRIAL DATE

Once the court has dealt with the pre-trial checklist (PTC) and any necessary pre-trial review or hearing, the court will then list the matter for trial. Once this has been done, it will then dispatch to all parties a notice of hearing, informing the parties of the trial date. There are a number of important matters that a legal representative needs to deal with and these are outlined below.

20.4.1 ISSUE WITNESS SUMMONSES

As soon as you receive the notice of hearing from the court, you will need to consider which witnesses and experts will be required to attend the trial, either to give oral evidence or to produce specified documents. You should already have, by this stage, permission from the court to rely on and adduce such evidence at trial. It is therefore extremely important that you prepare, issue, and arrange for the service of a witness summons in respect of each witness and expert in Form N20 (see the Online Resource Centre for a copy of the form). The purpose of the summons is to compel attendance at trial.

online resource centre

Professional Conduct

If a witness or expert subsequently fails to attend trial having been validly served with a witness summons, then they will either be fined if in the county court (County Courts Act 1984, s. 55(1) and (2)), or be found to be in contempt if in the High Court. If, however, you omit to deal with the issue and service of witness summonses, and one of your witnesses fails to attend court, you are likely to be in breach of Solicitors' Code of Conduct 2007, Rules 1.04 and 1.05, be the subject of a wasted costs order if the trial is adjourned, or be faced with a professional negligence action if the evidence of the absent witness was crucial to the success of the case.

In order for the witness summons to be valid, Form N20 must be correctly completed and sent to the court. You can decide whether you wish to serve the witness summons yourself, in which case, you will need to send three copies to the court. If you decide that you want the court to serve the summons, then the court requires only two copies. In either case, the summons will only be valid if you enclose a court fee and a sum of money in respect of the witnesses' reasonable expenses and compensation for loss of time (known as 'conduct money'—see CPR 34.7). Service must be effected at least seven days before the date of the trial (CPR 34.5).

 Practical Considerations

Some legal representatives prefer not to serve experts with witness summons, because they feel this is disrespectful, and that it is implied in the expert's duty to the court and acceptance of instructions that he will attend the trial of the matter. However, others believe that all witnesses giving oral evidence or producing documents to the court at trial should be summonsed to 'cover their backs' against the risk of a potential professional negligence claim should the expert fail to attend. We would recommend that a politely worded covering letter to the expert explaining the purpose and nature of the summons would alleviate any professional discomfort on the part of the legal representative, whilst affording him the protection that he and his client deserve. In any event, witnesses, such as the police, will not attend trial unless served with a witness summons. Further, witness summonsing your expert allows him to clear his diary and to prevent non-attendance by a supervening incident—particularly if a medical expert.

20.4.2 **CONTACT COUNSEL**

Unqualified practitioners are not permitted to act as trial advocates in fast-track or multi-track cases, although you may have the opportunity to undertake trial advocacy in small claims cases. You will need to ensure that you have the appropriate solicitor-advocate or barrister to undertake the advocacy. In this section, we refer to the trial advocate as 'counsel'.

 There is a chapter on the Online Resource Centre on drafting instructions to counsel.

 Professional Conduct

When considering this and advising the client, you are under a duty to act in the best interests of your client (Solicitors' Code of Conduct 2007, Rule 1.04, and Guidance Note 4 to Rule 11). For example, you may have chosen a competent, relatively inexpensive, but fairly inexperienced counsel to advise on prospects of success at the outset of the case, but you have managed the case without further input from this counsel. As the trial approaches, you will need to consider with your client whether counsel with more trial experience would be more appropriate, even if that would entail instructing a more expensive counsel. You will also need to consider the timing of the change of counsel. (See below for conferences with counsel.) Any change in counsel for this reason before trial for should be detailed in a written note on the file and a letter to the client.

Once you have the trial date from court, practitioners will have the task of booking counsel for the trial and considering with the client and counsel whether a pre-trial conference is required. The simplest and quickest way of booking counsel is to contact the counsel's clerk directly over the telephone or by email. Remember that you will have already sought counsel's general availability for the trial window when completing the PTC. The court may have taken several weeks to list the matter and dispatch the notice of hearing to you, so you will need to act expeditiously, because counsel may, in the interim, have other commitments.

Counsel's clerk will place the details of the trial in the diary and this secures counsel for the trial. At this stage, there is no need to send any papers to counsel or to agree a fee. The terminology for this, when you come to undertake them, is important: when sending papers to counsel to advise, draft, or attend a conference (if you are seeking a conference with a Queen's Counsel, then it is called a 'consultation'), you are said to be 'instructing counsel' and the papers are known as 'instructions to counsel'. When you send papers to counsel to attend any interim or final hearing, you are said to be 'briefing counsel' and the papers are known as 'a brief'. The key point with a brief is that, as soon as this is 'delivered' to counsel, the brief fee is incurred—and there will be a liability to pay for counsel whether or not the trial or hearing goes ahead. This is the reason why briefing counsel is only done a matter of days before the hearing, because settlement efforts are at a premium at that stage.

 Practical Considerations

It is always worth ensuring you have a good relationship with counsel's clerk, because if they are on your side, they will be more likely to waive a brief fee for an aborted or adjourned hearing, or to squeeze in an urgent conference. It is the clerk who is responsible for agreeing all fees and arranging conferences with counsel. These are never discussed with counsel.

The brief fee that you agree covers counsel's preparation for the trial, excluding the time spent at any pre-trial conference, plus his attendance at court for the first day of the trial no matter for how long he is there. If the trial is listed for more than one day, then the clerk will discuss a refresher fee with you, which represents a percentage of the brief fee. For example, if the brief fee is £3,000 and the trial is listed for three days, the refresher fee for each of the two remaining days could be £1,500 per day, making total counsel's fee for the trial £6,000.

20.4.3 LIAISE WITH YOUR CLIENT

Another immediate task that you must undertake is to contact your client to inform him of the trial date. Again, you will have already obtained his available dates and inserted them in the PTC. It would also be sensible to ask your client to keep his diary relatively free for the few days in the run-up to the trial for settlement negotiations and generally, to enable you to seek instructions from him without delay. There is no requirement to witness summons your client.

20.4.4 CHECK YOUR DIARY

The trial date needs to be inserted into your diary, with the weeks before left relatively clear to focus on the final preparations for the trial bundles (see below) and settlement opportunities. The run-up to trial is an extremely busy time for legal representatives, whose workload for the few days before the trial becomes almost exclusively taken up with the matter in hand.

 Practical Considerations

It is good practice to have a central diary scheme or departmental white board, on which details of the trial date and venue can be posted, so that others in the department are aware that a trial is coming up or is taking place. This will indicate that you will be busy and out of the office for extended periods of time. Delegation of tasks on other files may have to be considered if another file demands attention whilst you are unavailable.

20.5 PREPARATION FOR TRIAL

20.5.1 ADMINISTRATIVE TASKS

20.5.1.1 How is the evidence at trial to be given?

It is extremely important that the trial flows without a hitch in terms of presentation of the evidence to the judge. You do not want to irritate your judge for any reason, so it is worth spending some time considering, both at the PTC stage and directly before trial, how the judge will hear the evidence. Special requirements in relation to the presentation of the evidence at trial should have been set out in the PTC. (See Chapter 12, paragraph 12.7.3.3, for a discussion on the PTC.)

A witness or expert may be giving evidence by video link, for which permission of the court is required. You may have video or audio recordings to play to the judge, some documents may need to be displayed electronically, or you may need access to the Internet. Similarly, an interpreter may be required. You will need to arrange all of these for the day of the trial by ensuring that there is a working video link facility at court, a video or DVD player available, a laptop and projector, an Internet connection, and a variety of visual displays, such as flip charts. The choice and costs of the interpreter are also important.

20.5.1.2 Transcripts

In some lengthy trials, it may be appropriate to arrange for a daily transcript to be produced. There are two types of transcription service available: a daily transcript, which is available a few hours after the day's hearing has finished, and a realtime transcription, such as LiveNote. This is more expensive than the daily transcript, but allows you to follow the trial by reading the text on a laptop in court, which, in complex matters and lengthy cross-examination, allows you and your advocate to highlight salient points.

20.5.1.3 General arrangements

There are also a number of good general 'housekeeping' tasks for a legal representative to consider, such as ensuring that the court has sizeable and numerous conference rooms for meetings with counsel and the client before the trial starts and in which to debrief at the end of the day. Is there a canteen or restaurant at the court, and if not, what alternative arrangements can be made for lunch and general refreshments? Is the court near a railway station or car park (sometimes voluminous documentation is required to be taken to the court on the day of the hearing)?

20.5.1.4 Preparing your witness of fact for trial

Whilst witness summons have usually already been served in the run-up to trial, witnesses should be contacted shortly before the trial to firm up on final arrangements for meeting up at court, how to prepare for the trial, and what to expect when giving evidence. You should:

- ensure that the witness knows the location of the court and has made adequate travel arrangements;
- explain the layout of the court and where he will be giving evidence;
- advise him of the appropriate attire for his court appearance;
- outline what he should do to prepare to give evidence—he should be asked to review his and other relevant witness statements, and any relevant documentation; and
- advise him on giving his evidence. You should explain to him when and how long he is likely to be in the witness box, that he will be asked to take an oath or affirmation, how to address the judge, and remind him to address his answers to the judge, not counsel. It would also be useful to explain to him the process of cross-examination and re-examination, and to give him some tips on keeping calm in the witness box.

20.5.2 PREPARING THE TRIAL BUNDLES

20.5.2.1 What documentation goes into a trial bundle?

Trial bundles must be prepared for all trials and this is a task that usually falls to those new to practice. There are several points of reference to help you to decide when and what documentation is used to compile the trial bundles, as follows:

- the court order following the PTC and/or review or hearing;
- the Court Guides; and
- CPR 39 and its Practice Direction.

The trial bundles are prepared by the claimant's legal representative (CPR 39.5(1)), and getting the bundles right requires structured planning and attention to detail. They are very time-consuming to prepare and this should not be underestimated. The process begins with a review of all non-privileged documentation and the preparation of a trial bundle index. This should be sent to your counsel and opponent for approval before the actual documents are copied.

 Practical Considerations

When drafting the index, use your common sense as to what documents to include and in what order they should appear, remembering to exclude all privileged and without-prejudice documents, and to include only those that are necessary for the trial. For example, there is little point enclosing copy correspondence with the court, because this is unlikely to go to any issue in the case or the faxed duplicate version of a letter unless sending the letter by fax will help prove a point. Try to make the bundles as user-friendly as possible for the judge and counsel: a bundle that contains irrelevant, poorly copied, and obliterated material is unlikely to impress the judge.

The claimant must file the bundles between three and seven days before the start of the trial unless the court has made a different order (CPR 39.5, and PD 3.1 and 3.4). In more lengthy and complicated matters, the trial bundle can consist of a substantive bundle, an authorities' bundle, and a procedural bundle. Alternatively, depending on the amount of documentation, there may only be one substantive bundle, containing the following documents:

- the trial timetable* and statement of parties;*
- a schedule of issues;*
- a skeleton argument* and list of authorities* (plus a reading list, where appropriate);
- a case summary* and/or chronology,* where appropriate;
- the claim form and all statements of case;
- CPR 18 requests and replies;
- witness statements and summaries;
- notices of intention to rely on hearsay evidence and corresponding notices to attack credibility;
- notices of intention to rely on evidence, such as plans and photographs, under CPR 33.6;
- notices to admit;
- experts' reports;
- relevant orders for directions; and
- any relevant necessary documents.

* See paragraph 20.5.2.2 below.

20.5.2.2 Documentation specifically prepared for trial

The documents marked with an asterisk above are documents that are specifically prepared for the trial as a result of a court order or as per the requirements of the Court Guides. All of these documents, save for the skeleton arguments and list of authorities, are usually prepared by the claimant's solicitor and are usually agreed by the opponent.

- The trial timetable sets out what will happen in what order and for how long, on the day(s) of the trial. The judge does not always follow it. The statement of parties identifies who will be representing each party in terms of the legal team, including counsel, and details the party to the action and who will be attending on their behalf, if appropriate.

- The schedule of issues will list the main issues still outstanding between the parties on liability, causation, and quantum.

- The skeleton argument and list of authorities will be prepared by each party's trial advocate, and will set out in writing the legal basis for the party's case and the main submissions to be made on the day of the hearing. It may attach cases or statutes for the judge to read. Therefore, in line with the 'cards on the table' approach to litigation, both you and your opponent will have an outline of the major submissions to be made at trial.

- The case summary and chronology provide an outline of the case facts, and what is being claimed or refuted. Chronologies are not always necessary, but can be useful when dates and conduct are crucial to a case, such as in a breach of contract action.

20.5.2.3 The trial bundle index and the bundles

Once you have prepared, and your trial advocate has approved, the trial bundle index, this should be sent, usually by email, to your opponent's legal representative for agreement. Invariably, their counsel will want to approve the index too, so planning your preparation of the trial bundle index in advance is essential. It is not unusual for your opponent to request that additional documents be added to the index. The trial bundle is an agreed bundle, and it may take a little 'toing and froing' before agreement is reached.

Once it is agreed, the first bundles created can be paginated and the page numbering inserted in the index. Then, the copying begins. There should be a minimum of six duplicate bundles prepared: one each for the judge, yourself, and your counsel; one each for your opponent and his counsel; and one for the witness in court. It is probably a good idea to prepare a further trial bundle for your client and an extra copy to be left at the office. The copies for the judge and witness box must be filed within the deadlines stipulated above, but it is probably a good idea to liaise with the court clerk regarding the practical arrangements for delivery if the bundles are numerous or cumbersome.

 Practical Considerations

Questions often arise as to how best to deal with large documents, such as plans, poor-quality copies, hole-punching, and pagination. CPR 39 and its Practice Direction are helpful, as are the Court Guides, although most of the principles are based on common sense—for example:

- consider using separate files for very large documents, rather than including them in chronological order in the bundles;

- insist on the best copy quality and avoid copying from faxed versions;

- hole punch only where text will not be obliterated; and

- paginate where the number can be clearly seen and not omitted by the photocopier.

A final thought on the preparation of trial bundles is to focus on making the bundles as user-friendly as possible for the judge and counsel. Trial bundles that are too heavy, and overflowing with irrelevant materials and poor copies, are likely to frustrate your trial judge.

20.5.3 PART 36 OFFERS AND ADR

Now that most of the substantive matters in the action have been dealt with, you have attended to the filing of the PTC, and your trial preparation is in hand, this is another ideal time at which to continue your attempts to settle the case to avoid trial.

The 'Litigation train' diagram at the beginning of this chapter highlights that this is a good time to seek counsel's advice in conference for the purpose of defining views on liability, causation, and quantum, as well as for advice on making a well-pitched Part 36 offer or revised offer. In line with the overriding objective, it may now also be appropriate to reconsider ADR again (especially if you have not yet tried one of the processes). Counsel can also be asked for his views on which is the most suitable process.

20.5.4 **REVIEW FUNDING COVER**

Very often, there will be a need if your client is funded by insurance—whether after the event (ATE), before the event (BTE), or even a third-party funder—a trade union, or if your client is publicly funded, to report the pre-trial position to the funder and seek authority to proceed to trial.

20.5.5 **UPDATE DOCUMENTATION**

In some actions, from the initial preparation of documentation (particularly medical evidence and a variety of schedules) to trial, a significant amount of time has elapsed and the information contained in such documentation may need updating to ensure that the court has the most up-to-date and accurate information before it on the day of the trial. In the case of the medical report, for example, if the expert examined the claimant over a year before trial, you will need to check with the expert that the prognosis is still accurate, and he may need to re-examine the claimant and provide an up-to-date report. Similarly, if the schedule of losses in the particulars of claim has changed since issue (and this is very likely due to items being agreed or changed), this will also need revising, as will the defendant's counter-schedule.

 Costs

In the run-up to trial, costs are being incurred at a tremendous rate. Costs estimates will have been periodically prepared and updated for the court, and for your client, throughout the action. This is a final opportunity to consider—and discuss with your client—the overall costs of the action (with projected figures for the trial itself). In fast-track cases, Form N260 is required to be filed at least two clear days before the trial. In multi-track cases, there is no requirement to file a costs schedule, although it is best practice to have available up-to-date costs figures in any event.

20.6 **THE DAY OF THE TRIAL**

20.6.1 **MEETING UP**

Arrive at court early to ensure that you have a conference room for discussions with counsel and your client before the trial commences. As an alternative, if the court centre is local to either counsel or your firm's offices, this conference can take place at either of these locations, but ensure you allow ample time to make your way across to court in time for the 10 a.m. or 10.30 a.m. start. Once at court, you will need to keep an eye out for your witnesses as they arrive, and remind them that they are not allowed to discuss the case with either party and its respective legal team. It is part of your role on the day of the trial to ensure that the witnesses are prepared and ready to give evidence.

20.6.2 **TRIAL ETIQUETTE**

There are a number of important points to note and whilst some of these may seem elementary, the intensity of the run-up to trial and the trial day(s) can mean that these are sometimes overlooked.

• When the judge enters or leaves the room, the court usher will say 'Court rise'. Everybody must stand until the judge is seated or has left the room. The judge has his own private entrance to the courtroom and, on entering and leaving, he will bow to the court. Everybody must reciprocate. If you enter or leave the courtroom whilst the judge is sitting, then you should stand to face the judge and bow before sitting or leaving. It is important not to turn your back to the judge.

- Formal dress should be worn by all those attending court. Usually, dark-coloured suits are appropriate.

- All mobile phones and 'blackberries' should be switched off.

- If you must talk, this must be done as quietly as possible, only to communicate a message to your counsel or the court clerk, and only if urgent, otherwise you should wait until a break in the proceedings. Traditionally, legal representatives sitting behind counsel write a message and tug on counsel's gown to attract his attention to enable him to reach for the note. Take a pack of sticky notes in with you on which you can pass short notes to counsel.

 Practical Considerations

As the trial day progresses, there may be times during the day at which your counsel is making good progress in his cross-examination. It is very important for you, as well as your client, not to react in any way to evidence or submissions, because the judge sees all reactions. For example, if your counsel trips up your opponent's witness in your favour, under no circumstances should you laugh, or even smile. Similarly, if you disagree with what your opponent's counsel or witness is saying, then you are not to sigh or show signs of frustration.

20.6.3 A TYPICAL DAY IN COURT

The judge usually sits between 10 a.m. and 4 p.m., but, on occasions, he may sit later, depending on the progress of the trial and the availability of the court staff.

The usual format of the trial is as follows.

1. Opening submissions for the claimant.

2. Opening submissions for the defendant.

3. Any preliminary issues (these sometimes involve dealing with unforeseen events that arise on the morning of the trial—see below).

4. Claimant's witnesses of fact.

5. Claimant's expert evidence.

6. Defendant's witnesses of fact.

7. Defendant's expert evidence.

8. Closing submissions for the claimant.

9. Closing submissions for the defendant.

Depending on the nature of the case and the judge, opening submissions may be dispensed with if the skeleton arguments are sufficient. This is happening more frequently as it saves time on the day of the trial. Therefore, give thought to abandoning these opening submissions and discuss this with your trial advocate. In terms of all of the witnesses, they are subject to an examination-in-chief by their own counsel (although this is often limited to confirming their name, address, and that the witness statement in the trial bundle is their own), cross-examination by the opponent's counsel, and re-examination by their own counsel.

 Practical Considerations

The main function of the legal representative during the trial is to take detailed notes, irrespective of transcription services, and to be aware of any issue that needs to be brought to counsel's attention during trial. This is hard work, so ensure that you are alert and focused on what is being said in court at all times by all persons present. Ensure that you have enough paper; counsel notepads are often used by the legal team to make notes and an array of coloured pens is also useful to highlight the salient points that you may want counsel to consider at a break in the proceedings, or for the purposes of cross-examination. The notes can be reviewed at the end of the trial day.

20.6.4 UNFORESEEN EVENTS

On the eve of the trial, or even on the morning of the hearing, certain matters often arise, the most common of which are new evidence and attempts to amend statements of case on the part of your opponent. If something does arise, it is important to discuss it with counsel and your client, taking the time to assess the potential impact on your client's case, and whether and to what extent the late change should be opposed.

Occasionally, the trial will need to be adjourned, but this is really a last resort and clear costs orders will need to be made. If the trial is to go ahead, then you may wish to make the appropriate costs representations to the judge if the unforeseen event has an impact on your own client's costs, such as a new witness, which extends the length of the trial, or an amended particulars of claim, which requires an amended defence to be prepared.

20.7 AFTER THE TRIAL

There are a number of considerations that you will need to bear in mind when both parties have made their closing submissions and the trial has effectively finished. These are in relation to the judgment, costs, and appeals.

20.7.1 JUDGMENT

Fast-track trials or trials that have been relatively straightforward are more likely to have judgments available immediately after the completion of the closing submissions. In these cases, the judge may retire to his rooms to consider his judgment before coming back into the court to 'hand it down' to the parties' advocates. Once judgment has been given in these circumstances, then representations are made to the judge on the question of costs (see Figure 4.2 in Chapter 4 for the different types of costs order) and for permission to appeal. These are discussed in further detail below.

In most other cases, judgment is not usually handed down on the last day of the trial, because the judge requires time to evaluate all of the evidence heard and review any legal authorities. After closing submissions, the judge will inform the court that he will reserve judgment, and will fix a date, there and then, with the court clerk and the parties for the formal handing down of the judgment, which is frequently several weeks—or even months—from the completion of the trial.

 Practical Considerations

In some cases, clients have been waiting a long time for their case to come to trial. It is sensible to manage their expectations not only of the trial procedure itself, but also as to when they are likely to know whether they have substantially won or lost. The trial day(s) are the most expensive part of litigation and whether your client is under a conditional fee agreement (CFA), paying privately, or is funded by insurance, there may be additional legal fees and disbursements relating to the trial that need to be paid out before the judgment is handed down. A well-informed client is more likely to be patient and content during the period between trial and judgment.

Once the judge has prepared his judgment and the date that has been fixed for the formal handing down approaches, the judge may release his draft judgment to the parties. Draft judgments are technically confidential and should not be released to your client, although the judge may not, in every draft judgment, attach an embargo in this regard. Practice Direction 40E contains provisions dealing with how draft judgments should be treated.

Judgments are sometimes released in draft a day before the judgment is to be delivered to allow the parties time to consider whether they wish to seek any consequential orders or permissions to appeal, and to identify any typographical errors or other minor errors before the formal handing down, which is when the judgment becomes effective.

At the handing-down hearing, the judge will sit and recite his judgment, after which, the parties can make the various representations to the court, as highlighted above.

 Practical Considerations

In order to be prepared for the handing down of judgment hearing, which is only a short hearing, revisit the Court Guides on draft judgments and handing down, and be clear about what potential orders you may be required to make.

20.7.2 COSTS

Your client should have been given the requisite information on costs at the outset of your retainer with him and at appropriate intervals throughout his case. This information would include funding the litigation, the extent of costs recovery against the opponent, and the various costs orders that can be made by the court, including the basis upon which those costs are assessed. (See Chapter 3, paragraph 3.2, and Chapter 4, paragraph 4.3, for full details of your duty to your client in this regard.)

Therefore, by the time that the judgment is handed down, the costs consequences of winning or losing should come as no surprise to your client, even if the terms of the judgment do. The important feature here is to ensure that, at the hearing, you are in a position to do your best for your client when counsel is making representations to the judge on costs, either asking for an order for costs, or opposing an order for costs.

 Practical Considerations

You may wish to prepare in advance of the hearing a bundle for your counsel containing all of the Part 36 offers that have passed between the parties in the event that, should your client be successful, you have to hand information to help the judge decide whether any costs and interest enhancements should be made, or conversely, should your client have effectively lost, the bundle may assist the judge in deciding whether any penalties should be imposed as a result of your opponent not beating an offer.

Remember that, if it is a fast-track trial, then you should have prepared a statement of costs in a form similar to Form N260, as a summary assessment will be made. Fixed costs usually apply to fast-track trials (see Chapter 4, paragraph 4.7.2, and CPR 46).

20.7.3 APPEALS

An appeal is an application to a higher court requesting that all, or part, of the judgment made in the lower court be overturned. The current appeals system in the UK, from county court to Supreme Court, is set out in Chapter 1 at paragraph 1.7.3. In this section we are only going to look at the appeals process between county courts and the High Court as these are the type of appeals that you may come across as a junior practitioner. CPR 52 and its Practice Direction govern these appeals, along with the Access to Justice Act 1999, and concern decisions of the courts at interim hearings, as well as final hearings.

There are strict requirements for appeals in terms of the number of days from the judgment within which you can appeal and to which court. These must be observed, because there is no scope for either party to agree an alternative. In most cases, permission to appeal is required from the trial judge (or district judge or Master if an interim hearing) and you will need to persuade him that the actual appeal would have a real prospect of succeeding, or that there is another compelling reason why the appeal should be heard.

The application for permission to appeal must therefore be dealt with when judgment is given either on the last day of the trial, or at the handing-down hearing. This is done by oral submission alone.

 Practical Considerations

Should your client lose the trial, it may be worth considering making an application for permission to appeal in any event after judgment, even if you are unsure whether the appeal will eventually be lodged—it is more difficult and costly to apply for permission to appeal out of time.

There are two grounds of appeal: that the decision of the lower court was wrong, or that it was unjust because of a serious procedural or other irregularity. The appeal is filed on an appellant's notice in Form N161, and there are detailed requirements for the documentation to be filed with the N161 and for the appeal. Again, the Court Guides are also very useful to help you to prepare for the appeal.

In so far as costs are concerned for the appeal, the costs rules are generally the same as for other applications and hearings. However, it should be noted that the appeal court has a discretion over the costs of the appeal hearing, but also over the costs in the lower court. Your client will need to be informed of the cost implications before the appeal is launched. Part 36 offers can also be made in relation to costs hearings or the costs of an appeal.

20.8 CONCLUDING A CASE WITHOUT TRIAL

Parties can choose to settle their dispute either before proceedings are issued or during the litigation itself. Here, we look at how this can be done.

20.8.1 SETTLEMENTS REACHED BEFORE PROCEEDINGS

Settlements achieved without the need to issue proceedings are often as a result of an ADR process, such as negotiation or mediation.

However, once the terms of settlement have been reached, it is important to consider the cost provisions of the settlement, because there is no strict entitlement in the absence of an express agreement. As regards costs, the position is the same unless there is a contractual or statutory provision applicable. If the settlement concluded that one party would pay the other party's costs, but the terms of settlement have not confirmed the sum of those costs or a method by which they will be settled, then the receiving party can issue a Part 8 claim in respect of those costs under the provisions of CPR 44.12A.

20.8.1.1 Settlements generally

Once the terms of the settlement have been agreed, the agreement needs to be recorded in writing. Sometimes, it is sufficient for an exchange of correspondence between the parties to represent the agreement reached adequately. However, most legal representatives would prepare a separate document, commonly known as a 'compromise agreement', which would include all of the agreed terms. This compromise agreement, in effect, creates a legally binding contract between the parties that, if breached, enables a claim to be pursued for breach of the compromise agreement.

Practical Considerations

If a compromise agreement were to be breached, it is likely that the action that would follow would be commenced as a Part 7 claim in which a prompt application for summary judgment would be made. (See Chapter 14, paragraph 14.3, for details of a summary judgment application.)

20.8.1.2 Compromising a claim for a child or protected party

When a compromise of the action is reached before proceedings are issued on behalf of a child or protected party, then the party paying over the sum of the agreed settlement will not obtain a valid discharge unless the court has approved the settlement. Approval is sought by issuing a CPR Part 8 claim form (CPR 21.10(2)).

Practice Direction 21 sets out those documents that should be provided to the court. These are:

- a draft consent order in Form N292;
- a court funds Form 320; and
- the litigation friend's approval of the proposed settlement terms.

In personal injury actions, the following additional documents or details must be provided to the court:

- the circumstances of the accident;
- the (up-to-date) medical reports;
- the (up-to-date) schedule of loss and damage; and
- counsel's opinion (relating to the terms of the settlement).

If there is a claim for future pecuniary loss, the court must be satisfied that the parties have considered whether the damages should take the form wholly or partly as periodical payments.

Practical Considerations

The courts do not take 'infant approval settlements' lightly (also known as 'protected party settlements'). Common problems arise with a failure on the part of the legal representative to address minor important details and include: a failure to provide the birth certificate; failure to obtain a supplemental report where the child's injuries have persisted beyond the prognosis period outlined in the original medical report; a failure of the medical report to address certain issues that may impact on the amount of the damages that the child or protected party might be awarded. Usually, the child and his litigation friend will attend this hearing, and the judge will ask the child questions if he is old enough to understand and answer the questions put to him.

20.8.2 SETTLEMENTS REACHED AFTER PROCEEDINGS

20.8.2.1 Consent orders

If settlement has been reached during litigation, again by an ADR process, a consent order will need to be prepared (where both parties are legally represented) to record the terms of settlement of the dispute and the provision relating to costs. Care must be taken when drafting consent orders to ensure that all parties understand to what they are agreeing. An example of where this went wrong can be found in *Lucinda Newall v John Lewis* [2008] EWHC 910 (Ch). Once signed by both parties, the consent order is sent to the court for approval. In practice, it is rare for the court to interfere in the terms of settlement agreed between parties.

The term 'consent order' is a generic description for all orders that record settlements. As with pre-action settlements, the consent order is a legally binding contract and, if breached, the innocent party is entitled **to issue fresh proceedings** for breach of contract—that is, of the consent order.

A template consent order appears as Figure 20.1 at the end of this chapter.

20.8.2.2 Tomlin orders

In commercial claims, another piece of litigation on the back of the original claim may be frustrating, because a further action, even if short-lived, will be time-consuming, will necessitate the following of Protocols, and will incur costs and disbursements, during which time the breaching party may have absconded or become insolvent.

 Professional Conduct

You are likely to be in breach of Solicitors' Code of Conduct 2007, Rule 1.05, if you failed to draft a Tomlin order, but instead prepared a generic consent order, and your opponent subsequently disposed of its assets or became insolvent, rendering a recovery unlikely due to the time constraints of issuing fresh proceedings.

In an attempt to remedy this inconvenient position, a consent order can be drafted in a particular manner to **avoid the need to issue fresh proceedings,** and consequently shorten the overall timescale and costs implications for your client. This particular type of consent order is known as a 'Tomlin order'.

It is essentially split into two parts: the first part is the order itself, and the second part is the schedule (or sometimes a settlement agreement) annexed to the order. The schedule often contains a confidentiality clause, so that the terms of settlement remain confidential. However, even where confidential schedules are annexed to the order, there are occasions on which the court may order their disclosure (see *L'Oreal SA v eBay International AG* [2008] EWHC 313 (Ch)). There may, however, be instances where parties would be well advised to draft the order stating that the agreed terms in the schedule are confidential and are not to be filed at court. The court has, on occasions, kept a copy of the confidential schedule on the court file in a sealed envelope. This would prevent a non-party being able to obtain a copy under CPR 5.4C(1) (see *ABC v Y* [2010] EWHC 3176 (Ch)).

The order does not set out the details of the agreement between the parties, but merely states that:

- the parties have agreed terms of settlement;
- all further proceedings are stayed;
- the stay is based on the terms set out in the schedule being complied with;
- if the terms in the schedule are not complied with, then the innocent party can make an application to the same court in which the proceedings were issued and ask the court to allow it to enforce the terms agreed in the schedule (by way of one of the enforcement options set out in Chapter 21)—a procedure that is known as 'liberty to apply'; and
- there is a provision for the payment and assessment of costs.

The order essentially sets out all of the items that the court is able to order. The order must also be dated.

The schedule usually appears at the end of the Tomlin order and includes (where the agreement involves the payment of money):

- who is paying the money, how much, and when;
- that the agreement is in full and final satisfaction; and
- a default provision on interest should the monies not be paid.

The court has the power to vary the terms incorporated into the order but not to vary the terms of the schedule (except on the usual basis for interfering with a contract). The court only has the power to enforce the terms of the schedule if not adhered to by either party.

 Practical Considerations

Tomlin orders are frequently used in litigation to record settlement of terms. They are mainly used when a payment is to be made sometime in the future. Their main advantage is that, should the terms of the schedule be breached, then like a Part 36 settlement, there is no need to issue fresh proceedings for breach of the agreement; rather, you are permitted to go back into the original set of proceedings (by virtue of the liberty to apply clause in the order) and ask the court, by way of an application—probably without notice and hearing—for permission to proceed straight to enforcement.

A template Tomlin order appears as Figure 20.2 at the end of this chapter.

20.8.2.3 Compromising an action for a child or protected party

If an action on behalf of a child or protected party is compromised by settlement, the court must approve the settlement before it can be a valid settlement.

Here, the requirement to obtain the court's approval of the settlement is mandatory (whereas the reason to obtain approval in paragraph 20.8.2.1 above is in order that the payer obtains a valid discharge). The approval is sought by issuing an ordinary application notice. The information set out in paragraph 20.8.2.1 above should be provided to the court.

Whenever the court has made a judgment for the child or protected party in an action or is approving a settlement, the court will also give directions how the money shall be dealt with. In the case of large orders or settlements for a protected party, the court will usually direct that an application should be made to the Court of Protection to appoint a receiver and for the funds to be transferred to the Court of Protection. For orders or settlements for a child, or for smaller settlements or orders for a protected party, the court will administer and invest the funds.

The provisions for accepting a CPR Part 36 offer are the same as in paragraph 20.8.2.1, save in circumstances in which there has been a payment in the High Court. *John James Brennan (by Joy Brennan his Litigation Friend) v (1) Eco Composting Ltd (2) J Bascombe Contractors Ltd* [2006] EWHC 3153 confirmed that children or protected parties are entitled to the interest accrued on the payment from the date of valid acceptance and that this was from the date on which the court approved the settlement. The court also made it clear that it was the claimant's (or his litigation friend's) responsibility to make the application for court approval promptly.

20.8.3 DISCONTINUANCE OF PROCEEDINGS

CPR 38 governs the discontinuance of proceedings by a claimant.

At any point during proceedings, even at trial, a claimant can decide that he no longer wishes to pursue the whole, or any part, of his claim even though no settlement has been reached and the action is therefore ended. The usual reasons for discontinuance are that the defendant is no longer worth suing, or that the claimant no longer believes that his own claim will substantially succeed at trial.

Generally, the claimant can discontinue of its own volition, but provisions relating to when the claimant will need permission and multi-party claims are contained in CPR 38.2.

In order to discontinue, the claimant must file and serve a notice of discontinuance on all other parties to the action, and whilst the defendant can apply to have the notice set aside (where no permission was required by the claimant) within 28 days, this is rare.

The main feature of a claimant's entitlement to discontinue is that he is liable to pay the defendant's costs on the standard basis for the whole action or the part of the action that has been discontinued. It is therefore very important that this is explained to your client. However, in exceptional cases, the court will exercise its inherent discretion and reduce the claimant's costs' liability (see *Messih v Mcmillan Williams and Ors* [2010] EWCA Civ 844 and *Dhillon and Anor v Siddiqui and Ors* [2010] EWHC 1400 (Ch) where in this latter case the court was minded to use a different test in deciding costs by exercising its discretion by reference to CPR 44.3 rather than CPR 38.6).

KEY POINTS SUMMARY

- Issue and serve witness summons, and liaise with witnesses directly before trial.

- Book and brief counsel, and consider whether a pre-trial conference is appropriate with the client and any experts or witnesses.

- Allow plenty of time to prepare accurate and user-friendly trial bundles. Keep a spare one at court and at the office.

- Ensure that you are familiar with every aspect of the case before the trial commences.

- Put administrative arrangements in place for the smooth running of the trial.

- Keep in close contact with counsel and the client in the days running up to the trial.

- Be clear as to the arrangements for the handing down of judgment, and if a draft judgment is released, adhere to any embargo placed on it by the judge.

- Know the strict time limits for appeals and instruct counsel to be prepared to seek permission or to oppose an application for permission to appeal when the judgment is handed down.

- Understand the mechanics of settling before and after the issue of litigation.

- If settlement is concluded by a non-Part 36 offer, ensure that the correct consent order is agreed and drafted.

Case study *Andrew James Pike v Deep Builders Ltd*

All of the directions have now been complied with, and the PTC has been filed and served. You have now received a notice of hearing, listing the trial for three days. Acting for Andrew Pike, consider the following questions.

Question 1

To whom should you witness summons and why?

Question 2

Is it necessary to have a conference with counsel at this stage? Give reasons for your answer.

Question 3

If Andrew Pike does not beat Deep Builders' Part 36 offer of £20,000, what are the likely cost consequences for each party and how will the court deal with this?

Question 4

You have been instructed by your supervising partner to help prepare a trial bundle index for the trial of this matter. He informs you that all special damages have been agreed subject to liability, although medical evidence has not been agreed, because the defendants obtained an order seeking their own evidence. There is no order for expert oral evidence at trial.

The young practitioner who was helping your principal has departed on annual leave, but has left you his notes on what he would include in the bundles. These may or may not, be of assistance to you. These appear in the Online Resource Centre.

Based on your knowledge of the case for Andrew Pike and the information that your colleagues have provided, draft the trial bundle index.

Case study *Bollingtons Ltd v Mrs Elizabeth Lynch t/a The Honest Lawyer*

Question 1

The fast-track trial has been listed. As the day of the trial approaches, Mrs Lynch is getting nervous and asks you to attend the trial with her. What costs advice would you give her?

Question 2

Mrs Lynch lost the fast-track trial both on the claim against her and her counterclaim, the judge indicating in his judgment that he preferred the evidence of Mr Green. Permission to appeal was obtained. Consider what advice you would give to her on the prospects of successfully appealing and the costs implications.

Any documents referred to in these case study questions can be found on the Online Resource Centre—simply click on 'Case study documentation' to access the documents that you need for Chapter 20 and to be reminded of the questions above. Suggested answers to these case study questions can also be accessed on the Online Resource Centre by your lecturer.

FIGURE 20.1 TEMPLATE CONSENT ORDER

IN THE HIGH COURT OF JUSTICE   **201? 201?-P-3003**

QUEEN'S BENCH DIVISION

                DISTRICT REGISTRY

Between

                                                                       Claimant

                                            and

                                                                   Defendant

                                          CONSENT ORDER

Upon the Claimant and Defendant having agreed to settle this matter

By Consent it is ordered that:

1. The Defendant do pay the Claimant the sum of £ . . . . by Friday 25th January 201? 201? In full and final settlement of his claim

2. The CMC listed on 14th December 201? 201? be vacated

3. The Defendant do pay the Claimant's costs of the action to be the subject of a detailed assessment if not agreed.

We consent to the terms of this order

. . . .

For the Claimant

. . . .

For the Defendant

Dated . . . .

FIGURE 20.2 TEMPLATE TOMLIN ORDER

IN THE HIGH COURT OF JUSTICE   **201?-P-3003**

QUEEN'S BENCH DIVISION

                         DISTRICT REGISTRY

Between

                                                                                          Claimant

                                         and

                                                                                          Defendant

                               TOMLIN ORDER

Upon the Claimant and Defendant having agreed to the terms set out in the Schedule attached, By Consent it is ordered that:

4. All further proceedings in this action be stayed on the terms set out in the attached schedule to this order, except for the purpose of carrying the said terms into effect and for that purpose there is liberty to apply

5. There be no order as to costs

                                 Schedule

1. The Defendant do pay the Claimant the sum of £xxx with in xx days of the date of this order

2. The order is made in full and final settlement of claims subsisting or capable of subsisting between the parties

3. In event of late payment, the Defendant will pay interest on the sum of . . . . . . or any part thereof at a daily rate of . . . . %

Whilst there is no 'Litigation train' diagram to begin this chapter, enforcement is dealt with in the interactive 'Litigation train' diagram available on the Online Resource Centre, where this subject area can be looked at as a whole.

online resource centre

Relevant court forms relating to this chapter:

- N316 or N316A Information Hearing

- PF 53 (Writ of Fi Fa) and PF 86 (Praecipe)   High Court Execution

- N42 or N53 (Warrants of Execution) and N323 (Request Form)   County Court Execution

- N337 (Application) Attachment of Earnings

- N349 (Application) Third Party Debt Order

- N379 or N380 (Application)   Charging Order

- N208 (Part 8 Claim Form)   Order for Sale

21.1 INTRODUCTION

The legal practitioner is very often involved in the enforcement of judgments that arise from money debts for clients either as part of a litigation team or as part of the debt collection department. The legal practitioner is required to be aware of a range of enforcement methods. However, it is understanding which particular method or methods are most appropriate in terms of recovery of debt, costs outlay, and time, that will ensure that the legal practitioner works effectively in the recovery of money judgments.

Since the late 1990s, the Lord Chancellor's department has been considering some fundamental changes to the way in which the enforcement of money debts proceeds in England and Wales, as a result of which the Tribunals' Courts and Enforcement Act 2007 was created. The Act proposes, amongst other things, substantial amendments to many of the methods of enforcement detailed in this chapter. However, at the time of publication, there has been no indication of when these changes will be implemented. It is clearly an area that requires your careful monitoring as a legal representative in post-judgment work and we suggest that you keep abreast of changes via the Ministry of Justice website—http://www.justice.gov.uk.

The law, therefore, as presently stated, is contained in the Civil Procedure Rules 1998 (CPR), but these are still supplemented by the old High Court and County Court Rules (RSC and CCR respectively), reference to which is made throughout this chapter.

Remember that European payment order procedure (EPOP) and European small claims procedure (ESCP) judgments (see Chapter 9, paragraph 9.2.2) are recognized and enforceable in England and Wales (if obtained in another member state) without the need for a declaration or recognition of enforceability. They will therefore be treated, to all intents and purposes, as if they were secured in a domestic jurisdiction, because they are governed by the CPR on enforcement. The only requirement is that a copy of the EPOP or ESCP judgment is produced to the court to satisfy authenticity.

This chapter will consider:

- making the most of the judgment debt;

- ascertaining the judgment debtor's financial position;

- deciding which method(s) of enforcement are the most suitable; and

- foreign judgments.

 Professional Conduct

Enforcement proceedings are difficult to proceed with successfully. Consequently, there are a high proportion of unrecovered judgment debts. The legal representative must ensure that the judgment creditor client understands that despite the variety of enforcement methods available, there is no 'magic wand' to guarantee either a full or partial satisfaction of the judgment. This is important, because the judgment creditor will need to provide further funds in order to pursue investigations and enforcement proceedings. These costs are, for the most part, fixed, but whilst they are usually added to the judgment debt, if the debt is not recovered, these will not be recovered and the client will be even more out of pocket. It is therefore essential that the judgment creditor client does not have enhanced expectations and is aware of the cost outlay at the outset of enforcement proceedings.

21.2 INTEREST ON JUDGMENT DEBTS

21.2.1 HIGH COURT JUDGMENTS

A judgment obtained in the High Court attracts interest from the date of the judgment (if the judgment was a liability only judgment, then the interest will not begin to run until a judgment has been obtained in respect of damages), or consent order (Judgments Act 1938). The interest rate that applies is varied by statutory instrument, but is currently 8 per cent per annum. When calculating the interest due on a judgment debt—particularly one that has been outstanding for a number of years—it will be necessary to check the interest rate applicable to a given period during the lifetime of the judgment to ensure arrival at an accurate overall figure.

21.2.2 COUNTY COURT JUDGMENTS

The position in relation to interest on county court debts is more intricate. A judgment obtained in a county court will attract interest at 8 per cent per annum, on the same basis as a High Court debt, but only if the judgment is for £5,000 or more. Therefore, a debt of anything up to £4,999 will not accrue interest in the county court. There is an exception to this where the Late Payment of Commercial Debts Act 1998 applies to the sum against which the judgment was obtained.

There are also certain other provisos for judgments in excess of £5,000, as follows.

- If payment of the judgment is deferred or is to be made by instalments, interest will not begin to run until the deferred date or the instalment is due.

- If the judgment creditor elects to proceed by one of the enforcement methods detailed in paragraph 21.6 below, the judgment debt will not accrue interest unless the enforcement method chosen (including an information hearing) fails to make any financial return. Even if a small payment is recovered, this will stop any interest further accruing, effectively making the judgment debt interest-free.

- A judgment creditor can apply to enforce the interest accrued on a judgment debt. In order to do this, a certificate setting out the amount of interest claimed, the original sum upon which it is claimed, and the relevant dates, as well as the rate of interest, must be supplied to the court.

21.3 POST-JUDGMENT CONSIDERATIONS

21.3.1 THE JUDGMENT CREDITOR

The identity of the parties involved in enforcement proceedings is different from that in the main proceedings in which the judgment was obtained. The successful party pursuing the judgment is usually known as the 'judgment creditor' and the losing party against whom the judgment was made is usually known as the 'judgment debtor'.

Once a judgment is obtained in an action, the court will not automatically enforce it if it remains unpaid in breach of the order or judgment. This is a matter for the judgment creditor. How he enforces it will be largely dependent upon the amount of the judgment and the information relating to the judgment debtor's financial position. This latter point should have been considered with the client before proceedings were issued, because there is little point pursuing litigation or a form of dispute resolution when your opponent is a 'man of straw', or a financially insolvent company. Advice should also be given to the client to review this risk (that is, the ability of the defendant to pay any judgment awarded) during the course of an action. It would be included as part of the risk assessment carried out from time to time.

 Professional Conduct

Under the Solicitors' Code of Conduct 2007, Rule 1.03, you must act in the best interests of your client. A failure to consider with your client his opponent's ability to pay damages and costs, at the outset of the retainer, will render you in breach of this professional conduct rule if it transpires that the litigation has been worthless, because the opponent does not have the means to pay.

This is unlikely to be a problem if the judgment debtor is insured and his insurers have conducted the defence.

21.3.2 LIMITATION

The judgment remains in force for six calendar years from the date of judgment for most types of enforcement options. It would appear that the exceptions to this are third party debt orders (see *Westacre Investments Inc v Yugoimport SPDR* [2008] EWCA 801 (Comm)) and charging orders (see *Yorkshire Bank Finance Ltd v Mr. and Mrs. Mulhall* [2008] EWCA Civ 1156). If six years have elapsed since the date of the judgment and the judgment creditor wishes to enforce the judgment, he must apply to the court for permission to enforce, in accordance with Rules of the Senior Courts (RSC) Order 46 (CPR Sched. 1) and County Court Rules (CCR) Order 26, r. 5 (CPR Sched. 2). This limitation period is perhaps not such a bar to enforcement, as limitation periods can be under the Limitation Act 1980 in main actions. Applications are often successful, but the court will only exercise its discretion where it is just to do so and justice can be done to both parties (*Good Challenger Navegante SA v Metalexportimport* [2003] EWCA Civ 1668).

 Practical Considerations

The application for permission to enforce can usually be made without notice and consideration should be given, in order to effect a cost saving for the client, to whether it is appropriate in each case to proceed by way of a paper application.

If the judgment is paid within one month of the date of judgment, the court can be asked to cancel the entry in the Register of Judgments, Orders and Fines, which was created by the Register of Judgments, Orders and Fines Regulations 2005, SI 2005/3595. The Register includes High Court and county court judgments. Its purpose is to allow a public search of these judgments to assist in enforcement and responsible lending. The effect of the cancellation of the entry is that there will be no record that a judgment has ever been secured against the debtor. If it is paid after one month, the court can only be asked to mark the entry as 'satisfied', but it will still remain for six years. This effectively means that the fact that there has been a judgment, even though it has been satisfied, cannot be removed from the record until the six years has elapsed.

21.3.3 INITIAL ADVICE TO THE JUDGMENT CREDITOR

Once a judgment has been obtained, the judgment creditor will need to consider the following with his legal representative before identifying which method of enforcement he is to pursue:

* the whereabouts of the judgment debtor;
* the assets belonging either wholly or partly to the judgment debtor; and
* whether he is entitled to recover against those assets.

Once this has been considered, the legal representative may need to give some thought to whether it is appropriate for the judgment to remain in the court in which it was obtained or whether enforcement needs to be dealt with in another court.

21.3.4 TRANSFER OF PROCEEDINGS FOR THE PURPOSE OF ENFORCEMENT

There are three situations in which a judgment debt will need to be transferred to a different court:

* where a county court judgment is to be enforced in the High Court;
* where a High Court judgment is to be enforced in the county court; and
* where a county court judgment needs to be transferred to the debtor's home court for a particular type of enforcement.

21.3.4.1 County court judgment to be enforced in the High Court

Where a decision is made by the judgment creditor and his legal representative to enforce a county court judgment in the High Court (predominantly for the reason that debts over £600 only can be transferred and interest begins to accrue, or if the debt exceeds £5,000, execution must take place in the High Court, as detailed in paragraph 21.6.1 below), an application notice will need to be issued in the county court under the County Courts Act 1984, s. 42. Once the application has been granted, the judgment creditor is required to apply for a certificate of judgment under CCR Order 22, r. 8 (CPR Sched. 2). This certificate represents the order transferring the judgment to the High Court (CCR Order 25, r. 13, CPR Sched. 2).

21.3.4.2 High Court judgment to be enforced in the county court

If the High Court judgment is to be transferred to the county court for enforcement (usually only where an attachment of earnings order is sought, execution is sought on a sum of under £600, or a charging order is applied for on a sum less than £5,000, as detailed in paragraph 21.6 below), the judgment creditor and his legal representative must apply to the High Court for an order transferring the proceedings (CPR 70.3). However, the High Court does have the power, under s. 40(2) of the County Courts Act 1984, to order the transfer of proceedings to a county court even though the proceedings would otherwise fall outside the county court's jurisdiction (*National Westminster Bank plc v King* [2008] EWHC 280). Once the order has been made, the judgment creditor is required by Practice Direction (PD) 70.3 to file a number of documents with the county court, including a copy of the judgment.

21.3.4.3 Transfer of a judgment between county courts

Where a county court method of enforcement requires the process to be undertaken in the court in the jurisdiction of which the debtor resides or runs his business (usually in cases of a charging order, attachment of earnings order, and a judgment summons), CCR Order 25, r. 2 (CPR Sched. 2) provides for the transfer of the action from the court in which the main action proceeded to judgment to the debtor's home court.

The procedure is simple and requires no more than a letter to the court in which the judgment was obtained requesting the transfer. The court will notify all parties once it has approved the transfer request.

21.4 INVESTIGATING THE JUDGMENT DEBTOR

Few debtors are difficult just for the sake of it, but many are frustrated in their dealings with legal representatives who fail to pursue the most appropriate method of enforcement. In order to avoid this, before commencing enforcement proceedings, the debtor's whereabouts and assets need to be identified. The most common way of doing this is to instruct an enquiry agent. If this is to be done, the judgment creditor client will need to be made aware of the cost of the enquiry agent and what might be achieved, then provide instructions to proceed to appoint an enquiry agent. A limit should be placed on those costs, so that a disproportionate amount of money is not spent.

You could undertake again the suggested searches that you conducted after your first client interview (see Chapter 6 at paragraph 6.5.4). Enquiry agents can often discover assets or information that were not ascertained: for example, at an information hearing, as detailed in paragraph 21.5 below.

Most firms will have a number of established enquiry agents or private investigators that could be employed. Indeed, you may already have instructed one at the outset of the client retainer when considering with your client whether the opponent was worth suing. The agent or investigator will need to be instructed in writing with as much information as possible.

In order to make a cost saving for your judgment creditor client, there are a number of enquiries that a legal representative could make both where the whereabouts of the debtor is not known and where there is communication with the debtor, but he is not paying, either in advance of instructing an agent or potentially instead of employing one.

21.4.1 TRACING ELUSIVE ABSENTEE AND 'GONE AWAY' DEBTORS

The legal representative may wish to consider checking the following as part of his initial tracing steps:

- directories such as BT's *Phone Book*, the *Yellow Pages*, *Thomson Local*, and the telex directory;
- the Royal Mail tracing service—see http://www.royalmail.co.uk;
- Companies House—see http://www.companieshouse.gov.uk;
- statutory records;
- trade associations and clubs, such as the Chamber of Commerce and the Federation of Master Builders;
- the electoral roll or business rates listings; and
- the Land Registry.

These are enquiries that an enquiry agent would probably make, but which, if done internally, could effect a cost saving for the client.

21.4.2 HOW TO DEAL WITH DIFFICULT DEBTORS

If you are already in contact with the judgment debtor, before proceeding to enforcement, you may wish to secure payment of either the whole or part of the debt by agreement. The following are some practical considerations for the legal representative.

- Always try to maintain good accurate information.
- Consider negotiating concessions, such as extra time to pay.

- Think about your communication style: being thoughtful about the way in which you speak to the judgment debtor may impact on the results that you achieve.

- Plan your telephone call by reviewing the file in advance, noting whether any previous payments or offers have been made.

- Make effective telephone calls by overcoming the debtor's objection to payment and obtaining payment in full either by debit or credit card, payment by BACS, CHAPS, or cheque, on an agreed date.

- Know what makes debtors respond to debt recovery letters by having a variety of debt recovery letters and forms that get read, instead of ignored and thrown in the bin.

21.5 INFORMATION HEARINGS

If the judgment debtor does not pay immediately after the judgment has been obtained and the judgment creditor has been unable to obtain information about the nature of the judgment debtor's assets by way of the suggestions in paragraph 21.4 above, he can apply to bring the debtor before the court to be examined on his means. This is known as an 'information hearing' and can be used to secure information to enable you to undertake on behalf of your client one of the enforcement methods in paragraph 21.6 below. It is not classed as a method of enforcement.

PD 71 governs the information hearing.

21.5.1 THE APPLICATION

The judgment creditor must complete and file an application in Form N316, if the debtor is an individual. Form N316A is completed if the application is to question an officer of a company or other corporation, because it will be an officer of the company or corporation that will be brought before the court.

The notice must include:

- the name and address of the judgment debtor;
- the judgment or order sought to be enforced;
- the amount then owed; and
- any particular documents that the judgment debtor is to bring to court.

The court will then issue an order for the judgment debtor to attend court at a specified time. This will be indorsed with a penal notice warning him that if he does not attend, he may be sent to prison for contempt.

Unless the court orders otherwise, the order must be served personally within 14 days of the information hearing. If he fails to serve it, the judgment creditor must notify the court at least seven days before the hearing. If he is successful, he must file an affidavit of service not less than two days before the hearing.

The judgment debtor can demand in advance his expenses for travelling to and from the information hearing, and can request that, within seven days of service of the order, the judgment creditor pay a sum reasonably sufficient to cover those expenses.

21.5.2 THE HEARING

An officer of the court or, alternatively, a judge (if that is considered appropriate) conducts the hearing.

Where an officer conducts it, standard questions are asked, as set out in Appendices A and B to PD 71. The judgment creditor may attend the hearing and ask additional questions, but these should be set out in the application notice.

The officer makes a written record of the responses given by the judgment debtor, who is then invited to read and sign it at the end of the hearing. If a legal representative attends the hearing, fixed costs may be awarded (CPR 45.6).

When the hearing is before the judge, the standard questions are not used. The judgment creditor's legal representative asks the questions and the hearing is tape-recorded. CPR 44.7 provides the judge with discretion to make a summary assessment of costs at the end of the hearing.

If the judgment debtor fails to attend court or, having attended, refuses to answer questions, a committal order (PD 71.7.1) may be made against him that is likely to be suspended, effectively giving the debtor a second chance to comply. This is not however secured as a matter of course and will only be granted if the disobedience is unintentional and the order is appropriate in the circumstances. If the debtor fails again, then a committal order is likely to be made by the judge (CPR 71.8).

21.6 VARIOUS METHODS OF ENFORCEMENT

So far in this chapter, we have discussed pre-enforcement considerations. We now move on to look at the most common enforcement methods employed by the court.

 Costs

The rules in relation to each of the methods of enforcement are fairly straightforward. A legal representative needs to learn how to use each method to its advantage, and this may involve looking to combine some of the enforcement options, or considering the cost and timing implications of the methods chosen. The costs of each enforcement method usually gets added to the judgment debt. This is invariably a fixed cost, but the client pays for each method employed on the usual interim basis, as defined under the terms of the client retainer. The judgment creditor client needs to be kept updated as to the likely recovery of the debt and cost of enforcement in the same manner as in the main action.

21.6.1 THE WRIT OF *FIERI FACIAS* (HIGH COURT) AND THE WARRANT OF EXECUTION (COUNTY COURT)

The writ of *fieri facia* (in the High Court) is governed by RSC Order 46 (CPR Sched. 1) and the warrant of execution (in the county court) is governed by CCR Order 26, r. 1 (CPR Sched. 2) in the county court. They are the only methods of enforcement in this chapter that do not require a judicial decision.

This form of enforcement can be combined with other methods of enforcement in this chapter and seeks to recover the judgment debt by threatening to sell, or by selling, the judgment debtor's goods. This is currently the most popular method of enforcement. This can be done in both the High Court and the county court, and each court has its own procedure, although in neither court do you need permission to issue unless the judgment is more than six years old.

The court in which the judgment was obtained will usually be the court in which the execution will take place, subject to the following.

- If the proceedings to enforce are for a sum of £5,000 or more, art. 8 of the High Court and County Court Jurisdiction Order 1991, SI 1991/724, allocates all proceedings for enforcement against goods to the High Court.

- Where the sum to be enforced is more than £600, but less than £5,000, the judgment creditor can choose whether to proceed in the High Court or county court. His decision may be based on the type of other enforcement method available in each court, or the fact that interest will accrue on all High Court judgments, or that execution by High Court enforcement officers (HCEOs) is often considered to be more effective than execution by a county court bailiff. If it is the case that the judgment debtor elects to move from the county court to the High Court or vice versa, the judgment must be formally transferred, as detailed in paragraph 21.3.4 above.

- Enforcement against goods where the sum that it is sought to enforce is less than £600 can only be taken in the county court (High Court and County Court Jurisdiction Order 1991, art. 8(1)(b)).

The costs, usually fixed, of the execution are added to the writ or warrant.

  Practical Considerations

When advising a judgment creditor client on whether to execute in the High Court or county court, irrespective of the interest accrual in the High Court, you may wish to consider the practical difference between execution in each court. This relates to the fact that High Court execution is carried out by an HCEO, who is independent of the courts, whereas county court enforcement is carried out by a bailiff, who is employed by HM Courts Service. It is thought that, because the HCEOs are paid by fees and take a percentage of what they recover, they have a greater incentive to secure payment than the bailiffs and, as such, are more successful on execution.

21.6.1.1 Procedure in the High Court
Execution in the High Court is effected through producing the following to the court:

- two copies of the writ of *fieri facias*—otherwise known as a 'writ of fi fa' (Practice Form PF 53);
- a *praecipe*, otherwise known as a 'request for issues of the writ', with the court fee imprinted thereon (Practice Form PF 86);
- the judgment, or an office copy of it; and
- the order granting permission to issue (where required).

The writ is formally issued by being sealed by the court (RSC Order 46, r. 6, CPR Sched. 1) and a copy is returned to the judgment creditor, who forwards it to the HCEO, who will acknowledge receipt and send the writ to the officer for execution in the county in which the debtor's goods are situated. The writ is valid for 12 months.

21.6.1.2 Procedure in the county court
Execution in the county court also involves the production of the following to the court:

- the warrant of execution in Form N42 (or Form N53, if it is to be executed in a different county court);
- the payment of the fee prescribed; and
- a request in Form N323.

The warrant is executed by the bailiff of the court for the district in which it is to be executed. Before the warrant is executed, the court sends a notice in Form N326 to the debtor (CCR Order 26, r. 1, CPR Sched. 2) to inform him that a warrant has been issued and execution will follow.

21.6.1.3 What happens on execution?
Execution has essentially three stages:

(a) entry onto the debtor's premises;

(b) seizure of the goods; and

(c) securing of the goods.

21.6.1.3.1 *Attending the debtor's premises*

In executing the writ or warrant, the HCEO or bailiff attends the address specified and requests such of the debtor's goods as may be sufficient to realize the judgment debt and expenses.

In practice, the debtor's goods are not taken away there and then. The HCEO or bailiff will agree not to take away the goods on that day in return for the debtor agreeing not to dispose of them. This is known as 'walking possession' and is effectively used to give the debtor another opportunity to pay the judgment without the sale of his possessions. If the debtor does not pay by the date agreed between them, the HCEO or bailiff will return to the property, and physically remove the goods and sell them—most probably at public auction. In the meantime, the debtor is not allowed to dispose of them.

Once sold, the HCEO or bailiff will deduct expenses (and the HCEO will deduct an additional percentage fee), and the judgment creditor is then paid off in respect of the judgment debt, interest if accrued, and fixed costs. If there is any surplus, this is returned to the debtor.

21.6.1.3.2 *Lawful entry*

The whole issue of the HCEO or bailiff attending the debtor's premises has always gained much media attention in relation to 'lawful entry' and this is one of the areas under significant review in the Tribunals Courts and Enforcements Bill. As the law currently stands, doors must not be pushed open or broken, and there must be no forcible entry, although climbing over a wall or fence is permitted to gain entry.

21.6.1.3.3 *Items that can and cannot be seized*

There are a number of rules relating to what can and cannot be taken on execution. It is up to the debtor to satisfy the HCEO or bailiff that any item is 'necessary' for him to continue existing or running a business. It is very much a matter of common sense as to what can and cannot be taken. The debtor must give written notice that the goods are exempt.

Included in those items that can be taken are generally 'non-necessary' items, such as motor vehicles, money, furniture, and electrical items.

Those items that cannot be taken under the Senior Courts Act 1981, s. 89(1), and County Courts Act 1984, s. 89(1), are any items on hire or hire purchase, tools books, and any motor vehicles and other items of equipment that are necessary for use by the debtor in his job or business: for example, a vehicle that is used during the business day, not merely to get to and from work. Additionally, clothing, bedding, furniture, household equipment, and provisions as are necessary for satisfying the basic domestic needs of the debtor and his family cannot be taken away, although items such as CD players and microwaves are not considered to be necessary for basic living.

21.6.1.3.4 *Suspending the warrant*

The judgment debtor can ask the court to suspend the writ or warrant on the understanding that the debtor pays the judgment debts within a specified time. If the debtor fails to satisfy the writ or warrant within the agreed time, then the court will lift the suspension and the HCEO or bailiff will attend the debtor's premises to remove the appropriate goods.

21.6.2 ATTACHMENT OF EARNINGS

The attachment of earnings is governed by the Attachment of Earnings Act 1971 and CCR Order 27 (CPR Sched. 2).

It is an order that is made compelling an employer of the judgment debtor to make regular deductions from the debtor's earnings and pay them into court.

There are a number of important points to note when considering applying for an attachment of earnings order, as follows.

• It is only available as a method of enforcement in the county court and only for a debt of at least £50. Therefore, any High Court judgment that is to be enforced by way of an attachment of earnings order will need to be transferred to the debtor's county court (see paragraph 21.3.4 above for the procedure on transfer).

- Once an attachment of earnings order is made, the judgment creditor cannot use any other method of enforcement unless the court gives permission.

- No interest accrues on the judgment debt whilst the order is in force.

- An attendance order is only applicable to persons who are employed, so self-employed or unemployed persons cannot have an attachment of earnings order made against them.

 Practical Considerations

In view of the 'no interest' provision above and the exclusivity of the order made, an attachment of earnings order is not usually a first-choice method of enforcement; rather, it is a last-resort consideration by legal representatives.

21.6.2.1 Procedure

As with many methods of enforcement, the procedure is based on the completion and filing of standard forms, as follows.

- The judgment creditor must complete Form N337 and send it to the county court for the district in which the judgment debtor resides. If the judgment was made in a different county court, the proceedings must be transferred (see paragraph 21.3.4 for the procedure on transfer).

- The court will usually then serve a notice of application for an attachment of earnings order in Form N55 on the debtor, together with Form N56, which is a questionnaire that the debtor must complete detailing his statement of means.

- If the debtor completes and returns Form N56, the court staff may make an attachment of earnings order (Form N60), and send copies to the parties and to the debtor's employer.

- A hearing is not, however, necessary unless the court staff feel that there is insufficient information to make an order.

- In the event that the debtor does not return a statement of means within the time allowed, the court staff will automatically issue an order (Form 61) compelling him to do so. This is indorsed with a penal notice. The ultimate sanction for repeated disobedience would be arrest and imprisonment.

- If there is insufficient information contained in the Form N56, the court will convene a hearing before the district judge or Master, who will seek to obtain the necessary and relevant information for the purposes of making an order. The order will only be made if the court is satisfied that the debtor has sufficient means.

- The order, whether made by the court staff or the district judge, will specify the 'normal deduction rate' and 'the protected earnings rate', the latter being the amount that the court decides the debtor must be allowed to retain out of his earnings in any event. This is usually the amount that the debtor would receive for himself and his family if he were on Income Support.

 Practical Considerations

If acting for a debtor client, in order to avoid embarrassment to the debtor, it is possible to agree to an attachment of earnings order by consent or to ask the court to make a suspended order. The effect of these is that the employer will not be notified unless the debtor fails to make the agreed instalments promptly.

21.6.2.2 What happens after the order is made?

After the order is made, the costs are usually summarily assessed and added to the judgment debt (CCR Order 27, r. 9, CPR Sched. 2). The order is served on the debtor and the employer. Additionally, the employer also receives an explanatory booklet setting out how an attachment of earnings order works. It highlights to him, in accordance with the Attachment of Earnings Act 1971, s. 7, that he is entitled to levy an administration charge of £1 per monthly deduction.

The order will remain in force until the judgment debt is satisfied, but in the meantime, it is incumbent on both the employer and the debtor to notify the court of any changes to the employment.

21.6.3 THIRD-PARTY DEBT ORDERS

Third-party debt orders are governed by CPR 72 and cover the situation in which the court may order an independent third party, such as a bank, building society, or trade debtor who holds or owes money for or to the judgment debtor, to pay the outstanding sum directly to the judgment creditor. The order essentially allows the third party to 'leapfrog' payments due to the debtor and make them to the judgment creditor.

Third-party debt orders are a particularly effective method of enforcement where the debt to be attached is owed by a responsible body, such as a bank or building society, and there are specific provisions set out below regarding the information that the court is required to have if the application is to be successful.

However, there are three situations in which a third-party debt order would not be appropriate:

- where the debt emanates from a European Community (EC) country, the English courts will not make a third-party payment debt order, because the national courts of EC countries have exclusive jurisdiction in enforcement (*Kuwait Oil Tanker Co Sak v Qabazard* [2003] UKHL 31);
- where the debt emanates from non-EC countries, the English courts will not make a third-party payment debt order unless the English order will be recognized under the foreign law as discharging the liability of the third party (*Societe Eram Shipping Co Ltd v Compagnie International de Navigation* [2003] UKHL 30); and
- where the judgment debt is for less than £50.

Whilst third-party debt orders are a useful method of enforcement, they are the least used, because, evidentially, they are difficult to pursue successfully. However, they can be combined with another method of enforcement, if appropriate.

21.6.3.1 Procedure

Third-party debt orders follow a two-stage process: an interim order and a final order. Both stages are dealt with by a district judge in the court in which the judgment was secured.

21.6.3.1.1 *The interim order*

The first stage is made upon an application made without notice (CPR 72.3) on Form N349 by the judgment creditor. The notice will include the following information and is verified with a statement of truth.

1. The name and address of the judgment debtor.

2. Details of the judgment debt (and the amount remaining outstanding).

3. Whether the debt is payable by instalments and what sums are due.

4. The name and address of the third party, with details of the account or debt owed (or such as are known to the judgment creditor).

5. Confirmation that the third party is within the jurisdiction.

6. Whether there are any other persons who have a claim to the debt known to the judgment creditor.

7. Details of the source of the judgment creditor's information.

On receipt of this information, the judge will consider the information without a hearing (CPR 72.4(1)) and may make an interim order if he deems it to be appropriate in all of the circumstances. The interim order, usually in Form N84, will specify the sum to be retained and will include fixed costs. The matter will then be listed for a final hearing not less than 28 days after the interim order was made.

The interim order must be served on the third party not less than 21 days before the hearing date (CPR 72.5(1)(a)). The interim order is not binding on the third party until it is served (see Chapter 9, paragraph 9.7). The interim order directs the third party not to make any payment out that reduces the amount owed to the judgment debtor.

The interim order must also be served on the judgment debtor, but not until it has already been served on the third party—that is, not less than seven days after the third party has been served, but in any event, seven days before the hearing takes place (CPR 72.5(1)(b)). As evidence of service, the judgment creditor must either file a certificate of service not less than two days before the hearing or produce one at the hearing itself.

21.6.3.1.2 *The final order*

The second stage of the process is when the judge at the hearing considers making the interim order final. The burden is on the judgment debtor to show why the order should not be made final. The court, however, has a discretion to make the order final and will only do so if equitable. There are a number of possible orders that the court could therefore make—that is, a final order, a discharge of the interim order, or a decision regarding any matters in dispute between the third party and the judgment debtor relating to whether there are monies owed or held—but the order will not be made if the debtor is insolvent. It is a precondition of a third-party debt order that the third party be discharged from his liability to the judgment debtor in the amount that he pays directly to the judgment creditor.

If the order is made final (usually in Form N85), it is enforceable as an order to pay the sum specified to the judgment creditor. Once this has been effected, the third-party debt to the judgment creditor is discharged to the extent that it has been paid. If the third party refuses to pay the monies over to the judgment creditor, then the judgment creditor can enforce the third-party debt order as a judgment.

21.6.3.2 Objections to the interim and final order

The third party can object to the interim order if he claims not to owe the judgment debtor the sum specified or any sum. To do so, he must notify the court in writing within seven days of being served with the interim order. If the judgment creditor disputes this, then he must similarly serve written evidence of the grounds of his dispute.

Both the third party and the debtor can object to the interim order being made final. This must be again done in writing to the court not less than three days before the final hearing (CPR 72.8). The usual reasons for the objections are that someone else has a claim to the money specified in the interim order. If that is the case, the court will serve a copy of the application and hearing date on that person (CPR 72.8(5)).

21.6.3.3 Third-party debt orders against banks and building societies

Third-party debt orders are used most frequently against these deposit-taking institutions and have the highest success rate. It should be noted that the order made will only be in respect of a credit balance at the time of the interim order and cannot be made against joint accounts. The effect of the interim order is to freeze the account.

The following points should be noted when applying for a third-party debt order against a bank or a building society.

- The Form N349 must state whether the person signing the statement of truth knows the branch name and address (speculative applications will not be granted).

- The order must be served on the registered or head office, as well as the branch office.

- A bank or building society served with an interim third-party order is required to retain the sum ordered, and to search for and disclose details of accounts in the name of the judgment debtor. If it does not do so, then in the event that monies are paid out of the frozen account, the bank or building society may be held to be in contempt of court.

- Any order against a bank or building society cannot require payment that would reduce the account to less than £1.

- The bank or building society, if not objecting to the application, usually does not attend the final hearing, but merely writes to the parties and the court, denoting its agreement to comply with any order made.

- The bank or building society is entitled to deduct an administrative charge (currently £55) before paying the judgment creditor.

- The judgment debtor can apply for a hardship order with evidence of his needs and financial circumstances. What this means is that if he and his dependants are likely to suffer hardship in meeting the ordinary living expenses if a third-party debt order against a bank or building society is made final, then he can apply to the court in advance of the final hearing in accordance with PD 72.5.

21.6.4 CHARGING ORDERS

Charging orders are governed by the Charging Orders Act 1979 and CPR 73, and can be made in the High Court only if they are in respect of High Court maintenance orders or the judgment is for a sum exceeding £5,000. The county court has unlimited jurisdiction.

This method of enforcement does not affect the accrual of interest payable on High Court judgments or on county court judgments on which interest is payable.

21.6.4.1 Charging orders on land

Charging orders made over land are similar to the judgment creditor having a mortgage over land specified in the order. The judgment creditor becomes a secured creditor of the judgment debtor. A charging order can be made in respect of land owned both solely and jointly by the judgment debtor. If the order is obtained against jointly owned land, then the security is not over the land itself, but over the debtor's beneficial interest in the land.

 Practical Considerations

When advising a client on a charging order, it must be stressed to him that this method of enforcement only provides security for the judgment debt unless an order to enforce the sale of the property is applied for. The order for sale proceedings are notoriously difficult to succeed in and are detailed in paragraph 21.6.4.2 below.

21.6.4.1.1 *The procedure*

The general procedure for obtaining a charging order is similar to that of a third-party debt order in that it is in two stages: an interim order and a final order.

21.6.4.1.2 *The interim charging order*

The first stage is to obtain the interim order and, to do this, an application notice in Form N379 must be filed with the court, with the information contained in PD 73.1.2, which includes details of the judgment debtor, the judgment, the property to be charged, and particulars of any other person who has a prior charge on the property. The judgment debtor must also file a draft interim charging order.

An interim charging order is made without notice to the debtor and the court will usually make the interim order on Form N86 without a hearing. A judge will consider the application, and grant the interim order and fix a final hearing date at which the order may be made final (CPR 73.4).

Once the interim order has been made, this must be served on the debtor and any other such creditors as the court directs not less than 21 days before the final hearing. The judgment creditor must either file a certificate of service not less than two days before the hearing or produce one at the final hearing.

Whilst the interim charging order is being served, it is also suggested that the interim order is registered. If it is done at the interim stage, there is no need for it to be re-registered once the order has been made final. If the debtor is the sole owner of the land, the interim charging order can be registered at the Land Charges Department as an order affecting land (if the title is unregistered), or at HM Land Registry as a notice (if the land is registered).

If the land is jointly owned by the debtor, then the interim charging order is registered only against the debtor's interest in the land. Unfortunately, if the land is unregistered, the interim charging order is unregistrable, although an application can be made to register a pending action along with a caution against first registration and then a writ or order affecting land when the interim order is made. However, if it is registered land, it can be entered as a restriction on the Register.

 Practical Considerations

Before proceeding with the charging order application, it is essential to undertake an index map search and a search of the title to ascertain if the land is registered and who owns the land. Office copy entries should also be obtained, because this will additionally, for properties sold recently, denote the sale price of the property, which, in turn, will help you to make an early decision as to whether there is any available equity in the property worth securing. The office copies will provide you with the details of prior charge holders that the court will want to be served with the interim charging order. Further correspondence can be entered into with them to ascertain the current amount of loan outstanding, which will further assist you and your client in considering the security available.

21.6.4.1.3 *The final charging order*

The second stage of the procedure is to attend the hearing of the interim charging order. If the debtor or one of the prior secured creditors wishes to object to the interim order being made, written evidence must be filed and served not less than seven days before the hearing. Prior charge holders rarely attend the final hearing.

At the final hearing, the judge has a discretion as to whether to make the interim order final, to discharge it, or to decide any other issues. In accordance with the Charging Orders Act 1979, s. 1(5), the court must consider the personal circumstances of the debtor and whether any other creditor of the debtor would be likely to be unduly prejudiced by the order becoming final. The costs of the charging order are usually fixed and are added to the sum secured on the property. The final order will be made on Form N87.

Practical Considerations

Because a charging order is merely security for a judgment debt, consideration should be given to combining it with another enforcement method or payment by an instalment order. The latter can only take place if the charging order was obtained first (*Robaigealach v Allied Irish Bank plc*, LTL 12/11/2000).

21.6.4.2 Order for sale

Once the judgment creditor has his security over the property, he has the option of enforcing the sale of the property to realize his security. At present, there is no time limit within which this action can be taken. This is still a fairly draconian step to take, and successful orders for sale are few and far between.

Procedurally, an order for sale is achieved by commencing a CPR 8 claim.

- in the Chancery Division (if a High Court charging order (CPR 73.4.2)); or

- in any division of the High Court (CPR 73.10). The usual court is the Chancery Division but there may be cases where it is sensible and proportionate to issue in the Queen's Bench Division of the High Court; or

- in the county court (if a county court charging order, provided that the amount secured does not exceed the county court limit—which stands at £30,000 under s. 23 of the County Courts Act 1984).

The Part 8 claim should include the following written information, as set out under CPR 73.10:

- details of the charging order and the property to be sold;
- the amount of the secured charge and the amount due at the issue of the Part 8 claim;
- confirmation of the debtor's title to the property;
- if known, the names and addresses of any other prior charge holders and the amount owed;
- an estimate of the value of the property;
- the identity of anyone who is in possession of the property; and
- details of the land charge or Land Registry entry.

Costs

The cost outlay to the client who wishes to proceed to enforce an order for sale is significant and includes sizeable disbursements, such as the court issue fee and the cost of a 'drive-by' valuation of the property. The report can be appended to the Part 8 claim as evidence of available equity in the property if that is the case. Because this is a particularly difficult order to obtain, the client will need to be advised fully on the cost implications (even though the judgment creditor's costs will be added to the overall debt) and the prospects of success.

Because this is a Part 8 claim, the debtor is only required to file an acknowledgement of service, after which, the court will list the matter for directions. The court is likely to order that all of the prior charge holders be notified of the Part 8 proceedings, usually by copying the claim form and supporting evidence to them. Other likely directions include giving the debtor an opportunity to respond to the claim and to list the matter for a final hearing.

In exercising its discretion whether to make an order enforcing the sale of the property, the court will take into account the position of the creditors of the judgment debtor and also any trustee or person beneficially entitled to the land in question as well as the size of the debt. The court will also consider any human rights issues. If the order for sale is made, the judgment debtor is allowed one more chance to pay the debt, failing which the property will be sold.

21.6.4.3 Charging orders on securities

The procedure highlighted in paragraph 21.6.4.1 in respect of a charging order on land can be used where a judgment creditor requires a charging order on a judgment debtor's beneficial interest in securities, although the application notice to be filed with the court is in Form N380. Charging orders on securities are governed by s. 2(2) of the Charging Orders Act 1979.

The types of security are as follows:

- government stock;
- stock of anybody (other than a building society) incorporated in England and Wales;
- stock of anybody incorporated outside England and Wales, or of any state or territory outside the UK, being stock registered in a register kept at any place within England and Wales; or
- units of any unit trust in respect of which a register of the unit trust is kept at any place within England and Wales.

The order may, however, be extended to any interest or dividend payable in respect of the assets. Once the interim order is obtained, if the judgment debtor disposes of his interest in any securities, such a disposition will not be valid (CPR 73.6). A copy of the interim order must be served on the Bank of England or the company concerned.

21.6.4.4 Charging orders on a partner's interest in partnership property

Section 23 of the Partnership Act 1890 allows a judgment creditor to apply for a charging order over a partner's interest in the partnership property and profits in payment of the amount of the judgment debt and interest thereon, and may, by the same or subsequent order, appoint a receiver of that partner's share or profits.

The procedure is by way of a Part 8 claim, which must be served on the debtor and the other partners. If the order is made, the other partners are at liberty to redeem the interest charge or can purchase it if a sale is ordered.

21.6.5 OTHER TYPES OF ENFORCEMENT

21.6.5.1 Sequestration

Sequestration is a form of contempt proceedings that are available in both the High Court and the county court, and is governed by RSC Order 46, r. 5 (CPR Sched. 1).

This can be used only in respect of injunction-type orders and rarely concerns money judgments. It is the means of enforcement against the assets of an individual, corporate body, or trade union.

The relevant procedure is to issue an application in accordance with CPR 23 directly to the judge, seeking permission to issue a writ of sequestration. The writ appoints four 'sequestrators', and directs them to take possession of all of the real and personal property of the contemnor, and to keep that property until the contempt is cleared.

21.6.5.2 Judgment summons

A judgment summons is a procedure for punishing by a period of imprisonment a defaulting judgment debtor who could pay, but has chosen not to.

This method of enforcement is available only in the case of High Court maintenance orders and judgments, or orders of any court concerning payment of certain taxes or other sums or contributions due to the state.

The order can be suspended so long as stated instalments are paid. There are standard forms for the request for a judgment summons (Form 342) and for the request for a warrant of committal (Form 344).

21.7 **BANKRUPTCY, WINDING UP, AND DEBT RELIEF ORDERS**

21.7.1 **BANKRUPTCY AND WINDING UP**

Bankruptcy and winding-up orders are not methods of enforcement, and the detail of these procedures falls outside the scope of this book. However, in practice, judgment creditors often threaten insolvency proceedings as a means of compelling the debtor to 'pay up'. If they are successful, the business or company will fold, and with that may come financial and social disgrace for the judgment debtor. The outcome for the judgment creditor is not, however, necessarily beneficial, because by securing such an order, he simply stands in line with all of the other unsecured creditors; there is no expediting of payment of the judgment debt to him just because he successfully secured the bankruptcy or winding up of the debtor.

Insolvency proceedings are often a last resort after a number of methods of enforcement have been tried. Failure to pay a judgment debt is frequently evidence that the judgment debtor is insolvent. It may, however, mean that the judgment debtor is prepared to go to great lengths to avoid paying a judgment debt and thus the 'threat' or application to make the judgment debtor bankrupt or to wind up the company may be sufficient for them to pay the debt due.

If the judgment creditor wishes to pursue insolvency proceedings, the debt must be at least £750 in respect of an individual (Insolvency Act, s. 267(4)) and must exceed £750 in respect of a company (Insolvency Act 1986, s. 123).

The first step is usually to serve a statutory demand (which does not involve the court). There is a prescribed form for this and once this has been personally served, the debtor has 21 days in which to satisfy the demand, failing which the judgment creditor can issue either a bankruptcy petition against an individual or a winding-up petition against a company. The judgment creditor does not need to have obtained a judgment from the court to issue a statutory demand; there simply needs to be the minimum amount of an undisputed debt, as indicated above.

The issue of a bankruptcy petition or winding-up petition is effected on standard forms with an affidavit. The petition and affidavit are filed at court: in respect of a bankruptcy, at the debtor's local county court (in London, the correct court is the Bankruptcy Registry, which forms part of the Chancery Division); and in respect of a winding up, the Chancery Division of the High Court (Insolvency Act 1986, s. 117). There are three grounds upon which a bankruptcy petition can be issued (Insolvency Act 1986, ss. 268 and 276) and seven grounds in respect of a winding-up petition (Insolvency Act 1986, s. 122).

 Practical Considerations

In so far as advising the judgment creditor on pursuing such proceedings, the cost implications are significant due to the court issue fee. There is also an impact on enforcement procedures in other actions, because once the bankruptcy or winding-up proceedings have been commenced, the court has the power to stay any pending actions against the debtor. If a final order is made, then instead of continuing with the litigation, the creditor proves in the bankruptcy (Insolvency Act 1986, s. 285). If a judgment creditor had already commenced enforcement proceedings elsewhere, then, generally, he is allowed to keep what he has recovered, as long as the enforcement was completed before the date of the final order. These issues will need to be discussed with the client before litigation and/or enforcement proceedings are commenced. It is advisable to undertake a 'bankruptcy only search' in the Land Charges Register against the individual and a search of the Central Index of Petitions in the Companies Court in London against a company to check whether there are any existing insolvency proceedings.

21.7.2 DEBT RELIEF ORDERS (DROS)

The Tribunals, Courts and Enforcement Act 2007 introduced a new form of debt relief, which came into force in April 2009. They are designed to be an alternative to bankruptcy—especially for clients who have less than:

- £15,000 in unsecured debts;
- £300 in assets; and
- £50 per month disposable income.

Any creditor who is included in the debt relief order (DRO) will be prevented from taking any action to recover its debt. The debt is designed to be discharged at the end of one year.

As a legal representative, you act as an intermediary to help debtors to apply online for a DRO via the Insolvency Service website—http://www.insolvency.gov.uk. However, you will need to be trained to become an intermediary, because the Solicitors Regulation Authority is not an accredited body for this purpose.

21.8 THE ENFORCEMENT OF FOREIGN JUDGMENTS

There are a variety of provisions under which the English courts will recognize and enforce foreign judgments, as follows:

- at common law.
- under the Administration of Justice Act 1920;
- under the Foreign Judgments (Reciprocal Enforcement) Act 1933;
- under the 'European Regime', which consists of the following. These have broadly similar terms on jurisdiction and the recognition and enforcement of judgments in civil and commercial matters:
  - 1988 and 2007 Lugano Conventions
  - 1968 Brussels Convention
  - 2001 Brussels Regulation.

21.8.1 AT COMMON LAW

At common law, a foreign judgment can be enforced because it creates an implied contract to pay. There are exceptions to this, but all foreign judgments must be conclusive—particularly regarding the cause of action.

Proceedings are commenced in the appropriate English court, usually by a CPR Part 7 claim, followed by an application for summary judgment. There are defences available: for example, that the judgment was obtained by fraud, is contrary to public policy, or is contrary to human rights legislation.

However, for the proceedings to be successful, the defendant must have been present in the foreign country when the claim was issued in England and Wales, or agreed to submit to the jurisdiction of the foreign court.

21.8.2 THE ADMINISTRATION OF JUSTICE ACT 1920

The Administration of Justice Act 1920 permits Commonwealth judgments to be registered in England and Wales within twelve months of the date of the judgment. The court has a discretion whether to register the judgment and there are defences available in line with those available at common law (see paragraph 21.8.1 above).

The procedure is governed by CPR 74.

21.8.3 THE FOREIGN JUDGMENTS (RECIPROCAL ENFORCEMENT) ACT 1933

The 1933 Act permits the registration of judgments obtained in all EU countries with which England and Wales have entered into a reciprocal enforcement arrangement within six years of the date of the judgment. As with paragraphs 21.8.1 and 21.8.2 above, there is a range of defences available.

21.8.4 THE LUGANO CONVENTIONS

The Civil Jurisdiction and Judgment Regulations 2009, SI 2009/3131, brought into force the new 2007 Lugano Convention on 1 January 2010, which now includes Denmark, Norway and Switzerland. At the time of writing, Iceland has yet to ratify the new convention. The 2007 Lugano Convention replaces the 1988 Lugano Convention brought in under the Civil Jurisdiction and Judgments Act 1982. Until such times as Iceland ratifies the new Convention, the 1988 Lugano Convention will apply.

These conventions are important because the Civil Jurisdiction and Judgments Act 1982 (as amended by the Civil Jurisdiction and Judgments Act 1991) at s. 4, permits a judgment of a contracting state under the Lugano Conventions to be registered in this country (and subsequently enforced through the courts by means already discussed in this chapter).

21.8.5 THE BRUSSELS CONVENTION 1968 AND 2001 REGULATIONS

The Brussels Regulation has not only largely replaced the 1968 Convention, but has also replaced the provisions on enforcement under the 1988 Lugano Convention. The 2007 Lugano Convention's provisions will however be aligned with the provisions of the Brussels Regulations, which state as follows.

Article 34 provides four possible defences:

- if it is contrary to public policy (Art. 34(1));
- where the judgment was obtained in default of appearance of the defendant (Art. 34(2));
- where the judgment is irreconcilable with a judgment between the same parties in the state in which the recognition is sought (Art. 34(3)); and
- where the judgment is irreconcilable with an earlier judgment in another regulation state (Art. 34(4)).

The drafting of these Conventions and Regulations is somewhat confusing. Essentially most of their terms are materially the same on many jurisdictional and enforcement issues: a claimant who has secured a judgment from a member state can enforce it in any other member state without issuing fresh proceedings. This only applies to court judgments (including Tomlin orders), but not currently arbitral awards.

Closer scrutiny of this 'European Regime' will however be required should you find yourself in the position of having to enforce a foreign judgment.

21.9 ENFORCEMENT OUTSIDE ENGLAND AND WALES

Once a judgment has been secured in England and Wales, if a debtor has assets outside the jurisdiction, it may be appropriate to try to enforce the judgment outside the jurisdiction. How this is done very much depends on whether the judgment was obtained as a result of a contested or uncontested claim.

21.9.1 CONTESTED JUDGMENTS

Contested judgments concern judgments that have been secured as a result of a contested action in which a defence was filed and the matter proceeded to trial.

Consideration will need to be given as to whether the court for the country in which enforcement proceedings are to be brought will recognize any English judgment. If there is no reciprocal enforcement procedure in the country concerned (see paragraph 21.8.3 above), then, to enforce an English judgment in such a country, fresh proceedings on the judgment will have to be taken there.

21.9.2 UNCONTESTED JUDGMENTS

EC Regulation No 805/2004 creating a European Enforcement Order for uncontested claims allows those who have an uncontested judgment in England and Wales to obtain a European enforcement order (EEO) certificate from the courts, which allows the judgment to be transferred to an EU member state for enforcement. This avoids the need to have the judgment formally recognized by the courts of another member state under the Brussels Regime, although the judgment creditor will be bound by the enforcement procedures available in that member state.

The EEO has been an option for judgment enforcement for all uncontested judgments since 20 January 2005. What this means is that this procedure can only be used where the proceedings involving the defendant proceeded on the basis that the defendant either admitted the debt, agreed to judgment by consent, failed to file a defence, or filed a defence, but failed to attend the hearing.

On receipt of the uncontested judgment, the application for the EEO is on paper and is made to a master or district judge in the court in which the judgment was secured (CPR 74 and its Practice Direction). This process is simple, and quicker and cheaper than under the Brussels Convention.

21.10 ENFORCEMENT OF AGREEMENTS RESULTING FROM CROSS BORDER MEDIATION

So far, this section has discussed the enforcement of a foreign judgment in England and Wales. With the implementation of the EU Mediation Directive, the CPR have now been amended, where relevant, to permit the enforcement in England and Wales of agreements resulting from cross-border mediation whilst maintaining the confidentiality of the agreement.

21.11 HOW TO ADVISE A JUDGMENT DEBTOR

Whilst there is no 'Litigation train' diagram to begin this chapter, enforcement is dealt with in the interactive 'Litigation train' timeline available on the Online Resource Centre, where this subject area can be looked at as a whole.

The following represents a non-exhaustive list of considerations that should be borne in mind if advising a judgment debtor.

• Negotiate with the judgment creditor for payment of the debt by instalments, whilst agreeing to a charge on land to secure the debt.

• Are there any grounds for having the judgment debt set aside?

• If the judgment is in the county court, the debtor may be able to apply for an instalment order (CCR Ord 22, r. 10, CPR Sched. 2).

- The debtor may wish to apply for an administration order. Administration orders are a court-administered debt management scheme for those who are unable to pay their debts. They are governed by s. 6 of the County Courts Act 1984. Currently, the scheme is restricted to the county court for those with at least one judgment debt and whose debts total no more than £5,000. What this effectively means is that a schedule of creditors is prepared, detailing the amounts owed to each, and the debtor is ordered to pay the total amount by instalments directly to the court. The court then apportions the received amounts between the creditors pro rata to the debts. Whilst this type of order is in force, any other type of enforcement proceedings cannot be taken and interest does not accrue.

- Negotiate a settlement of the judgment debt of a lesser amount. Often—particularly in the case of banks or other lending institutions, or with a judgment creditor who is tired of the struggle (and costs) of seeking to recover a due debt—the judgment creditor will agree a lesser figure without further action being needed.

KEY POINTS SUMMARY

- Know the fundamental principles and procedures of the different types of enforcement method and how they interrelate.

- Be prepared to give your judgment creditor client pragmatic advice about enforcement prospects and costings.

- Keep an eye out for some potentially fundamental reforms on enforcement in England and Wales.

- Remember that many of the rules relating to enforcement are still contained in the old RSC and CCR.

Case study *Bollingtons Ltd and Mrs Elizabeth Lynch t/a The Honest Lawyer*

Judgment was obtained against Elizabeth Lynch in the sum of £10,000 plus VAT, interest, and costs. The defendant's counterclaim was dismissed.

Mrs Lynch did not pay the amount stipulated within the time limit set out in the judgment. Your enquiries have revealed that Mrs Lynch is still living in the flat above The Honest Lawyer, which she owns jointly with her husband and upon which there are two mortgages. She is still trading at all three pubs. There is a county court judgment recently registered against her. She has a current account with the local branch of her bank.

Question 1

List briefly the possible means of enforcing the judgment, and the possible advantages and disadvantages of each in relation to this case study.

Question 2

Consider also whether you may require further information and how this could be obtained.

Question 3

Consider whether you could use a combination of enforcement methods and, if so, which ones.

---

online resource centre

Any documents referred to in these case study questions can be found on the Online Resource Centre—simply click on 'Case study documentation' to access the documents that you need for Chapter 21 and to be reminded of the questions above. Suggested answers to these case study questions can also be accessed on the Online Resource Centre by your lecturer.

APPENDICES
COURT FORMS

Claim Form

In the

for court use only

Claim No.

Issue date

Click here to clear your data after printing

Claimant

SEAL

Defendant(s)

Brief details of claim

Value

Defendant's name and address

	£
Amount claimed	
Court fee	
Solicitor's costs	
Total amount	

The court office at

is open between 10 am and 4 pm Monday to Friday. When corresponding with the court, please address forms or letters to the Court Manager and quote the claim number.

Printed on behalf of The Court Service

Claim No.

Does, or will, your claim include any issues under the Human Rights Act 1998? ☐ Yes ☐ No

Particulars of Claim (attached)(to follow)

Statement of Truth
*(I believe)(The Claimant believes) that the facts stated in these particulars of claim are true.
* I am duly authorised by the claimant to sign this statement

Full name _____

Name of claimant's solicitor's firm _____

signed _____ position or office held _____
*(Claimant)(Litigation friend)(Claimant's solicitor)   (if signing on behalf of firm or company)
*delete as appropriate

Claimant's or claimant's solicitor's address to which documents or payments should be sent if different from overleaf including (if appropriate) details of DX, fax or e-mail.

| Click here to reset form | Click here to print form |

Response Pack

You should read the 'notes for defendant' attached to the claim form which will tell you when and where to send the forms

Included in this pack are:

- either **Admission Form N9A** (if the claim is for a specified amount) or **Admission Form N9C** (if the claim is for an unspecified amount or is not a claim for money)

- either **Defence and Counterclaim Form N9B** (if the claim is for a specified amount) or **Defence and Counterclaim Form N9D** (if the claim is for an unspecified amount or is not a claim for money)

- **Acknowledgment of service** (see below)

Complete

If you admit the claim or the amount claimed and/or you want time to pay ▶	the admission form
If you admit part of the claim ▶	the admission form and the defence form
If you dispute the whole claim or wish to make a claim (a counterclaim) against the claimant ▶	the defence form
If you need 28 days (rather than 14) from the date of service to prepare your defence, or wish to contest the court's jurisdiction ▶	the acknowledgment of service
If you do nothing, judgment may be entered against you	

Acknowledgment of Service

Defendant's full name if different from the name given on the claim form

In the	
Claim No.	
Claimant (including ref.)	
Defendant	

Address to which documents about this claim should be sent (including reference if appropriate)

	if applicable	
	fax no.	
	DX no.	
	Ref. no.	
Tel. no. Postcode	e-mail	

Tick the appropriate box

1. I intend to defend all of this claim ☐

2. I intend to defend part of this claim ☐

3. I intend to contest jurisdiction ☐

(My) (Defendant's) date of birth is [D D M M Y Y Y Y]

If you file an acknowledgment of service but do not file a defence within 28 days of the date of service of the claim form, or particulars of claim if served separately, judgment may be entered against you.

If you do not file an application to dispute the jurisdiction of the court within 14 days of the date of filing this acknowledgment of service, it will be assumed that you accept the court's jurisdiction and judgment may be entered against you.

Signed

(Defendant)(Defendant's solicitor)(Litigation friend)

Position or office held
(if signing on behalf of firm or company)

Date

The court office at

is open between 10 am and 4 pm Monday to Friday. When corresponding with the court, please address forms or letters to the Court Manager and quote the claim number.

N9 Response Pack (04.06)   HMCS

Check here to clear your data after printing

Admission (specified amount)

- You have a limited number of days to complete and return this form
- Before completing this form, please read the notes for guidance attached to the claim form

Name of court	
Claim No.	
Claimant (including ref.)	
Defendant	

When to fill in this form

Only fill in this form if:

- you are admitting all of the claim **and** you are asking for time to pay; or
- you are admitting part of the claim. (You should also complete form N9B)

How to fill in this form

- Tick the correct boxes and give as much information as you can. **Then sign and date the form.** If necessary provide details on a separate sheet, add the claim number and attach it to this form.
- Make your offer of payment in box 11 on the back of this form. **If you make no offer the claimant will decide how much and when you should pay.**
- If you are not an individual, you should ensure that you provide sufficient details about the assets and liabilities of your firm, company or corporation to support any offer of payment made in box 11.
- You can get help to complete this form at **any** county court office or Citizens Advice Bureau.

Where to send this form

- **If you admit the claim in full**
  Send the completed form to the address shown on the claim form as one to which documents should be sent.
- **If you admit only part of the claim**
  Send the form **to the court** at the address given on the claim form, together with the defence form (N9B).

How much of the claim do you admit?

- ☐ I admit the full amount claimed as shown on the claim form **or**
- ☐ I admit the amount of £ _____

1 Personal details

Surname	
Forename	

☐ Mr ☐ Mrs ☐ Miss ☐ Ms

☐ Married ☐ Single ☐ Other *(specify)* _____

Date of birth [D D M M Y Y Y Y]

Address

Postcode _____

Tel. no. _____

2 Dependants *(people you look after financially)*

Number of children in each age group

under 11 ☐ 11-15 ☐ 16-17 ☐ 18 & over ☐

Other dependants *(give details)* _____

3 Employment

☐ **I am employed as a** _____
My employer is _____

Jobs other than main job *(give details)* _____

☐ **I am self employed as a** _____

Annual turnover is............................ £ _____

☐ **I am not** in arrears with my national insurance contributions, income tax and VAT

☐ **I am** in arrears and I owe........... £ _____

Give details of:
(a) contracts and other work in hand
(b) any sums due for work done

☐ **I have been unemployed for** _____ years _____ months

☐ **I am a pensioner**

4 Bank account and savings

☐ **I have a bank account**
  ☐ The account is in credit by........ £ _____
  ☐ The account is overdrawn by.... £ _____

☐ **I have a savings or building society account**
  The amount in the account is.......... £ _____

5 Residence

I live in ☐ my own house ☐ lodgings
☐ my jointly owned house ☐ council accommodation
☐ rented accommodation

N9A Form of admission (specified amount) (04.06)   HMCS

6 Income

My usual take home pay *(including overtime, commission, bonuses etc)*	£	per
Income support	£	per
Child benefit(s)	£	per
Other state benefit(s)	£	per
My pension(s)	£	per
Others living in my home give me	£	per
Other income *(give details below)*		
	£	per
	£	per
	£	per
Total income	**£**	**per**

8 Priority debts *(This section is for arrears only. Do not include regular expenses listed in box 7.)*

Rent arrears	£	per
Mortgage arrears	£	per
Council tax/Community Charge arrears	£	per
Water charges arrears	£	per
Fuel debts: Gas	£	per
Electricity	£	per
Other	£	per
Maintenance arrears	£	per
Others *(give details below)*		
	£	per
	£	per
Total priority debts	**£**	**per**

7 Expenses

(Do not include any payments made by other members of the household out of their own income)

I have regular expenses as follows:

Mortgage *(including second mortgage)*	£	per
Rent	£	per
Council tax	£	per
Gas	£	per
Electricity	£	per
Water charges	£	per
TV rental and licence	£	per
HP repayments	£	per
Mail order	£	per
Housekeeping, food, school meals	£	per
Travelling expenses	£	per
Children's clothing	£	per
Maintenance payments	£	per
Others *(not court orders or credit debts listed in boxes 9 and 10)*		
	£	per
	£	per
	£	per
Total expenses	**£**	**per**

9 Court orders

Court	Claim No.	£	per

Total court order instalments	**£**	**per**

Of the payments above, I am behind with payments to *(please list)*

10 Credit debts

Loans and credit card debts *(please list)*

	£	per
	£	per
	£	per

Of the payments above, I am behind with payments to *(please list)*

11 Offer of payment

☐ I can pay the amount admitted on

or

☐ I can pay by monthly instalments of £

If you cannot pay immediately, please give brief reasons below

12 Declaration   I declare that the details I have given above are true to the best of my knowledge

Signed

Position or office held *(if signing on behalf of firm or company)*

Date

click here to clear data after printing

Defence and Counterclaim (specified amount)

- Fill in this form if you wish to dispute all or part of the claim and/or make a claim against the claimant (counterclaim).
- You have a limited number of days to complete and return this form to the court.
- Before completing this form, please read the notes for guidance attached to the claim form.
- Please ensure that all boxes at the top right of this form are completed. You can obtain the correct names and number from the claim form. The court cannot trace your case without this information.

How to fill in this form

- Complete sections 1 and 2. Tick the correct boxes and give the other details asked for.
- Set out your defence in section 3. If necessary continue on a separate piece of paper making sure that the claim number is clearly shown on it. In your defence you must state which allegations in the particulars of claim you deny and your reasons for doing so. **If you fail to deny an allegation it may be taken that you admit it.**
- If you dispute only some of the allegations you must
  - specify which you admit and which you deny; and
  - give your own version of events if different from the claimant's.

Name of court	
Claim No.	
Claimant (including ref.)	
Defendant	

- If you wish to make a claim against the claimant (a counterclaim) complete section 4.
- Complete and sign section 5 before sending this form to the court. Keep a copy of the claim form and this form.

Community Legal Service Fund (CLSF)

You may qualify for assistance from the CLSF (this used to be called 'legal aid') to meet some or all of your legal costs. Ask about the CLSF at any county court office or any information or help point which displays this logo.

Community Legal Service

1. How much of the claim do you dispute?

☐ I dispute the full amount claimed as shown on the claim form

or

☐ I admit the amount of £ [   ]

If you dispute only part of the claim you must **either**:

- pay the amount admitted to the person named at the address for payment on the claim form (see How to Pay in the notes on the back of, or attached to, the claim form). Then send this defence to the court

or

- complete the admission form **and** this defence form and send them to the court.

☐ I paid the amount admitted on *(date)* [   ]

or

☐ I enclose the completed form of admission

(go to section 2)

2. Do you dispute this claim because you have already paid it? *Tick whichever applies*

☐ **No** *(go to section 3)*

☐ **Yes** I paid £ [   ] to the claimant

on [   ] *(before the claim form was issued)*

Give details of where and how you paid it in the box below *(then go to section 5)*

3. Defence

HMCS

Defence (continued)

Claim No. [   ]

---

4. If you wish to make a claim against the claimant (a counterclaim)

If your claim is for a specific sum of money, how much are you claiming? £ [   ]

I enclose the counterclaim fee of £ [   ]

My claim is for *(please specify nature of claim)*

[   ]

- To start your counterclaim, you will have to pay a fee. Court staff can tell you how much you have to pay.

- You may not be able to make a counterclaim where the claimant is the Crown (e.g. a Government Department). Ask at your local county court office for further information.

What are your reasons for making the counterclaim?
If you need to continue on a separate sheet put the claim number in the top right hand corner

[   ]

---

5. Signed
(To be signed by you or by your solicitor or litigation friend)

*(I believe)(The defendant believes) that the facts stated in this form are true. *I am duly authorised by the defendant to sign this statement

*delete as appropriate

Position or office held
(if signing on behalf of firm or company)

[   ]

Defendant's date of birth, if an individual   [D D] [M M] [Y Y Y Y]

Date [   ]

Give an address to which notices about this case can be sent to you

[   ]

Postcode

Tel. no. [   ]

	if applicable
fax no.	
DX no.	
e-mail	

| Click here to reset form | Click here to print form |

Admission (unspecified amount, non-money and return of goods claims)

In the	
Claim No.	
Claimant (including ref.)	
Defendant	

- Before completing this form please read the notes for guidance attached to the claim form. If necessary provide details on a separate sheet, add the claim number and attach it to this form.
- If you are not an individual, you should ensure that you provide sufficient details about the assets and liabilities of your firm, company or corporation to support any offer of payment made.

In non-money claims only

☐ I admit liability for the whole claim
(Complete section 11)

In return of goods cases only

Are the goods still in your possession?
☐ Yes ☐ No

Part A Response to claim (tick one box only)

☐ I admit liability for the whole claim but want the court to decide the amount I should pay / value of the goods

OR

☐ I admit liability for the claim and offer to pay [   ] in satisfaction of the claim
(Complete part B and sections 1 - 11)

Part B How are you going to pay the amount you have admitted? (tick one box only)

☐ I offer to pay on (date) [   ]

OR

☐ I cannot pay the amount immediately because (state reason)

[   ]

AND

I offer to pay by instalments of £ [   ]
per (week)(month)
starting (date) [   ]

1   Personal details

Surname	
Forename	

☐Mr ☐Mrs ☐Miss ☐Ms
☐Married ☐Single ☐Other (specify) [   ]

Date of birth [D D M M Y Y Y Y]

Address [   ]
Postcode [   ]
Tel. no. [   ]

2   Dependants (people you look after financially)

Number of children in each age group

under 11 [ ] 11-15 [ ] 16-17 [ ] 18 & over [ ]

Other dependants
(give details)
[   ]

3   Employment

☐ **I am employed as a** [   ]
My employer is [   ]

Jobs other than main job (give details) [   ]

☐ **I am self employed as a** [   ]

Annual turnover is.......................... £ [   ]

☐ **I am not** in arrears with my national insurance contributions, income tax and VAT

☐ **I am** in arrears and I owe........... £ [   ]

Give details of:
(a) contracts and other work in hand [   ]
(b) any sums due for work done [   ]

☐ **I have been unemployed for** [years] [months]

☐ **I am a pensioner**

4   Bank account and savings

☐ **I have a bank account**
☐ The account is in credit by........ £ [   ]
☐ The account is overdrawn by.... £ [   ]

☐ **I have a savings or building society account**
The amount in the account is.......... £ [   ]

5   Residence

I live in ☐ my own property ☐ lodgings
☐ jointly owned house ☐ rented property
☐ council accommodation

N9C Admission (unspecified amount and non-money claims) (04.06)   HMCS

6 Income

My usual take home pay *(including overtime, commission, bonuses etc)*	£	per
Income support	£	per
Child benefit(s)	£	per
Other state benefit(s)	£	per
My pension(s)	£	per
Others living in my home give me	£	per
Other income *(give details below)*		
	£	per
	£	per
	£	per
Total income	**£**	**per**

7 Expenses

(Do not include any payments made by other members of the household out of their own income)

I have regular expenses as follows:

Mortgate *(including second mortgage)*	£	per
Rent	£	per
Council tax	£	per
Gas	£	per
Electricity	£	per
Water charges	£	per
TV rental and licence	£	per
HP repayments	£	per
Mail order	£	per
Housekeeping, food, school meals	£	per
Travelling expenses	£	per
Children's clothing	£	per
Maintenance payments	£	per
Others *(not court orders or credit debts listed in sections 9 and 10)*		
	£	per
	£	per
	£	per
Total expenses	**£**	**per**

8 Priority debts *(This section is for arrears only. Do not include regular expenses listed in section 7)*

Rent arrears	£	per
Mortgage arrears	£	per
Council tax/Community Charge arrears	£	per
Water charges arrears	£	per
Fuel debts: Gas	£	per
Electricity	£	per
Other	£	per
Maintenance arrears	£	per
Others *(give details below)*		
	£	per
	£	per
Total priority debts	**£**	**per**

9 Court orders

Court	Claim No.	£	per

Total court order instalments	**£**	**per**

Of the payments above, I am behind with payments to *(please list)*

10 Credit debts

Loans and credit card debts *(please list)*

	£	per
	£	per
	£	per

Of the payments above, I am behind with payments to *(please list)*

11 Declaration   I declare that the details I have given above are true to the best of my knowledge

Signed

Position or office held

Date

(if signing on behalf of firm or company)

Click here to reset form | Click here to print form

Defence and Counterclaim
(unspecified amount, non-money and return of goods claims)

In the	
Claim No.	
Claimant (including ref.)	
Defendant	

- Fill in this form if you wish to dispute all or part of the claim and/or make a claim against the claimant (a counterclaim)
- You have a limited number of days to complete and return this form to the court.
- Before completing this form, please read the notes for guidance attached to the claim form.
- Please ensure that all the boxes at the top right of this form are completed. You can obtain the correct names and number from the claim form. The court cannot trace your case without this information.

How to fill in this form
- Set out your defence in section 1. If necessary continue on a separate piece of paper making sure that the claim number is clearly shown on it. In your defence you must state which allegations in the particulars of claim you deny and your reasons for doing so. **If you fail to deny an allegation it may be taken that you admit it.**
- If you dispute only some of the allegations you must
  - specify which you admit and which you deny; and
  - give your own version of events if different from the claimant's.

- If the claim is for money and you dispute the claimant's statement of value, you must say why and if possible give your own statement of value.
- If you wish to make a claim against the claimant (a counterclaim) complete section 2.
- Complete and sign section 3 before returning this form.

Where to send this form
- send or take this form immediately to the court at the address given on the claim form.
- Keep a copy of the claim form and the defence form.

Community Legal Service Fund (CLSF)
You may qualify for assistance from the CLSF (this used to be called 'legal aid') to meet some or all of your legal costs. Ask about the CLSF at any county court office or any information or help point which displays this logo.

Community Legal Service

1. Defence

Defence (continued)

Claim No.

2. If you wish to make a claim against the claimant (a counterclaim)

If your claim is for a specific sum of money, how much are you claiming?   £

I enclose the counterclaim fee of   £

My claim is for *(please specify)*

- To start your counterclaim, you will have to pay a fee. Court staff can tell you how much you have to pay.

- You may not be able to make a counterclaim where the claimant is the Crown (e.g. a Government Department). Ask at your local county court office for further information.

What are your reasons for making the counterclaim?
If you need to continue on a separate sheet put the claim number in the top right hand corner

3. Signed

(To be signed by you or by your solicitor or litigation friend)

*(I believe)(The defendant believes) that the facts stated in this form are true. *I am duly authorised by the defendant to sign this statement

*delete as appropriate

Position or office held

(if signing on behalf of firm or company)

Defendant's date of birth, if an individual

D D M M Y Y Y Y

Date

Give an address to which notices about this case can be sent to you

Postcode

Tel. no.

if applicable

fax no.

DX no.

e-mail

Notice of funding of case or claim

Notice of funding by means of a conditional fee agreement, insurance policy or undertaking given by a prescribed body should be given to the court and all other parties to the case:

- on commencement of proceedings
- on filing an acknowledgment of service, defence or other first document; and
- at any later time that such an arrangement is entered into, changed or terminated.

Click here to reset form	Click here to print form

In the

The court office is open between 10 am and 4 pm Monday to Friday. When writing to the court, please address forms or letters to the Court Manager and quote the claim number.

Claim No.	
Claimant (include Ref.)	
Defendant (include Ref.)	

Take notice that in respect of

☐ all claims herein

☐ the following claims

☐ the case of *(specify name of party)*

[is now][was] being funded by:

(Please tick those boxes which apply)

☐ a conditional fee agreement
  ⌐Dated

which provides for a success fee

☐ an insurance policy issued on
  ⌐Date   ⌐Policy no.

  Name and address of insurer

Level of cover

Are the insurance premiums staged?

☐ Yes   ☐ No

If Yes, at which point is an increased premium payable

☐ an undertaking given on
  ⌐Date

by
  Name of prescribed body

in the following terms

The funding of the case has now changed:

☐ the above funding has now ceased

☐ the conditional fee agreement has been terminated

☐ a conditional fee agreement
  ⌐Dated

which provides for a success fee has been entered into;

☐ an insurance policy
  ⌐Date

has been cancelled

☐ an insurance policy has been issued on
  ⌐Date   ⌐Policy no.

  Name and address of insurer

continued over the page ◨⇨

N251 Notice of funding of case or claim (09.09)

© Crown copyright 2009

Level of cover

Are the insurance premiums staged?

☐ Yes   ☐ No

If Yes, at which point is an increased
premium payable

☐ an undertaking given on

Date

has been terminated

☐ an undertaking has been given on

Date

Name of prescribed body

in the following terms

┌Signed

Solicitor for the (claimant) (defendant)
(Part 20 defendant) (respondent) (appellant)

┌Dated

Click here to print form

Click here to clear text after printing

Claim Form
(Additional claims-CPR Part 20)

In the	
Claim No.	

Claimant(s)

Defendant(s)

Part 20 Claimant(s)

Part 20 Defendant(s)

Brief details of claim

Value

SEAL

Defendant's name and address

	£
Amount claimed	
Court fee	
Solicitors costs	
Total amount	
Issue date	

The court office at

is open between 10 am and 4 pm Monday to Friday. When corresponding with the court, please address forms or letters to the Court Manager and quote the claim number.

N211 - w3 Claim Form (CPR Part 20 - additional claims)(4.99)

Printed on behalf of The Court Service

	Claim No.	

Particulars of Claim (attached)

Statement of Truth

*(I believe)(The Part 20 Claimant believes) that the facts stated in these particulars of claim are true.

* I am duly authorised by the Part 20 claimant to sign this statement

Full name _____

Name of Part 20 claimant's solicitor's firm _____

signed_____ position or office held_____

*(Part 20 Claimant)('s solicitor)(Litigation friend)   (if signing on behalf of firm or company)

*delete as appropriate

Part 20 Claimant ('s solicitor's) address to which documents or payments should be sent if different from overleaf. If you are prepared to accept service by DX, fax or e-mail, please add details.

Click here to reset form	Click here to print form

Allocation questionnaire

To be completed by, or on behalf of,

who is [1ˢᵗ][2ⁿᵈ][3ʳᵈ][   ][Claimant][Defendant] [Part 20 claimant] in this claim

Name of court
Claim No.	
Last date for filing with court office	

Please read the notes on page six before completing the questionnaire.

You should note the date by which it must be returned and the name of the court it should be returned to since this may be different from the court where the proceedings were issued.

If you have settled this claim (or if you settle it on a future date) and do not need to have it heard or tried, you must let the court know immediately.

Have you sent a copy of this completed form to the other party(ies)?   ☐ Yes   ☐ No

---

A   Settlement

Under the Civil Procedure Rules parties should make every effort to settle their case before the hearing. This could be by discussion or negotiation (such as a roundtable meeting or settlement conference) or by a more formal process such as mediation. The court will want to know what steps have been taken. Settling the case early can save costs, including court hearing fees.

For legal representatives only

I confirm that I have explained to my client the need to try to settle; the options available; and the possibility of costs sanctions if they refuse to try to settle.   ☐

For all

Your answers to these questions may be considered by the court when it deals with the questions of costs: see Civil Procedure Rules Part 44.3 (4).

1. Given that the rules require you to try to settle the claim before the hearing, do you want to attempt to settle at this stage?   ☐ Yes   ☐ No

2. If Yes, do you want a one month stay?   ☐ Yes   ☐ No

3. Would you like the court to arrange a mediation appointment?   ☐ Yes   ☐ No
   (A fee will be payable to the mediation provider appointed by the National Mediation Helpline.)

4. If you answered 'No' to question 1, please state below the reasons why you consider it inappropriate to try to settle the claim at this stage.

Reasons:

N150 Allocation questionnaire (09.10)   1   © Crown copyright 2010

B Location of trial

Is there any reason why your claim needs to be heard at a particular court? ☐ Yes ☐ No

If Yes, say which court and why?

C Pre-action protocols

You are expected to comply with the relevant pre-action protocol.

Have you done so? ☐ Yes ☐ No

If No, explain why?

D Case management information

What amount of the claim is in dispute? £

Applications

Have you made any application(s) in this claim? ☐ Yes ☐ No

If Yes, what for?
(e.g. summary judgment,
add another party)

For hearing on

Witnesses

So far as you know at this stage, what witnesses of fact do you intend to call at the trial or final hearing including, if appropriate, yourself?

Witness name	Witness to which facts

Experts

Do you wish to use expert evidence at the trial or final hearing?

☐ Yes ☐ No

Have you already copied any experts' report(s) to the other party(ies)?

☐ None yet obtained
☐ Yes ☐ No

Do you consider the case suitable for a single joint expert in any field?

☐ Yes ☐ No

Please list any single joint experts you propose to use and any other experts you wish to rely on.
Identify single joint experts with the initials 'SJ' after their name(s).

Expert's name	Field of expertise (eg. orthopaedic surgeon, surveyor, engineer)

Do you want your expert(s) to give evidence orally at the trial or final hearing?

☐ Yes ☐ No

If Yes, give the reasons why you think oral evidence is necessary:

Track

Which track do you consider is most suitable for your claim? Tick one box

☐ small claims track
☐ fast track
☐ multi-track

If you have indicated a track which would not be the normal track for the claim,
please give brief reasons for your choice

3

Disclosure of electronic documents

If you are proposing that the claim be allocated to the multi-track:

1. Have you reached agreement, either using the Electronic Documents Questionnaire in PD31B or otherwise, about the scope and extent of disclosure of electronic documents on each side? ☐ Yes ☐ No

2. If No, is such an agreement likely? ☐ Yes ☐ No

3. If there is no agreement and no agreement is likely, what are the issues about disclosure of electronic documents which the court needs to address, and should they be dealt with at the Case Managment Conference or at a separate hearing?

E Trial or final hearing

How long do you estimate the trial or final hearing will take?

days	hours	minutes

Are there any days when you, an expert or an essential witness will not be able to attend court for the trial or final hearing? ☐ Yes ☐ No

If Yes, please give details

Name	Dates not available

F Proposed directions *(Parties should agree directions wherever possible)*

Have you attached a list of the directions you think appropriate for the management of the claim? ☐ Yes ☐ No

If Yes, have they been agreed with the other party(ies)? ☐ Yes ☐ No

G Costs

*Do **not** complete this section if you have suggested your case is suitable for the small claims track **or** you have suggested one of the other tracks and you do not have a solicitor acting for you.*

What is your estimate of your costs incurred to date? £

What do you estimate your overall costs are likely to be? £

In multi-track cases these questions should be answered in compliance with CPR Part 43.

H Fee

Have you attached the fee for filing this allocation questionnaire? ☐ Yes ☐ No

An allocation fee is payable if your claim or counterclaim exceeds £1,500.

Additional fees will be payable at further stages of the court process.

I Other information

Have you attached documents to this questionnaire? ☐ Yes ☐ No

Have you sent these documents to the other party(ies)? ☐ Yes ☐ No

If Yes, when did they receive them?

Do you intend to make any applications in the immediate future? ☐ Yes ☐ No

If Yes, what for?

In the space below, set out any other information you consider will help the judge to manage the claim.

Signed

[Counsel] [Solicitor] [for the][1st][2nd][3rd][   ]
[Claimant] [Defendant] [Part 20 claimant]

Date

Please enter your name, reference number and full postal address including (if appropriate) details of telephone, DX, fax or e-mail

	If applicable	
	Telephone no.	
	Fax no.	
	DX no.	
Postcode	Your ref.	

E-mail

Click here to reset form | Click here to print form

Notes for completing an allocation questionnaire

- If the claim is not settled, a judge must allocate it to an appropriate case management track. To help the judge choose the most just and cost-effective track, you must now complete the attached questionnaire.
- If you fail to return the allocation questionnaire by the date given, the judge may make an order which leads to your claim or defence being struck out, or hold an allocation hearing. If there is an allocation hearing the judge may order any party who has not filed their questionnaire to pay, immediately, the costs of that hearing.
- Use a separate sheet if you need more space for your answers marking clearly which section the information refers to. You should write the claim number on it, and on any other documents you send with your allocation questionnaire. Please ensure they are firmly attached to it.
- The letters below refer to the sections of the questionnaire and tell you what information is needed.

A Settlement

Under the Civil Procedure Rules parties should make every effort to settle their case before the hearing. This could be by discussion or negotiation (such as a roundtable meeting or settlement conference) or by a more formal process such as mediation. The court will want to know what steps have been taken. If you think that it would be worthwhile you and the other party trying to negotiate a settlement at this stage you should tick the 'Yes' box. The court may order a stay, whether or not all the other parties to the claim agree. Even if you are requesting a stay, you should still complete the rest of the questionnaire.

More information about settlement options is available in the Legal Services Commission leaflet 'Alternatives to Court' free from any county court or the LSC leaflet line on 0845 3000 343. If you would like to find out more about mediation, and the fees charged, contact the National Mediation Helpline on 0845 60 30 809 or go to www.nationalmediationhelpline.com. Although you may appoint a mediator of your choice, if you would like the court to arrange a mediation for you please tick 'Yes'. By ticking this box you are consenting to your contact details being passed via the Helpline to an accredited external registered provider.

B Location of trial

High Court cases are usually heard at the Royal Courts of Justice or certain Civil Trial Centres. Fast or multi-track trials may be dealt with at a Civil Trial Centre or at the court where the claim is proceeding.

C Pre-action protocols

Before any claim is started, the court expects you to have complied with the relevant pre-action protocol, and to have exchanged information and documents relevant to the claim to assist in settling it. To find out which protocol is relevant to your claim see: http://www.justice.gov.uk/civil/procrules_fin/menus/protocol.htm

D Case management information

Applications

It is important for the court to know if you have already made any applications in the claim, what they are for and when they will be heard. The outcome of the applications may affect the case management directions the court gives.

Witnesses

Remember to include yourself as a witness of fact, if you will be giving evidence.

Experts

Oral or written expert evidence will only be allowed at the trial or final hearing with the court's permission. The judge will decide what permission it seems appropriate to give when the claim is allocated to track. Permission in small claims track cases will only be given exceptionally.

Track

The basic guide by which claims are normally allocated to a track is the amount in dispute, although other factors such as the complexity of the case will also be considered. Leaflet EX305 - The Fast Track and the Multi-track, explains this in greater detail.

E Trial or final hearing

You should enter only those dates when you, your expert(s) or essential witness(es) will not be able to attend court because of holiday or other commitments.

F Proposed directions

Attach the list of directions, if any, you believe will be appropriate to be given for the management of the claim. Agreed directions on fast and multi-track cases should be based on the forms of standard directions set out in the practice direction to CPR Part 28 and form PF52.

G Costs

Only complete this section if you are a solicitor and have suggested the claim is suitable for allocation to the fast or multi-track.

H Fee

For more information about court fees please go our website www.hmcourts-service.gov.uk or pick up a fees leaflet EX50 from any county court. If you cannot afford the fee, you may be eligible for remission of the fee. More details can be found in the leaflet EX160A, which can be downloaded from our website or you can pick up a copy from any county court.

I Other Information

Answer the questions in this section. Decide if there is any other information you consider will help the judge to manage the claim. Give details in the space provided referring to any documents you have attached to support what you are saying.

6

Listing questionnaire
(Pre-trial checklist) [Click here to clear all fields]

To be completed by, or on behalf of,

who is [1st][2nd][3rd][   ][Claimant][Defendant]
[Part 20 claimant][Part 20 defendant] in this claim

In the

Claim No.

Last date for filing
with court office

Date(s) fixed for trial
or trial period

This form must be **completed** and **returned** to the court no later than the date given above. If not, your statement of case may be struck out or some other sanction imposed.

If the claim has settled, or settles before the trial date, you must let the court know immediately.

Legal representatives only: You must **attach** estimates of costs incurred to date, and of your likely overall costs. In substantial cases, these should be provided in compliance with CPR Part 43.

For multi-track claims only, you must also **attach** a proposed timetable for the trial itself.

A Confirmation of compliance with directions

1. I confirm that I have complied with those directions already given which require action by me. ☐Yes ☐No

   If you are unable to give confirmation, state which directions you have still to comply with and the date by which this will be done.

Directions	Date

2. I believe that additional directions are necessary before the trial takes place. ☐Yes ☐No

   If Yes, you should attach an application and a draft order.

   *Include in your application all directions needed to enable the claim **to be tried on the date, or within the trial period, already fixed.** These should include any issues relating to experts and their evidence, and any orders needed in respect of directions still requiring action by any other party.*

3. Have you agreed the additional directions you are seeking with the other party(ies)? ☐Yes ☐No

B Witnesses

1. How many witnesses (including yourself) will be giving evidence on your behalf at the trial? *(Do not include experts - see Section C)*

Continued over ⇨

N170 Listing questionnaire (Pre-trial checklist) (12.02)

Printed on behalf of The Court Service   1 of 3

Witnesses continued

2. If the trial date is not yet fixed, are there any days within the trial period you or your witnesses would wish to avoid if possible? *(Do not include experts - see Section C)*

Please give details

Name of witness	Dates to be avoided, if possible	Reason

Please specify any special facilities or arrangements needed at court for the party or any witness (e.g. witness with a disability).

3. Will you be providing an interpreter for any of your witnesses? ☐ Yes ☐ No

C Experts

You are reminded that you may not use an expert's report or have your expert give oral evidence unless the court has given permission. If you do not have permission, you must make an application (see section A2 above)

1. Please give the information requested for your expert(s)

Name	Field of expertise	Joint expert?	Is report agreed?	Has permission been given for oral evidence?
		☐ Yes ☐ No	☐ Yes ☐ No	☐ Yes ☐ No
		☐ Yes ☐ No	☐ Yes ☐ No	☐ Yes ☐ No
		☐ Yes ☐ No	☐ Yes ☐ No	☐ Yes ☐ No

2. Has there been discussion between experts? ☐ Yes ☐ No

3. Have the experts signed a joint statement? ☐ Yes ☐ No

4. If your expert is giving oral evidence and the trial date is not yet fixed, is there any day within the trial period which the expert would wish to avoid, if possible? ☐ Yes ☐ No

If Yes, please give details

Name	Dates to be avoided, if possible	Reason

D Legal representation

1. Who will be presenting your case at the trial? ☐ You ☐ Solicitor ☐ Counsel

2. If the trial date is not yet fixed, is there any day within the trial period that the person presenting your case would wish to avoid, if possible? ☐ Yes ☐ No

If Yes, please give details

Name	Dates to be avoided, if possible	Reason

E The trial

1. Has the estimate of the time needed for trial changed? ☐ Yes ☐ No

If Yes, say how long you estimate the whole trial will take, including both parties' cross-examination and closing arguments ☐ days ☐ hours ☐ minutes

2. If different from original estimate have you agreed with the other party(ies) that this is now the **total** time needed? ☐ Yes ☐ No

3. Is the timetable for trial you have attached agreed with the other party(ies)? ☐ Yes ☐ No

Fast track cases only

The court will normally give you 3 weeks notice of the date fixed for a fast track trial unless, in exceptional circumstances, the court directs that shorter notice will be given.

Would you be prepared to accept shorter notice of the date fixed for trial? ☐ Yes ☐ No

F Document and fee checklist

Tick as appropriate

I attach to this questionnaire -

☐ An application and fee for additional directions

☐ A draft order

☐ Listing fee

☐ A proposed timetable for trial

☐ An estimate of costs

Signed	Please enter your [firm's] name, reference number and full postal address including (if appropriate) details of DX, fax or e-mail
[Counsel][Solicitor][for the][1ˢᵗ][2ⁿᵈ][3ʳᵈ][ ] [Claimant][Defendant] [Part 20 claimant][Part 20 defendant]	
Date	Postcode

Tel. no.	DX no.	E-mail
Fax no.	Ref. no.	

Certificate of service

Name of court	Claim No.
Name of Claimant	
Name of Defendant	

On the ....*(insert date)*

the .... *(insert title or description of documents served)*

a copy of which is attached to this notice was served on *(insert name of person served, including position i.e. partner, director if appropriate)*

....

Tick as appropriate

- [ ] by first class post or (with effect from 6th April 2006) an alternative service which provides for delivery on the next working day.
- [ ] by Document Exchange
- [ ] by delivering to or leaving at a permitted place *(see notes overleaf)*
- [ ] by personally handing it to or leaving it with *(please specify)*
- [ ] by fax machine (.....................time sent) *(you may want to enclose a copy of the transmission sheet)*
- [ ] by other electronic means *(please specify)*
- [ ] by other means permitted by the court *(please specify)*

at *(insert address where service effected, include fax or DX number, e-mail address or other electronic identification)*

being the [ ] claimant's [ ] defendant's [ ] solicitor's [ ] litigation friend:

- [ ] usual residence
- [ ] last known residence
- [ ] place of business
- [ ] principal place of business
- [ ] last known place of business
- [ ] principal office of the corporation
- [ ] principal office of the company
- [ ] other *(please specify)*

The date of service is therefore deemed to be .... *(insert date - see overleaf for guidance)*

I believe that the facts stated in this Certificate are true.

Full name _____

Signed _____ **Position or office held** _____

(Claimant)(Defendant)('s solicitor)('s litigation friend)   (if signing on behalf of firm or company)

Date _____

N215 Certificate of service (01.06)   Click here to clear all fields   Click here to print form   HMCS

Notes for guidance
Please note that these notes are only a guide and are not exhaustive
If you are in doubt you should refer to Part 6 of the rules

Where to serve

Nature of party to be served	Permitted place of service
Individual	• Usual or last known residence
Proprietor of business	• Usual or last known residence; or • Place of business or last known place of business
Individual who is suing or being sued in the name of a firm	• Usual or last known residence; or • Principal or last known place of business of the firm
Corporation (incorporated in England and Wales) other than a company	• Principal office of the corporation; or • any place of within the jurisdiction where the corporation carries on its activities and which has a real connection with the claim
Company registered in England and Wales	• Principal office of the company or corporation; or • any place of business of the company within the jurisdiction which has a real connection with the claim

Personal Service - A document is served personally on an individual by leaving it with that individual. A document is served personally on a company or other corporation by leaving it with a person holding a senior position within the company or corporation. In the case of a partnership, you must leave it with either a partner or a person having control or management at the principal place of business. Where a solicitor is authorised to accept service on behalf of a party, service must be effected on the solicitor, unless otherwise ordered.

Deemed Service - Part 6.7(1). A document which is served in accordance with these rules or any relevant practice direction shall be deemed to be served on the day shown in the following table.

Method of service	Deemed day of service
First class post or (with effect from 6ᵗʰ April 2006) an alternative service which provides for delivery on the next working day.	The second day after it was posted
Document exchange	The second day after it was left at the document exchange
Delivering the document to or leaving it at a permitted address	The day after it was delivered to or left at the permitted address
Fax	If it is transmitted on a business day before 4 p.m., on that day, or otherwise on the business day after the day on which it was transmitted
Other electronic method	The second day after the day on which it was transmitted

• If a document is served personally after 5 p.m. on a business day, or at any time on a Saturday, Sunday or a bank holiday, the document shall, for the purpose of calculating any period of time after service of the document, be treated as having been served on the next business day.

• In this context "business day" means any day except Saturday, Sunday or a bank holiday; and "bank holiday" includes Christmas Day and Good Friday.

Service of documents on children and patients - The rules relating to service on children and patients are contained in Part 6.6 of the rules.

Claim Forms - The general rules about service are subject to the special rules about service of claim forms contained in rules 6.12 to 6.16.

Request for judgment
and reply to admission
(specified amount)

Click here to reset form	Click here to print form

In the

Claim No.	
Claimant (including ref)	
Defendant (including ref)	

- Tick box A or B. If you tick box B you must complete the details in that part and in part D. Make sure that all the case details are given. Remember to sign and date the form. Your signature certifies that the information you have given is correct.

- If the defendant has given an address on the form of admission to which correspondence should be sent, which is different from the address shown on the claim form, you must tell the court.

- Return the completed form to the court.

A ☐ **The defendant has not filed an admission or defence to my claim**

Complete all the judgment details at D. Decide how and when you want the defendant to pay. You can ask for the judgment to be paid by instalments or in one payment.

B ☐ **The defendant admits that all the money is owed**

Tick only **one** box below and complete all the judgment details at D.

☐ **I accept the defendant's proposal for payment**

Say how the defendant intends to pay. The court will send the defendant an order to pay. You will also be sent a copy.

☐ **The defendant has not made any proposal for payment**

Say how you want the defendant to pay. You can ask for the judgment to be paid by instalments or in one payment. The court will send the defendant an order to pay. You will also be sent a copy.

☐ **I do NOT accept the defendant's proposal for payment**

Say how you want the defendant to pay. Give your reasons for objecting to the defendant's offer of payment in the space opposite. (Continue on the back of this form if necessary.) Send this form to the court **with defendant's admission N9A.** The court will fix a rate of payment and send the defendant an order to pay. You will also be sent a copy.

C

☐ Defendant's date of birth is not stated in the form of reply but is known to the claimant as

D	D	M	M	Y	Y	Y	Y

☐ Defendant's date of birth is not stated in the form of reply and is not known to the claimant.

D Judgment details

I would like the judgment to be paid

☐ (immediately)

☐ (by instalments of £ [____] per month)

☐ (in full by [____])

Amount of claim as admitted (including interest at date of issue)	
Interest since date of claim (if any)	
Period from ____ to ____	
Rate ...... %	
Court fees shown on claim	
Solicitor's costs (if any) on issuing claim	
Sub Total	
Solicitor's costs (if any) on entering judgment	
Sub Total	
Deduct amount (if any) paid since issue	
Amount payable by defendant	

I certify that the information given is correct

Signed [____]

(Claimant)(Claimant's solicitor)(Litigation friend)

Position or office held [____]

(if signing on behalf of firm or company)

Date [____]

The court office at

is open between 10 am and 4 pm Monday to Friday. When corresponding with the court, please address forms and letters to the Court Manager and quote the Claim number

N225 Request for judgment and reply to admission (specified amount) (04.06)   HMCS

Notice of Part Admission
(specified amount)

Click here to reset form	**Click here to print form**

Name of court

To the Claimant['s Solicitor]

Claim No.	
Claimant (including ref)	
Defendant (including ref)	
Defendant's date of birth	
Date	

The defendant has partly admitted your claim (see the attached forms N9A and N9B)

- **Please tell the court what you wish to do by completing the lower half of this form and returning it to the court on or before[   ]**
  At the same time you must send a copy to the defendant. If you do not return this form to the court by the date shown, your claim will be stayed. No further action will be taken by the court until the form is received.
- You must tick box A or B. If you tick box B you must also complete the details in that part and part D.
- Remember to sign and date the notice.

A ☐ I DO NOT accept the defendant's part admission

If you tick this box the claim will proceed as a defended claim. If the defendant is an individual and lives in, or carries on business in, another court's area, the claim may be transferred to that court. You and the defendant will be sent an allocation questionnaire and the date by which it must be returned to the court. The information you give will help a judge decide whether your case should be dealt with in the small claims, fast or multi-track. Leaflets telling you more about the tracks are available from the court office. You will be sent a notice of allocation setting out the judge's decision.

B ☐ I ACCEPT the amount admitted by the defendant in satisfaction of my claim

Tick only **one** box and follow the instructions given.

☐ **I accept the defendant's proposal for payment**

Complete all the judgment details at D. The court will enter judgment in accordance with the offer and will send the defendant an order to pay. You will also be sent a copy.

☐ **The defendant has not made any proposal for payment**

Complete all the judgment details at D. Say how you want the defendant to pay. You can ask for the judgment to be paid by instalments or in one payment. The court will send the defendant an order to pay. You will also be sent a copy.

☐ **I do NOT accept the defendant's proposal for payment**

Complete all the judgment details at D and say how you want the defendant to pay. Give your reasons for objecting to the defendant's offer of payment in the space opposite. (Continue on the back of this form if necessary.) The court will fix a rate of payment and send the defendant an order to pay. You will also be sent a copy.

C

☐ Defendant's date of birth is not stated in the form of reply but is known to the claimant as

D	D	M	M	Y	Y	Y	Y

☐ Defendant's date of birth is not stated in the form of reply and is not known to the claimant.

D Judgment details

If you are not accepting the defendant's proposal for payment, say how you would like the judgment to be paid.

I would like the judgment to be paid

☐ (immediately)

☐ (by instalments of £   per month)

☐ (in full by   )

Amount of claim as admitted	
Court fees entered on claim	
Solicitor's costs (if any) on issuing claim	
Sub Total	
Solicitor's costs (if any) on entering judgment	
Sub Total	
Deduct amount (if any) paid since issue	
Amount payable by defendant	

I certify that the information given is correct

Signed .... **Dated** ....

N225A Notice of part admission (specified amount) (04.06)

Click here to print form

Request for judgment by default
(amount to be decided by the court)

| Click here to reset form | Click here to print form |

In the	
Claim No.	
Claimant (including ref)	
Defendant	

To the court

The defendant has not filed (an acknowledgment of service)(a defence) to my claim and the time for doing so has expired.

I request judgment to be entered against the defendant for an amount to be decided by the court and costs.

Defendant's date of birth (if known) | D | D | M | M | Y | Y | Y | Y |

Signed
(Claimant)(Claimant's solicitor)(Litigation friend)

Position or office held
(if signing on behalf of firm or company)

Date

Note: The court will enter judgment and refer the court file to a judge who will give directions for the management of the case including its allocation to track.

The Court Manager

The court office at

is open between 10 am and 4 pm Monday to Friday. When corresponding with the court, please address forms or letters to the Court Manager and quote the claim number.

N227 Request for judgment by default (amount to be decided by the court) (04.06)   HMCS

Application notice

For help in completing this form please read the notes for guidance form N244Notes.

Name of court	
Claim no.	
Warrant no. (if applicable)	
Claimant's name (including ref.)	
Defendant's name (including ref.)	
Date	

Click here to reset form **Click here to print form**

1. What is your name or, if you are a solicitor, the name of your firm?

2. Are you a   ☐ Claimant   ☐ Defendant   ☐ Solicitor

   ☐ Other *(please specify)*

   If you are a solicitor whom do you represent?

3. What order are you asking the court to make and why?

4. Have you attached a draft of the order you are applying for?   ☐ Yes   ☐ No

5. How do you want to have this application dealt with?   ☐ at a hearing   ☐ without a hearing

   ☐ at a telephone hearing

6. How long do you think the hearing will last?   ☐ Hours   ☐ Minutes

   Is this time estimate agreed by all parties?   ☐ Yes   ☐ No

7. Give details of any fixed trial date or period

8. What level of Judge does your hearing need?

9. Who should be served with this application?

10. What information will you be relying on, in support of your application?

☐ the attached witness statement

☐ the statement of case

☐ the evidence set out in the box below

If necessary, please continue on a separate sheet.

Statement of Truth

(I believe) (The applicant believes) that the facts stated in this section (and any continuation sheets) are true.

Signed _____ Dated _____

Applicant('s Solicitor)('s litigation friend)

Full name _____

Name of applicant's solicitor's firm _____

Position or office held _____
(if signing on behalf of firm or company)

11. Signature and address details

Signed _____ Dated _____

Applicant('s Solicitor)('s litigation friend)

Position or office held _____
(if signing on behalf of firm or company)

Applicant's address to which documents about this application should be sent

	If applicable
	Phone no.
	Fax no.
Postcode	DX no.
	Ref no.

E-mail address _____

2

Click here to print form

Application Notice (Form N244) – Notes for Guidance

Court Staff cannot give legal advice. If you need information or advice on a legal problem you can contact Community Legal Service Direct on 0845 345 4 345 or www.clsdirect.org.uk, or a Citizens Advice Bureau. Details of your local offices and contact numbers are available via their website www.citizensadvice.org.uk

Paying the court fee
A court fee is payable depending on the type of application you are making. For example:

- To apply for judgment to be set aside
- To apply to vary a judgment or suspend enforcement
- To apply for a summons or order for a witness to attend
- To apply by consent, or without service of the application notice, for a judgment or order.

No fee is payable for an application by consent for an adjournment of a hearing if it is received by the court at least 14 days before the date of the hearing.

What if I cannot afford the fee?
If you show that a payment of a court fee would involve undue hardship to you, you may be eligible for a fee concession.

For further information, or to apply for a fee concession, ask court staff for a copy of the combined booklet and form EX160A - Court fees - Do I have to pay them? This is also available from any county court office, or a copy of the leaflet can be downloaded from our website www.hmcourts-service.gov.uk

Completing the form

Question 3
Set out what order you are applying for and why; e.g. to adjourn the hearing because..., to set aside a judgment against me because... etc.

Question 5
Most applications will require a hearing and you will be expected to attend. The court will allocate a hearing date and time for the application. Please indicate in a covering letter any dates that you are unavailable within the next six weeks.
The court will only deal with the application 'without a hearing' in the following circumstances.

- Where all the parties agree to the terms of the order being asked for;
- Where all the parties agree that the court should deal with the application without a hearing, or
- Where the court does not consider that a hearing would be appropriate.

Telephone hearings are only available in applications where at least one of parties involved in the case is legally represented. Not all applications will be suitable for a telephone hearing and the court may refuse your request.

Question 6
If you do not know how long the hearing will take do not guess but leave these boxes blank.

Question 7
If your case has already been allocated a hearing date or trial period please insert details of those dates in the box.

Question 8
If your case is being heard in the High Court or a District Registry please indicate whether it is to be dealt with by a Master, District Judge or Judge.

Question 9
Please indicate in the box provided who you want the court to sent a copy of the application to.

Question 10
In this section please set out the information you want the court to take account of in support of the application you are making.
If you wish to rely on:

- **a witness statement,** tick the first box and attach the statement to the application notice. A witness statement form is available on request from the court office.

- **a statement of case,** tick the second box if you intend to rely on your particluars of claim or defence in support of your application.

- **written evidence** on this form, tick the third box and enter details in the space provided. You must also complete the statement of truth. Proceedings for contempt of court may be brought against a person who signs a statement of truth without an honest belief in its truth.

Question 11
The application must be signed and include your current address and contact details. If you agree that the court and the other parties may communicate with you by Document Exchange, telephone, facsimile or email, complete the details

Before returning your form to the court
Have you:
- signed the form on page 2,
- enclosed the correct fee or an application for fee remission,
- made sufficient copies of your application and supporting documentation. You will need to submit one copy for each party to be served and one copy for the court.

Click here to clear text after printing

Witness Summons

To

In the	
Claim No.	
Claimant (including ref)	
Defendant (including ref)	
Issued on	

You are summoned to attend at *(court address)*

on   of   at   (am)(pm)

(and each following day of the hearing until the court tells you that you are no longer required.)

☐ to give evidence in respect of the above claim

☐ to produce the following document(s) *(give details)*

The sum of £   is paid or offered to you with this summons. This is to cover your travelling expenses to and from court and includes an amount by way of compensation for loss of time.

This summons was issued on the application of the claimant (defendant) or the claimant's (defendant's) solicitor whose name, address and reference number is:

Do not ignore this summons

If you were offered money for travel expenses and compensation for loss of time, at the time it was served on you, you must –

- attend court on the date and time shown and/or produce documents as required by the summons; and

- take an oath or affirm as required for the purposes of answering questions about your evidence or the documents you have been asked to produce.

If you do not comply with this summons you will be liable, in county court proceedings, to a fine. In the High Court, disobedience of a witness summons is a contempt of court and you may be fined or imprisoned for contempt. You may also be liable to pay any wasted costs that arise because of your non-compliance.

If you wish to set aside or vary this witness summons, you may make an application to the court that issued it.

The court office at

is open between 10 am and 4 pm Monday to Friday. When corresponding with the court, please address forms or letters to the Court Manager and quote the claim number.

N20 Witness Summons (09.02)   *Printed on behalf of The Court Service*

Certificate of service

Claim No.	

I certify that the summons of which this is a true copy, was served by posting to _____

(the witness) on _____ at the address stated on the summons in accordance with the request

of the applicant or his solicitor.

I enclosed a P.O. for £ _____ for the witness's expenses and compensation for loss of time.

Signed _____
Officer of the Court

Statement of Costs
(summary assessment)

Click here to clear your data after printing

Judge/Master

In the	
	Court
Case Reference	

Case Title

[Party]'s Statement of Costs for the hearing on *(date)*   **(interim application/fast track trial)**

Description of fee earners*

    (a) *(name) (grade) (hourly rate claimed)*

    (b) *(name) (grade) (hourly rate claimed)*

Attendances on   *(party)*

    (a) *(number)*   hours at £   £   0.00

    (b) *(number)*   hours at £   £   0.00

Attendances on opponents

    (a) *(number)*   hours at £   £   0.00

    (b) *(number)*   hours at £   £   0.00

Attendance on others

    (a) *(number)*   hours at £   £   0.00

    (b) *(number)*   hours at £   £   0.00

Site inspections etc

    (a) *(number)*   hours at £   £   0.00

    (b) *(number)*   hours at £   £   0.00

Work done on negotiations

    (a) *(number)*   hours at £   £   0.00

    (b) *(number)*   hours at £   £   0.00

Other work, not covered above

    (a) *(number)*   hours at £   £   0.00

    (b) *(number)*   hours at £   £   0.00

Work done on documents

    (a) *(number)*   hours at £   £   0.00

    (b) *(number)*   hours at £   £   0.00

Attendance at hearing

    (a) *(number)*   hours at £   £   0.00

    (b) *(number)*   hours at £   £   0.00

    (a) *(number)*   hours travel and waiting at £   £   0.00

    (b) *(number)*   hours travel and waiting at £   £   0.00

                                       Sub Total £   0.00

IMPORTANT: This form has been revised to show the four grades of fee earner which have been agreed between the Supreme Court Costs Office and the Law Society and with the concurrence of the Head of Civil Justice. It is being introduced in advance of the formal amendment in the December update to the Civil Procedure Rules. THIS MESSAGE WILL NOT PRINT OUT.

Brought forward £ [0.00]

Counsel's fees *(name) (year of call)* [   ]

      Fee for [advice/conference/documents]   £ [   ]

      Fee for hearing   £ [   ]

Other expenses

      [court fees]   £ [   ]

      Others   £ [   ]
      (give brief description) [   ]

Total   £ [0.00]

Amount of VAT claimed

      on solicitors and counsel's fees   £ [   ]

      on other expenses   £ [   ]

Grand Total   £ [0.00]

The costs estimated above do not exceed the costs which the *(party)* [   ]
is liable to pay in respect of the work which this estimate covers.

Dated [   ]   Signed [   ]

                                   Name of firm of solicitors [   ]
                                   [partner] for the *(party)*

---

* 4 grades of fee earner are suggested:

(A) Solicitors with over eight years post qualification experience including at least eight years litigation experience.

(B) Solicitors and legal executives with over four years post qualification experience including at least four years litigation experience.

(C) Other solicitors and legal executives and fee earners of equivalent experience.

(D) Trainee solicitors, para legals and other fee earners.

"Legal Executive" means a Fellow of the Institute of Legal Executives. Those who are not Fellows of the Institute are not entitled to call themselves legal executives and in principle are therefore not entitled to the same hourly rate as a legal executive.

In respect of each fee earner communications should be treated as attendances and routine communications should be claimed at one tenth of the hourly rate.

List of documents: standard disclosure

Notes

- The rules relating to standard disclosure are contained in Part 31 of the Civil Procedure Rules.
- Documents to be included under standard disclosure are contained in Rule 31.6
- A document has or will have been in your control if you have or have had possession, or a right of possession, of it **or** a right to inspect or take copies of it.

In the	
Claim No.	
Claimant (including ref)	
Defendant (including ref)	
Date	

Click here to clear all fields

Click here to print form

Disclosure Statement

I, the above named

☐ Claimant   ☐ Defendant

☐ Party (if party making disclosure is a company, firm or other organisation identify here who the person making the disclosure statement is and why he is the appropriate person to make it)

state that I have carried out a reasonable and proportionate search to locate all the documents which I am

required to disclose under the order made by the court on (date of order)

☐ I did not search for documents:-

☐ pre-dating

☐ located elsewhere than

☐ in categories other than

☐ for electronic documents

☐ I carried out a search for electronic documents contained on or created by the following:
(list what was searched and extent of search)

N265 Standard disclosure (10.05)

HMCS

☐ I did not search for the following:-

☐ documents created before [   ]

documents contained on or created by the ☐ Claimant ☐ Defendant

☐ PCs   ☐ portable data storage media
☐ databases   ☐ servers
☐ back-up tapes   ☐ off-site storage
☐ mobile phones   ☐ laptops
☐ notebooks   ☐ handheld devices
☐ PDA devices

documents contained on or created by the ☐ Claimant ☐ Defendant

☐ mail files   ☐ document files
☐ calendar files   ☐ web-based applications
☐ spreadsheet files   ☐ graphic and presentation files

documents other than by reference to the following keyword(s)/concepts
(delete if your search was not confined to specific keywords or concepts)

[   ]

I certify that I understand the duty of disclosure and to the best of my knowledge I have carried out that duty. I further certify that the list of documents set out in or attached to this form, is a complete list of all documents which are or have been in my control and which I am obliged under the order to disclose.

I understand that I must inform the court and the other parties immediately if any further document required to be disclosed by Rule 31.6 comes into my control at any time before the conclusion of the case.

☐ I have not permitted inspection of documents within the category or class of documents (as set out below) required to be disclosed under Rule 31(6)(b)or (c) on the grounds that to do so would be disproportionate to the issues in the case.

[   ]

Signed [   ]   **Date** [   ]

(Claimant)(Defendant)('s litigation friend)

List and number here, in a convenient order, the documents (or bundles of documents if of the same nature, e.g. invoices) in your control, which you do not object to being inspected. Give a short description of each document or bundle so that it can be identified, and say if it is kept elsewhere i.e. with a bank or solicitor

I have control of the documents numbered and listed here. I do not object to you inspecting them/producing copies.

List and number here, as above, the documents in your control which you object to being inspected. (Rule 31.19)

I have control of the documents numbered and listed here, but I object to you inspecting them:

Say what your objections are

I object to you inspecting these documents because:

List and number here, the documents you once had in your control, but which you no longer have. For each document listed, say when it was last in your control and where it is now.

I have had the documents numbered and listed below, but they are no longer in my control.

Notice to admit facts

Click here to clear your text after printing

In the	
Claim No.	
Claimant (include Ref.)	
Defendant (include Ref.)	

I (We) give notice that you are requested to admit the following facts or part of case in this claim:

I (We) confirm that any admission of fact(s) or part of case will only be used in this claim.

Signed _____
(Claimant)(Defendant)('s Solicitor)

Position or office held
(If signing on behalf of firm or company)

Date _____

- -

Admission of facts

I (We) admit the facts or part of case (set out above)(in the attached schedule) for the purposes of this claim only and on the basis that the admission will not be used on any other occasion or by any other person.

Signed _____
(Claimant)(Defendant)('s Solicitor)

Position or office held
(If signing on behalf of firm or company)

Date _____

The court office at

is open between 10 am and 4 pm Monday to Friday. Address all communication to the Court Manager quoting the claim number

N266 - w3 Notice to admit facts (4.99)

Printed on behalf of The Court Service

Notice to prove documents at trial

Click here to clear your text after printing

In the	
Claim No.	
Claimant (include Ref.)	
Defendant (include Ref.)	

I (We) give notice that you are requested to prove the following documents disclosed under CPR Part 31 in this claim at the trial:

Signed

(Claimant)(Defendant)('s Solicitor)

Position or office held
(If signing on behalf of firm or company)

Date

The court office at

is open between 10 am and 4 pm Monday to Friday. Address all communication to the Court Manager quoting the claim number

Printed on behalf of The Court Service

INDEX